The

Second Spring

The Community of St. John Baptist
in America
1940–2020

Valerie Bonham

2022

Published by CSJB Books
Community of St. John Baptist, PO Box 240, 82 West Main St., Mendham, NJ 07945

Text © Valerie Bonham 2022
Logo © CSJB
First edition

Typeset by Books to Treasure
Cover design by Sr. Monica Clare CSJB

ISBN 978-0-9981483-1-1

The author and Community of St. John Baptist gratefully acknowledge the generosity of the Episcopal Church Women's History Project for their grant which has enabled the publication of this book.

Also by Valerie Bonham:
In the Midst of the People (1983) (out of print)
A Joyous Service: The Clewer Sisters and their work (1989 and 2nd revised edition 2012)
A Place in Life: The Clewer House of Mercy, 1849–83 (1992)
Sisters of the Raj: The Clewer Sisters in India (1997)
Living Stones: The Community of St. John Baptist in America, 1874–1939 (2016)
Various articles in the *Oxford Dictionary of National Biography* (Oxford 2004 and later)

By Valerie Bonham & Julie Dexter
A Good Foundation: Holy Trinity Coleford (2009)

Edited by Valerie Bonham:
A Tribute to Maurice Bond (1984)
Windlesora (The Journal of the Windsor Local History Group) Numbers 4–7 (1985–88)

The Sisters in 2018 with Christmas Crèche and Jennie.
Left to right: Sr. Barbara Jean, Sr. Monica Clare, Sr. Eleanor Francis, Sr. Laura Katharine, Sr. Linda Clare, Sr. Margo Elizabeth, Sr. Pamela, Sr. Victoria Michelle, Sr. Mary Lynne, Sr. Deborah Francis, Sr. Suzanne Elizabeth

*This book is dedicated to the greater glory of God
and in thanksgiving for the
Community of St. John Baptist in America,
and for all the Sisters, past, present and future.
And for Sr. Margaret Helena, of whom it was written at the time of her death:
"She spanned the old and new eras of Community history, striving always to adjust
to new times and new situations. The Community of St. John Baptist has been
shaped by her presence and will continue in her spirit."*

"God calls and promises to be with those he calls—that means every one of
His children. Our prayer is that we all may seek and find His presence. He does
not promise life without problems or success in our ventures—He promises His
presence—our true peace."
Mother Margaret Helena, 1976.

"We are primarily a group of praying women who were called together by God. From
our prayer springs our work for God, but it springs *from* our prayer and is *not* instead
of prayer."
Sister Elizabeth Anne, when elected Mother Superior in 1979,
quoting from Mother Annys of Clewer

CONTENTS

List of illustrations · · · I

Author's Preface · · · IV

Community Preface by Sr. Monica Clare, CSJB · · · VI

Foreword by Dr. Mary Sudman Donovan · · · VII

A word about words · · · XI

Acknowledgments · · · XII

Introduction: Looking back in thankfulness: the story so far ... XV

1. The Winds of Change—the Community 1940–44 · · · 1

2. With no lack of love—the Community 1945–49 · · · 23

3. From "out West" to "down South"—
   from Portland, Oregon to Corsicana, Texas · · · 48

4. Broad and sound foundations—
   St. John Baptist School, 1940–59 · · · 61

5. "Let our living be thanksgiving"—the Community 1950–55 · · · 73

6. "Varied and unending"—the Community 1956–59 · · · 91

7. "On the frontier"—the early years in Jersey City, 1951–59 · · · 100

8. Widening horizons ... —the Community 1960–64 · · · 120

9. ... And building bridges—the Community 1965–69 · · · 134

10. A tough assignment—Jersey City in the 1960s · · · 148

11. "Our common heritage"—the Community 1970–74 · · · 176

12. Challenge and change—the Community 1975–79 · · · 194

13. A complication of circumstances—
    the final decade in Jersey City · · · 258

14. Showing forth the Kingdom of God—
    the Community 1980–84 · · · 302

15. To receive all as Christ— the Community 1985–89 · · · 324

16. All gifts differing—the Community 1990–94   342

17. Work for the Lord—the Community 1995–99   360

18. Share the Vision—the Community 2000–04   380

19. Renewing our Ministry—the Community 2005–09   406

20. From Cornerstones to Living Stones—
    the Community from 2010 onwards   430

APPENDIX 1 Mothers and Sisters Superior   470

APPENDIX 2 Sisters who have entered into rest since 1940   471

APPENDIX 3 Letters from an Indian reservation   472

APPENDIX 4 A tribute to the late Sr. Jane Mankaa   484

LIST OF ILLUSTRATIONS

The Sisters in 2018 with Christmas Crèche and Jennie	*frontispiece*
Sr. Jeannette Louise	220
Sr. Florence Teresa, Mother Superior 1915–42	220
Sr. Alice Ursula, Superior 1942	220
Sr. Waldine Lucia, Superior	220
St. John Baptist Church, Corsicana, TX	221
Sr. Margaret Helena, Superior 1949–79	221
Sr. Adela	221
St. John Baptist House, Corsicana, TX	222
St. John Baptist School students, 1940	223
St. John Baptist School students, 1940s	223
Aerial view of St. Marguerite's and convent	224
Cornerstone of St. John Baptist School, now lost	224
St. John Baptist School students in their old Chapel, late 1940s	225
Sr. Elizabeth Marion	225
Sr. Eleanor Lucy	225
Sr. Catherine Vera	226
Sr. Mildred Eleanor, December 1964	226
Sr. Agatha Louise	226
Sr. Jane Patricia	226
Sr. Mary Barbara	227
Sr. Julia Frances	227
Solemn High Mass at Mendham on June 28, 1952	227
The convent chapel in ruinous condition before restoration	228
William Cordingley's proposed chapel for St. John Baptist School	229
Children at Grace Church, Jersey City, with Sr. Agatha Louise	230
Children at Jersey City with Sr. Elizabeth Anne	230
Sr. Julia Frances's 60th anniversary of Profession, May 23, 1959	231
Group of Sisters, December 1963	232

Ground-breaking ceremony for St. John Baptist School Chapel   233

Lowering the spire on the new chapel at St. John Baptist School, 1965   234

St. John Baptist School students in the tower of the new chapel   235

Sister and students in the new chapel at St. John Baptist School   235

Sr. Agnes Genevieve, Sr. Katharine Veronica, and Sr. Winifred Agnes   236

St. Luke's School, NYC, with Sr. Agnes Genevieve, Sr. Katharine

     Veronica, and Fr. Weed   236

Sisters in St. Christopher's House, Jersey City   237

Sr. Katharine Veronica at St. John Baptist House   238

Sr., formerly Mother General, Dorothy Frances   238

Sr. Laura Katharine, Sr. Barbara Jean, and members of other Communities   238

Builders fixing the Cross   239

Sr. Mary Lynne, 1979   240

Sr. Susinne Paula, 1985   240

Sr. Suzanne Elizabeth, Superior   240

Sr. Elizabeth Anne, Superior   240

Mother Suzanne Elizabeth with some of the English Sisters at Clewer   241

Sr. Barbara Jean's ordination as deacon   242

Sr. Barbara Jean at the time of her ordination as a priest   243

Sr. Barbara Jean, Superior   243

Sr. Margo Elizabeth welcoming Pony   243

Sr. Margaret Helena and Pony   244

Sr. Linda Clare at work in the Garden of Hope   244

At the old St. John Baptist House   245

Sr. Pamela and Sr. Linda Clare in the Garden of Hope   246

Sr. Margaret Helena and Sr. Mary Lynne   246

Restoration of the convent roof and chimneys, 2010   247

Sr. Monica Clare signing the Register of Superiors   247

Sr. Eleanor Francis at the time of her ordination as a priest   248

Sr. Eleanor Francis, Superior   249

Sr. Mary Lynne meeting Sr. Jane Mankaa at Newark airport in 2012   250

Sr. Lura Grace   250

Sr. Laura Katharine with Jennie   250

Sr. Laura Katharine and Sr. Deborah Francis   250

Sr. Deborah Francis handing out soup kitchen vouchers in NYC   251

The Cornerstone of the convent   251

Sr. Margo Elizabeth leaving for a Celtic Journey, 2015   252

Sr. Mary Lynne and Sr. Jane Mankaa in Cameroon   252

Sr. Victoria Michelle   252

Sr. Pamela and Sr. Monica Clare at the first CSJB golf outing   252

Sr. Eleanor Francis, Sr. Pamela, and Sr. Monica Clare with the Rt. Revd. Carlye Hughes, Bishop of Newark   253

Sr. Pamela, Sr. Suzanne Elizabeth, Sr. Eleanor Francis, Sr. Barbara Jean   253

Sr. Linda Clare, Commemoration Day 2016   254

Sr. Suzanne Elizabeth   255

Sr. Barbara Jean celebrating Palm Sunday Eucharist, 2018   256

Sr. Barbara Jean celebrating the 50th anniversary of her Life Profession   256

Sr. Laura Katharine celebrating the 50th anniversary of her Life Profession   256

Sr. Victoria Michelle outside the Church of the Messiah, Chester, NJ   257

Deaconess Marian Brown   472

AUTHOR'S PREFACE

MANY SECOND SPRINGS

THIS is the second of my two books on the history of the Community of St. John Baptist in the USA. The first book, *Living Stones*, published in 2016, began with the arrival in New York City of the first three Sisters from Clewer, UK, in 1874, and ended in 1939. This second volume takes up the story from 1940 until 2020. The beginning of the 1940s saw a major change in the Sisters' work and ministry, away from the older institutional work. As new work and new challenges unfolded, the Community underwent a time of renewal—a "Second Spring."

The idea for the title *The Second Spring* came to me one day during one of my spring research visits to the convent at Mendham. I was sitting in the cloister looking across the front lawn, and there in front of me was the Magnolia tree in full flower. This elderly tree undergoes a transformation every springtime when it bursts into flower and becomes a thing of beauty. And so it is for the Community. The time of their "Second Spring," spanning the eighty years from 1940 onwards, has been a time of continued renewal, as old work has been surrendered and new work has been undertaken.

The more I researched those eighty years, and spoke to, and listened to, the present-day Sisters, the more I understood that there has not been just one "Second Spring" but many. The Sisters have never been afraid to withdraw from a ministry when the time has come to do so. And usually it has been followed by new ministry, another "Second Spring." Sometimes this has been in parishes, sometimes traveling out to spread the news about the Community, and other times at the convent offering a ministry of welcome, hospitality and spiritual guidance. It has spanned parish work in Texas, New York City, Jersey City, work in schools, Celtic Journeys, supporting young people recovering from addiction, supporting work with orphans in Cameroon, mission work on a native American reservation, and so much more, as these pages will recount.

But the underlying work is that of prayer, the daily office, and the sacraments. It is what empowers the Sisters in their visible ministry, and the

iv

"powerhouse" is the chapel. Many people judge Religious Communities by what they can see them doing. But as a Sister once said to me, "We are human *beings*, not human *doings*." In other words, it is the life of prayer, of being still in the presence of God which lies at the heart of all they do, that is the most important aspect. If the day ever comes when the Sisters are unable through age or illness to do outside ministry, the life of prayer will continue. And at a time when a formerly unknown virus is sweeping across the globe, killing thousands and forcing the closure of public meeting places, including places of worship, it is this life of prayer that may be acknowledged as the most important. As will be seen at the end of the final chapter, even in the face of a pandemic, when the Sisters were prevented from welcoming guests and groups to the convent and retreat house, they have found new ways to engage in ministry through modern technology—yet another Second Spring.

All my work for CSJB, spanning over thirty years in the UK and USA, has been a joy and privilege—a labor of love. And it has not just been a case of working on the archives, but also joining with the Sisters in worship, fellowship at mealtimes, walks, talks, and simply being with them. Like the Magnolia tree, the Community of St. John Baptist has been at Mendham for many years, and by the grace of the Holy Spirit it is something beautiful for God.

Valerie Bonham
Wells, Somerset, UK

COMMUNITY PREFACE

VALERIE BONHAM'S series of books detailing the history of our Community from its very beginning in England in 1852, through the founding of the American Community of St. John Baptist in 1874 and now through the present time, is an invaluable service to the Church and to all who are associated with the Community of St. John Baptist. Her vivid, entertaining and heartfelt rendering of the many changes and challenges our Community has survived provides wisdom and inspiration not only to us Sisters in the present day, but also to any who might be called to ministry.

From the very beginning, Religious Communities in the Church of England faced tremendous obstacles and yet somehow, through the grace of the Holy Spirit, overcame them to minister to God's people. *The Second Spring* tells the story of how the Sisters of CSJB in America have continually redefined our ministries to meet the needs of modern times while keeping the dreams of our Mother Foundress Harriet Monsell alive today and for future generations.

We are deeply inspired by the stories of the many CSJB Sisters who have gone before us. We constantly reap what they planted while sowing new dreams for the Sisters who will come after us. Our story is far from over. We know with certainty that God will provide many more opportunities for us to practice mercy and grace in a world that is crying out for justice and compassion.

We give thanks to Valerie Bonham for keeping our story alive.

Sister Monica Clare, CSJB
Sister Superior, the Community of St. John Baptist, Mendham

FOREWORD

WHAT a marvelous gift Valerie Bonham has given us in this portrait of the Community of St. John Baptist! We are initially invited into the convent grounds near Mendham, NJ, allowed to gaze on the verdant surroundings of this peaceful setting. As we move up the road, we encounter first a modern school building, bustling with the activities of its teenaged students, then a stone cemetery, silent with the memories of so many souls who have served this Community. Around the corner is the retreat house welcoming visitors from many parts of the world who come seeking spiritual solace or a deeper understanding of many facets of the Christian faith. And then at the center is the convent itself, serene in its walls of white stucco and pointed slate roofs. What Valerie has done is to fill these walls with the rich history of so many of the persons who passed through this site, shaping an extensive array of ministries and connections that reach out in extraordinary ways to the huge complex of human life that surrounds the convent walls.

It is the extensive array of ministries that captures our imagination. For we quickly learn that the Sisters who have inhabited these walls have in no way been cut off from the world around them. Listing the various Community issues they have encountered over the years would correct any such notion. Throughout the years there is the consistent theme of caring for children: providing a safe home for orphaned or discarded children in St. Marguerite's Home, offering St. Anna's as a haven for girls whose antisocial behavior might well have led to criminal acts, maintaining St. John the Baptist School and St. Helen's Hall in Oregon to provide quality high school and junior college education to young women. All of these ministries involved steady concern, creative solutions and generous love and care from many Sisters over the years.

By the 1950s, Episcopal Churches in many US cities were struggling to find ways to deal with the problems of the inner-city, using church buildings erected in more prosperous times as centers for community rehabilitation and renovation. Sisters from Mendham joined this process, working at St. Luke's Chapel in Greenwich Village, New York, and Grace Church, Jersey City. Dealing directly with the immediate problems of clients well below the poverty line led the Sisters into complex confrontations with law enforcement officials, city regulatory boards, community organizers and crusading politicians. Though this work was certainly not for the faint of heart, the Sisters' long and faithful presence at both locations brought healing and courage to those with whom they worked. Less lengthy work at St. Elizabeth's and St. John's Churches in Elizabeth, NJ, in the early 1990s drew upon the learnings of the work at Grace Church and St. Luke's. Eventually those learnings were also transferred to work at the Church of St. Mary the Virgin, especially focused on the massive work with the homeless in that part of mid-town Manhattan.

The ordination of women to the priesthood was another crucial issue in the wider community that quickly made its way through the convent walls at Mendham. While many women's Communities were hesitant about the ordination of women to the priesthood, the CSJB welcomed the movement. Just after the 1976 decision by the Episcopal Church to allow women's ordination, the Sisters celebrated the ordination of one of their Associates, Abigail Painter, to the priesthood in early 1977 with Mother Margaret Helena preaching the sermon at St. Paul's Church in Morris Plains. Two weeks later, a former St. John Baptist School student, Martha Blacklock, was ordained priest in the school chapel. For the next two decades, the Sisters wrestled with the possibility of the ordination of one of their own members. Finally, on February 19, 1994, Sr. Barbara Jean was ordained to the priesthood in the CSJB Chapel. Symbolic of the complicated issues this ordination evoked was the fact that both Mother General Jane Olive and Sr. Marjorie from the Clewer Community in England attended, though some Sisters in their Community remained opposed to women's ordination. The second ordination in 2008 of Sr. Eleanor Francis testified to the Community's continued support of women priests.

The scourge of drug addiction that seemed ever more present in New Jersey in the 1980s presented yet one more opportunity for ministry. The closure of the St. John Baptist School had left the buildings for the residential school vacant—the perfect setting for a residential treatment center for drug addicted teenagers. The 1992 opening of Daytop, a residential program for drug addicted teenagers that included high school studies, counseling and family therapy, presented an innovative program for healing and spurred informal contacts between the Sisters and the young residents there.

The Sisters also wrestled with the structure of the Sisterhood itself. In 1940 they cast off the category of "mission sister" or "lay sister" that had been integral to the original vision of Sister Frances Constance as she shepherded the Community's move from England to New York in the 1870s. At a moving service on Easter day, 1940, the three remaining Mission professed Sisters were welcomed into the full fellowship of the Community, discarding the last vestiges of class discrimination exemplified by the separate orders. In later years, careful attention was paid to the development of a program for Associates, people who provided prayer, organizational and financial support for CSJB's work. Building off that work in the 1980s, an Oblate program invited dedicated career women in the nearby community to a deeper commitment of prayer and study. One of the Oblates lauded the program for helping "bring to our work the love and sympathy which promotes healing and wholeness."

So many other world-wide issues made their way to the Community's doorstep. Several Sisters joined the relief work at St. Paul's Chapel in New York City after the bombing of the World Trade Center in 2001. With fire fighters and police and volunteers from all walks of life, they shared the common task of restoring hope to a beleaguered city. Further afield, the welcome CSJB provided to Sister Jane Mankaa from West Africa led to the development of a huge ministry to HIV orphans in Cameroon, with Mendham Sisters traveling to Africa to share in that healing. Celtic Journeys led by Sisters to Ireland and Scotland inspired modern pilgrims. As Sister Suzanne Elizabeth testified, "Resting in the 'thinness' of these places gave us a sense of 'peace that passes all understanding' and brought balm to our aching spirits."

Living in a monastic Community can never be easy. The daily schedule of worship services must at times feel arbitrary and invasive, demanding a period of attention when one would so much rather be doing something else. It is difficult to commit oneself to live with decisions made by Community vote and to live joyfully and acceptingly with those decisions even when one is convinced that her solution to a particular problem has far more merit than that determined by the majority. There are times that one must commit herself to accomplishing a task simply because she knows that task must be completed for the Community's well-being. And there are always those moments when the outside world crashes in on the ordered life with intensive demands for a whole new kind of response, demanding that one rearrange her life in a totally new direction.

In Jesus's parable of the talents, the person who invests those talents reaps the greatest reward. Somehow, the willingness of this long line of women to submit themselves to a life ordered and inspired by a steady pattern of daily worship has enabled those women to reach out into areas that individually they might never have considered. And that reaching out, that exploration, has reaped blessings on the neighborhood of Mendham, the Episcopal Dioceses of Newark and New Jersey and New York and Oregon and even Cameroon. The talents of this transforming Community have indeed been invested wisely and well. Our world is a better place because of their efforts.

Mother Margaret Helena closed her 1976 Newsletter to the Associates with the following words:

"With all the stresses and strains of government and Church, life goes on with the daily renewal of Communion and prayer. God calls and promises to be with those He calls—that means every one of His children. Our prayer is that we all may seek and find His presence. He does not promise life without problems or success in our ventures—He promises His presence—our true peace."

Mary Sudman Donovan
Denver, Colorado

A WORD ABOUT WORDS …

All historians have difficulty over words: meanings change within the space of a generation. This applies especially to words and phrases associated with religion, racial origins and gender identity and equality. I have made every effort to avoid using words that are no longer politically correct. This is especially appropriate in relation to the work undertaken by the Sisters amongst girls and women who did not have a good start in life, and who might otherwise have been rejected by society. The difficulty arises when quoting from contemporary documents, because while it is necessary to maintain the integrity of the original sources, it is also important to avoid causing offence to the modern reader. I hope I have managed to avoid falling into a trap either way!

Furthermore, since I began writing the present book the Black Lives Matter movement has arisen in response to injustice towards people of color. When I was writing the chapters on the Sisters' ministry in Jersey City I became aware of how much racism there was during those three decades. The Sisters unconditionally welcomed all who came to their door, and many did so, a large number of whom were people of color. Irrespective of racial origin, all of those people were in dire need; and the Sisters were always there to help, console and comfort them. In describing the ministry of the Sisters I have tried to bear in mind the changing use of language over the succeeding decades.

Also, as an English historian writing for American readers, I am aware of subtle differences in our common language. My manuscript has been proof read by both American and English proof readers and I hope, therefore, that the resulting book will be acceptable to readers on both sides of the Atlantic.

Valerie Bonham
2021

ACKNOWLEDGMENTS

AS this second book for the Community of St. John Baptist is published I am very much aware of the help given me by so many people. Firstly, there are the Sisters themselves, and I cannot thank them enough for their love and trust. It is a truly stupendous thing to allow someone who is not a member of the Community to have access to their archives and to write what inevitably is my own interpretation of the life and ministry of that Community. But the Sisters have done much more than that, by their welcoming and generosity, and by their readiness to share their life with me. Each Sister has given me valuable insights into their work and ministry in the Community.

Maureen Woods, the business manager at the convent, has helped with my travel arrangements on several occasions, and I am grateful for her assistance. Many of the archive photographs in this book were restored through the expertise of Sr. Monica Clare, who has also designed the cover. Sr. Linda Clare took me to Holy Cross Monastery at West Park, in upstate New York. And Sr. Suzanne Elizabeth organized the famous visit to Grace Church (Van Vorst), Jersey City, referred to in Chapter 13. She also provided the photograph on the back cover. It has been very helpful to visit Episcopal Churches in New Jersey and to join them for worship—Messiah in Chester with Sr. Victoria Michelle; St. Mark's, Mendham, with Sr. Barbara Jean; an ordination at Christ Church, Short Hills, with several Sisters; and the licensing of the Revd. Diana Wilcox at St. Luke's, Montclair, with Sr. Eleanor Francis and Sr. Pamela. Also it was good to visit Grace Lutheran Church in Mendham with Sr. Victoria Michelle. Sr. Barbara Jean has shared many memories of her early life in Community. Sr. Suzanne Elizabeth has been the Community editor of both the first book, *Living Stones*, and this present book, and I am grateful to her for all her comments, memories, and encouragement, and for answering my many questions.

Several former students of St. John Baptist School have given me their memories. It was quite by chance that I discovered that Lynn Wilder Mullin was a former student there. She was in the Chapter Room gift wrapping prizes for the Golf Outing while I was working on the archives when she happened to say she was a student from 1962–65. I immediately got out my notebook and she provided me with her memories. Christine

Brodeur MacClellan also gave me memories of her time at the school from 1968–72. And Christine Chrystal sent me her memories from 1956–60. The memories of Kitty King Rockwell (1938–41) and Marjorie Wysong (1935–41, now Sr. Marjorie Raphael, SSM) were included in *Living Stones*, but the group photograph of St. John Baptist School students in 1940 includes them both. I am grateful to Associate and former St. John Baptist School student Mary Ann Renn for sending a large file of photographs of the Navajo mission to Sr. Monica Clare. Knowing I would be interested, Sr. Monica Clare shared them with me and I have included a photograph of Deaconess Marian Brown in Appendix 3.

The Revd. Canon Elizabeth Geitz has been helpful regarding Sr. Jane Mankaa and the work of the Good Shepherd Home, Cameroon, and the Good Shepherd Academy. Her book, *I am That Child*, has been very helpful. Sr. Mary Lynne has spent much time with me showing photographs and giving me information about Sr. Jane's ministry. I am grateful to the Revd. Canon Joseph Ngijoe for insights into life in Cameroon at a time of political unrest.

Dr. Mary Donovan has once again provided the Foreword as well as joining with me in providing programs for the Sisters. Her knowledge of the Episcopal Church and the role of women within it is unsurpassed. Marnie Robinson has read parts of the manuscript and saved me from using words which are "un-American."

In the UK, Ruth Jolly and in Australia, Adrianne Fitzpatrick have both excelled themselves with their proof reading, indexing and typesetting skills. This is the fourth book they have prepared for me and I am truly grateful for all their hard work.

I am, along with the Sisters, deeply grateful to the Episcopal Church Women, whose History Project has given a generous grant for the publication of this book. I am also tremendously grateful to Sr. Pamela, who has done the administrative work to secure this grant.

The publication of this book has been delayed by the Covid-19 pandemic, which has also prevented my annual research visits to Mendham. Personal bereavement has also been a factor in the delay. I hope 2022 will find me at the convent once again—a place I have grown to love since my first visit in 2013.

My family continue to show interest in my writing, and look forward to each book as it is published. My daughter Louise has known the UK Sisters all her life and first visited them at Clewer as a newborn baby. And lastly, my late husband Fred Bonham always gave his quiet support, and was looking forward to this latest book. It is something like 38 years since I first began researching and writing CSJB history. At that time we lived in the parish of Clewer, UK, five minutes' walk from the Sisters' convent. His interest and support never diminished even though I have had to travel much further to do my research. His sudden death on February 16, 2021, has left a void in my life, but completing this book has brought a measure of healing.

Valerie Bonham
Wells, Somerset, UK

INTRODUCTION

LOOKING BACK IN THANKFULNESS:
THE STORY SO FAR …

SIXTY-FIVE YEARS had passed since the momentous day, February 5, 1874, when three Sisters of the Community of St. John Baptist, Clewer, near Windsor, UK, had first arrived in New York City. Sr. Frances Constance, Sr. Fanny and Sr. Emma had left England with the blessing of the Warden[1] and co-Founder, Canon T. T. Carter, and with the prayerful support of Mother Harriet Monsell, co-Foundress. The enterprise had been made possible through the generosity of Helen Stuyvesant Folsom, who as Sr. Helen Margaret had been professed in July 1874.[2] She had financed the Sisters' work in New York from her own inheritance, and had made the Folsom mansion at 220, Second Avenue available for the Sisters.

The three Sisters soon made their mark on the Episcopal Church, and as soon as the Community seemed established and enquirers began to arrive seeking admission, the two English Sisters returned to Clewer.[3] Meanwhile the Sister Superior, American-born Sr. Frances Constance, continued to build up the small but growing Community. Sr. Helen Margaret transferred from Clewer to New York in 1875 and it was largely through her kindness and compassion that the Sisters began their first major work—ministry to the German immigrants living in the tenements on the Lower East side. This in turn became the Holy Cross Mission and, as a direct result of this work, the men's Order of the Holy Cross was founded in 1881. Holy Cross Church was consecrated in 1885. Although she has rightly been described as the American Foundress, Sr. Helen Margaret never held any particular office such as Superior or Novice Mistress. She had struggled with her health before joining the Community at Clewer and had at last been well enough to be professed. To do so, and to return to America, her homeland, was for her the greatest joy.

In 1881 the Clewer Chapter[4] agreed to the work in New York becoming an affiliated house with its own Chapter and Warden. Sr. Frances Constance now became Mother Superior, and while novices still spent several months of their novitiate at Clewer, they returned to New York for profession. Even so, the last word in many matters still rested with the Clewer Chapter and Warden. But even this rather limited degree of independence was a huge affirmation for the American Community so soon after their arrival in New York, and there can be no doubt that this was due to the wise leadership of Sr. Frances Constance.

Sr. Helen Margaret's death in 1882, probably from tuberculosis, was the first loss sustained within the American Community. Her death was greatly mourned by the German mothers who had benefited from her ministry both in New York City and in the summer rest house, known as St. Anna's, at Farmingdale, Long Island. It was they who paid for her memorial brass in Holy Cross church. The brass is now on the floor of the choir in the main chapel at the convent in Mendham, NJ.

The first three Mothers Superior had each brought distinctive gifts to the Community and these served for the mutual up-building of all. Mother Frances Constance brought wisdom, compassion and clarity of vision. She inspired confidence in her novices and won affection from all who encountered the Sisters. Religious Communities were still relatively new within the Episcopal Church, and there were many obstacles in the early days. She overcame them through a combination of tact, diplomacy and firmly standing her ground. Her successor as Superior, Mother Gertrude Verena, built upon those solid foundations. She built up the interior spiritual life of the Community. Her own great devotion to the Blessed Sacrament and the Divine Office was translated in practice into the depth of spiritual formation she gave to the Sisters. She laid the foundations of the spiritual life and practice of the Community to the present day. The third Mother Superior, Mother Mary Angela, has been remembered for her legal mind. She quickly rose to the challenge when it came to settling legal matters which, if neglected, would have placed the Community at a great disadvantage and possible financial loss. This cleared the way ahead for the Community's eventual relocation to Mendham. But also, Mother Mary Angela had a great sense of empathy with the German immigrants, and with the novices whose vocations she nurtured with care and compassion. She has been remembered as the "trainer" of the Community.

The early years in New York saw the increase in numbers of Sisters and in their work and ministry. The earliest and longest lasting work was St. John Baptist School, begun in 1880. By this time the Sisters had moved from 220, Second Avenue, NYC, to their new, purpose-built Mother House at 233, East Seventeenth Street, opened in 1877. The school was accommodated in St. John Baptist House but from the start it was very crowded, and in 1883 the buildings were extended. Other work followed, some of which, such as Christ Church Home, South Amboy, and St. Hilda's, Morristown, was fairly short-lived, and some had to be refused. An invitation to take charge of the Midnight Mission in 1883 was accepted as it gave a real opportunity to help women and young girls who were abused and rejected by society. Often with nowhere else to go or no one to turn to, they ended up on the streets of New York with all the attendant moral dangers. It was tough work but in 1887 the Trustees of the Mission decided to open a country branch at Mamaroneck in Westchester County, New York, and the Sisters were invited to take charge. Although they withdrew from the Midnight Mission after a few years, the Sisters remained in charge of St. Michael's Home, Mamaroneck, until 1937.

A strong feature of CSJB in the UK had been the ability to take different types of work, even though the original work had been of a similar nature to the Midnight Mission. CSJB in New York began to follow that pattern with work in education, moral rescue work, and in 1886 the opening of St. Andrew's Convalescent Hospital, NYC. Unlike St. Andrew's Hospital, Clewer, where the Sisters ministered to women, men and children, the hospital in New York City was much smaller and for women only. But it served a great need and continued until 1950.

During their twenty-six years in New York City the Sisters had witnessed great changes. By 1900 much new building was happening and the city was becoming increasingly noisy, busy and over-crowded. A legacy from Sr. Frances Constance, who had died in 1901, made it possible to consider leaving the city. It had already been necessary to abandon St. Anna's summer rest house at Farmingdale, Long Island, due to an outbreak of typhoid, and after a nomadic existence for a year or two, it became possible for St. Anna's to transfer to Mendham. This happened in 1902. A year previously, the Community had purchased ten acres of land adjoining the new St. Anna's for their own future use. The new convent would eventually be built on this site.

A new challenge awaited the Sisters in 1904 when they accepted an invitation to take charge of St. Helen's Hall, a large school for girls at Portland, Oregon. Geographically it was almost as far away from New York as the English Sisters' convent at Clewer, near Windsor, UK. But also, there were no Religious Communities in Oregon, and indeed the Episcopal Church had only been there a few decades. It was real pioneering work. The Sisters rose to the challenge and gradually won the hearts and minds of their critics. A disastrous fire in 1914 seemed to spell the end of the school, but phoenix-like it rose out of the ashes with the Sisters still in charge. And there was heroism, too. In 1918 when Spanish influenza hit Portland, Sisters Waldine Lucia, Alice Ursula and Marie Elisabeth volunteered to help nurse the victims in the emergency hospital. Their own welfare was overseen by Sr. Mary Angela, by now no longer Mother Superior, but Sister Superior in Portland. All the Sisters survived and the school went from strength to strength under their leadership.

The site at Mendham acquired a new building in 1908. This was St. Marguerite's, a home for girls who were either orphaned or had one parent who was unable to look after them through illness, poverty or other reasons. It was run by the Sisters and continued into the 1940s, by which time it had become more of a home school. Former pupils and teachers cherish memories of it into the 21st century.

Soon St. Marguerite's would no longer be alone at the top of the hill. The Cornerstone of the new convent was laid on April 30, 1913, and by September 1915 the Sisters were able to move into the still uncompleted building. It was dedicated on June 8, 1916. With the move, St. Anna's summer rest work came to an end and in 1916 St. John Baptist School moved from New York into the former St. Anna's rest house at the foot of the hill. Possession of the new convent enabled the Sisters to open within it a new rescue home for girls and women. This was to be called St. Anna's in tribute to the house at the bottom of the hill where the girls and women had lived temporarily from 1913 until the convent was completed.

The 1880s and 1890s had seen the largest numbers of professions and this trend continued until the First World War. Numbers peaked in 1917/18, with forty-five Sisters including novices. After this time there was a gradual fall in numbers as older Sisters passed to their rest and vocations slowed down. At Clewer, where numbers were calculated in hundreds rather than in tens, the same trend was happening but was less noticeable. Although the United States was not drawn into the First World War until 1917, there was an impact on the Community. Communication between Mendham and Clewer was hindered by U-boats operating in the Atlantic. Also, the financial strictures brought by the war began to impinge on the Sisters' work, as benefactors found themselves less able to give as generously as previously.

The 1920s would bring fresh challenges but also new opportunities as the Community adapted to changing needs. 1924 marked the golden jubilee of the Sisters' arrival in New York City. June 26 was kept as

"Commemoration Day"—a great day of thanksgiving for the blessings of the past fifty years. A commemorative booklet was produced and widely distributed to Associates and other friends. Meanwhile St. John Baptist School was still at the bottom of the hill and the building was increasingly inadequate. Throughout the 1920s Sr. Elisa Monica, Sister Superior of the school, begged, borrowed and cajoled until splendid new school buildings halfway up the hill opened in 1929. Also in the 1920s Mother Florence Teresa had encouraged Sr. Elisa Monica to write her early memories of Community life and together they also compiled short biographies of all the departed Sisters.[5]

The Wall Street crash on October 29, 1929, sent shock waves throughout the world's financial markets. And it would have serious consequences for the Sisters' work and ministry as once wealthy benefactors found themselves bankrupt. Throughout the 1930s the Community struggled to maintain the work in the branch houses as before. But there were the inevitable casualties. Appeals for funds were made for the so-called "charitable works"—St. Anna's, St. Marguerite's, and St. Michael's. Other work going back to the beginning had to close. It was with great reluctance that Holy Cross Mission was closed in 1934 and the church soon after. Great sadness was felt by the Sisters when in 1937 the Trustees closed St. Michael's Home, Mamaroneck, against the wishes of the Community. But other work continued against all the odds—St. Helen's Hall, St. John Baptist School, St. Andrew's Hospital, St. Anna's, and St. Marguerite's.

There were signs of hope, too. Mother Florence Teresa had been in office since 1915 and had been continually re-elected with no other candidate standing. Although she was again elected in November 1939, this time there were two other candidates. Her health was failing and she was increasingly deaf and had failing eyesight, so the time was fast approaching for a change of leadership. That change did not happen in 1939, but the scene was being set for new leadership in the next decade.

The world was hurtling into another war and this would have significant repercussions for CSJB as once again communications between Mendham and Clewer were severely curtailed. There would be a greater chasm opening up between them, as issues which had been simmering throughout the 1930s gradually assumed greater importance. The Japanese attack on Pearl Harbor on December 7, 1941, brought the United States into the conflict; and with it, a sense of solidarity between Mendham and Clewer. But those Community issues still had to be addressed and it would take several years, even after the War had ended, before a solution was reached. That was just one challenge, though it was the most serious, that the Sisters at Mendham would face in the 1940s. The solution would set the course for the Community for the next generation.

Throughout all the difficulties of a fast-changing world, the Sisters remained faithful to their life of prayer, the sacraments and the recitation of the daily office, all in the context of their vowed life. It was what has undergirded all their life, their work, their ministry, from the beginning up to the present day.

As the Sisters entered the 1940s they were ready to face all the challenges that came their way. Challenges and changes. The result would be the surrendering of some older work and the acceptance of new work and ministry, and a new sense of identity. It would not be without pain but the result would be a Second Spring.

And so the story continues …

─────────────────

[1] Most women's Religious Communities founded in the nineteenth century were overseen by a clergyman, often the founder, who styled himself as Warden. In the case of the Community of St. John Baptist, the Warden from its beginning in 1852 until his death in 1901 was the Co-Founder, the Revd T. T. Carter (Canon after 1870). He had not only a pastoral oversight, but also directed the Community in their decisions and from time to time exercised the power of veto. When the Community in the US became an affiliated house, he was styled Warden General, over the US Warden. Even after Carter's death, the role of Warden remained unchanged until the late twentieth century.

[2] Helen Stuyvesant Folsom's maternal grandmother, Judith Stuyvesant, was descended from Peter Stuyvesant, one of the founding fathers of the Dutch colony of New Amsterdam, later New York. It is more than likely that Helen's fortune, which she so readily expended on bringing CSJB to New York and establishing them there, was derived from her Stuyvesant ancestry.

[3] Sr. Fanny had been admitted as a postulant at Clewer on October 1, 1866, and professed on November 29, 1870. At the time of her death on January 21, 1933, she was described in the Clewer Community Annals as the senior Sister of the Community, i.e. she had been professed the longest. It was also noted that she had done parish work until a few years before her death, but no further details are given. Her funeral was on January 24, 1933.

More is known about Sr. Emma. She was admitted on November 6, 1869, and professed on February 7, 1872, with Canon Carter's niece, Sr. Alice. The main focus of Sr. Emma's ministry was St. Augustine's Home, Clewer—a home for destitute boys. Shortly before her death on March 22, 1909, Sr. Emma provided Cecil Sharp with twenty-five English folk songs passed down to her from her mother and nurse. Cecil Sharp was traveling all over England collecting English folk songs in order to save them from being lost.

For more about Sr. Emma and St. Augustine's Home, see Bonham Valerie, *Scamps reclaimed: St. Augustine's Home, Clewer* in Windlesora, no. 12, 1993. Also, Bonham, Valerie *A Joyous Service* (rev. ed. 2012) Chapter 5. And for more about her folk songs see Bonham, Valerie *A Joyous Service* op. cit. Appendix 2, Sister Emma and her songs.

[4] The Community Chapter consisted of all choir Sisters who had been professed more than five years. All decisions relating to Community life had to be made by the Chapter; and in major decisions, more than one vote was taken. The US Chapter was represented on the Chapter at Clewer by just one vote, even when the decision related directly to the American Sisters or to overall Community policy. This became an increasingly contentious issue after 1940.

[5] Sr. Elisa Monica was eighteen years old when the Sisters first arrived in New York, and she lost no time in paying them a visit. Soon she was a postulant but then had to withdraw in order to take care of her father and brother following the death of her mother. She kept in touch with the Sisters and after ten years was able to join the Community. See Chapter 2 of *Living Stones* for her earliest memories of the Community in New York.

The *Early Memories* file and *Sisters' Biographies* written at the invitation of Mother Florence Teresa gave me vital information for *Living Stones*.

THE WINDS OF CHANGE

The Community 1940–44

FAITH, PRAYER AND SACRAMENT. These were the infrastructure on which the Community of St. John Baptist was founded, and they undergirded every aspect of community life during some of the most challenging years the Sisters had yet known.

The end of the 1930s had seen the winds of change beginning to stir within the Community. Financial hardship had been greatly eased by a legacy which the Sisters had not hoped to receive due to the Great Depression. To their immense relief this became a reality at the end of January, 1940, thus saving the Community from the threat of bankruptcy. The way ahead suddenly seemed clearer and more positive. But the new decade would bring its own challenges, together with changes to the Community, and life would never be quite the same again.

But some things never change—winter 1940 was harsh. The Sisters were accustomed to severe weather up on top of the hill at Mendham, but the winter weather lasted intermittently from February 14 until early in March. The Community Record Book noted that there was "a heavy snow storm all night and day with high wind … No one able to come here from the school after the morning, as the storm increased steadily and the snow drifted."

Next day there was no Mass as the roads were impassable so no priest could get through. But the Sisters managed to get across the lawn to St. Marguerite's home. "Mr. Cullen made a path up the road with his small motor plow to bring 1 quart of milk. It took him two hours to do it!" The road from Morristown to Mendham was in a bad condition and there were deep drifts on the convent drive. To crown it all there was an outbreak of "grippe" [influenza] at the school which affected children and Sisters. Then, on March 3, the snow returned. "Bad storm of rain, snow, sleet and hail. Sisters from the school had to walk up convent hill as Thompson's car could not make it … Girls could not get to Mendham church."

Next day things were worse than ever. "Storm continuing—no lights or telephone. Everything covered with ice," and the following day, "Much danger from falling ice. Many trees destroyed or badly broken, several houses in Mendham damaged by falling trees. Walking very bad. Still no lights [but] telephone working intermittently."

A major change was made at Easter 1940. Mother Florence Teresa (Hoopes) made the following entry in the Community Roll Book: "On Easter day 1940, at Mass, Sr. Francina, Sr. Lillian Christine and Sr. Jeannette Louise, the last three of the professed mission Sisters, after the vote in two successive Chapters held at the Convent of St. John Baptist, on December 1, 1939, and on January 4, 1940, became choir Sisters, wearing the choir Sisters' habit, in full fellowship with the Community, and taking their places in the order of profession." The decision had not been made easily, there being a discussion lasting two-and-a-half hours at the December meeting of the Chapter. But finally the decision was made, though with the proviso that the three Sisters should undergo a period of instruction, plus an oral examination before their profession. According to the Community Record Book the three Sisters made their confession and renewed their vows in the presence of the Warden in Holy Week and took their places in choir in the order of profession. On Easter Sunday 1940 (March 24), they put on their choir habits and on Easter Tuesday (March 26), Bishop Washburn,[1] the Community Visitor, came to take a service of blessing. They were conducted to the altar by Mother Florence Teresa, where they knelt and shared the renewal of profession promises and received the bishop's blessing.

The decision to discontinue the category of mission Sister and to bring them into choir was several years ahead of the decision of the Motherhouse at Clewer to discontinue lay Sisters. There had only been eight professed mission Sisters in America whereas at Clewer numbers of lay Sisters had peaked in the years before World War 1 at 62 (choir Sisters numbered just over 200). By 1946 when the decision was made at Clewer to bring the lay Sisters into choir there were c. 48 and just over 100 choir Sisters.[2]

It was Sr. Frances Constance who had introduced the category of mission Sister in the early years. At first she had introduced a "Second Order" because she sensed that some of the women coming to test their vocation in New York would not be equal to the rigors of a year in the Clewer novitiate.[3] But the Chapter at Clewer decided there should be a category for these women within the First Order. The problem lay in what to call them. When the Affiliation was formed in 1881, this was solved—they were to be called mission Sisters. The few Second Order Sisters became either mission or choir Sisters. The class-oriented stigma surrounding the title "lay Sister" which Sr. Frances Constance (Mother after the Affiliation was formed) had no doubt sensed at Clewer was thus avoided.

Sr. Francina's (Vesbeck) profession as a mission Sister in May 1913 had been the last profession in St. John Baptist House, NYC. Dutch by birth, she had lost an eye when she was 14 in a sledding accident but this did not prevent her admission to the convent. Her main ministry had been at Holy Cross House, NYC, and later at St. Anna's Home, Mendham, where she worked in the kitchen, and, being a gifted cook, taught her skills to the girls and women there.

Sr. Lillian Christine (Naser) and Sr. Jeannette Louise (Dyke) were professed together as mission Sisters in June 1922. Sr. Lillian Christine was orphaned as a young child and would have had a natural empathy with the girls and women at St. Anna's Home and Holy Cross House. She had a similar ministry there to that of Sr. Francina, and as another gifted cook, taught her skills to the girls. Sr. Jeannette Louise first knew CSJB through working at St. Helen's Hall, Oregon, on the housekeeping staff. After her profession she worked at Holy Cross House and when it closed in 1934 she came to assist at St. Marguerite's Home in Mendham, where her talent at knitting and crochet was much appreciated. As well as making beautiful things for sale, she also taught the girls her skills. A photograph of Sr. Jeannette Louise in the early 1940s shows her wearing the habit of a choir Sister.

Although the legacy from Mrs. Sydney Webster had saved the Community from the threat of bankruptcy, there were still financial concerns, especially regarding property other than that at Mendham. But at the end of May the Sisters learned they were to receive a legacy of $2,000 from the late Miss Louisa Floyd-Jones, the sister of the late Sr. Henrietta Mary.

At last the chapel walls were being plastered. Earlier photographs show the bare walls, simply whitewashed over the exposed terracotta bricks.[4] The work began on April 23, 1940, and the Sisters were unable to have a choral Mass for St. Mark's day two days later. The work took several weeks, during which time the Sisters worshipped in the Chapter room. Other work was being undertaken to repair roof tiles damaged during the winter storms. And then the ceiling in the office at St. Marguerite's fell in during the night. All this was unanticipated expense in financially straitened times.

Despite her increasing deafness and concerns about her failing eyesight, Mother Florence Teresa made her annual visit to St. Helen's Hall in Portland, Oregon, and found all very encouraging. It was a much-needed boost to morale, there being so much illness among the Sisters at Mendham that it was easy to be discouraged. But St. Helen's Hall was in good shape. The previous year had seen an enrollment of 406, of whom 225 were in the Junior College. There had been an inspection in the spring and the school had been rated "Superior." Twenty-nine students had graduated from the High School and 34 from the Junior College. A number of nurses from the Good Samaritan Hospital Training School received certificates for their science work in the Junior College. The Lake House at Lake Oswego was still a great success, providing a means for the girls to escape the city at weekends or vacations. And there was an innovation—driving lessons! This was for girls over sixteen under State auspices and was very popular.

News of the war caused the Sisters much concern. The Community Record Book noted: "War news appalling. Surrender of King Leopold of Belgium. Italy's likelihood of going against the Allies soon. Ireland's disloyalty—all terrible." And the Short Record Book for the same period stated: "Italy went into the War. Canada declared War on Italy. *Awful* state of the World." Although the United States had not yet entered the war, the Sisters were prayerfully concerned about the work of CSJB at Clewer and at the many UK branch houses, some of which had already closed or had evacuated to safer locations. One of the main impacts of the war was the lack of communication between Mendham and Clewer—enemy U-boats were creating havoc in the Atlantic and mail was being lost. This would become an increasing problem as the war progressed. All the Sisters could do was pray, and this they did.

On Sunday May 26, 1940, the Catholic Congress Cycle of Prayer asked to have a service in the convent chapel. This took the form of a Day of Prayer for Peace, concluding with Vespers and Benediction of the Blessed Sacrament. It was poorly attended, and Mother Florence Teresa noted in the Community Record Book that "It was a foggy, dark, damp day, [which] may have accounted for the few present."

Vocations to the Community were by now few and far between, a sign of the changing world since the end of the Great War. So it was no surprise, though still a matter of sadness, when another novice left in July 1940, after finding she had no vocation. And two Sisters who had been professed in the late 1930s also left within a year or two of making their vows.[5] However, on November 7, 1940, Sr. Alice Madeline and Sr. Katharine Veronica were professed, and these Sisters would stay. It was a joyous occasion with many guests and a large number from the school.

Sr. Alice Madeline (Cranmer) was a former student at St. John Baptist School, as was her mother before her. She graduated in 1937 and wanted to join the Community, but first took a college course in nursery school techniques. She then ran a small nursery school at home in Wilmington, NC, for three years before joining the Community. She worked at St. John Baptist School from time to time but her main work was at St. Marguerite's, where her nursery training would have been put to good use.

Sr. Katharine Veronica (Finch) trained as a nurse at St. Luke's Training School for Nurses, NYC, and then, after a time as a private nurse, worked for nine years as a visiting nurse, which included visiting patients in Bergen Pines sanatorium. At some point during that time she met Sr. Lillian Christine, and it was through their friendship that she entered the Community of St. John Baptist. During part of her novitiate she was school nurse at St. John Baptist School, but after profession worked at St. Anna's, where she had a rapport with the girls and women and kept in touch with many of them after they left. From 1943–45 she worked at St. Marguerite's and at St. Andrew's Hospital, NYC. Much of Sr. Katharine Veronica's work lay in the new ministries taken by the Community after 1945, and there will be more about these later. Almost all of those ministries saw her active there—St. John's Parochial School, Corsicana, Texas; Christ Church, Newark; school nurse again at St. John Baptist School, Mendham; St. Luke's Chapel, NYC. Later she returned to the convent, where she held various offices. It was said of Sr. Katharine Veronica that she had a wonderful gift for making friends and that all ages loved her, from small children in the primary grades through to the elderly at St. Luke's Chapel, where she organized a lunch program. This continued long after she left. She corresponded with many people from all walks of life and continued to keep in touch with several of her childhood friends.

On November 8, 1940, the day after the profession, Sr. Adela (Sharpe) had a stroke. Professed in May 1890, she was the second longest surviving professed Sister.[6] She was English by birth, and had had a sister (Sr. Sophia

Agnes) at Clewer who had died there in 1938. Sr. Adela had worked in all the Community branch houses, including St. Helen's Hall in Oregon. Throughout 1940 her health had been failing and giving cause for concern. Following the stroke on November 8, she lingered until shortly before midnight on Saturday, November 16, when she died peacefully. Mother Florence Teresa noted in the Short Record Book that "her eyes were wide open and a beautiful expression on her face as though she saw Our Lord and all the Blessed." In her letter to the Sisters, Mother Florence Teresa wrote of how Sr. Adela had taught many pupils at St. Marguerite's. "In all weathers she and Sr. Catherine Faith would plod back and forth to St. Marguerite's and the School to teach their spiritual pupils." She summed up Sr. Adela's life in Community: "[She] had great faithfulness to duty, loyalty and devotion to her Community and to her Superiors, and much brightness. We rejoice in her deliverance from much suffering, but we shall miss her sorely." She was laid to rest in the Community cemetery on Tuesday, November 19, after the usual rites and ceremonies.

February 1941 saw the arrival of Sr. Eudora from the UK Community work in Barbados. Six months after her profession at Clewer in 1933 she had been sent to the Community work in India, which she fell in love with, and remained so for the rest of her life. But in 1938 she was withdrawn from there, and after a brief respite at Clewer was sent to Barbados.[7] It was difficult work. During her time in the West Indies she visited the island of St. Vincent where the rumor was spread that she was a German spy, which later appealed to her sense of humor, but was alarming at the time. Having overcome that misunderstanding, she returned to Barbados aboard an oil tanker. The only way she could get a passage was by signing on as the ship's cook! But all this had taken its toll on her health, and as it was impossible to return to Clewer because of the Battle of the Atlantic, the decision was made that she should fly to Trinidad and then get a passage to the US on an American ship. So it was that on February 2, 1941, Mother Florence Teresa and Sr. Alice Ursula met her at the New York docks and took her to St. Andrew's Hospital, where she was to recuperate before going to the convent at Mendham. Her American experience was to last two-and-a-half years. She later wrote, "I can still picture the welcome [at Mendham] with the Sisters assembled in the hall and everything so homelike and CSJB."

The Sisters were looking for ways to improve and update their charitable work. They were advised by the social workers who were responsible for sending girls to St. Anna's to open a high school course, and as a result, more girls were being admitted. Also, St. Anna's Guild was formed for "old girls," and this was a great success, meeting four times a year. No doubt the visits of these former residents encouraged the new girls to persevere in their training. And at St. Marguerite's, the ethos of a school, rather than an orphanage, had taken shape over the past few years. But for both St. Anna's and St. Marguerite's time was running out, no matter how much the Sisters tried to modernize their methods and facilities.

And funding was difficult, too. Since 1936 Sr. Elisa Monica had managed the St. Marguerite's Maintenance Fund, when income from the St. John the Baptist Foundation had ceased. She had begged and appealed from all and sundry and had been able to give Sr. Julia Frances $500 a month. Many older benefactors had died and although some left legacies, such as the $2,000 left to St. John Baptist School by Celestine Pinckney, who had died in 1940, legacies were rarely left for the charitable work. But there was an exception in the legacy left by Fr. Clarence Dunham, which was divided between the school and St. Marguerite's.

Winter weather—deep snow and communications cut off was the usual recipe for late February and early March 1941. But the St. Anna's girls enjoyed a sled ride, and so by all accounts, did Sr. Eudora!

Fr. William Osborn Baker, for many years the Warden, finally resigned due to ill health in April 1941. He had given notice of his resignation in June 1939, but had continued on light duties, and other priests deputized for him. Mother Florence Teresa asked him to remain as "nominal" Warden until they had found a successor. On June 12, Mother and Sr. Alice Ursula visited Fr. Baker for what would be the last time. He was clearly dying but gave them his blessing as well as a relic of the True Cross.[8] He wept as the Sisters left, and they did not see him again. He died peacefully on July 10, and several Sisters attended his funeral at Trinity Church, Princeton. A requiem was said at the convent as well as the Office for the Dead.

Amidst this time of sadness there was also a time of joy when Sr. Jane Patricia (Freeland) was elected for profession. Meanwhile, the question of a new Warden had been very much in the minds of all the Sisters. Mother and several Sisters had been greatly impressed by the retreat given earlier in the year by Dom Paul Severance, OSB,[9] and were keen to appoint him as Warden. He was elected on August 20 and instituted on September 8, 1941, immediately before Sr. Jane Patricia's profession. Also at this time there was a new Community chaplain, Fr. Edward Noble, who would serve for several years.

Another old friend of the Community, Bishop Stearly, formerly Bishop of Newark, died on November 8, 1941. He had been the Visitor to the Community and had laid the Cornerstone of the school in 1928 and had blessed the new building in 1929. Mother Florence Teresa and several Sisters attended his funeral at Trinity and St. Philip's Episcopal Cathedral, Newark, NJ.

On November 30, 1941, the nave of the Cathedral of St. John the Divine, NYC, was opened for the first time, and on December 4 there was a great service of dedication. Mother Florence Teresa and Sr. Alice Ursula (Strickland) attended. The music was very grand and the congregation numbered 15–16,000! Three days later, on December 7, 1941, the Japanese Navy Air Service attacked the US naval base at Pearl Harbor, Hawaii. This act of aggression brought the United States into the war. England, Canada and five other countries declared war on Japan, as did the United States. Next day, December 8, both President Roosevelt and Winston Churchill made speeches on U.S. radio. At the convent each Sister was given air raid duties and training by Mr. Gardner, the Defense Inspector, who also advised the Chapter about "black-out" precautions.

Mother Florence Teresa summed up the Christmas celebrations for 1941 in the Community Record Book: "A really lovely Xmas in spite of heavy hearts and grave anxieties." And as they had done for so many years, those Sisters who were able to do so prayed the old year out and the New Year in. The next eighteen months would bring many changes but the Sisters would take them all in their stride, trusting in God at all times.

Sr. Eudora was very anxious to get home to England, but this was impossible while the German U-boats were wreaking havoc in the Atlantic. Meanwhile she worked first in the Church Workroom, but by her own admission was "found wanting"![10] She then worked in most of the Community houses, wherever she was needed most; with so many Sisters constantly ill, she was in great demand.

Sr. Eudora had much in common with Sr. Fanny Helen (Andrew), now aged 80, who was English by birth and had been received as a novice in New York in 1888. All her professed life had been with the American Affiliation.

Communication with Clewer was minimal, letters were lost at sea, and there was a huge sense of abandonment through no fault of the Sisters either side of the ocean. When news came by cable of the death of Sr. Eliza Faith at Clewer, it was the first communication received in a year.

Early in May 1942 food rationing began; but the strictures of war did not impinge upon the devotional life of the Sisters, who observed Lent and Holy Week in the usual way. Fr. Noble, their Chaplain, assisted by other visiting clergy, led all the Holy Week rites and ceremonies. Holy Week was followed by the Community retreat. Other retreats were held too—the annual ladies' retreat which had been held for many years, and the girls' day of devotion for St. Anna's and older girls, which took place at St. Marguerite's. But numbers attending the ladies' retreat were fewer, possibly due to illness, lack of money, and the many other retreats now being held.

At this time Fr. Noble became an Associate; his wife had been received some weeks earlier. Since at least 1858 the Sisters at Clewer had used for their daily offices *The Day Hours of the Church of England*. A new edition had now been published, and on March 16, 1942, the Sisters at Mendham received 50 copies at a cost of $100, which was paid by a friend of the Community.

A statue of the Blessed Virgin Mary holding the infant Jesus was blessed by Fr. Noble on May 1, 1942, in memory of Fr. Aitkins, former Warden and Chaplain. This was placed in the entrance to the chapel where it stands today. It was given by Dorothy Lyon Smith and bore the inscription:

In Memoriam
James Fley Aitkins, Priest, Chaplain,
Warden of the Community of St. John Baptist
1915–1937

Fr. Frank Aitkins and his sister also attended as well as a number of other friends.

St. Andrew's Hospital, NYC, was still fulfilling its role as a safe haven for women to convalesce after illness before returning to the demands of family life. But despite a legacy of $10,000 left by Mrs. Hicks Arundel, who had left a similar legacy to the Community, the hospital was in deep financial trouble. In June Sr. Elisa Monica's brother, Mr. Lawson Purdy, came to discuss Foundation matters including St. Andrew's with Mother Florence Teresa and Sr. Alice Ursula. The Ladies' Committee had grown tired of fund-raising and were critical of what they called the old-fashioned methods of Sr. Mary Katharine (Cuzzens), who had been in charge for some years. The Short Record Book notes: "Wanted to close the hospital—sell the house or give it over to the Government. It was a very sad and painful interview. We resolved to fight for St. Andrew's— to keep it and the house." What is not clear from this is whether it was the St. John the Baptist Foundation that wanted to close the hospital, or the Ladies' Committee. Nor is it clear exactly where Mr. Purdy stood on the issue. Always loyal to the Sisters, he may have been placed in a very difficult position if he could see that the hospital was untenable. A further meeting a month later saw his resignation and that of most of the Trustees, and it was noted that some of the Sisters would be made Trustees, and management of the hospital would be in their hands.

Wednesday, June 10, 1942, saw the death at Glens Falls, NY, of Olive Frances Rheinelander, formerly Sr. Olive Frances. She had left the Community in 1927 and until that time had inscribed many beautiful manuscripts which are still in the possession of the Community.[11] After leaving the Community she continued this work and many are now in the Morgan Library, NYC.[12] It was a sign of the changing attitude towards former Sisters that a requiem was celebrated by Fr. Noble on June 16. Twelve of the older Sisters who remembered her attended it.

News came through from Clewer on June 21, 1942, of the death of Sr. Evelyn at St. Raphael's Home, Torquay. She had been Mother Superior at Clewer (Mother General) from 1907–28 and had been present at the blessing of the new buildings for St. John Baptist School, Mendham, in June 1929. Upon returning to the UK from that visit she had become Sister Superior at St. Raphael's Home, a convalescent home for women, until her death.

On September 28, 1942, Sr. Mary Katharine died very suddenly at St. Andrew's Rest, Woodcliff Lake. She had a major heart attack and died almost immediately. She had been admitted as a postulant in March 1897 and professed in June 1900. The ministry with which she was always associated was at St. Andrew's Hospital, NYC, and its summer rest home at Woodcliff Lake. She had made both places welcoming and comfortable for the patients and for the Sisters, who stayed at Woodcliff Lake for their summer rests if they had no family to go to. On the day of her death she rang the Angelus and about 40 minutes later Miss Lafferty (one of the nursing staff) thought she heard her call, but on reaching the Sister's room found she had died. Her Community Biographer noted that "a bright and loving spirit was added to our treasure in heaven." Mother

Florence Teresa described her death as "a great shock and loss," and "all were much broken up. Sr. Mary Katharine was much beloved by many." After all the usual requiems and offices for the dead Sr. Mary Katharine was laid to rest in the convent cemetery on October 1.

The end of 1942 saw some far-reaching changes. Sr. Elisa Monica, who was now 86, had been Sister Superior of St. John Baptist School since 1914. Her health had been failing for several years and now it was thought appropriate that she should step down. Her place was taken by Sr. Alice Ursula, who had been Assistant Superior of the Community since April 1937. But soon it was "all change" once again because Mother Florence Teresa resigned as Mother Superior on October 25, 1942, after 27 years in office. Sr. Alice Ursula was elected in her place on December 15, 1942, and installed two days later. Mother Florence Teresa remained in office until the day of the installation. She wrote to the Sisters, "When I have had a period of freedom from responsibility after many years in Office, I shall hope to serve the Community in some small way, though I realize my many disabilities." Sr. Florence Teresa had been the only Mother Superior many of the Sisters had known and so this change in leadership was a momentous one.

Other elections had to be held at this time. Sr. Florence Teresa now became Novice Mistress; Sr. Ellen Juliana (Somerly) became Assistant Superior; Sr. Agnes Genevieve (Brooks), Sr. Superior at St. John Baptist School. Sr. Julia Frances (Hobbie) remained Sister Superior at St. Marguerite's and Sr. Waldine Lucia (Scratchley) remained Sister Superior at St. Helen's Hall in Portland, Oregon. Within a few months it would be "all change" again.

St. Andrew's Day, November 30, 1942, was kept with Mass at 7.00am and 8.40am. It was a special day as it marked the 90th anniversary of Harriet Monsell's profession at Clewer and thus the birth of CSJB. As the year drew to a close with no end to the war in sight, the Sisters kept the usual festivities both in and out of chapel. Twelve St. Anna's girls took part in a Christmas pageant at St. Mark's, Mendham, and the children at St. Marguerite's enjoyed their Christmas tree, though fewer guests came, no doubt the result of fuel rationing. The life of prayer and sacrament continued throughout all the changes and chances of a troubled world, and the New Year was prayed in with a spirit of hopefulness.

Nineteen forty-three began relatively uneventfully. There were the usual illnesses among the Sisters, some of whom were in hospital. There

was measles at the school which resulted in quarantine, and there was the
usual bad weather with heavy snowfalls. Sr. Elisa Monica gave cause for
concern by having a cold which threatened to develop into pneumonia.
Mother Alice Ursula spent several nights at the school in order to
administer medication every four hours. True to form, Sr. Elisa Monica
made a good recovery.

Mother Alice Ursula had been failing in health for some time with
constant colds. And there was the ongoing anxiety about St. Andrew's
Hospital. So many Sisters were ill during Holy Week that the Short Record
Book noted: "We had to omit Nocturnes—only four or five Sisters in
chapel on whom all the pressure fell." Mother Alice Ursula had been in
bed with a cold during the previous week, but on Wednesday in Holy Week
she got up but did too much and was ordered back to bed by the doctor.
But she took part in the Maundy Thursday Watch before the Blessed
Sacrament from 10.00 until 12.00. Several of the St. Anna's girls watched
all day in the Lady Chapel, and some watched all night. On Easter Day
1943 (April 25), Mother Alice Ursula collapsed at the second Mass but the
doctor said it was indigestion, not a heart attack as the Sisters had feared.
A note in the Community Record Book in Sr. Florence Teresa's writing
declared: "It probably *was heart.*" It was an anxious time but Mother got
up for the Warden's visit in Easter week, during which time he received
seven senior students from St. John Baptist School as Associates.

The doctor had recommended a time of rest and change for Mother
Alice Ursula and so on May 3, 1943, she left for San Antonio, TX, where
she had a happy visit with her sister, Anne. She then traveled on to St.
Helen's Hall, Portland, OR, arriving there on Monday, May 21. It was the
first time she had been back there since 1925 and she found the school
buildings much changed. On the Wednesday the boarders gave a special
tea in her honor and invited those alumnae who would have remembered
her. Next morning she went to Mass and breakfast but left the breakfast
table feeling unwell. She walked up two flights of stairs to her room and
said she had chest pains. The doctor was called but she died within 45
minutes of leaving the breakfast table.

Mother Alice Ursula's death was a great shock to the Sisters, but its
happening so far from Mendham compounded their grief. On that day
when she left the convent for her time of rest and recuperation, no one
thought they would never see her again. Her Community Biographer
wrote: "It was a time of great trauma in the Community … Her sudden

death was hard to accept." News reached Mendham by telegram at 1.45pm: "Mother passed away 9.30am today." There was no easy way of breaking the news. The bell was tolled and the Litany was said in the chapel and at St. John Baptist School. There was an irony in that Mother Alice Ursula, who as a 37-year-old Sister had risked her life to care for Spanish influenza victims at Portland in 1918, should return there 25 years later and die of a heart attack.[13]

The immediate question was, where should the burial take place? It had always been CSJB practice to bury Sisters where they died: thus in the UK, departed Sisters lie at rest in many places. Sr. Ellen Juliana, the Assistant Superior, consulted each Sister individually and the decision was reached by nineteen votes to four that the funeral and burial should be at Portland. She telegraphed the decision back to Sr. Waldine Lucia in Portland. Sr. Florence Teresa noted in the Short Record Book: "A terrible shock, great blow, and serious loss to the Community." So it was that Mother Alice Ursula, who had held office for just six months, was laid to rest in Riverview Cemetery, Portland, next to Sr. Katharine Angela. The burial took place on Friday May 28, 1943, following the requiem and burial offices celebrated by Bishop Dagwell, Fr. Ayres and Fr Simmonds.

Back at Mendham all the usual rites and ceremonies for the funeral of a Sister were held, except the burial. Although there was no coffin, the Holy Cross bier and the Community pall and requiem lights were used, the latter lit only during the services due to the blackout.

Among the many messages and letters of condolence, the Sisters especially appreciated the letter from Bishop Washburn, their Visitor, so much so that it is preserved in the Community Record Book. He wrote, "I know something of the sorrow which fills your hearts on the heavy tidings from Portland. Mother Alice Ursula seemed so full of life and hope and joy; it is hard to think of the Community without her radiant personality. We shall all miss her, though … we shall continue to have her prayers for us all as she lives in the nearer presence of Our Blessed Lord." A letter dated May 27, 1943, from the Warden, Dom Paul Severance, promised a requiem next day. Dom Paul was not in residence at Mendham, but at this time was living at Valparaiso, Indiana, where he was hoping to establish a Benedictine priory. He had been the Sisters' Warden only since September 1941. A letter dated May 28 came from Fr. Edward Schlueter, vicar of St. Luke's Chapel, NYC (1909–45), whom the Sisters had known since he was a boy. "I know of nothing that has shocked me as much as the word over the telephone last night about the Reverend Mother Alice Ursula. I feel that I know her better than most of the younger Sisters and she always seemed altogether well and ready for work. I know it must mean for you and the Sisters an almost staggering sorrow. I said a requiem this morning and shall continue to pray for the Sisters that God may do what He always does if we let Him, turn our sorrow into joy. Whenever God sends us an especially heavy cross, it means that He is preparing us for some special blessing."

Ascension Day 1943 was observed with an outdoor procession on the eve, as well as solemn Vespers and Benediction, and on the day itself a solemn Mass followed by a picnic lunch at St. John Baptist School. It was a very hot day with temperatures over 80°F. But uppermost in everyone's mind was the forthcoming election of the new Mother Superior. The Sisters were still grieving the loss of Mother Alice Ursula only a month previously. "Everyone is strained, under shock, sorrow and grave anxiety. [It is] the greatest crisis in the Community," wrote Sr. Florence Teresa in the Record Book.

Summer activities continued unabated. On June 11, St. Anna's and St. Marguerite's high school had their Commencement. There were three graduates, and Fr. Noble gave them their diplomas in chapel. Printed invitations had been sent out, but few people came, due to increased fuel restrictions. Next day, St. John Baptist School had its Commencement at St. Peter's, Morristown. As so often happened the guest speaker spoke for too long, but Bishop Washburn kept his speech short. Tributes were paid to the late Mother Alice Ursula and to Sr. Elisa Monica (Purdy), no longer Sister Superior. Lawson Purdy (Sr. Elisa Monica's brother) and Kenneth Strickland (Mother Alice Ursula's brother) were both present. The patronal festival, the Nativity of St. John Baptist, was deferred by the Warden for one day as Corpus Christi fell on June 24th, but next day all the usual festivities took place. There was Mass at 7.00am and again at 8.40am. At 3.00pm there was a tea party in the cloister and supper at 6.00 on the lawn. True to tradition they had ice cream and cookies for tea—made by Sr. Eudora. It was a very hot day with the temperature reaching 96°F.

On July 1, 1943, the nominations were sent out for the office of Mother Superior. Three Sisters were nominated—Sr. Waldine Lucia, Sr. Agnes Genevieve and Sr. Margaret Helena (Forney). Fr. Noble had been delegated by the Warden to take the Chapter of Election on July 22. Sr.

Waldine Lucia was elected and she left Oregon on a one way ticket on July 30. Her installation took place on August 10, 1943. Also on August 10, Sr. Margaret Helena had her blessing as Assistant Superior. Sr. Waldine Lucia had worked at St. Helen's Hall for over 30 years and had been Sister Superior since 1922. She was one of the three Sisters who had heroically nursed patients during the Spanish influenza epidemic in 1918.

There is a saying that "a new broom sweeps clean." Mother Waldine Lucia was that new broom. Although she had returned to Mendham at intervals for Community Chapter meetings, she had not lived in the convent for many years. Upon her return she could see exactly what needed to be swept away in order for the Sisters, many of whom were elderly and in poor health, to have time to really *live* the Religious Life and to enable themselves to concentrate on work that was viable. In time, they might even be able to undertake new work, more appropriate for modern times—a Second Spring. But that still lay a few years ahead.

Sr. Mildred Eleanor (Blodgett) succeeded Sr. Waldine Lucia as Sister in Charge at St. Helen's Hall, and it fell to her to break the news to the Rt. Revd. Benjamin Dagwell, Bishop of Oregon, that due to the shortage of Sisters in the East it would be necessary for the Community to withdraw from St. Helen's Hall in June 1944. The bishop was greatly distressed and would do his utmost over the next few months to dissuade the Sisters, but he would be unsuccessful. Ironically, St. Helen's Hall was the Community work that was the most successful at that time. If it had been situated in the East it might not have been necessary to withdraw, but it was almost 3,000 miles from Mendham.[14] Also, there were five Sisters still in Oregon and they were sorely needed at Mendham. Mother Waldine Lucia noted in the Community Record Book that "the Hall has to be sacrificed for the works and for the lives of the Sisters." St. John Baptist School was full but only had three Sisters, though there were secular teachers; and St. Marguerite's needed another Sister.

Nearer home, the first work that Mother Waldine Lucia swept away was St. Anna's Home. The Sisters had tried valiantly to modernize their methods by creating the high school at St. Anna's, but by late 1943 this clearly was not working. In the early years many of the girls had been sent by the Probation service as an alternative to detention for offences such as petty thieving. In more recent years girls had been sent to the Sisters by the social services. But in some cases, where several girls of varying ages came from one family because they were orphaned or had no one to care for them, the younger ones would go to St. Marguerite's and the older ones to St. Anna's.

By the early 1940s, the social workers were sending some really difficult girls to St. Anna's who were having a bad influence on others. Some were running away and when this happened the police had to be called out. Now, as Mother Waldine Lucia wrote in the record book, "[The police say] we are taking too wild a girl for our set up. [There is] some truth, I fear in their complaint." The social workers were no help to the Sisters after the girls had been placed. The facilities at St. Anna's were overcrowded and should have been housed in a separate building to comply with modern standards, but there was no funding for it. Furthermore, the girls' quarters were fairly near those of the Sisters,[15] and violent, disruptive behavior was very unsettling for those who were elderly or infirm. Mother Waldine Lucia told the Consultative Council on September 30, that "we have to close either St. Anna's or St. Marguerite's … We have not the trained Sisters for that type of work as it has to be run today." The Council decided that St. Anna's should close and a few days later Mother Waldine Lucia told the Sisters at Conference—many seemed relieved.

Bishop Washburn made a last ditch attempt in mid-October to salvage St. Anna's by offering $30–40,000 to build new quarters. Mother Waldine Lucia turned it down on the grounds that even such a large sum would be inadequate to build and equip premises that would meet modern-day standards. But her main reason was lack of Sisters able to undertake such demanding work. So it was that after 30 years, St. Anna's closed. The last girl had been admitted on September 13, 1943, at age 13. She went to a children's home in New Brunswick, NJ. Others returned to the social workers for new placements or to their families. During the three decades of its existence, St. Anna's had provided a fresh start for many girls and young women. It had been an important Community work and the number of former residents who kept in touch with the Sisters is a lasting testimony to its value.[16] But Mother Waldine Lucia had the wisdom to know when the time had come to withdraw, and although it was a sad decision, it was also liberating for the Sisters. The good news was that St. Marguerite's was able to remain open for a few more years even though the finances were far from healthy.

War conditions continued to bite. The coal shortage had now become serious and heating the large convent building was a problem. The decision was made to close the chapel for the winter and to move upstairs and use the library as a chapel. This made life easier for the older, infirm Sisters. A small organ brought from Oregon was to be used there.

Sr. Eudora had been in America for two-and-a-half years and was anxious to go home to Clewer. But there was still great danger from U-boats. Eventually she secured permission to make the journey, having been called out of Compline to take a phone call from the British Consulate in New York. Everything moved rapidly with hardly time to say goodbye to the Sisters—the phone call had come on Friday and she sailed on Sunday. The ship sailed to Halifax, Nova Scotia, and from there joined a convoy of 83 ships. "Destroyers and Frigates on all sides gave us a great feeling of security. It was only when they dashed up close that we got to know when we were in danger."[17] One night they found themselves alone, the rest of the convoy "having melted away in the night." She recalled her worst moment was standing by the lifeboat station for hours not knowing whether the noise they could hear meant they were being attacked or were attacking. The voyage took three weeks and they finally landed in Scotland. Arriving in London she found an air raid in progress. Having left England for India in peacetime, this was a new and frightening experience. Finally she arrived safely at Clewer, and later brought her memoirs to an end with the words "here ends my first ten years."

As the year turned into 1944 it brought the usual bad weather, illnesses and wartime difficulties, but nothing out of the ordinary. A letter from Bishop Dagwell implored the Sisters to reconsider their decision to leave St. Helen's Hall, but his request had to be refused. Everything he said about the importance of the work and the impact the Sisters had made was true, which made it all the more difficult for Mother Waldine Lucia to stand firm. But stand firm she did, though with a heavy heart.

Nearer to home, there were financial worries regarding St. John Baptist School, where the mortgage still stood at over $53,000. Sr. Elisa Monica's fundraising days were over by now, due to her frail health, but she still took an active part in Community life when she was able. On Maundy Thursday evening she took her usual hour of the Watch from 7.00–8.00 and came to Mass, but after returning to the school she was taken ill. The doctor was called and she was taken by ambulance to All Souls' hospital with suspected pneumonia, but she made a good recovery. There were now two car drivers in the Community—Sr. Jane Patricia who was a driver before coming into Community, and Sr. Margaret Helena, who had passed her driver's test recently, at the first attempt. This made hospital visits easier as the Sisters did not have to rely on outside help.

In June 1944 Mother Waldine Lucia left for Oregon for the final winding up of the Community's work there. On June 24, the Nativity of St. John Baptist, Fr. Ayres celebrated Mass in the chapel at St. Helen's Hall—"our last one." The Sisters were given many farewell gifts of flowers and candy. After a few days' break, Mother and Sr. Agatha Louise left Portland on July 6 for the last time, arriving back at Mendham on July 11. Sr. Agatha Louise (Weiss) had worked at St. Helen's Hall as a novice from 1925–26, and after her profession from 1928–44. Sr. Elizabeth Marion (Case) had left to travel east on June 1, having served from 1930–31 as a novice and after profession from 1933–44. Sr. Margaret Helena had returned in 1943, and Sr. Eleanor Lucy (Cowan), who had served as a novice from 1935–36, and after her profession from 1938–44, also returned east. Sr. Mildred Eleanor had served from 1929–44 and succeeded Sr. Waldine Lucia as Superior at the Hall. She remained there for a few more weeks to manage the final business of withdrawal and arrived back at Mendham on July 30, 1944. "That wonderful chapter in our history now closed" was Mother Waldine Lucia's final sad word in the Record Book.[18]

While the work in Oregon was finally ending there had been a great development regarding the war. On June 6, Allied troops had landed on the Normandy beaches. "D Day—Very exciting, and much news on radio" was how it was reported in the Community Record Book. This marked a turning point in the war in Europe as five Allied beach-heads were established. Two of those five—Utah and Omaha—were stormed by US forces who sustained heavy losses. But from now on the tide had turned and there was hope that the war would soon end.

There were developments at the various Community works at Mendham, the most radical one being the proposal to send the girls from St. Marguerite's to the local public school. This had worked well for the boys from a local home and it was thought it would give the girls a wider education and also help them to interact with other children. There was also a financial consideration in that the Sisters could no longer afford to pay the wages of the number of secular teachers required at St. Marguerite's. The Consultative Council agreed to this change in policy. However, the County Superintendent questioned the right of the children to attend the public school. It all depended on whether or not the work was a charitable institution. Even so, the children had their first day at the public school and came back very happy. All's well that ends well—in November 1944 the ruling came through that St. Marguerite's was a charitable institution and that it would be permissible to send the girls to the local public school.

In September 1944 Mother Waldine Lucia received a letter from Mother Dorothy Frances at Clewer, asking her to come over to discuss Community matters. But to cross the Atlantic was still dangerous even though D Day had turned the tide of the war. And there was the expense which could hardly be spared because there were so many other calls on the Community funding. For instance, the property at the foot of the hill that had once served as St. Anna's summer rest house, and had later housed St. John Baptist School, was now in bad repair. The Sisters wanted to sell it and eventually did so. St. Marguerite's also had ongoing problems with the lack of secular helpers, and the building was also becoming in great need of repairs.

On October 13, Mother Waldine Lucia had an appointment with Mr. Strickland (brother of the late Mother Alice Ursula) about the finances and in particular St. John the Baptist Foundation. He reported that they "were in bad shape" and that they "ought not to keep those very old New York houses." And Mother noted: "I agree with him." St. Andrew's Hospital was in such a bad state of repair that it was fast becoming untenable. Also, there were no maids to help with the work there and no man to stoke the boiler, so the house had been closed for two months. It was estimated that $25,000 would be needed to put the building in good order. Mother Waldine Lucia also noted that Mr. Strickland was helping over the Incorporation in New Jersey—"a very important thing for us to do—we ought to have done it years ago. In order to be exempted from taxes the NJ law requires all institutions or business to be Incorporated in NJ. Had a two hours talk with [him]." In the midst of all these difficulties it was impossible for Mother Waldine Lucia to even contemplate a visit to Clewer. But this request from Mother Dorothy Frances (Mother General) was just the tip of an iceberg that would loom very large in the second half of the decade.

Meanwhile the Sisters continued to keep the feasts and fasts of the Church year, even when many were too poorly to get to chapel. Nothing was omitted and despite the strictures of wartime there was still much to celebrate. The Sisters' retreats often hosted members of other Communities and this was a good means of sharing in prayer and in the common calling to the Religious Life. And those Sisters who were able went out and about to spread the word about Community life. Sr. Margaret Helena in particular made this a part of her ministry by going to churches in the vicinity of Mendham to talk about the Religious Life. It opened the eyes of many people who previously knew nothing about it. And her winning personality was amply suited to attract interest and answer people's questions.

Mother Waldine Lucia had initiated several changes since her installation on August 10, 1943. It had not been an easy time for her or for the Community, but her powers of discernment had shown her what needed to be done and she had shown great courage by standing firm and doing what was required. As 1944 gave way to 1945 there would be more changes. And in particular, the relationship with Clewer would require much tact and diplomacy. Old work would continue to close, much to the distress of some Sisters, but gradually the first tentative shoots of new work would appear. It would mark the beginning of the Community's "Second Spring."

---

[1] The Rt. Revd. Benjamin Washburn was Bishop of the Episcopal Diocese of Newark, NJ, 1935–58.

[2] The criterion at Clewer had been education. Choir Sisters had a complicated Daily Office, most of which was sung, and many lay Sisters would not have had the educational ability to cope with this. Also the lay Sisters lived by a simpler Rule and wore a much simpler habit. They did much more manual work than the choir Sisters. In the early years at Clewer many of the choir Sisters had been titled ladies in secular life, whereas many of the lay Sisters had previously been in domestic service. To a 21st-century reader this may sound very "class-ridden," but so was Victorian England, where keeping one's "place in life" was important.

[3] At this time, novices in the American affiliation had to spend a year in the novitiate at Clewer.

[4] See the photograph on page 203 of BONHAM, Valerie *Living Stones*. Some of the internal corridors and passages leading to the chapel were never plastered and remain so today.

[5] These were Sr. Elisa Mary, who left in 1942, and Sr. Hilda Mary, who left in 1944, neither of whom should have been professed, but perhaps if temporary vows had been in place, their lack of vocation would have been detected earlier.

[6] The longest was Sr. Elisa Monica, professed in 1886.

[7] In 1926 the Community was invited to work in Barbados and they accepted. It was in fact

a huge mistake because numbers of Sisters were decreasing at an alarming rate, with older Sisters dying and fewer new vocations. The only way in which the Barbados work could be sustained was to take Sisters away from India. In 1921 there were 199 professed choir Sisters at Clewer including those in India, but by 1939 the number had fallen to 123, i.e. 83 less than in 1921. The question of falling numbers of vocations at Clewer did not seem to be addressed, and there was a sense of denial about it.

[8] The Short Record Book states that "a Reliquary receptacle" was made in the high altar to house Fr. Baker's gift. It was placed there on October 8 by Fr. Mayo, OHC. Also at this time the Short Record Book notes that the monstrance lent or given by Mother Mary Angela to Fr. Wallis, Rector of St. Paul's, Staten Island, was to be given back to the St. John the Baptist Foundation, as it was bought with money given by the Holy Cross congregation. The foundation then asked permission to give it to the Community to be used at the convent or to be lent to the School.

[9] Dom Paul Severance, OSB, was born in Willsboro, New York, in 1892. He was ordained priest in 1921 and served as Assistant Priest at St. Mary the Virgin, NYC, before going to the Philippines until 1925 when he returned to the US and was Assistant Priest at St. Clement's, Philadelphia. From 1926–34 he was Professor of Apologetics at the Anglo-Catholic seminary, Nashotah House, Wisconsin. In 1935 he returned to St. Clement's but along with a like-minded group of clergy wrote to the Abbot of the Benedictine Community at Nashdom, near Burnham, UK, asking if someone would come over to the US to train them for the monastic life. The abbot, Dom Martin Collett, invited the group to England in order to enter the Nashdom novitiate. The six priests arrived at Nashdom and Fr. Severance was clothed in 1936, making his first vows in 1937. The threat of war led him to return to America to establish the Benedictine life there and eventually he was joined by three of the brethren and they opened St. Gregory's Priory, Valparaiso, IN. In 1941 he made his life profession along with Dom Francis Hilary Bacon. But at Valparaiso they had looked after three missions and this impinged on their Religious Life, and so in March 1946 they moved to Three Rivers, MI, where Dom Paul became the Prior. In November 1946 he had a cerebral hemorrhage and never fully recovered. Meanwhile, in 1947, Dom Augustine Morris had been elected Abbot of Nashdom and in 1949 he visited St. Gregory's. Upon his return to England he took Dom Paul with him, where he was cared for at Nashdom. He died peacefully on November 2, 1949, and was buried in the monastic cemetery at Nashdom.

Nashdom Abbey had a reputation as the most extreme Anglo-Catholic religious order for men in the Church of England. Until the late 1960s the Divine Office was sung in Latin and the Conventual Mass was also in Latin and followed the Roman rite. All Masses celebrated by individual monks were also in Latin and according to the Roman rite. It was only after the vernacular was adopted after Vatican II that vocations began to dwindle, as Nashdom lost its individuality and became like many other men's Communities. The ultra-Romanism of Nashdom was well known throughout the Anglican Communion and for this reason Bishop Washburn was initially unhappy at the Sisters' choice of Dom Paul as their Warden.

Sources: *Singing God's Praises: the first sixty years*. St. Gregory's Abbey 1998. Also, *The Jubilee Book of the Benedictines of Nashdom 1914–64*. Faith Press 1964. And my own personal knowledge of Nashdom from the mid-1960s onwards.

[10] Sr. Eudora Memoirs—*From Barbados to USA and Home to Clewer*.

[11] Most of the framed illuminated manuscripts on display in the front hall of the convent at Mendham were the work of Sr. Olive Frances. She also painted the angels which decorate the tabernacle on the high altar in the main chapel.

[12] In June 2016 I visited the Morgan Library accompanied by Sr. Suzanne Elizabeth and Sr. Mary Lynne, where we saw many MSS inscribed by her.

[13] For details of her heroism in 1918 see BONHAM, Valerie *Living Stones* Chapter 16.

[14] There will be more about St. Helen's Hall in Chapter 4, "From out west to down south."

[15] St. Anna's quarters were where the guest wing at the convent is today.

[16] For an account of St. Anna's see BONHAM, Valerie *Living Stones* Chapter 14 "Redeeming the past."

[17] Sr. Eudora Memoirs op. cit.

[18] It was the ending of a chapter, but not the end of all contact. Sr. (later Mother) Margaret Helena had family in the west and visited them every year. She also visited St. Helen's Hall every year until she was in her nineties.

WITH NO LACK OF LOVE
The Community 1945–49

NINETEEN FORTY-FIVE opened in the usual way—Board meetings which caused financial concern, bad weather which made getting out and about difficult, and growing anxiety about the health of older Sisters, especially Sr. Elisa Monica (Purdy) who was once again in hospital.[1] Others included Sr. Catherine Vera (Jones) and Sr. Lillian Christine (Naser), who were both frequently confined to hospital. The question of transferring the Incorporation to New Jersey rather than New York was ongoing.

In 1933–34 and again in 1939 the Chapter at Clewer had revised the Constitution and there had been some tension because the Sisters at Mendham had not been fully consulted,[2] and had only one vote in the Clewer Chapter. This was to be cast by the American Mother Superior on behalf of her Sisters. Further revisions were begun in 1945 and Mother General Dorothy Frances was very anxious that Mother Waldine Lucia should travel to Clewer. However, the war had made such a journey impossible, as well as the expense involved. The point was made by Sr. Florence Teresa (Hoopes), whose long memory went back to the early years, that Mother Frances Constance (Paine) only went to the first Chapter at Clewer after the Community had been established in America. Even so, Mother Waldine Lucia, Sr. Margaret Helena (Forney) and Sr. Mildred Eleanor (Blodgett) set to work on the revision of the Constitutions.

The Rule had not been revised since 1907 and much had changed since that time, and so early in 1945, the Chapter at Clewer set about revising the Rule in addition to the Constitution. There were several major issues which were not relevant to the Community at Mendham: for instance, the incorporation of lay Sisters into choir. This had already been addressed at Mendham in 1940 with the incorporation of the three remaining mission Sisters into choir. And then at Clewer, a Third Order, to be known as the Society of St. John the Forerunner, was to replace the Magdalens. The Sisters would have their own Rule, distinctive habit, and bronze Cross, and the old chapel would be designated for their use as the Chapel of the Forerunner.

But there was one issue in particular that did affect the Community at Mendham—temporary vows for possibly three years before life profession. At Clewer the suggestion of temporary vows was accepted, but not at Mendham. Sisters on both sides of the Atlantic were surprised if not shocked to discover that their Warden Founder, Canon Carter, had written to the Chapter at Clewer in 1891 advocating a renewal of the promises made at profession after five years, and suggesting that only then might Sisters be allowed a vote in Chapter, instead of after two years.

There was good news at St. John Baptist School, where the evaluators had given it a good report. They spoke well of Sr. Eleanor Lucy's (Cowan) work plan and schedule, but said the domestic science course was too elementary.

And the Sisters had a good report too! The Warden (Dom Paul Severance, OSB) had made a visit and said in his address that he saw real progress in the Community, with mutual co-operation and much pulling together, even though some older Sisters were finding change difficult. This was encouraging at a time when the Community needed real affirmation.

April 9, 1945, saw a great service at the Cathedral of St. John the Divine, NYC, to commemorate the centennial of the restoration of the Religious Life in the Anglican Church. Nearly all the Religious Communities were represented and nineteen CSJB Sisters were present.

When the Sisters were in Oregon they had the benefit of a holiday cottage at Seaside, given to them by Catherine Percival. Now the work was over, they no longer needed it, so they proposed selling it and using the proceeds to buy a house at Manasquan, NJ. This was approved by the Board of Directors on April 23, 1945. The Sisters took possession of the house on June 22, and named it St. Alban's, as it was that saint's feast day. It was a real help to the Sisters, especially those who did not have families to visit for their rests.

But things were not so good at St. Marguerite's home, where there had been an inspection of the building by some social workers. The building was in bad shape and they wondered how it could have got into such a condition. Work needed to be done to the floors and walls and the toilets needed upgrading. In June, the St. John the Baptist Foundation decided to use the funds from the sale of the property at the foot of the hill to make the repairs to St. Marguerite's. The house had at last been sold a month previously. Some older girls had recently been sent to St. Marguerite's by the social workers, and early in May two of them ran away during a tea party, which ruined the fun for the younger girls. When they returned soon afterwards, Mother Waldine Lucia sent for the social workers and told them very firmly that those particular girls should not have been placed with them. The girls were taken back and sent elsewhere.

From time to time the Sisters would be offered new work and usually had to refuse it. One such offer came in May 1944 for the Sisters to run a children's home at Taft, California. This was a town with a population of 3,200 situated in an oil and gas producing area, and with a desert climate. The Sisters had quite rightly turned it down. But in July 1945 there came the offer of work in St. John's parochial school in Corsicana, TX, 60 miles south of Dallas. Mother Waldine Lucia, who was a Texan, was clearly excited at the prospect of this new challenge. She brought the subject to the Consultative Council, who were in favor and asked her to visit Corsicana. "I shall take two Sisters with me—Sr. Mildred Eleanor and Sr. Agatha Louise (Weiss)," she noted in the Community Record Book. At a Chapter meeting on July 30, a vote was taken and out of 30 Sisters present, 25 voted in favor and only two against; presumably the other three votes were either spoiled papers or abstentions.

The next step was to consult the Visitor, Bishop Washburn, who presumably raised no objection, because the three Sisters drove to Corsicana on August 12, 1944, spending ten days there. Mother Waldine Lucia and her companions met several priests from Dallas, and she gave an address there about the Religious Life. Clearly this was a much-needed affirmation for the Community after all the financial anxiety and problems relating to their older work. Mother wrote enthusiastically in the Community Record Book, "The priests want us in Dallas, a way may be opened for us there later on as aspirants come." This might have been over-optimistic, but the prospect of brave new work was greatly needed. Although this particular new opportunity did not last many years, it proved to the Sisters that despite all the difficulties with the older work, they were still able to face and accept new challenges. This was the first tentative sign of the Second Spring of the Community.[3]

Also, the war finally came to an end. On May 8, 1945, the war in Europe had ended, but in the Far East it continued until August, and many US troops were still fighting. Now, with the Japanese surrender, all hostilities ceased. Having won the war, the Allied heads of state now had to win the peace.

Back at the convent, Sr. Florence Teresa had resigned as Novice Mistress, having become blind, and Sr. Elizabeth Marion (Case) had been appointed in her place. People continued to be inspired by the Sisters and all that they stood for, and hopes were being raised by the admission of a postulant. In July 1945 the Sisters had received a surprise visit from Fr. Paul Wessinger, SSJE.[4] Fr. Paul had recently made his life profession in the Society of St. John the Evangelist. He told the Sisters that he had found his Religious vocation through seeing the Sisters at St. Stephen's parish church, Portland, Oregon, and he had frequently called on them as a young student.

Meanwhile as the year drew to a close, there were the usual concerns about St. Andrew's Hospital, which was only taking a few patients because the elevator needed expensive repair work. And there were the continuing problems relating to the constitutional revisions being made at Clewer. Elevators can be fixed, but the widening gap between Mendham and Clewer was ongoing and it seemed there would be no quick fix. A Committee of six Sisters was formed at Mendham to discuss the proposed changes to the Rule and Constitution, of most of which they were not in favor. The snow and ice and violent storms that saw the old year out seemed to symbolize the increasing chill with the UK Mother House. And yet, this was not how either part of CSJB wanted it to be, and so in January 1946 Mother Waldine Lucia agreed to visit Clewer.

There were some bright spots as 1946 arrived. Although St. Andrew's summer rest house at Woodcliff Lake closed, the altar was brought to Mendham. (When the convent was renovated in 1960 it was placed in the new upstairs chapel dedicated to St. Michael.)[5] On February 5, the anniversary of the first Sisters' arrival in New York, there was a novice clothing in the main chapel. Mother Waldine Lucia commented that it was "a bright, lovely day, service went beautifully." Fr. Hall and Fr. Noble were present and the Warden presided. There were a number of guests including the mother of the new novice, Sr. Frances Agatha, who "seems very happy—I hope she proves to have a good, true vocation," wrote Mother.[6] Girls from the school and seven older girls from St. Marguerite's were there and Mother noted that the "singing of the girls was lovely." Later in the year two more postulants would be received.

Nineteen-and-a-quarter acres of the Farmingdale property had been sold for a good sum and the money had gone to the Foundation. The Board of Directors was trying to get the rest of the property tax exempted. As noted above, the house at the bottom of the hill at Mendham had at last been sold for $6,000, and the money was designated for restoring St. Marguerite's, though nothing had been done yet due to the difficulty of getting estimates from builders, plus the number of strikes and unsettled labor conditions.

The only way Mother Waldine Lucia could be assured of a return date from England was to fly both ways, but it was expensive. The cost was the equivalent of two ocean trips in 1934, which was the last time anyone had traveled from Mendham to Clewer in peacetime. But if the Affiliation with Clewer was to be saved then it was necessary to make the visit.

There were good reasons, quite apart from the wartime constraints, why communication had broken down to such an extent. Although Mother Dorothy Frances had been in the Community since 1911 (professed in 1913), she had been in India from 1931–39 (as Sister Superior 1931–37, and Mother Provincial from 1938–39). She was called back to Clewer when she was elected Mother General in 1939 and would remain in office until 1958. During the crucial years when the Clewer Chapter had begun revising the Constitutions, Sr. Dorothy Frances was absent in India. She therefore had no contact with the American Affiliation, and did not understand America and the difficulties following the Wall Street crash and the Great Depression, followed by the War and the difficulty in trans-Atlantic travel. Mother Waldine Lucia had been in Oregon for most of *her* Community life, and so with one in India and the other in the far west of America, the two future Mothers Superior were geographically as far apart as CSJB work allowed.

As part of her preparation for her visit to Clewer, Mother Waldine Lucia held an informal discussion with the Sisters about the issues involved, in particular about asking to become a Congregation rather than an Affiliated House. Such status would give more freedom. But there were other issues, too, such as changes to the habit and the ongoing question of temporary vows. There was much concern that temporary vows might undermine the importance of final vows, or that it would make for lack of stability. The consensus of opinion was against temporary vows. By the time of Mother Waldine Lucia's visit to England the Clewer Chapter was already discussing the motion "to consider for the first time and vote upon the resolution that the American Affiliation be constituted a

Congregation." This made it all the more important for the visit to Clewer to take place as soon as possible. And so on June 25, 1946, Mother Waldine Lucia, accompanied by Sr. Margaret Helena, flew to England. Sr. Elisabeth Roberta (Gernand) was appointed Assistant Superior for the time of Sr. Margaret Helena's absence.

They were met at Windsor by Mother Dorothy Frances and Sr. Eudora and stayed for what Mother Waldine Lucia described as a very difficult four weeks. The Community at Clewer was in bad shape—"war worn" was how Mother Waldine Lucia described it. There was still extensive food rationing and their visits to St. Stephen's College and other Community branch houses gave them a shock. "All on *very* old fashioned lines—heads all old … Clewer now has only one novice and a junior professed." (As noted in the previous chapter, by 1946 there were just over 100 choir Sisters at Clewer, whereas just before World War I there had been just over 200. The optimum years at Mendham had been 1917/18 with 45 Sisters including novices). Also, the Indian work had come to an end. It was always the intention to hand the work over to Indian Christians when the country gained independence from Britain, and the last two Sisters (Sr. Georgina and Sr. Lilian Mary) had arrived back in England in April 1946. But the withdrawal from such prestigious work was a bereavement for those who had known and loved it. It was not good for morale at Clewer. In addition, the decision had been made to withdraw from Barbados as from November 1946. All this weighed very heavily on the Sisters at Clewer. From being the largest and fastest growing Anglican Community, they had reached a point where the future was not looking good. All these factors had a bearing on life at the English Mother House, and Mother Waldine Lucia and Sr. Margaret Helena found the reality of life at Clewer depressing.

On August 6, 1946, they left for their return journey, which they had managed to convert to a sea passage. A cheerful letter from Sr. Eudora, written on August 5, accompanied them. "I trust you are well over any pangs of sea sickness. Soon you will be hailing the skyline of New York. Don't forget England. Our love and prayers follow you—we shall miss you." Conditions on board ship were dreadful, not at all what Sr. Eudora had envisaged for them, and they were glad to finally reach New York on August 13. But they had much food for thought. "Clewer has gone down greatly" was the remark in the Record Book, and the sense of grief is tangible. But at a personal level their visit had done much to boost the morale of the Clewer Sisters, as letters to Mother Waldine Lucia testify. For instance, Sr. Anna Patience, who was based at St. Basil's Home, Oxford (a home for elderly ladies), wrote to Mother Waldine Lucia shortly before she returned to Mendham with Sr. Margaret Helena: "Your visit, I'm sure has meant much to us all, a real strength and happiness; drawing us all so much closer together … It is wonderful how God has raised you both up to help us through these difficult days."

On September 13, 1946, Mother Waldine Lucia went to All Souls' Hospital, where Sr. Elisa Monica was dying. Fr. Noble was sent for but Sr. Elisa Monica had already passed to her rest in the early hours of Holy Cross Day—Mother and Sr. Margaret Helena were with her. It was an appropriate day, as she had been at the consecration of Holy Cross Church, NYC, on September 14, 1885. She was 90 years old at the time of her death and had known the Community since their first arrival in New York in 1874 when she was eighteen years old. Her body was taken back to the convent and the requiem and burial offices were said. Mr. Cordingley, faithful as ever, together with a workman, got the cemetery in good order, and George Thompson dug the grave. Three hymns were sung at the graveside on what was a very warm day. There were many flowers—and tributes.[7]

Lawson Purdy, her brother, wrote to Sr. Agnes Genevieve in Corsicana: "Thank you for your kind and understanding letter. Sister said goodbye to me on August 30. She said, 'I have lived ninety years and have had a very interesting life.' My wife and I were privileged to attend the Requiem, the service for the Sisters and the Committal. The sun was shining, the air was soft and sweet and the spiritual atmosphere was serene. I think Sister was there and was satisfied."[8]

A letter dated September 19, 1946, came from Sr. Margaret at Clewer. "Dearest Mother Waldine Lucia, We had the Requiem for Sister Elisa Monica this morning … I think I am the only one left here who knew her. We were in the novitiate together so had opportunities of seeing each other. I remember one little incident which we shared which always amuses me. At the Conference after tea one Sunday (do you remember the Sunday tea Conference in the old days?) Sister Jane Frances, who was Mother then, said in her majestic manner that she wished to speak to both of us. When we arrived at Mother's door to wait for her, Sr. E. Monica whispered to me, 'What have you been doing?' I could only say I did not know! But it had not struck me that we had been in some mischief together for which Mother wished to speak to us, and which we should certainly have heard about from Sr. Elizabeth! [the Novice Mistress at Clewer]. However, Mother only wanted me for some message and I do not know what Sr. E.M. was wanted for. I expect only a friendly talk with Mother!"[9]

Access to the convent at Mendham had always been difficult and by September 1946 urgent work needed to be carried out. It would cost at least $2,000 to patch the road up and so the decision was made to build a new straight road from the convent to the school. It would cost $4,500 but would be easier and less expensive to maintain. Work began on October 15, 1946, and the school also had their road patched up and resurfaced.

November 5, 1946, saw the re-election of Sr. Waldine Lucia as Superior. She had just returned from a visit to Corsicana, where she found all well with 58 pupils in St. John's School. The Community Warden, Fr Paul Severance, OSB, was taken ill with a brain hemorrhage on the way to the convent for Mother's election and was taken to St. Luke's Hospital, NYC. His duties as Warden were delegated to Fr. Noble as Acting Warden until further notice. Next day, November 6, Sr. Waldine Lucia was installed as Mother Superior. Also, Sr. Margaret Helena had her blessing as Assistant Superior, Sr. Elizabeth Marion as Novice Mistress, Sr. Mildred Eleanor as Sister Superior at St. Andrew's Hospital and Sr. Mary Barbara as Sister Superior at St. John Baptist School, Mendham.

St. Marguerite's, the former orphanage, later a home school, had closed in October 1946. In its time it had been a great work and many young lives had been given a secure and loving home life and education. But times were changing and the tide of opinion was turning against "institutional" work of this type. Social workers were favoring sending individual children out to foster care, or to specialized homes which the Sisters were not qualified to run. Even some of the clergy were now saying the Sisters' methods were outdated and they should withdraw. So it was that after nearly 40 years of caring, the Sisters had to close St. Marguerite's. At the same time as the withdrawal, the Sisters were able to make a start on the long catalog of repairs there. The St. John the Baptist Foundation had given $10,000 for immediate repairs to the roof and a new oil furnace. That was good news, and it enabled the Sisters to use St. Marguerite's as a guest house for women and girls who needed a quiet time of rest or retreat.

Christmas in the chapel was cold and icy, and outside there was deep snow. But all went well with the festival despite some Sisters being ill, and news that the Warden, Fr. Severance, would never be well again. Illness spread through the Community like wildfire in the first few days of January 1947 and it lasted most of the month.

In England the country was in the grip of one of the coldest winters on record. Sr. Eudora wrote from Clewer to Mother Waldine Lucia on February 7, 1947: "We trust that you are warmer than we are. Our electricity and coal situations have never been so desperate … I cannot imagine anything icier than this convent." Food rationing was still in force and Sr. Eudora, who was kitchen Sister at the time, was finding it very difficult to make ends meet. Mindful of this situation, the Sisters at Mendham regularly sent food parcels, and indeed had done so throughout the War, though many had been lost in transit. In the same letter Sr. Eudora wrote: "What a wonderful act of Providence that your generous and lovely parcels—three of them—came. Every single article was appreciated and made the most of but particularly did I say a heartfelt thank you for the 6lbs of cheese, providing as it did three glorious breakfasts rich in Vitamin A! … I cannot tell you how grateful we are for the extra food in this bitter weather. The Sisters were able to have a whole slab of Baker's chocolate, and didn't they enjoy it. For several days Sisters kept popping in to [ask me] to thank our American Mother for the lovely parcels." Despite the difficulties over the revision of the Rule and Constitution, there was a great depth of friendship at a personal level between the two parts of the Community.

In the midst of all the winter conditions, a bishop from the Philippines offered the Mendham Sisters work there. They had to refuse it, but regretfully. "Wish we could take it, that is what this Community needs," wrote Mother Waldine Lucia in the Community Record Book. But distance and the lack of younger Sisters prevented them from accepting the challenge. On February 24, 1947, the two postulants were received as novices—Sr. Ora Mary and Sr. Ellen Elisabeth.

A letter from Dom Francis Hilary Bacon, OSB, informed the Sisters that the Warden would be unable to fulfill any further duties and therefore must resign. The search for his successor now began in earnest. And soon after Easter a former Warden died—Fr. Warren K. Damuth was described in the Community Record Book as "a good, holy Warden." A requiem was offered for him on April 19, 1947.

St. Andrew's Hospital, NYC, had to be temporarily closed to enable work to be done on the building. The combination of workmen, Sisters, patients, dust, and the smell of paint did not mix well. Fr. Shirley Carter Hughson, OHC, whom the Sisters had known and trusted for many years, strongly recommended that the Sisters should give up smaller works such as St. Andrew's. In his view, institutional work could now be far more effectively and efficiently run by seculars because State and Federal funds were available. He felt that such work was too expensive for the Sisters to run, and was "a waste of Sisters."

Meanwhile the search for a new Warden continued. The Sisters took advice from the many priests who knew them and celebrated the Eucharist with them. But it was their old friend Fr. Edward Schlueter who solved the problem. He recommended Fr. Paul Weed, who was also highly recommended by Fr. Hughson, OHC, who said that he would infinitely prefer to see Fr. Weed as Warden of the Community. "Very high praise," commented Mother Waldine Lucia in the Community Record Book. Mother duly visited Fr. Weed and asked him to consider becoming their Warden. He spoke very highly of the Religious Life. In June he led the Sisters' retreat and on July 12, 1947, was unanimously elected as Warden.

Fr. Weed was installed on September 4, 1947, the start of a long ministry with the Sisters, lasting 30 years. At the time of his election he was 40 years old. Mother Waldine Lucia commented that "the Mass was most beautifully sung." There were fourteen priests and the bishop in the sanctuary, and all the Sisters were present including those from Texas. After the guests had left, Sr. Mildred Eleanor had her blessing as Sister Superior of the work at Corsicana, TX, in succession to Sr. Agatha Louise. Then she left for Texas with Sr. Eleanor Lucy and Sr. Katharine Veronica. Several Sisters left for various destinations after the service, including Sr. Margaret Helena, who set out for Oregon to visit her family. She arrived home at the convent on October 2, after a traumatic journey in which the train she was traveling on was wrecked in an accident. Two people were killed on her train (the engineer and fireman), but more were killed on the other train. She was not badly injured.

The situation with Clewer continued to be ongoing. Earlier in the year the Chapter at Mendham had taken just twenty minutes to vote in favor of petitioning the General Chapter at Clewer for the status of a Congregation.[10] Mother General Dorothy Frances had replied favorably saying that once the new Warden was installed, the Mendham Chapter would be able to begin work on the Constitution "and definitely settle that we are only to be bound together by the Rule if you accept it." Fr. Weed took the view that the Customary and Constitution could be changed without changing the Rule, and wrote to Mother General.

Offers of new work continued to be made. At the Chapter on July 12, the Sisters had voted in favor of working one day a week in the parish of St. Uriel the Archangel, Sea Girt, NJ, not far from the Sisters' rest house at Manasquan.[11] The work began in the church school on October 15, 1947, with 40 children—only 25 had been expected but it was thought that some would drop out. Sr. Margaret Helena and Sr. Ellen Elisabeth were in charge of the work, and drove down each time. Also in October, Canon Leslie of Newark asked whether the Sisters could help in Christ Church parish. This was a very poor, but flourishing, parish in East Newark. "It is the type of work the Sisters need," wrote Mother Waldine Lucia in the Community Record Book. On December 11, the Chapter decided in favor of the work at Newark. Mother Waldine Lucia thought the work would be "a good experience, for few Sisters have done parish or mission work."

There seemed to be a breakthrough at the end of 1947 regarding St. Andrew's Hospital, NYC. The head of the House of the Holy Comforter[12] had made "a splendid offer" of $59,000 for St. Andrew's. But the Sisters were unable to accept it for the time being as they had no place to transfer the work of caring for the convalescent patients from St. Andrew's. Mr. Henry, a priest on the Diocesan Housing Board, advised the Sisters to move out of the city up to Poughkeepsie in New York State, where they were much needed. "It seems very perfect on paper but will need much investigation," was Mother's comment. The idea of moving to Poughkeepsie was a ray of hope in what had been an ongoing problem.

The Sisters on their hilltop site were accustomed to harsh winters and being snowed in, but the winter of 1947–48 was one of worst in living memory. The snow began on Christmas Eve, but did not prevent the Sisters from visiting friends nearby with gifts of fruit and candy. By the Feast of St. John the Evangelist (December 27), the road was blocked by high drifts; and next day, taking Sr. Lillian Christine back to Bergen Pines hospital in North Jersey, where she was being treated for tuberculosis,[13] involved a five hour round trip, only to find the road closed again. The convent car was stowed safely in Mr. Gunther's garage and he then drove Mother back to the convent over the snow drifts in his jeep. On the same day Sr. Jane Patricia went out on foot for the mail, not realizing until too late just how deep the snow was. The expedition took several hours and she arrived back exhausted. Mother decreed that no Sister must go out alone in such conditions. The snow plow finally came on December 30, but the telephone line was still down.

As the old year was prayed out and 1948 was prayed in the Sisters must have hoped for better weather too. But January 4 saw an even greater storm with high winds, ice and snow, no lights or telephones and much damage to trees and property. Looking back in the Associates' Newsletter, Mother Waldine Lucia recalled that they were without light or telephone for thirteen days, "forcing us to use candles and oil lamps which produced indeed an aesthetic 'dim religious light.' This however, was not very satisfactory for reading or finding our way after dark around this big house with its many winding stairs." The snow plow had to dig the Sisters out no fewer than thirteen times. The Sisters maintained their daily office through all this, though not always able to sing due to the number of Sisters who were ill. And the Mass was celebrated as and when Fr. Noble or any other priest could get through the snow to the convent. But there were respites in the storms, and on February 1, several Sisters were able to attend the Centennial service at Christ Church, Newark. Bishop Washburn and Canon Leslie told Mother Waldine Lucia how pleased they were with the Sisters' work in the parish. They had made many pastoral visits in the short time since they began working there.

Despite continuing bad weather, there was a St. John the Baptist Foundation meeting in New York at which Mother Waldine Lucia asked for funding for renovations to the infirmary building at St. Marguerite's. She wanted to add two more rooms in order to make the building into a residence for the clergy. Fr. Noble lived in Mendham and other clergy lived further away, and it was necessary to have some place where clergy could stay. Mr. Purdy supported the suggestion and also said it was very necessary for St. Marguerite's to be Incorporated in New Jersey in order to be exempt from taxes. It was also decided not to sell the houses in New York as they were now in good order and bringing in good rents.

It was not just at the infirmary building at St. Marguerite's that work needed to be done: the convent needed urgent repairs too. Some painting and decorating had been done in the past year, but much more needed doing. Mother Waldine Lucia now asked the Board of Trustees for their permission to use the proceeds of a legacy[14] for repairs to the chapel and laundry and other necessary work.

On April 10, 1948, Mother Waldine Lucia sent a letter of formal resignation of the work at Corsicana after the 1948–49 school year (see Chapter 3). At the end of May Mother received a telephone call from Fr. Barrow at Albany Cathedral in New York State, asking the Sisters to undertake work in their parochial school. "It sounded most interesting." It was good for the Community's morale to have these offers of work even when, as in this instance, it had to be refused. With the tide turning against the traditional ministries of Religious Communities, it was good to have positive requests. It showed them that some clergy still had faith in them.

There was an important Chapter meeting on June 7, 1948, to discuss the Clewer revised Rule for the first time. After much discussion the Sisters voted—17 against, 9 in favor and 1 vote spoiled. Two Sisters were too ill to vote. At Clewer in December, 1947, the Sisters had voted 68 in favor, 15 against and 1 vote spoiled. As a result, the Chapter at Mendham petitioned the Clewer Chapter to be allowed to retain the Rule presently in use, i.e. that of 1907.

At the end of the Chapter meeting on June 7, the Sisters had a Conference about the future of St. Andrew's Hospital. All except one were in favor of selling the New York property and moving to Poughkeepsie. Mother Waldine Lucia commented in the Community Record Book, "We are greatly wanted there and there seems to be a need for that type of work. The various social workers, both City and County, and all the churches in Poughkeepsie, also the St. Barnabas Hospital fund will back up St. Andrew's." An offer of $60,000 cash for the St. Andrew's building was made in July 1948, but frustratingly, there were insufficient members of the Board of Trustees present at the meeting on July 26 in order to obtain the necessary two-thirds majority. It would have been an ideal solution to the problem of St. Andrew's Hospital especially as the outstanding mortgage stood at only $5,000. The hospital was closed at the end of August and on September 16, a Court order was obtained approving the sale of the property. A suitable house at Poughkeepsie had been found after much searching and an offer of $25,000 in cash had been made as work would need to be done on the property.

Also on July 26, 1948, Sr. Florence Teresa fell down the stairs from the second floor at the convent and broke her arm. A few days later, on July 31, she was much worse with a high temperature and none of the usual doctors were available. Finally she was taken to All Souls' Hospital in the Mendham ambulance. Next day, August 1, she passed to her rest. Many people came to her requiem and many praised the singing. "I am sure Sister's prayers helped us—she loved singing," wrote Mother Waldine Lucia. She was laid to rest in the Community cemetery next to her collaborator in Community history, Sr. Elisa Monica. Together with Sr. Julia Frances, Sr. Florence Teresa was one of the last two living Sisters professed in the 19th century. She had led the Community as Mother Superior from 1915 until 1942. Her last years had been a trying time as she coped with deafness and blindness, and she lived to see the post-War fall in vocations. But although she did not live to know about the full flowering of the Community's Second Spring in the next decade, she had known of its first stirrings with the work in Texas, and nearer home in Newark. So now she joined that great body of Living Stones, joining her continued prayers with theirs in the nearer presence of God.

The dominant event at the end of 1948 was the visit from Clewer of the Mother General, Dorothy Frances, accompanied by Sr. Hilda Frances. They arrived on October 22, and were met by Mother Waldine Lucia, finally arriving at the convent about 4.45pm. "Joy bells rang and Sisters all assembled in cloister and hallway to greet them." The Warden (Fr. Weed) and Fr. Schlueter came to the convent two days later in order to meet Mother General. She told the Warden she had thought as long ago as 1934, when she was in India, that the American Affiliation should separate from Clewer, and wondered why it had taken so long. Fr Weed told her very firmly that in the event of a separation the American Sisters should keep the Rule and name.

At a meeting of the Consultative Council on October 26, all the Sisters spoke "very plainly and splendidly." Mother Waldine Lucia asked that the Clewer Chapter would "let us go with their blessing." She also emphasized that the American Community had a legal right to their Name, Rule and Cross. The Chapter met on November 2, with Mother General and Sr. Hilda Frances present, and Mother General called for a vote regarding the separation. Only two Sisters voted against it. A Conference was held on the same day and after addressing the Sisters, Mother General allowed them to speak freely. One Sister summed up the feelings of many when she said that she was "professed in the Community as it is now, and I expect to live and die in it." The point was also made that some priests were not sending prospective aspirants to the Community at Mendham because they were still tied to England. Instead they were sending them to Communities that they considered to be wholly American. This surely was as good a reason as any to separate from Clewer.

Events moved fast now. On December 3, 1948, the Consultative Council changed the agenda for the next Chapter so that a resolution could be sent to the Clewer Chapter stating "our desire for a separation." Mother Waldine Lucia wrote in the Community Record Book: "In other words freedom from the jurisdiction of Clewer." Voting figures in the Clewer Chapter were not recorded in the Mendham Community Record Book, but in reply Mother General had a cable from Clewer: "Sorrowful but send love and sympathy. Keep dedication etc., but not the Cross." Mother Waldine Lucia confided to the Community Record Book, "We intend to keep the Cross." And indeed they did.

Mother General's return to Clewer was delayed because of serious storms and another dock strike. Meanwhile, it was Thanksgiving, and Mother Waldine Lucia noted that "we gave the English an American Thanksgiving dinner." The Chapter at Mendham voted on December 3, and resulted in 24 Sisters voting in favor of the separation and three against. Finally the two English Sisters sailed home on December 6, 1948, laden with gifts for the Sisters at Clewer. It would be many years before they would meet the American Sisters again.[15] The second Chapter on the resolution to separate was held on December 29, 1948, and the Sisters at Mendham voted overwhelmingly in favor, only one voting against. "Now the die is cast," Mother Waldine Lucia wrote in the Community Record Book.

On December 15, 1948, Sr. Amy Grace wrote from Clewer to Mother Waldine Lucia following the Mother General's arrival home. "How generous you have all been to them and to us. We had a display of all your gifts last evening and feel we cannot say 'thank you' enough for it all. And both Mother and Sr. Hilda Frances say your kindness and goodness to them has been more than they can say ... I do trust we shall remain united—and more than ever [united] in love. As you keep the Founder's primitive Rule and Constitutions I shall always feel you remain *the true unchanged CSJB*. I remain wholly with you, thank God—but am too old now to do more than wait here to join the rest of the dear Community gone before ..."[16] [my italics]

On January 6, 1949, Mother Waldine Lucia wrote to Mother Dorothy Frances regarding the resolution to separate. "The resolution represents long and prayerful study of the needs and the position of the Community of St. John Baptist in the United States. In 1881, our Warden Founder [Canon Carter] wrote a letter to Chapter in which he said that with the experience of time and distance he thought it would be wise to make the American House an Affiliated House with as little delay as possible. He gave as reasons … the difficulty of distance, the difference in government, the autonomy of the American Church, and pointed out that the American Bishops were unwilling to recognize works which were particularly English. As the years have gone by those differences have remained and the development of the American House has been more and more distinctly American, just as the English Community has developed along more distinctively English lines. No doubt this was inevitable and follows the pattern of our respective Church and State governments. Therefore the resolution is sent to the Mother House in full confidence that the Chapter will understand that it is an action taken after prayerful consideration, *and with no lack of love* or veneration for our common heritage, or for lack of affection for the present members of the Community." [my italics]

If there was a note of regret or sadness it is highly understandable. To sever a tie originating in Mother Harriet's Community founded in 1852, and guided by the Rector of Clewer, T. T. Carter, was a major development. And that is how it should be seen—a development, a liberation, rather than a great divorce. And it did not in any way obliterate the past ties with the Founders, Mother Harriet and T. T. Carter, nor with Mother Frances Constance, the first Superior in New York. It was a natural process, one which the Clewer Chapter had not been able to see, but which maybe Mother Dorothy Frances had seen. So now CSJB in the USA was free to fly solo without having to gain permission from Clewer to do whatever their Chapter considered right for the Community. Some Sisters on both sides of the Atlantic would feel a sense of bereavement, but at that stage in the life of the US Sisters, the Affiliation had to die so that the Community might live. It was an important factor in the Second Spring of the Community. Sr. Margaret Helena wisely commented, "I have not understood this as a 'break.' It is rather a separation—like the Churches—the American Church is completely autonomous."[17]

Mother Dorothy Frances' visit had another rather disconcerting effect besides the separation. She had been taken to Boston, Mass., to see the Sisters of the Society of St. Margaret, and had talked to their Superior, Mother Mary Agnes, about the future of CSJB on its hilltop site at

Mendham. Then Bishop Washburn had been to visit Mother Dorothy Frances and she had talked to him about it, and the process continued with talks with the Warden and other clergy. The general opinion was that the Sisters should move from their hilltop site or they would die out within a few years.[18] The Bishop wanted the Sisters to do more parish work, though not outside his diocese as he didn't want to lose them. Mother General advocated moving to Poughkeepsie, where St. Andrew's Hospital was about to be re-located. Mother Waldine Lucia's reply to the bishop was, "Send us good vocations then we can undertake more work." All this negativity coming on top of the stressful situation regarding the relationship with Clewer was not helpful. But the seed of doubt had been sown.

Nineteen forty-eight had been a traumatic year but it ended with a joyous celebration of Christmas, despite it being very cold with much snow. The Sisters received "beautiful letters" from Bishop Washburn and Canon William Leslie about the Sisters' work at Christ Church, Newark, NJ. It was just what they needed to affirm them as they sought to find new forms of ministry whilst living out their vowed life in the accustomed manner. A new year beckoned, with new challenges and the continuing stirrings of a Second Spring. And on January 4, 1949, Elizabeth Anne Franklin was clothed as a novice, taking the name Sr. Elizabeth Anne. She had trained as a teacher, and then in 1943 came to teach at St. Marguerite's shortly before its closure. She then entered St. Luke's School of Nursing, NYC, and graduated in September 1947. "We hope she has a good, true vocation, a sense of the sacrificial side of the life … The service was beautiful as usual and many compliments about the singing," wrote Mother Waldine Lucia. By now there were three novices and the Sisters felt encouraged by this.

On January 18, 1949, the move from New York to the new premises for St. Andrew's Hospital at Poughkeepsie began. It took three days and involved four vans, some Sisters and the three novices. The novices were there for ten days and one of them, Sr. Ora Mary (Synnes), was to stay there for several months. Sr. Agatha Louise was appointed Sister in Charge.

Later in February, there came a request from Fr. MacLaury, the president of Canterbury College, Danville, Indiana,[19] to take on the supervision of a girls' dormitory there. The college authorities thought it would help the girls to know the Sisters and would help the Sisters get vocations. Mother Waldine Lucia wrote sadly in the Community Record

Book: "We have not, under the circumstances, the Sisters to send there for such a worthwhile work. It's a grand opportunity, not only for us, but the possibility of doing some work with that age of girl. He then said if he paid us the railroad fare would we send two Sisters to spend five days or a week on the campus? I said yes." On March 3, 1949, Sr. Margaret Helena and Sr. Elizabeth Marion left for Canterbury College to spend five or six days there meeting the students and giving addresses on the Religious Life. Both Sisters were ideal for this mission, having worked at St. Helen's Hall, Oregon, and therefore knowing how to approach girls and young women in a way that they could relate to. They returned on March 10, declaring it a very worthwhile visit.

There were developments at St. John Baptist School. The Sister Superior, Sr. Mary Barbara (Schroeder), wanted to include men on the School Board, but this would require consent by the Chapter as it involved a change in Community policy. At St. Andrew's Hospital, Poughkeepsie, the work was a great improvement on the old building in New York, being lighter and with much more space between the beds. Like the former hospital in New York City, the hospital at Poughkeepsie was small and admitted only convalescent patients. A Women's Auxiliary had been formed to support the work of the hospital.

Meanwhile the convent building was causing concern. The chapel roof[20] was examined by experts but they would not give an estimate for repairs—they declared it not worth mending as it was so poorly constructed. Outside, the Shrine wall had been patched up, but the rest was "going to pieces fast." The new road had still not been completed, but following a Board of Directors meeting in May the work was finished and Mother considered it to be "a splendid road." The Sisters were also pleased that many rooms and bathrooms at the convent had been painted by Mr. Grier.

On May 25, 1949, St. John Baptist parochial school at Corsicana, Texas, closed and the Sisters flew home. But as one door closed another opened, with an offer of ministry in New York City. Fr. Schlueter had retired from St. Luke's, Hudson Street, New York City,[21] and was replaced by Fr. Weed, the Sisters' Warden. He invited some of the Sisters to live and work in the Mission House. They would teach in the Sunday School and do pastoral visiting and chapel work, but no school work. It was a tempting offer but needed careful and prayerful consideration. The Sisters were very concerned about whether they should accept work under their

Warden. It seemed like a blurring of boundaries. Also, they feared his expectations might be greater than they could meet, especially with parish visiting. On August 18, 1949, there was a Chapter meeting regarding the revised Constitutions, which were passed. At the same meeting a vote was taken regarding the work at St. Luke's. Nineteen Sisters voted against taking the work and seven in favor. Fr. Weed was very disturbed at the Sisters' refusal and quoted Fr. Schlueter as saying "I should think you would sacrifice everything to take up new work, or you will *die* out on this hill," and Fr. Weed added, "I agree as Warden and Priest."

Mother Waldine Lucia was clearly coming to agree about the necessity of moving. She wrote in the Community Record Book, "He asked me if I thought we could do it by [the following] January. I said I didn't know, but that the picture would have to greatly change for us. This big place [meaning the convent] had to be gotten rid of with all the work involved, and great expense of keeping it up. The physical work required many Sisters, and we had few equal to it, so that new work, as things are at present, cannot be considered if we are to live our Rule of Life. He did not like it, but seemed extremely annoyed." But it was the living of the vowed life that was all-important—the life of prayer, daily office and the Mass was what defined the Sisters, and distinguished them from secular parish workers or missionaries.

Even though the Sisters were hesitant at taking work outside the convent, plenty of people found their way to the Sisters and enjoyed the beauty of their hilltop site. For instance, on May 21, 1949, the Sunday school from the Congregational Church at Chatham came on a visit to see what a convent was like. They enjoyed a picnic in the grounds near the woods. Next day, about 53 people from Christ Church, Newark, came to the convent for a picnic, but the weather was cold and wet, so after Evensong they all had supper at St. Marguerite's. Canon William Leslie brought the Sisters 100lbs of potatoes and a large ham.[22] Individual people also came for quiet days. And although the work at Corsicana had ended, two ladies from there had become Associates and wanted to continue the connection. There were also Associates in Portland, gained when the Sisters worked there at St. Helen's Hall, who continued to meet faithfully. They were greatly encouraged by Sr. Margaret Helena's annual visits.

On June 21, 1949, St. Andrew's Hospital, Poughkeepsie, was blessed and over 300 people were present on a very hot day. By July 4, there were ten convalescent patients, but many more would be needed if the hospital was going to pay its way. By the Fall, concern was being expressed at the lack of patients. The hospital was equipped for 25 but rarely exceeded ten. In the New York days, most of the patients would have come from there and would have been unable to have afforded to stay in a private nursing facility while recovering from illness or surgery. Benefactors, who were often known to the Sisters, subscribed to the upkeep of the hospital, thus enabling the patients to stay there at a greatly reduced rate. And those patients who could not afford to donate were never turned away.[23] By moving to Poughkeepsie, the hospital lost a valuable connection with the city. In fact the hospital's days were numbered and it had to be given up early in 1950. It was the end of an old work which had tried valiantly to renew itself, but without adequate funding and with too few patients nothing more could be done to save it.

On September 8, 1949, Sr. Ora Mary was professed in the presence of many guests and priests. Mother Waldine Lucia declared it to have been "a very beautiful service. Everything went so well—many singing practices helped … The Sisters worked so hard on all details." It had been a day of joy following an anxious time. A novice (Sr. Ellen Elisabeth) had left earlier in the year, and more recently another Sister (Sr. Margaret Raphael), who had been professed in 1930, also left. Sometimes vocations are lost or were never real, but they always bring sadness at their ending.

Fr. Weed was still hoping the Sisters would have a change of heart about St. Luke's; and on September 18, he came to the convent accompanied by Fr. Schlueter. He said it wasn't just that he wanted the Sisters to work there, but reminded them that when the Israelites were about to be engulfed by the Red Sea, the Lord said to Moses, "Go on." The Holy Nativity Sisters wanted to work at St. Luke's, but Fr. Weed was still hopeful that CSJB would accept the challenge. The same evening Fr. Schlueter spoke to a small group of the Sisters—Sr. Margaret Helena, Sr. Elizabeth Marion, Sr. Mary Barbara, Sr. Mary Joan and Sr. Julia Frances. Mother Waldine Lucia recorded his words in the Community Record Book. "When a Community is down that is not the time to retrench but to make a bold move to go on, take up new work, have great faith and courage. Get out of this big house—it's a palace. Move to St. Marguerite's if that will, as some think, save the cost of fuel and workers. This may or may not be the help you are looking for … Sell the convent; if you can't sell it then let it go to pieces; it gives a wrong impression."

On the evening of Sr. Ora Mary's profession (September 8) Mother

Waldine Lucia had given the Warden, Fr. Weed, her resignation as Mother Superior. Now, on September 19, he gave "a splendid address," telling the Sisters to be guided by the Holy Spirit in the election of the new Mother Superior.

St. John Baptist School made a good start to the new academic year with 32 boarders and four day girls. There were several new teachers, a new house mother, and all seemed to promise well. By now Sr. Eleanor Lucy was working at the school in addition to Sr. Mary Barbara, who was still Sister Superior, and Sr. Jane Patricia, who seemed to work there at times in between working at the convent.

There was an important Chapter meeting on October 6, 1949, when the Sisters were to consider whether they should move to St. Marguerite's as suggested by Fr. Schlueter, and whether to take up the offer of work at St. Luke's Chapel, New York City. The Sisters voted unanimously in favor of accepting the work at St. Luke's. They also voted to move to St. Marguerite's, which was no longer being used as a home or school, and was therefore available for use by the Sisters.

A great deal of work needed to be done to make it suitable for the Sisters to live and work in. The old class-room was converted into a chapel, and the altar and pews from St. Marguerite's chapel were moved into the new chapel. Benches from the Chapter room at the convent were brought across and it was said to look "all very churchly."[24] Mother Waldine Lucia, Sr. Margaret Helena and Sr. Katharine Veronica moved to St. Marguerite's to prepare it and then all the Sisters except for Sr. Fanny Helen (Andrew) moved there on foot. Sr. Fanny Helen was moved on a stretcher, being too ill to walk there. When the Sisters' old friend Fr. Granville Mercer Williams, SSJE,[25] was told about the move, he remarked, "I have always thought that building [the convent] a very unfortunate one, very inconvenient and poorly constructed."[26]

As for St. Luke's, there seemed to be some uncertainty as to what exactly the Sisters would do there. The first offer had been for Sunday school work and chapel work but no school work. Now it seemed to have changed to chapel work, and teaching three classes in the school as well as the Sunday school. A letter from Fr. Weed on October 10, 1949, stated that the first priority would be to "set up a convent, live the Religious Life and pray. The work and opportunities in the parish we can work out later." And the terms of work seemed to change frequently before the Sisters began it.

On Monday, November 7, 1949, the Chapter met to elect the new Mother Superior. There were three nominations—Sr. Margaret Helena, Sr. Mildred Eleanor and Sr. Mary Barbara. The election was held after a novena (nine days) of prayer, and Sr. Margaret Helena was duly elected. The installation was on Wednesday, November 9. There were no guests, it being a private service for the Community, but the girls from St. John Baptist School came in after the installation. Sr. Julia Frances and Sr. Waldine Lucia walked up to the altar with the Mother elect. The service was in the convent chapel, which was still being used, and the reception afterwards was at St. Marguerite's. On the same day Sr. Mildred Eleanor had her blessing as Assistant Superior; Sr. Agatha Louise as Sister Superior of St. Andrew's Hospital, Poughkeepsie; and Sr. Mary Barbara as Sister Superior of St. John Baptist School.

On November 10, the day after Sr. Margaret Helena's installation as Mother Superior, Sr. Marie Elizabeth died. She had recently begun to show signs of dementia and it had been necessary to admit her to hospital. She was professed in January 1908, between the death of Sr. Gertrude Verena and the funeral. Sr. Marie Elizabeth was one of the Sisters who had nursed the Spanish influenza victims at Portland, Oregon, in 1918. It was said of her at the convent that wherever there was sickness she was there to help, and she fulfilled the role of Assistant Superior, infirmarian and clothes Sister all at the same time.[27] Her time in hospital during her last illness was mercifully short. Mother Waldine Lucia recounted that her last words were, "God bless the Sisterhood." Her Community Biographer noted that she had lived a long life filled with many good works. Sr. Marie Elizabeth's funeral was on November 12, 1949, and following the usual rites and ceremonies, she was laid to rest in the convent cemetery.

And so, as Sr. Marie Elizabeth began her new life in the nearer presence of God, so too the Sisters began their new life at St. Marguerite's, with a new Mother Superior to lead and guide them. Mother Waldine Lucia had served the Community as Superior for six difficult, challenging years. It is hardly surprising that she resigned after a fairly short term of office. No other Superior up to that time had been tasked with guiding the Community through so many challenges. The surrender of old, much loved work had not come easily, especially to the older Sisters who had once been in charge of those works in younger, more flourishing times. The most painful aspect of the 1940s was the separation from Clewer, but the Affiliation would live again a quarter of a century later. The challenge of maintaining the convent was sapping the energy of those Sisters who were able to keep it going. But there were good signs too. The work in Corsicana may have been short lived but it was the first blooming of the Second Spring. Other work, especially at Newark, and the promise of new work in New York and also in Jersey City would see the Second Spring burst into full flower. But without the wisdom and sound common sense of Mother Waldine Lucia, the Community might well have given up hope and turned in on itself.

Now there was a new Mother Superior. Sister Margaret Helena had already shown she was able to take on any challenge. The great challenge now would be to lead and guide the Community as it took on new work, new ministries, and found new life. Only she had the wisdom, the pastoral skills and the personal magnetism to bring the Community back to life.

---

[1] There was also a stern warning in the Community Record Book that "No Sisters must have cats in the refectory, bedrooms or chapel." Nothing was said about dogs! The Short Record Book specifies "School Sisters," which makes more sense, as Sr. Elisa Monica loved cats and had at least two.

[2] Some notes in the archives at Mendham state that in 1933 the Chapter at Clewer revised the Constitutions, but the revision did not receive the sanction of their Visitor, the Rt. Revd. Thomas Banks Strong, Bishop of Oxford. Therefore it was never brought to the Chapter at Mendham.

[3] There will be more about the work in Corsicana in Chapter 3 "From out west to down south."

[4] Fr. Paul Wessinger, 1915–2009, became Superior of the American Province of the Society of St. John the Evangelist 1972–83. His death on May 22, 2009, was in the 95th year of his life, the 65th year of his profession, and the day before the 69th anniversary of his ordination to the priesthood.

[5] At this time the Sisters had begun to close the main chapel during the winter because it was so expensive to heat it. The Community Record Books indicate that they used the library as a winter chapel. It is not clear whether the altar from Woodcliff was used there before St. Michael's chapel was formed.

[6] Sr. Florence Agatha later left through ill health.

[7] So passed the first historian of CSJB in America. Without Sr. Elisa Monica's Early Memories and the Sisters' Biographies that she wrote, I would have had great difficulty writing Living Stones, as these provided me with major sources. She died less than a year before I was born and I feel that she passed the mantle of US CSJB history on to me—or so I like to think.

[8] There will be more tributes to Sr. Elisa Monica in a later chapter.

[9] This all rings very true! Mother Jane Frances may well have had a majestic manner. She was the maternal granddaughter of the 2nd Lord Erskine, and her sister married Lord Archibald Campbell, second son of the 8th Duke of Argyll. She spent her rests at Inverary Castle in Scotland. In 1881 she became Mother Superior (Mother General) until 1889, when she became Sister Superior in India until 1918. It was always said of her at Clewer that she was very unhappy in the office of Mother Superior and would leave her study door open in order to see who would pass by. The Sister would then be called in for a talk, so it is perfectly believable that she wanted a friendly talk with Sr. Elisa Monica. Sr. Margaret was clothed in 1885 and professed in 1887. She had served in India from 1884–1900, and returned there after a brief furlough at the end of 1900 until 1905. She returned to India again on January 2, 1919, having succeeded Sr. Jane Frances as Sister Superior in India and remained in office until 1931, when she was succeeded by Sr. Dorothy Frances. She died at a great age in 1954.

[10] A Congregation was defined as "a branch of the original Community having its own complete organization and government, limited only as to the completeness of its autonomy by the statutory conditions of its creation."

[11] There are no records of this work in the Community archives at Mendham apart from a brief mention in the Community Record Book.

[12] The House of the Holy Comforter was a small convalescent home in NYC for women with chronic illnesses. CSJB had worked there from 1884 until 1891.

[13] In 1948, Sr. Lillian Christine was given new treatment for her tuberculosis (possibly one of the new antibiotics). This arrested the illness and she was able to return to live at the convent.

[14] Mother Waldine Lucia's handwriting in the Community Record Book is not always easy to read! The legacy in question looks like "the Cozzens Estate." If so this could be from Sr. Mary Katharine, whose family name was Cuzzens (note different spelling) and who died in 1942. Or it might have been from a relative. She came from a distinguished family—see BONHAM, Valerie *Living Stones* Appendix 3 "Sisters' families and American history," pages 370–71.

[15] Both Mothers, by then out of office, would live to see the two parts of CSJB re-Affiliated. When Sr. Barbara Jean visited Clewer in 1973, a year before the re-Affiliation, Sr. Dorothy Frances told her that the separation was the greatest regret of her life. She also said that she had prayed daily for each Sister at Mendham by name since 1949.

[16] Sr. Amy Grace was formerly Amy Hyde Parker and came from a long line of naval officers. She was born on December 27, 1864, the daughter of naval Captain Sir William Parker, 9th Baronet, and his wife, Sophia Mary Barnardiston. The ancestral home was Melford Hall, Long Melford, Suffolk, UK, which was partly destroyed by fire in 1942 when it was requisitioned by the Ministry of Defence as an Officers' Mess. Sr. Amy Grace was received as a novice at Clewer on December 7, 1894, at 30 years of age, and was professed on June 18, 1897. She died on October 17, 1956, at age 91. (Melford Hall was restored and is presently in the care of the National Trust.)

[17] This was at a Conference on the Rule held at Mendham on November 2, 1948, in the presence of Mother General Dorothy Frances and Sr. Hilda Frances. At the same Conference Sr. Julia Frances commented that she would always have love and gratitude in her heart for Clewer, a feeling shared by many of the Sisters.

[18] The ultimate irony was that it was the UK Community who eventually had to leave their vast Victorian Mother House at Clewer in September 2001, whilst the US Sisters are still on their hilltop site at Mendham in their restored convent.

[19] In the Weekly Letter to the Sisters, Sr. Margaret Helena, Assistant Superior, wrote that Canterbury College, Danville, IN, was taken over by the Church in 1946. It was formerly a teacher training college. Out of 400 students, 38 were postulants for Holy Orders and others were aspirants. Several of the girls were Associates of Religious Orders.

[20] This was still the original flat roof.

[21] St. Luke's in the Fields, Hudson Street, NYC, was founded in 1821 on a site donated by Trinity Church, Wall Street, and soon became known as a center of Anglo-Catholic worship within the Episcopal Church. In 1891 it became a chapel of Trinity Church and was known as St. Luke's Chapel. After the Sisters left St. Luke's in 1976, the church became independent of Trinity, Wall Street, and is now known as St. Luke's in the Fields.

[22] This seems like an enormous amount of potatoes, in addition to the ham, but no explanation was given as to where he had obtained them.

[23] For more about St. Andrew's Convalescent Hospital, NYC, see BONHAM, Valerie *Living Stones* Chapter 9.

[24] Sr. Margaret Helena, Assistant Superior, writing in the Weekly Letter to the Sisters, Wednesday, October 19, 1949.

[25] Fr. Granville Mercer Williams, SSJE, was fifth rector of the Church of St. Mary the Virgin, NYC, from 1930–39. In 1939 he was elected Superior of the American Province of the Society of St. John the Evangelist.

[26] Although William Cordingley has always been referred to as the architect of the convent, it was Durr Friedley who had the original idea for a much larger convent and invited Cordingley to collaborate with him. Neither of them had any previous experience in architectural design, but it was Friedley who chose the rather fragile terracotta bricks for the main construction around the steel frame. See: BONHAM, Valerie *Living Stones* Chapter 11.

[27] A story about Sr. Marie Elizabeth relates that the convent had a dog called Teddy who used to go to the surgery after dinner with Sr. Marie Elizabeth and cough—she would then give him a cough drop!

❧ 3 ❧

FROM "OUT WEST" TO "DOWN SOUTH"

From Portland, Oregon to Corsicana, Texas

IN MAY 1903 the Community of St. John Baptist had accepted the offer to take charge of St. Helen's Hall, a large school for girls in Portland, Oregon. It was not their foundation and had evolved from a small school established in 1869 with its own distinctive rules and traditions.[1] It had always been a hope cherished by Mother Frances Constance, the first Superior in the US, that one day the Sisters' ministry would extend beyond the Rocky Mountains, and with this in mind the Sisters had readily accepted the challenge. And indeed it was a daunting prospect from the very beginning. Religious Communities were an unknown quantity at that time in the far west, and at first the Sisters had to cope with suspicion about their way of life and opposition to their methods of running the school. Ever open to a challenge, Sr. Elisa Monica, the first Sister Superior at the school, defeated all opposition and soon the school had made a name for itself as a center of excellence in girls' education.

In July 1914 Sr. Elisa Monica returned east to help move St. John Baptist School from New York City to temporary accommodation at Bernardsville, NJ, and shortly afterwards there was a disastrous fire at St. Helen's Hall. This might have been the end of the story, and indeed the Sisters thought very seriously about giving the work up. But this would not be in the spirit of the Community and so they resolved to continue. In 1916 Sr. Mary Angela, having resigned as Mother Superior at Mendham, became Sister Superior at St. Helen's Hall, and the rebuilding began.

It was in 1918, during the time that Sr. Mary Angela was Sister Superior, that the Spanish influenza epidemic reached Portland and the school had to be temporarily closed. Three Sisters, under Sr. Mary Angela's supervision, volunteered to help nurse the influenza victims and did so heroically.[2] One of them, Sr. Waldine Lucia, succeeded Sr. Mary Angela as Sister Superior at St. Helen's Hall in 1922. Little by little the school was rebuilt over the next few years, like a phoenix rising from the ashes, and new buildings were added throughout the 1920s and early 1930s. The Wall Street crash of October 1929 and subsequent economic depression resulted in a number of parents being unable to afford the school fees, but the school survived when many others did not. The great event of the 1930s was the opening of the junior college in new purpose-built premises in March 1934. It was the first accredited junior college in Oregon. This greatly widened the scope of the school and gave girls the chance of a higher level of education. But the greatest sadness of the 1930s was the sudden death of Sr. Katharine Angela on June 2, 1935. She had worked at Portland since 1921 and was devoted to the school and the students, and they were devoted to her. Hers was the first death from within the Community in the far west and she was buried in the Riverview Cemetery at Portland.

On June 8, 1939, the Bishop of Oregon, the Rt. Revd. Benjamin Dagwell, wrote an encouraging letter to Mother Florence Teresa following the Commencement ceremonies for the school and junior college. "The Diocese of Oregon and the patrons of St. Helen's [Hall] are under great obligation to your Order. Sister Waldine Lucia, with her usual zeal and thoroughness, [has] led us through another year. I hope that she and the other wonderful Sisters will find rest and refreshment this summer. The heavy responsibilities you carry as the head of a great Order must be somewhat lightened by the realization of the gratitude of your many beneficiaries." On the same day he had written a personal letter to Sr. Waldine Lucia. "The more I see and hear of the work the more I appreciate the extent of your burdens. You and your Sisters are doing a grand job as educators and missionaries. I am proud to have a small share in your work and I want you and your associates to know that it is deeply appreciated."

By the beginning of the 1940s St. Helen's Hall was thriving and was the most successful of all the CSJB work at a time when the older, more institutional work was coming to an end. When in August 1940 the bishop asked the Sisters to take charge of Ascension Chapel[3] Sunday school, the Sisters felt they could not refuse even though it was a big undertaking in addition to all they already had to do. Sr. Agatha Louise and Sr. Margaret Helena took on the work, assisted by some of the senior students.

St. Helen's Hall went from strength to strength, with an evaluation ranking it as "Superior" and with an enrollment of over 400 in September. The Sisters were asked to be on the Curriculum program project under the State Department of Education. Much maintenance work was done on the buildings, and extra accommodation was taken for the boarders.

Nineteen forty-one saw the school laboring under the economic effects of the war. In August the enrollment was down on the previous year and this affected the funds, so much so that the main building was not heated after 3:00pm. Also, there were only two men to drive the car and bus, no chaperone, and only six maids. And then on December 7, 1941, the Japanese attacked Pearl Harbor, thus bringing the United States into the war. This of course affected the Mother House at Mendham, but even more immediately St. Helen's Hall, as Oregon was geographically much closer to the Pacific theater of war. The school was immediately put onto a war basis—black-outs; no radios allowed; and the school was tied in with the public school alarm system. Evacuation plans were made ready in case of need. Sisters and girls began taking First-Aid classes and there was great anxiety about possible air raids. The Fall saw shortage of fuel stopping the much-loved excursions to the house at Lake Oswego.

On June 21, 1942, the war came too close for comfort when a Japanese submarine (1-25) shelled the Oregon coast near Seaside, where the Sisters had their summer rest cottages. Sr. Mildred Eleanor and Sr. Agatha Louise were there at the time, and although the Sisters and the cottages escaped unscathed, it was a timely reminder of the perils of war.

The Sisters spent two days at the Diocesan Convention in May, where they gave meditations. October 1942 had seen the resignation of Mother Florence Teresa after 27 years in office as Mother Superior at Mendham. Sr. Alice Ursula was elected Mother Superior on December 15, and was installed at Mendham two days later. Numbers in the school slowly began to increase and the winter of 1942–43 saw a large enrollment of boarders despite severe weather, food rationing and lack of fuel.

It had become customary for the Mother Superior to make an annual visit to Portland, and Mother Alice Ursula was particularly excited about her visit in May 1943, having worked there until 1925. There had been many changes since the rebuilding of the school after the fire. Sr. Alice Ursula, as she was then, had been one of the Sisters who had inspected the Portland Academy building, and had helped make the decision to move the school there in 1920.

Writing an account of the work in Portland some years later, Sr. Waldine Lucia recalled Mother's visit in May 1943. "It was intensely interesting and gratifying to her to see how the school and property had developed. Everything she saw and did delighted her." Mother Alice Ursula's sudden illness and death on May 26 has been written about at some length in Chapter 1. The St. Helen's Hall Record Book stated: "May 20, Mother

Alice Ursula arrived." And the brief entry for May 26, "Mother died," speaks volumes about the sense of shock and grief which was felt by the whole Community, east and west, and by the students at the Hall and the many Associates. In accordance with the CSJB custom to bury Sisters where they died, Mother Alice Ursula was buried in Portland next to Sr. Katharine Angela.

In due course Sr. Waldine Lucia was elected Mother Superior and left Portland for her installation at Mendham, which took place on August 10, 1943. She had worked at St. Helen's Hall for over 30 years and it must have been a great wrench to buy that one-way ticket. But the Community had elected her, and in obedience she traveled east to take up the challenge of her new office. She left Portland on July 30, and Sr. Mildred Eleanor (Blodgett) now took up office as Sister Superior. One of the last entries made by Sr. Waldine Lucia in the Portland Record Book related to the future of the Sisters at the school. "Much talk of giving up the Hall in the East. The time may be here to do so because of the shortage of Sisters … School in a splendid financial condition—and prospect for the coming year is good. Must look to God for guidance."

On August 24, 1943, Bishop Dagwell visited St. Helen's Hall and was told by Sr. Mildred Eleanor and Sr. Agatha Louise that the Sisters would, with much regret, withdraw from the school in June 1944. The bishop was very distressed by the news. May 1944 saw the 75th anniversary of the school, and the *Sunday Oregonian* of May 21, 1944, ran a double page illustrated article about the school throughout its historic years. Bishop Dagwell paid tribute to the Sisters' leadership: "We hoped and prayed that circumstances making this decision necessary might change, but that has been impossible and now we must look to others for the leadership and direction of the Hall."

Meanwhile, life at the school went on as usual under the supervision of the Sisters until they left on July 26, 1944, when they began their final journey east. They had left St. Helen's in good order with a large enrollment, $50,000 in the savings account and a similar amount in War Bonds. The Sisters would not be forgotten, nor would they forget. In the early years they were pioneers of the Religious Life in Oregon and throughout those 40 years of service had influenced bishops, clergy, and the Diocesan Convention, as well as inspiring the girls in their care. When they left, St. Helen's Hall was the oldest Episcopal school west of the Rocky Mountains. A letter to the Sisters from the Mothers' Club of the junior college, dated 1944, expressed their regard for the Community. "For the years of service given to St. Helen's Hall, and particularly the Junior College; for that serene beauty of the soul which comes with close companionship with God and which has touched the lives of all with whom you have come in contact; for the example of service … which you have given to our daughters and which we know will never be forgotten, we express our humble thanks and appreciation."

Bishop Dagwell never ceased to miss the Sisters and early in 1945 he became an Associate. Writing just before Christmas 1945, he said, "We miss you constantly but especially at this Christmas season. The school runs along with the momentum provided through the forty years of devoted direction given by your Order. The [junior] College seems to be running down. It may stop at the year's end. I shall be thinking of you tonight at Evensong and at the Christmas Dinner which I shall have with the boarders. Please give my greetings to your Sisters and use the small check for some of your good works." In an undated reply, but from early 1946, Mother Waldine Lucia wrote, "I am not surprised at what you write about the College. It met a need at the time it was established and has done good work, and filled a small niche in the educational and religious world that will have repercussions in years to come, I am sure." Later in January 1946 the bishop wrote again saying the decision had been made to continue with the Junior College in the hope of building up the enrollment. "Needless to say, we miss you at every turn of the road." The Junior College continued until 1947, when it closed; by this time it needed improved premises which would have involved much expense.[4]

So as one door closed, another opened, and Mother Waldine Lucia had some surprising news to tell Bishop Dagwell in the undated letter of early 1946 quoted above. "You were probably surprised to read in the Church papers that we had taken up work in Texas. We were surprised ourselves and Texas of all places! But the call was very persistent, and after the third one, plus the arrival of a postulant, we felt we had to make the venture of faith. Much to the surprise of the so-called Catholics of that part of the world (near Dallas), a supposedly Low-Churchman asked our Community to help him establish a Parochial School. We responded by sending Sisters who could do that type of work, provided it was kept on a small scale. We had to make this provision simply because we do not have the Sisters to do a larger work. The School is a great success thus far, the applications exceeded the number they could take. But, the road is not all as flowery as one might think." She went on to explain that the town of Corsicana was in the midst of the Southern Baptist "Bible belt." "At first the Sisters were not very welcome, but now they are beginning to win their way. Whether we shall keep the work beyond two years remains to be seen. At any rate we have put the Parochial School on the map in that part of Texas. The young Priest in charge of the Parish, under whom the Sisters work, is very enthusiastic, and most dynamic and easy to work with, he has been lovely to the Sisters. Do pray for this work, for it seems to be greatly needed in that town *and has brought new life and hope to us as well.*" [my italics]

A few months earlier, in September 1945, Deacon Joseph Turnbull had written to Mother Waldine Lucia. Together with Fr. Paul Wessinger he had visited the convent at Mendham in July 1945. Now on September 25 he wrote to Mother telling her about his four far-flung mission parishes in Montana, and how he longed for his priestly ordination so that he could celebrate the Eucharist. He also asked whether the work at Corsicana had "materialized." "I was so impressed with your spirit and do hope and pray that God will send you many aspirants to the Religious Life." He continued: "Oh how I wish we had some Sisters out here to help … If the day ever arrives that you have so many Sisters you don't know what to do with them, let me know and we'll put them to some real mission work." He concluded by saying once again how impressed he was when he visited the convent, and asked for prayers.

Mother Waldine Lucia responded in a caring and pastoral way. "Remember this, that the lonely outposts are God's challenge to us." After some counsel about the value of spiritual communion, and the promise of prayer for him, she continued, "I would love to send some Sisters out to such a work and many would love to go too, but our numbers are too few at present. Yes, the work in Texas has 'materialized'—I went down there in August and looked at the field. One or two Sisters went with me. The whole set up seemed so promising that I left the two Sisters there and sent a third one last week. [St. John's] Parochial School was opened from October 1, [1945]. So remember us in your prayers for this is a great venture of faith, and takes much courage on our part because of conditions here in the East, and our shortage in numbers. Corsicana, Texas, is about 60 miles from Dallas. St. John's parish is a small one, but there are many young married people [who are] devoted to their Church.

That section … seems to be so alive. I gave a talk on the Religious Life … in Dallas—never had I met such a dynamic group of young people or priests. The new bishop is a good Churchman and the priest seems very happy to have him. That is indeed a very alive Diocese. They want us in Dallas and we want very much to go there too, but not in school work. Those of us who have been in school work for many years, long for parish or mission work of a different type … We hope in time to be able to work among the colored people [sic] in Corsicana—the Church does little for them." Explaining that the school was in a predominantly Baptist locality, Mother Waldine Lucia commented that "The Sisters' habit causes much comment." She concluded her letter with the assurance of prayer: "I pray that God's richest blessing may rest upon you and your work … our Workroom is closed for lack of workers but we might be able to help in a small way."

Mother Waldine Lucia was accompanied on her initial visit to Corsicana by Sr. Mildred Eleanor and Sr. Agatha Louise. At first the work did not seem promising. The house where the Sisters would live was not ready, the priest was absent on his wedding trip, and everything was disorganized. But soon things began to improve and people from the church were very helpful.

Sr. Katharine Veronica (Finch) was the first Sister to go to Corsicana after work was officially accepted, leaving the convent on September 17, 1945, and she went with much eagerness and enthusiasm. The others to work there were Sr. Agatha Louise (Weiss), Sr. Agnes Genevieve (Brooks), and Sr. Eleanor Lucy (Cowan). Sr. Katharine Veronica was a gifted teacher and enjoyed working with small children. Sr. Agatha Louise had previously worked at St. Helen's Hall, where she was in charge of the lower school, which had flourished under her care. She had great enthusiasm and the ability to inspire others. Sr. Agnes Genevieve had previously worked at St. Marguerite's and at St. John Baptist School. She got on well with people wherever she worked and remained in Texas throughout the short life of the school. The children in the second grade were especially fond of her. Sr. Eleanor Lucy was described as deeply joyous, and a superb teacher, who always looked at a problem from the children's need. Although her lasting work would be in Jersey City, she approached the work in Texas with the same spirit of dedication. A note in the Corsicana Record Book stated that "white habits were allowed as the heat is great and very prolonged." In fact the white habits were not successful and they were replaced by grey cotton habits in September 1947, which the Sisters declared were cooler and more practical.

The parish priest was the Revd. Robert Kennaugh, who, together with his wife, Betty, and Mr. and Mrs. Doyle West, was a great source of support throughout the Sisters' time at the school. Sr. Agatha Louise was the first Sister Superior, until 1947. The initial enrollment at the school (which was an elementary school) was 28 and it was hoped that numbers would increase, but in view of these small numbers a Sunday school was added to the Sisters' work. The school soon got into an ordered routine although there seemed to be a large number of Committees for such a small work. In October 1946 Mother Waldine Lucia made her first visit since the Sisters took up the work, and shortly before Christmas Sr. Margaret Helena also visited. Mother Waldine Lucia was pleased with all the work and reported in the Community Record Book that the school was "doing well, 58 students, and all rooms freshly painted. Sisters' house painted—the chapel very [smart?] and churchly. The parish and school gave a reception. We went to the West's the next day—fear he and others are wanting younger Sisters."

From their first arrival the Sisters had been impressed and encouraged by the kindness of many people from the parish who shared hospitality with them and gave them gifts of food and household commodities. It is not clear from the records whether there were any secular teachers at first, but given the fairly small enrollment, it is unlikely. The Sisters gave parties for the children at Halloween, St. Valentine's Day and at Carnival time. When the school was visited by the County Education Supervisor in May 1947 for its second-year accreditation, it received a high rating. This was encouraging for the Sisters, but before they left to return to Mendham at the end of May, when the school closed for the summer, they attended two meetings of the School Board. It seemed that although there was a good educational standard the school was in debt. Mr. Doyle West, the treasurer, said that $3,000 would be needed to cover the present debt and pay for repairs and the equipment required before the school reopened in the Fall.

The Sisters left for the summer on June 3, 1947, arriving back east two days later.

The work was continuing to pose problems; and not just the financial ones highlighted at the end of May. The Sisters had been approached about adding a fifth grade, but this was impossible without the help of trained secular teachers. In their initial enthusiasm, the Sisters had added a pre-school instead of keeping to the original plan of beginning with a Kindergarten and possibly a first grade, then adding a grade each year up to the sixth grade. It was a mistake easily made, for the initial enrollment had been low, but as soon as it began to increase problems arose. The Sisters had over-stretched themselves and now it all seemed overwhelming. Mother Waldine Lucia responded to the offer of two secular teachers and no more, by suggesting that CSJB should withdraw and be replaced by the Sisters of the Community of the Teachers of the Children of God, an Episcopalian educational order founded in 1935 in Tucson, AZ, who could do the work more cheaply as they were wealthier. But the CSJB Sisters continued for the time being.

Sr. Agatha Louise was replaced as Sister Superior by Sr. Mildred Eleanor (who had returned to Mendham following the initial visit to Corsicana). Sr. Mildred Eleanor had her blessing as Sister Superior of the work in Corsicana on September 4, 1947, the same day that Fr. Paul Weed was installed as Warden of the Community. She then left for Texas, accompanied by Sr. Eleanor Lucy and Sr. Katharine Veronica.

The situation about staffing was still causing anxiety when the school started back in the Fall and on October 21, 1947, Mother Waldine Lucia flew to Texas, a journey of nine hours. This was her second visit since the Sisters had taken the work. The problem was that the School Board wanted only Sisters in the school and no secular teachers, but this was over-stretching the Sisters' resources. Mother felt that the school had expanded too fast and that was the root of the problem. The School Board had invested several thousand dollars in founding the school, and therefore the Sisters could not pull out of the work immediately.

But an added problem was that the State Board of Education had raised the standards required and the Sisters could not meet these in the upper grades. If there had been more Sisters at the convent who had the right qualifications for the work, solving the problem might have been easy. But back at Mendham there were so many elderly Sisters who were now in poor health. They had been young and dynamic when they joined but now they were wearied by age and illness, and their effective working days were over. Fewer women were coming to test their vocations, and of those who came, few stayed. An important letter had been sent to Fr. Kennaugh in February 1946 which had not been answered. In it Mother Waldine Lucia had stated that there would have to be secular teachers.

The Sisters did not pursue the matter, so it was "our fault for part of the difficulty at present," wrote Mother in the Corsicana Record Book. "We straightened out the problem after a fashion and some concessions were made. This year the school has three secular teachers, big salaries etc. Next year the school will take only four-year old children and there will be no expansion beyond the 5th grade." Mother returned by plane to Mendham on November 8, 1947. She said the flight was "a splendid trip on a clear day."

The main decision coming from Mother Waldine Lucia's visit was that the Sisters would not withdraw during the coming academic year (1947/8). This was encouraging news for everyone, but the Sisters were then discouraged by the news that Fr. Kennaugh might be combining his duties at Corsicana with working at National Council Headquarters in New York City. This would take up a considerable amount of his time and left the Sisters feeling very unsupported. Also there was an ongoing question relating to the school buildings. These were generally agreed to be inadequate but no one seemed willing to address the problem. It was beyond the Sisters' terms of reference to take any action and certainly beyond them financially.

Shortly after Easter 1948, Fr. Kennaugh announced he would be leaving the parish for the post in New York at the end of April. It seemed that he would leave the parish altogether: the distance between Corsicana and New York was too great to combine both roles. This was a great blow to the Sisters and to those involved with the school, especially the Wests, who did so much for it. Mother Waldine Lucia decided that the Sisters would have to withdraw after the next academic year (1948/49), and sent her letter of resignation on April 10, 1948. In mid-April the Wests flew to New York to talk about the future of the school with her. Apparently there was a faction opposed to the school—not to the Sisters, but to a private school where they were having to pay fees for their children's education. Sr. Mildred Eleanor wryly commented in the Corsicana Record Book: "… very few of them realize what religion must do for their little ones though they really love the Sisters!"

Fr. Kennaugh left on April 28, 1948, and Fr. Robert Moore of St. Paul's, Waxahachie, was to minister to the Sisters. Fr. Clarence Westapher was due to take up office as Rector at St. John's in June. Meanwhile the idea of parochial schools had caught on, and Fr. Thomas Carson of St. James, Texarkana, came to see the Sisters about running a parish school.[5]

As the academic year closed in May 1948, the School Board decided to continue the school for the next year with the four Sisters and two secular teachers. Doyle West was jubilant and hoped against hope that the Sisters would stay. By the time the Sisters arrived back in Corsicana ready for the new academic year, the bishop had told Fr. Westapher that he wanted him to stay in his parish, which was still at an early pioneering stage. Fr. Kennaugh was recalled and continued to hold office until the beginning of February 1949, when he finally resigned. Meanwhile the parochial school had made a good start up to 5th grade, and the Sisters continued to be an encouraging presence within the diocese.

In February 1949 the bishop asked Sr. Mildred Eleanor to be on the Committee for Diocesan Schools, i.e. the Cathedral School and parochial schools. But Doyle West took her place because the Sisters knew they would not be in Texas beyond the end of the 1949 academic year. The bishop was far from happy at the prospect of the Sisters leaving the diocese even if they left the school, and continued to hope that the school would continue. He was convinced of the value of such schools to the church and the wider community. Requests continued to come in from clergy wanting the Sisters to start parochial schools in their parishes—the latest came from Fr. William Fox of Irving, TX, asking the Sisters to join his mission parishes. The new rector of St. John's, Fr. William Acosta, made a preliminary visit to the parish in March 1949, declaring he was favorable to the Sisters but did not know they were leaving.

Meanwhile, the time for the withdrawal from Corsicana was getting close, and in February 1949 Mother Waldine Lucia received what she called a sad letter from Sr. Mildred Eleanor saying that the bishop and priests were "making such a fuss" about them leaving. But the decision had been made and it had to be kept. On April 26, 1949, the President of the Board of Education announced to the Parent Teacher Association that the school would not go on after the Sisters left. "Doyle West made a very fine speech in which he paid [the] Sisters a tribute and said we should also remember Bob Kennaugh without whose vision the school would not have been. He ended by saying the school had not been in vain, for besides the results they all knew in individual children, it had also done much for Texas in improving teaching methods. It has started the ball rolling in establishment of parochial schools. It has done something which will live on."[6]

Meanwhile, the Sisters continued to give talks about the Religious Life as well as about parochial schools. And Associates were received from Corsicana as a result of the Sisters' ministry and they would continue to keep in touch long after the Sisters left.

As the end of May 1949 approached there was "Open House" at the school. It seemed to provide the solution to all the groups who wanted to say goodbye to the Sisters. There were over 100 people in the afternoon and a large number in the morning. Ice cream and cookies were provided by various willing helpers, including the school mothers. Sr. Mildred Eleanor noted in the Corsicana Record Book that "Doris and Doyle West and several others were considerably comforted by the 'blaze of glory' in which the school is going out." But it was not before the institution of Fr. William Acosta as rector of St. John's by the bishop. The school closed at noon as there was a grand reception in the parish house for the new rector with many people present. Next day, May 29, 1949, the Sisters left Corsicana for the last time, their airfare to New York being paid by friends from the parish.

How did the Sisters feel about leaving the school? The Corsicana Record Book sheds very little light, but some letters from individual Sisters to Mother Waldine Lucia, whilst deferring to the decision, were tinged with regret. In February 1949 Sr. Eleanor Lucy wrote, "I am pulled in two over it. I care much about our being free to relieve strain at home—I dislike to see us leave Texas when we are the only Community working here now. And I care for the Corsicana work, and even if it is at a low ebb would like to see it rise from the ashes." Another Sister[7] wrote, "Fr. Kennaugh feels the school had had very definite good results … He feels that the establishment of other Parochial Schools is in part due to the signal success of this one and to the fact of our being in Texas."

And so the Sisters came home and were soon deployed in other new work being offered to the Community. It was an occasion of sadness to leave Texas, but not one of defeat. Mother Waldine Lucia could discern many positive aspects in the presence of the Sisters there, even over such a short time. Writing in the Community Record Book on February 15, 1949, she noted: "We were the first [Sisters] in Texas to have a parochial school. Now within three years there are many throughout the State. Several priests have asked us to help them start one here and there— splendid offers too. We *prepared the way* [my italics] and in a measure made the Religious Life known in that section of the Country. So we have accomplished something—not much can be done in a place in less than five years. Now in our fourth we are beginning to be known and sought after. We now need the Sisters in the East, though we are turning our backs on a splendid opportunity in a field where there are no Sisters. The priests and bishop must teach and preach vocations ..."

A Community with St. John Baptist as the patron had surely lived up to his teaching to "prepare the way of the Lord" in a place where Sisters were unknown. There was always a sense of sadness when a work had to be given up, but Mother Waldine Lucia was right to see the positive side of what had been achieved. The work in Corsicana was the first flowering of the Second Spring, and it prepared the way by giving the Sisters the confidence to know that amidst all the old work that was dying, there was new life and new work.

---

[1] See BONHAM, Valerie *Living Stones* Chapters 12 and 18.

[2] Ibid. Chapter 16.

[3] This is one of the oldest original church buildings still being used for religious services in Portland. It began in 1889 when the Rt. Revd. Benjamin Wistar Morris II, missionary Bishop of Oregon, laid the Cornerstone for Ascension Chapel. Later the whole building was moved by a team of horses to its present location on Southwest Spring Street. It was designated as a "chapel of ease," then later served as a Sunday school affiliated with Trinity Church, which later became the Cathedral in northwest Portland. In 1968, Ascension became a mission church with a full-time vicar, and by 1984 gained full parish status with a rector and its own elected vestry.

[4] St. Helen's Hall continued until 1972 when it merged with Bishop Dagwell Hall, an all-boys school, and took the name Oregon Episcopal School (OES). It is now a leading school with a research-based science program.

See www.oes.edu See also STOUT, Sally Read *St. Helen's Hall: the first century, 1869–1969.*

[5] St. James Day School opened in Fall 1948 and still flourishes.

[6] Corsicana Record Book.

[7] Only the first part of this typewritten letter has survived, so the writer is unknown.

4

BROAD AND SOUND FOUNDATIONS

St. John Baptist School, 1940–1959

A S THE OLDER institutional work of the Community drew to a close, St. John Baptist School seemed to go from strength to strength. The 1940s would bring a number of changes, but as the new decade opened thoughts were focused on the 60th anniversary of its founding. The St. John Baptist School Association had met on December 30, 1939, at the Waldorf Astoria in New York City, to plan the celebrations. Sixteen classes were represented, beginning with Mrs. Katharine (Hovey) Seabury from the class of 1894, and ending with six from the class of 1939. Letters of encouragement were received from absentees "all heartily in favor of making this anniversary year a big one and pledging cooperation in whatever plans were made."[1] Plans were laid for an anniversary dinner in New York sometime in April with distinguished speakers, with the expectation that Sr. Elisa Monica would be there. She had been Sister Superior at the school since 1914. Also, plans were made to publish a large Alumnae number of the school Yearbook *The Satura*; and to give an anniversary dance in New York for younger members sometime in May 1940. Most ambitious of all was the plan to raise $10,000 for payment on the school mortgage "as a testimony of appreciation for all that Sr. Elisa Monica has done for the school during the many years that she has been connected with it."[2] None of this could be done without the active support of alumnae and friends, which included fundraising for the various events. Mother Florence Teresa was able to report in the Associates' Newsletter of summer 1940 that the dance held after Christmas and the tea dance in the spring had both been very successful.

On May 31, 1940, seven school girls were received as Associates of the Community—good news indeed as older Associates were becoming fewer. June 1 was the School prize giving and Commencement, and for the first time it was held at St. Peter's, Morristown. This was at the request of parents and friends who felt that more guests could be accommodated there, and it proved to be a great success. The service was held in the church and the luncheon and meeting in the parish house. The Sisters' luncheon was held in a separate room. About 250 people attended and there were 200 at the luncheon. Mother Florence Teresa's only criticism was that while the two speeches were good they were *"very long."*

Although the United States had not yet joined the war, one way in which the school was able to help the war effort, and show solidarity with the English Sisters, was by taking in girls who had been evacuated from England. On September 27, 1940, Sr. Elisa Monica and Sr. Margaret Raphael went to Whippany to discuss the possibility. The first girl, Patricia Boucher, arrived on October 26, 1940, and three more arrived early in 1941. These were Jean Allen and Jean Mary Wood who arrived on January 17, and Mary Crossland who arrived in February. Other girls came later, [3] but soon the Battle of the Atlantic would make the crossing too dangerous. Once the United States entered the War, following the Japanese attack on Pearl Harbor on December 7, 1941, a number of former students of the school joined the various women's services. Marian Wysong,[4] who had entered the school in 1930, graduated in 1935 and then joined the teaching faculty, now left to join the Red Cross Motor Corps and saw service in North Africa.

The Community and the School had been saddened by the death of Miss Celestine Pinckney of Morristown, who had done much fundraising for the new school building in the 1920s. *The Satura* of 1941 paid tribute to her and from it we learn that she had known about the school since its days in New York when her cousin, Anna Parker, graduated in 1898. But it was only since 1923, when she was in her thirties, that she had formed a connection with the school at Mendham. From that time onwards her commitment had been wholehearted. This was all the more remarkable as she was very disabled by arthritis, being unable to walk and with little use in her arms and hands. But she had the gift of enthusiasm and was able to enthuse others. She knew exactly who to contact for funds and who to enlist in her campaign to raise enough to build the new school at Mendham. When the school was blessed on June 5, 1929, she was carried in her wheel chair to the ceremony and shown all over the new building. But her commitment did not stop there. She continued to organize concerts and sales and to attend Commencement. While visiting relatives at Charleston, SC, she developed a coronary thrombosis and died soon afterwards. The tribute in *The Satura* of 1941 concluded with the words that "she died leaving us the memory of her heroic, unselfish life and faithful friendship." But that wasn't all. She left $1,600 to be paid towards the outstanding mortgage, and a further $2,000 which was used for the same purpose.

In 1939 Mr. William Cordingley had given part of his house at the foot of the hill to the school. It had been named St. Hilda's Lodge and was used partly for teachers' accommodation, and partly for an art studio and domestic science facilities. Now in September 1941 it was transformed into a preschool and primary school, as a lower school for day pupils, but this was fairly short-lived.

Nineteen forty-two saw the resignation of Sr. Elisa Monica as Sister Superior of the school. She had been in office since 1914, but now, at age 86 and in failing health, she stepped aside and moved back to the convent.[5] The girls might be forgiven for feeling shocked. Sr. Elisa Monica had become so identified with the school that it was difficult to think of it without her. But she was after all a St. John Baptist Sister and knew when the time had come to "decrease" in favor of her successor. Writing in the school history,[6] former student Charlotte Urquhart, who graduated in 1943, recalled: "Whenever you were with her you liked yourself. When you came away from her you felt proud … The school was a good place to be … There she sat twinkling out at you from under her two-toned veil, her hands moving back and forth on Pash, her cat … [Her] eyes were still beautiful and the most piercing blue. When she looked at you she saw YOU."[7]

Sr. Elisa Monica's successor at the school was Sr. Alice Ursula (Strickland). But as already noted in Chapter 1, Mother Florence Teresa resigned as Superior at the convent in October 1942 and Sr. Alice Ursula was elected in her place. And so for the second time in the same year St. John Baptist School had yet another Sister Superior. This was Sr. Agnes Genevieve (Brooks), who had been professed since 1931 and had previously worked at St. Marguerite's. She would remain in office until 1946 when she was one of the Sisters chosen to take up the challenge of starting a parochial school in Corsicana, Texas.[8]

As noted at length in Chapter 1, Mother Alice Ursula's sudden death on May 26, 1943, while visiting St. Helen's Hall in Portland, Oregon, came as a great shock to the Community and to all who knew her. This sense of shock was felt no less at St. John Baptist School and a requiem was offered at the school. The 1944 edition of *The Satura* was dedicated to her memory with the words: "To Sister Alice Ursula. In loving memory and gratitude for all she has done for the school and especially for her individual care and devotion to each and every one of us, we dedicate this our Year Book." There followed a poem written by one of the girls on behalf of all, in which the Sister was referred to as "beloved Sister [and] friend."

Sr. Elisa Monica continued to have an interest in the school even though she was no longer Sister Superior, and was an honored guest on special occasions. On January 8, 1944, she wrote to the alumnae expressing her regret at not being able to attend their meeting. "My dear Alumnae. It is with great regret that I [will] miss your meeting. The reason is Hitler and his war; for the war makes gasoline scarce so that we cannot run a car to New York, and I am not allowed to travel by train. But I hope that you will have a very successful meeting. Seven of last year's class are in seven different colleges, two have returned to England, all the rest are working. This year the school is full as never before. We are glad to help parents who are fighting or working for our country, so we have put in extra beds and a seventh table in the dining room, and we seem to go on very well. We have a graduating class of ten, good teachers, and three of our girls are on the State hockey team reserve. So we are keeping up our record. We count on the loyalty and interest of our Alumnae. Very affectionately, Elisa Monica, Sr. CSJB."

The new Sister Superior, Sr. Agnes Genevieve, soon endeared herself to the girls, who showed their appreciation by dedicating the 1945 edition of *The Satura* to her with the words: "In affectionate and grateful recognition of all the love and kindness she has shown us, all the worthwhile lessons she has taught us, and the many personal sacrifices she has willingly given to us, we dedicate our Yearbook."

On May 19, 1945, the Chairman [sic] of the Board of Directors of the St. John Baptist School Association, Judith Meylan Henderson, paid tribute to Sr. Elisa Monica in a letter to the alumnae. "Do you know that this is the 65th year of St. John Baptist School and that Sister Elisa Monica has been connected with the School for 47 years? Many of us have had the great privilege of knowing her and being guided by her. Others who have not personally been in contact with her know her as one of the great personalities of St. John Baptist School. Her love for the school and her steadfast faith and devotion to the high ideal of establishing the school on a firm, worthwhile foundation, have long been known and appreciated ..." She then went on to relate the financial difficulties at the school, chiefly concerning the outstanding mortgage, and appealed to the alumnae to contribute generously to pay this off "in honor of Sister

Elisa Monica. Many of us want very much to present as large an amount as possible, to her personally, while she can receive it. This will give her more happiness than anything that we can ever do in the future." Mrs. Henderson expressed a hope that Sr. Elisa Monica would be present at Commencement on June 2, even though she had suffered two attacks of pneumonia during the past two winters. [It is not clear whether she did in fact attend.] Mrs. Henderson summed up her tribute and appeal with the words: "Sister Elisa Monica has lived and dreamed St. John Baptist School for all these years and [she] has been one of the biggest factors in making it what it is today. Let us now while we can, show her our very great appreciation."[9]

Sr. Elisa Monica's mother (formerly Susan Bard Johnson) had left property in Brooklyn, known as the Johnson estate, to her. The shares had been invested for the use of the Community, some of the interest being used for St. John Baptist School, and some for St. Helen's Hall in Portland, Oregon, when the Community had charge of it. In November 1945 Sr. Elisa Monica had written to Mother Waldine Lucia, stating that the City of New York had voted to acquire a tract of land in Brooklyn for public buildings, including the Johnson land. Both the Community and St. John Baptist School held shares in the Johnson estate and the sale of these would enable the mortgage on the school to be paid off, and still leave a reserve fund of $4,500. Sr. Elisa Monica did not live to see this business concluded shortly before Christmas 1946, but doubtless she would have rejoiced when the mortgage was finally cleared.

Sr. Mary Barbara (Schroeder) was appointed Sister Superior of the school in 1946 in succession to Sr. Agnes Genevieve, following the latter Sister's move to Texas. Sr. Elisa Monica's death on September 14, 1946, Holy Cross day, has already been referred to in Chapter 2, but mention must be made here of the loss felt by the school. Blanche T. Bigelow, a former student, wrote to the Sister Superior, Sr. Mary Barbara: "… If ever rest was earned *she* has earned it. With her goes the last of those who gave me early influences of faith and churchmanship. Her influence, however, as you say, will never die."

The St. John Baptist School Association announced that on November 23, 1946, there would be a Memorial Service for Sr. Elisa Monica at the Church of the Ascension, NYC, followed by lunch in honor of Sr. Mary Barbara, the new Sister Superior. "We who owe so much to Sr. Elisa Monica, and the School which was her life, can best pay our debt by

supporting Sr. Mary Barbara and her plans for carrying on the School."
Two Sisters attended the service as well as about 50 alumnae.

The 1947 edition of *The Satura* carried a long tribute to Sr. Elisa
Monica by Elspeth Hart from the class of 1943. "… It was a tradition
at the school that this, and only this, Sister would lead us downstairs to
Sunday dinner … She trudged past the statue of St. John Baptist, her two
pets—cats—following her as if in procession … 'Hush, hush, quiet girls,'
she would say with a nodding head or a shaking finger. Visible respect
evinced itself on the faces of those fifty odd students as they gazed at
the old Sister. Softly then they padded down the stairs and into the dining
room. Happy was the person who sat next to Sister, and pointed were the
conversations that sought to draw a word or two from her. She never did
say much … Two years before this Sunday I had caught my first glimpse
of her. She was walking from the convent to the school. Hunched over,
face hidden, hands folded, seemingly oblivious of the stiff wind that
whipped across the Mendham hills. I marveled that she didn't blow away;
she seemed so fragile and small. Yet on she came with her habit blowing
in the wind … During those two years, certain portraits of Sister will
remain unforgettable. Like the day I saw her walking among the gardens,
her gardens, slowly she would bend over and pluck out a few weeds. Then
on she would amble to a clump of buttercups and pick a tiny bouquet …
She paused a moment to watch the girls set up the archery target, then
drawing her habit closer to her slight figure, she would stroll on. Or like
the day I saw her pick up the aged cat, Claude, and stroke him fondly.
Then her peace-making to the other cat, 'Now Pash, it isn't that I like
Claude any better, but he's been sick.'"

The war had brought about many changes at St. John Baptist School
and the rather sheltered, isolated existence from the wider world came to
an end. Newspapers, radio, and, much later, TV became part of everyday
life and the discussion of current affairs was encouraged in the history
curriculum. Engaging with the post-War issues began to be seen as
appropriate for young women, many of whom would go on to college
and university. Thus towards the end of 1946 the girls were shocked into
action after seeing Save the Children Fund's film *Children of Tragedy*, and
decided to sponsor a school at Rensel, Holland, that had been shattered
by the war, for a year. The school was run by the Sisters of Charity and
was an elementary school of 140 girls. Boxes of clothing, school supplies
and funding for specific needs were to be sent.

School life went on as usual under the leadership of Sr. Mary Barbara, who would be Sister Superior for the next 25 years. It was said of Sr. Mary Barbara in her Community Biography that everything she did prospered, and indeed the school now settled down to a time of steady growth, and in the next decade, further change and expansion of the buildings. Some of the lay members of the teaching faculty stayed for a number of years. These included Miss Marian Wysong, who returned after the war until 1961, and Miss Florence Barber, who taught English. Miss Barber had joined the staff during the war and remained at the school until her death in 1957. The 1958 edition of *The Satura* bore an affectionate tribute to her.

The academic work continued to a high standard, but it was not all work and no play. Sports activities flourished, especially hockey and tennis, under Miss Wysong's guidance. Concerts were held at the school, some of which were "home grown" and others were performed by visiting artistes. And there were visits off the campus, a notable one being to the UN Security Council. This soon became an annual event.

A new brochure for the school throughout the 1950s set out the objectives, amongst which were "to help students to develop a clear, wholesome philosophy of life, through the sacramental teaching and influence of the Church … that they may be able to meet the demands of our constantly changing era with courage and vision; to lay broad and sound foundations of scholarship that they may appreciate and enjoy the culture of the ages, and relate both to modern life; to encourage each student's own special capacities, by careful, individual supervision and guidance …; to train girls to be ready to bear their share of the burden of the future, having a definite standard of faith and morals, girls who will make good wives and good mothers, good friends and good citizens."

The major project which dominated the 1950s was the provision of a new gymnasium in memory of Sr. Elisa Monica. The new school, opened in 1929, had no gym and the students had continued to use the gym in the old school at the bottom of the hill until the property was sold. Then the school rented the gym of a neighboring school but this facility was withdrawn when the hosting school grew in numbers. Provision of a new, purpose-built gym would be a huge effort of fundraising due to post-war austerity. In November 1953 an ambitious illustrated brochure was produced outlining the school's history and the plans for the new building. This included photographs of school life and the architect's impression of how the new building would look. The construction was to be of cinder block with laminated arches and the building would be at a lower level than the school so as not to detract from the main building. A glass-enclosed passageway would connect the two buildings. It was estimated that the new building could not be completed for less than $150,000.

Although the school was now out of debt on the original mortgage, the new work could not begin until much of the new target had been reached. A loan of $60,000 had been obtained early in 1957, but Mother Margaret Helena had made it clear that the present school building and property would have to be given as collateral for the loan, and not the convent or convent property.[10] On March 1, 1957, the ground was broken for the new building, and on October 6 it was dedicated by the Bishop of Newark, the Rt. Revd. Leland Stark, in spite of early snow. Mother Margaret Helena declared it was "a lovely service." Lawson Purdy, Sr. Elisa Monica's brother, attended and gave an address. Known as the Sister Elisa Monica Field House, the new building was much more than a gym. It also contained a stage for performing drama and concerts, and downstairs there was a science laboratory, a classroom and a music room. The architect was James S. Jones of Morristown.[11] When the school had been at the bottom of the hill there had been a pond, and in 1958 a new pond for swimming and skating was constructed below the new gym.

Many former students kept in touch with the school and with the Community long after they left.[12] The school had instilled a sense of loyalty and a bond of friendship which has lasted through the years. Former student Chris Chrystal regularly visits the convent and during her visit cleans the memorial stones in the Community cemetery. She recalled her schooldays: "I was there from 1956–60, my high school years. It would have been classed as a private high school, or private preparatory school. In 1956 the school had seventh and eighth grade as well as the four high school grades (9th, 10th, 11th, and 12th). Seventh graders were twelve years old, eighth graders were thirteen, freshmen in high school were fourteen, sophomores were fifteen, juniors were sixteen, and seniors, seventeen. But the school dropped the seventh and eighth grades while I was there, so then we only had the high school grades. As I recall, there were about eighty or so students while I was there, including fifty-six boarders and the rest day students. They came from middle and upper class homes. Many of the girls came from very nice homes [and] most were from homes that were economically comfortable, and some were wealthy. A number of girls came from broken homes or homes where the mother had died or left, and had been sent [to the school] to provide stability, often by a relative or guardian. It was not a 'snobby' school as were a number of prep schools, because the Sisters maintained strict discipline and did not permit us to do much besides study, sport and chores. We were allowed to go into town (Mendham) on Saturday afternoon, but several shops where we might encounter local boys were off limits to us."[13]

Chris Chrystal recalled Sr. Katharine Veronica, who was a trained nurse before coming into Community, and was the school nurse from 1955–62. "She was kind and friendly with a big smile she used often. She tried to teach algebra to Betty Ambler and me … We could not learn algebra. Somehow we both graduated without grasping this subject, and never needed to know it through our whole professional lives. Most of the girls called Sister Katharine Veronica 'Katy V.' She used to write to me in the summer when she was on vacation at the Jersey shore. I will always remember her fondly." Sr. Katharine Veronica had worked at St. John's Parochial School, Corsicana, TX, before coming back to work at Mendham. Her Community Biographer wrote: "She had a wonderful gift for making friends." It was said of her that all ages loved her, from the little children in the primary grades at Corsicana, through the older girls at St. John Baptist School, to the elderly people amongst whom she ministered later at St. Luke's Chapel, NYC.

Sr. Elizabeth Marion's Community Biographer noted that she had a great gift for organizing people and the various work she did in Community. She had previously worked at St. Helen's Hall until the Sisters withdrew, and upon her return joined the teaching faculty at St. John Baptist School. Chris Chrystal remembers her fondly. "She taught Latin and seemed very scholarly. I was taking Latin and French at the same time and got them mixed up all the time! Poor Sister—she tried. Her nickname was 'Lizzie Fizz.'"

Chris Chrystal noted that the girls did not know the Sisters at the convent very well because they only saw them from time to time. The "school Sisters" who taught the girls every day all had nicknames. For instance, Sr. Mary Barbara was known amongst them as "Soupy" because she was the Sister Superior! The girls thought the Sisters didn't know but maybe they had their suspicions! Although Sr. Agatha Louise was not on the staff at St. John Baptist School, some of the Sisters gave spiritual guidance to the girls. Chris Chrystal remembers her in this role. "She was a very sweet and kind person; light-hearted, and she made it fun. A few of us in my class (1960) had her for this and we nicknamed her 'Sally' for her initials—SAL." Her Community Biographer noted that Sr. Agatha Louise was much loved wherever she worked. Sr. Susinne Paula also gave spiritual direction. Chris Chrystal remembers her as "very cute and had a sweet little face and personality to match. She was known to the girls as 'Suzie' but not to her face of course."

Sr. Jane Patricia was second Sister at the school. Chris Chrystal recalls her vividly. "She taught Old Testament and some languages and was known as 'JP'. She was very strict and shook her big roll of keys at us when she was in silence and was angry about something we did. She was good at catching us who broke the regulations but we got away with a few stunts. One was putting the wooden mallet that was used to hit the gong in the morning and at dinner into her shoe in her closet. I did not do it, but I did set an alarm clock to go off at midnight and stuffed it into a balloon, which I then blew up and put on the shelf in the school infirmary. It went off as planned and Sister scurried around looking for it until she found it ringing away inside the balloon. We thought that was pretty funny! In those days, the late fifties, we were pretty tame! This was before drugs, when having Pepsi in your room during the week could get you impounded for the weekend."

Summing up her memories, Chris Chrystal remarked, "As a youth, I saw the Sisters as 'magical' people who were beyond the weaknesses that plague the rest of us. I saw them as models of near perfection, to be respected and obeyed without question. They were women of God— beyond us. As I aged I was surprised to learn that Sisters got sick, went to the dentist, had various ailments and personalities similar to other people, but better restrained. It still shocks me to see them in secular clothes. When they wore full habits with starched white 'headgear' and long veils, all one ever saw of them was their face and hands. We didn't know how old they were and never saw any hair that might suggest age. To me it seemed they were not concerned about petty things but were focused wholly on prayer and good works. I still believe they are the soul of goodness and that they try every day to be all that they promised. As teenagers, we schoolgirls were not always as tolerant and understanding as we hopefully tried to become as we aged. I did not know that Sisters had feelings. It occurred to me that when I graduated in 1960, I might have thanked each Sister for all she had done for me and to my benefit.

Cleaning their tombstones is the least I can do for the wonderful spiritual life they have given me."[14]

As the school prepared to enter the eighth decade of its existence there was much to be thankful for. The school was housed in a fine new building, blessed in 1929; there was now a new gym which was everyone's pride and joy, and there was even a new pond. The one thing lacking was a purpose-built chapel. Mr. William Cordingley had planned an ornate Gothic building but presumably the funding had run out for it was never built. The only existing clue to how it would have looked is in a photograph of the architect's model, which is itself now lost. It would have looked entirely out of keeping with the main school building, which even in the 21st century looks surprisingly modern. And so, as the 1960s dawned, the next major project—the provision of a chapel, always dreamed of—now became a reality. This will feature in a later chapter.

Meanwhile much was happening at the convent under the leadership of Mother Margaret Helena. So it is necessary to return to the 1950s.

---

[1] Letter to Alumnae and Friends of St. John Baptist School Association, February 1940.

[2] Ibid.

[3] These were Suzanne and Gabriella Turnay, who had come to England from Poland; Alison Hunter; and later, Jill Dundas and Gillian Savory, who came under special arrangements as they were too young to attend regular classes. Source: PRICE, Margaret M. *St. John Baptist School 1880–1980*.

[4] Marian R. Wysong, 1917–92. The 1951 edition of *The Satura* was dedicated to her "in grateful appreciation for the loving aid and inspiration you have given us."

Other former students who served in World War II from 1941–46 were: Constance Anderson; Blythe Bailey; Margaret Bailey; Marian Fisher; Barbara Greey; Emily Harris; Joantre Hawkins; Dorothy Howell; Gilberta Lyon; Mary Ann McConahay; Julie Pullman; Ellen Wilson; Markie Wilson; Patricia Wilson; Ruth Wilson; Jean Wood. In addition, Alice McIlvaine, class of 1928, entered the WACS (Women's Army Corps) in 1945, shortly before the War ended and served for twenty years; Louise Roberts, class of 1941, and Frances Casey, class of 1935, both served in the WAVES (the women's branch of the US Naval Reserve). Source: PRICE, Margaret M. op. cit. p.36.

[5] Sisters who worked at the school lived there although they returned to the convent for special occasions.

[6] Price op. cit. Chapter 4.

[7] The girls affectionately called Sr. Elisa Monica the "two-toned nun." Her black habit had faded to grey over the years and she had repaired her veil with a strip of newer black material, giving a two-toned effect!

[8] See Chapter 3.

[9] Mrs. Henderson, as Judith Meylan, had a long association with St. John Baptist School, having graduated in 1916. In her letter to the Alumnae quoted above she wrote, "We older Alumnae, who go back to the days on Stuyvesant Square [NYC] and the New York of thirty and forty years ago, and those who lived through the transition period of the trek to Bernardsville and World War I, as well as the rather subdued and modest days of the little grey house at the foot of the hill, and finally the Alumnae of recent years who have enjoyed the fine, new school building on the top of the hill with its sunshine, broad views and high living—all cherish in one way or another certain very strong memories of our St. John Baptist School days. And we are today what we are, to a very definite extent, because of the impressions received, the trainings learned and the knowledge acquired, from those old SJBS experiences."

[10] Community Record Book January 23, 1957. According to the Minutes of the Community Chapter on December 10, 1957, the mortgage was $40,000. The Minutes of the Chapter held on December 17, 1959, stated that it was only necessary to put a mortgage of $30,000 on the school property and that this had been paid in full in September. In 1955 the school had received a legacy of $30,000 from an old graduate who was a relation of Sr. Elisa Monica.

[11] James Suydam Jones, architect, of Morristown, died at age 86 in a nursing home in Chester, NJ, on November 13, 2000. He had his own architectural firm in Morristown for over 40 years and was a member of the American Institute of Architects.

[12] The school memories of Marjorie Wysong, now Sr. Marjorie Raphael, SSM, (1935–41) and Kitty King Rockwell (1938–41) are in BONHAM, Valerie *Living Stones* Chapter 19 pp.324–325.

[13] Information from Chris Chrystal by email to Valerie Bonham, April 2020.

[14] Chris Chrystal wrote these memories in 2015 and sent them to me via Sr. Suzanne Elizabeth when she visited the UK.

5

LET OUR LIVING BE THANKSGIVING

The Community 1950–55

A S 1950 DAWNED, the Sisters entered not only a new decade but also a new era in Community life. As already noted in Chapter 2, on October 6, 1949, shortly before Mother Waldine Lucia finished her term of office, the Community Chapter had voted in favor of closing the convent and moving across the lawn to the now disused St. Marguerite's. The resolution before the Chapter was a radical one and the move to St. Marguerite's was intended to be temporary. The resolution acknowledged that "the cost of operating the property of this Community at Ralston and Mendham, NJ, is beyond the resources of the Community, the main building being in very bad repair … It appears that it would be to the best interest of the Community to sell the entire property, if a sale could be consummated to advantage."[1] It was therefore resolved that "an effort be made to dispose of the Ralston, Mendham, property with the view of re-locating where the work of the Community could be conducted on a more economical basis."[2]

It was a difficult decision to make. Although the convent building was less than 40 years old, and there were several older Sisters who remembered re-locating from New York,[3] it was the Mother House. And although it may be said that it was just bricks and mortar, its status as "Mother House" singled it out from other branch houses that had already been closed. It was also the Sisters' *home*—the place where they lived and prayed, and to which they returned after outside ministry and family visits. The prospect of living within sight of the Mother House and watching it deteriorate further was potentially painful.

There was much discussion, centering mostly on how the proposal would affect both the novitiate and the spiritual life of the Sisters. As already noted in Chapter 2, the Chapter had refused the offer of parish work at St. Luke's Chapel, NYC, where the priest, Fr. Paul Weed, was also their Warden. Now the proposal to work at St. Luke's came before Chapter again on October 6, 1949, where it was linked up with the question of whether to dispose of the convent building. The initial refusal had been on the grounds that the Community could not undertake further work unless the Sisters were freed from the burden of manual labor in the convent. They had been strongly advised to dispose of the buildings, move elsewhere and take new outside work.[4] After much discussion the Chapter voted in favor of disposing of the convent and re-locating elsewhere, and to undertake the work at St. Luke's Chapel.[5]

So it was that as Mother Margaret Helena took up the reins of office, she also faced the huge challenge of selling the Mendham property and re-locating elsewhere. This would occupy several years before its final resolution.

Mother Margaret Helena had been in office less than two months when the new decade dawned and she had seen many changes in the Community since her arrival as a postulant in February, 1933, preceded by five years as a secular teacher at St. Helen's Hall in Portland, Oregon. Her Community Biographer wrote of her that "more than any other Sister she spanned the old and new eras of the Community, striving always to adjust to new times and new situations. CSJB has been shaped by her presence and will continue in her spirit." During her Community life so far, she had seen the withdrawal from Oregon (a work which was close to her heart), the adoption of work in Texas and subsequent withdrawal, the closure of the older institutional work, and the separation from Clewer, and now the challenge to their very presence at Mendham. There were other challenges and changes, too: older benefactors had died. In 1939 the Community had been saved financially by a substantial legacy[6] which had enabled the Sisters to continue their work. Although St. John Baptist School had received several legacies in the 1940s, the Sisters knew that they could no longer rely on the benevolence of Associates and other friends, because since the Wall Street crash the economic climate had changed forever. Also, vocations were fewer. There was no shortage of "would-be" novices but few made it past the postulant stage and only Sr. Elizabeth Anne would make her life profession (in 1951). At the start of this new decade there were twenty-six professed Sisters.

A Newsletter to the Associates, dated thirteenth Sunday after Trinity, 1950, gave the latest news of the Community and the Sisters' ministry. Three older Sisters had died during the year: Sr. Fanny Helen (Andrew) on January 31, Sr. Catherine Vera (Jones) on May 25, and Sr. Virginia Dorothea (Appleton) on July 7. Between them, these three Sisters had worked in all the Community houses.

Sr. Fanny Helen was, in her heyday, eminently practical and had been in charge at most of the Community houses. She had gained a reputation at the convent of being a very good cook. Her Community Biographer wrote that "she could make a pudding of most anything 'perhaps a piano leg' when unexpected guests arrived"! She also did beautiful sewing and "had a magic touch with gardens." She had a deep influence on the girls at St. Michael's Home, Mamaroneck, and many years after Sister's death a former girl said she still used the prayers Sr. Fanny Helen had taught her. Born in England, she was received as a novice in New York in 1888, and died a faithful Sister 62 years later.

Sr. Catherine Vera, who died on May 25, was Canadian and remembered for her nursing skills. Wherever a nurse was needed she was sent to help. Thus when Sr. Katharine Angela (Brooks) was taken ill at Portland in 1934, Sr. Catherine Vera was sent out there to bring her home. She had been in the Community since her reception as a novice in 1911.

Sr. Virginia Dorothea was received as a novice in 1897 and her main Community work was at Holy Cross House, New York, where she became Sister in Charge. Mother Margaret Helena wrote of these three Sisters: "each one had lived a long and useful life in the Community and had contributed much to our 'treasure in heaven'. May they go from strength to strength in that larger life." All the usual rites and ceremonies took place in the main chapel, followed by burial in the Community cemetery.

In the same Newsletter, Mother Margaret Helena reported the closure of St. Andrew's Hospital, Poughkeepsie, less than a year after the removal from New York City. During that time nurses' salaries had doubled, and then salaries of other workers had to be increased proportionately. This factor, together with the lack of patients, spelled the end of this older work. After several months of uncertainty the hospital was closed to patients in April 1950, and the final removal of furnishings took place on August 15.[7] The Sisters who had worked there returned to the convent.

If this news was tinged with sadness, there was also plenty of good news in the Newsletter. In Mother Margaret Helena's words, "Let us go on to the blessings and joys." And these were plentiful as the Community's Second Spring flowered abundantly.

Following the decision by the Community Chapter to take up the work at St. Luke's Chapel, NYC,[8] the Sisters lost no time. On January 9, 1950, Sr. Elizabeth Marion (Case) received her blessing as Sister in Charge. She had many organizational skills. Meanwhile, Sr. Agnes Genevieve (Brooks) and Sr. Susinne Paula (Ruby) were to accompany her in this new work. Sr. Agnes Genevieve had taught at St. Helen's Hall, St. Marguerite's, and at St. John Baptist School, before going to Corsicana, TX. Her Community Biographer described her as "a very loving, and lovable person who got on well with people. She was much loved at St. Luke's." When the Community took work in Jersey City, Sr. Elizabeth Marion moved there from St. Luke's and was appointed Sister Superior, and Sr. Agnes Genevieve became Sister in Charge at St. Luke's. Sr. Susinne Paula served for a time at St. Luke's but her great work was in Jersey City and there will be more of this in a later chapter.

Other Sisters would also work at St. Luke's Chapel during the next 24 years. A house—90, Barrow Street—was taken nearby and was opened on Wednesday January 11, 1950, as St. John Baptist House. Fr. Weed celebrated the first Mass in the house and reserved the Blessed Sacrament the day after the Sisters moved in. Although there had been some confusion as to what they would undertake within the parish, the Sisters were soon drawn into all aspects of parish life: supervising sacristy work; parish visiting, especially amongst the sick and poor; teaching sacred studies in the parochial school; helping in the Sunday school and Vacation Bible School; and preparing candidates for confirmation. So it was that after a space of thirty-five years, CSJB returned to New York City and opened another St. John Baptist House. Many of the children taught by the Sisters came from families of Afro-Caribbean origin who had settled in this racially diverse area. There are many photographs in the Community archives showing Sisters with groups of children obviously thrilled to be in the picture with Sister.

The parish work at Christ Church, Newark, NJ, was now in its third year. The Sisters did not have a Community house there due to lack of funds, but they traveled there two days a week and their ministry was much valued. In 1950, for the second year running, the Sisters helped at the Vacation Bible School at Christ Church. In 1949, seventeen children had turned up and the Sisters were pleased, but in 1950, 54 children came, and the Sisters were amazed! The days consisted of attendance at the 9:30 Mass, followed by a pottery class. Then there was a Bible class, followed by lunch, then some games and dismissal. A Presbyterian friend fired the children's pottery, which they were able to proudly take home later. On the Sunday after Ascension Day, 93 members of Christ Church parish came to the convent for Solemn Evensong and supper.

Nearer home, the Sisters continued to teach in the Sunday School at St. Mark's, Mendham.

A valuable ministry lay in the conducting of Quiet Days and Retreats at the convent, for various groups and individuals. The main chapel at the convent was still used for these events and remained a valuable resource. It was a serious factor in the Sisters' deliberations about moving, but the die had been cast and the task of finding suitable property was ongoing. Also, various Sisters, including Mother Margaret Helena, continued to go far and wide addressing groups, young and old, about the Religious Life.

Although the older Associates were departing this life, new ones continued to be admitted, including ten in 1949–50. Even so, there were still a few Associates who had been received at the Mother House in New York City before the Sisters re-located to Mendham. The oldest were Mrs. Florence Jayne Gates, admitted in 1883, a former student of St. John Baptist School in its very early days; Miss Caroline Runtz-Rees, admitted in 1889; and Miss Helena Appleton, sister of Sr. Virginia Dorothea, admitted in 1894. But Fr. Schlueter always claimed a longer connection as the Sisters had been present at his baptism in 1877![9]

Of the ten new Associates admitted in 1949–50, five were admitted in Texas before the final departure of the Sisters. Leaving a work did not necessarily mean severing ties, as the Texas Associates showed by keeping in touch and making visits when in the New York and New Jersey areas. Also, there was a strong body of Associates in Oregon and the numbers continued to increase with regular meetings, corporate Communions, and the annual visit from Mother Margaret Helena. All in all, the support and ministry of the Associates was a great help to the Sisters—and still remains so.

Mother Margaret Helena finished her Newsletter with the following words: "Religious Orders as well as everyone else are feeling the strain and stress of life in a troubled world. To us it is a source of comfort and encouragement to find our Associates so eager for a closer spiritual tie with the Sisters, and to feel the power of your prayers and interest in our behalf. We pray it will be an equally great source of spiritual strength for you … We beg you to keep us in your prayers, as you are in ours."

As 1951 dawned there was a chilling note in the Community Record Book[10] stating that "the Mayor of Mendham, Dr. Thompson, came to see whether the convent could be used as an Emergency Hospital in case of bombing."[11] The threat of war was looming large in America at this time.

The so-called Cold War between the USA and USSR had begun almost as soon as the Second World War had finished. The first major conflict began in June 1950 with the invasion of South Korea by Soviet backed troops from North Korea. A month later, American troops entered the conflict on behalf of South Korea. By this time the Soviet Union had developed its own nuclear bomb and this raised the threshold of fear to a global level. The Korean War came home to Mendham when Mother Margaret Helena received a telegram on December 8 that her older brother, Colonel Frank Forney, had been killed in action on November 29, 1950.[12]

Two Sisters went to their eternal rest in 1951. Sr. Alice Madeline (Cranmer) died on April 16, and Sr. Ada Marian (Whittingham) on December 4. Sr. Alice Madeline had only been professed since 1940 and had poor health from the beginning. A fall during the move to St. Marguerite's resulted in her returning to Wilmington, NC, in 1950 for a medical consultation set up by her father, who was a physician. A cancerous tumor on her spinal cord was diagnosed, with a very limited prognosis. She was aged 36. She remained at her parents' home and passed to her rest on April 16, 1951, shortly before Mother Margaret Helena and Sr. Waldine Lucia arrived. It was decided to have the funeral and burial in Wilmington with Mother and Sr. Waldine Lucia present. The Community funeral pall was placed over the coffin along with Sr. Alice Madeline's vows and New Testament. The committal was 162 miles away at Windsor, NC, where four other siblings were buried. Sister's wooden Cross was put on the coffin. This was the first funeral of a Sister entirely away from the Community work.

Sr. Ada Marian, who died on December 4, 1951, was the third former student at St. John Baptist School to have joined the Community, and was professed in 1904. Her Community Biographer wrote of her gentleness, and how young children were attracted to her like a magnet. Maybe it was because she was a small person, so small children were immediately drawn to her. She worked at St. Helen's Hall in the kindergarten, and the son of the Cathedral Dean used to tell of how he was sent to a girls' school and sat on Sr. Ada Marian's lap!

On May 3, 1951 (Ascension Day), there was Mass in the main chapel at which the girls from St. John Baptist School were present. Then at 3:00pm there was a confirmation in the convent chapel and eight of the school girls were confirmed by the Rt. Revd. Benjamin Washburn, Bishop of Newark. Tea for the guests followed at the school, during which the bishop made an exciting proposal. He was convinced that the way forward for the Community was to undertake parish work and was pleased about their work at Christ Church, Newark, and at St. Luke's Chapel, NYC. Now he wanted the Sisters to work in the parish of Grace Church (Van Vorst) in Jersey City. This was a challenging project and Mother went to see Fr. Weed, their Warden, to discuss the matter. Also, on May 26, the School Commencement service was held at the convent for the first time and was declared a great success.

On June 22, 1951, Sr. Elizabeth Anne was professed on "a lovely bright day." And indeed it *was* a lovely bright day, a day to renew hope for the future of the Community. There were about 30 guests, including Judge Osborne and his wife. The judge had been very supportive to the Community on legal matters for several years.

Four days later, Associates' Day was held and was well attended by both lay and priest Associates. Fr. Paul Moore, Rector of Grace Church (Van Vorst) was among the clergy present and Bishop Washburn preached a stirring sermon. He spoke of the Community's "foundation" work in America as being "that of parish and parish school work, and that now we had gone back to our original work, and that he was glad and thankful to have us doing such fine work."[13] Further talks took place with Fr. Moore in July. "All promises well," was the comment in the Record Book. On August 23, 1951, the Community Chapter voted in favor of taking the work in Jersey City.[14]

Although St. Marguerite's had closed as a home school some years previously, there were still funds in its name. In August 1951, at a Board meeting, the decision was made to combine all the small accounts together and use the interest to help poor children. For several years the Sisters helped to finance a boy from Christ Church, Newark, at St. Bernard's School. This funding came from the St. Marguerite's funds. Also, the Community funded a scholarship for a high school boy in the Holy Cross mission in Bolahun, Liberia.

Similarly, although St. Andrew's had closed as a hospital, the Board still met as the funds had not been dispersed. At a meeting on March 10, 1951, it was decided to give St. Luke's Hospital, NYC, $2,000 from the interest on St. Andrew's account. The Community Record book noted: "this to be done until St. Andrew's re-opens or work of like nature [is taken] by the Community."[15] Writing to the Associates in Lent 1952, Mother Margaret Helena informed them that "we have not been able to re-open St. Andrew's but we have participated in the convalescent work of St. Luke's Hospital in New York." The donations to St. Luke's Hospital were particularly appropriate as several Sisters had trained as nurses there before joining the Community, and this would continue into the 1960s when the future Sr. Suzanne Elizabeth trained there.

The Sisters' chaplain, Fr. Noble, suffered a serious stroke just before Lent 1951, and for several months other clergy from neighboring parishes celebrated Mass at the convent. But due to his slow progress he resigned and the Sisters appointed Fr. Elmer J. Templeton. He took up his duties at the beginning of September 1951.

On September 18, 1951, Mother Margaret Helena and Sr. Waldine Lucia had a serious car accident on the way back from the Jersey shore. Sister Waldine Lucia described what happened in the Community Record Book. "A large car shot across the highway and we ran into it. Our car was wrecked, the other car much damaged, and two were hurt. Mother had her front teeth knocked out, and her face much bruised. Her Cross saved her from a crushed chest—the Cross was badly bent. Sr. Waldine Lucia was badly bruised. The Sisters came home in an ambulance." The Sisters gave thanks that despite their injuries, no lives had been lost.

Throughout 1951 and 1952 negotiations to sell the Mendham property were being conducted, and every time the Sisters' hopes were raised, they were subsequently dashed. Bishop Washburn was fully supportive of the Sisters' intention to move. He said, "I think it is the right thing to do, doubtless there will be heartaches, but it is the life and inner spirit that counts."[16] Rumors abounded and eventually Mother Margaret Helena issued a statement in the 1952 Newsletter to Associates (there had been no Newsletter in 1951). "For several years we have thought we should try to dispose of the large buildings and land we are not able to use or maintain. Last spring we received an offer from Esso Standard Oil of New Jersey for the convent, St. Marguerite's, the caretaker's house and the guest house. They wanted it for an emergency headquarters in case of a national disaster. It seemed a wonderful solution to a very grave problem for us. We found a house near Morristown and started the legal procedure ... which was denied after a wealthy Episcopalian stirred up objections. The argument was that if we were allowed to buy and occupy a single family dwelling, it would make it easier for another institution to acquire [property]. After that denial we found several suitable houses but each time in a restricted zone. On what seemed like good advice we tried again in Montclair and met with even more opposition than in Morristown. There it was plainly obvious that the objection to us was because we are Religious." The refusal from Montclair was particularly disappointing because the residents clearly expressed a prejudice against Religious Communities, and in particular a fear that the Sisters would take in so-called "wayward girls" which would lower the tone of the exclusive residential area. They need not have feared—the Sisters had given up this type of work a decade ago. The Sisters appealed against the ruling, but their appeal was dismissed.

Even though all efforts to sell the convent and re-locate had been thwarted, Mother Margaret Helena did not lose heart. "We have now abandoned the hope of finding a suitable place, for the present, at least. I hope you will pray most earnestly that God will show us what to do." Meanwhile, the Sisters had fully embraced parish work, not only at St. Luke's Chapel, NYC, Christ Church, Newark, and in Jersey City, but also in short-term work in a number of parishes. Thus the Vacation Bible School at St. John's Church, Dover, NJ, was added to the growing list, and during the winter the Sisters were helping with an experimental school of religious education at St. Paul's Church, Morris Plains, NJ. The summer Vacation Bible School at St. Uriel's, Sea Girt, continued to be held with the Sisters commuting from their beach house at Manasquam. The Sisters had also been elected to serve on the Diocesan Board of Religious Education.

Mother Margaret Helena was full of enthusiasm as she wrote to the Associates about the work which had begun in September 1951 in Jersey City. At first the Sisters commuted from the convent. "I am sure Grace Church needs no introduction. The eyes of the whole American Church are watching that great experiment in the reclamation of a depressed and spiritually deserted neighborhood. We are very fortunate indeed, to have a share in this work. In the early summer [1952] we hope to have a house in the parish and three Sisters will be in residence." Mother concluded her letter to the Associates on a hopeful and positive note. "For all of these opportunities of service; for four hundred or more children it has been our privilege to teach; for those who have asked our prayers; for our Associates who have helped us by their prayers, time and gifts, we are humbly grateful. So in the face of disappointment, perplexity and uncertainty *let our living be thanksgiving*." [my italics]

The great event of 1952 for CSJB on both sides of the Atlantic was the Centennial celebration of the founding of the Community at Clewer.

On June 28 there was a Solemn High Mass at Mendham, held outside under the trees. Over 500 people were present from far and wide on a most memorable day. Bishop Washburn was present and the sermon was preached by the Rt. Revd. Robert Campbell, OHC. A choir was provided by the boys of Grace Church (Van Vorst), Jersey City. The day was captured by a splendid set of photographs. After the Mass there was a picnic lunch and the Sisters gave guided tours of the chapel, and a group of graduates showed visitors round St. John Baptist School. The day was given full coverage in the *Morristown Daily Record* of June 30, 1952, and two weeks previously, on June 19, there had been an article about the Community and the forthcoming celebration. Two days later, on June 30, there was a meeting for the Associates and about eighteen attended.

Two Sisters who did not live to celebrate the Centennial were Sr. Laura Claire (De Cormis), who died on April 22, and Sr. Lillian Christine (Naser), who died on May 6.

Sr. Laura Claire was professed in 1895 and her Community Biographer described her as "very small in stature. She had snapping black eyes and dark eyebrows giving her a very bright face." She was described as "a devoted Sister." She had worked in a number of branch houses and after returning to the convent when she was elderly she continued to sew chapel linens. In the summer months she would sit in the cloister sewing and singing hymns. She was very faithful at the Offices and prayer time. Her death at age 92 was peaceful after 57 years in life vows.

Sr. Lillian Christine was a mission Sister, professed in 1922, and one of the three last mission Sisters who were professed as choir Sisters in 1940. She had worked at St. Anna's, Holy Cross House, NYC, and St. Andrew's Hospital, but in her later years she developed tuberculosis and spent a long time in hospital. When she died, her Community biographer wrote that "she was loved and mourned by many 'old girls' and the many people with whom she had been associated. Her ministry had been very rich indeed."

Sometimes a work reaches its conclusion, and at the beginning of August 1952 the Sisters withdrew from teaching Sunday School at St. Mark's, Mendham. Otherwise, there was much summer activity—Sisters going for their rest, others taking Vacation Bible School in the various parishes, and changing of personnel in the different Community work. And then St. Marguerite's began to show its age. Emergency repairs to the gables costing $1,700 had to be made. The Sisters could ill afford it, but it was a great necessity.

Towards the end of August 1952, Mr. Wysong, legal advisor, came to discuss a proposal from the bishop: for the Sisters to take on, and partly finance from St. Andrew's funds, the Diocesan Rest Home for elderly ladies. He advised the Sisters against it as the Community would lose its identity in such a combined work. They wisely heeded his advice.

With the coming of the Fall, Sr. Mildred Eleanor (Blodgett) had her blessing as Sister in Charge of the Jersey City work, and Sr. Agnes Genevieve as Sister in Charge at St. Luke's Chapel.

On September 6, Mother Margaret Helena, Sr. Katharine Veronica, Sr. Waldine Lucia and Sr. Eleanor Lucy set out in the convent car for Boston, Mass., to attend the triennial General Convention of the Episcopal Church. All the Communities were represented and helped at the Religious Orders' booth. Bishop Benjamin Dagwell of Oregon was amongst the many people whom they met. He was still grieving the loss of CSJB from St. Helen's Hall in Portland, declaring that only the Sisters had the answer to what he perceived as problems at the school. The Sisters also attended the Conference of Religious Orders before returning to the convent on September 15.

The Sisters had been commuting to Jersey City several times a week, but accommodation had now been found for them. It consisted of a top floor apartment of ten small rooms and "a lovely chapel." On October 27, 1952, the furniture van pulled up outside what would become St. Christopher's House, just a hundred yards or so away from Grace Church. On November 27, Thanksgiving Day, after the Solemn High Mass in the church, all the priests, Sisters, choirs and people processed along the street to St. Christopher's for the blessing of the house by Bishop Washburn. After the blessing there was coffee and cheese crackers! Then all the Sisters returned to the convent for the Thanksgiving dinner.

And indeed there was much to give thanks for. Just two weeks previously, on November 10, 1952, there had been the election of the Superior, and Sr. Margaret Helena had been re-elected in what the Warden, Fr. Weed, described as "a wonderful election." Mother was installed on November 12, and other officers had their blessings—Sr. Katharine Veronica as Assistant Superior, Sr. Waldine Lucia as Novice Mistress, Sr. Agnes Genevieve as Superior of St. John Baptist House, NYC, Sr. Mary Barbara as Sister Superior of St. John Baptist School, and Sr. Mildred Eleanor as Sister Superior of St. Christopher's House, Jersey City.

As 1952 drew to a close, the Morristown telephone operators gave a party for 60 Grace Church children. The Community Record for December 20 noted that it was "a lovely party and nice gifts. Some children had never seen Evergreen trees growing before." The Sisters celebrated Christmas in the usual way and 1953 came in with heavy snow and ice. Some things never change! At the tea party on New Year's Day Mother read some of the biographies of older Sisters long departed. "All very interesting and precious" was the note in the Community Record Book.

The Affiliated status with Clewer had ceased in 1949 but there was still friendly contact between CSJB in England and in America. The Weekly Letter to the Sisters sent by Mother Margaret Helena often contained news from Clewer. Food rationing was still in force in England until July 1954, and gifts of food from Mendham continued to be a great help. The Mendham Community Record for February 19, 1953 (the day after Ash Wednesday), noted that "Mother sent cheese to England for Easter." This would have been greatly appreciated.

Towards the end of 1952 Canon Leslie from Christ Church, Newark, announced his forthcoming retirement, and the Sisters decided to withdraw from the parish when he left. In fact they stayed on for a few months under his successor but finally withdrew in October 1953. Requests for the Sisters to undertake new work continued to flow in. A tempting offer, which they resisted, came from Bishop Mason, asking the Sisters to work at a school in Dallas, TX. Although it had been several years since they withdrew from Corsicana, the memory of the Sisters, and the impact they had made, was still fresh in the Episcopal Church in Texas. And indeed Mr. Doyle West continued to beg them to return to Corsicana. The Sisters knew when to say "no"—fortunately.

There can be no doubt that the Sisters' presence and ministry was greatly appreciated wherever they went. At Jersey City, Fr. Robert Pegram spoke to Mother Margaret Helena about the Sisters and their work, saying how much their presence, and what they stood for, was appreciated. And at the end of the Vacation Bible School at St. Uriel's Church, Sea Girt, NJ, the Sisters were given a large basket of fruit and $100, much to their surprise. They declared it to be "a lovely gift."

June 24, 1953 (the Nativity of St. John Baptist), was kept in the usual joyful way with lovely weather as a bonus. In the evening all the Sisters came in from the branch houses and a few Associates were also present for the picnic supper on the lawn. Next day, more Associates arrived and there was a special Mass of Thanksgiving, during which five new Associates were received. At the meeting which followed the Mass, a letter of congratulation was written to Mrs. Florence Jayne Gates, who had been an Associate for 70 years. Plans were laid for an Associates' Quiet Day in the Fall.

Mother Margaret Helena frequently went to parishes to speak about the Religious Life, but in September 1953 she went to Christ Church, Elizabeth, NJ, to speak about altar work and altar guilds. Her audience was "a nice group of young girls." This would be an increasing topic for talks and programs over the coming years. But none of this activity could happen without the undergirding of the daily office, private prayer, and the daily Eucharist. This, as always, was what gave the Sisters the spiritual strength to go out to the parishes and show how the Religious Life is lived. And this is what people saw when they encountered the Sisters because, unlike social workers doing a job, the Sisters were *living* their vowed life in the midst of all the difficulties they encountered.

Winter came early in 1953 with heavy snow and a bad storm on November 6. There was much damage to property throughout New Jersey, including the beach house at Manasquam. Fortunately the new service road from the school to the convent had been completed, as the old road was by now in a poor condition. The St. John the Baptist Foundation had given financial help towards this.

Nineteen fifty-four began with the publication of an attractive booklet, written by Mother Margaret Helena, with the title *A Message from the Community of St. John Baptist*. It was illustrated and gave a brief account of the Community from the arrival of the Sisters in New York on February 5, 1874.[17] Mother's introductory letter in the booklet outlined the daily life of the Sisters, emphasizing the spiritual life undergirding all the activity. There was a copy of the address given to Associates by Fr. Raymond Miller at their annual Mass in 1953; a résumé of the years activities; and a more detailed account of St. John Baptist School, St. Luke's Chapel, NYC, and Grace Church (Van Vorst), Jersey City.

In early June 1954 an old tradition was revived. The Warden was conducting the Sisters' retreat, during which a service was held at the Community cemetery. This was much appreciated, especially by the older Sisters who remembered it from past years. At the same time Bishop Washburn was at the school, where he was conducting his usual annual retreat for seminarians. He decided to call in to see the Sisters and arrived just as the procession to the cemetery was about to begin, and so he joined in with them.

Groups from churches far and wide continued to come to the convent and a note in the Community Record Book for September 14, 1954, noted that "27 colored [sic] people from St. Phillip's Church, Bronx here for a picnic—supposed to be 45, but [we were] thankful for only 27 as it was a bad cold, rainy day and much fog all day." How disappointing, as it was their first visit to the convent and all the Sisters had come in from New York and Jersey City especially to welcome them. The visitors had brought their own luncheon and the Sisters provided tea and coffee. The Altar Guild was present in the convent parlor to show them the historic vestments. The day finished with Evensong.

By 1954 the Sisters had been working at St. Luke's Chapel for four years. During that time they had seen how St. Luke's was a "solid Rock for many storm-tossed souls."[18] No one was turned away from St. Luke's, whether it was a priest asking to celebrate Mass, or a troubled soul needing a listening ear and a kind word. The Sisters were involved at all levels of parish life, from preparing the altar for Mass to teaching sacred studies in the parochial school. Also they visited the sick in their homes and generally helped the poor and needy. Mother Margaret Helena wrote modestly that "there is nothing spectacular about the Sisters' work: they are part of the kaleidoscopic life of the parish—sorrowing with those who sorrow and rejoicing with those who rejoice."[19] But many people would have said that they made a huge difference.

In a similar way the work in Jersey City was also changing people's lives and the Sisters were very much a part of this transformation of what was a very socially deprived area. Mother Margaret Helena wrote: "There are disappointments as well as joys, but more and more those who come to Grace Church are learning the way of life, and if they fail they know the way back to God."[20]

The Oregon Associates were going from strength to strength. Mother Margaret Helena met with them on October 2, 1954. Four new Associates were received at Mass, followed by a business meeting and lunch. There were 32 at Mass, including some Associates from other Communities. No doubt the annual visit by Mother Margaret Helena (which she combined with a family visit) helped the Oregon Associates to continue to flourish.

The Community Record Book had a joyous entry for October 28, 1954. "A great day for us. The Warden Founder [Canon Carter] must have prayed

for us, for the bishop signed the new Constitution at last—'Approval'."
It was an auspicious day for gaining approval as it was Canon Carter's
anniversary. The Sisters had been wrestling with the new Constitution
for several years, and Bishop Washburn had not made it easy for them.
He had misunderstood the clause referring to "Bishop's approval" and
had assumed the Sisters needed his approval for all new work. In fact his
approval was only required for new work within the Diocese of Newark.
He had also attempted to insist that all funds and buildings would revert
to the Episcopal Church in the USA in the event of the Community
coming to an end. The Sisters had resisted this very firmly and the new
Constitution stated that in the event of the Community coming to an
end, all property etc. would revert to the St. John the Baptist Foundation.

On New Year's Eve, 1954, Mother Margaret Helena received a letter
from the Bishop's Committee of St. Mark's Church, Honolulu, Hawaii,
thanking the Sisters for the gift of a large bell. The Sisters believed it had
come from St. Helena's Chapel at the summer rest house at Farmingdale,
and it had been in the cellar at the convent for 40 years. The bell was rung
72 times in thanksgiving when the church was consecrated on November
29, 1954. A request had come from Fr. Joseph Turnbull at St. Mark's for
the Sisters to take up work in Honolulu as from September 1955.[21] This
was another request that had to be reluctantly turned down.

As 1954 came to an end, the Post Office at Ralston closed its doors on
December 31. Henceforth the Sisters' address would now be Mendham.
Thus their address was changed without them moving, but many people
were saddened at what was perceived as a loss of identity, as the old place
name passed into history.

The first few months of 1955 passed fairly uneventfully. There were
the usual retreats for the Sisters, quiet days for groups who appreciated
the peaceful surroundings, and in many cases the chance to escape from
the noise and "busyness" of town and city.

On May 14, 1955, Helena Appleton died. By this time she was the
senior Associate, having been received on September 17, 1894, and she
was referred to in the Community Record Book as "our most faithful
Associate." Her sister was the late Sr. Virginia Dorothea, who had died in
1950. Helena Appleton was the daughter of the Revd. Richard P. Appleton
and his wife Mary. He was the rector of St. John's Episcopal Church,
Boonton, NJ. Helena lived for most of her adult life in East Orange,
NJ, and worked as a librarian at Orange Free Library. After her father's

death she lived with her mother until the 1930s, when she moved to New York City. She then became an active member of St. Mary the Virgin, NYC, and shortly before her death was appointed supply Secretary for the Women's Auxiliary there.[22]

The 1955 hurricane season began in June, which was early. Many of the great storms did not affect New Jersey, but on August 14, Hurricane Connie rampaged its way up the east coast and hit New Jersey. Fortunately the Sisters had bought a generator in order to keep the refrigerators going. But the severe storm didn't spare them and their lights were out for thirty-six hours. They had hardly recovered from the storm damage when Sr. Sara Josephine (Lucy) died, on August 19, 1955. Sr. Sara Josephine was a graduate from Bryn Mawr College in math and science, and following her profession in 1902, taught math at St. Helen's Hall. She was described as "a good and faithful Sister, and a dependable worker, [which is] the greatest contribution one can make." Her funeral took place on August 22, and almost all the Sisters were present.

On September 8, there was the reception of a novice, Sr. Mary Carol. This was good for Community morale as a number of postulants had come and gone without entering the novitiate. So there were high hopes for Sr. Mary Carol, although in the long term she did not fulfill them. On a more positive note, there was a Chapter of Election for the Superior on October 3, following a novena (nine days) of prayer. Sr. Margaret Helena was elected once again and, following the usual custom, all the Sisters went to the Chapter Room to greet the Superior. There were a few changes to other offices: Sr. Elizabeth Marion became Assistant Superior, Sr. Waldine Lucia was re-appointed Novice Mistress, Sr. Mary Barbara remained Sister Superior of St. John Baptist School, Sr. Agnes Genevieve was to be Sister Superior at St. Luke's Chapel, and Sr. Agatha Louise Sister Superior at Jersey City. The installation by the bishop took place on October 4.

And so 1955 passed into another New Year. The Sisters had much to give thanks for. If they had felt thwarted in their attempt to sell the convent and move elsewhere, they were by now beginning to perceive God's will in their staying on their hilltop site, even if their address had changed from Ralston to Mendham! Soon, thanks to the generosity of the late Helena Appleton, it would be possible to move back into the convent.

As noted above, at the tea party on New Year's Day 1953, Mother Margaret Helena had read to the Sisters some of the Community

Biographies of departed Sisters. There can be little doubt that those departed Sisters would have rejoiced at the new forms of ministry now being exercised. Numbers may have been less than in their day, and they might have been surprised to find the Community living at St. Marguerite's, and the institutional work that that they had known now closed, but they would have rejoiced that their beloved Community was now in its Second Spring.

---

[1] Chapter Minutes October 6, 1949.

[2] Ibid.

[3] Sr. Fanny Helen (Andrew), Sr. Laura Claire (De Cormis), Sr. Julia Frances (Hobbie), Sr. Virginia Dorothea (Appleton), Sr. Sara Josephine (Lucy), Sr. Ada Marian (Whittingham), Sr. Waldine Lucia (Scratchley), Sr. Catherine Vera (Jones), Sr. Francina (Vesbeck), Sr. Beatrice Clare (Pelz) and Sr. Mary Joan (Gleason).

[4] See Chapter 2.

[5] The voting was as follows: 23 in favor and three against moving out of the convent; 22 in favor, three against and one abstention on the motion to dispose of the convent; 26 in favor and none against taking the work at St. Luke's Chapel.

[6] For details of the Hamilton Fish Webster legacy see BONHAM, Valerie *Living Stones* Chapter 20, pp.358 & 360.

[7] The altar and reredos would later be used in St. Michael's Chapel in the restored convent. For a photograph of the altar and reredos *in situ* at St. Andrew's Hospital, NYC, see BONHAM, Valerie *Living Stones* p.189.

[8] St. Luke's Chapel was one of eleven chapels founded from Trinity, Wall Street, NYC. Its correct title is St. Luke's in the Fields, Greenwich Village, reflecting the more rural setting of the original church in 1820. It was destroyed by fire in 1886 and was rebuilt in 1892. In 1976 Trinity, Wall Street, divested itself of all but one of its chapels, and St. Luke's again became an independent parish. The church burned down in another fire in 1981, and after it was rebuilt it was renamed St. Luke's in the Fields.

[9] A favorite story told by the Sisters was that when he was a small boy, Edward Schlueter said he wasn't sure whether he wanted to be a Sister or a Priest when he grew up!

[10] Community Records, June 8, 1948–71. Entry for January 4, 1951.

[11] Although no further reference was made in the Community Record Book, the convent did become a shelter in case of a nuclear attack. Fortunately, it was never brought into use. Information given by Sr. Suzanne Elizabeth, CSJB.

[12] Colonel Frank Hartman Forney (1906–1950) graduated from West Point in 1929. He was a veteran of World War II. In Korea he commanded the 19th Engineer Combat Group, and was killed in action while attached to the IX Corps fighting along the Ch'ongchon River. His body was not recovered and his name is inscribed on the Courts of the Missing, Court 6, at the Honolulu Memorial. Amongst his many decorations he was awarded posthumously the Silver Star for "conspicuous gallantry and intrepidity in connection with military operations against the enemy." The Forney Bridge monument was built after the Korean War to commemorate Colonel Forney and was later re-located to a more accessible site. Sources: http://valor. militarytimes.com Also https://abmc.gov Also https://www.army.mil/article/136478

[13] Community Record Book op. cit. Entry for June 26, 1951.

[14] There will be much more about the work in Jersey City in later chapters.

[15] Since their re-location to Ripon College, Cuddesdon, the UK CSJB Sisters have been financially supporting charitable organizations that reflect their original work of rescuing women and girls from situations of grave moral danger. Human trafficking and prostitution are as rife in 21st century UK as in the 19th. This is on very similar lines to the Sisters at Mendham, whose financial help to poor children and to one of the great New York teaching hospitals reflected the same philanthropic ideal.

[16] Community Record Book op. cit. Entry for June 2, 1951.

[17] There is always something new to learn! In her short account of the Sisters' early work, Mother Margaret Helena noted that when the first Sisters arrived in New York, they were met by Mr. George Winthrop Folsom (Sr. Helen Margaret's bother), Dr. Stuyvesant Fish Morris, and Miss Annie Ogden. I had not previously discovered who met the Sisters on their arrival, but the first two are no surprise. Dr. Stuyvesant Fish Morris was a nephew of Hamilton Fish Webster (see note vi above), and his mother was a Stuyvesant. But I have been unable to trace Miss Annie Ogden.

[18] *A Message from the Community of St. John Baptist* p.8.

[19] Ibid.

[20] Op. cit. p.9.

[21] Fr. Joseph Turnbull was an old friend of the Sisters.

[22] Op. cit. p.6. Additional information provided by Sr. Monica Clare, CSJB.

6

VARIED AND UNENDING

The Community 1956–59

THE SECOND HALF of the 1950s was a period of consolidation. The new work begun a few years previously continued against the background of the liturgical year, and of the Sisters' vowed life. Winter weather lingered on—Easter Sunday on April 1, 1956, saw deep snow, but both the Masses were celebrated in the main chapel. On April 10, Mother Margaret Helena started out for Oregon, where her father was very ill, but sadly he died two days later, shortly before her arrival. The Sisters continued to travel far and wide and on May 10, Mother Margaret Helena and Sr. Agatha Louise left for the Community of the Transfiguration at Glendale, Ohio, to attend the blessing of "the St. John Baptist window, dedicated to our Community."[1] Groups continued to visit the convent from the parishes where the Sisters worked, and also from parishes where the priest knew of the Sisters.

There were two new developments at this time. Firstly, when Mother Margaret Helena, or any other Sister, went to a parish to talk about the Religious Life, she often took a slide show with her so that her audience could see the convent and its surroundings for themselves. Secondly, there was an increasing number of groups from Young People's Fellowships. This post-War decade was a time when the church tried to reach out to young people by giving them a place to meet, discuss faith-related topics, and have someplace to play team games. In June 1956 the YPF from St. Clement's, Philadelphia, came for a picnic and tour of the chapel.

During 1956, what had previously been a dim hope of renovating the convent began to seem more like a possibility. The late Helena Appleton, who had died in May 1955, left a substantial bequest to the Sisters, and other bequests also helped. In November 1956, Sr. Waldine Lucia noted in the Community Record Book that "repair men are working on the convent—a very expensive job costing over $30,000, but necessary if we are to save the convent." It was a long and tedious process, and by March 1957 the work was still in progress. "Men working on the convent, trying to make it waterproof—a very expensive job."[2] It would be several years before the convent was habitable.

Living so close to the convent—just across the lawn—and seeing it gradually deteriorating, must have been disheartening for the Sisters. It must also have provoked comments, even criticism, from the many groups of visitors who came for retreats, quiet days and parish picnics. Conditions in St. Marguerite's were probably not ideal for the Sisters' way of life. It was, after all, built as an orphanage, with large dormitories. These were converted into individual rooms or cells for the Sisters and for a limited number of female guests. But it was not purpose-built as a convent, and although there was a chapel in the house, the Sisters had to go across to the main chapel for large functions—in all weathers. Perhaps it is not a coincidence that there were no life professions after that of Sr. Elizabeth Anne (June 22, 1951) for the duration of the Sisters' residence at St. Marguerite's. Other postulants and novices arrived and left during that time, but when the future Sr. Suzanne Elizabeth came to the Community as a postulant in November 1963, the Sisters were once again living in the convent. The state of the convent in 1949, however, was such that desperate measures had to be taken, and the large, empty former orphanage was the obvious answer. As already noted, this was meant to be a temporary measure until new accommodation could be found. That these efforts were thwarted was by no means the fault of Mother Margaret Helena, but no doubt there was great relief when the Community moved back to the renovated convent.

The other building project at this time, already discussed in Chapter 4, was the building of the new gymnasium at St. John Baptist School. The contract was signed on February 15, 1957, and the ground was broken on March 1. Work proceeded rapidly and the new building was dedicated on October 6, 1957, in the snow. All present were greatly pleased with the gym, which the Sisters pronounced to be "splendid."

There was still a certain amount of contact with Clewer. On March 19, 1957 (the feast of St. Joseph), the Community Record Book noted that some "very handsome white vestments" made at Clewer were worn for the first time. An older set of white vestments were then sent back to Clewer for refurbishment in the Church Workroom.[3]

Nineteen fifty-seven was a year of loss for the Sisters when several clergy passed to their rest. The first of these was Fr. Edward Schlueter, who died on April 2.[4] He was one of the Sisters' oldest friends, having been known to them since he was a baby. There was a requiem for him on April 5, and the next day fourteen Sisters attended his funeral at St. Luke's Chapel, NYC. The church was very full. On September 11, Fr. Noble, former chaplain to the Sisters, died peacefully. He had resigned his chaplaincy in 1951 but the Sisters had kept in touch with him. They had visited him on Christmas Day 1956, and he was very pleased by their visit. His funeral took place in the Sisters' chapel and he was laid to rest in the Associates' area of the Community cemetery. Mrs. Noble came to live at the convent. Finally, on October 8, Fr. Frank Aitkins died and was buried in the Community cemetery.

A new ministry in the shape of evaluating Sunday schools is evident from the Community Record book in 1957. Mother Margaret Helena and Sr. Waldine Lucia belonged to the special Committee of the Diocesan Department of Christian Education. The evaluation consisted of the priest and superintendent of the Sunday school coming to the convent for an interview, followed by a visit to the parish by the two Sisters, during which other interviews might be conducted. It is not clear from the Sisters' records how many parishes took advantage of this ministry. The Diocesan Department of Christian Education continued to hold meetings at Mendham. The day would begin with Mass in the main chapel, and the meeting would end at 4:00pm. Another innovation at this time was a summer program where young girls would come to the convent to help out during their vacation. They would help with care of guests.

Many years previously the convent had been famed for the illuminated manuscripts produced by a few Sisters in the Church Workroom. In more recent years this was a skill taught in the novitiate but the work was not done on a large scale. Sisters would illuminate cards to give to each other at festival times. But in the summer of 1957 Sr. Elizabeth Marion worked on an illuminated guest book for the Morristown Neighborhood House.[5] Sr. Waldine Lucia commented in the Community Record Book, "a very lovely piece of work—our contribution for that cause."

Throughout the latter part of 1957 and into 1958 there was growing concern for Sr. Mildred Eleanor,[6] who had four major operations for cancer. But even though she had been close to death several times, she recovered from her ordeal and lived another ten years.

Nineteen fifty-eight was an uneventful year in many ways, but the Sisters' spiritual life undergirded all they did—whatever the weather! In March their long retreat was held in the chapel at St. Marguerite's. Two

Sisters from the Order of St. Anne[7] and two from the Society of St. Margaret, Boston, Mass., also attended. There was heavy non-stop snow for 43 hours. The snow plows had difficulty clearing it, but the retreat was uplifting.

St. John Baptist-tide in June 1958 followed its usual pattern with two Masses—one in St. Marguerite's and the choral Mass in the main chapel. There was a tea party at 3:00pm, Vespers at 4:00pm and picnic supper on the lawn at 5:00pm. A few friends were present, such as Fr. Templeton and his growing family, the Grier family, and Gertrude Gleckler, who had been received as an Associate in 1953. All the Sisters were present too, though several had to return to New York and Jersey City at the end of the day. On June 28, Commemoration Day, the Sisters hosted about 60 visitors, and all had lunch in the refectory at St. Marguerite's. In August a group of eighteen people came for a day retreat from Elizabeth, NJ, the parish where Miss Gleckler lived, thus forging a new parish connection with the Sisters.

The Community Record Book failed to note that, after nineteen years in office at Clewer, Mother Dorothy Frances resigned in 1958. She was succeeded by Sr. Annys, who was installed on September 15, 1958, and would hold office for twenty years. Mother Annys and Mother Margaret Helena had an instant rapport which would bode well for the future relationship between the two halves of CSJB.

Bishop Benjamin Washburn retired as Bishop of Newark on November 1, 1958.[8] Although at first he had viewed the Sisters with some hesitation, and indeed he was not the first bishop to do so, he proved to be a good friend and supporter. In his opinion the Sisters should have been out in the parishes, doing pastoral work and teaching the faith. At first he had little understanding of what is known as "the hidden life"—the life of prayer, the living of the vowed life away from the "busyness" of the wider world. He saw their role as engaging in activity, whilst visible in parish life. And to a certain extent the Sisters took on this role, but never at the expense of their life of prayer and the sacraments. This was what fueled their active work—the chapel was the powerhouse, and in time Bishop Washburn came to understand this. Without that spiritual thread running throughout their life, they would have been severely compromised.

On October 22, 1958, six Sisters went to the consecration of Donald MacAdie[9] as Suffragan Bishop of the Diocese of Newark. They were pleased to be in the procession. On November 1, 1958, Bishop Leland

Stark was installed as Bishop of Newark and five Sisters were in the procession. A new episcopal relationship was about to be forged, and on February 8, 1959, Mother and Sr. Katharine Veronica took part in the bishop's Youth Rally in Newark.

Requests for the Sisters to take on extra work continued to flow in from far and wide. On January 19, 1959, Bishop James Pike[10] of California invited the Sisters to work in his diocese. They declined the offer. An interesting request came to the Sisters in April 1959, when they were invited to help in the work of the Rose Bud Mission to the Lakota people of the Sioux Nation in South Dakota. The Sisters rather reluctantly declined this offer—there was illness in the Community and thus no Sisters could be spared for this work. But a few years later, Sisters were able to assist at the Navajo Mission in Arizona.[11]

The Sisters had been at St. Luke's Chapel[12] almost ten years. When they had first arrived there they were told by the man who ran the local drugstore, "This is not New York—this is Greenwich Village." The Sisters rapidly came to understand what a varied and colorful place it was, and they soon found ample scope for their ministry. St. John Baptist House in Barrow Street was a convenient stopping place for Sisters on their way to and from the convent, or for meetings of the St. John the Baptist Foundation. And it was a convenient base for the Sisters, whose spiritual life was centered on the chapel there.

St. John Baptist House closed for a month each summer to allow the Sisters to have their rests, and they were never sure what they would find when they returned. There was a great deal of vandalism in the area and the Sisters were not immune from being targeted. On one occasion they returned from their summer rest to discover that someone had taken the door knob and knocker!

But there were many good things too. St. Luke's School, recently opened, had gained a reputation as an outstanding parish school, and the Sisters taught some of the classes in religion as well as in the Sunday school and weekday catechism class. There was also a thriving junior altar guild, supervised by the Sisters, as well as parish visiting and maintaining a presence at the various adult groups and guilds. Photographs taken at the time show the Sisters surrounded by happy groups of children. St. Luke's was one of the many parishes that came to Mendham for picnics, but in May 1959 there was nearly a disaster. Two elderly ladies set the woods on fire while trying to kill caterpillars, and the local fire engine had to be called out! Fortunately the fire was contained before it spread and got out of hand.

In a Newsletter to the Associates dated Advent 1959, Mother Margaret Helena described the work at Jersey City[13] as "varied and unending," but that description could equally apply to all the work and ministry carried out by the Sisters at this time. In the same Newsletter she described Sr. Julia Frances' 60th anniversary of profession on May 23, 1959. It was "a wonderful day" with 100 guests, many of whom were former girls from St. Marguerite's, where Sr. Julia Frances had ministered for so long and so faithfully. Two "old girls," Marguerite Dennis and Ruth De Lagerberg, had spent nearly a year tracking down former residents of the home. And they came in droves, with husbands, children and grandchildren, for the picnic on the lawn. There was a special anniversary cake and everyone had cake and ice cream. The day ended with Evensong in the chapel at which Bishop Washburn preached. He had confirmed many of the guests when they were children. Mother Margaret Helena wrote, "We all had happy memories of his many visitations. It was a beautiful day, and the only thing Sr. Julia Frances wished was that she had had time to sit down with each 'child' and hear of all that had happened since she left St. Marguerite's!"

There was another significant anniversary on St. Alban's day, June 22, 1959, when Sr. Waldine Lucia celebrated the 50th anniversary of her profession. There is no entry for this in the Community Record Book— the entries were still being made by Sr. Waldine Lucia, who would not call attention to herself. However, Mother Margaret Helena wrote about it in the Associates' Newsletter for Advent 1959. "It wasn't possible to have a party for all the St. Helen's Hall girls!" She summed up these two anniversaries as "sixty years and fifty years of devoted service are indeed the cause for thanksgiving."

On June 19, 1959, just a few days before Sr. Waldine Lucia's anniversary, there came a phone call from Rockland State Hospital to say that Sr. Jeannette Louise had died. She had been increasingly ill since the day in the summer of 1956 when she had set out for Oregon to visit her sister. Four days into the journey she had become confused and was assisted by a Holy Nativity Sister, who recognized the CSJB habit and Cross. Mother Margaret Helena and Sr. Waldine Lucia took a helicopter to La Guardia airport and flew to Butte, Montana, and fetched her home by rail. The Sisters did everything possible to keep her safely at the convent, but eventually she needed the total care that could only be given in hospital. She had been visited faithfully by Mother and various Sisters until just a few days before her death, when she no longer recognized anyone. Her Community Biographer wrote, "The death certificate said 'premature senility' but today it might say Alzheimer's. Sr. Jeannette Louise had given all she had to her Lord and the Community—who can measure or identify the blessing that long, weary illness brought to everyone including Sister herself." The requiem was celebrated on June 23, and Sister was laid to rest in the Community cemetery.

And so Community life continued—next day about 60 people came for St. John Baptist's day and eight new Associates were received. Afterwards, some Sisters went to Manasquan for their summer rest, but others continued the work of hospitality at the convent. A typically busy day took place on August 8, when 87 people came from St. Mary the Virgin, NYC. There was a service in chapel, then luncheon, and their day ended with the Litany. But the Sisters' day had not ended. At 3:00pm the staff from Grace Church, Jersey City, Vacation Bible School came to the convent for a service followed by supper out of doors.

An old friend of the Community, Dr. Lawson Purdy, died on August 30, 1959, in his 96th year. He was the brother of the late Sr. Elisa Monica and had faithfully served the Community as legal and financial advisor for over 60 years. He trained as a lawyer and was well known in New York for his campaigns for tax reform and also to provide better living conditions for the tenement dwellers on the lower East Side. His death was the ending of an era for the Community.

"Mr. Raymond Julian, who is an architect, drew the plans for the addition we put on the Chaplain's house this summer, also for the alterations which are being made at the convent. After many years, and with large legacies, we are about to complete enough repair work to make the large convent building habitable. The whole exterior has been repaired and refinished, and much of the interior plaster has been replaced. We are making a small chapel on the second floor and are reducing the size of the kitchen. We are planning to move back into it, but at present cannot set a date." This was very welcome news for the Associates when they received the Advent Newsletter at the end of 1959.

As the 1950s gave way to the new decade there would be much to give the Sisters hope and confidence for the future, even though several of the older Sisters would pass to their rest. Soon they would move into the renovated convent; there would be new novices who had real vocations; St. John Baptist School would have its long-awaited chapel; and the new Mother Superior at Clewer would begin to extend the hand of friendship towards the Sisters at Mendham. A brighter dawn was breaking.

———————————————

[1] Community Record Book entry for May 10, 1956. Two windows on the south side of the chapel depicted the Revd. Dr. John Mason Neale, founder of the Society of St. Margaret, and Mother Harriet Monsell, foundress of CSJB. The windows were dedicated on May 11, 1956. Further information: Sister Monica Mary Heyes, CT, *Women of devotion. History of an Anglican Religious Community* 2014. I am grateful to Karen Corbett, Parish Administrator of Christ Church, Glendale, and to Sr. Suzanne Elizabeth, CSJB, both of whom pointed me in the direction of the Community of the Transfiguration for the location of the CSJB window. And to Kimberley Fonner, Administrative Assistant to the Superior of the Community of the Transfiguration, Glendale, Ohio, for providing photographs of the window.

[2] Community Record Book entry for March 13, 1957.

[3] The Church Workroom at Clewer was known far and wide. At first it was established in London in the 1860s, moving from Soho to Gower Street in 1883. In 1937 it moved to Clewer and was one of the last Community works before the Sisters left Clewer in September 2001.

[4] Fr. Schlueter was vicar of St. Luke's Chapel, NYC, from 1909 until 1945. During those first years the neighborhood was crowded with poor tenement dwellers. His great inspirations were Fr. James Huntington, OHC, and the Sisters of the Community of St. John Baptist. His friendship with the Sisters was life-long.

[5] The Morristown Neighborhood House is a non-profit agency dedicated to improving the lives of families in the surrounding communities. There was a special exhibit in 1957 to celebrate the opening of a new building. The organization kept its Centennial in 1998.

[6] In her book about Grace Church (Van Vorst), Jenny Moore tells a story about Sr. Mildred Eleanor. She was talking on the sidewalk to Fr. Paul Moore and his wife, Jenny, when a small boy shouted, "Father, Father, one of the new kids is peeing off the roof!" Before Fr. Paul could answer him, Sr. Mildred Eleanor patted the boy's head saying "Boys will be boys. I bet you used to do things like that all the time, Father." Source MOORE, Jenny *The people on Second Street* 1968 p.176.

[7] Order of St. Anne was founded in 1910 at Arlington Heights, Boston, MA, to care for children. The Sisters still live there, their convent now being known as the Bethany House of Prayer.

[8] Bishop Benjamin Washburn became Coadjutor Bishop of Newark in 1932 and Diocesan Bishop from 1935–8.

[9] Bishop Donald MacAdie served from 1958–63 under Bishop Leland Stark, who served as Bishop of Newark 1958–74.

[10] Bishop Pike was a controversial man, promoting social issues ahead of his time, but more seriously questioning the basics teachings of Christianity. He had heresy charges brought against him several times during his episcopacy but was never taken to court. He probably knew of the Sisters because from 1952 he was Dean of the Cathedral of St. John the Divine, NYC. In 1958 he became Bishop Coadjutor of California, succeeding to the See a few months later. He was succeeded as bishop in 1969 by the Rt. Revd. Chauncey Kilmer (Kim) Myers, who had worked with the Sisters during their early years in Jersey City until moving to lower East side in Fall 1952.

[11] See Appendix 3, Letters from an Indian Reservation.

[12] St. Luke's Chapel burned down in 1981, a few years after the Sisters left, and presumably the parish records perished. There are no detailed Record Books at the convent relating to the work at St. Luke's and so this very important Community work is relatively unrecorded.

[13] There will be much more about the work in Jersey City in Chapters 7, 10 and 13.

7

ON THE FRONTIER

The Early Years in Jersey City, 1951–59

JERSEY CITY HAS undergone many changes, economic, social and demographic, since the founding of Grace Church in 1847. At that time the area was mostly populated by white, well-to-do families whose business was in New York City, but who chose to live away from the increasing noise and congestion there. The first service, held in a temporary wooden church building, was on April 26, 1847; and on May 18 the parish was incorporated under the names of the Rector, Wardens and Vestrymen of "Grace Church in Van Vorst." On May 24, Fr. Albert C. Patterson was appointed Rector and on May 26, 1847, the parish became part of the Diocese of New Jersey.[1] Fr. Patterson resigned on October 1, 1848, and his successor as Rector was the Revd. Milo Mahan.[2] Under Fr. Mahan's guidance the new parish flourished and the congregation increased to such an extent that he decided to build a permanent stone church to seat 500 people. Many of the wealthy parishioners gave generously, not least Mrs. Sarah Van Vorst and three of her adult children, who gave three lots of land at the corner of Erie and South Seventh Street (later called Second Street), in memory of her husband Cornelius Van Vorst (1794–1852). Fr. Mahan left for St. Mark's, Philadelphia, in June 1850 and the church building project was completed by his successor, the Revd. David Macurdy. The Cornerstone was laid on December 6, 1850, and the building was consecrated on May 18, 1853, by the Rt. Revd. George Washington Doane, Bishop of New Jersey.[3]

The first years in the new church saw a rapid turnover of clergy until the appointment of the Revd. George Stephen Bennit in 1887, who served there until his death in 1915. During his incumbency a bonded debt of $13,500 was liquidated, an endowment fund of almost $40,000 was set up, and the communicant list almost doubled. In 1912 the church tower was built, finally giving Grace Church the appearance it has today. By 1915 the exodus from the neighborhood of white, wealthy Episcopalians had begun. In April 1918 Canon Henry Bryan, a former curate, became Rector and stayed until 1933. He improved the church's finances but the

Wall Street crash and the onset of the Great Depression left the parish increasingly impoverished.

Following Canon Bryan's departure, Grace Church lost its independent status as a parish and came under the jurisdiction of the bishop. The finances continued to plunge as more well-to-do families moved away and more immigrants, mostly of Afro-Caribbean or Hispanic origin, moved into Jersey City. These new families were poor people who found it difficult to get employment. No longer able to afford a full-time priest, the parish was served by the Church Army from 1947–49. In 1947 the church celebrated its centennial.

In spite of all the efforts of the Church Army, the church finances continued to decline as well as numbers in the congregation. The one remaining Church Army worker was assigned to work in the Midwest and all seemed to point to the end of Grace Church. And then there was light in what had become a dark place thanks to the open mind of the Rt. Revd. Benjamin Washburn, Bishop of Newark.

In the summer of 1949 Bishop Washburn was approached by two priests and a seminarian at General Theological Seminary, NYC. They sought ministry in a failing church amongst underprivileged people who had become alienated from "religion." This may have seemed like a naïve request, but Bishop Washburn immediately thought of Grace Church (Van Vorst) and decided to take up their offer. There was little to lose. The two priests were Fr. C. Kilmer (Kim) Myers and Fr. Robert Pegram. The seminarian was Paul Moore, who was ordained to the priesthood at Grace Church in 1949. The three moved into the dilapidated rectory in June 1949 along with Paul Moore's wife Jenny and their growing family.[4] As they were moving in they saw a visual parable in the shape of two signs at the lych-gate. One displayed a verse from psalm 100:3—"Enter His gates with thanksgiving"; the other was a crudely painted sign saying "Keep out." The second sign was quickly torn down but it indicated the huge task that awaited their ministry.

Grace Church was clearly going to be a challenge. There were the few remaining well-to-do parishioners, most of whom no longer worshipped at Grace Church, and the impoverished immigrant community who felt excluded and "unchurched." The author of the Commemoration booklet wrote of the impact made by the three clerics. "From the moment of their arrival in June 1949, this team made the life and problems of the people of the community their own, reaching out to people of all races and backgrounds, many of whom, newly arrived from the South, were struggling to keep afloat in depressed and often hostile surroundings. In time the devotion, warmth, and hard work of this new team ministry built up a strong and vibrant congregation, which has given Grace Church renewed life and a renewed sense of purpose."

In May 1951 Bishop Washburn had suggested to Mother Margaret Helena that CSJB should undertake work at Grace Church. Having already begun work at St. Luke's Chapel, Greenwich Village, they found the prospect of further work an exciting challenge. In September 1951 Sr. Agatha Louise and Sr. Eleanor Lucy began the work, at first commuting from the convent, but on October 27, 1952, the Sisters were able to move into the house at 278, Second Street, acquired for them by the clergy, finally living there from the following day. A faint note in pencil in the Jersey City Record Book states that four Sisters moved in that day: Sr. Mildred Eleanor (Blodgett) (Sister Superior), Sr. Agatha Louise (Weiss), Sr. Elizabeth Marion (Case), and Sr. Eleanor Lucy (Cowan).

On October 31, the first Mass was celebrated by Fr. Pegram in the Sisters' chapel and later the same day Bishop Washburn came to see the Sisters in their new house. On November 7, it was decided that the house would be known as St. Christopher's, and it remained the focus of the Sisters' work throughout their long ministry in Jersey City. In fact this was the third St. Christopher's House, the first having been the Sisters' summer rest house next to St. Anna's, Farmingdale, and the second at Mendham, serving a similar purpose until it was torn down to make way for the convent. As noted in Chapter 5, St. Christopher's was blessed by Bishop Washburn on November 27, 1952. Just how the 200 guests were accommodated for refreshments after the service remains a mystery, but also a sign of hope for the future.

The exact nature of the Sisters' duties was noted in the Jersey City Record Book kept by the Community throughout their ministry. "Settled day for staff meetings (Friday, later changed). Sisters are to have meetings with elementary Sunday school teachers and the girls assisting. Also to go to some of the activities, meetings, guilds, from time to time, e.g. play practices, Sunday evening youth group etc. The Fathers emphasized the fact that they do not wish to interfere with our Rule of Life but they do want us to be a real part of the parish life in all age groups." After the meeting the Sisters drove back to the convent at Mendham for singing practice (some things never change!). This was for the installation of

Mother Margaret Helena, who had been re-elected as Mother Superior.

There was much coming and going between the Sisters at St. Luke's Chapel and Jersey City as well as to and from the convent. Sr. Eleanor Lucy gave an insight into this in her Community memoir written in the 1970s. In some ways this jumps ahead of the immediate early years but it shows just how difficult it is to know which Sisters were working there at any given time. "On September 7, 1951, Sr. Agatha Louise and I went to Jersey City for the first time. We spent Fridays and Sundays at Jersey City, teaching the younger Church School children on Sunday and visiting Church School families on Fridays … The Community came into residence on October 28, 1952. Sr. Mildred Eleanor was Superior and Sr. Agatha Louise, Sr. Elizabeth Marion and I were the workers. Sr. Agatha Louise became Superior, I believe, in the Fall of 1953. During the first few years there were changes from time to time. I went to St. Luke's [Chapel], Hudson Street, after my retreat in 1955 and didn't return [to Jersey City] until 1957. At that time Sr. Mildred Eleanor was again appointed Superior, and Sr. Elizabeth Anne and I were the workers. That was the year of the Asian flu and then serious illness for Sr. Mildred Eleanor. I became Sister in Charge in December 1957. In 1958 I was made Sister Superior and I received my blessing at the time of Mother's re-election. Sr. Susinne Paula had come to take my place while I had the Asian flu. When Sr. Mildred Eleanor became ill she continued with us here in Jersey City. Ever since, I have been here in Jersey City, at Grace Church. Sr. Elizabeth Anne continued until made Assistant Superior in 1970. Sr. Susinne Paula, with short stays at the convent, has worked here continuously since 1957. The young Sisters have all worked here at various times in the capacity of extra workers for Church School, bazaars, toy sales, etc."

When the decision was made to accept the work at Grace Church, Sr. Eleanor Lucy was the ideal choice. Although she was plagued by poor health, she always rose above it, putting the ministry first. A time at St. Helen's Hall in Portland, Oregon, and later at St. John's parochial school, Corsicana, TX, had shown what a good teacher she was. At Grace Church she needed not just teaching skills, but compassion for those poor, often hungry and ill-clothed, children. Her Community Biographer recalled how one winter she brought a group of children into St. Christopher's, where they would be warm. She had found them outside on the street in the bitter cold. She gave them an impromptu painting lesson, much to their enjoyment. Sr. Eleanor Lucy was always able to look at a problem from the children's point of view and meet their needs. This also applied to helping the mothers find warm clothing and shoes for the children. There was always a supply ready to hand out at St. Christopher's. And it was appreciated by young and old. One little girl, who had just been given a warm coat, said, "Sisters, you have done so much for me, what can I do for you?" Sr. Eleanor Lucy gave her the important task of sorting out the Sunday school crayons!

Sr. Agatha Louise had trained to be a teacher and had taught at St. Marguerite's before coming into Community. Like Sr. Eleanor Lucy, she had worked at St. Helen's Hall in Portland, Oregon, and at the school in Corsicana. The contrast between these schools and work at Grace Church could not have been greater, but it was work she enjoyed and she remained at Jersey City until her health failed, making it necessary to return to the convent. Sr. Elizabeth Marion had similar Community experience to Sr. Agatha Louise, having worked at St. Helen's Hall, where she remained until the Community withdrew in 1944. She then taught Latin at St. John Baptist School and after several other positions in Community, including that of Assistant Superior, she worked briefly at St. Luke's Chapel, NYC, before going to Grace Church. Sr. Mildred Eleanor had also worked at St. Helen's Hall and at Corsicana before going to St. Luke's Chapel, NYC. Her final Community work was at Grace Church.

These then were the first four Sisters who pioneered the Community work at Grace Church (Van Vorst). Doubtless it came as a culture shock after earlier work in Oregon or at St. John Baptist School, though the work at Corsicana was similar to Grace Church. Even so, the Sisters, in true CSJB spirit, saw the need and answered it. All were moved with compassion when they encountered the poverty there. Other Sisters, such as Sr. Ora Mary (Synnes) and Sr. Katharine Veronica, would fill in at times, and yet others, some of whom were not yet in Community, would follow later. There would be times of success and times of failure but the presence of the Sisters meant a great deal more than they knew. In the words of Jenny Moore, author of *The People on Second Street*, "We learned in our first year on Second Street that it is not enough to become familiar with poverty's face, for after that comes frustration as you find how little its features can be changed."[5] And while she was referring principally to the clergy team, it is equally appropriate to the Sisters.

It was tough work in a tough area. At first the remaining white people protested to the bishop about the new regime at Grace Church. The idea of a ministry team was alien to them, whilst the Church Army workers did not pose a challenge. And there was interracial tension too. The clergy called an interracial meeting, attended by the bishop, and all went smoothly with no outbursts. But a few weeks later, when a colored boy claimed to have been insulted by a white boy, there was almost a riot. A white gang approached Grace Church intending to beat up any people of color they could find. Once again, the clergy acted as mediators and the gang disbanded. Gradually the message came through to the young people at Grace Church that there was a better way than violence. Some formidable weapons were handed in to the clergy, who locked them away.[6]

The work in Jersey City, described by Mother Margaret Helena as "a great experiment in the reclamation of a depressed and spiritually deserted neighborhood," slowly began to improve the lives of those in the immediate area. Jenny Moore graphically described how the clergy team had to contend with hostility and suspicion from all quarters (and presumably this applied to the Sisters too, though she does not mention them).[7] The local inhabitants had become so accustomed to violence, physical and verbal abuse, poverty, and living quarters that were unfit for human habitation, that it took a huge effort to win their trust and for them to believe that Grace Church was there for them.

During their first few months at St. Christopher's House the Sisters received many visitors brought by the bishop or by one of the clergy team. Thus on March 1, 1953, "Fr. Moore brought the Vicar of All Hallows, London, to see our chapel." This was Fr. P. (Tubby) Clayton, founder of the international organization Toc H, who was on a fund-raising tour to rebuild his church, All Hallows by the Tower, which had been destroyed in the Blitz.[8] Later in the year Miss Van Vorst visited the Sisters and stayed for Mass in their chapel. She would visit from time to time, thus maintaining the link established by her family almost a century previously.

The Sisters soon settled into the work at Grace Church and their spiritual life was centered partly in public worship in the church, but also in the chapel at St. Christopher's. Life was busy. For instance on March 26, 1953, there was a staff meeting, then secretarial work on the Holy Week notices; then at 4:00pm three Sisters attended the Way of the Cross for children; and finally there was a Women's Guild meeting at the rectory. Throughout Holy Week the Sisters attended the full program of services in church. On Easter Sunday the Sisters went to 8:00am Mass in church, after which there was a procession along Second Street to St.

Christopher's to restore the Blessed Sacrament.[9] The procession consisted of Fr. Moore, acolytes, Sisters and children. The ancient hymn *Tantum Ergo* was sung as the Blessed Sacrament was placed in the aumbry. Then all returned to church for Sunday school and Mass. In the afternoon the Sisters called at the rectory and then went out to visit the elderly who could not go out to church. Soon the Sisters would be visiting new families, a sure sign of growth.

There were comings and goings to and from the convent at Mendham as well as St. Luke's Chapel, NYC. St. Christopher's was a convenient port of call (in addition to St. John Baptist House, 90, Barrow Street, NYC) for Sisters from Mendham attending special services and for meetings of the Consultative Council. Mother Margaret Helena visited frequently, usually accompanied by Sr. Waldine Lucia. It was an important exercise in maintaining Community life with the Sisters based away from the convent. Several Sisters came for the funeral of Fr. W. F. Venables, for 32 years a priest in the Diocese of Newark, on May 9. On June 9, 1953, Sr. Agatha Louise and Sr. Elizabeth Marion went to the consecration of Bishop Leland Stark for the Diocese of Newark, and two weeks later, on June 14, Sr. Agatha Louise and Sr. Eleanor Lucy went by bus with the Grace Church people for Bishop Ludlow's farewell service.[10]

With the help of the Sisters the pastoral work at Grace Church was increasing. On Wednesday July 22, 1953, the Assistant Superior, Sr. Mildred Eleanor, and Sr. Agatha Louise went to the first meeting of the Mothers' Club: thirteen mothers were present. Mrs. Anderson from the Newark Diocesan Youth Consultation Service spoke on "How mothers can help their children." It seems that the mothers were very interested. On a more familiar note, the end of July and beginning of August brought the Vacation Bible School. Sr. Mildred Eleanor was in charge of the eight-year-old boys, and Sr. Katharine Veronica (who had come from New York) had charge of the seven-year-old girls and boys. Numbers attending were not recorded. Sr. Susinne Paula came from the convent to look after St. Christopher's and to provide meals for the Sisters each day. Saturday August 29 was "Field Day." The Jersey City Record Book states: "Mother Superior, Sr. Mary Joan and Sr. Jeannette Louise came [from the convent] to the service—had lunch with the Sisters and we all drove to the park to see the Field Day." Later the three visitors returned to the convent. But "Sr. Mildred Eleanor and Sr. Agatha Louise and mothers had the younger [children] on the playground from 4:00 to 5:15. At 5:15

went to the Parish House for movies (gave out candy on the way out)."

As 1953 gave way to 1954, there had been the usual round of parties for the mothers and children in addition to the services in church. On January 10, there was a pageant given by the children at the 11:00am Mass to the growing congregation. Several Sisters came from the convent or from New York: Sr. Katharine Veronica, Sr. Beatrice Clare (Pelz), Sr. Elisabeth Roberta (Gernand), Sr. Francina and Sr. Jeannette Louise. They brought sandwiches so as not to stretch the resources at St. Christopher's House and left after lunch. On February 21, the Young Peoples' Discussion Group celebrated its second anniversary with a service in church followed by a social. The Sisters' Record Book noted that they "went to the service and stayed a very short time for the social—left as the dancing began."

Vacation Bible School took much organizing; and on June 14, 1954, the Sisters went to help with a Jersey City Conference for Vacation Bible School teachers. The conference lasted from 9:00am until 3:00pm. At Grace Church the Bible School opened on July 26, and about 150 children enrolled, much to the surprise and delight of the Sisters.

As Christmas approached there was much activity preparing gift packages for families and toys for the children. Other churches had donated gifts, especially toys, but the Sisters had to wrap them all. Also, there were food parcels, mostly canned food. All of these parcels were delivered to needy families by the clergy or by the Sisters. But this was not all. Presents were needed for the various parties.

On Christmas Day the Sisters went to the rectory after the 10:00am Mass to give and receive greetings. Then they took the 12:00 train to Morristown and were met by Mother and Sr. Ellen Juliana (Somerly) who took them to the convent. They returned to Jersey City later the same day by car but two days later returned to Mendham for the Community tea party.

Nineteen fifty-four had been very much of a routine year, but in her letter to the Associates[11] Mother Margaret Helena had written very optimistically about the work in Jersey City. No doubt she could see improvements during her regular visits with Sr. Waldine Lucia. She wrote: "Everyone is happy and grateful to God for the growth of the past year. The seed sown is beginning to bear fruit in a growing sense of corporate responsibility and parish life. The people have formed a council which works with the staff on parish projects. They have contributed to the parish budget, and are vitally concerned with increasing adult membership."

She continued: "The children are a joy. This year the Sunday school attendance has been more regular, and behavior and response have improved accordingly. There were 375 children at the Children's Mass on Easter [Sunday], and 238 in Church on Ash Wednesday. We still have problems of children who can't come because they don't have shoes or a proper coat. The clothing our good friends send has been a tremendous help. One little girl was to have a new pair of shoes for Confirmation, and all the way to the store she kept reminding the Sister not to get them 'too tight round the waist.' The old ones were too short and hurt her instep. This year the Sisters have directed the seminarians and other workers in the Sunday school. They have written the material and prepared the handwork. This has been time-consuming but unbelievably rewarding. The children treasure the little things they can make and take home. There are disappointments as well as joys, but more and more those who come to Grace Church are learning the way of life, and if they fall they know the way back to God. The priests in charge say that the 'team' is not complete without the Sisters, and we are glad and thankful for the privilege of being part of the 'team.'"

There had been some changes to the clergy team. Fr. Myers had left Grace Church for similar work on the Lower Eastside in the Fall of 1952. This left Fr. Moore and Fr. Pegram, but in the summer of 1954, Fr. James Parks Morton came to the parish. In June 1955 Ledlie Laughlin was ordained deacon and joined the team. His ordination to the priesthood took place at Grace Church on January 1, 1956.

Winter 1955 brought the usual severe weather but the Sisters battled their way through to the convent for their regular retreats, confessions and keeping in touch with their Community life. Back in the parish they supported by their presence the three Lent suppers in the rectory. These were held for parishioners and all found a welcome. The Sisters also found time to meet old friends such as Doyle and Doris West from Corsicana, who were visiting at St. John Baptist House, 90, Barrow Street, in New York. A surprise visitor came in March—Mildred Lewis, a former resident at St. Marguerite's who had seen an entry for "Sisters of St. John Baptist" in the telephone directory.

Nineteen fifty-five and 1956 were fairly routine years, if indeed life at Grace Church could ever be described as routine! But the usual round of parish activities followed its course with the Sisters very much in evidence. In addition to work in the parish, the Sisters also went out and about to nearby parishes to speak about the Religious Life and also about the work in Jersey City, which was by this time attracting a good deal of interest. In October 1955, Sr. Ora Mary came to work at Grace Church, but after a few months her duties were cut back to the weekends as she was needed at the convent. She was a gifted musician with a lovely singing voice and was a great asset at festivals, and also for the daily singing of the Divine Office.

When St. Christopher's was re-opened at the end of August 1956, after the summer break, Sr. Mildred Eleanor, Sr. Elizabeth Anne and Sr. Agatha Louise took up residence. Sr. Elizabeth Anne has been described by her Community Biographer as "a hardworking, conscientious Sister who could fill in any place and do it well, and was loved by those with whom she worked." She had trained as a teacher and had taught at St. Marguerite's before entering St. Luke's School of Nursing, NYC. She finally came to the Community and was clothed as a novice in January 1949, and professed in June 1951. After profession she worked at St. Luke's Chapel and at Grace Church, where her previous experience was a much-needed asset.

In the spring of 1957 Fr. Paul Moore received a call to be Dean of Christ Church Episcopal Cathedral in Indianapolis, and left Jersey City together with his wife and family in the Fall of that year.[12] A few years after leaving Jersey City, Jenny Moore received a visit from a young man whom they had known as a small boy. "Before you came," he said, "we had very little hope, but you started a chain of things."[13] That could equally apply to the Sisters and their work at Grace Church.

Meanwhile, parish life went on with Fr. Pegram, Fr. Morton and Fr. Laughlin together with the Sisters. From August 5–16, 1957, the annual Vacation Bible School took place. Sr. Katharine Veronica was in overall charge, Sr. Elizabeth Anne helped with supervision and Sr. Ora Mary helped with the teaching. Two college students, Anne and Katherine, came to help and commuted daily from St. John Baptist House, NYC. Katherine had charge of the music and Anne taught the seven-year-olds. A total of 434 attended the Bible School. No sooner had the Bible School ended at Grace Church than Sr. Katharine Veronica and Sr. Ora Mary, together with the two girls, commuted by car to Christ Church, Newark, to help with the Bible School there. On August 28, there was a Baptism service at Grace Church, during which 125 were baptized as a result of the summer program.

After the summer break, during which St. Christopher's House was closed as usual, the Fall season made a good start with Sr. Elizabeth Anne assuming responsibility for the Women's Auxiliary and their meetings. There was also by now a Spanish group, over which Sr. Eleanor Lucy assumed responsibility. On October 12, 1957, there was the first session of the Saturday Church School and 150 children attended. They received teaching on Saturdays and then attended the Church service on Sundays. A week previously, on October 6, the Sisters had all traveled to the convent on the 2:00pm train for the blessing of the new gymnasium at St. John Baptist School. Next day the Warden, Fr. Weed, gave an address to the Community and Sr. Mildred Eleanor had her blessing as Sister Superior of St. Christopher's House.

As Sr. Eleanor Lucy noted in her memoir (see above), Asian flu struck towards the end of October 1957. Sr. Mildred Eleanor, Sr. Elizabeth Anne and Sr. Eleanor Lucy were all afflicted, and Mother brought Sr. Susinne Paula out from the convent to help at Grace Church. The clergy also fell ill, so there were fewer services for several days. Just at this time there was a clothing sale in one of the first-floor rooms at St. Christopher's. No one was well enough to take charge, so the church women did it all themselves and the sale was a great success, helping many who could not afford to buy new clothes for themselves or their children. It would become a regular event. Thanksgiving food boxes were delivered to needy families, the contents having been donated by the congregations of St. Paul's, Chatham, and Holy Cross, North Plainfield. A donation from Ascension Church, Bogota, was used to stock the food pantry.

On Thanksgiving Day the Sisters left for the convent after lunch, together with the New York Sisters, and stayed there overnight. As with all major festivals, the whole Community was able to celebrate together. Meanwhile, the clergy had introduced a corporate Communion for men, followed by breakfast, and there were 42 men present at the first one on December 1, 1957, which was Advent Sunday.

Despite illness, the work progressed with the help of some faithful women helpers, so that sales of clothes and the annual bazaar proceeded, the latter bringing in over $300. Advent was always a busy time because not only were there the spiritual preparations for Christmas, but also a seemingly continuous run of parties. Also, the Confirmation class began on December 4, but because of a bad snowstorm attendance was low. Sr. Susinne Paula had just three girls in her class and Sr. Elizabeth Anne had none at all. No one attended the Women's Auxiliary meeting, and only two came to the Spanish Auxiliary, along with two children.

In the midst of illness and bad weather, Fr. Morton brought a surprise visitor to see the Sisters. The Jersey City Record Book states "a lady, a friend of Fr. Morton, grand-niece of Mother Harriet at Evensong and came up to our house." Alas, her identity is not given, so it must remain a mystery.[14]

In 1957 Sr. Mildred Eleanor had the first of several operations for cancer, but recovered. Even so, she now had to remain at the convent for much of the time and so Sr. Eleanor Lucy was appointed Sister in Charge on December 21. The other Sisters at St. Christopher's House were Sr. Susinne Paula, Sr. Katharine Veronica and Sr. Ora Mary. Sr. Katharine Veronica was based in New York and just came as temporary help with all the Christmas activities. But Sr. Susinne Paula now became a regular worker at Grace Church. Her Community Biographer wrote of her: "Her longest service was at Grace (Van Vorst) in Jersey City. She loved that work and was never too tired to answer the door bell. It might be a man off the street asking for a sandwich or a little girl asking for a coat on a cold morning. The Christmas toy sale was a joy. Parents would come and buy a script for each child for twenty-five cents if they could afford it. If they couldn't afford it, the Sisters gave them the script. It entitled each child to two presents, one for fifteen cents and another for ten cents. The toys were donations from many sources: churches, organizations and individuals. Many were secondhand but they were carefully examined to determine if they were in good condition and clean. Throughout the year people brought used dolls for Sr. Susinne Paula. She cleaned and rehabilitated them and made exquisite clothes for them. By Christmas they looked like brand new dolls. Almost every time we went to St. Christopher's House there were pieces of dolls' arms, legs, heads and torsos soaking in the bathtub!"

As 1957 passed into 1958 the Sisters were busy with arrangements for the children's parties. Invitations had to be written and delivered but the Sisters had some help with this from members of the congregation, including teenagers from the Young Peoples' Fellowship. Ninety-eight children came to the party on December 28 (136 had been invited), and then all the children who had not been to another party were invited to one on New Year's Day. One hundred and twenty-five children came and all had a present.

Although the Sisters had a car at the convent, and another in New York, which made the frequent journeys much easier, they were also helped considerably by Mr. Grier and his son. They often visited Grace Church and the New York Sisters, fetching and carrying items to and from the convent, and also helping out when things needed fixing. Mr. Grier lived very near to the convent and had been an invaluable help for many years.[15]

February 10, 1958, saw a state of emergency being declared in Jersey City due to an underground burst water main which was losing water at a rate of 1,300,000 gallons hourly. Schools, factories and other workplaces were closed. At one stage water pressure was so low that firefighters could not have fought a blaze if it had occurred. The Sisters noted the state of emergency in the Jersey City Record Book but otherwise seemed unperturbed. Of greater concern was the bad weather a week later—a blizzard resulting in deep snow.

On April 19, 1958, Fr. Laughlin was married at Camp Schlueter.[16] Despite the bus breaking down, everyone arrived in time. Fr. Moore celebrated the nuptial Mass in the morning in the Camp Schlueter chapel and at 4:00pm Fr. Morton married them in the Community Church nearby. Next day Fr. Moore and Jenny visited Grace Church. He preached at the Mass, greeted the children and met the people at coffee hour. The church was full. At 3:00pm they visited the Sisters before flying back to Indianapolis. On May 18, Fr. Laughlin gave a reception for the parish at 4:00pm and all three Sisters went for a time.

The last week of May 1958 was full of activity. On May 25, Bishop Washburn came for a Confirmation. It was his last official visit before his retirement and the church was full. A new red frontal and fall was used, having been blessed at the first Mass that day. There was a reception in the parish hall for the bishop after the service. He must have seen a great difference in Grace Church since 1949. And then on May 28, there was the Church School Open House at 8:00pm. The Sisters and helpers spent all day preparing certificates and diplomas. These were for: the first group to complete teacher's training; 48 upper school completing 20 weeks of attendance or more; and 27 primary completing 15 weeks or more. Also there were pictures for boys' class, girls' class and primary class having the best percentage of active enrollment since February 1. There were exhibits and class parties in the classrooms.

On Sunday June 1, 1958 (Trinity Sunday), Sr. Eleanor Lucy, Sr. Susinne Paula and Sr. Elizabeth Anne went to Trinity, Wall Street, to celebrate their feast of title with them. They walked in the procession, preceding the Sisters of the Society of St. Margaret. After the Mass they went to St. John Baptist House in Barrow Street for dinner. Prize night and Commencement at St. John Baptist School, Mendham, on June 6 brought Sr. Susinne Paula back to the convent for an overnight stay, whilst Sr. Eleanor Lucy and Sr. Elizabeth Anne, together with Sr. Ora Mary, drove to Tuxedo Park, Orange County, for the Educational Fellowship Conference on Teacher Training. On June 20, several Sisters from New York and Jersey City went to Mass at Patterson to hear Archbishop Joost de Blank of Cape Town. He was an outspoken opponent of South Africa's apartheid policy and challenged the Dutch Reformed Church to repudiate it.[17]

On June 23, the Eve of St. John Baptist day, all the Sisters from Jersey City and New York[18] went to the convent for the Patronal Festival celebrations, arriving in time for first Vespers of the feast. Next day there was Mass, choral Mass, lunch, tea party and then supper at 5:00, after which all seven Sisters returned by car. The three Jersey City Sisters arrived at 7:30pm, in time for choral Mass and sermon—in Spanish.

There was a Stewardship campaign to help the church finances and on June 29, 1958, Bishop Stark came to give an address. To help things along a Strawberry Festival and "High Evensong" were held, closing the campaign for the payment of pledges. The result was not noted in the Sisters' Record Book.

With the coming of August there was the usual Vacation Bible School, which was well attended, with over 200 children. And then on August 17 there was the church picnic. After Mass at 8:00am the people went in the church bus and private cars to Watchung Reservation in Union County, NJ. The Record Book noted that it was an experiment but does not say whether it was successful.

It had been a busy summer; but before the Sisters could close St. Christopher's for their summer break there was the Open House day on August 24 (St. Barnabas). Mother Margaret Helena, Sr. Waldine Lucia and Sr. Mildred Eleanor arrived in time for Morning Prayer and Baptism at which 40–50 persons were baptized. Mother took photographs. The service was followed by an exhibit of all the things the children had made. Afterwards, six Sisters and five girls who were helpers had lunch at St. Christopher's. "We had TV dinners, ice cream and cookies." Next day, Sr. Katharine Veronica came over from New York to help close up the house for the summer vacation. A packed car with the Sisters, two helpers, and the baggage left St. Christopher's in pouring rain at 11:00am. They arrived at the convent in time for a late lunch at 1:00pm after a difficult journey due to the heavy downpour and difficult driving conditions.

On September 26, Mother Margaret Helena was installed at the convent by Bishop Washburn, having been re-elected as Superior. The Warden, Fr. Weed, gave his address at 11:30 and after an early lunch he left with the New York Sisters. Mother and Sr. Waldine Lucia brought the three Sisters back to Jersey City, leaving the convent at 1:30 and arriving at 3:10. Sr. Eleanor Lucy had received her blessing as Sister Superior and she was accompanied by Sr. Susinne Paula and Sr. Elizabeth Anne. A decision had been made that the Sisters were not required to attend Evensong in church (which was now to be at 8:00pm) unless it was part of the meeting of any organization with which the Sisters were involved. They would say Vespers in the chapel at St. Christopher's.

The classes made a good start in the Fall of 1958, with 172 children at the first Saturday Church School on October 4, and 164 children present at Mass next day. Various seminarians came to help with the Church School and the Sisters had helpers at St. Christopher's, notably Mrs. Mitchell, whose name appears frequently in their Record Book.

As noted in Chapter 6, on October 22, 1958, Donald MacAdie was consecrated as Suffragan Bishop of Newark at Trinity Cathedral, Newark.[19] Mother Margaret Helena, Sr. Waldine Lucia, Sr. Elizabeth Marion, Sr. Mary Barbara, Sr. Agnes Genevieve, and Sr. Eleanor Lucy attended what they described as a beautiful service, and they walked in the procession. A few days later, on October 26, the three Sisters were back at the Cathedral for a service of thanksgiving to mark Bishop Washburn's retirement. He had been Coadjutor Bishop of Newark for three years and Diocesan Bishop for 23, as well as being the Community Visitor.[20]

Meanwhile, parish life continued in its usual busy fashion; and on November 1, the church bazaar took place from 3:00–9:00pm. The Sisters made roast chicken and cookies as their contribution and on the previous evening helped supervise the setting up of the stalls. Mother and Sr. Waldine Lucia came for a time and the Sisters helped until it was time for Vespers, after which they helped again until 8:45pm.

Nineteen fifty-eight ended at Grace Church with a Mass to see in the New Year—not as popular as the Christmas Midnight Mass, but there were 30 communicants. It was a good way to end what had been a good year, for the church, for the Sisters, and above all for Jersey City.

Mother Margaret Helena visited on the evening of January 1, 1959, to wish the Sisters a happy New Year. Rehearsals for the pageant occupied the first few days of 1959 and there was much pressing of angels' costumes. In the midst of it all, Pauline, a former St. Anna's girl, brought her little boy to see Sr. Katharine Veronica: Sister had worked at St. Anna's from 1937–38 during her novitiate, and after her profession in 1940 until the closure of the home in 1943. It was said of her that she had a wonderful gift for making friends, and she kept in touch with many of the former girls from St. Anna's, who never forgot her kindness to them.

On January 4, 1959, the pageant took place after the Creed during the 10:30 Mass. The Sisters and three helpers dressed the children in their costumes, and all appeared except one little girl who had mumps! A last-minute substitute was found and all went well. Mother, Sr. Waldine Lucia, Sr. Elisabeth Roberta, and an Associate, Miss Gertrude Gleckler, came from the convent for the pageant and stayed for dinner. The costumes had a second usage on the following Sunday when they were borrowed by Sr. Ora Mary for a play she was to give at St. Luke's Hospital, NYC.

Bishop Stark officiated at a Confirmation on February 8, 1959, and confirmed 101 candidates. It was a long but impressive service, and the number surely reflects the progress made by clergy and Sisters in making Grace Church a welcoming place for all. Three days later, on Ash Wednesday, all three Sisters attended the 7:00am Mass, and a "goodly number" were there. These included many children, and after Mass they were given breakfast at St. Christopher's.

Bishop Stark was impressed by the progress of the work at Grace Church. As noted above, the church had lost its parish status in 1933 and came directly under the jurisdiction of the bishop. On February 17, 1959, the Sisters' noted in their Record Book that "the bishop expects to restore us to parish status in the Fall if we meet certain conditions, i.e. 75% of pledges paid up." On March 3, at a meeting of 100 people, the bishop explained about working for real parish status. In a letter to the CSJB Associates later in the year, Mother Margaret Helena thought it likely that Grace Church would be an "aided parish" for some time to come. Even so, "Friends in and out of the Diocese continue to help support the program and are very generous indeed. With five hundred children on the Church School list, I am sure you can realize how dependent we must be."[21]

Whitsunday 1959 (May 17) was kept as the patronal festival and at 6:30pm there was Solemn Evensong with sermon preached by Fr. Laughlin. It was a grand service, with special music accompanied by a new organ, trumpets, violins and drums. There was also a strawberry festival and exhibit. The Sisters attended the service and then went down to the exhibit in the basement and stayed there to supervise until 9:30pm.

As noted in Chapter 6, May 23, 1959, was a great day at the convent, where Sr. Julia Frances was celebrating the sixtieth anniversary of her profession. Not all the Jersey City Sisters were free to attend the celebrations, but Sr. Susinne Paula managed to be there, arriving back at St. Christopher's after supper at the convent.

On May 31, there was a special coffee hour to greet three young women who were to be in the NAACP Cotillion.[22] The Sisters attended for a short time. On the same day, the Sunday school teachers went to the Watchung Reservation after church and had a picnic lunch and were joined by the Sisters. On June 13, the sixth annual Day of Witness took place at the Cathedral of St. John the Divine, NYC, and this was strongly supported by the Sisters. Mother Margaret Helena, Sr. Waldine Lucia, Sr. Eleanor Lucy and Sr. Elizabeth Anne traveled from the convent; Sr. Elizabeth Marion, Sr. Katharine Veronica and Sr. Susinne Paula went from Jersey City; and Sr. Agnes Genevieve and Sr. Ora Mary came from the New York house. The theme was "One Family in Christ—Christ for the City." There was a long procession through Manhattan to the Cathedral, in which it was estimated 5,000 people joined. The Sisters did not join the procession but sat in choir, and in addition to CSJB Sisters there were Sisters from the Society of St. Margaret, the Order of St. Helena and brethren from the Order of the Holy Cross.

A sadder event attended by the Sisters was the funeral of Sr. Jeannette Louise at the convent on June 23, 1959. It was sad, but also a joy to know her long, confused illness was past, and now she would join her many departed Sisters.

Next day was the feast of the Birth of St. John Baptist and there was much to do at Grace Church before returning to the convent to celebrate the festival with the Sisters there. Fr. Morton celebrated Mass in the chapel at St. Christopher's and there were several parishioners present. After breakfast, 36 boys left for St. Paul's summer camp. The Sisters set off soon after, and they arrived back at the convent in time for dinner. As usual, there was the tea party at 3:00pm and supper on the lawn after Solemn Evensong. The New York Sisters returned before supper but the Jersey City Sisters stayed at the convent overnight. Next day, St. John Baptist House in Barrow Street was closed up for the summer recess, but at Grace Church there was still a busy month before the closure of St. Christopher's at the end of August. Vacation Bible School took up a lot of time and was well supported as usual.

Opening up on September 23, 1959, after the summer vacation, was a combined operation. Sisters Eleanor Lucy, Susinne Paula and Elizabeth Anne traveled to Newark with Mother and Sr. Waldine Lucia, and then went by bus to Jersey City, arriving at about 10:00am. Close behind was Mr. Grier with all the baggage, plus clothes for the clothing room. Then as soon as the house was in order, parish work began in earnest. And a new phrase entered the Record Book—"buzz groups" to describe small discussion groups. The ones held on October 6 were reported as being "good."

Visits to the convent continued to be a feature of parish life. On October 10, St. Teresa's Guild for Spanish parishioners had an afternoon visit, stopping first at St. Peter's, Morristown, and arriving at the convent at 3:30pm. They saw round the first floor of St. Marguerite's, where the Sisters were still residing, then went walking in the grounds. Spanish Evensong followed at 4:45 before supper under the trees. They left at 6:00pm and arrived home an hour later.

On October 30, Sr. Eleanor Lucy and Sr. Susinne Paula, together with staff members, went to Evensong at General Theological Seminary in NYC where the Archbishop of York (UK), the Most Revd. Michael Ramsey, preached the Matriculation sermon.

The arrival of Advent saw the usual preparations for Christmas, both spiritual and material. On December 22, 1959, the first "Thrift Sale" was held and around 119 families came. It lasted from 1:00pm until 9:00pm and raised $137. The Sisters and other staff members helped. The usual parties took place for both children and adults, and stretched into the New Year.

Mother Margaret Helena had written a Newsletter for Associates and Friends which they received in Advent. Of the work at Grace Church, she wrote: "Across the Hudson at the end of the Holland Tunnel is another parish in which it is our joy and privilege to live and work. As you all know, it is *on the frontier* of urban parish work, and there is very little one can say without the fear of being accused of exaggeration. [my italics] There is no place more arduous, more heart-breaking, more joyous or more rewarding.

It is an arduous task to try to convince poor and neglected people of the love of God and the reality of redemption. The failures of those who know the way but are overwhelmed by temptation are heart-breaking, but there is joy in those who persevere and when those who have gone astray do come back and make a fresh start. Many things have changed since the beginnings at Grace Church." Those things have been described in this chapter. The team work of clergy, Sisters and lay helpers may well have been arduous and heart-breaking, but also it was a joyous service, and rewarding to see this parish, which had been so deprived, come back to life—a true resurrection.

----

[1] The Life and History of Grace Church (Van Vorst). A Commemoration booklet written for the 125th Anniversary 1847–1972.

[2] By 1869 Dr. Mahan was Rector of St. Paul's, Baltimore, and had become a highly controversial figure on account of his extreme Anglo-Catholicism. He approached the CSJB Sisters at Clewer, UK, requesting them to take charge of St. Paul's orphanage in his parish. This was before the first Sisters from Clewer came to work in NYC. He died in 1870 soon after the Sisters' arrival at Baltimore, and soon there was trouble with his successor, who did not favor having Sisters in his parish. The so-called Baltimore episode dragged on for several years. For further details see BONHAM, Valerie *Living Stones* pp.8–9.

[3] He was the father of the Rt. Revd. William Doane, later the first Bishop of Albany, who suggested that Frances Paine should visit Clewer. This led to her joining the Community of St. John Baptist as Sr. Frances Constance, and eventually becoming the first Mother Superior of CSJB in New York.

[4] Jenny Moore wrote a vivid account of their years in Jersey City, but it does not mention the ministry of CSJB except in passing (pp.175–6). MOORE, Jenny The People on Second Street 1968.

[5] MOORE, Jenny ibid. p.196.

[6] Information from SONTAG, Frederick In the Church a candle burns in The Living Church June 10, 1951.

[7] MOORE, Jenny op. cit.

[8] The Revd. Tubby Clayton had been an Army chaplain in World War 1 and had founded Talbot House in Poperinghe, Belgium, as a refuge for Allied troops of all ranks.

[9] The Blessed Sacrament was traditionally removed on Maundy Thursday from its place of reservation in order to symbolize Christ's passion and death. It was then restored on Easter Sunday to symbolize His resurrection.

[10] The Rt. Revd. Theodore R. Ludlow had been Suffragan Bishop of Newark 1936–53.

[11] A Message from the Community of St. John Baptist … 1954

[12] The Revd. Paul Moore served as Dean of Christ Church Episcopal Cathedral, Indianapolis, from 1957 until 1964 when he was consecrated as Suffragan Bishop of Washington, DC. In 1970 he was elected as coadjutor Bishop of New York and was installed as Bishop of New York in 1972. He held office until 1989. Construction work on the Cathedral of St. John the Divine, NYC, had come to a halt during World War II, and in 1982 Bishop Moore was instrumental in resuming the work. A few years later it stalled due to lack of finance, and the Cathedral remains unfinished. Jenny Moore, his first wife and mother of his nine children, died of cancer in 1973.

[13] MOORE, Jenny op. cit. p.217.

[14] Earlier in the same year, 1957, Sr. Sheila, CSJB (Sheila O'Brien), great-great-niece of Mother Harriet, was professed in first vows at Clewer. Her life profession was on Ascension Day 1961, 110 years after Mother Harriet's clothing on Ascension Day 1851. I knew Sr. Sheila well and she provided me with much information about the O'Briens. She was very proud of her ancestry and in particular the link with Mother Harriet. She died on August 21, 2010, in the 93rd year of her life and the 53rd year of her profession.

[15] His son still worships at St. Mark's, Mendham.

[16] In 1915 the vicar of St. Luke's Chapel, Fr. Edward Schlueter, bought a farm in West Cornwall, CT. (St. Luke's was a chapel founded from Trinity Wall Street.) At that time St. Luke's neighborhood was very impoverished, with many overcrowded tenements. Fr. Schlueter opened the farm as a summer camp for boys and in 1925 he added facilities for girls. On his retirement in 1945 he sold the farm to Trinity Church, to ensure that the camp would continue as an Episcopal ministry. Trinity Church renamed it Camp Schlueter and modernized and expanded the facilities. A year-round conference center opened in 1954. Source www.trinitywallstreet.org

[17] Archbishop Joost de Blank, 1908–1968, was born in the Netherlands. He was Archbishop of Cape Town from 1957–63 and was known as "the scourge of apartheid." Previously he had been Bishop of Stepney in the London Diocese, UK, 1952–57. In 1963 he suffered a stroke and resigned from office, returning to England, where he became a residentiary Canon of Westminster Abbey. He is buried in Westminster Abbey.

[18] At this time the Sisters in New York were: Sr. Katharine Veronica, Sr. Agnes Genevieve, Sr. Julia Frances and Sr. Ora Mary.

[19] The Rt. Revd. Donald MacAdie was Suffragan Bishop of Newark 1958–63.

[20] During his time at Newark, Bishop Washburn had confirmed nearly 32,000 persons and had ordained 169 to the priesthood. Source: The Living Church November 9, 1958, p.7.

[21] Newsletter to Associates and Friends, Advent 1959.

[22] National Association for the Advancement of Colored People.

8

WIDENING HORIZONS …

The Community 1960–64

I F THE WINDS of change were blowing through the Community in the 1940s they were certainly doing so with the dawn of the 1960s. "It seems to me that almost at once the winds of change entered our life just as they were blowing in the Church." This was the considered opinion of Sr. Margaret Helena, writing her memories many years after leaving the office of Mother Superior.[1]

As the new decade dawned there was an air of excitement, as the long-awaited move back to the convent became a reality. An entry in the Community Record Book for January 25, 1960, noted: "Bought new kitchen ranges for the convent—work almost finished in the convent." On February 18, "got material for refectory curtains," and on February 25, "new upstairs chapel furniture arrived—very lovely. Men cleaning the convent, a big job—many problems." The move back into the convent was gradual and not without hitches, such as problems with the telephone line across the lawn. But on May 9, 1960, the Community Record Book noted: "The vans here for the great move back into the convent from St. Marguerite's." The sense of relief and joy is tangible. However, the building took some getting used to again, especially the stone stairs, as Sr. Ellen Juliana discovered when she fell on the front stairs, cutting her head badly.

In the midst of all the preparations for the anticipated move, Community life went on as usual. It had been a bad winter, with ice storms, deep snow and bitter cold continuing into March. Even so, the familiar round of daily office, Mass and prayer continued without interruption. In February 1960, the Sisters who were working at St. Luke's Chapel, NYC, went to Trinity Church, Wall Street, to the Diocesan Jubilee celebration for the Guild of St. Monica.[2] According to the Community Record Book, the guild had been started by CSJB in the mission house at 3, Morris Street in 1877.[3]

The Sisters continued to be in great demand to talk and give slide-show programs about the Religious Life. Word spread, and the number of parishes increased to include St. Paul's Westfield, Christ Church Hackensack, St. John's Passaic, and St. Stephen's Plainfield, to name just a few. In addition, the Sisters' ministry of hospitality continued, with groups visiting the convent from several parishes, for retreats, quiet days or more informal visits and picnics. One such parish was St. Peter's Church, Washington, NJ, where the Rector was the Revd. Henry F. Folsom. He was the sixth cousin of Sr. Helen Margaret, CSJB, Foundress of the Community in the USA.[4]

In June 1960, 63 Methodist ministers met at St. John Baptist School for a weekend conference—a sure sign of the dawn of more ecumenical times. Associates continued to be received, including Fr. Morton and Fr. Laughlin from Grace Church (Van Vorst), Jersey City. And others had passed to their rest, including Gertrude Gleckler, who had been an Associate for a few years, and was a faithful supporter of the Community. Her relative, Ann Gleckler, shared her enthusiasm for the Community and continued to visit and help. With so many ministries and with such great demands on their time for spiritual guidance, the Sisters could not have functioned effectively had it not been for various secular helpers who came to the convent to ensure its smooth running. Some were employed and others were voluntary helpers, including young people from Jersey City.

The graduating class of St. John Baptist School dedicated the annual *Satura* of 1960 to Mother Margaret Helena, who had been Mother Superior of the Community since 1949. "We, the eightieth graduating class, dedicate our yearbook to an individual who has been a great inspiration to us all in all our works. A person who has guided and enriched us both in material and immaterial ways and yet has always done these things indirectly. In appreciation for these things we wish to express our profound feelings in the only way in which we know. Sister Margaret Helena, Mother Superior to many of us, we thank you."

Towards the end of 1960, several postulants had been received but few made it into the novitiate and none were professed. Even so, it was a hopeful sign, because now that the Sisters were back in the convent the whole "ambience" of the place was more conducive to nurturing vocations. One young woman who visited for the first time from September 2–5, 1960, was Barbara Packer, the future Sr. Barbara Jean. Recalling that first visit, Sr. Barbara Jean has written: "I was eighteen and due to start at teachers' college about a week later. My experience that weekend was unforgettable. Sr. Katharine Veronica took me and another inquirer to a conference on Religious Life at St. Helena's convent in New York State, where we met representatives of most of the Episcopalian convents. But what stayed with me was CSJB. I felt the call then, but didn't come to stay till four years later, after I had become a teacher and worked a year in a school. During the years in between, I visited as often as I could. Coming from near Philadelphia, it was only a two-hour drive." As will be seen, she would be one of the three novices received in the 1960s who were later professed.

Nineteen sixty finished in much the same way that it had started, with heavy snow. The Midnight Mass was described as "lovely." On St. Stephen's day (December 26), there was a tea party with all the Sisters present, including those from New York and Jersey City, who managed to make the journey in spite of more deep snow. Several Sisters and guests kept the customary Watch to pray the old year out and the New Year in. There was a carol service in the main chapel and later, New Year's carols in the library with guests present.

The Sisters may have been back in residence at the convent but much more work needed to be done. For several weeks they were living surrounded by painters, electricians and other workmen. First the chapel bell was moved upstairs so that the Sisters could hear it better. The cellar floor was being painted, followed by the upstairs halls, bathrooms and cells. And the new lights in the refectory were very helpful.

Life continued in the midst of it all, and in April 1961 fourteen members of the Latin class from St. John Baptist School were given a tour of the convent. Also, twelve girls from the school Altar Guild were shown the vestments and the relic of the True Cross given to the Community by Fr. Baker in 1941, shortly before his death. 1961 would see a continued upward trend in numbers at the school, with 57 boarders and fifteen day students. Overseas students would increase in numbers over the coming years as well as a growing number of secular teachers. Sr. Mary Barbara continued to be Sister Superior, a position she had held since 1946, assisted by Sr. Jane Patricia. Sister Mary Barbara has been described as "not democratic in her attitudes by present-day ideas, but she was always consistent and always fair."[5]

Nineteen sixty-one saw the retirement of Marian Wysong from teaching at St. John Baptist School, but did not sever her ties with the Community. As already noted in Chapter 4, she was a former student, graduating in 1935, and was one of the first class of students at the new school buildings.

Former student Chris Chrystal has described her as "perhaps the most notable of all the graduates, ever." Certainly her devotion to the school and Community cannot be questioned. After her service in the War as a Red Cross ambulance driver in North Africa, she returned to the school in 1946. Chris Chrystal remembered her well: "Besides being coach for all our sports, field hockey, basketball and lacrosse, she taught drivers education and health and hygiene. We learned important life lessons from her, such as good sportsmanship, which applies to all sorts of life experiences ... She was a very kind, honest, fair, capable, and inspiring individual, and a favorite teacher of the student body."[6]

A wet morning did not dampen the spirits of the Sisters or their guests on St. John Baptist Day, June 24, 1961. Forty-five guests, mostly Associates, were at the Mass when the address was given by Bishop Washburn. The rain cleared in time for the afternoon but luncheon was taken in St. Marguerite's and supper in the cloister. Mother Margaret Helena gave a "general report—a good one." All in all it was a "lovely friendly day." On July 4, Fr. Morton brought 80 people from Grace Church (Van Vorst). They brought their own lunch but the Community Record Book noted that "we gave them supper—'a cook out.'" A few days later "a nice group" of 27 from St. Mary the Virgin, NYC, came for a picnic.

Still more work was needed on the convent and on July 14, 1961, an extensive plumbing job was being done on the north side of the house involving taking up some of the floors. The flat roof of the main chapel was being repaired by Mr. Robinson, which took well over three months, followed by cleaning and plastering the walls. Also, the Record Book notes that "a new room was built on the third floor of the convent." This probably refers to the division of the former St. Anna's dormitory into rooms for guests. The Community Record Book notes that the chapel was out of use until the beginning of October, when it was used for the first time on the 8th, even though the plaster was not quite dry and the painting still had to be done. It is unclear whether this means the main chapel or the new upstairs chapel. Many of the beautiful illuminated manuscripts, the work of Sr. Olive Frances before she left the Community in 1927, were restored and framed at this time.

Mother Margaret Helena continued to make her yearly visit to Oregon to see family and to keep in touch with Oregon Associates from St. Helen's Hall days. But by this time traveling was so much easier. When the first Sisters went out to Oregon in 1904 it involved a five-day train journey with several changes. Now in 1961 it was an easy flight. The Community Record Book noted on September 15: "Sr. Waldine Lucia took a plane to Chicago, met Mother there who came from Oregon, and both went to Racine, Wisconsin, for a Conference of Superiors and Novice Mistresses. A very splendid conference."

On October 4, there was a Chapter of Election at which Mother Margaret Helena was re-elected as Superior. Next day there was the installation service at 9:00am at which Fr. Weed, Fr. Templeton and Fr. Brown (the new rector of St. Mark's, Mendham) were present. It was an exceptionally cold day, with the thermometer registering 32°F, and after the installation service all went to the parlor for coffee. At 10:45am the special blessings took place: Sr. Waldine Lucia as Novice Mistress, Sr. Mary Barbara as Sister Superior of St. John Baptist School, Sr. Eleanor Lucy as Sister Superior of St. Christopher's House, Jersey City, and Sr. Agnes Genevieve as Sister in Charge of St. John Baptist House at St. Luke's Chapel, NYC.

On October 16, 1961, the Community Record Book noted that there was a bomb scare at St. John Baptist School. In fact three schools in the Mendham area were evacuated after a housewife in Mendham Borough had an anonymous phone call which the local press reported in the manner of a script from a gangster movie! "Lady, you'd better get your kids outta school because a big bomb is going off at 2:30." "What school do you mean?" she asked. "St. Joe's," he replied. "Do you mean St. John's?" "Yeah, that's the one." And with that he hung up. As the exact location was uncertain, word soon spread and all possible schools were evacuated, but the housewife had no idea why she was chosen to receive the call. Next day things became clearer. The bomb scare story was hatched in order to keep the police occupied while the Mendham bank was being robbed. No doubt the real-life story of cops and robbers proved an interesting diversion for all the scholars who had a day off lessons, not least the girls from St. John Baptist School.

Former residents from St. Marguerite's often visited the Sisters and many still kept in touch with Sr. Julia Frances. On November 7, 1961, Irene Icke, a former St. Marguerite's girl, married David Davis in St. Marguerite's chapel. Sisters continued to keep in touch with former students from St. John Baptist School, and on November 24, three girls visited the convent to tell the Sisters about their college experiences. Earlier in the year, several Sisters went into New York to meet a former girl from St.

Michael's Home, Mamaroneck, now married, with a son who was a priest.

As the year drew towards its close the Sisters continued to be in demand at conferences and meetings. On November 8, Mother Margaret Helena was on the staff of the Buck Hill Conference of Women of the Church. Sr. Waldine Lucia noted in the Community Record Book that it was "a wonderful experience." Mother had the largest number in her group.[7] A week later Sr. Agatha Louise and Sr. Katharine Veronica went to Gallaudet College, Washington, DC, to a meeting for Episcopal Workers for the deaf where they were asked to give a workshop.[8]

The year 1961 ended on a note of sadness with the sudden death on December 16 of Sr. Beatrice Clare. She was professed in 1913 and her main Community work had been at St. Michael's Home, Mamaroneck, where she was greatly loved by the girls. In later years at least one former girl named her daughter for Sister. After its closure in 1937 she returned to the convent and was a great help to Mother Florence Teresa. When Mother Florence Teresa began to lose her sight, Sr. Beatrice Clare would read books and newspapers to her. She had a great sense of humor and her Community Biographer noted that she could see a joke in any situation. On the day of her death she went to her room to fetch her handiwork for recreation. When she did not appear she was found lying on the floor, having died suddenly from heart failure. On December 18, her body was brought to the chapel and a watch was kept. Outside there was heavy snow and an ice storm. Next day her Requiem took place at 9:00am and Sr. Waldine Lucia noted in the Community Record Book that the Mass was lovely and the singing splendid. There was no singing at the graveside due to the extreme cold. Her grave in the Community cemetery was fairly near that of Sr. Florence Teresa.

After praying the old year out and the New Year in there was a tea party at 3:30pm followed by Vespers and Benediction. Next day Sr. Francina was taken ill. She had been in frail health for several years, but was taken to All Souls' Hospital in Morristown on January 9, 1962, when her condition worsened. Her death came suddenly and peacefully on January 13. Sr. Francina, Dutch by birth, was a former mission Sister, having been admitted as a postulant in 1906 and professed in 1913. She was the last of the three remaining mission Sisters to be professed as a choir Sister in 1940. Sr. Francina had worked first of all at Holy Cross Mission House, NYC, and then at St. Anna's at the convent, where she taught the girls how to cook meals, and also bread and pastries. Her Community Biographer wrote: "One of the favorites was doughnut holes. I don't remember round doughnuts, but mounds of doughnut holes were provided for novice receptions, professions and other functions." She also taught the girls how to scrub and clean.[9] At her death she "had a most radiant expression on her face which remained at the funeral. It was a happy homecoming for Sister who was truly a loving child of God."

There were the usual meetings to attend and visits from parish groups. On January 25, 1962, 29 girls, mostly from St. John Baptist School, came for an overnight retreat which was described as very splendid. Three of them stayed on until the Sunday with Mother giving them meditations. (Elizabeth) Lynn Wilder Mullin was a student at St. John Baptist School from 1962 until 1965 and has good memories of those years. She entered as a 10th grade student and continued through 11th and 12th grades, graduating in 1965. Like many new entrants, she was homesick for a time and didn't get home very often, having entered in September and made her first home visit at Thanksgiving. She was home for Christmas and then again at the end of February. Students had to be back in the school by Sunday night. On Saturdays the senior girls were allowed to walk into Mendham, but there were restrictions. For instance, they were not allowed to visit the pizza restaurant! The secular teachers lived in part of the house Mr. Cordingley had built at the bottom of the hill.

By the 1960s the school was changing. Lynn remembers that some of the girls "came from families with sadness," i.e. from broken homes. The uniform was blue, white and red plaid. The day began with Sr. Jane Patricia banging a Chinese gong at 6:30am. Then she would go from door to door and pull the covers off the sleeping girls and pull them out of bed! Lynn does not have good memories of the food, but maybe many other schools had similar diets. In the dining room there were six long tables and Sr. Mary Barbara, the Sister Superior, sat at the head of the middle one. There were other Sisters at the school at that time besides Sr. Mary Barbara and Sr. Jane Patricia—Sr. Agatha Louise who taught New Testament, and Sr. Elizabeth Marion who taught Latin. At Christmas the senior students would wear red nightdresses with SJBS embroidered on them and would go through the dormitories by candlelight singing carols to the juniors. St. John Baptist was a small school but a good one and Lynn has remained friends with several of her classmates, one of whom was maid of honor at her wedding.[10]

Towards the end of February, it was good to report that the main chapel and passage leading to it were now all painted. At a meeting of the St. John the Baptist Foundation, funds were given for more painting and for an elevator. Work began on installing the elevator early in April, but it was not finished until mid-June, when it was declared to be a great help.

On March 16, 1962, Sr. Waldine Lucia noted in the Community Record Book: "Suzanne Jackson, a student nurse from St. Luke's, NYC, here. May have a vocation—a nice girl." The future Sr. Suzanne Elizabeth would be the first of the inquirers to be professed in the 1960s. As older Sisters passed to their rest it was encouraging to know that new vocations were being sown.

On March 26, 1962, Sr. Elisabeth Roberta passed to her rest at Wayside Home, Mendham. She was professed on February 5, 1920, along with Sr. Ellen Juliana, and because of a heavy snowstorm the bishop had to be brought from Morristown by sled.[11] Sr. Elisabeth Roberta had a lovely singing voice and was often Precentress. After a time at St. Helen's Hall she had a ministry at St. Michael's Home, Mamaroneck. It was said of her that "she enjoyed the structured life at St. Michael's and brought it with her when she was in charge of St. Anna's." After St. Anna's she was Community Bursaress and kept impeccable records. She was laid to rest in the Community cemetery.

An epoch-making event took place from May 10 until June 7, 1962, when Mother Margaret Helena and Sr. Agnes Genevieve visited Clewer. The bishop sent Mother a generous check so they were able to fly. It was the first step in healing the rift between the two halves of CSJB. Mother Annys and Mother Margaret Helena had both been in Community at the time of the separation and were now in a position to begin the healing process. This was Mother Margaret Helena's first visit to Clewer and the first time that she had met Mother Annys, although there had been communication between them. They found an instant rapport which was a great asset.

By this time Community at Clewer was much diminished in numbers. In 1944, the Clewer Community had numbered 151 Sisters, consisting of 103 choir Sisters and 48 lay Sisters. The lay Sisters had been brought into choir in 1946, but by the 1960s the total number of Sisters at Clewer was possibly around 100.[12] The coming of the Welfare State had deprived the UK Community and many others of the moral rescue work for which they had been founded, and also of the work with convalescent patients and orphaned girls. And the 1944 Education Act had raised the standards for secondary education. Thus many of the UK branch houses had closed and some buildings, such as St. John Baptist School at Newport in south Wales and St. Andrew's Convalescent Hospital, Clewer, were later demolished.

More retreat work was being introduced as well as ecumenical links. And St. Stephen's College, Broadstairs, in Kent, was still a major Community work.[13] Mother Annys had been Sister Superior there before her election as Mother Superior at Clewer, and so she took Mother Margaret Helena and Sr. Agnes Genevieve to visit the College from May 21–23. This visit also involved an extensive tour of Canterbury given by Sr. Gladys, CSJB; and a brief visit to St. Mary's Abbey, West Malling, Kent, where Sr. Mary John (formerly Anne Marshall) was a novice. She was American and had visited Mendham before deciding to test her vocation as a Benedictine.[14]

The main objective of the visit to Clewer was to establish closer ties, and if all went well to lay the foundations for a more formal link, possibly re-affiliation. This still lay some years ahead after much negotiation, but a good start had been made. There were many letters to the Sisters at Mendham from Sisters at Clewer with greetings for St. John Baptist day on June 24.[15]

Meanwhile, Sr. Waldine Lucia and the Sisters from Jersey City went to St. Luke's Chapel, NYC, for the service for Religious Orders on June 3, 1962. According to Sr. Waldine Lucia it was a "glorious day with a fine sermon on the Religious Life by Fr. Chambers of the Community of the Resurrection." After the service "we served supper to all the women Religious at Barrow Street." And then on June 16, there was a picnic at the convent for 65 people from Newark Cathedral including the Dean. It was "a lovely day and the school pond was much used."

In September the Sisters received a lovely new set of green vestments from the Clewer workroom. And on October 2 a new Communion rail was put in the main chapel as a gift from Mr. George Turner and family, in memory of his wife Ruth, who had once been a novice in the Community.

October 30, 1962, saw the tenth anniversary of the Sisters' ministry in Jersey City, and Mother Margaret Helena visited the Sisters and spent the night at St. Christopher's House. So much had been achieved in that time. However, a problem now arose for the work there, as Sr. Susinne Paula was ill in hospital and her capacity for work would be limited for a time. Also, when the Sisters returned to 90, Barrow Street from the convent they found someone had tried to break in, not for the first time.

The year went out with widespread illness within the Community and for the first time in many years no one was well enough to be in chapel to pray the old year out and the New Year, 1963, in. Even so, the New Year arrived and the life of prayer, daily office, Mass and regular retreats would continue unabated. It was, as always, what had undergirded all the activity, the talks and programs, the hospitality and the ministry of presence to so many people.

Although St. Andrew's Hospital had closed several years previously, the Board still continued to meet and there were still funds. At their meeting on January 31, 1963, at Barrow Street, the Board voted in favor of giving $500 to St. Mary's Hospital for Children, NYC.

Nineteen sixty-three proceeded in much the same manner as previous years. Various parish groups came to see the convent and were shown the vestments. This was a valuable opportunity for the Sisters to teach about the meaning and use of the vestments as well as for the visitors to admire the beautiful needlework. Old friends kept in touch and visited from time to time. A few months previously, in the Fall of 1962, the West family from Corsicana, TX, had visited the Sisters at Barrow Street. Now in May 1963 a Mr. and Mrs. Adams Jnr, cousins of the late Sr. Frances Maude, came to the convent. She had died in 1938 and had been in the Community since 1893. It was Sr. Frances Maude who had worked closely with the architects on the design and building of the convent. Later in the year, during October three visitors from Oregon came for what Sr. Waldine Lucia described as "a lovely visit."

Improvements were still being made to the convent and its surroundings. The painting of the main chapel was at last finished in May. The many visits to parishes, as well as the need to transport Sisters to and from Jersey City and Barrow Street, necessitated more transport. In April, Mother had acquired "a secondhand small truck for hauling big things—a very useful machine." At the end of May, new additions were made to the garage and a car port was built at the back door. Also the Community Record Book noted that "a new Chevy" had been bought.

June 16 brought a group of 60 Sunday-school children and their parents from Fr. Folsom's parish. They stayed for Vespers and Benediction. On St. John Baptist's day, June 24, the Community Record Book noted: "Lovely bright day. 7:00am Mass in house chapel [St. Michael's], choral Mass 9:00 in main chapel. We had supper in the cloisters." Down the hill at the school there was a Methodist conference.

Two days later, on June 26, Sr. Mary Barbara and Sr. Jane Patricia started out for Europe, thus missing Commemoration Day at the convent on June 29. There was a High Mass for Commemoration Day with eight priests in the sanctuary in the main chapel. The chapel was full of guests at what was described as "a beautiful service." Ten new Associates were received. There was also a bad storm during which all the lights went out but in true CSJB spirit "the service went on." The schoolgirls playing the pipe organ quickly changed seats to the pump organ and continued playing.

The Suffragan Bishop of Newark, the Rt. Revd. Donald MacAdie, died on August 1, 1963, and Mother Margaret Helena and Sr. Waldine Lucia attended his funeral on August 3. On a happier note, Mother and Sr. Agatha Louise left on August 5 for a Conference at the University of Notre Dame du Lac, South Bend, Indiana. This was a conference for Roman Catholic Religious, but Anglican Religious were invited as observers, a sign of warmer ecumenical relations in the light of Vatican II. Nearly 2,000 RC Religious attended. The fact that Anglican Religious had been invited to a Roman Catholic conference was hugely significant, but Mother Margaret Helena made no comment about it in the Community Record Book other than reporting their presence.

After making several visits since her first in March 1962, Suzanne Jackson was received as a postulant on November 4, 1963. It was a sign of hope for the future of the Community. November 22, 1963, saw Mother Margaret Helena and Sr. Waldine Lucia at Jersey City for the bazaar at Grace Church.

A brief note in the Community Record Book, which is very easy to miss with the faded handwriting, states "President Shot." The shot that killed President John F. Kennedy echoed around the world but was reported in just two words.

On Thanksgiving Day, November 28, all the Sisters were home at the convent until the next day. On St. Andrew's Day, two days later, there was a bad snowstorm, the first of the coming winter. But next day there was "a nice visit" from three RC Sisters including a Mother Superior. They were shown over the convent and stayed for tea. Perhaps this was a result of bonds forged at the conference in Indiana.

The boiler for the heating system started a bad leak at the beginning of December, just as the cold weather set in. A new oil-powered furnace had to be installed and meanwhile, the old coal furnace continued to heat the building. The new system was not operational until the end of January. Fortunately, the St. John the Baptist Foundation helped with the funding.

Christmas had been celebrated "as usual" according to the entry in the Community Record Book. This meant the usual combination of Mass, the office, singing carols and welcoming guests. Shortly before the festival, Barbara Packer had written saying she would like to enter the novitiate in the Fall of 1964. She was received as an Associate on January 26, 1964. After Christmas, on December 28, Mother, Sr. Waldine Lucia, Sr. Katharine Veronica and Sr. Ora Mary went to a conference on vocations hosted by the RC Sisters of Christian Charity at Mallinckrodt Convent, Mendham. And so the year 1963 ended with joyful hope of new vocations, with seeds of ecumenical co-operation having been sown, and with the growing friendship with Clewer.

On March 6, 1964, the Rt. Revd. George Rath was consecrated Suffragan Bishop of Newark.[16] Meanwhile at Jersey City, Fr. Laughlin, priest in charge since 1961, had moved to Newark, NJ, where he had been appointed Dean of Trinity Cathedral. He was succeeded as priest in charge at Grace Church by Fr. John B. Luce. On March 7, he conducted a quiet day at the convent for members of Grace Church.

Mother Margaret Helena was endeavoring to maintain closer ties with St. John Baptist School, and on March 8, twenty school girls came to the convent for a talk and slideshow followed by Vespers and Benediction. The evening concluded with supper and was deemed a "great success." Both Mother Margaret Helena and Sr. Waldine Lucia understood schoolgirls from their earlier years at St. Helen's Hall, Portland, Oregon.

The Community Record Book noted on May 14, 1963, that Suzanne Jackson had begun her retreat prior to her reception as a novice on May 18, when she took the name Suzanne Elizabeth. She was the latest in a long line of Sisters who, before coming into Community, had trained as nurses at St. Luke's Hospital, NYC. The service was at 9:00am and all went well. Afterwards all the schoolgirls and teachers came up to the convent. Next day, Mother, Sr. Waldine Lucia, Sr. Agatha Louise, Sr. Agnes Genevieve, and Sr. Suzanne Elizabeth went to West Park, NY, for the ground-breaking ceremony for the new wing at Holy Cross monastery.

July and August 1964 was a time of racial tension in the US and on August 2, rioting broke out in Jersey City, lasting three days and nights. Mother and Sr. Waldine Lucia had visited the Sisters there on July 29 and had noted the tension. Grace Church was unharmed but the whole city was frozen in fear and confusion.

On a more positive note, two groups of foreign Christian exchange students came to stay at St. Marguerite's. The first group arrived on July 1 and the second on July 29. Each group consisted of 25 girls staying for four nights. Ecumenical visitors continued to come to Mendham, including a Japanese priest, a Russian bishop, a Syrian bishop and four RC Sisters.

But the great event of Fall 1964 was when Mother Annys and Sr. Catherine[17] arrived from Clewer on September 15. They stayed for a month and had a full schedule. On September 22, Mother Margaret Helena took them to visit a public school, knowing Mother Annys' interest in education. A four-day visit to 90, Barrow Street included some sight-seeing in New York City. This was followed by Jersey City, where they attended a service at Grace Church and stayed for dinner with the Sisters. There was an Associates' lunch at Hyde Park and on the way there Mother Margaret Helena took them to visit St. Helena's convent. A few days later Mother took them to Boston to visit St. Margaret's convent, where they stayed overnight. On October 4, Mother Margaret Helena was re-elected Mother Superior. On October 12, 1964, Barbara Packer was received as a postulant and next day the two English Sisters left for Clewer. It had been a memorable visit.

The English Sisters had returned home before the ground-breaking ceremony for the new chapel at St. John Baptist School on October 16. Mr. Cordingley's original plan had been for a Gothic style chapel but this was never built. A photograph of the model of the school (now lost) shows what the chapel would have looked like, and it did not match the style in which the school was built. The new chapel was designed by James S. Jones Jr. of Mendham and reflected the modern style popular in the 1960s. A photograph of the ground-breaking ceremony shows Mother Margaret Helena, Sr. Mary Barbara (Sister Superior of the school), Melvin Windsor, contractor, the Revd. Norman Post of St. Mark's Basking Ridge, and James S. Jones Jr, architect. Fr. Templeton, the school chaplain, was ill and Fr. Post substituted for him.

On October 21, 1964, Laura Weller visited the convent with a view to testing her vocation, and on December 7, she was received as a postulant. The Community now had a novice and two postulants and as 1964 gave way to 1965 there was much to be thankful for and much to hope for.

[1] Sister Margaret Helena, CSJB, *Memories of Community Life* 1999.

[2] Guild of St. Monica—a group for women. Archives of the guild from 1910–76 are held at Trinity.

[3] CSJB had worked in the parish of Trinity, Wall Street, until 1880.

[4] The Revd. Henry F. Folsom served as curate at St. James, Upper Montclair, before becoming Rector of St. Peter's, Washington, NJ, on April 1, 1959. Source: The Living Church February 1, 1959.

[5] PRICE, Margaret M. *St. John Baptist School 1880–1980* p.40.

[6] After retiring from the school, Marian Wysong devoted herself to public service. She created and ran the Mendham First Aid Squad and served as a Township Committee member. Also, she served for two terms as Mayor at a time when it was unusual for a woman to serve in this capacity. I am grateful to Chris Chrystal for this information and for her further memories in this chapter.

[7] At this time the role of women was being explored in depth within the Episcopal Church. It would eventually lead to the first ordinations to the priesthood in the mid-1970s. In this respect the Episcopal Church was decades ahead of the Church of England. Mother Margaret Helena was a strong supporter of women's ministry, having herself trained as a deaconess, though she was not commissioned.

[8] Gallaudet College (now University) is a federally chartered private university for the deaf and hard of hearing. It was founded in 1864 as a grammar school for deaf and visually impaired children.

[9] The girls at St. Anna's called Sr. Francina "Dutch cleaner" after a cleaning product. It is unlikely that she knew but it is still remembered within the Community!

[10] Information given by Lynn Wilder Mullin to Valerie Bonham at the convent in 2018.

[11] See BONHAM, Valerie *Living Stones* pp.244–5.

[12] The manuscript notebook which was in the Clewer archives (now dispersed) stopped at 1944 and no figures were entered after that date.

[13] It finally closed in 1991.

[14] Sr. Mary John, OSB, was still at West Malling Abbey at the time of writing in 2018. Source: *Anglican Religious Life 2018–2019*. Sr. Suzanne Elizabeth writes: "I met her before she entered. Later, I met her at West Malling a few times."

[15] One Sister whom the American visitors may not have met on this visit was Sr. Eudora, who was Sister Superior of St. Mary's Retreat House, Salisbury. It had been St. Mary's Home, the Salisbury Diocesan House of Mercy, run by the Clewer Sisters until they withdrew in 1947. Sisters from the Community of St. Peter the Apostle, Laleham on Thames, took it over until they withdrew in January 1959. After a refurbishment it reopened as a retreat house in September 1959 with Sr. Eudora in charge. It closed in 1971.

[16] The Rt. Revd. George Rath was Suffragan Bishop of Newark 1964–70, Coadjutor Bishop 1970–74 and Diocesan Bishop 1974–79.

[17] Sr. Catherine was from a different Community.

9

… AND BUILDING BRIDGES

The Community from 1965–69

O N JANUARY 15, 1965, St. Luke's Montclair Vestry Conference, consisting of twelve men and four women, took place at the convent. Ten days previously, on January 5, 1965, the Episcopal Church Women had had a Leadership Conference at Mendham. It is hardly surprising that the Community hosted these meetings, as Mother Margaret Helena was a supporter of women's ministry in the Church.[1] Later that month, on the 27th, Mother and Sr. Waldine Lucia traveled to Washington, DC, for the Installation of the new Presiding Bishop, the Rt. Revd. John E. Hines, formerly a diocesan bishop in Texas. Sr. Waldine Lucia noted in the Community Record Book: "We walked in the great procession—a glorious service. We spent the night at the YWCA." On February 6, Mother and three Sisters went to St. Luke's Montclair for the Centennial service of the Community of St. Mary.

April and May saw a time of rejoicing for the Sisters, closely followed by one of deep sadness. On April 5, 1965, Barbara Packer was received as a novice, taking the name Sr. Barbara Jean. A few days later, on April 16, Sr. Julia Frances was taken ill at the convent and was admitted to hospital. May 27 was Ascension Day and there was "a beautiful Mass." Later that day Sr. Julia Frances passed to her rest; two days later her body was "brought home." Her funeral took place on May 31, and not surprisingly there was a large crowd with several priests and many old girls from St. Marguerite's, which had been her great work.[2] She was laid to rest in the Community cemetery at Mendham. With the passing of Sr. Julia Frances the last link with the early days of CSJB in America also passed away. She was the second former student of St. John Baptist School to join the Community, having been a pupil in the 1880s. She was a cousin of Sr. Waldine Lucia and was the last Sister to have known Sr. Frances Constance, the first Superior in New York. Professed with Sr. Florence Teresa on May 26, 1899, in the chapel at St. John Baptist House, 233, East Seventeenth Street, NYC, she now passed to her rest on the day after her 66th anniversary of profession.[3]

The day before Sr. Julia Frances' funeral, on May 30, 1965, the new chapel at St. John Baptist School was dedicated by the Rt. Revd. Leland Stark, Bishop of Newark. The new building measured 35 x 75ft and had a tall pyramidal roof. It was of block construction with brick flooring and wooden interior arches. There was a separate tower and steeple, 70ft high, connected to the chapel by a 20ft corridor. The area at the base of the tower housed a baptistery. The chapel was connected to the school building by a corridor and was designed to seat 170. The east wall behind the altar was of clear glass. The former chapel in the main school building would now revert to its original use as a library. When St. Michael's Home, Mamaroneck, closed, the Stations of the Cross had been brought back to the convent and had found a home in the chapel at St. John Baptist School. But they did not fit into the new chapel at the school and so they were returned to the convent once more. Mother Margaret Helena put them in the chapel at St. Marguerite's, by then a flourishing retreat house, and the Community Record Book noted that "they are lovely there."

On June 7, 1965, Laura Weller was received as a novice, taking the name Sr. Laura Katharine. She had been educated at St. Katharine's School, which had been founded by the Community of St. Mary (Western Province) but was by then a diocesan school. Sr. Laura Katharine came to the Community with two music degrees.

St. John Baptist-tide went well. The day itself, June 24, was a lovely day, and as usual they had supper on the cloister. Commemoration Day two days later was described in the Community Record Book as "a wonderful day; many guests here; supper at St. Marguerite's; 20 Associates received."

Later that day Mother Margaret Helena and Sr. Agatha Louise left for England, though their flight was greatly delayed. They arrived home on July 24, after a lovely visit, though no details were recorded. Sr. Helen Muriel[4] came to Mendham with them for a short visit, flying home on August 12. During her stay Sr. Helen Muriel gave a talk to fifteen RC Sisters and two priests from St. Joseph's RC Church, Mendham, about her ecumenical travels in Europe. Earlier, on August 5, Sr. Katharine Veronica and Sr. Agnes Genevieve had arrived back at the convent after working for two weeks of their summer rest at Fort Defiance amongst the Navajo Indians.[5] They had been working with Deaconess Marian Brown, who had been ministering amongst the Navajo and Arapahoe Indians for more than 25 years. This new ministry for the Sisters would continue for three summers.

A last link with the early years of the convent at Mendham was severed by the death of William Cordingley on Saturday November 20, 1965. The Morristown *Daily Record* of November 22 reported that he was "crossing the street in front of the Black Horse Inn, where he had just eaten dinner, when he was struck by a car … He was walking towards his car that was across the street." Three Sisters went to his funeral and afterwards five family members came to the convent for luncheon. He was laid to rest in the cemetery of St. Joseph's RC Church, Mendham. He had served as a Justice of the Peace in 1925 and 1931, and as Mayor of Mendham in 1935–36 and 1941–42. Mr. Cordingley had been a faithful port of call for the Sisters in times of crisis over many years. The convent building and St. John Baptist School stand as his memorials within the Community.

As the year 1965 drew to a close there were three important events. First, Fr. William V. Albert was instituted as Rector at Grace Church (Van Vorst) on December 10, and several Sisters attended the service. Second, on December 14, Mother Margaret Helena, Sr. Waldine Lucia, Sr. Agnes Genevieve and Sr. Agatha Louise went to Holy Cross Monastery, West Park, NY, for the dedication of the new wing and blessing of the Cornerstone.

The third, and most important, of the events was the Chapter meeting on December 16, 1965. Following on from previous discussions, an important constitutional change was made. Article twelve was deleted and the following new one was adopted: "If the Chapter by a two-thirds majority shall vote in her favor, the novice as soon as may be, may make her profession in first vows in the chapel of the Mother House before the Visitor." The question of first vows was one of the stumbling blocks with the Community at Clewer in the 1940s leading to the severance of the Affiliation. At that time the Sisters at Mendham did not see the necessity for first vows, thinking it would somehow take away from the solemnity of life vows. But now as time had moved on this was no longer seen as an obstacle. It was a highly important change and one which would help pave the way for re-affiliation with Clewer, though that was still several years away.

And so 1965 drew to a close. Christmas Day was on a Saturday, so the parish Sisters were unable to come to the convent because of preparing for Sunday duties. It had been an eventful year full of contacts with parish groups, individuals seeking spiritual guidance, and generally making the message of God's love available to all. The three novices brought hope for the Community's future and the growing bond with Clewer was a great encouragement to Sisters on both sides of the Atlantic.

On January 19, 1966, Fr. Templeton celebrated the 25th anniversary of his ordination as priest. There were eight priests in the sanctuary at the Mass and a reception afterwards. Fifteen years of his 25 had been spent as Chaplain at St. John Baptist School and in service to CSJB. Girls from the school and many guests were present to join in the celebrations.

The resolution concerning first vows was voted on at a second Chapter on March 2, 1966, and reached the required majority. Consequently, there was a Chapter of election on April 18, and on May 1, Sr. Suzanne Elizabeth was told she was to be "brought forward for profession in First Vows." This took place on May 26, 1966, and all the Sisters were present. Sr. Waldine Lucia declared it to have been "a lovely service," and it was a joyous one, too. Officiating in the sanctuary were Bishop Stark, Fr. Weed (Warden), Fr. Templeton, four other priests and three Franciscan friars. There was a large number in the congregation and after the service refreshments were served.

There was a good enrollment at St. John Baptist School in 1966 and the new chapel was fully in use and fully paid for. Also, the space now created for the library was a helpful addition. The school Commencement service, held on June 4, was another lovely day with a big crowd in attendance, and Bishop Rath gave the address. Fifteen girls graduated and all of them were accepted for college or other training.

On June 8, 1916, the new convent had been dedicated and Sr. Mary Joan professed. Now, fifty years later, the golden jubilee of both was celebrated. Writing to the Associates on the Octave of St. John Baptist, Mother Margaret Helena noted: "We are most thankful that the whole building has been repaired and restored. After our years of anxiety and perplexity over it, God has given it back to our keeping, as it seems in almost a miraculous way." The Community Record Book has no entry for June 8, 1966, but doubtless the anniversary was kept on St. John Baptist Day (June 24) and Commemoration Day next day. Over the two days many guests were welcomed and 126 were seated at luncheon on Commemoration Day. Bishop Rath was present and pontificated at the High Mass. Bishop Stark and his wife came for the early Eucharist on the feast day and were both received as Associates.

The prayerful and supportive role of Associates was greatly valued by the Sisters. Six had died in the past year, nine had been received in the first half of 1966, and another 23 were received on Commemoration Day, bringing the number on the roll to 260. Mother Margaret Helena particularly noted in the Newsletter two of the longest serving Associates: Mrs. Pemberton Hollingsworth (Laura Albert), received in 1902, who was a great-aunt of Sr. Suzanne Elizabeth; and Mrs. Allen Tucker, received in 1905 and now aged 95.

At the end of Commemoration Day, Sr. Katharine Veronica and Sr. Agnes Genevieve arrived in Arizona to work for six weeks on the Navajo reservation with Deaconess Brown. Their main work was in the Vacation Church Schools, and on the first Sunday morning they were greeted by many of the children they had worked amongst the previous year. They were due back at the convent on July 27, but were delayed due to an airline strike.

On August 17, 1966, a new postulant was received and the new Clewer "Office for the reception of a Postulant" was used for the first time. This was a sign of the growing co-operation between Mendham and Clewer, enhanced no doubt by the reciprocal visits by Mothers and Sisters of both houses.

On October 19 the funeral took place at Newark Cathedral of Bishop Benjamin Washburn, former Visitor to the Community. The Community Record Book does not state whether any of the Sisters attended, but as he had been a good friend to the Community it is likely that CSJB would have been represented. But Mother was unavailable as she was at a conference in Racine, Wisconsin. Fr. Weed was re-elected Warden in the Fall of 1966, and was finally installed on November 10, Bishop Rath having been taken ill en-route for the original date of installation.

There was a sign at this time of changing attitudes to former Sisters. On November 11, 1966, Margaret Smith, formerly Sr. Margaret Raphael, wrote requesting restoration to the Community, having left in 1944. After leaving she had returned to live with her mother and had taken a nursing course. She qualified as a Licensed Practical Nurse and Visiting Nurse. Her request was not dismissed, nor was the decision for her restoration taken lightly. Mother Margaret Helena visited her and found her to be "a frail old lady." Then Mother went to consult with the bishop and with the Warden. Finally, after she had petitioned Chapter, a vote was taken and it was decided that Margaret Smith should have a six months probationary period, wearing the habit and using her Community name, but occupying the lowest professed place.

Work on the convent seemed never ending. On November 25, 1966, all the windows were being painted as they were "very nasty." The year 1966 came to a close with heavy snow on December 16, but it did not prevent Sr. Barbara Jean and Sr. Laura Katharine being sent to Jersey City that day to work for a week. The snow got deeper and by Christmas the storm was so bad that the School Sisters could not get up the hill to Midnight Mass nor to the Mass at 8:00am. But on December 28 there was a reception at the school for guests and teachers.

As 1966 gave way to 1967, there was growing concern for Sr. Ellen Juliana, who was in Morristown Memorial Hospital. But there was good news too. On January 3, Mother told Sr. Barbara Jean she was to be brought forward to Chapter for election in first vows. Chapter met on January 24 and Sr. Barbara Jean was duly elected.

Early in January 1967 the library was painted, as "it needed it badly." The convent roads were in bad shape again and in the following April the St. John the Baptist Foundation gave money for their repair.

Mother Margaret Helena had informed the Associates that "many good and useful things are happening at St. Marguerite's."[6] And indeed the retreat ministry there was going from strength to strength. Between September 1965 and June 1966, 35 retreats or conferences had been held there, most of them over one night and some for a full weekend. This was not counting the numerous individual visitors, nor groups coming for parish picnics and a tour of the convent. She estimated that 1,435 names were entered on the guest list for 1966. Now, in 1967, the retreat ministry and that of hospitality to friends and strangers alike continued. Among the varied groups of Religious, clergy, young people's fellowships, Episcopal Church Women, seminarians, and parish groups, the Community Record Book noted on several occasions meetings of Civil Rights groups.[7] While they did not participate in political activities, there can be little doubt that working at St. Luke's Chapel, NYC, and in Jersey City had made the Sisters more aware of the socio-economic division and discrimination between white people and people of color in those areas and throughout the United States.

Sr. Ellen Juliana passed to her rest on January 29, 1967, and was buried in the Community cemetery on February 1. Professed in 1920 with Sr. Elisabeth Roberta (who died 1962), Sr. Ellen Juliana was a graduate of Radcliffe College and was a gifted musician, singer and needlewoman. She did much repair work on the vestments as well as making new ones, and learned to do very fine painting and illuminating, thus continuing a Community tradition. Earlier in her Community life she had been school Sister at St. Helen's Hall in Portland, and then worked at St. Michael's Home, Mamaroneck, until it closed in 1937.

By February 1967 three new postulants had been received, two of whom had been postulants in other Communities (one for just two weeks). Perhaps not surprisingly they did not advance into the novitiate. But maybe it is a sign of Mother Margaret Helena's broadness of mind that she gave them a chance to test their vocation rather than rejecting them because of previous failures.

Winter weather persisted well into March. Sr. Barbara Jean's profession in first vows had been set for March 17, but there was such a bad snowstorm that the bishop could not get to the convent. The Warden, who had arrived the night before it, received her vows. Just a few days before this, on March 13, Sr. Mildred Eleanor passed to her rest. Professed in 1922, Sr. Mildred Eleanor became Sister in charge of St. Anna's before replacing Sr. Ellen Juliana at St. Helen's Hall. She remained there until the Community withdrew in 1944, and from there went to Corsicana. When that work was given up she worked at St. John Baptist House, NYC, and at Jersey City. She had survived surgery for cancer in the 1950s and continued to lead an active life in Community despite increasing ill health in her final years. Her last words were: "It be to be done." They were words from Mother Harriet and she was a true CSJB Sister to the last.

The Feast of Corpus Christi on May 25 was kept with four priests concelebrating the Mass. This was the first recorded concelebration at the convent, where the priests, gathered round the altar, joined together in saying the Prayer of Consecration.[8] Next day was also a day of celebration as Sr. Suzanne Elizabeth renewed her vows.[9] The bishop was unable to come and so the Warden (Fr. Weed) presided.

Summer was as hot as the winter had been cold and St. John Baptist Day was no exception. There is no record of Commemoration Day for 1967, but on June 26 Mother left for England for a conference and returned early in August, bringing Mother Annys with her. Sr. Katharine Veronica went to the Navajo reservation in Arizona for the third year running, taking Sr. Barbara Jean with her.

At the end of her six-month probationary period, Chapter voted that Sr. Margaret Raphael should be reinstated and renew her vows. She was then placed in choir according to her former seniority and all rights and privileges of a professed Sister were restored to her. This took place on August 15, 1967. Her Community Biographer wrote: "The Sisters were pleased to have her place occupied once more." Despite her frailty, Sr. Margaret Raphael served faithfully for another ten years until her death.

Immediately after Sr. Margaret Raphael's restoration a novice was received, and also an Associate, a seminarian working at Grace Church (Van Vorst).

On September 8, 1967, Sr. Laura Katharine was professed in first vows. There were now three Sisters professed in first vows and three in the novitiate, although one withdrew later in September, having no vocation.

Ecumenical relationships continued to prosper and on September 11, 1967, the Community welcomed a large number of RC Sisters for a conference. Supper was had in the Chapter room and the bishop gave an address of welcome. Many Associates helped meet the visiting Sisters at the airport.

Fall 1967 was a busy time for the Sisters with the usual round of meetings, teaching, spiritual guiding, and hosting groups large and small. But as usual the Sisters also took time throughout the year to nurture their own spiritual lives by means of their regular retreat days and their long retreats, the latter often attended by Sisters from the Society of St. Margaret, Boston. The daily office, Mass and prayer time punctuated each day. The chapel was always the "powerhouse" which nurtured all the Sisters did. From their life of prayer came their work for God. And so, as the Fall gave way to winter, the Sisters weathered all the storms, be they ice and snow or difficulties in the parishes.

The first quarter of 1968 may best be described as months of activity tinged with changes. Ecumenism was still a strong feature; and on January 21 there was a Christian Unity service in the main chapel which was attended by a big crowd, including many RC nuns. On February 16, the Community Record Book noted: "Had the New Rite this morning." It gives no clue to how this was received.[10] From February 18–20, various ministers of different denominations held meetings using the convent facilities. And groups of Lutherans began having regular meetings at the convent. Earlier in the month more work was being carried out on the convent buildings with the painting of the visitors' dining room and the pantry.

Sadly, Sr. Ora Mary left the Community on March 4, 1968, and was released from her vows by the Presiding Bishop. She had been professed on September 8, 1949, and was a talented musician. Shortly before leaving she had gained an MA.[11] On a more positive note, Sr. Barbara Jean renewed her first vows on March 19, and Sr. Suzanne Elizabeth renewed hers on May 27. And a brief note in the Community Record Book for April 2, "Mother read the Epistle," gives a clue to continuing liturgical change. Until this time the Sisters would be present at Mass and receive Holy Communion but would not have been permitted to take an active role, but times were changing rapidly. And so too the habit began to be reformed with narrower sleeves and bands. All the Sisters put on their new collars and bands on Whit Sunday (June 2) "as a try out!"

Mother Margaret Helena continued to cultivate closer relations with St. John Baptist School and invited the English History class up to the convent to see her slides from her visits to Clewer and elsewhere in England. On May 26 the Baccalaureate Sunday service was held in the new chapel at the school for the first time, and on June 1, 1968, there were twenty-two graduates at the school Commencement day.

As the summer dawned so too the number of visiting parish groups increased, including 55 people from All Saints', Millington. St. John Baptist Day (June 24) saw all the Sisters at the convent except for two Sisters who were working at Hoboken. Several girls from St. John Baptist School came for the Mass. Commemoration Day on June 29 was "a wonderful day" with 126 guests, plus the bishop and nine Franciscan novices. It was a "lovely service" with many priests present.

It was not just parish groups who came for picnics. On July 7, 16 junior professed RC Sisters and two professed Sisters of Christian Charity attended Vespers, followed by a picnic on the lawn and on the cloister. All declared it to be "a lovely party."

On August 2, 1968, Sr. Katharine Veronica and Sr. Barbara Jean returned from working for five weeks in Hoboken. This was a new work for the Community in a socially deprived area. The Community Record Book simply notes the work taking place but Sr. Barbara Jean has recalled it in some detail. "It was an ecumenical six-week program involving churches of different denominations, and included Christian education, field trips, sports and reading instruction. Sr. Katharine Veronica and I lived in the RC convent next door, ate with other volunteers at the Episcopal Church and taught Church School at the Lutheran Church. RC Sisters who were school teachers did the reading instruction. I believe Presbyterians and Methodists were also involved. I remember taking the children in buses to a park with a lake and a large zoo. It was at the height of the ecumenical movement and I think about 75–100 children were involved. I also think there was a lunch provided by the government, which does even now have lunch programs for needy children."

Older, more established work, such as the summer Vacation Bible School at St. Uriel's, Sea Girt, continued. This opened on August 12 for two weeks, with Sr. Agatha Louise and Sr. Barbara Jean in charge of it and Sr. Waldine Lucia keeping house for them at Manasquan. On August 11, Sr. Suzanne Elizabeth and Sr. Laura Katharine went to help with the school work and stayed at Manasquan. On returning to the convent, Sr. Laura Katharine renewed her vows on September 9, 1968.

On November 2, 1968, Sr. Eleanor Lucy and Sr. Katharine Veronica represented the Community at the laying of the Cornerstone of the new educational building at St. Paul's Morris Plains. Writing in the Community Record Book, Sr. Waldine Lucia noted that "the two Sisters helped to start the Sunday school there years ago. One of our Associates' medals was put in the Cornerstone." On November 17, Mother and Sr. Barbara Jean went to Gladstone for the laying of the Cornerstone for the new church building.

In November there was a chapter of accidents. Sr. Agnes Genevieve fell and broke her arm, and then on the same day (November 12), Sr. Agatha Louise fell and hurt her arm and hand. Tests revealed a sprained knee and finger and cracked shoulder. On November 27, Sr. Margaret Raphael fell and broke her wrist and a finger.

Early in the New Year Muriel Blue, one of the Sisters' most dependable resident helpers, fell on the ice and broke her arm in two places. All the schools were closed due to the snow and ice. Nineteen sixty-nine had begun with more work in the convent, with painting in the upper halls and Sisters' cells and new lighting fixtures in the cells which were a great help. With such a large building there would always be some work to be done. And this was not confined to the interior. In March 1969 the Cemetery wall had to be rebuilt, as the fragile terracotta bricks and stucco did not weather well.

St. Helen's Hall in Portland, Oregon, was due to celebrate its centennial later in the year and the Sisters had been asked to write the history of their forty years at the Hall. Sr. Waldine Lucia set about the task, using the Records of the work kept by the Community in addition to her own experience there and that of Mother Margaret Helena. The manuscript was completed by the beginning of March and sent to Sally Reed Stout, who was writing the centennial history.[12]

Ecumenical links with other Christian denominations continued to be strong. During the Week of Prayer for Christian Unity (January 18–25), a group met at the convent, and on March 7, Mother and Sr. Waldine Lucia went to a service held during a day of prayer at the Congregational Church in Mendham. A few days later Mother and Sr. Agatha Louise went to Trenton, NJ, to a Sisters' Formation Conference and took three RC Sisters with them. Soon after Easter a large group of Lutheran women came for an overnight stay at St. Marguerite's. On May 8, Mother Margaret Helena and Sr. Agnes Genevieve went to St. Gregory's Abbey, Three Rivers, MI, for the installation of Dom Benedict Reid as the first Abbot of the Benedictine Congregation in America.[13]

At home, all the Sisters were present for Sr. Barbara Jean's renewal of her vows towards the end of March 1969. Then Sr. Suzanne Elizabeth made her profession in life vows on May 26, 1969. The service took place at 7:30am, followed by breakfast to which the guests were invited to stay. This was the first profession in life vows since that of Sr. Elizabeth Anne on June 22, 1951.

On June 29, 1969, the senior students from the School were invited to the convent for dinner with the Sisters. Sr. Suzanne Elizabeth had been working at the School as house Sister and school nurse. She was popular with the girls and they dedicated the 1969 edition of the Yearbook *The Satura* to her. The dedication stated that "she has been our friend and guide during our years here. By her understanding and patience, she has helped us all through many a major crisis. Who among us has not said, 'Sister can I talk to you?' or 'Sister, are you busy?' No matter how trivial the problem, she has put aside what she was doing to listen and help. In leaving St. John's we will take with us what we have learned from her about perseverance and friendship. It is to you, Sister Suzanne Elizabeth, that the Senior Class dedicated this book *The Satura '69*, to which you gave so much of yourself."

A reflection of the never-ending circle of Community life may be seen in four events in 1969: Sr. Barbara Jean's renewal of her first vows, followed closely by Sr. Suzanne Elizabeth's profession in life vows, and then on June 22, a party to celebrate Sr. Waldine Lucia's sixtieth anniversary of her profession. The fourth event took place on September 8, when Sr. Laura Katharine renewed her first vows. The progression through the novitiate to first vows and from thence to life vows and then the glorious thanksgiving of a life-long dedication to God is to be seen repeatedly in the life of the Community.[14]

On July 5, four Sisters flew to England—Sr. Katharine Veronica, Sr. Elizabeth Anne, Sr. Suzanne Elizabeth and Sr. Barbara Jean. While they were away, the Community Record Book noted on July 20 that "the astronauts landed on the moon—a giant leap for man." Next day's entry noted that they had "left the moon safely." Back on planet Earth, on July 21 the Community Record Book reported that the four Sisters were "having a wonderful time." Details of their itinerary were not given except that "they will go to Clewer for six days before returning to New Jersey."[15] During their absence in England, Fr. David Leech, Headmaster of St. Helen's Hall and of Bishop Dagwell Hall, came to the convent for "a delightful visit."

The Community was accustomed to answering all kinds of pastoral need and on August 25, 1969, the Sisters were roused from their beds by the Methodist pastor, who asked them to take in a homeless family for the night. There were three children and their mother. The Sisters opened up St. Marguerite's for them, there being no other guests there.

The St. Helen's Hall centennial was celebrated in November 1969. Mother, Sr. Waldine Lucia, Sr. Eleanor Lucy, Sr. Elizabeth Marion and Sr. Agatha Louise, all of whom had worked at the school, went to the celebrations. Upon returning home they declared it to be "a grand, glorious visit."

The three junior Sisters and Sr. Suzanne Elizabeth went to Jersey City on December 20, 1969, to help with the sale, which as noted in Chapter 7 was a major undertaking. Meanwhile, there were a number of funerals of old friends. Alice Dennis, a former St. Marguerite's and St. Anna's girl, passed to her rest, and on December 11 her funeral was attended by Mother Margaret Helena and Sr. Waldine Lucia. On December 29, four Sisters attended the funeral of Theo Hobbie, a relative of both Sr. Julia Frances and Sr. Waldine Lucia.

The 1960s had been a decade of change, of a widening of Community horizons and of building bridges. Changes within the Episcopal Church were reflected in the adoption of liturgical change in worship, cautious at first, but later more extensively. The ecumenical movement had been embraced with enthusiasm. The growing bonds with Clewer reflected a new desire for healing old wounds. And the presence of new, young Sisters brought hope for the future. As the decade came to a close, the ice and snow did not prevent Mother Margaret Helena, Sr. Waldine Lucia and the junior Sisters from praying the old year out and the New Year in. It was a time-honored custom, part of the tradition of CSJB. There can be no doubt that the tall white building at the top of the hill at Mendham stood as a sentinel in a dark world and as a sign of hope and stability to those who sought peace and healing.

---

[1] The mid-1960s were to see ground-breaking changes in the governance of the Episcopal Church, starting at parish level, which ultimately led to the ordination of women to the priesthood a decade later. But in the mid-1960s women were still not permitted to serve on parish vestries in most dioceses. In 1967 the General Convention voted to allow women to serve as deputies for the first time, but it was not until the next General Convention in 1970 that they took their seats.

[2] For more about Sr. Julia Frances's ministry at St. Marguerite's see BONHAM, Valerie *Living Stones* Chapter 13.

[3] The two novices, Sr. Suzanne Elizabeth and Sr. Barbara Jean, together with the postulant who would become Sr. Laura Katharine, all still in Community at the time of writing (2020), provide an unbroken link via Sr. Julia Frances to the earliest days in New York in the 1880s.

[4] Sr. Helen Muriel, CSJB, was professed at Clewer in 1920. She had served in the Community work in India from 1920–26 and 1927–29; also at St. Stephen's College, Broadstairs, 1933–60, and as Novice Mistress from 1960–67. In 1963 she and Sr. Eudora had been on an ecumenical visit to Europe, staying at RC, Lutheran, and Russian Orthodox convents, and attended several conferences in France for Novice Mistresses.

[5] See Appendix 3, Letters from an Indian Reservation, from their visit in 1966.

[6] *Newsletter to Associates and Friends* Octave of St. John Baptist 1966.

[7] The Civil Rights Movement in the US had been increasing in momentum from the mid-1950s.

[8] Concelebration was revived in the 1960s in the Roman Catholic Church following Vatican II, and the practice spread into the Anglican Church. Its origin lay in the early Apostolic Church, where the Bishop would preside at the Eucharist surrounded by the other priests joining in the words of the Consecration.

[9] First or Temporary Vows may be renewed annually for at least three years. At the end of that time a Sister may be elected to Final Profession. Source: https://www.csjb.org/becoming-a-sister.html

[10] In 1967 the General Convention had approved an updated Eucharistic Rite for trial use. Between 1967 and 1979, when the new *Book of Common Prayer of the Episcopal Church* was officially adopted, many parishes experimented with the new rite. Source: HEIN, David and SHATTUCK, Gardiner H. Jr. *The Episcopalians* 2004 p.147.

[11] Sr. Ora Mary (Carmen Ora Synnes) returned to the Community briefly and was professed again on April 8, 1991, but left finally on July 27, 1992. She was born on August 14, 1925, and died on November 6, 2009, at 84 years of age. Her last known place of residence was San Marcos, California. Source: www.genalogybank.com

[12] Sally Reed Stout *St. Helen's Hall: the First Century 1869–1969* Portland, Oregon.

[13] St. Gregory's Abbey was founded from Nashdom Abbey in the UK. See: *Singing God's Praises: The First Sixty Years.* Three Rivers 1998.

[14] There was a further profession in first vows on July 2, but Sr. Ellen Marie did not proceed to life vows.

[15] Sr. Suzanne Elizabeth writes: "We had ten days to visit ten Cathedral cities, and after one free day, ten days' study at Canterbury. Then six days with the Clewer Sisters." Source—note to Valerie Bonham, Mendham, 2019.

10

A TOUGH ASSIGNMENT

Jersey City in the 1960s

WITH THE DAWN of the 1960s the work at Grace Church (Van Vorst) was by now well established, and the team of clergy and Sisters were beginning to see positive results in the shape of growing numbers of adults and children in the congregation and attending the various programs. This was encouraging as it signified that the people from the parish were beginning to understand that Grace Church was "their" church irrespective of their ethnic or economic background. Indeed the Hispanic congregation were having Mass in Spanish and there was a Spanish-speaking women's group.

January 31, 1960, was a great day in the life of the parish. At 10:30am there was a solemn High Mass and Confirmation by the Rt. Revd. Donald MacAdie, Suffragan Bishop of Newark, followed by a reception for the bishop and Confirmation class in the parish hall. The Confirmation class had lunch at St. Christopher's House, and then at 2:30pm the parish bus, the station wagon and the Volkswagen left for a trip to the Cathedral of St. John the Divine, NYC, with members of the Confirmation class. The three Sisters (Eleanor Lucy, Susinne Paula and Elizabeth Anne) went in the station wagon and all were back by 6:00pm.

At the beginning of February there was a special vestry meeting to decide whether to allow a concert by the Prairie View Agricultural and Mechanical College, TX.[1] They voted in favor of the concert going ahead, although the Jersey City Record Book does not note whether it took place. Even so, it was another sign of the increasing inclusiveness of Grace Church at a time when racial intolerance was a growing problem in wider society and the civil rights movement was at its height.

The 1960s would be a decade of increasing liturgical changes and there was a foretaste of this on March 9, 1960, when Fr. William Sadley preached at evening Mass. He had been a seminarian in 1955 and had visited the Sisters. The introduction of evening Mass was controversial in some quarters because it implied a shortening of the Eucharistic fast. It proved a popular innovation at Grace Church and the Sisters noted that there was "more than one altar rail" at the next evening celebration on March 16.

Numbers were flourishing at Grace Church, especially with the children's activities, for which the Sisters had special responsibility. For instance, on March 12, 1960, there were 225 children at the Saturday Church School, the second largest attendance of the year. Such large numbers are difficult to comprehend more than half a century later, but there may have been a number of reasons. The children, and indeed their parents, were glad of somewhere they could go that was safe and (in the winter) warm. There were no public parks or play areas except for the streets, and gangs of youths posed a threat to young children, especially those of color. The Sisters themselves were welcoming, and they answered every need as it arose. Thus children with no warm clothes were given coats and shoes, and those who had no breakfast were fed. No one was ever turned away because of race, color, or social status. There were secular helpers who were trained by the Sisters, but it was the Sisters themselves who provided the key to this vital work amongst the poor and neglected because of their self-dedication in their vowed life.

As well as attending services in Grace Church, the Sisters also had their own chapel at St. Christopher's, where they recited the daily Office and where one or other of the clergy would celebrate Mass. There was close contact with the convent at Mendham, with Sisters going back and forth in order to refresh their own spiritual lives by means of retreats and Community celebrations. And Mother Margaret Helena frequently visited the Sisters in Jersey City and New York in order to maintain a sense of continuity and community. Also, the Sisters would go back to the convent when extra help was needed there. Thus the three Sisters went over from May 9–11, to help with the removal back into the newly restored convent building after the decade-long stay at St. Marguerite's.

In July 1960 the Revd. Roland Bigrigg arrived at Grace Church as the new "acting" curate. He had formerly ministered in the Diocese of Grafton, Province of New South Wales, Australia, and would live at the Rectory, 268, Second Street. Meanwhile, the Rector of Grace Church, the Revd. Ledlie Laughlin Jr., was on study leave in order to do graduate work at St. Augustine's College, Canterbury, UK, until July 1961.

On October 10, 1960, Fr. Morton brought a great-nephew of Mother Harriet to Jersey City, but alas, he was not named in the Record Book.

As the year proceeded in its course the Jersey City Record Book logged

many familiar events, not least Thanksgiving. For two or three days before
the festival the Sisters packed boxes of food for those in need who would
not otherwise afford to celebrate. Then on the day itself, the Sisters
had a Mass in their chapel at 7:30am, celebrated by Fr. Morton, before
attending the Mass in church at 10:30. After a light lunch they caught
the 1:00pm train and were met by Mother Margaret Helena, who drove
them to the convent. The New York Sisters were driven to the convent
by the "aspirants" (not named). Clearly the convent was still undergoing
renovation (as noted in Chapter 8) because there was a tea party at 3:00pm
"in the temporary Community room."

The coming of Advent brought many visitors to St. Christopher's
bearing gifts of toys for the Thrift sale. The weather was appalling, with
snow and ice, so that the Sisters found themselves giving hospitality to
the visitors. "Fr. Edler and his three little daughters came with toys from
Trinity, Irvington. They were chilled so we gave them all tea." "New
Canaan toys came—a curate, his wife and child came—it was snowing
and we gave them coffee and sandwiches. We spent the day (December
19) receiving people and gifts." The Sisters and their helpers spent many
hours wrapping the toys, until long after Compline, but it was all worth
the effort. The next day the Thrift sale took place and was attended by
155 families with 606 children! The sale brought in $170.25 and this was
put into a discretionary fund for children's clothing, and to buy Christmas
food for the needy. All but a few toys went in the sale.

The work did not end when the sale closed. Next day, Sr. Susinne
Paula fixed stockings for families who hadn't come for gifts, and the other
Sisters contacted mothers to come for Christmas clothing. They arrived
at St. Christopher's on the 23rd and the Sisters were busy all day. "We
had some shoe expeditions," was the note in the Record Book. On the
morning of Christmas Eve, people came for food boxes consisting of
"hamburgers, rice or spaghetti, corn or peas, canned peaches, according
to size of family. Also bread and margarine."[2]

Christmas Eve afternoon saw the Sisters traveling to 90, Barrow Street,
NYC, for their confessions to the Warden (Fr. Weed) followed by tea
with the Sisters. Then it was back to St. Christopher's for Vespers and
Compline at 6:00pm, Mattins at 9:00pm and Midnight Mass in church
starting at 11:30pm, when the Sisters made their Communions. Next day
the Angelus was rung at 7:00am, Prime and Terce was at 7:30, and after
breakfast there was Sext and Nones. The Mass in church was at 10:30am,

after which the Sisters greeted the Rectory family, and following a quick lunch boarded the 1:00pm train for the convent. The New York Sisters also came to the convent, so the whole Community was once more together for the great festival. Both groups of Sisters stayed overnight, returning to New York and Jersey City the next evening.

Once they were back at St. Christopher's the Sisters were busy again, preparing for the various children's parties which were held in the last week of the year, and for the Epiphany pageant.

As so often happened, January was bitterly cold, with deep snow which brought all transport to a standstill. Trouble with the furnace meant everyone shivered and even the Saturday Church School was canceled. Sr. Waldine Lucia was still maintaining the Community Record Book at Mendham and she noted a deed of heroism by the Sisters at Jersey City which they had not recorded in their own JC Record Book. It states that on February 2, 1961, "there came near to being a great tragedy in the Murphy [?] family in Jersey City. A call came for help as the family was in trouble. Sr. Elizabeth Anne was sent. Later another call came and Sr. Eleanor Lucy went—found some members of the family on the floor in a faint, others sick. Sister knew at once what the trouble was. It was gas. She opened windows, called a doctor—the firemen came too. The firemen found the chimney almost blocked by ice. God was good to that family." Without the rapid action of the Sisters the whole family might have perished.

February 5, 1961, was Confirmation day. There had been another blizzard the day before this and Bishop Stark had a difficult journey by taxi, train, tube and on foot. Seventy-five out of 91 candidates managed to reach the church on foot.

Meanwhile next day, the Sisters bought warm coats for a needy family. By mid-February the cold conditions had improved in time for Lent, and there were over 300 children at the Saturday Church School on the 18th. In addition to the parish work, the Sisters also went out to neighboring parishes to give talks on the Religious Life and on the work at Grace Church.

On Palm Sunday (March 26), there were 485 people in church of whom over 200 were children. On Maundy Thursday the Blessed Sacrament was removed from the church and brought to the Sisters' sacristy in case there was an emergency.[3] The Sisters went into silence from 6:00pm. Mattins followed at 7:15pm and then they went to the church for the

Mass at 8:00pm, followed by Lauds. The Sisters' Good Friday timetable shows how they combined their Community devotions with the corporate observances in church. The day began early with the Angelus at 5:30am, followed by Watch in church; then Prime and Terce, followed by Way of the Cross in church. Sext was at 11:30am and then from 12:00 until 3:00pm there was the Three Hours' Devotion in church, followed by Nones. Lunch was at 3:30pm and then there was a break until Vespers and Compline at 6:00 followed by supper at 6:30. Mattins was at 7:15pm and then a service in church at 8:00pm followed by Lauds. On Easter Sunday the church was packed at the 10:30am Mass with 891 people of whom around 500 were children. It was standing room only until the children left as usual after the Creed.

There was a tragic note in the Jersey City Record Book for May 30, 1961, when the Sisters heard of a tenement fire in which a mother and six of her nine children perished. The Sisters knew the family and it was a reminder of the terrible conditions in which many of the parishioners still lived.

On August 20, Bishop Stark came and baptized 82 children and confirmed eleven adults. Mother and Sr. Waldine Lucia came for the service and stayed for dinner. Then at 2:00pm St. Christopher's House was closed for a month for the summer break.

Time flies, and it was soon time to re-open for the Fall season; and on September 21, Mother Margaret Helena, accompanied by Sr. Waldine Lucia, brought Sr. Eleanor Lucy, Sr. Susinne Paula and Sr. Elizabeth Anne back to St. Christopher's, arriving at 3:00pm. One of their faithful helpers (Mrs. Bober) had been in and vacuumed the house and put up the curtains. The Jersey City Record Book noted that their arrival was "delayed by the hurricane" but gives no more detail. This was "Hurricane Esther" and had the dubious distinction of being the first tropical cyclone to be discovered by satellite imagery.[4]

The Sisters were on hand to help when pastoral emergencies happened, such as on October 13, 1961, when they heard news of a suicide. The man was taken to hospital but his life could not be saved. Sr. Eleanor Lucy and Sr. Elizabeth Anne spent most of the morning at the house with his family. They attended his funeral in church three days later.

It seems as if there had been a loss of communication between the clergy and the Sisters. On October 24, there was a conference "with the Fathers, the first in four years." Mother and Sr. Waldine Lucia also attended, and out of the two-hour meeting came the following decision. "We are to have more help from the parish to free Tuesday and Thursday afternoons for calling." After this, things began to improve and a week later the Record Book noted that all three Sisters went calling following a staff meeting in the morning.

And so the year proceeded very much as usual with observance of feast days, travels to and from the convent and participation in all the many parish activities. In the midst of preparations for the annual Thrift sale, Sr. Beatrice Clare died suddenly at the convent on December 16. Next day the Sisters worked on preparing the sale items until almost the last moment, then after early dinner took the 6:00pm train, arriving at the convent in time for the 7:30pm service in chapel. The funeral took place next day, December 19, in very bad weather, and faithful worker Muriel Blue drove the Sisters back to New York and Jersey City immediately after the committal. She then stayed at St. Christopher's to help the Sisters until after the sale. Within the first hour of their return, people from five churches brought gifts of toys for the sale. December 21 saw the sale taking place with the usual large measure of success, followed next day by clearing up, and the day after that by distributing food and clothes.

Christmas Eve 1961 fell on a Sunday and so instead of the usual 10:30am Mass there was a service of nine lessons and carols. That day the Sisters began using their new office books for First Vespers of Christmas. The weather was bad but it did not prevent a considerable number of people attending the Midnight Mass, which began at 11:30pm. The Sisters also attended and received Holy Communion. On Christmas Day the Sisters traveled by train to the convent after attending church in the morning and, along with the New York Sisters, stayed until the following evening. And then it was back for the children's parties and after these had finished it was the Epiphany pageant. Thus 1961 passed into 1962.

Nineteen sixty-two began with the death at All Souls' Hospital, Morristown, of Sr. Francina on January 13, and the Sisters from Jersey City left for the convent on the 2:00pm train on the 15th. Her funeral was next day and the Sisters traveled back immediately afterwards. On a more cheerful note, Bishop MacAdie came to Grace Church on January 21 and confirmed 99 children, 42 of whom had been prepared by the Sisters, and the rest (mostly boys) by the clergy.

There was a degree of excitement on February 20, 1962, when Colonel John Glenn[5] orbited the Earth aboard the Mercury Friendship 7 spacecraft. He was the first American to orbit the Earth, circling it three times. These were the early days of the so-called "space race" and Glenn became the fifth person and third American in space. The Sisters at Grace Church noted in their Record Book: "Staff meeting—TV of orbiting man-guided space capsule—also followed on radio in pm."

Back at Mendham, Sr. Elisabeth Roberta passed to her rest on March 26, and the Sisters traveled to the convent for the funeral on March 28. They returned after the committal. Otherwise, the work in Jersey City had fallen into a familiar routine. Even so, it is still a matter of surprise that so few Sisters could do so much work and ministry, not just within the parish but also reaching out to other parishes with their talks and programs. They had secular helpers but the incentive came from the Sisters. The source of their strength was their daily, ordered spiritual life centered on the chapel in St. Christopher's.

In April 1962, Sr. Susinne Paula left Grace Church to work at St. John Baptist School and was replaced by Sr. Katharine Veronica, who came in from the New York work. But Sr. Susinne Paula returned to Jersey City after the summer break. In May, Fr. Morton left the parish in order to work on the Executive Council of the Episcopal Church. There was a thanksgiving service for his faithful work among them at the Saturday Church School on May 19, and next day in church.[6] He was replaced in the clergy team by Fr. John B. Luce on June 4.[7]

As the year passed there was a high point on October 31, when the Sisters gave thanks for ten years of "blessings and privileges" at St. Christopher's House. The thanksgiving Mass was celebrated by Fr. Laughlin, and Fr. Luce was there too. Mother Margaret Helena and Sr. Waldine Lucia had arrived the previous evening for Vespers and a festive dinner with the Sisters. They stayed overnight and left next day after the Mass and Terce. It was indeed a ministry to give thanks for.

Next day was All Saints, and Fr. Laughlin celebrated Mass at 7:00am in St. Christopher's Chapel. There was an evening Mass in church at 7:00pm attended by the Sisters. This was followed by coffee hour and a discussion on the spiritual needs of the parish.

On November 2, All Souls' Day, there was Mass in church and Fr. Luce read the names of those who had died in the past year, and also "such people as we thought ought to be remembered who had no one to remember them." There was a tragic note in the Jersey City Record Book for November 3: "little baby found in vestibule [at church], was baptized and taken to hospital." The past ten years had seen many changes in the parish and in the church community, but it was still a tough assignment for the three Sisters, as testified by such entries. Who knows what tragic story lay behind the abandonment of that tiny baby. But the mother who was driven in her desperate need knew her baby would be rescued by the kindness of clergy and Sisters.

And so the year drew towards its close—Thanksgiving came and went in the usual way and was soon replaced by the "busyness" of end-of-year sales, and then the great festival of Christmas. If the Sisters were exhausted they didn't admit it. Instead they simply continued giving to God a joyous service. Their Foundress, Mother Harriet Monsell, would have recognized it and would have been proud of her Sisters so many years later.

New Year's Day 1963 found the Sisters traveling to St. John Baptist House in Barrow Street for dinner with the Sisters there. The weather was very cold, registering 10°F on the thermometer. Even so, the Epiphany pageant went ahead as planned but not before rigorous rehearsals and the usual search for costumes. No one came from the convent due to the extreme cold, but Mother and Sr. Waldine Lucia came for the Epiphany party on January 16, and stayed overnight.

On February 5, Fr. Laughlin was elected as Dean of Newark Cathedral. He announced his appointment to the church congregations on February 17.

One aspect of the Sisters' ministry at Grace Church which receives little attention in their Record Book is the summer camping program. The Sisters did not attend the summer camps but they made an annual appeal for funding. Thus on March 12, 1963, they sent out 306 appeal letters in one mailing. The target for 1963 was $5,000 and through the generosity of their friends and supporters a total of $5,472.70 was raised. As a result, 207 children had "happy, refreshing vacations and we are grateful to each person who helped us to bring this about."[8] Most children went either to Forest Lake, NY,[9] or to Elko Lake, NY,[10] but a smaller number went to Edgewater Creche, Englewood, NJ, and other smaller camps. The camps were run by the New York Episcopal City Mission Society and the aim was very similar to the fresh air work undertaken by the Sisters in their early years in New York City.[11]

Holy Week and Easter 1963 were observed in the usual way, but on Palm Sunday there was an outdoor procession from the church, down the street, across, and up the other side. Fr. Laughlin's last Sunday was on April 21, and Mother and Sr. Waldine Lucia came from the convent. The previous day the church children had said farewell to him and he was given a book and cope. He was installed at Newark Cathedral as Dean on May 19, and the service was attended by the three Jersey City Sisters along with Mother Margaret Helena, Sr. Waldine Lucia, Sr. Elizabeth Marion, and Sr. Agatha Louise. They declared it was "a beautiful service."

St. John Baptist Day and Commemoration Day found the Sisters briefly back at the convent. But soon they returned to Jersey City to supervise the departure of the children to Elko Lake on July 1, and to Forest Lake on July 2. One little girl arrived late, which involved a frantic chase by a Sister and the hopeful camper—all was well that ended well. The Forest Lake send-off involved a 4:30am breakfast for Sr. Eleanor Lucy and Sr. Elizabeth Anne. A late night saw the two Sisters waiting up until 1:00 am for the campers' return. Throughout August, the Sisters were busy sending off various groups to the summer camps involving early mornings and late nights, but towards the end of the program the secular staff took over.

On July 22, there was a day trip for the staff at Grace Church—Sisters, clergy and secular helpers. They all left the church at 11:00am in the yellow bus belonging to the church and had a mid-day picnic at the Lewis Morris Park at Morristown. They reached the convent at 2:30. Vespers and Benediction of the Blessed Sacrament in St. Michael's Chapel was attended by all, and afterwards the secular staff went swimming at the school. There was a formal dinner in the visitors' dining room at 6:00pm. After a good day everyone returned to Jersey City.

On July 30, 1963, the Sisters heard that Mrs. Weed, the Warden's mother, had died. The New York Sisters returned early from their summer vacation in order to attend her funeral next day. The three Sisters from St. Christopher's House also attended. Later that day Fr. Francis Xavier Walter[12] arrived to replace Fr. Laughlin on the clergy team and began his ministry next day, August 1. Also on August 1, Bishop MacAdie died, and his funeral at St. John's Church, Passaic, on August 3, was attended by Fr. Walter, Fr. Luce, Sr. Eleanor Lucy, Sr. Susinne Paula, Mother Margaret Helena and Sr. Waldine Lucia. Fr. Weed was re-elected as Warden on October 2, and re-installed next day at the convent by Bishop Stark. All the Sisters from New York and Jersey City attended.

As the Fall program got under way Sr. Eleanor Lucy set out their needs in an appeal letter.[13] "We are starting the Fall with the usual emergency needs of people pressing upon us. We have been receiving clothes regularly but the Pantry shelf is practically bare and we have no discretionary funds as yet with which to carry on. Twice already we have been asked for warm coats for little girls. The first cold day will bring boys knocking at the door for warm jackets. Children's underwear is in constant demand. Girls' school dresses and boys' school clothing is needed as well as children's shoes and sneakers … These articles are most urgent."

Moving on to the Thrift Sale, Sr. Eleanor Lucy explained what was needed. This also shed some light on the housing conditions in which people lived. "Books should be easy reading, for the majority of our children do not read well. Because in most cases too many people live in too few rooms, large picture puzzles are not welcome—there is no space to set up a card table and too many little fingers to scatter pieces around. Little children's puzzles in a frame they do care for. The boys like construction kits. However, because of the misuse of Duco and like cements they should be snap together kits or be supplied with a harmless glue … Games and various craft sets are welcome."

Sr. Eleanor Lucy continued her appeal: "Each year some of you give us gift clothing at Christmas time. In that too, we rejoice. Our children, like yours, enjoy wearing something bright at Christmas. The weeks fly and Thanksgiving and Christmas will soon be here. At Thanksgiving we try to be sure all will have a Thanksgiving Dinner; at Christmas we stress toys; at Easter we try to see that the children have proper Easter clothing."

The appeal was successful and donations of toys and clothing poured in, especially throughout December, from churches and individuals. On the day of the sale (December 20), about 700 children were provided for. Next day used toys and clothes were given out to the neighborhood people who were too poor even to come to the sale. On December 23, parents on the "clothing list" came for new clothing for their children. Christmas Eve saw the Sisters giving out twenty Christmas dinners, including turkeys, to people in the neighborhood, until 9:30pm. Then they said Mattins and went to church for the service of lessons and carols at 10:30pm followed by Midnight Mass. On Christmas Day the Sisters arrived at the convent in the afternoon and stayed overnight. Then it was back to all the parties; faithful helpers did much of the preparation. The Sisters did not attend the New Year's Eve Mass at 11:30pm but Sr. Elizabeth Anne kept the Watch in their chapel.

As ever, the first two weeks of January 1964 brought extreme weather. The pageant went ahead on January 12, but no one was able to come from the convent. Next day, there was a blizzard and several parish parties had to be canceled. Fortunately the weather improved sufficiently for the Sisters to attend the consecration of Paul Moore as Suffragan Bishop of Washington at the National Cathedral in Washington, DC. The three Sisters left at noon on January 24 and met Sr. Agatha Louise in Newark, arriving in Washington at 4:40pm. The service of consecration took place next day. The Sisters sat in choir next to the Moore family. Many of his former parishioners at Grace Church had traveled in the Church busses for the ceremony.[14]

The year flew by fairly uneventfully. On St. John Baptist Day (June 24), the Sisters went to the convent and then arrived back at Grace Church in time for the dedication of the parish hall by Bishop Stark. A large number of secular staff was taken on to help with the Vacation Bible Schools and summer camps.

The summer of 1964 saw widespread civil disobedience. A note in the Jersey City Record Book for July 17, 1964, states: "Fr. Walter and staff demonstrated at City Hall over housing and tearing down of condemned buildings. They dumped garbage from Whiton Street by station in front of City Hall. Fr. Castle[15] [and staff from his church, St. John's, Summit Avenue, Jersey City] took part too. Some of our staff just picketed but Fr. Walter [and others] were arrested for dumping garbage without a permit and in an inappropriate place. Fr. Castle and six staff members were also arrested. They were in jail some hours, the men longer than the girls. Bail was set at $100." The object of the garbage dumping was to bring the bad housing to the notice of the authorities. While not directly involved themselves, the Sisters loaned the bail money. This happened during the absence of Fr. Luce who was on vacation in Paris. Upon his return on July 29, the Record Book noted: "Trouble with Fr. Walter broke." The trial of Fr. Walter, Fr. Castle and nine summer staff (three from Grace Church and six from St. John's) took place on July 31. They were each fined $10 plus costs, for littering. Fr. Walter's involvement was brought before the bishop and on August 10, there is a note in the Record Book "Bishop's decision—both priests to be reconciled and stay." But it was clearly a difficult relationship which impinged upon the work of the ministry team.

Meanwhile, the Sisters continued with their ministry of pastoral care in what must have been a difficult time. There was more racial tension too, and this erupted on August 2, 1964, when the police arrested a

26-year-old woman on a charge of disorderly conduct. When a man tried to intervene on her behalf, he too was arrested. That evening a riot broke out and lasted intermittently until the morning of August 5. This was just one incident in a summer of increasing racial tension throughout New Jersey and also in Harlem, Brooklyn and other parts of New York City.[16]

After the summer break the Sisters re-opened St. Christopher's, and on September 23 noted that a Church Army worker (Louise Brown) had been to see Grace Church with a view to working there one day a week. A few days later, on September 27, Mother Margaret Helena brought Mother Annys, who was on a visit from Clewer, to see the work at Grace Church. They arrived in time for the children's Mass and were also at the 10:30 Mass when there were four baptisms. Afterwards there was coffee hour with an informal reception to welcome the two Mothers. They left for the convent at 2:15 following a Community dinner. There was another opportunity to meet Mother Annys on October 13, this time at St. John Baptist House, Barrow Street, NYC, for a farewell dinner.

As the year drew to an end there were the usual activities in preparation for the Thrift sale, the many parties, and the giving of much-needed food and clothing. The Sisters could not have done this without the generous support of many parishes and other friends in the diocese and in New York. The organizational skill required for the smooth running of all these events was phenomenal, especially as there were only three Sisters, although other Sisters came to help at busy times. It was of course fueled by their spiritual life, which undergirded everything they did. It had been a difficult year in Jersey City, and at Grace Church. The presence of the Sisters brought a sense of stability and faithfulness into the life of the church and the wider community.

Nineteen sixty-five began with Fr. Luce flying off to Puerto Rico on January 5, and Fr. Walter going to Washington to the College of Preachers on the 11th. Various clergy came to celebrate Mass during their absence, one of whom robed in a surplice, but Fr. Castle wore vestments.[17]

From January 20–23 the three Sisters and Mother Margaret Helena attended a training conference, though the Jersey City Record Book fails to state the location. As well as a number of clergy, 27 Sisters from seven Communities were present. Despite another absence by Fr. Walter, who was in Alabama, and Fr. Luce being ill, the Confirmation by Bishop Stark went ahead on January 31. Five children were baptized beforehand, the

Sisters standing as sponsors. On February 1, Sr. Katharine Veronica and Sr. Elizabeth Anne went to Fr. Garfield's installation as Rector of St. Mary the Virgin, NYC.

Early in February 1965 Sr. Susinne Paula came down with influenza and, following an alarming rise in her temperature, was admitted to Christ's Hospital, Jersey City. Sr. Suzanne Elizabeth came from the convent to help and returned to the convent with the Sisters for their retreat, at the end of which she went back to Jersey City, staying until early in March. There was a parish Mission from March 7–11, conducted by the Rt. Revd. Chandler Sterling, Episcopal Bishop of Montana.[18] The Mission began with a service at 8:00pm, followed by coffee hour. Next day he conducted a quiet day at the convent for clergy, returning to Jersey City in the evening. On the final day the bishop celebrated in the chapel at St. Christopher's at 7:00am and then stayed to talk with the Sisters. Meanwhile, Fr. Luce had gone to Selma, Alabama, to join the protest march called by Martin Luther King Jr. against racial segregation.[19]

The general atmosphere of unrest both in the parish and in the troubled relationship between the clergy may have influenced the behavior of the children. There were frequent absences by both priests, and the Sisters continued their workload with little support from them. Their Record Book noted bad behavior by the children at the Saturday Church School on March 13, so they decided there would be no Church School the following week. Instead, there was a meeting with the teachers on March 20 from 9:30–12:15, and the decision was made to lock the church and use the parish hall instead.

During the intervening week Sr. Eleanor Lucy and Sr. Elizabeth Anne went by train to Pennsylvania for a speaking engagement at Trinity Episcopal Church, Easton. They stayed overnight with a church member. Next day, March 19, there was Mass at 7:00am for the feast of St. Joseph, after which the Sisters had breakfast at the Rectory with Fr. Harvey, the parish priest, his wife and their five children. Then followed a meeting with a group doing remedial tutoring for underprivileged children. They were then driven back to Jersey City by Fr. Harvey.

The season of Lent sped by and there was the usual Palm Sunday outdoor procession. But on Good Friday there was no service in church until 7:30pm. The Sisters kept a Watch from 12:00–3:00 as usual. On Holy Saturday the Easter Vigil was celebrated at 7:30pm with the blessing of the New Fire, blessing of the Paschal Candle and several baptisms. Next day, after the parish Mass, the Sisters went to the convent by car along with the New York Sisters, and stayed overnight.

A Liturgical Conference took place in New York from April 26–28 at the Waldorf Astoria. It was attended by Sr. Eleanor Lucy, Sr. Elizabeth Anne and the three New York Sisters. Also, four Sisters from the Society of St. Margaret, Boston, were there. The Sisters from CSJB were pleased to see Bishop Paul Moore, and also Fr. Pegram, who was by this time Rector of St. James Episcopal Church, Mount Airy, MD. On the second day there was a Mass at which the Bishop of Southwark, UK, the Rt. Revd. Mervyn Stockwood, presided, assisted by twelve priests and deacons. There were more than 900 Communicants. In the midst of it all the Jersey City Sisters were "whisked off" to give an evening talk about their work to a parish group, but afterwards returned to St. John Baptist House where they were staying during the conference. Next day, the conference ended with a Mass in the Cathedral of St. John the Divine followed by a buffet lunch in the crypt.

Back at Grace Church, Sr. Suzanne Elizabeth was called back to the convent in order to nurse Sr. Julia Frances, who was seriously ill. Sr. Barbara Jean, recently received as a novice, came to Grace Church in her place, temporarily. As noted in the previous chapter, Sr. Julia Frances passed to her rest on May 27 (Ascension Day), and her funeral on May 31 was attended by the Sisters from Jersey City. They had traveled back to the convent the day before the funeral in order to be at the dedication of the new chapel at St. John Baptist School.

Problems with the clergy team continued during May 1965, and there were meetings between Fr. Luce and the vestry members, followed by meetings with the bishop, who in turn had a meeting with Mother Margaret Helena. In the midst of it all the Sisters continued with their ministry, registering all who would attend the summer camps, as well as speaking to parish groups near and far about CSJB and the work at Grace Church. On Sunday June 6, the Sisters traveled back to the convent in the afternoon, and next day Laura Weller was received as a novice, retaining her baptismal names (Laura Katharine). On the same day (June 7), there was a Chapter meeting to vote for the second time on changes to the daily office, reducing the seven offices to five.[20]

The decision had been made to dissolve the team ministry and June 13, 1965, saw Fr. Luce's and Fr. Walter's final Sunday in the parish.[21] On Sunday July 4, Fr. William V. Albert[22] officiated on his first Sunday in the parish, having been appointed by the bishop as locum tenens.

Summer camps went on as usual with help from Captain Stein of the Church Army. The Vacation Church Schools went ahead too with help from Sr. Barbara Jean and Sr. Laura Katharine. After returning from their summer break the Sisters were visited by Fr. Albert, who told them the vestry had unanimously elected him and called him as Rector. The church was then reconstituted as a parish but would continue to receive some financial support from the diocese. On September 28, 1965, Mother Margaret Helena, Sr. Waldine Lucia and the three Jersey City Sisters attended a special parish meeting with the Archdeacon at which Fr. Albert's call was announced, to take effect on December 1. During the intervening weeks he was absent from the parish several times, and early in November he was quite seriously ill and was at the hospital for two weeks. Fortunately, he was sufficiently recovered for his installation on December 1. Mother Margaret Helena, Sr. Waldine Lucia, Fr. Weed, the three New York Sisters and the Jersey City Sisters were present. Bishop Paul Moore also attended unofficially and came to see the Sisters before dinner.

As 1965 gave way to a new year, the Sisters hoped that a new Rector would bring a fresh start to the parish and much-needed healing. There was no Midnight Mass to welcome the New Year but Fr. Albert promised the Sisters that there would be one the following year. Nineteen sixty-six began with a Mass at 7:00am in the chapel at St. Christopher's House, followed by a Mass for the Saturday Church School at 9.30. This was followed by the class parties, divided into age groups. The Sisters noted in their Jersey City Record Book that there were toys, mittens and socks for all. On the Feast of the Epiphany (January 6), Fr. Albert gave a party for the Spanish-speaking neighbors of the church.

The Sisters had several meetings with the new Rector; the pageant went ahead as usual after much rehearsing; and there was much coming and going between the convent and Grace Church by the three novices (Sr. Suzanne Elizabeth, Sr. Barbara Jean and Sr. Laura Katharine). Back at Mendham, Fr. Templeton celebrated the 25th anniversary of his ordination to the priesthood on January 19, and the three Sisters from Grace Church attended his Mass and reception. A week later, the Sisters were back at the convent for a Leadership Conference from January 26–29, along with several clergy, two St. Margaret's Sisters and a total of nine CSJB Sisters.

There was a Mission early in February 1966 aimed specifically for the Spanish-speaking people in the parish. On February 4, Fr. Wipfler[23] arrived and there was a meeting with the Sisters and Fr. Albert, who then went out into the street and gathered in Spanish people living close by. The Mission began on February 7, with the arrival of the other two priests, Fr. William Frey[24] and Fr. Luis Ducet.[25] There was a dinner attended by 108 people followed by a service in church. The Sisters were involved with the mission, including parish visiting in the daytime and helping with children's activities in the evening, while the adults attended the mission service—Sr. Eleanor Lucy had 36 children for painting and Sr. Susinne Paula with Sr. Elizabeth Anne had the children for games. One hundred and eleven adults attended the mission on the second day and were shown moving pictures of the Passion of Our Lord. February 9 was the last day and there was an evening Mass for adults and children followed by coffee hour and an opportunity for people to ask questions. The three mission priests left that night.

On March 3, 1966, the Rectory at Grace Church was robbed at about 6:00pm. A tape recorder, some clocks, a food mixer, and an overcoat were stolen. Next day the police were at the Rectory and in the evening there was a special vestry meeting about the robbery. Nothing more was noted in the Sisters' Record Book. In August, Fr. Albert's Buick station wagon was stolen in the night. It was found a few days later by Sr. Elizabeth Anne on Bay Street. The battery was stolen from it but otherwise the car was unharmed. Two weeks later it was stolen again.

On Palm Sunday (April 3), 300 people took part in the outdoor procession as part of the main service. Later that day Fr. Albert became ill with a cold and high temperature and so there were no weekday Masses until Wednesday, when there was a Mass in the Sisters' chapel. On Maundy Thursday there was a Mass at 8:00pm with procession to the Altar of Repose. On Good Friday the Sisters kept a Watch between 5:00 and 9:30am; and between 12:00–3:00pm there were the Three Hours Devotion, preceded at 11:00am by the Way of the Cross. On Holy Saturday in the evening there was the blessing of the New Fire and 12 baptisms. On Easter day the Sisters, together with the New York Sisters, traveled to the convent after lunch, staying until the following evening. On the Tuesday after Easter there was a tenement fire at 212, 214 and 216 Second Street. The Sisters noted it in their Record Book but did not comment on the extent of the damage, nor whether there were casualties or fatalities.

Ecumenical meetings continued to be held and the three Sisters attended two in close succession during April. In their Record Book the Sisters described the second one, which was held at the Rectory, as "a hot meeting." It was decided that Upper Jersey City and Lower Jersey City would become two united projects each with their own identity.

On April 17, 1966, Fr. Albert flew to Chicago to meet with Monsignor Quinn, Mr. Saul Alinsky (who fought to improve living conditions for African Americans) and others. He returned on April 23. A new assistant priest, Fr. Sotolongo, arrived with his family on April 26, the Sisters having worked all afternoon to get the apartment at St. Christopher's ready for their occupation. It is not clear whether this was a temporary placement or whether it just did not work out. Fr. Albert had many absences from the parish, mostly to Massachusetts, and this may have caused tension, but whatever the reason, Fr. Sotolongo told the Sisters in October that he would be leaving on November 1. Fr. Albert was away on vacation so the Sisters made a long distance call to tell him the news.

On May 26, Sr. Suzanne Elizabeth made her profession in First Vows at the convent and all the Sisters were there, returning to Grace Church after lunch. On Whitsunday (the feast of Pentecost), there was no Patronal celebration at the church, a disappointment for the Sisters. Later they accompanied Fr. Albert, Fr. Sotolongo, some young people, and the choir, to Holy Trinity, Brooklyn, the Church Army Headquarters, for the admission of Cadets and CA Sisters. On June 4, Fr. Albert, the Sisters and helpers took 53 10–12-year-olds to Bear Mt., for a picnic. The Sisters noted in their Record Book that "the children were good and the occasion successful." The sense of relief is tangible! Next day there was tea and dedication of a plaque in church in memory of Miss Mary Van Vorst.

The Sisters spent St. John Baptist Day (June 24) at the convent, having arrived the night before, and they stayed on for Commemoration Day on the 25th. Fr. Sotolongo and his family came for Commemoration Day along with many other guests, including Bishop Rath. Fr. Albert was away but he telephoned the Sisters while they were at the convent to tell them that the National Executive Council had asked him to represent the Episcopal Church on the Mississippi March against Fear.[26] He returned from the March on June 28. Meanwhile, the summer activities at Grace Church continued thanks to the hard work of the Sisters, Fr. Sotolongo and their secular helpers.

After their return to St. Christopher's in September following the summer break, the Sisters made some changes to their routine. Lauds and Prime were said before Mass with Terce at 9:30, Sext and Nones at 11:45, Vespers at 5:00 and Compline at 9:00. On Saturdays and Sundays Lauds and Prime were said before breakfast, with Terce and Sext after Church School, and Nones at 2:30.

On October 19 Sr. Eleanor Lucy and Sr. Elizabeth Anne went to Newark Cathedral for Bishop Washburn's funeral.

As 1966 drew to a close there were the familiar activities—the sales and the parties. As usual toys and gifts flooded in from near and far and the Sisters, the novices, and all their helpers worked extremely hard to ensure the success of these events and to make sure that everyone who was in need was catered for. Christmas Eve brought a heavy snowstorm and the congregation was very small in number at Midnight Mass. Next day the Sisters went to New York for dinner with the Sisters there, but had great difficulty getting from North Street station to Barrow Street. They stayed overnight in order to be at Mass on St. Stephen's Day, Fr. Albert having gone away again. The Saturday Church School parties took place on New Year's Eve, but despite Fr. Albert's promise to the Sisters, there was no Midnight service. It had not been an easy year in many ways but the Sisters never once wavered in their commitment to their ministry and mission in this difficult but immensely rewarding parish.

January 6, 1967, the Feast of the Epiphany, saw 275 people at Mass in church followed by a party for the Spanish-speaking children. Two hundred bags of toys were given out and the children enjoyed ice cream and cookies. Entertainment was provided by a Pakistani magician. The novices had come from the convent to help out and stayed until after the pageant on January 8. All the Sisters returned to the convent on January 23 for the Chapter of Election when Sr. Barbara Jean was elected for profession in First Vows.

As so often happened, a day of joy became tinged with sadness when on the day of the parish Confirmation (January 29), Mother phoned with news of the death of Sr. Ellen Juliana. The Sisters had just finished Lauds and immediately said the Litany for the Departed for their Sister. All went to the convent for her funeral on February 1.

Blizzard conditions starting on February 7 disrupted travel and attendance at church next day, which was Ash Wednesday. Despite the weather, the painting of St. Christopher's went ahead and took nine days to complete.

On March 13, 1967, Sr. Mildred Eleanor died at Morristown Memorial Hospital. The three Sisters from Grace Church were already at the convent for their March retreat and so they stayed on for the funeral on the 15th, but only Mother, Sr. Eleanor Lucy and the new postulant (Patricia) walked to the cemetery in a torrential rainstorm. Two days later, on March 17, Sr. Barbara Jean made her profession in First Vows, but due to yet another blizzard which prevented Bishop Rath's presence, Fr. Weed was authorized to receive her vows.

The March vestry meeting at Grace Church, which took place on Tuesday in Holy Week, was stormy. The Sisters noted in the Jersey City Record Book: "Fr. Albert met the revolt head on with arguments from the Diocesan Canons and the Prayer Book." No further explanation was given but this could be related to his frequent absences from the parish and reliance on services being taken by other clergy, or cancellation of services. The rest of Holy Week and the Easter services proceeded as usual with the Sisters attending them all, as well as the offices in their own chapel, and working in the church to prepare for Easter. On April 1, Grace Church hosted an Archdeaconry Corporate Communion for men and boys (the church women cooked breakfast for 105!). The Sisters did not attend the Mass but did all the altar work.

It is difficult to keep track of which of the newly professed Sisters and novices were working at Grace Church, as they tended to come from the convent for short stays or to help at especially busy times. Amidst all the parish work, the Sisters continued to visit parishes far and wide to speak about the Religious Life and about the work in Jersey City, sometimes staying overnight. For instance, in April they visited Holy Cross, North Plainfield, and Christ Church, East Orange. Meanwhile Fr. Albert continued to embrace issues of social concern and on April 23, 1967, went to New York to take part in a march commemorating the Armenian genocide in 1915. Next day he went to Trenton to hear the Governor of New Jersey proclaim Armenian Day.[27]

The month of May 1967 was extremely busy. On the 18th, Sr. Eleanor Lucy, Sr. Elizabeth Anne, and Sr. Barbara Jean went to the Diocesan Convention. On May 21, Fr. Albert and the three Sisters went to the Church Army graduation. Then two days later, Sr. Eleanor Lucy, Sr. Elizabeth Anne and Sr. Barbara Jean went to St. Boniface RC Church, Jersey City,[28] to see a film on narcotics, after which the Sheriff spoke on the increasing drugs problem. On May 25, Fr. Albert and the Sisters went to the Centennial of the Confraternity of the Blessed Sacrament (C. B. S) at St. Paul's Chapel, NYC. (The C. B. S. had been founded by the Revd. [later Canon] T. T. Carter of Clewer in the UK, Co-Founder of CSJB, to promote a greater reverence for the Eucharist.) Preparations for the summer camps and Vacation Bible School went ahead in between all the outside visits and meetings. Then there was a tragedy when the eldest son of a church member shot and killed three women and then himself on June 21. His body and that of one of the women (his cousin) were brought into church on the evening of June 23.

Between July 12 and 15, 1967, there were major race riots in Newark—one location of 159 such riots throughout the United States that summer in response to the assassination of Martin Luther King, Jr., on April 4, at Memphis, TN. Twenty-six people died and over 700 were injured in the Newark rioting, the immediate cause being a white police officer beating an African American taxi driver. The unrest spilled over into Jersey City and affected attendance at church services. Only 47 people came to the 9:30am Mass at Grace Church, preferring to stay safely at home rather than venture out onto the streets. A staff dinner went ahead on July 25, but Bishop Stark was unable to come as he was exhausted by the riots and the "Black Power" Conference.

On September 22, 1967, Fr. Albert married Anne Perkins at Grace Church. Fr. Castle officiated at the ceremony and the best man was Fr. Hemsley.[29] After the ceremony the couple left for Massachusetts. Following their return on October 7, the parish gave a "pot luck" dinner and reception which was declared a success. Ten days later, Sr. Eleanor Lucy and Sr. Elizabeth Anne took them to 90, Barrow Street to meet the Sisters and to see St. Luke's. Later in October Jenny Moore and her publisher made a surprise visit to Grace Church and called on the Sisters. Her book *The People on Second Street* would be published the following year.

On November 13, Sr. Eleanor Lucy and Sr. Elizabeth Anne, together with Fr. and Mrs. Albert, attended a special meeting organized by the bishop about the new liturgy, and on November 17 it was used for the first time in the chapel at St. Christopher's House, and then in church on December 3. The Midnight Mass at Christmas saw the new liturgy in use in bi-lingual form (American/Spanish).

The usual parties took place around Epiphany-tide 1968. The Spanish Mass was Choral with a procession and a congregation of about 225. Afterwards, all went to the parish hall for ice cream, sandwiches and gifts.

The Sisters had worked hard preparing tickets for the gifts and it went much better than the previous year. Sr. Barbara Jean and the new novice, Sr. Ellen Marie, came to help, returning to the convent afterwards. The Ecumenical movement was still in full swing and on January 23, Grace Church hosted a meeting. This was attended by about 300 people—clergy, laity and 60 Sisters from several RC Communities as well as CSJB. Next day, January 25, Sister Edna Brooks of the Church Army joined the staff at Grace Church.

A spate of petty crime broke out at this time. In the evening of January 25, 1968, some boys broke into the church but gave themselves away by talking into the loudspeaker! A few days later on February 5, the boys broke in again, this time through a window by the Nativity chapel. The police were called. Two days later at about midnight there was a fire in a basement flat and the house owner (Mr. Oglesby) heard boys running away. Next day, February 8, boys broke into the church bus by the emergency door. A day later the Sisters noted in their Record Book: "About 10:30 Edna [Church Army] called. Boys were in church. Sr. Elizabeth Anne and Sr. Eleanor Lucy went over with her to inspect and relock. We asked Mr. Oglesby to come with us. Meanwhile Fr. Albert had arrived home and joined us."

But it wasn't all petty crime and chasing would-be thieves! From February 9–16, some girls from Purnell School, a private school in New Jersey, came to Grace Church on a social science project. With all the ongoing problems in Jersey City this was the ideal parish for them to gain experience and they spent much time with the Sisters. On February 10, Sr. Eleanor Lucy and Sr. Elizabeth Anne took them to a housing meeting at St. John's African Methodist Episcopal Church, at Lafayette. On February 15, the girls went with the Sisters to the General Theological Seminary in NYC. Several seminarians had spent time at Grace Church and the Sisters noted that "Richard Markham and Kevin Maguire had a very high tea with all our Seminary friends there." Earlier the same day Sr. Eleanor Lucy had taken the girls to a meeting of the Y. C. S. (Youth Consultation Service, which had been started by the Episcopal Church in the Diocese of Newark.) On their final day Fr. Albert took the girls to the Court and to see the jail before they left later in the afternoon. There was a "Young People's Happening" at the convent on March 8–9, and five went from the Grace Church congregation. They were driven there and back by Sister Edna, CA.

On March 14, there was a note of alarm in the Jersey City Record Book when Sr. Eleanor Lucy was admitted to Christ Hospital with pneumonia. Reinforcements came in the shape of Sr. Laura Katharine from New York and Sr. Barbara Jean with Sr. Ellen Marie from the convent. On March 24, Sr. Eleanor Lucy was allowed to leave the hospital but first went to the convent before returning to Jersey City on April 2.

An invitation for the Sisters to travel to Vermont to speak to the Diocesan Episcopal Church Women was accepted, and Sr. Eleanor Lucy and Sr. Elizabeth Anne made the journey from May 13–16. They returned to Second Street on the 16th just as thieves were breaking into a neighboring house!

The year proceeded fairly uneventfully with all the usual feasts, fasts and other activities. Fr. Albert, his wife and new baby continued to take regular breaks at New Salem, MA, relying on other priests to cover the services.

The spate of petty crime involving break-ins at the church was not confined to Grace Church. Of a more serious nature was the bombing of a car in front of St. Mary's RC Church at 254, Second Street, on October 21. But parish life went on, and the Sisters continued to work hard to keep the activities happening, along with living their own vowed life. Links with other denominations continued to be valued—this was at the height of the Ecumenical Movement. And it was not simply a case of attending conferences, but also of hosting groups for tours of Grace Church and St. Christopher's. Thus on October 29 and November 7, two Methodist groups came to see the work. Links with other Episcopal churches continued to be valued and indeed the work amongst the poor in Jersey City could not have happened without the many contributions from these generous congregations. So it was a great pleasure for Sr. Eleanor Lucy and Sr. Katharine Veronica to attend St. Paul's, Morris Plains, on November 2, for the dedication of the sanctuary and education building.

On November 11–12, Sr. Eleanor Lucy and the Church Army Sister attended a conference at Buck Hill Falls, PA. Several bishops were there including Bishops Stark and Rath. The Sisters' Record Book noted that it was "an excellent conference and Grace Church received $145 for youth work." On November 19 there was a vestry meeting preceded by dinner cooked by Fr. Albert. Alas, the mince pies were stolen by a well-known local lad and his gang! Perhaps their need was the greater.

As 1968 gave way to 1969 the usual activities took up a great deal of

time. In addition, there was a teachers' strike starting on January 27, and
Sr. Eleanor Lucy came out of her retreat to help with the neighborhood
children, teaching an English class. Next day she taught all day, including
taking 27 children on a trip to Coney Island Aquarium. On January 28,
Sr. Elizabeth Anne taught several little children. The second week of
February saw blizzard conditions for several days bringing all transport
to a halt. But it did not prevent a boy breaking in to St. Christopher's
House on the night of February 15.

During Lent 1969 a series of exchanges with St. Mark's, Mendham,
church school took place. On March 1, the Mendham 4th grade class
came to visit the Grace Church nine- and ten-year-olds. They went to
the class and then had lunch together, the children from both churches
having brought their own sandwiches. Cocoa was provided for all by
the Sisters. Next day the Grace Church nine- and ten-year-olds went to
Mendham, first to St. Mark's and then to the convent. Sister Edna, CA,
accompanied them. The visits continued until March 16.

The ongoing problem of bad housing was tragically brought home on
March 6, 1969, when a terrible fire ripped through a tenement block at 65,
Mercer Street and nine people were killed. A woman and three children,
known to the Sisters, got out safely from the fourth floor. On March 23
(Passion Sunday), there was a march in memory of the fire victims from
Ninth Street, Second Street and Mercer Street. This was an ecumenical
gathering and there was an agape service followed by speeches. Two
days later, on March 25, there was a fire in Woodward Street in which a
woman known to the Sisters and her seven-month-old baby died. Their
funeral took place on March 31, conducted by Fr. Albert. It was attended
by Sr. Susinne Paula, who came in from the convent, and also Sr. Eleanor
Lucy, Sr. Margaret Raphael, and Sr. Elizabeth Anne. The burial took
place at Tonnele Avenue Cemetery, Hoboken. On May 14, there was a
fire in First Street over a furniture store. A married couple (Mr. and Mrs.
Colon) and their two children lost everything and another couple were
evacuated from their apartment for safety. Four CSJB Sisters, two RC
Sisters, people from St. Boniface RC Church, and Fr. and Mrs. Albert
were all involved until 2:00am helping give temporary accommodation
to those made homeless by the fire. Sixteen people slept in rooms on the
second floor at St. Christopher's House, and the Colon family stayed for
two weeks while looking for rooms.

On May 25, 1969, the Sisters, together with the New York Sisters, returned to the convent for Sr. Suzanne Elizabeth's profession in Life Vows next day. This took place at the Choral Mass at 7:30am. The Jersey City Record Book noted that there was wedding cake at lunch. But before this, there was the Chapter of Election for Sr. Ellen Marie's profession in First Vows.

Change was in the air in Jersey City in the form of merging parishes. It was not a popular idea, parishioners preferring to keep their individual identities, especially the poorer parishes whose vestry members feared it would lead to their closing. On June 10 there was a vestry meeting at Grace Church to discuss and vote on the merger. The outcome was that Grace Church vestry members decided against the scheme, nor did they want Fr. Albert to work elsewhere. On June 12, there was a meeting at the Church of the Incarnation, Jersey City, at which Fr. Albert made it known about Grace Church's withdrawal from the plans.

The month of June 1969 was always busy with preparations for the summer camps and Community celebrations. Thus all Sisters from Jersey City and New York arrived at the convent on June 23 in time for Vespers, and stayed overnight for St. John Baptist's Day. There was the usual Choral Mass, dinner, tea party in the afternoon and supper on the cloister. In the early evening all returned by car but with some changes. Sr. Susinne Paula replaced Sr. Margaret Raphael, and Sr. Laura Katharine came to take over Sr. Elizabeth Anne's work. It was not long before Sr. Laura Katharine (who had two music degrees) was playing the organ in church in addition her other duties.

On June 28, everyone was back at the convent for Commemoration Day. Then the first group went off to Elko Lake summer camp later that day, so there was no lingering at the convent. July 2 saw the Sisters at the convent again for Sr. Ellen Marie's profession in First Vows. Unfortunately Sr. Eleanor Lucy broke her ankle in chapel just before the service and after the reception she was taken to All Souls' Hospital in Morristown where it was set in a cast. She stayed behind at the convent to recuperate and returned to Jersey City after the summer break. The Jersey City Record Book noted that "Sr. Ellen Marie looked very nice as a professed Sister." Alas, it was not to last, and she did not proceed to Life Vows.

On July 5, 1969, the Jersey City Record Book noted: "excitement over 280, Second Street, but our papers were signed and passed and we had the key." On June 13, Fr. Albert had given the lawyers an order to go ahead on buying the property, which was next to St. Christopher's House. The house, which was to be called St. Martin's, was dedicated on December 14. It would be the cause of much expense and difficulty, but that lay ahead in the next decade, and in a later chapter.

As noted in previous chapters, there was a growing warm relationship with the UK CSJB at Clewer, with reciprocal visits between Sisters from the English and American convents. On July 5, Sisters Katharine Veronica, Elizabeth Anne, Suzanne Elizabeth and Barbara Jean left for a visit to England. Following their return they were in demand to give talks and show their pictures of CSJB in England.

Fires were still endemic and on November 18, the Red Cross Director, Mr. Sharf, visited the Sisters to ask whether they would receive fire victims on a temporary basis. The answer of course was "yes" and on December 1, as the Sisters returned from a Chapter meeting at the convent, there were needy people seeking refuge. The fire victims were at St. Christopher's over a period of three weeks.

And so the year 1969 came to an end in the way so familiar from years past. It was also the end of the decade. Much had changed since the Sisters had come to work at Grace Church in 1951. There had been changes in the clergy, the liturgy, and the area surrounding Grace Church. Horizons had widened, and ecumenical links had been forged. Other things did not change—the grinding poverty which still oppressed so many, the unsafe tenement houses in which they lived, and the continuing struggle for civil rights. All this would continue into the next decade. And in the midst of it all there were the Sisters who were always there to pick up the pieces when life in Jersey City seemed to be falling apart. Non-political, non-partisan, but always inclusive, never turning anyone away—the presence of the Sisters was the one sign of stability in a sea of poverty, grief and uncertainty.

---

[1] Now known as the Prairie View A&M University, the college was founded in 1876 in the aftermath of the Civil War by two former slaves who became leading political figures. Historically it catered for people of color and it is the second oldest public university in the State of Texas. Source: en.m.wikipedia.org

[2] It seems that the modern idea of food pantries (food banks in the UK) was being pioneered in Jersey City by the Sisters from the 1950s onwards. The sad part is that in the 21st century there is still a need for them on both sides of the Atlantic.

[3] If someone was dying and needed the last sacraments.

[4] Hurricane Esther started on September 10, and reached hurricane force on the 12th. New Jersey did not have the full force of it but the strong winds and coastal flooding were disruptive enough. It weakened as it went up the New England coast and finally dissipated on September 27. Source en.m.wikipedia.org

[5] Colonel John Glenn died on December 8, 2016, at age 95.

[6] When the Revd. Paul Moore became Bishop of New York in 1972, Fr. Morton became Dean of the Cathedral and held office for 25 years. He founded the Interfaith Center of New York and was an early leader in the "green movement."

[7] Fr. Luce (1930–2012) had studied at Harvard and trained for ministry at Nashotah House, WI, and at the College of the Resurrection, Mirfield, UK.

[8] Letter from Sr. Eleanor Lucy to Mrs. Mason, October 5, 1963. [I am not sure who Mrs. Mason was, but clearly she was a great friend and supporter.]

[9] Forest Lake camp opened in 1926 for boys. In 1990 the camp admitted girls.

[10] Elko Lake was a summer camp for many years until it was developed for residential use in the 1990s. It catered for boys and girls.

[11] See BONHAM, Valerie *Living Stones* Chapter 5 Times never to be forgotten—the "fresh-air" work at Farmingdale.

[12] Fr. Francis Xavier Walter was born in Mobile, Alabama. He was ordained priest in the Episcopal Church in 1957 and spent the next two years as a fellow and tutor at General Theological Seminary, NYC. He then served in Jersey City at Grace Church (Van Vorst), where he became increasingly aware of social injustice, especially racism. Source: revmoore. blogspot.com

[13] Letter to Mrs. Mason, October 5, 1963. Op. cit.

[14] Paul Moore served as Suffragan Bishop in the Diocese of Washington, 1964–70, then as Coadjutor Bishop of New York, 1970–71, and then as 13th Bishop of New York, 1972–89.

[15] Fr. Robert Castle (1929–2012) was Rector of St. John's Episcopal Church, Summit Ave, Jersey City from 1960–68. He was a well-known civil rights activist, having marched with Martin Luther King Jr. and others. He was arrested on multiple occasions during that time while lobbying for cleaner and safer streets. The garbage dumping incident was long remembered and made its way into his obituary notices. After leaving St. John's, his notoriety resulted in his being unable to find another parish in the diocese of Newark and he moved to Vermont. He then became Rector of St. Mary's Episcopal Church in Harlem, 1987–2000. St. John's Church was closed in 1994 and work began in 2016 to convert the building to apartments.

[16] The Jersey City riot of August 1964 was one of the first race riots to occur after the passage of the Civil Rights Act, 1964. The Civil Rights Act, 1964, was intended to end segregation in public places and to ban employment discrimination on the grounds of race, color, or religion. It was first proposed by President Kennedy and signed into law by his successor President Johnson. It did not solve the problem of racial discrimination, but it was a beginning.

[17] The priest who robed in a surplice would have been Evangelical or Low Church, whilst Fr. Castle was an Anglo-Catholic, as indicated by his wearing Eucharistic vestments.

[18] Chandler Winfield Sterling, 1911–84, was ordained deacon in 1938 and priest in the same year. He had several parish ministries and then in 1956 became Coadjutor Bishop of Montana. Later in 1956 he became Bishop of Montana until 1968. From 1968–76 he was Assisting Bishop of Pennsylvania. His diary, entitled *Riding the Circuit*, described his ministry traveling around Montana between 1957–67. He died on March 3, 1984, and his grave is in the cemetery at Nashotah House, Wisconsin.

[19] The march was part of the ongoing civil rights campaign and followed unsuccessful attempts to register black voters in the South. King called for a peaceful march from Selma to the State capital, Montgomery, a distance of 54 miles. They marched round the clock for three days and met with violent opposition. In August 1965 Congress passed the Voting Rights Act which guaranteed the right to vote to all African Americans and banned the literacy tests formerly required. It was a milestone in civil rights history.

Source www.history.com

[20] This is the present (2020) practice at the convent, the offices being: Lauds, Terce, Noonday, Vespers and Compline.

[21] It is not clear who made the decision to dissolve the team ministry, but presumably it had the agreement of the bishop and vestry.

[22] Fr. William V. Albert served as assistant priest at Grace Church, Monroe, LA, then as priest in charge of the Redeemer Mission, Brookhaven, MS, from 1947. Source: *The Living Church* November 23, 1947. He was Rector of Grace Church (Van Vorst), Jersey City, 1965–75, and died in October 1979.

[23] Fr. William Wipfler served as a missionary in the Dominican Republic and Costa Rica. He was very involved in the struggle for human rights for people of Latin American origin and was a friend of Archbishop Oscar Romero, who was assassinated in 1980.

[24] Fr. William Carl Frey was ordained in 1956 in Colorado. He served as a missionary in Latin America from 1962 and was made missionary Bishop of the Episcopal Diocese of Guatemala in 1967.

[25] Fr. Luis Ducet was received into the Episcopal Church as a deacon on September 7, 1963, by Bishop Richards of Central America. He was Spanish by birth, for a number of years was a Jesuit in the Roman Catholic Church, and had worked in Latin America for the past 15 years. Prior to his reception as an Episcopalian he had studied privately under the direction of Fr. William Frey and at the time of his reception as deacon was placed in charge of the Mission San Pablo, Guadalupe, San Jose, Costa Rica. Source: *The Living Church* October 20, 1963.

[26] The March against Fear was begun by James H. Meredith, a former serviceman in the US Air Force, who had been the first African American to attend the University of Mississippi. He had been walking from Memphis, TN, to Jackson, MS, in an attempt to encourage voter registration by African Americans in the South. But he was shot by a sniper on June 6, one day after setting out on his lone march. Other civil rights leaders, including Martin Luther King Jr. and Stokely Carmichael, arrived to continue the March, and Meredith recovered sufficiently to rejoin it. The marchers reached Jackson on June 26. It was during this March that Stokely Carmichael coined the phrase "Black Power."

[27] 1.5 million Armenians were slaughtered by the Turks in 1915. In 1967 a memorial was erected in Yerevan, the capital of Armenia, and on April 24 Armenians world-wide remember those who died.

[28] St. Boniface Church, Jersey City, opened in 1866 to serve the German population. In 1996 it became part of the parish of the Resurrection, and the church finally closed in 2006.

[29] Possibly Fr. Bernard Hemsley of St. James, Long Island, NYC.

11

"OUR COMMON HERITAGE"

The Community 1970–74

THE DECADE BEGINNING in 1970 would see many changes in the Community at Mendham. There would be sadness as well as joy, gains and losses, changes in leadership, and the withdrawal from well-established branch work. But as Christine Brodeur MacClellan has said, "The core of CSJB is stability."[1] And it is that sense of stability that has informed all Community decisions from its foundation.

The Community Record Book noted in its entry for January 11, 1970, that it was twenty years since the Sisters had first gone to work at St. Luke's Chapel, NYC, and had subsequently taken up residence at 90, Barrow Street, which they named St. John Baptist House.

On February 9, Sr. Mary Joan (Gleason) passed to her rest. She was the last novice to be received at the original St. John Baptist House, NYC, and the first to be professed at Mendham.[2] A trained nurse, she had then followed her vocation as a Religious Sister despite parental objection, and after her profession had been sent to St. Helen's Hall, Portland, Oregon, because she was "young, active and an excellent nurse." Later she became house Sister at St. John Baptist School and afterwards worked at St. Andrew's Convalescent Hospital, NYC. Her Community Biographer noted that "all the School girls, both in the West and East, loved her." She was described as having a "merry disposition, and was always good company with good stories to tell." But even young, active Sisters eventually grow older and Sr. Mary Joan passed very gently to her rest in her 88th year of age and the 54th year of her profession. She was laid to rest in the convent cemetery on February 12, 1970.

Some things never change and extreme weather was one of them. On Good Friday (March 27) 1970 there was a heavy snow storm, but the services were held as usual. By Easter Day there was another bad storm and none of the Sisters from New York or Jersey City could get to the convent.

Sr. Barbara Jean made her solemn profession on March 31, 1970, in what was described as "a lovely service." Having trained as an elementary school teacher, she could teach grades six to eight, and now went to work at St. John Baptist School. She continued to assist with other Community work in the vacations.

The end of May and the month of June was a busy time. The Baccalaureate service took place in the school chapel on May 31, and then on June 6 there was the Mass on Commencement Day, which was also in the school chapel. There had been a certain "distancing" between the school and the convent which Mother Margaret Helena tried to overcome by inviting some of the girls to the convent for Sunday tea, and also for Mass on Fridays. June 24, St. John Baptist Day, was "a happy time" at the convent with all the Sisters present and 20 guests. Commemoration Day was on June 27, and there were 150 guests. Fr. Maitland[3] gave a splendid address and there were many priests present, including Bishop Stark. Also, nine Associates were received. It was a dark, cold day but lunch was had on the cloister.

Sr. Laura Katharine made her profession in Life Vows on September 8, 1970, and would fulfill every ministry in the Community except that of Superior. On October 1, Mother Margaret Helena was once again elected as Superior. The installation service took place next day and was described in the Community Record Book as "a lovely service." Sr. Elizabeth Anne was appointed Assistant Superior and Sr. Suzanne Elizabeth Novice Mistress.

During the Fall of 1970 St. John Baptist School joined with St. Bernard's School, Gladstone, for certain courses for juniors and seniors. This turned out to be a short and unsuccessful experiment and the program was soon discontinued.

Nineteen seventy ended on an anxious note as Sr. Mary Barbara underwent major surgery for cancer. She had succeeded Sr. Alice Ursula as Sister Superior of St. John Baptist School in 1946. Christine Brodeur[4] was a student at the school from September 1968 until June 1972 and recalls Sr. Mary Barbara having taught her Church history. Close at hand was Sr. Jane Patricia, who was school Sister and taught Christine Greek for two years. Christine was the only student to take Greek at this time. Sr. Jane Patricia was a scholar who specialized in medieval literature. According to the history of St. John Baptist School[5] Sr. Mary Barbara "insisted on going about her duties as usual. She believed in uncomplaining acceptance of what was inevitable, whether it was the weather or serious illness. Her deep Christian faith sustained her as she serenely faced her suffering."

There was still a culture of protecting the schoolgirls from the unpleasant realities of life and this may not always have been helpful. Thus they were not told about the severity of Sr. Mary Barbara's illness, and when she died it was a huge shock, all the more so for the lack of preparation. There was also a spirit of rebellion creeping into the school in 1970/71. This is hinted at in the school history.[6] "The demands by college students everywhere for greater freedom, fewer restrictions, more control over their own lives, have been echoed by younger students testing the limits to which they can stretch their own privileges, regarding themselves as adults in a way previous generations never thought of themselves, and with some legal basis for their contentions." But causing a bomb scare was beyond all reasonable limits! Christine Brodeur MacClellan recalled: "Yes, I do remember being brought into the chapel … I think it was in the Fall and we had been through a series of fire drills both daytime and night time. I know the fire department responded. It was before lunch and we were kept in the chapel for about an hour. I can't remember the girls involved, [but I] think at that time the school was starting to get some girls who had issues. This era was the beginning of the drug culture and big times of protest. The war in Vietnam did not help either. I know in 1969 there was an attempt for the schoolgirls to have a peace protest and sit-in. Well, that got squashed too."[7] The three girls who caused the bomb scare were expelled in January 1971.

There had been reciprocal visits for several years between the Mothers and Sisters at Clewer and Mendham. As the relationship became closer, the idea of re-affiliation became more of a possibility. On December 11, 1970, all the Sisters and the Warden (Fr. Weed) had a conference at Mendham to discuss the possibility of re-affiliation with Clewer. This was favorably received and on January 9, 1971, Mother Margaret Helena wrote to Mother Annys. "This year we have put some thought into a suggestion of instituting a request for some form of affiliation with Clewer; because of our great love for you and our common heritage, and for the purpose of preserving that heritage with a tangible link. We have talked of many aspects of the situation: the very happy relationship we have now; the reasons for which the affiliation was dissolved in 1949; the many changes in the Christian world—better understanding—movements towards reunion—that we and Clewer belong to the same family; what might be involved in a new affiliation; most important of all—would the Clewer Sisters want it, or is our present relationship the best solution?

This last question is the key and the question we are really asking. If you should answer in the affirmative, how would you suggest it might be effected?" She then expanded on the question of what might be involved. Regarding a common Rule, she asked, "What would happen if you or we thought it should be further revised?" And regarding a common Office book, "Would we be able to maintain a sevenfold Office?" Finally, she explained: "We do not envision any great change in status. We are well aware of the differences of custom and place, but we would see this in terms of spiritual rather than material value."

Mother Margaret Helena's letter was well received and was discussed at the Clewer Chapter meeting on March 17, 1971. Mother Annys lost no time and replied immediately after the meeting. "At the Chapter today we unanimously agreed that we should like to have closer links with you all, and one senior Sister asked me to add that we did this 'with great joy.'[8] We also agreed that the only essential link was a common Rule; that a common Office was not essential. We hope that when Sister Suzanne Elizabeth and Sister Eleanor Lucy come over in April that they may have some details to suggest." The Mendham Community Record Book noted on March 24, "Clewer wants re-union with them as much as we do—hope it comes soon."

On March 29, 1971, the Mendham Sisters had a discussion about re-affiliation and the following points were agreed: there should be a common Rule, and the Clewer Rule would be discussed in Chapter at Mendham. The Mother Superior at Clewer should take precedence in the affiliated house and she would have a pastoral but not executive position. The Constitution and Customary would be as similar as place and state laws allow. The silver Cross would be the symbol of the Community, but the style of habit could vary. If particular problems arose regarding the Rule, Constitution or Customary they would have to be settled by mutual agreement. These suggestions were taken to Clewer by Sr. Suzanne Elizabeth[9] and Sr. Eleanor Lucy on their spring visit.

Mother Annys wrote to Mother Margaret Helena on April 2. "Thank you very much for your suggestions about the future—Chapter will now have a look at them: they seem to me to be what is needed." Evidently the Sisters were making the most of their visit and with characteristic humor Mother Annys noted, "Your two are getting on alright—they are gallivanting in London today, and we have a mammoth outing planned for Friday! … We are going to have the Jersey City slides on Saturday. I am trying to hatch a trip to Cambridge[10] sometime, but it may be addled! English weather is excelling itself now, and we are having more sun than in August, so I think the Sisters are not cold." The two Sisters arrived back at Mendham on May 4, 1971. A good start had been made towards re-affiliation, but it would take several Chapter meetings on both sides of the Atlantic over several more years before it became a reality.

Amidst all the planning and discussion with the Sisters at Clewer, the varied work at Mendham continued as usual. Groups from many parishes continued to visit the convent or stay at St. Marguerite's, and Sisters went far and wide to speak about the Religious Life. Between June 1970 and June 1971 a total of 1,893 guests had been received.

A long-standing work came to an end in June 1971. This was at St. Uriel's Church, Sea Girt, NJ, where the Sisters had worked since 1947 for one week in the summer Vacation Bible School. Now after 24 years the Sisters withdrew, following the retirement of Fr. Miller. There were strong links with St. Mark's, Mendham, at this time and Sr. Suzanne Elizabeth prepared the candidates for the Confirmation that took place there on June 20. She read the Epistle at the service.

There was growing concern for Sr. Mary Barbara, who by the end of July was critically ill. Sr. Katharine Veronica, a trained nurse, was sitting with her at night time and she passed to her rest on August 2, 1971. Her body was brought from the school to the convent chapel on August 4 and she was laid to rest in the convent cemetery the following day. She was succeeded as Sister Superior at St. John Baptist School by Sr. Jane Patricia. Thus the school students came back after their summer vacation to learn that Sr. Mary Barbara had died and there was a new Sister Superior. The older girls probably had some idea of the severity of Sister's illness, and it must surely have been obvious to all that she was very ill, especially following surgery at the end of the previous December.

At a Chapter meeting held on October 20, 1971, the Sisters considered for the first time that a formal request should be made to the Chapter of the Community at Clewer to re-establish an affiliation. The American Chapter would rescind the 1907 Rule presently in use and adopt the 1967 revision in use at Clewer. The Constitution would be as nearly like that of Clewer as Church and State laws allowed. Changes to the Rule must be submitted to both English and American Chapters and must be passed by the specified majority in two successive Chapters in both countries. The Mother Superior of Clewer would be the Mother General and take precedence in the Affiliated House. The Warden of Clewer would be the Warden General. These would be honorary but not executive positions. Finally, the silver Cross would be the symbol of the Community though the style of the habit might vary. These resolutions, based on the ideas outlined to Mother Annys earlier in the year, were discussed and passed by the 15 Sisters at Mendham who had voting rights.

Fr. Paul Weed retired as vicar of St. Luke's Chapel, NYC, in the Fall of 1971 but remained as Warden to the Sisters. He was succeeded as vicar of St. Luke's by Fr. Laughlin.[11] Several Sisters went to his installation on December 19, which they described as a "long, but lovely service." There were changes too at Trinity, Wall Street, where the Revd. Dr. Robert R. Parks was installed as the 15th Rector of the parish on January 26, 1972. Mother Margaret Helena and Sr. Suzanne Elizabeth went to the installation service. Dr. Parks would bring in changes to the parish structure which would directly affect the Community work at St. Luke's Chapel.

Back at the convent, Christmas Day 1971 was "a beautiful, bright day with all the Sisters home."

As 1972 dawned, the Sisters were looking towards the Centennial of the arrival of the Community on February 5, 1874. To this end, a history of CSJB in America was planned and on January 21, 1972, Fr. James Simpson and Fr. Edward Story made their first visit to the convent to begin their research. They also visited Clewer in July, Mother Annys commenting in a letter to Mother Margaret Helena: "I have just unloaded all the records we possess … and hope they have got enough to occupy them for some time!"

Ever since the convent had been built, the main Chapel and part of the cloister had not had a pitched roof. The flat roof, meanwhile, gave an unfinished appearance and it had always been hoped that the building would be completed. Thus on February 21, 1972, a Chapter meeting was held and all but two of the Sisters voted in favor of having the walls built up prior to the construction of a pitched roof. The work was not completed until the following year.

On May 4, Mother gave a meditation at the House of the Good Shepherd, Hackettstown, and four days later left for England to continue talks about the re-affiliation. She returned on May 30, accompanied by Mother Anna Maria of the Anglican Community of St. John Baptist in South Africa, known as the Baptistine Sisters. In July 1970 the Sisters at Mendham had voted to help the Baptistine Sisters financially. After sharing in the St. John Baptist Day celebrations and Commemoration Day, Mother Anna Maria left for England again on July 11.

Disaster struck St. John Baptist House in Barrow Street during the Sisters' absence in July, when a broken water pipe did much damage. Furniture had to be removed and a great deal of mopping and cleaning up was done by Mother, Sr. Agnes Genevieve and Sr. Katharine Veronica. New furniture had to be bought and it was several months before the Sisters were able to move back. Then in August a bath tub on the fourth floor at the New York house overflowed and water went through two ceilings into the chapel ceiling.

On a more cheerful note, Mother and seven Sisters went to the Cathedral of St. John the Divine, NYC, on September 22, for the installation of the Rt. Revd. Paul Moore as diocesan bishop, having previously served as Suffragan bishop since 1970. Fr. Paul Weed was reinstalled as the Community Warden on October 4, 1972.

Several Episcopal Communities were keeping important milestone anniversaries. Thus on November 4, Mother Margaret Helena and Sr. Elizabeth Anne went to Catonsville, MD, for the Centennial of the All Saints' Community. On March 2, the following year they went to the Community of the Transfiguration for their 75th anniversary.

The most important event, as 1972 drew to a close, was the Chapter meeting on December 7, at which the Sisters voted for the second time on the proposals for re-affiliation with Clewer. Of the fifteen Sisters eligible to vote only one voted against each of the resolutions. Now all that remained was for the Chapter at Clewer to vote on the proposals. On March 12, 1973, the Community Record Book noted triumphantly, "Received cablegram from Clewer—'affiliation unanimous, much love, Mother.'"[12] The sigh of relief was discernable on both sides of the Atlantic. Mother Annys had lost no time in sending the good news, the Chapter having met the same day. All the Sisters at Clewer with voting rights (i.e. 45 Sisters) had voted unanimously in favor.

Many of the Sisters both at Clewer and Mendham had passed to their rest in the years between the separation and re-affiliation. In 1947, the year after lay Sisters were amalgamated into choir at Clewer, the Community there numbered 145. Thus the number of professed Sisters at Clewer had fallen by 100 in the 25 years between the separation and re-affiliation.

One Sister at Clewer who did not live to see the reunion was Sr. Amy Grace. She had written to Mother Waldine Lucia in December 1948 expressing the hope that the Community would remain united.[13] Professed in June 1897, she passed to her rest on October 17, 1956, at the age of 91, just six months short of the 60th anniversary of her profession. There had been 31 Sisters at Mendham at the time of the separation. Eighteen Sisters had passed to their rest between 1947 and 1973.

Holy Week 1973 was kept with all the usual observances. On April 19, Maundy Thursday, there was "a beautiful Mass" and as the school students had gone home for the weekend, the two Sisters from the school (Sr. Jane Patricia and Sr. Barbara Jean) were able to be at the convent. The Community Record Book reported that it was "the first warm day of the year, nearly 80° F." All the Sisters and their guests took part in the Maundy Watch.

Easter Day was equally beautiful and all the Sisters were present for Vespers and dinner. The flowers in the chapel were especially lovely. Next day there was the usual Easter tea party with all Sisters present. Later in the evening the New York Sisters left, but the Jersey City Sisters stayed until next morning.

St. Mark's Day was transferred from April 25 to April 30 to avoid the Easter octave. It was of special importance in 1973, being the Centennial anniversary of St. Mark's, Mendham. Bishop Rath confirmed thirteen children at 7:00pm, followed by Holy Communion and a buffet supper. The Sisters declared, "Everything very beautiful."

On May 31, Mother Margaret Helena and Sr. Suzanne Elizabeth went to meet the Warden General, Fr. F. P. Coleman,[14] at the airport. During his visit he conducted the Sisters' long retreat, beginning on June 4, in addition to various preaching engagements and meeting other Religious. St. John Baptist Day was a great day with Fr. Coleman celebrating Mass in the main chapel and four Sisters singing at the crossing during the offertory. Two hundred people were present at Vespers and for the picnic supper. Nine new Associates were received and Bishop Rath was present too.

On June 26, Sr. Barbara Jean flew to England to work with the Clewer Sisters for a month. During that time she met Sr. Dorothy Frances, formerly Mother General at the time of the separation. Now very old and infirm, Sr. Dorothy Frances told her that the separation was the greatest regret of her life.[15] It was a blessing indeed that both she and Sr. Waldine Lucia lived long enough to see the two parts of CSJB reconciled and re-affiliated. Sr. Barbara Jean returned to Mendham on July 27, and Fr. Coleman returned to Clewer on July 3.

On September 2, 1973, Sr. Waldine Lucia celebrated her 93rd birthday. There was a party with the Sisters and friends to celebrate this milestone. Another Community anniversary took place on September 14, when the Society of St. Margaret, Boston, celebrated the centennial of the Sisters' arrival from East Grinstead, UK. Mother and several Sisters went to Boston for the celebrations. There had been a close connection over the years between CSJB and SSM, with Sisters from the latter Community often joining the Community retreat at Mendham. Earlier in the year (May 6), Mother had attended a celebration at Trinity, Wall Street, NYC, to commemorate the SSM centennial.[16] Five hundred people were in the congregation, along with Mother, Sr. Eleanor Lucy and the three Sisters from Barrow Street.

On September 30, St. Mark's, Mendham, had a folk Mass in the convent chapel followed by a picnic outside. Sr. Barbara Jean directed the music group of school girls to accompany the Mass. This was still the era of liturgical change and experimentation, and folk Masses were popular at this time.

On September 25, Mother Margaret Helena and Sr. Suzanne Elizabeth flew to Glendale, Ohio, for a conference on the Religious Life hosted by the Community of the Transfiguration. They returned on September 28. On October 3, 1973, Mother Margaret Helena was re-elected as Superior. It was a busy day, with a visit in the afternoon by the Bishop of Lincoln, UK, the Rt. Revd. Kenneth Riches, and his wife. Several Associates came to help prepare for their visit. Vespers was at 3:00pm, followed by the bishop's address on St. Francis. All the Sisters were present, having been at the convent for the Chapter of Election in the morning.

Mother Margaret Helena was re-installed on October 15 at 7:00am with the Rt. Revd. Kenneth Anand[17] presiding because the Visitor, Bishop Stark, was in hospital. The Service for the Installation of a Mother Superior was taken from the Old Rule Office Book and took place after the Gospel and before the Creed, using the Rite II Eucharist of the trial Book of Common Prayer, currently being revised in the Episcopal Church. Afterwards all the other office holders were re-appointed. Later that morning, eight Sisters including Mother Margaret Helena went to the Cathedral of St. John the Divine for the memorial service for Jenny Moore, wife of Bishop Paul Moore and author of *The People on Second Street*. About 1,000 people were present. She had died of cancer on October 3, at age 50, and her funeral had taken place on October 5 at the National Cathedral in Washington, DC.

The Fall season continued to be one of activity, with Sisters attending meetings or giving quiet days near and far. Ecumenical hospitality continued. Thus on October 16, Sr. Barbara Jean conducted a quiet day for a group of women from Hill Top Presbyterian Church, Mendham. A week later, Sr. Katharine Veronica hosted a picnic at St. Marguerite's for 72 senior citizens from St. Luke's Church, NYC. In December, a group of thirteen Lutheran Church women with their pastor came to St. Marguerite's for an overnight retreat. There were also meetings on vocation for Religious at various venues, which the Sisters endeavored to attend, as well as engaging in discussions on "Christianity and Social Welfare." The Church was changing and the Sisters at this time did all they could to be part of the ongoing process. The Diocese of Newark was about to undergo change too, with the retirement of Bishop Stark, who had held office since 1958. Mother, Sr. Elizabeth Anne, Sr. Susinne Paula and Sr. Eleanor Lucy attended his farewell dinner on November 9, along with an estimated 1200 other people.

As the year 1973 drew to a close there had been a warmer relationship with St. John Baptist School, with reciprocal visits. The school year had begun on September 11, with Mother and four Sisters attending the School Mass. The Community Record Book noted: "The Kiss of Peace given with a card from Sr. Jane Patricia, and flowers from Mother for girls and teachers. A happy beginning of a New [School] Year." November 17, 1973, was the day of the sale at the school and several Sisters went to buy items and to see old girls. They went back in the afternoon for a musical performed by the girls which they declared to be "very good." On December 19 Sr. Jane Patricia brought some of the girls to the convent to sing carols, and on December 23 there was a tea at the school for alumnae, which was attended by about 30 people.

And so 1973 ended and the old year was prayed out and the New Year prayed in by Mother and four Sisters. Despite increasing frailty, Sr. Waldine Lucia joined them in chapel at 11:30pm. It was a time-honored CSJB tradition, amidst all that was new.

On January 28, 1974, Sr. Elizabeth Marion and Sr. Suzanne Elizabeth drove to Kennedy airport to meet Sr. Jane Olive, Sr. Letitia and Sr. Catherine Mary, who were visiting from Clewer. They reached the convent at 6:00pm and joy bells rang to greet them. The Record Book noted: "Right after dinner after seeing a small bit of the house, they were sent to bed. A good trip and safe arrival. Mother Annys was cabled." Next day they were taken by Sr. Suzanne Elizabeth and Muriel Blue to a fish and chip dinner at St. Mark's, Mendham. "Very much like an English one."

The purpose of the English Sisters' visit was to join in celebrating the Centennial of the founding of CSJB in America on February 5 [1874]. It was to be combined with a seminar for Religious and there was much preparation at the convent and St. Marguerite's in order to accommodate over 50 male and female Religious.[18] They arrived on February 3, and seventeen Orders were represented despite the gasoline shortage which prevented some from attending. New Jersey was worst hit by the shortage.[19] The seminar finished in the morning of February 5, and was followed at noon by the Thanksgiving Mass. Two hundred people were expected, but only about 175 were able to make the journey. The Community Record Book noted, "A beautiful Mass, choir filled with Religious. Monks and clergy filled the sanctuary. Almost 100 school girls, teachers, friends and Associates in the nave. A young Associate, Margaret Hackman, played the trumpet, another one was boat *girl* in place of a boy who was ill. Clergy and Religious processed in with trumpet fanfare; school girls sang at the offertory; plainsong Te Deum was sung at the end. The second service for trial use was used. A catered luncheon followed at about 1:30. A beautiful day was had by all on the 100th Anniversary of the American Founding of CSJB." A chartered bus helped many to get to their next destination.

On February 7, two of the English Sisters (the Record Book does not say which) went to New York City by train and the third joined them next day after giving a talk at the school Mass. The Sisters were to tour New York City and visit Jersey City, spending time in both branch houses. Also, they were to visit the Community of St. Mary, Peekskill, staying for one night. The Sisters at Mendham had only enough gas in the cars for emergency use, and February 8 saw deep snow. The English Sisters returned to Mendham on February 14 after "an interesting and exciting time." On February 15, several teachers from St. John Baptist School came to tea at the convent in order to meet the English Sisters, and Bishop Anand and his wife came to dinner. As Bishop Anand was Punjabi by birth, Sr. Catherine Mary was especially pleased to meet them, having worked as a medical doctor in Assam before joining CSJB.

All too soon the visit was over and on February 20, the Sisters caught the 10:00pm flight back to England, Sr. Suzanne Elizabeth and Muriel Blue having driven them to JFK Airport. The Community Record Book noted: "Everyone very sad at their going—a very happy visit from all sides." Next day, Mother Annys sent a cable: "Loving thanks for visit, all safely home. Love, Mother."

A former resident of St. Anna's (Betsy) called at the convent on February 21. She prayed in St. Michael's Chapel and talked with Sr. Margaret Raphael. Years previously she had been baptized and Sr. Katharine Veronica and Sr. Eudora had been her sponsors. Then on March 13, a group of thirteen high school girls from East Orange came for a tour of St. John Baptist School and the convent and stayed to Vespers and supper.

On March 23, 1974, Bishop Rath was installed as Bishop of Newark, having previously served as Suffragan Bishop from 1964 and as Coadjutor Bishop since 1970. Mother Margaret Helena, Sr. Barbara Jean and Sr. Laura Katharine went to the service.

"Doing things for others" was the theme for a Lent project for Sunday School children in 1974. In response to this, Sr. Barbara Jean's class went to visit a nursing home, and Sr. Suzanne Elizabeth's classes (4th through 8th grade) went to the Matheny School for children with cerebral palsy and other disabilities.[20] On April 7, Sr. Suzanne Elizabeth and Sr. Eleanor Lucy went to Essex County Mental Hospital for the Palm Sunday Masses (both Episcopalian and Roman Catholic) at the request of Fr. Milligan, a CSJB Associate.

The Community had always contained several Sisters who had previously been trained nurses. On April 19, 1974, Sr. Katharine Veronica, Sr. Elizabeth Anne and Sr. Suzanne Elizabeth, all graduates of St. Luke's, went to the St. Luke's Hospital graduation at the Cathedral of St. John the Divine, NYC. There was a reunion of graduates during the weekend and the three Sisters were to attend class seminars and luncheon on the Saturday. On May 30, Sr. Elizabeth Marion went to Wellesley College for her 60th college reunion, having graduated in 1914.

Relations with St. John Baptist School continued to flourish, and on May 9 the three senior students attended dinner at the convent. The Community Record Book noted that "we all sat at the visitors' table with a fire in the fireplace—flowers, candles and tablecloths. A lovely evening." The previous day, Sr. Jane Patricia had flown to a Cistercian conference in the mid-West to give a paper about a medieval manuscript she had been loaned and had worked on translating. Medieval studies would increasingly occupy her interests from this time onwards. Meanwhile, on May 11, Mother Margaret Helena attended the parents' luncheon at the school. On May 29 Mother, accompanied by three other Sisters, gave out the sports awards at the school. The Record Book noted that she "received a kiss and hug from each student—a very affectionate and grateful group of girls."

The major event of the summer of 1974 was the visit by Mother Annys (Mother General), Sr. Eudora, Sr. Marjorie, and Sr. Monica. They arrived on June 4, having been met at JFK airport by Mother Margaret Helena and Sr. Suzanne Elizabeth. Before retiring to bed at 9:00pm they had ice cream, but the tour of the convent and grounds waited until next day. On June 7 they went to New York City and Jersey City to greet the Sisters in the branch houses. In the evening they attended prize night at the school with Mass and supper. Bishop Anand presented the diplomas at the school graduation on June 8, which took place at St. Peter's, Morristown. Most of the Sisters attended and stayed to the lunch afterwards.

June 10, 1974, saw the installation in the National Cathedral, Washington, DC, of the Rt. Revd. John Allin[21] as the 23rd Presiding Bishop of the Episcopal Church. Mother Margaret Helena and Mother Annys attended the service. A few days later the English Sisters were driven to Washington, DC, by Mrs. Templeton, the chaplain's wife, for a sight-seeing trip, returning next day, having had "a wonderful time." June 22 was Sr. Waldine Lucia's 65th anniversary of profession. She was by now frail in health, but the day was no less joyous. On the same day there was the annual meeting of the Confraternity of the Blessed Sacrament at Paterson, NJ, and ten Sisters from CSJB attended the Mass and luncheon. The Community Record Book noted that "banana splits in honor of the English Sisters were eaten on the way home." (!)

June 23, Commemoration Day, dawned with rain, but the Community spirit was not dampened. Two hundred and thirty-five people were expected, of whom about 200 came. Eleven new Associates were admitted at a service of reception, followed by Vespers and sermon given by Fr. Henry F. Folsom, a direct descendant of the family of Sr. Helen Margaret Folsom CSJB, the Foundress of CSJB in the USA. A "box supper" took place in the convent and on the cloister, followed by addresses by both Mothers. All the Sisters were present and it was declared to have been a wonderful day.

It was announced that Sr. Jane Patricia would not be at the school in the next academic year. She would be studying for her doctorate and traveling whilst deciding on her future. On June 25 the Board of Directors of the school gave a dinner party for her. And on July 2 Sr. Jane Patricia flew to St. Gregory's Abbey, Three Rivers, Michigan, having formally resigned as Sister Superior of St. John Baptist School.

The English Sisters' visit was almost over. On June 27 Sr. Marjorie and Sr. Monica flew back to England but Mother Annys and Sr. Eudora stayed on until July 7. During this time they visited Jersey City and New York City and were able to join in the July 4 celebrations. They arrived home at Clewer on July 8, and cabled to say they had had a safe journey and were now back in their refectory after extensive restoration.[22] Soon afterwards, on July 25, Sr. Elizabeth Anne, Sr. Katharine Veronica and Sr. Laura Katharine left for a three-week visit at Clewer.

Back at the convent, there were Vacation Bible Schools which involved Sr. Suzanne Elizabeth and Sr. Barbara Jean, firstly at St. Dunstan's Episcopal Church, Succasunna, NJ, and then an ecumenical one in Mendham. These took a great deal of preparation. Also, since the departure of Sr. Jane Patricia, Mother Margaret Helena stepped in as headmistress of St. John Baptist School until further notice, in addition to her role as Mother Superior at the convent. At the end of August 1974 there was a reassignment of Sisters at the branch houses due to the shortage of Sisters at the school. Thus Sr. Agnes Genevieve and Sr. Katharine Veronica returned to Barrow Street, NYC, and Sr. Agatha Louise was to be there temporarily and then be at the school. Sr. Laura Katharine was to replace her at Barrow Street. When the school opened on September 9 there were 32 students. Mother was to spend part of each day there and Sr. Barbara Jean and Sr. Agatha Louise were to live there with the students.

On September 8, 1974, the last of the Centennial celebrations began with a seminar on the Religious Life. There were fourteen participants and the seminar began with Vespers at 5:30 in the main chapel. After dinner for all at 6:30 at St. Marguerite's, the first session started at 7:30. Fr. Weed chaired the group and Fr. Templeton gave three addresses. Next day at 12:00 noon in the main chapel there was a Thanksgiving Mass for 100 years of ministry. Sr. Waldine Lucia, who had celebrated her 94th birthday a few days previously, was able to be present. The seminar closed after the 3:00pm session and the New York Sisters returned to Barrow Street. The Jersey City Sisters stayed at the convent for a few more days before returning to St. Christopher's House, along with Judy their dog.

Six Sisters attended the 90th anniversary celebration of the Order of the Holy Cross at the Cathedral of St. John the Divine, NYC, on September 14, 1974 (Holy Cross day). And at the end of September Fr. Arthur Pederson was instituted as Rector of Grace Church (Van Vorst) in Jersey City, Fr. William Albert having resigned on health grounds earlier in the year. Another Centennial celebration was coming up—the Diocese of Newark, NJ, and a plea for help was sent to the Sisters from the Diocesan Altar Guild. They needed help in making vestments for the celebration in November. Sr. Suzanne Elizabeth and two women went to Newark to do some sewing and brought back some for others to do. By November 10 all was well, and the great service of Thanksgiving for the Diocese was held at Seton Hall University, South Orange, NJ. An estimated 5,000 people were present including seven CSJB Sisters. It was "a beautiful service and day."

On November 5, 1974, there was a great celebration for Mother Margaret Helena's 70th birthday, and especially for the 25th anniversary of her election as Mother Superior. All the Sisters were present until the following day, and also present at lunch were Mother's niece, her husband and child. An album, made by the Sisters, was presented to Mother commemorating her years as Superior. She was "surprised and overwhelmed." It was a very happy day. Mother Margaret Helena would serve several more years before finally resigning as Mother Superior in 1979.

Nineteen seventy-four drew to a close with the death of Sr. Agnes Genevieve on December 8. She had been experiencing heart trouble for a short time, and had returned to the convent from Barrow Street on November 30. On December 7 she was feeling unwell and the doctor was called. Next day, after Vespers, Mother found her on the floor of her cell, having passed away very suddenly and peacefully. The Litany for the Departed was said in chapel; and the Sisters at the branch houses, and at Clewer, were informed. Sr. Agnes Genevieve's funeral was on December 12, and about 50 people were present. Many came from New York City, where she had worked for 25 years. Amongst the many letters received there was one from the Rector of Trinity, Wall Street, as St. Luke's was a chapel of the parish. Many people were grateful for all she had done.

Sr. Agnes Genevieve had been Sister in Charge at St. Luke's Chapel and this was how many people would remember her. But before that time she had worked at St. Marguerite's when it was a home school; then she served as Sister Superior of St. John Baptist School, 1942–46. She was one of the Sisters who worked at the short-lived school in Corsicana, TX, from 1946–49. Her first introduction to CSJB was when she worked as a secular teacher in the Lower School at St. Helen's Hall, Portland, Oregon under Sr. Elisabeth Roberta. In common with several Sisters she faced strong parental objection to her becoming a Sister, but followed her vocation. In 1962 she had visited Clewer with Mother Margaret Helena in the early days of nurturing the friendship that would lead to rebuilding the affiliation. And together with Sr. Katharine Veronica, she had given up her summer rest to work on the Navajo reservation with Deaconess Brown. Her contribution to the life and ministry of CSJB was boundless.

The Sisters were still hoping and praying for more vocations. The branch work was struggling to keep going and during the following year decisions would need to be made about the work in New York. Women did still express an interest in the Religious Life and on December 18, 1974, a postulant was received. Alas, she left on January 3.

Despite influenza striking several Sisters on New Year's Eve, all members of the Community were together as they prepared for another year.

---

[1] Conversation with Valerie Bonham, May 2017.

[2] Sr. Mary Joan's profession at Mendham took place on June 8, 1916, on the same day that the new convent was blessed.

[3] Fr. Robert Maitland was Rector of the Church of the Savior, Denville, NJ. He gave the annual retreat to the School students. Mother Margaret Helena was a mentor to him and other young clergy during this period.

[4] Christine Brodeur was received as an Associate on January 10, 1973.

[5] PRICE, Margaret M. *St. John Baptist School 1880–1980*.

[6] PRICE, Margaret M. op.cit.

[7] Christine Brodeur MacClellan by email to Valerie Bonham, March 2018.

[8] This might have been Sr. Eudora, who had spent several years at Mendham during the War when she was unable to return safely to Clewer from the Community work in Barbados. Or it might have been Sr. Dorothy Frances, Mother General at the time of the separation in 1949.

[9] During the UK visit Sr. Suzanne Elizabeth also attended a Novice Directors' Conference.

[10] In 1964 the UK CSJB took over Neale House, Cambridge, from the Society of St. Margaret. It was a small house where students could stay and from where the Sisters did pastoral work within the student body as well as parish and hospital visiting. It was given up in the early 1970s and the house was bought by Fitzwilliam College in 1976.

[11] The son of Dean Ledlie Laughlin, who was formerly Rector of Grace Church (Van Vorst), Jersey City.

[12] The cablegram is preserved in the Community Record Book at Mendham.

[13] See Chapter 2.

[14] Fr. Coleman was Warden at Clewer from 1968–79.

[15] As recounted to me by Sr. Barbara Jean.

[16] The SSM Sisters were working at Trinity, Wall Street. In 2020, three SSM Sisters live at Neale House in Manhattan and exercise a variety of ministries from Trinity Church, Wall Street.

[17] The Rt. Revd. Kenneth D. W. Anand was an Assistant Bishop in the Diocese of Newark, 1974–76, and was also Vicar of the Church of the Transfiguration, Towaco, NJ. He was Punjabi by birth and was ordained to the priesthood in 1942, working for several years in Bombay. He then studied in England and was called to work as a priest at St. Paul's Cathedral, Calcutta. He was then appointed as the second Bishop of Amritsar at age 45, following his consecration at St. Paul's, Calcutta on December 6, 1959, and his enthronement the following Sunday in his Cathedral at Ambala. He died on July 27, 1975, while having a vacation in India. A library was founded in the Newark Diocesan House, NJ, in his memory.

[18] It is not clear whether there were any members of Roman Catholic Communities at the seminar, or whether it was just for Episcopalian Religious.

[19] During the 1973 Arab-Israeli War, Arab members of the Organization of Petroleum Exporting Countries (OPEC) imposed an embargo against the United States in retaliation for the US decision to re-supply the Israeli military. The embargo was also extended to other countries that supported Israel. The US economy was put under severe strain. The embargo was lifted in March 1974. Source https://history.state.gov/milestones/1969-1976/oil-embargo

[20] Founded in 1946 by Walter and Marguerite Matheny, the school, situated at Far Hills, NJ, now has a hospital in addition to its special education facility, and runs programs for children and adults with medically complex developmental disabilities.

[21] The Rt. Revd. John Maury Allin (1921–1998) was Bishop Coadjutor of the Diocese of Mississippi 1961–66 and Diocesan Bishop 1966–74. He was very involved in the civil rights movement, helping to create the Committee of Concern, an alliance of ecumenical and civil rights leaders that helped rebuild more than 100 black churches that had been bombed by white supremacists in Mississippi. He was the last Presiding Bishop to have opposed women's ordination and to have been pro-life on abortion. In 1978 he offered to resign because of his viewpoint on women priests but was persuaded to stay in office. He retired in 1985. Source https://en.m.wikipedia.org

[22] The great Victorian convent at Clewer, designed by Henry Woodyer, underwent extensive

restoration work from 1970–74, including redesigning the kitchen. With characteristic humor Mother Annys had written in the Clewer *Associates' Newsletter* of July 1967: "If Henry Woodyer had had to do any cooking, he would not have designed his own kitchen after the style of the Abbot's kitchen at Glastonbury, as he did the convent one."

12

CHALLENGE AND CHANGE

The Community 1975–79

AFTER ALL THE excitement of 1974 (the Centennial year) and the reciprocal visits with the Clewer Sisters, it is hardly surprising that 1975 was a more routine, even mundane time. Even so, it was a year of important milestones, and as always, the Sisters lived their vowed life within the context of the daily round of prayer and sacraments.

From time to time students stayed with the Sisters; and on January 5, 1975, Christine Brodeur came to stay at the convent for three weeks as part of her college work, helping in a nursery in the mornings and helping the Sisters at other times.

January 11 marked the 25th anniversary of the Sisters' work at St. Luke's Chapel and school in New York. No celebrations were planned. However, on February 2 (the Feast of the Purification of the Blessed Virgin Mary), Mother Margaret Helena and several Sisters went to St. Luke's Chapel for the evening Mass in the presence of the Presiding Bishop. Mother gave him a Crucifix made from nails from a parish where he had once been Rector. Also present were some Sisters from the Community of St. Mary, Peekskill, celebrating 110 years since their foundation.

Discussions had been going on for some time about the future of St. John Baptist School, made all the more urgent by the death of Sr. Mary Barbara (Schroeder) and the departure of Sr. Jane Patricia on study leave. On February 6 it was finally decided not to merge with another school. The Community Record Book noted that "SJBS must remain a conservative boarding and day school for girls." But the question of the headship remained unresolved. Clearly, Mother Margaret Helena would be unable to continue in this role indefinitely together with the office of Mother Superior at the convent.

At the end of February Sr. Winifred Agnes underwent major surgery and although she made a good recovery, she was unable to be at the New York house for some time. Three weeks later, on March 22, Sr. Katharine Veronica fractured her arm and was temporarily relieved of her duties in New York by Sr. Agatha Louise. But the greatest concern at this time was for Sr. Waldine Lucia, who was failing rapidly. Easter came early for Sr. Waldine Lucia, whose final decline began on Palm Sunday, March 23. But she was peaceful and was lovingly attended by the Sisters and Visiting Nurse, so that on March 26, Mother went into New York for a morning meeting at 90, Barrow Street and stayed to lunch. By 2:00pm it was clear that Sr. Waldine Lucia's passing was getting near. Sr. Suzanne Elizabeth and Sr. Barbara Jean stayed with her, holding her hands, but she was asking for Mother. A message got through to the New York house and Mother arrived back at the convent at 3:00pm. Sr. Waldine Lucia died very peacefully at 3:30pm on Wednesday, March 26, 1975.[1] The bell was tolled and the Litany of the Dead was said.[2]

The Sisters now had to prepare for the funeral and also keep the observance of the Sacred Triduum, the three days leading to Easter. On Maundy Thursday Sr. Waldine Lucia's body was placed in the nave of the main chapel with a short service. On Easter Monday, March 31, at 7:30pm, there was a service in the main chapel during which the coffin was brought into choir and the Office of the Dead was said. The best white frontal was on the altar and the flowers "were simple but beautiful." Next day, April 1, the requiem Mass was offered with the Bishop presiding and the Warden celebrating, wearing white vestments. The music was that composed for Sisters' requiems by Fr. Nancrede (chaplain 1878–92). It was a mild, sunny day and about 50 people attended the requiem and lunch afterwards. Everyone followed to the cemetery for the committal. Mr. Grier tolled the bell. The Community Record Book noted: "Many letters, calls and memorial gifts have come, Sister having been widely known in the diocese and in Oregon. Three of her relatives were able to be present. The Mass was glorious and all went well."

Sr. Waldine Lucia's death marked the end of an era. She was clothed as a novice in 1906 and, although she was not strong physically, was professed in 1909. Her cousin was Sr. Julia Frances, whom she greatly admired. At the time of her death she was the last remaining Sister to have been professed in the chapel at the old St. John Baptist House (233 East Seventeenth Street) in New York. As Sister Superior for 23 years at St. Helen's Hall in Portland, Oregon, she saw the school grow in size and competency. Her Community Biographer described the school's success: "The dynamo was a tiny Sister with bright blue eyes, a quick mind and a visionary perception of her task." She also showed great courage. The first manifestation of this was when, as a young Sister, she nursed victims of the Spanish influenza at Portland in 1918. She was the last of those three Sisters to pass to her rest.[3] But during her time as Mother Superior she showed courage in other ways: by withdrawing the Community from St. Helen's Hall, a work she loved; by understanding and acting upon the need to separate from Clewer; and by closing St. Anna's home and St. Marguerite's home school, thus freeing the Community to serve in new ways.[4] In all this she helped bring about the Second Spring of the Community.

Sr. Waldine Lucia was held in high esteem by many people. Thus when St. Helen's Hall celebrated its Centennial in 1969, there were more than 600 alumnae at the dinner and they gave her a standing ovation and prolonged applause. In October 1975 a plaque in her memory, given by the alumnae of St. Helen's Hall, was placed in St. John Baptist Cathedral, Portland, Oregon. Sr. Waldine Lucia passed to her rest in her 95th year of age, 69th year in Community and 66th year of Religious profession.

On April 30, 1975, the appointment was announced of Fr. Edwin Cromey[5] as headmaster of St. John Baptist School. A tea party was given which was attended by most of the Sisters and the teaching faculty. This was a departure from "tradition" designed to inject new life into the school. Fr. Cromey was principal speaker at the school prize night and dinner on June 6, an event which was well attended by most Sisters and many alumnae as well as families and friends. Graduation day next day was equally well attended, notably by about 30 former students. Schoolgirls continued to be invited to the convent for dinner from time to time, and school exchanges with English students from St. Stephen's College, Broadstairs, also took place. This was a boarding school for girls owned and run by the Clewer Sisters.

The grounds surrounding the convent, retreat house, and school continued to be greatly appreciated by visiting groups. Such a large space was a great asset to the Sisters in their various ministries. Thus on June 8, 1975, the Community Record Book noted: "About 150 people on our grounds today!" These consisted of various groups: St. Mark's, Mendham, for a Eucharist and picnic, though the poor weather drove them into St. Marguerite's; the Episcopal group from Linden for a picnic; St. Peter's, Morristown, for a picnic in the school grounds; and the Lutheran Church Women's Executive Council, who were staying overnight at St. Marguerite's. Sisters also continued to go out and about speaking about the Religious Life. And Sr. Suzanne Elizabeth began a long-term ministry with the Diocesan Altar Guild, giving talks and training.

Sixteen new Associates were received on Commemoration Day, June 28, 1975, and there were about 175 guests at the Solemn High Mass followed by lunch on the cloister. It was "an especially pleasant time for everyone." After summer rests for several Sisters, the Vacation Bible Schools took place in several parishes with help from the Sisters. All went well despite very bad weather. On August 1, 1975, Fr. Cromey officially took up his position as the new head of St. John Baptist School and there was a Mass in the school chapel. About 20 people attended including two Sisters, the staff and faculty, and other friends. There was much to be discussed about the running of the school, and two days later Fr. Cromey came to the convent for dinner and a conference with Sr. Barbara Jean and Sr. Laura Katharine. On August 3, 150 people from Grace Church (Van Vorst) had a Mass followed by a picnic on the convent grounds. They were probably very glad to have this day out as Jersey City had been without water the day previously. Later in August there was the "worst electric storm in many years." Over two inches of rain fell in a very short time and there was a power outage for four hours.

The new academic year began on September 8, 1975, with 38 students. Sr. Barbara Jean and Sr. Laura Katharine had moved from the convent to the school the previous day. The first week passed happily, boding well for the future. But as Mother Margaret Helena wrote in a letter to the Associates, "Our great need is students and a larger income."

The Fall season brought groups to St. Marguerite's as usual. In the words of Mother Margaret Helena: "St. Marguerite's continues to be a surprise and joy." Clearly there was a great need for a place where people of all ages and all traditions could come to "search for a better understanding and love of God, and responsibility towards their fellow men [sic]."

But the branch work in New York City and Jersey City was by this time beginning to cause some concern as to its future. On September 21, Mother had a conference with Fr. Laughlin, Rector of St. Luke's Chapel, about the work in New York. Part of the concern about the branch work was not of the Sisters' making. There had been a financial crisis in New York City which had repercussions far and wide. Trinity Church, Wall Street, was badly hit and the Rector, the Revd. Dr. Robert R. Parks, decided to put into effect the results of a parish analysis that called for self-governance by the congregations of Trinity Church and its five dependent chapels, of which St. Luke's was one.

Since the death of Sr. Agnes Genevieve it had not been possible to have three Sisters at St. Luke's all the time. On September 10, 1975, Sr. Agatha Louise had fallen backwards down the stairs at Barrow Street and been taken to hospital for tests. At first it was thought that no bones were broken but when her progress seemed to be very slow it was discovered she had three broken ribs. Clearly she would be unable to return to New York. Sr. Katharine Veronica had carried on a ministry to senior citizens at St. Luke's and had been greatly supported by an Associate, Mrs. Marion Burger. The decision by the Rector of Trinity to "set the chapels free" did not come into effect until the following year, but, combined with the problem of shortage of Sisters to work at St. Luke's, the painful decision was made to give up 90, Barrow Street. Sr. Katharine Veronica would continue her ministry, commuting from Jersey City. And then there was a twist in the tale. An inspection of St. Christopher's House in Jersey City resulted in a report that it was unsafe and a fire hazard. The Sisters had to move. Therefore, the decision was made to use 90, Barrow Street as a base from which the Sisters would commute to Jersey City.[6]

On September 14, 1975, Pope Paul VI canonized Mother Elizabeth Ann Seton, the first American-born person to be officially recognized as a saint. The Sisters watched the ceremony on TV at the convent. On September 21, three Sisters went to the Sisters of Charity of St. Elizabeth for a celebration in honor of their foundress.[7] A few weeks later, on November 23, Mother, Sr. Elizabeth Anne, Sr. Elizabeth Marion and Sr. Laura Katharine went to Elizabeth, NJ, for Evensong in honor of St. Elizabeth Ann Seton. Ecumenism was still alive and well.

On November 2, 1975, there was a service at St. Luke's Chapel, NYC, in thanksgiving for the Sisters' work there over 26 years. The Warden, Fr. Weed (recently re-elected), preached the sermon. Mother Margaret Helena, Sr. Winifred Agnes, Sr. Agatha Louise and Sr. Elizabeth Marion attended from the convent. The Community Record Book noted that it was "a sad and happy occasion." On November 5 all the branch house Sisters came to the convent for Fr. Weed's re-installation as Warden next day. Bishop Rath celebrated at the Choral Eucharist, and Fr. Templeton and Fr. Cromey served as acolytes.

Former residents and workers at the Sisters' homes continued to visit and remember times past. On November 15 Roseanna Dennis, an old St. Marguerite's girl, paid a visit. A few weeks previously a former cook at St. John Baptist School, now aged 82, had visited. She remembered Sr. Margaret Raphael from forty years earlier. On November 14, the

Community's oldest Associate, Mrs. Teresa Wilson, died at age 95. She had been an Associate since 1912. Mother Margaret Helena and Sr. Suzanne Elizabeth attended her funeral in St. John's Church, Boonton, where her husband had once been Rector.

On November 26 there was an Eve of Thanksgiving service at Hilltop First Presbyterian Church, and a good many townspeople were there. Next morning all the Sisters, plus four St. Margaret's Sisters, were at the convent for a Choral Eucharist for Thanksgiving Day at 8:00am. A tea party at 3:00 was followed by Vespers at 4:00 and dinner at 5:00. Fr. Weed was present and at 8:00pm the Sisters went into silence for next day's retreat and colloquium on the Religious Life. The introduction of a colloquium into the retreat was judged to have been very acceptable. "The discovery of common interests and problems, as well as blessings, brought a strong feeling of solidary and strength."[8]

Next day, November 29, the Sisters celebrated First Vespers of Advent. The Advent wreath was put in the refectory, and before the grace the first candle was lit and prayers were said. On Advent Sunday, November 30, there was a Mass at St. Mark's, Mendham, to dedicate the enlarged sanctuary and side chapels. Bishop Rath celebrated and former vicar Fr. Elwood Boggess[9] preached the sermon. It was a beautiful service and the church was crowded for both the service and the reception which followed. Mother and Sr. Suzanne Elizabeth attended.

As Christmas approached it was time to put into action the painful decisions made earlier about the branch work. On December 10, Sr. Elizabeth Anne and Sr. Eleanor Lucy moved from St. Christopher's House to 90, Barrow Street, from where they would commute to Jersey City daily. Sr. Susinne Paula was in poor health and would remain at the convent, but would still do sewing for the Jersey City work. Even so, she went to Jersey City ten days later, along with Sr. Laura Katharine and Sr. Suzanne Elizabeth, to help prepare for the toy sale. Mr. Grier had two journeys with the truck loaded with donated toys for the sale.

St. John Baptist School had a Christmas sale on December 13, which was not too well attended, but the Sisters enjoyed meeting many old friends and former students. On December 19 there was a Christmas program in the school chapel, after which the girls went home for the Christmas vacation. Most of the Sisters attended what they described as "a very nice program." Next day the school Sisters came back to the convent for the Christmas vacation.

On Christmas Eve, Vespers and Benediction took place in St. Michael's chapel at 4:00pm after which Sr. Barbara Jean and Sr. Suzanne Elizabeth went to the pageant at St. Mark's. There were about ten guests at the Midnight Mass and sung Lauds, starting at 11:30pm. All went very well. Christmas Day saw all the Sisters home by the afternoon in time for Vespers and Benediction at 4:00pm, followed by dinner at 5:00pm. There was a tea party at the convent for St. John Baptist School alumnae on December 28. About 37 former students were present. The Community Record Book noted: "Very nice time and glad to see some old students not present in a long while." And on December 29, Fr. Cromey and his wife invited all the Sisters for dinner. It was a very nice evening and indicative of the new relationship between the convent and the school. In the midst of concerns about the rest of the Community work, the school seemed set fair for survival.

Nineteen seventy-six was a year of change not only for the Community but for the wider Episcopal Church, and as so often happens, "change" can bring pain as well as joy. Even so, the year began with the reception of a postulant, and another would be received later in January. It was a sign of hope for the Community, although in the long term, neither of them would make life vows. Meanwhile, on January 7, Mother Margaret Helena and Sr. Elizabeth Anne met with the bishop and the Diocesan Mission Committee to discuss the future of Grace Church and the Sisters' work there. The various ecumenical services for the Week of Prayer for Christian Unity were poorly attended, although several Sisters, plus some RC Sisters, went to a number of them.

On February 4, 1976, there was a catastrophic earthquake in Guatemala with a magnitude of 7.5. The death toll was estimated at 23,000 and approximately 76,000 people were injured. The Sisters had financially "adopted" a child called Marguerita through Christian Aid and there were fears that she had not survived.

On a more positive note, a movie had been made about the Diocese of Newark and the Sisters had been featured. On February 28 the movie was shown at St. Marguerite's and most of the Sisters viewed it. The Community Record Book noted: "It is beautifully put together, much of it photographed in front of the convent and the Sisters in Jersey City are also in the film."

July 4, 1976, was the bi-centennial of the US Declaration of Independence in 1776. There would be great celebrations nearer the day, but some churches began early. Thus on February 29, Sr. Barbara Jean and Sr. Suzanne Elizabeth went to St. Luke's, Montclair, as special guests at their 1776 Eucharist at which the 1662 Book of Common Prayer was used. Many people were present dressed in the clothing of that period, and the food at the reception was of that period too. Somewhat ironically, the guests of honor were the British Consul and his wife! A month later, on March 28, St. Mark's, Mendham, held a 1662 Prayer Book service and Sr. Suzanne Elizabeth's Church School children attended, noting the differences in the liturgy and ceremonial.

On March 5, Fr. James Simpson and Fr. Edward Story brought to the convent the first two copies of *Stars in His Crown*, the long-awaited history of the Community up to 1974. They presented the book to Mother and it was admired by all the Sisters. It would be read at recreation during Lent, which had begun two days previously. On the same day at 6:00pm a vigil of prayer was begun for the election of the Bishop Coadjutor of the Diocese of Newark, due to take place the following day. Mother Margaret Helena had nominated Fr. Robert Maitland, friend and Associate of the Community, and he remained in the running until the seventh and final vote, at which the Revd. John Shelby Spong was elected. He was formerly Rector of St. Paul's Church, Richmond, Virginia.

Negotiations were continuing regarding the work in New York City. On March 15 Mother called a meeting of the Consultative Council to decide about leaving St. Luke's Chapel in June. The Community was now being asked to pay for rent, repairs and insurance, beyond their means, and felt it was not justified in continuing the work there.

Mother Margaret Helena celebrated the fortieth anniversary of her profession on March 25, the Feast of the Annunciation of the Blessed Virgin Mary (and the anniversary of Mother Harriet Monsell's death in 1883). As usual on feast days, there was a Choral Mass.

Holy Week 1976 saw the Warden, Fr. Weed, at the convent for the first time in over 27 years in office. On Palm Sunday the temperature dropped to 22°F but by Easter Day it had soared to 96°F and it was the hottest place in the USA. The Community Record Book noted that the fruit trees blossomed instantly and the bulbs all came up. All went well with the Holy Week rites and ceremonies. On Maundy Thursday after the Mass the Sisters kept a Watch at the Altar of Repose. The School students went home that day, and so Sr. Barbara Jean and Sr. Laura Katharine came back to the convent for the remainder of Holy Week and the Easter weekend.

On Good Friday Fr. Templeton led the Three Hours Devotion. And on Saturday the lighting of the Paschal Candle took place at 5:30pm.

Life at the convent continued to be very active within the context of the Sisters' vowed life. Quiet days, retreats, conferences and hospitality were all part of the rich tapestry of Community life. Sr. Suzanne Elizabeth had been a member for some time of the Diocesan Communications Committee, which met at various venues. On April 26, there was a Confirmation with a Eucharist at St. Mark's, Mendham, at 6:00pm, followed by dinner. Sr. Suzanne Elizabeth presented her Confirmation class and read two lessons. Sr. Agatha Louise and Sr. Elizabeth Marion also attended. On May 29, 1976, Christine Brodeur graduated from Drew University. Her parents, plus Sr. Suzanne Elizabeth and Sr. Laura Katharine, attended the ceremony, which was followed by lunch.

In 1967 the General Convention of the Episcopal Church had opened the diaconate to women and recognized deaconesses as deacons, the same year that women were made eligible for election as Convention deputies. (This latter constitutional change did not come into effect until the 1970 General Convention.) But women were still prevented from ordination to the priesthood, and it would be some years before this barrier was removed. In June 1976, Martha Blacklock, an Associate and a graduate of St. John Baptist School, was ordained as a deacon. Sr. Jane Patricia returned to the convent from her travels overseas in order to be Martha Blacklock's presenter at her ordination on June 5, and to read the Epistle.

June 5, 1976, was also graduation day for St. John Baptist School and most of the Sisters attended the ceremony at St. Peter's, Morristown. Deacon Martha Blacklock preached at St. Mark's, Mendham, next day. Meanwhile, Sr. Jane Patricia resumed her overseas traveling. On June 6, there was a service at Trinity Wall Street, NYC, in honor of the Religious who had worked in the parish during the past 100 years. It was attended by Mother Margaret Helena, Sr. Agatha Louise, Sr. Elizabeth Marion, Sr. Eleanor Lucy, Sr. Katharine Veronica and Sr. Laura Katharine. Many CSJB Associates attended and Mother Margaret Helena read a lesson. Also present were Sisters from the Society of St. Margaret and the Community of St. Mary who had worked in the parish, as well as brethren from the Order of the Holy Cross. After the service there were refreshments in the parish house and grateful speeches for all the work and ministry over the years.

June 11 was a day of joy when both postulants were clothed as novices at the 9:00am Choral Eucharist. They took the names of Sr. Karen John and Sr. Martha Clare, having been prepared by the Novice Mistress, Sr. Suzanne Elizabeth. About 50 guests were present and there was a reception in the parlor after the service.

Next day, June 12, 1976, at 11:00am, the Bishop Coadjutor elect (the Revd. John S. Spong) was consecrated in the Sacred Heart Cathedral (RC) in Newark. Mother, Sr. Elizabeth Anne, Sr. Susinne Paula, Sr. Eleanor Lucy, Sr. Suzanne Elizabeth and Sr. Laura Katharine attended. Fr. Pederson, Rector of Grace Church, brought the Jersey City Sisters and some parishioners. The Sisters took part in the procession. The Community Record Book noted that "it was a perfectly beautiful day, warm, sunny, breezy. The service was lovely (over at 2:00pm)."

After so much activity the Sisters were probably thankful for their long retreat from June 13–18, conducted by Fr. Weed. And thankful too for the novices who "held the fort," doing most of the work, thus shielding the professed Sisters from interruptions to their quiet time.

An unusual event took place on June 19 at St. John Baptist School, when Deborah Almy, a school graduate, married Fr. James Ransom, chaplain for the past two years. The ceremony, including a Nuptial Mass, took place in the School Chapel and a tent was pitched outside for the reception. Fr. Philip Cato, Associate Rector of St. Peter's, Morristown, and Fr. Ledlie Laughlin, Rector of St. Luke's Chapel, NYC, officiated. Six Sisters, including Mother, attended the service.

A wedding party of seventeen people stayed overnight at St. Marguerite's on June 25. The wedding was next day in the School Chapel, though the Community Record Book does not name the happy couple. Also staying at the School was a Transcendental Meditation[10] group numbering about 55. But the great event on June 26 was Commemoration Day, kept both at Mendham and at Clewer. The Sisters woke up to a beautiful day with a clear sky, and the temperature soared into the 80s. There was no early Mass, just the Solemn High Mass at 11:00am, at which all the Sisters received Holy Communion with the Associates and other guests. Bishop Rath officiated, the Warden, Fr. Weed celebrated, and Fr. Maitland was deacon. Bishop Stark was present in the congregation. The acolytes were Fr. Simpson and Fr. Story, the authors of the Community history. Fr. Laughlin preached on vocation. The Community Record Book noted: "200 guests were expected and they came! It was a beautiful service followed by catered luncheon on the cloister." Mother gave a speech, followed by a word from the Bishop and Warden. Sixteen new Associates were received, including five from St. Mark's, Mendham, a woman deacon and two priests. Everyone had left by 3:00pm and the Sisters' day returned to its usual timetable.

On June 27, 1976, Mother Margaret Helena, Sr. Elizabeth Marion, Sr. Agatha Louise and Sr. Laura Katharine went to Trinity, Wall Street, for the last service of the Sisters working in the parish at St. Luke's Chapel. It was "a little service of setting apart for new work, and a blessing was given to Sr. Katharine Veronica and Marion Burger who were leaving the Chapel." Afterwards there was a reception. Next day, Sr. Suzanne Elizabeth took the two novices to New York to pack up everything for moving back to the convent. Mr. Grier went into New York the following day to supervise the move. In the afternoon he brought Sr. Katharine Veronica, Marion Burger and Alex the cat back to the convent.

Trinity News, the newsletter for the parish of Trinity, Wall Street, carried a tribute to the Sisters' work at St. Luke's in its issue of May/June 1976. Under the headline "St. John Baptist leaves enriched lives at St. Luke's," the article paid tribute to the work of the Sisters over a period of 26 years, and especially to Sr. Katharine Veronica, who had worked there for the past fourteen years. "Its work has been a witness to the flexibility of a Religious Order that has been interested in meeting felt needs." During that 26 years the Sisters had been involved in religious education in St. Luke's School for nursery and kindergarten, Vacation Bible School, Confirmation instruction, junior Altar Guild for girls of five to eight years, volunteers in the Greenwich Village Nursing Home, hospital and home visits, Episcopal Church Women, quiet days, sacristy work, and the senior citizens' lunch club. The Sisters would be greatly missed but not forgotten. Writing to CSJB Associates in December 1976, Mother Margaret Helena said: "They were very happy years and we are grateful for them. Our love and work live on in the hearts and work of our Associates in the parish."

Visitors from summer camps came for tours of the convent during July and other Sisters went to help at Vacation Bible Schools in the area. On August 2 the Mendham Vacation Bible School began with more than the expected numbers. Sr. Barbara Jean taught music to all 104 students. And on the same day, August 2, 1976, Lynne Pfitzinger came to stay for a week—the first visit by the future Sr. Mary Lynne. She joined the novices at recreation and next day went to help at the Mendham Vacation Bible School, and a few days later at the VBS at Succasunna, NJ.

A former St. Anna's girl, Iris, had visited the Sisters and asked whether

her granddaughter could be baptized in the convent chapel. Her son, the baby's father, was Sr. Katharine Veronica's godchild. The baptism took place on August 4, 1976, and the baby was named Monique Elizabeth. Fr. Cromey performed the service, which was attended by several Sisters. There were about ten other guests including the four grandparents.

As often happened in the summer months, several Sisters were traveling to see family and friends. Mother Margaret Helena returned from her annual visit to Oregon on August 5. She combined visiting family with meeting the Oregon Associates. About 22 Associates had attended the meeting at Portland on August 4. There had been a Mass celebrated by Bishop Hal R. Gross, Suffragan Bishop of Oregon. He also provided lunch for the group. On Monday August 9, 1976, Sr. Katharine Veronica, Sr. Suzanne Elizabeth and Christine Brodeur had hoped to fly to England to visit the Sisters at Clewer. Despite a hurricane warning, they were assured the flight would leave from JFK airport as planned. Having arrived at the airport, they found the flight was canceled, but after returning to the convent overnight the travelers finally were airborne next day at 11:30am. A telegram from Clewer, sent at 1:50am UK time, gave news that all three had arrived safely. The storm was not severe at Mendham although large branches were broken off several trees. After a stay of just over two weeks the travelers returned on August 31. There was a traffic jam on the way to the airport and car trouble coming home, but finally they reached the convent at 6:15pm.

With all her many years in Community there was not much that Mother Margaret Helena didn't know, especially about past Sisters. But there was one story which had her mystified. She noted in the Community Record Book on August 24, 1976, "Sr. Winifred Agnes in retreat—told me a fantastic tale about wearing out some red things at St. Michael's." This related to Sr. Julia Bernardine, who died on February 16, 1922. Sr. Winifred Agnes was not professed until 1926 so may not have known Sr. Julia Bernardine personally, but many of her contemporaries would have known her. Apparently when she was working at St. Michael's Home, Mamaroneck, Sr. Julia Bernardine fell down the back stairs. When she was rescued she was found to be wearing a silk petticoat and explained that she thought it more in line with poverty to wear it out than to give it up! Her Community Biographer, Mother Florence Teresa, did not specify whether or not the petticoat was red, so maybe the story was "embroidered" over the years.

A highlight of the Fall season of 1976 was the visit of an orchestra from Holy Trinity School, Port-au-Prince, Haiti. They arrived on September 4, "a little before 8:00pm, tired and hungry. They had driven 550 miles. Fifty-five in the group. Very pleased with St. Marguerite's, and everyone with a bed!" The concert took place in the evening of September 5, at Mallinckrodt convent, Mendham, and there were 600 people in the audience. Mother Marjorie Raphael, SSM, and Sr. Anne Marie, SSM, were traveling with the orchestra. Mother Margaret Helena remarked in her Associates' Newsletter for December 1976 that the concert was beautiful.

Next day was Labor Day, a public holiday, and the musicians "spent the entire day playing ball on the lawn and packing their three hundred pieces of luggage in their truck." Mother Marjorie Raphael and Sr. Anne Marie took the opportunity to meet Mother Marjorie Raphael's cousin, Marian Wysong, former teacher at St. John Baptist School.[11] At six o'clock on Tuesday morning the Sisters "waved goodbye with the full moon in the west and the sun rising in the east and the Haitians were on their way to JFK airport and home." In the Weekly Letter to the Sisters Mother Margaret Helena remarked that "the manners and demeanor of all the young people were a witness to the influence of St. Margaret's Sisters in Haiti."

The other momentous event of Fall 1976 was the General Convention, which met at Minneapolis. Sr. Suzanne Elizabeth and Sr. Elizabeth Anne attended the meeting. Sr. Suzanne Elizabeth was sent by the Newark Diocesan Altar Guild to the meeting of the National Altar Guild Association, running concurrently with the General Convention. There were two main items on the agenda: the ordination of women to the priesthood and the adoption of the new, revised *Book of Common Prayer* to replace that of 1928. There had been growing impatience within parts of the Episcopal Church regarding the lack of progress towards ordaining women to the priesthood. On July 29, 1974, three bishops in Philadelphia had ordained eleven women as priests. But their orders were considered "irregular" as they were ordained without the sanction of General Convention. There had been much campaigning in the interim period and on September 23, 1976, the General Convention approved the ordination of women to the priesthood and episcopate. The first ordinations would take place after January 1, 1977. The Orders of the so-called "Philadelphia 11" were also regularized. Also, the new Prayer Book was authorized for use. It was a tumultuous few days and Sr. Suzanne

Elizabeth has remarked that many tears were shed on both issues from all viewpoints.[12]

Although Fr. Cromey had made some improvements at St. John Baptist School there was still concern for its future. It had never had a large intake of students, but with only 40 at the start of the academic year in Fall 1976, the future looked increasingly bleak. It was running at a financial loss and the generous benefactors of previous generations had by now passed to their rest. By the end of 1976 Mother Margaret Helena was able to report to the Associates that they hoped to have 50 students in the New Year. The Board of Trustees had therefore put off making a decision about closing the school. "If we could add another thirty students we would be very near balancing the budget." By the end of October the enrollment had continued to increase and Mother was able to report to the Sisters that "there is a healthy and happy spirit over there."

On October 6, 1976, Sr. Margaret Helena was re-elected Superior for the ensuing three years. This would be her final term of office. She was installed on October 7, and later in the morning Sr. Elizabeth Anne was re-appointed Assistant Superior, Sr. Suzanne Elizabeth Novice Mistress, and Sr. Eleanor Lucy Sister Superior of St. Christopher's House, Jersey City.

Having become independent from Trinity, Wall Street, St. Luke's Chapel had reverted to its earlier name of St. Luke in the Fields, and Fr. Laughlin now became its Rector. He was inducted into office on Monday, October 18, 1976. Mother Margaret Helena attended the service with the Sisters from Jersey City and Sr. Katharine Veronica, as well as Marion Burger and Helen Brelsforth, from the convent. Writing to the Sisters in the Weekly Letter[13] dated October 20, Mother remarked: "The very impressive service lasted over two hours; many 'old timers' were there, as well as Bishop Moore, the Laughlins, [and] the Mortons. Fr. Morton remarked that Jersey City certainly erupted, meaning that the original team and ourselves were there."

"Seminary for a Day," a training event for Church School teachers, had been introduced a few years previously. October 30, 1976, saw an attendance of 60 with six courses on offer, each participant having a choice of three. Amongst the speakers were Bishop Spong and Deacon Martha Blacklock. A week later, a conference on Prayer was held at St. Marguerite's with 36 people attending, including a former student from St. Helen's Hall.

News came from Clewer of the death of two Sisters one month apart from each other. Sr. Agnes Jean died at Clewer on October 25, 1976, the 60th anniversary of her profession. On November 30 (St. Andrew's Day) Sr. Dorothy Maude died at Clewer. Both Sisters were professed together on October 25, 1916, and on January 30, 1926, they both sailed for Barbados to take up the new Community work there. They worked at Barbados for the next 20 years and returned to Clewer on November 7, 1946, when the Community withdrew from the work.

Mother Margaret Helena had always been a supporter of women's ordained ministry, but she was aware that some Associates might be troubled by the decision regarding women priests (and also the new Prayer Book). And there were Sisters at Clewer who were opposed to women's ordination.[14] Thus in her Newsletter to Associates dated December 30, 1976, she attempted to steer a pastoral course. She wrote: "For many reasons this new year seems to be a threshold into something significant and new. Especially this is true of the Church. Someone described the Church as in a 'swirl of controversy.' It is very hard to differentiate fact from fear, theology from emotion, tradition from opportunity. General Convention has left us with all these possibilities and confusion. There are many honest and prayerful people in disagreement with the decisions of General Convention, and many others who disagree with them and feel the way has opened to new dimensions and new life. One thing we see emerging is the individual responsibility of Church members. The Church is not the responsibility of the clergy only, but each of us has a priesthood to share the good news, to be a witnessing member of Christ's kingdom."

Mother Margaret Helena closed her 1976 Newsletter to the Associates with the following words: "With all the stresses and strains of government and Church, life goes on with the daily renewal of Communion and prayer. God calls and promises to be with those He calls—that means every one of His children. Our prayer is that we all may seek and find His presence. He does not promise life without problems or success in our ventures—He promises His presence—our true peace."[15]

As 1977 dawned, many women were eagerly anticipating their ordination to the priesthood. Among them were two CSJB Associates, Deacon Abigail Painter and Deacon Martha Blacklock. Abigail Painter was ordained to the priesthood at St. Paul's Church, Morris Plains, on January 5, 1977, and Mother Margaret Helena preached the sermon. Writing to the Sisters in the Weekly Letter dated January 13, Sr. Elizabeth Marion passed on the following message from Mother: "Whatever one thinks (or feels) about the ordination of women, the service at St. Paul's Church was beautifully planned and carried out. Hundreds attended; there was standing room only. Many old friends were there, and Abby herself was most edifying." Then, expressing her own opinion, Sr. Elizabeth Marion continued: "Mother's sermon was beautiful, applying the Epiphany theme to the occasion; every word could be heard."

In the same Weekly Letter, January 13, Sr. Elizabeth Marion added: "Martha Blacklock's ordination on the 18th will be a different kind of occasion. Instead of a sermon some people who have been in the Workshop on Ministry will state what they think this ministry should be." The ordination took place in St. John Baptist School Chapel and was well attended despite bad weather. Martha Blacklock was a former student at the school and chose for the Epistle "Whatsoever things are true" (Philippians 4:8), which was the school motto. It was read by Mother Margaret Helena, and Martha Blacklock's father read the Gospel.

At the end of February 1977 the Sisters had a visit from a very distinguished guest, Bishop Desmond Tutu. The Weekly Letter gives no details except that all enjoyed his visit very much and that the Sisters "found him a delightful and most friendly guest." At this time he was Bishop of Lesotho and was already well known as an anti-apartheid campaigner.[16]

Sr. Katharine Veronica was about to go to Washington, DC, on March 12, to speak about the Navajo people amongst whom she had worked for two summers several years previously (see Appendix 3). When she returned home to the convent she had much to tell the Sisters. Her hostess in Washington was Jane Traugott, who had been one of a group of people held hostage by a Muslim group from March 9–11. Three buildings had been seized with 149 hostages, many of them Jewish. Two men were killed, including a police officer, and several injured, but the group surrendered after 39 hours and the hostages were freed. Jane Traugott was unharmed. She was able to accompany Sr. Katharine Veronica on a tour of the National Cathedral.

At Clewer, Mother Annys was in poor health. The Sisters at Mendham had invited her to come over for the Superiors' Conference to be held at Peekskill from April 24–28. She had joyfully accepted the invitation and hoped to arrive on April 21 and stay for three weeks. At the end of March she had major surgery but still hoped to be well enough to make the journey. Alas, on April 20 Mother Margaret Helena received news that Mother Annys was unable to come after all.

Lynne Pfitzinger had made several visits to the convent and she was received as a postulant on May 25, 1977. The Sisters came over from Jersey City so all the Community were present. The Warden, Fr. Weed, assisted by the Chaplain, Fr. Templeton, received her before Vespers. Later in the year, on November 7, she was received as a novice, taking the name Mary Lynne.

The Weekly Letter for June 1, 1977, contains a notice of the death of Fr. E. J. Templeton, suddenly, from a heart attack. He had been Chaplain at the convent and school since 1950. His funeral was on June 4, with all the Sisters present as well as Bishop Rath. Bishop Stark did the committal at the graveside.

On December 13, 1977, Sr. Eleanor Lucy (Cowan) had a chill and went to bed but was up and about next day doing mailings for the Grace Church Thrift Sale. By December 16 she was no better and was admitted to Morristown Memorial Hospital, but she passed to her rest early in the morning of December 17. It was a great shock to the Community and to the people of Grace Church, where she had ministered for 25 years. In the midst of it all Mother Margaret Helena was taken ill and admitted to hospital, where she had surgery. She was unable to be at Sr. Eleanor Lucy's funeral on December 21. The Sisters had kept a Watch by the coffin from 9:00am until the funeral Mass began at 11:00am. Bishop Rath officiated and Fr. Weed celebrated. Several other priests were in the sanctuary including Fr. Cromey, Fr. Watters and Fr. Pederson. Bishop Moore and Bishop Spong were in the congregation, as well as 40 other people, including children from Jersey City and members of Sister's family. At 7:30pm there was a memorial service for Sr. Eleanor Lucy at Grace Church and about 50 people were in the congregation.

Mother Margaret Helena, who wrote Sr. Eleanor Lucy's Community Biography, said of her that "she was deeply joyous as a novice, and all through her life as a Sister." Health issues plagued her throughout her Community life but "in all these she survived, overcame and lived a very busy life." Having been educated at the Sorbonne in Paris and at Radcliffe College, she was a superb teacher with a real rapport with the children in her care. Although her great work was at Jersey City, Sr. Eleanor Lucy had also worked at St. Helen's Hall in Oregon and at Corsicana, TX. She was immensely practical, too. Mother Margaret Helena recalled how Sr.

Eleanor Lucy advised the Jersey City Sisters to put on their best habits during the racial riots because if St. Christopher's House was set on fire and the Sisters were saved, the habits would be saved too! "Sister was very much beloved by the people with whom she worked and she loved them." The Sisters received many tributes including one from the Archdeacon for Missions in the Diocese of Newark (the Venerable Sydney Grant). "The Department of Missions unanimously expressed its great love and gratitude for the valuable work that was so compassionately done by Sr. Eleanor Lucy in the program at Grace Church (Van Vorst). We are also aware of her influence in other areas of the Diocese and of the Church." Meanwhile, the Sisters at Grace Church were resolved to continue the work they had been called to do there, which was so close to Sr. Eleanor Lucy's heart and to theirs. Thus all the Advent and Christmas activities which she had planned went ahead as usual. Her death would put a strain on the viability of the Sisters' work there, but for the time being they remained in the newly renovated St. Christopher's House. (There will be more about the work in Jersey City in the next chapter.)

Writing her annual Newsletter to the Associates in Advent 1978, Mother Margaret Helena commented that it had been "a year of change and a kaleidoscope of activity." She had made a good recovery from the surgery at the end of 1977, but the death of Sr. Eleanor Lucy had necessitated some "personnel" changes. Thus Sr. Elizabeth Anne, who had been in Jersey City as Assistant Superior of the Community, now became Sister Superior of the work in Jersey City, and Sr. Katharine Veronica was appointed Assistant Superior at the convent.

On April 26, 1978, Mother, Sr. Elizabeth Marion and Sr. Susinne Paula traveled to England for three weeks. Sr. Elizabeth Marion spent some of the time visiting relatives, but Sr. Susinne Paula spent the whole three weeks at Clewer. The two Mothers went to a Superiors' Conference which lasted a week. This would be Mother Annys' last Superiors' Conference, as she had decided to resign from office after 20 years. After a busy visit the three Sisters returned to Mendham on May 16. Later, on August 10, 1978, Sr. Edna Frances was installed as Mother Superior (Mother General) at Clewer. Mother Annys had been the Superior through tumultuous times. Her two greatest achievements were the re-affiliation between Clewer and Mendham and the restoration of the convent at Clewer.[17]

The summer program began soon after the Sisters' return. One of the three novices was professed in first vows on May 25, though she did not proceed to final vows. Meanwhile, there was much preparation for the Vacation Bible Schools. Sr. Barbara Jean and Sr. Katharine Veronica taught at St. Mark's, Mendham, and Sr. Barbara Jean and Sr. Mary Lynne taught at Christ Church, Middletown, NJ. This was Sr. Mary Lynne's first experience of teaching in a Vacation Bible School, and as it was thought there would be only five or six in the pre-school class, she was not given a helper. To everyone's surprise 28 small children arrived on the first day! Next day she was given a helper.

Writing of Grace Church (Van Vorst), Mother Margaret Helena described it as "always a place of joy and hard work." The renovations at St. Christopher's House were completed and the Sisters held an "open house" during the first week of May. There was also a new van which provided much-needed, reliable transport. The summer program at Grace Church was one of the best in recent years, with 100 children sent to camp and 150 children enrolled for the church activities.

Commemoration Day 1978 was celebrated on Sunday June 25, with Vespers, an address by Bishop Rath, the reception of 12 Associates, and supper on the cloister. At Portland, Oregon, there was a day for Associates on August 15. The Mass, which was attended by 29, was celebrated by Bishop Gross, and 26 stayed for luncheon. Although Bishop Gross was retiring, Mother Margaret Helena expressed the hope that he would continue to care for the Portland Associates.

Meanwhile, St. John Baptist School "seems to be recovering its past excellence." Fifty-eight students were enrolled at the opening of the academic year and the boarding department was full. It was hoped that some more day students would enroll. "Best of all," wrote Mother "we have students interested in study, as well as some outstanding athletes. Sr. Barbara Jean and Sr. Laura Katharine work at the school but live at the convent. They have time for their 'Prayer time' before they go, and nearly always, are able to return for Vespers."

St. Marguerite's continued to have a full schedule of conferences and retreats with an average of about 2,000 guests each year. In September 1978 the Conference for Major Superiors of the American and Canadian Religious Orders took place at St. Marguerite's. Twenty-seven Superiors, all of whom were Anglican, attended. The Presiding Bishop, the Most Revd. John Allin, came one evening for dinner and addressed the conference. Five Bishop Visitors also attended one afternoon and discussed the role of a Bishop Visitor, and what they expected of Religious.

Sr. Margaret Raphael (Smith) died on September 2, 1978, after an illness of only three hours. Since her restoration to Community in 1967 she had made every effort to be a helpful member of CSJB. She had worked in Jersey City for a year and was very happy there. But she became increasingly frail and came back to the convent. After the usual funeral rites she was buried in the convent cemetery.

The latter part of 1978 was full of resignations and retirements. Fr. Paul Weed, Warden of the Community since 1947, announced his retirement, but was received as an Associate, so his connection with the Community would continue but on a different level. "He has been the faithful, wise and prudent shepherd for whom we are most grateful," wrote Mother. Another old friend of the Community, Fr. Paul Wessinger, SSJE, was elected as Warden and installed by Bishop Rath on October 28. He had first encountered the Sisters in Portland, Oregon, as a teenager when he was invited to the girls' prom there. By the time he became Warden he was the Superior of the American Congregation of SSJE, and, having lived in England, knew the Sisters at Clewer. The Sisters at Mendham had known Fr. Wessinger since his first visit to the convent in July 1945 when he had recently made his life profession in SSJE and had just been ordained to the priesthood.[18]

Bishop Rath was retiring as of January 1, 1979. "He too has been a good friend and faithful pastor and we are grateful for his ready help and good will," wrote Mother Margaret Helena. He would be succeeded as diocesan bishop by Bishop John Shelby Spong who had indicated his willingness to accept the office of Visitor and would make his first Visitation in February 1979.

Mother Margaret Helena concluded her Associates' Newsletter at the end of 1978 with the words "With all the 'chances and changes' of our life, the Divine Office, the daily Eucharist and the Sisters' life of prayer have been the constant, and is the true meaning of our lives. We are ever conscious of the support and strength pouring in from our Associates and friends prayers and service, and we are most grateful."

Saturday January 13, 1979, saw the installation in Newark Cathedral of the Rt. Revd. John Shelby Spong as Diocesan Bishop. The Sisters attended and walked in the procession. For the presentation of symbols they brought an illuminated manuscript written by a Sister, and the Rule and Constitution of the Community. As Visitor of the Community the bishop would be the guardian of the Rule and Constitution. In her

Weekly Letter to the Sisters on January 17, Mother Margaret Helena noted that "the celebrations of Bishop Spong's 'New Ministry' are now at Convocation level, and ours will be tomorrow at St. Peter's Church in Morristown. The television and newspaper coverage of all these services has been very good." The following week (January 24), she was able to report that "the celebration last Thursday of a New Ministry, for the Convocation of Morris, was a beautiful service. St. Peter's Church was full. We walked in the procession with one of the 'symbols'; our gift was the New English Bible from Morris Convocation." On February 6, the bishop came for his first Visitation, staying overnight to learn about the life of the Community. Meanwhile it snowed heavily but did not prevent the Jersey City Sisters from coming over. But it did prevent the school students from returning from a long weekend.

The ministry of hospitality continued to go from strength to strength and a large attendance was expected for a day for the clergy to be led by the Revd. Dr. Morton Kelsey.[19] About 50 clergy registered for the day, which took place on February 23. The main chapel was used and lunch was served in the convent.

Five Sisters attended the installation of the Revd. Edgar Fisher Wells as Rector of St. Mary the Virgin, New York City, on February 18, 1979. Mother reported that it was a glorious service with Bishop Moore and six priests concelebrating the Mass.

Fr. Coleman, the Warden General, came from Clewer for a visit on March 1, accompanied by the Warden, Fr. Wessinger, who had been visiting the UK. While at Mendham, Fr. Coleman conducted the Sisters' retreat. This would be Fr. Coleman's final visit as Warden General, having resigned at around this time. At Clewer, the Sisters unanimously elected Fr. Austin Masters, SSM, as Warden and he was installed on September 21.

Holy Week and Easter 1979 were celebrated in the usual way, with one exception. The Palm Sunday service was shared with the school students, using the main chapel. The procession started in the cloister with the blessing of the palms. On Easter morning the Sisters telephoned the English Sisters, and spoke to Mother Edna Frances, Sr. Annys and Sr. Monica. Mother Margaret Helena described it as "a joy." It was the start of a tradition still observed in the 21st century. A tradition was revived when a few days later, on April 25, Sr. Mary Lynne arrived at Heathrow airport for a month-long novice visit at Clewer. She was the first American novice to do so for many years. Before the original affiliation, novices would spend several months or even a year at Clewer. On May 3, Mother Margaret Helena was able to report to the Sisters that "Sr. Mary Lynne writes very happily about her experiences in England. Sr. Monica and Christine met her at the airport. One day she and Christine walked to Windsor to explore the 'Queen's Doll House'; then they had tea, went to Evensong in St. George's Chapel and walked home again. Sr. Monica has taught Mary Lynne how to lead the Choir procession after dinner and None." She arrived home at the convent on Friday, May 25.

Meanwhile, Mother and Sr. Suzanne Elizabeth traveled to Toronto for the triennial meeting of the Conference on the Religious Life. They returned on May 2 and reported that it was a much larger Conference than ever before. A number of guests from new or experimental Communities were there as well as the older established ones.

St. John Baptist School was very active at this time. The seniors went to dinner and their annual tour of the convent on May 9, and on May 15, the 7th and 8th grade students entertained the Sisters at a formal tea. This was organized by Sr. Laura Katharine "and was beautiful—pretty girls in pretty dresses and with pretty manners!" Even so, Sr. Barbara Jean overheard one girl remark to her friend that the manners went with the dress and she was going to take them off! The Latin classes had set up a Roman Forum in preparation for their imaginary trip to Pompeii in AD79, complete with visual aids such as maps, graffiti, a model villa and scrolls of Pliny's letters. After all the activity, the Commencement service took place on June 2 in the school chapel and this went well.

Commemoration Day 1979 took place again on a Sunday (June 24) which was also the Birth of St. John Baptist. Once more there was a fuel shortage[20] but a good number came to the convent to join the celebrations. The main chapel was full and extra chairs had to be brought in. Bishop Spong preached about the ministry of St. John Baptist and the Community's choice of its patron saint. Fourteen new Associates were received, and eight others had been received since the previous June. It was a chilly, overcast day so supper was served indoors.

Summer passed in the usual way with well-attended Vacation Bible Schools, summer camps from Jersey City, and afterwards, the Sisters' summer rests. During the last week of August the Sisters embarked on a new project—The Search Program. Although they still had novices and Sisters in first vows, numbers in the Community were falling rapidly as older Sisters passed to their rest. In recent years the Sisters had worked hard to make the Religious Life known by going out to address parish groups and others about their way of life. Audiences were appreciative but the number coming forward was minimal. It was not simply a CSJB problem—all Communities were facing the same challenges, and now that women could be ordained, the priesthood offered another, alternative choice of vocation. The Search Program[21] invited participants to gain a closer insight into the Religious Life by coming to the convent and learning in situ. It had been advertised in *The Living Church* so that a wide readership would know about it. The small group of searchers were very appreciative and returned to their homes with much food for thought and prayer.

An era lasting thirty years came to an end on Wednesday October 3, 1979, when Mother Margaret Helena wrote in her Weekly Letter: "All the Sisters were here for the Chapter; the Jersey City Sisters will stay through Thursday for the Superior's installation." Mother Margaret Helena was standing down from her long-held office as Mother Superior and Sr. Elizabeth Anne was elected in her place. Bishop Spong, the Visitor, presided over the Election Chapter because Fr. Wessinger could not get out of Boston due to the crowds there to welcome Pope John Paul II. The Installation was next day, October 4, and was an impressive and inspiring service. The Mass readings and music were those of the Feast of St. John Baptist but the Visitor preached on the election of Matthias. The Warden, Fr. Wessinger, was by now able to get away from Boston and he celebrated the Mass. About 25 close friends and Associates were present as well as the newly appointed vicar of Grace Church (Van Vorst), the Revd. Elisha John Gwynn. The Sisters in England sent a telegram and there were many other warm messages. Later the same morning Sr. Katharine Veronica was appointed Assistant Superior, Sr. Margaret Helena Novice Mistress and Bursaress, and Sr. Suzanne Elizabeth Sister Superior of St. Christopher's House, Jersey City. In addition, the Warden appointed Fr. Thomas Cure, SSJE, as Sub-Warden.

An undated and unattributed newspaper cutting with the headline "Sister Elizabeth Anne elected" gives details of the Community work. When the reporter (Rose B. Stewart) asked what the Community did, Mother Elizabeth Anne quoted Mother Annys. "We are primarily a group of praying women who were called together by God. From our prayer springs our work for God but it springs from our prayer and is not instead of prayer."

On October 22, Mother Edna Frances and Sr. Gina arrived from Clewer. Sr. Annys was not well enough to come, having had more surgery recently. They were met at JFK airport by Mother Elizabeth Anne, Sr. Margaret Helena and Sr. Mary Lynne. Following their arrival at the convent there was "a joyful reunion in the cloister." On October 24, Sr. Mary Lynne began her profession retreat and on All Saints' Day (November 1) she was professed in first vows. Mother Elizabeth Anne gave an account in her Weekly Letter of November 7, 1979. It was "a glorious occasion. The School girls came, and many Associates and friends, including Sister's family and several members of her parish, All Saints', Princeton, NJ. The Rector, Fr. Schwartzentruber, and her former minister Dr. Fearon, participated in the service. Bishop Spong received her vows, and Fr. Cure the Sub-Warden celebrated the Eucharist. It was a joy to have the Mother General and Sr. Gina here for the profession … When they leave for England on Sunday evening, Sr. Margaret Helena will be going with them for a visit at Clewer until December 19."

On December 5, Mother Elizabeth Anne reported to the Sisters: "We have had word from Clewer that the Sisters celebrated Thanksgiving Day (for the first time on English soil?) with turkey and trimmings—another reverberation of the Sisters' visit here! And Sr. Margaret Helena writes that she is 'living the life of Reilly'!"

Fr. Gwynn was installed at Grace Church (Van Vorst) on December 16, and some of the Sisters went to the service. On December 19, Sr. Margaret Helena arrived home in the middle of a snowstorm. The Christmas festival was kept in the familiar way with Sisters and some friends and guests.

Thus CSJB passed from one decade into another. There had been many challenges and changes but the Sisters had remained faithful to their calling and would go ahead into the future trusting that all would be well.

[1] Mother Harriet Monsell, Foundress of CSJB with the Revd. T. T. Carter, died on March 25, 1883. As well as being the Feast of the Annunciation to the Blessed Virgin Mary, it was also Easter Sunday. Harriet Monsell is celebrated in the Church of England *Common Worship* Calendar on March 26.

[2] Sr. Waldine Lucia had outlived Sr. (formerly Mother) Dorothy Frances at Clewer by just a few months, Sr. Dorothy Frances having died in April 1974.

[3] See BONHAM, Valerie *Living Stones* Chapter 16

[4] This also enabled the part of the convent building formerly used for the St. Anna's girls to be adapted as guest accommodation. The closure of St. Marguerite's home school enabled it to be used to accommodate the Sisters during the decade that the convent was closed, and later to be adapted as a retreat house.

[5] Fr. Edwin Cromey graduated from General Theological Seminary, NYC, in 1962. Before his appointment to St. John Baptist School, Mendham, he held several posts as headmaster or administrator in schools in Long Island and Jersey City, his last being Principal Administrator of Lutheran Parochial Schools in Jersey City.

[6] There will be more about this in the next chapter.

[7] St. Elizabeth Ann Seton (1774–1821) was the first American-born person to be canonized by the Catholic Church. She was canonized by Pope Paul VI on September 14, 1975.

[8] Mother Superior's Weekly Letter to the Community, December 5, 1975.

[9] St. Mark's was a mission church of the Diocese of Newark for many years. On December 7, 1956, under the leadership of Fr. Elwood Boggess, St. Mark's achieved parish church status within the diocese. In 1963 Fr. Philip S. Watters became vicar of St. Mark's and in 1975 began improvements to the building.

[10] Transcendental Meditation, or TM, was/is a meditation technique first developed in 1965 by the Indian guru Maharishi Mahesh Yogi. It became very popular in the 1960s and '70s, especially in the UK and USA, after the Maharishi was visited by the English pop group The Beatles. I remember on one of my early visits to Clewer, soon after moving into the parish in 1975, Sr. Eudora telling me that the Sisters at Clewer were "doing TM." I looked quite blankly at her, never having heard of TM until that day. She was not impressed at my ignorance!

[11] Mother Marjorie Raphael, SSM (Marjorie Wysong), was a former student at St. John Baptist School, and some of her school memories are in BONHAM Valerie *Living Stones* Chapter 19. The Society of St. Margaret still has a branch house at Port-au-Prince, Haiti. It was destroyed in the earthquake in 2010 but the Sisters remain there working amongst the many poor and homeless.

[12] Conversation with Valerie Bonham during one of my research visits to the convent.

[13] The Community Record Books stop abruptly in mid-September 1976. The Weekly Letters were written by a Sister on the instructions of the Mother Superior.

[14] In the Church of England women were not ordained as deacons until 1988. General Synod did not authorize women priests until November 1992, and the first ordinations followed in April 1994. But General Synod did not authorize women bishops until November 2014, and the first woman bishop was consecrated in January 2015.

[15] This is reminiscent of Julian of Norwich: "He did not say you will not be tempted; you will not be troubled; you will not be distressed; but He said you will not be overcome." *Revelations of Divine Love* Chapter 68.

[16] Bishop Tutu became Bishop of Johannesburg 1985–86, and Archbishop of Cape Town 1986–94. After retiring from office he chaired the Truth and Reconciliation Commission 1996–98 in post-apartheid South Africa, and has continued to embrace issues of social justice.

[17] Even though the UK Sisters eventually left Clewer because of reduced numbers, the restoration initiated by Mother Dorothy Frances, and continued by Mother Annys, made it possible for the Sisters to remain there for another 25 years.

[18] See Chapter 2 and endnote iv.

[19] The Revd. Dr. Morton Kelsey (1917–2001) was an Episcopal priest, Jungian therapist, counselor and religious writer.

[20] The fuel shortage in 1979 was due to decreased oil output in the wake of the Iranian Revolution. Widespread panic resulted in driving oil prices sky high. The situation would worsen in 1980 following the outbreak of the Iran–Iraq War when oil production in Iran almost stopped and Iraq's oil output was severely curtailed. Economic recessions were triggered in the US and other countries.

[21] The Search Program still continues twice a year at the time of writing (2019).

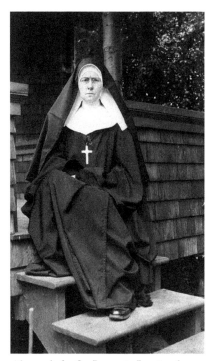

Above left: *Sr. Jeannette Louise, former mission Sister, in her habit as a choir Sister, 1940*

Above right: *Sr. Florence Teresa, Mother Superior 1915–42*

Below left: *Sr. Alice Ursula, Superior 1942*

Below right: *Sr. Waldine Lucia, Superior 1943–49. Photographed later in life*

Above: *St. John Baptist Church, Corsicana, TX*
Below left: *Sr. Margaret Helena, Superior 1949–79*
Below right: *Sr. Adela*

St. John Baptist House, Corsicana, TX

St. John Baptist School students, 1940
Back row: M. Wilson, G. Handy, M. Wysong, L. Roberts, F. Shaffer
Front row: E. Snedaker, E. Wilson, L. Livingston, C. King

St. John Baptist School students, 1940s

Above: *Aerial view of St. Marguerite's and convent, 1940s/50s. Note the flat roof over the convent chapel*

Below: *Cornerstone of St. John Baptist School, now lost*

Above: *St. John Baptist School students in their old Chapel, late 1940s. The altar is now in St. Mark's Episcopal Church, Mendham*

Below left: *Sr. Elizabeth Marion*

Below right: *Sr. Eleanor Lucy*

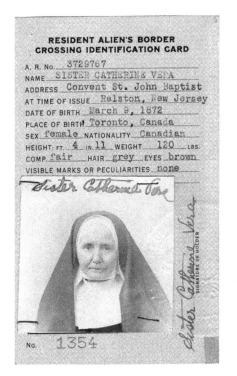

Above left: *Sr. Catherine Vera*

Above right: *Sr. Mildred Eleanor, December 1964*

Below left: *Sr. Agatha Louise*

Below right: *Sr. Jane Patricia*

Above left: *Sr. Mary Barbara*   Above right: *Sr. Julia Frances*

Below: *Solemn High Mass at Mendham on June 28, 1952, to celebrate the founding of CSJB in 1852 at Clewer, UK*

The convent chapel in ruinous condition, late 1950s, before restoration

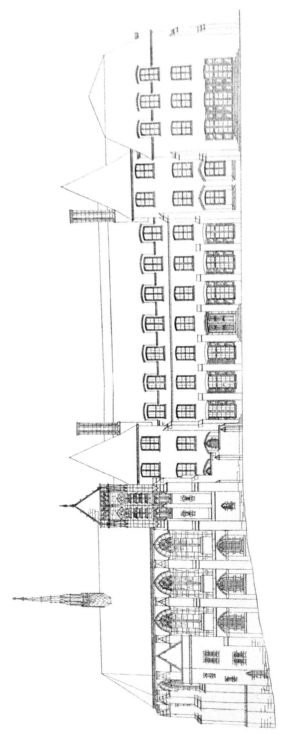

FRONT ELEVATION

William Cordingley's proposed chapel on left, for St. John Baptist School. Note the difference in the proposed school from the one which was built. Cordingley's proposed chapel was not built.

Above: *Children at Grace Church,
Jersey City, with Sr. Agatha Louise*

Left: *Children at Jersey City with Sr.
Elizabeth Anne*

Sr. Julia Frances's 60th anniversary of Profession, May 23, 1959

Left to right: Mother Margaret Helena, Sr. Francina, Sr. Waldine Lucia, Sr. Ora Mary, Sr. Agatha Louise, Sr. Elizabeth Marion, Sr. Julia Frances, Sr. Katharine Veronica, Sr. Mary Joan, Sr. Ellen Juliana, Sr. Agnes Genevieve, Sr. Mildred Eleanor, Sr. Susinne Paula

Group of Sisters, December 1963
Left to right: Sr. Mary Joan, Sr. Agatha Louise, Sr. Ellen Juliana, Mother Margaret Helena, Sr. Waldine Lucia

Ground-breaking ceremony for St. John Baptist School Chapel, October 16, 1964, with Mother Margaret Helena and Sr. Mary Barbara

Lowering the spire on the new chapel at St. John Baptist School, 1965

Left: *St. John Baptist School students in the tower of the new chapel*

Below: *Sister and students in the new chapel at St. John Baptist School*

Above: *Sr. Agnes Genevieve, Sr. Katharine Veronica, and Sr. Winifred Agnes outside St. John Baptist House, 90 Barrow Street, NYC, 1964*

Below: *St. Luke's School, NYC, with Sr. Agnes Genevieve, Sr. Katharine Veronica, and Fr. Weed*

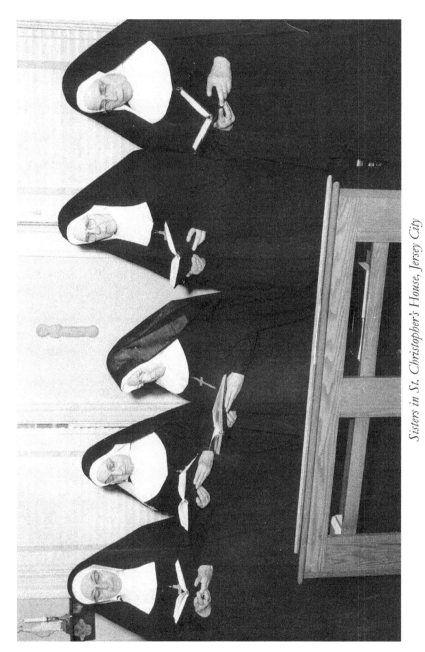

Sisters in St. Christopher's House, Jersey City

Mother Margaret Helena, Sr. Agnes Genevieve, Sr. Waldine Lucia, Sr. Winifred Agnes, Sr. Katharine Veronica

Above left: *Sr. Katharine Veronica at St. John Baptist House, 90 Barrow Street, NYC*

Above right: *Sr., formerly Mother General, Dorothy Frances on right. Photographed at Clewer, UK, by Sr. Barbara Jean in 1973*

Below: *Sr. Laura Katharine on left, Sr. Barbara Jean on right, and members of other Communities, with guitars, 1968*

Builders fixing the Cross on the new pitched roof of the main Chapel at the convent, 1973.

Above left: *Sr. Mary Lynne, 1979*
Above right: *Sr. Susinne Paula, 1985*
Below left: *Sr. Suzanne Elizabeth, Superior 1983–97*
Below right: *Sr. Elizabeth Anne, Superior 1979–82*

July 1985. Mother Suzanne Elizabeth (seated center) with some of the English Sisters at Clewer

Left to right: Sr. Gina, Sr. Elizabeth Jane, Sr. Pamela, Sr. Moira, a Sister of the Community of the Reparation to Jesus in the Blessed Sacrament, Sr. Beatrice Kitchener, Society of St. John the Forerunner, Sr. Esther Mary, CRJBS, Sr. Letitia, Sr. Eudora, Sr. (formerly Mother) Annys, Sr. Sheila. Seated in front: Mother Edna Frances, Sr. Zoë, Sr. Mary Theresa

Sr. Barbara Jean's ordination as deacon, Trenton Cathedral, PA, June 10, 1989

Above left: *Sr. Barbara Jean at the time of her ordination as a priest, February 1994*
Above right: *Sr. Barbara Jean, Superior 1997–2009*
Below: *Sr. Margo Elizabeth welcoming Pony*

Above: *Sr. Margaret Helena and Pony*
Below: *Sr. Linda Clare at work in the Garden of Hope*

At the old St. John Baptist House, 233, E. 17th St., Manhattan, NYC, November 1984, marking the 100th anniversary of the founding of the Order of the Holy Cross. Left to right: Sr. Katharine Veronica, Sr. Laura Katharine, Sr. Mary Lynne, Sr. Susinne Paula, Sr. Barbara Jean, Mother Suzanne Elizabeth

Above: *Sr. Pamela and Sr. Linda Clare in the Garden of Hope*

Below: *Sr. Margaret Helena and Sr. Mary Lynne at the Oregon Episcopal School (formerly St. Helen's Hall) for the 125th anniversary of its foundation, 1993*

Opposite top: *Restoration of the convent roof and chimneys, 2010*

Opposite bottom: *Sr. Monica Clare signing the Register of Superiors after her installation, December 11, 2019, in the presence of the Rt. Revd. Allen Shin, Visitor to the Community*

Sr. Eleanor Francis at the time of her ordination as a priest, December 13, 2008, with Sr. Barbara Jean and the Rt. Revd. Mark Beckwith, Bishop of Newark

Sr. Eleanor Francis, Superior 2010–19

Above left: *Sr. Mary Lynne meeting Sr. Jane Mankaa at Newark airport in 2012*

Above right: *Sr. Lura Grace*

Below left: *Sr. Laura Katharine with Jennie*

Below right: *Sr. Laura Katharine and Sr. Deborah Francis at the Church of St. Mary the Virgin, NYC*

Above: *Sr. Deborah Francis handing out soup kitchen vouchers in NYC*
Below: *The Cornerstone of the convent*

Above left: *Sr. Margo Elizabeth leaving for a Celtic Journey, 2015*

Above right: *Sr. Mary Lynne and Sr. Jane Mankaa in Cameroon*

Below left: *Sr. Victoria Michelle*

Below right: *Sr. Pamela and Sr. Monica Clare at the first CSJB golf outing,*
         April 27, 2015

Above: *Sr. Eleanor Francis, Sr. Pamela, and Sr. Monica Clare with the Rt. Revd. Carlye Hughes, Bishop of Newark*

Below: *Sr. Pamela, Sr. Suzanne Elizabeth, Sr. Eleanor Francis, and Sr. Barbara Jean*

Sr. Linda Clare, Commemoration Day 2016

Sr. Suzanne Elizabeth at the book launch for Living Stones, *January 2017* (above left), *enjoying the CSJB golf outing, 2018* (above right), *and celebrating the 50th anniversary of her Life Profession, May 26, 2019* (below)

Above: *Sr. Barbara Jean celebrating Palm Sunday Eucharist, 2018*

Below left: *Sr. Barbara Jean celebrating the 50th anniversary of her Life Profession, March 31, 2020*

Below right: *Sr. Laura Katharine celebrating the 50th anniversary of her Life Profession, September 8, 2020*

Sr. Victoria Michelle outside the Church of the Messiah, Chester, NJ

A COMPLICATION OF CIRCUMSTANCES

The Final Decade in Jersey City

THE NEW DECADE—the 1970s—dawned at Grace Church (Van Vorst) with all the usual activities around the Epiphany season despite the bad weather. On the feast day itself, the Sisters had an early Mass in their chapel at St. Christopher's House and in the evening there was Mass in church for the Spanish-speaking neighborhood. This was followed by a Walt Disney movie, "Run, Appaloosa, Run," attended by 150 children. The same day, Fr. Albert brought home a new blue Ford station wagon. It had cost 1,500 books of trading stamps plus $1,000 borrowed from church funds until the last 500 books were collected. A few days later he brought back a new bus.

January 11, 1970, was the day of the pageant and it was seen by 150 people, including 25 from St. Matthew's Church, Paramus, NJ, brought there by their parish priest Fr. Hobbs. Afterwards the whole congregation had lunch in the parish hall, consisting of hot dogs, sandwiches, cookies and peppermint sticks.

On a more serious note, another tenement fire had made a number of people homeless. A mother with four children and a family of six were temporarily housed at St. Christopher's. There were several more fires over the next few weeks, with the Sisters always helping by giving shelter to those rendered homeless.

January 27, 1970, was an important day both at the convent and at Grace Church. The Sisters returned to the convent for the Chapter of election for Sr. Barbara Jean, who was duly elected for final vows. Later that day, Sr. Eleanor Lucy and Sr. Elizabeth Anne spoke about the work recently taken up at Christ Church, Elizabeth, NJ. Back in Jersey City, at 12:00 noon, Anne Albert was commissioned in the Church Army. On February 1, after the bi-lingual Mass, there was a reception in Anne Albert's honor at which she made a speech. Fr. Albert continued to be erratic in his time keeping, not appearing at church at all on February 2 (the Feast of the Purification of the BVM), and arriving 40 minutes late to Mass on February 13, having been at a meeting with Bishop Rath.

On March 31, 1970 (Tuesday in Easter Week), Sr. Barbara Jean made her final vows at the convent during the Choral Mass, Bishop Stark receiving her vows.

On May 8, 1970, the Rt. Revd. Paul Moore was installed as Suffragan Bishop of New York and the three Sisters from Grace Church, together with the New York Sisters, went to the service at the Cathedral of St. John the Divine. Fr. Albert and Fr. Laughlin represented the Diocese of Newark and the Sisters walked in the procession.

Jersey City saw further rioting in June following alleged police brutality towards a Puerto Rican man. The trouble began on June 10 and lasted until the 14th. Some of the Sisters were at the convent for the long retreat but Sr. Katharine Veronica was at St. Christopher's. The worst night was June 12, when the Jersey City Record Book noted: "Riots in this area 11:00pm–2:30am. Molotov Cocktails thrown, windows broken all around, fire engines … Fr. Albert hit by a stone." Even so, parish and Community life went on—the Sisters returned from their retreat; a baby was baptized; there was a Pew Rally followed by a reception; and Fr. Albert went to New Salem, MA. At St. Martin's House (next to St. Christopher's and owned by the parish), painting and decorating was about to be carried out, and then the painter didn't come! The work was eventually completed early in July, including painting in the church.

Meanwhile all the usual summer activities took place, such as Vacation Bible School in various locations, and sending the children off to summer camp. The fact that the wheels all ran so smoothly is down to the hard work of the Sisters and their secular helpers. Sr. Eleanor Lucy wrote in her annual report: "This year for the first time during our own Vacation Church School we had a regular session from 9:00 to 11:30 and then left on the bus for trips returning around 5:00pm. The children loved it and expected there would be a trip every Saturday in the winter." She continued: "About 130 children went to camp. The children at Elko Lake had three weeks each instead of two." The total enrollment at Saturday Church School had been 170, and the number of children who had attended church was 166.

Sr. Eleanor Lucy gave an insight into the hard work of their supporters. "St. Teresa's Guild and St. Monica's Guild still carry on the Clothes Room, especially Mrs. Bober who has given hours of time to it for years assisted by very loyal friends. Mrs. Flores has opened it once a week and Mrs. Maria Colon has opened it frequently as well as one of the ladies on the block.

If we could open it regularly it would be a real source of support for the Church." Concluding, she wrote: "The Sisters have been involved in most of the parish happenings. It has been a tremendously busy year, but we think you all know how much the Community cares for the work here."

On August 14 the *Jersey Journal* published an illustrated article on the summer program under the headline *Grace Church has Recipe for Joy*. "Put 60 kids, a stack of paper, pots of paint, scissors and glue in a room. Add a handful of tender loving care. Mix well for two weeks. Yield: five dozen well rounded, happy youngsters … The two-week session filled with arts and crafts, country bus rides, songfests and film reels of Bible stories … and the tender loving care of the priests, nuns and summer staffers is more than enough to go around." The long report told of the efforts to replace the old bus, and of the summer camp program. The reporter was clearly impressed by what she saw and heard and finished her article with the words: "Are all these good intentions paying off? Ask the children. It's summed up by one smiling little boy who says, 'Do I like it? I love it!'"[1]

Fall 1970 saw two important events for the Community. On September 8 Sr. Laura Katharine made her final vows before Bishop Stark. And then on October 1 all returned to the convent for the Chapter for the election of the Mother Superior. Unsurprisingly, Sr. Margaret Helena was re-elected and re-installed the following day. This was followed by the appointment of Sr. Elizabeth Anne as Assistant Superior, and other office holders including Sr. Eleanor Lucy as Superior at St. Christopher's House, Jersey City. Afterwards, Sr. Eleanor Lucy, Sr. Susinne Paula and Sr. Elizabeth Anne returned to Jersey City. Next day, Sr. Laura Katharine went there to stay permanently as second worker, replacing Sr. Elizabeth Anne.

More temporary refugees were taken in during October when a fire escape on one of the tenements collapsed. And there was so much vandalism and petty crime in the area that the Sisters were advised to get a dog. Thus on October 28, 1970, the 18th anniversary of the blessing of St. Christopher's House, the Sisters went to the pound with Fr. Albert and came back with "Judy." They made a donation of $5 for her.

On November 3, the Sisters went to the convent for a Consultative Council meeting followed by a birthday party for Mother and others who were having anniversaries. Upon their return to St. Christopher's next day they found the basement had been broken into, the clothing room opened, and tools including a drill and sander had been stolen. Such petty crime, as well as being disturbing for the Sisters, was a great inconvenience because the clothes were used to help the needy. Thus when there was a disastrous fire nearby on November 28, and 47 families were burned out of their homes, the Sisters gave them refuge and helped with food and clothing. Such was the seriousness of the fire that it received extensive coverage in the *Hudson Dispatch* for November 30. The fire started in a shed on First Street belonging to a printing firm and quickly spread, causing much damage. "Later [the victims] were taken to Grace Church (Van Vorst) Episcopal Church … They were given food, blankets and toilet facilities, while the babies were given hot milk."

A few days earlier, on November 25, 1970, *The Jersey Journal* had reported that "interior demolition will begin on the first of six buildings to be renovated in the downtown section of Jersey City, a spokesman for Grace Church (Van Vorst), the project sponsor, said today." One of Fr. Albert's great interests was in housing and this project was his brainchild. The report continued: "When the project is completed 44 apartments will be completely refurbished … The entire project is expected to be completed within seven months." The contractors intended to hire up to ten unemployed men from the neighborhood to work on the project.

The year drew to a close with all the usual parties, and the Sisters returned to the convent on Christmas afternoon. As always it was a brief overnight visit and then back to New York and Jersey City next day. Parties and the 1971 Epiphany pageant all went ahead in spite of the church furnace flooding, which meant no hot water in the rectory and no heating in the church or parish hall. The children's Epiphany party was held in the parish hall of St. Boniface RC Church with about 250 present. The Sisters had just four party bags left over at the end! This was followed on January 10 by the pageant, which the Jersey City Record Book reported "was largely Spanish speaking." St. Martin's House, next to St. Christopher's, was the venue for another Epiphany party attended by 32 women, 14 children and 12 men. The Sisters noted in the Record Book that it was very crowded and there was racial tension between "the Puerto Ricans and the negroes [sic]."

The Sisters continued to go outside the parish to talk about the work in Jersey City, which was becoming well known as an example of how a dedicated team of clergy, Sisters and lay workers could turn around a seemingly impossible situation of racial tension, poverty and disillusionment. There was, of course, no magic formula—just sheer hard work and continuous prayer. And while the Sisters might be primarily identified as the people who prayed, they also did a great deal of the hard work. Nor was it easy. There are frequent entries in the Jersey City Record Book about bad behavior at Saturday Church School, but they never gave up on those children.

As noted in Chapter 11, discussions were being held on both sides of the Atlantic regarding re-affiliation with Clewer. The Sisters at New York and Jersey City were fully involved with this. In April Sr. Eleanor Lucy and Sr. Suzanne Elizabeth made the journey to Clewer, arriving back home on May 4. Holy Week services proceeded as usual but at 3:30pm on Good Friday (April 9), Fr. Albert and others marched to the Margaret Hague Maternity Hospital where they held a service on the steps to protest about its planned closure. The Sisters were not involved and he was back in time for a service in church at 7:30pm.[2]

On May 23 there was a thanksgiving service at St. Luke's Chapel, NYC, to mark Fr. Weed's forthcoming retirement in the Fall. This was attended by the Sisters from Jersey City and from St. Luke's and everyone stayed to the luncheon afterwards. It was followed by a strawberry festival, which was enjoyed by all. But it was not the end of his long association with the Sisters as he would continue as their Warden after leaving the parish.

The first of the renovated buildings, 564–568 Jersey Avenue, was now ready for habitation. But the Sisters noted in their Record Book on June 28 that "we had a bad time on account of the delay over moving people into 564–568. The apartment was not ready and we had a battle with cockroaches."[3] Publicity regarding Fr. Albert's endeavors on behalf of impoverished families continued with an article in *The Jersey Journal* of September 30, 1971, under the headline *"Church helps family of 11 to buy a home of their own."*

Summer activities went ahead as usual followed by the Sisters' return to the convent for their break at the end of August. Upon their return for the Fall season the station wagon was stolen. The police soon found it, minus spare tire and battery. On a more cheerful note, Fr. Arthur Pederson joined the staff at Grace Church on October 1, 1971, and began by celebrating Mass. He took up residence in the apartment at St. Christopher's House, and over the next few years would be a great help and support to the Sisters.

On October 29 the first of the renovated houses was blessed at 5:45pm (see note iii below). Archdeacon Grant represented the Diocese of Newark. This was followed at 7:30 by dinner at the Plaza which was attended by the Sisters, including Sr. Elizabeth Anne, who had come from the convent. The work with the housing had by this time been consolidated as the Grace Church Rehabilitation Foundation, the President of which was Fr. Albert, and Fr. Pederson was listed as Assistant Rector and Counselor. The Sisters were listed as staff members, and many of the lay members of the church were listed as members of the Board.[4]

There had been growing co-operation between Grace Church and St. Matthew's Church, Jersey City, and this continued during 1972 with joint Church School sessions. On January 24 the Trinity Institute began with a Mass at the Lincoln Center. Organized and sponsored by Trinity, Wall Street, the aim was to equip clergy and lay people for leadership roles in the Church.[5] Sr. Laura Katharine and Sr. Eleanor Lucy attended the sessions from January 24–26, 1972. Fr. Albert attended the institution of Fr. Parks at Trinity Church, Wall Street, NYC, on the 26th, but first took the two Sisters to meet the Archbishop of Canterbury, the Most Revd. Michael Ramsey. They were photographed with the Archbishop.

On April 24 the Sisters attended a service at the Armenian Cathedral, NYC, to commemorate the victims of the Armenian massacre in 1915.[6]

May 21, 1972, was the 125th anniversary of Grace Church's incorporation as a parish. There was a special service at 4:00pm at which Bishop Anand represented the diocesan bishop and officiated. This was followed by a strawberry festival. At 7:30pm there was a buffet supper for the district clergy wives and staff of Grace Church (seventeen in all) with coffee, rolls, cold cuts, potato salad, jello and cookies. Mother Margaret Helena was in England, so missed the Grace Church celebrations.

On June 22 another renovated apartment block (346 Jackson Avenue) was dedicated. The Mayor cut the ribbon and Archdeacon Grant represented the bishop. This was the second year of the Rehabilitation Foundation and there were plans for taking over more buildings on the other side of the block. On the same day a stereo was stolen from 566 Jersey Avenue, one of the renovated apartments. Someone saw a man come out with it, so the stereo was recovered, but Fr. Albert decided to press charges.

Life went on and the summer program continued to reach out to children from poor backgrounds. More than a hundred went to summer camp for at least two weeks, some for longer. The summer staff volunteers took children on bus trips four days a week and assisted in the distribution of free lunches provided by the government. Nineteen seventy-two was the second year that the gym at Grace Church had been used as a center for the government's free lunch program. For so many children this meant the difference between being fed or going hungry in the summer vacation, as their parents could not afford to feed them. And the Saturday Church School and daily Vacation Bible School continued as usual.

There was a tragedy when two sixteen-year-old boys were drowned at the beginning of July. Sr. Elizabeth Anne and Sr. Eleanor Lucy went to the service at the funeral parlor. It was an Ecumenical service shared between Fr. Albert and the Roman Catholic priest.

As the summer program proceeded the Sisters began to have "trouble" with some of the helpers. They noted in the Record Book on July 24, "We discovered that the girls were going out with the 'guys' across the street." Two days later, at the staff meeting after dinner, Fr. Albert told the girls they must tell the Sisters where they were going, with whom, and when they would return. On July 27, after Evensong, the girls were each given written rules. The sixteen-year-olds, in addition, were told that the Sisters must have written or telephoned permission from the parents before the girls were allowed out with young men.

In a spirit of defiance, that same night two of the girls went out with two of the young men across the street. It was discovered when the mother of one of the girls telephoned to speak to her and she could not be found. Sr. Elizabeth Anne and Sr. Eleanor Lucy sat up all night to await their return. The Sisters had cabled the mothers to inform them about the new rules. By 3:00am next morning the Sisters found out that the boys' car had broken down at Paterson but the girls were there and were safe. At 7:00am Fr. Albert called the police at Paterson who picked the girls up and took them to the police station. Fr. Pederson went over to fetch them. Meanwhile, the girls' parents had been called and they arrived about noon. The Sisters sent the girls home in disgrace.

In spite of troubles with girl helpers, life went on and on July 27 the Sisters celebrated St. Christopher's Day. Mother Margaret Helena and the Sisters from New York called by to wish them a blessed day. Mother had been at 90, Barrow Street to help salvage furnishings after a burst water pipe had done much damage.

On July 29 the staff picnic took place at the convent. It was a welcome escape from Jersey City. Several staff members went swimming in the school pond with Billy Grier acting as lifeguard. It was a happier occasion than the Vacation Bible School's trip to Thompson's Park on August 8, when a gang tried to beat up one of the adult male helpers, who called the police. Many of the gang members were well known to the Sisters and clergy. A second picnic at the same venue on August 13 passed peacefully enough but when they returned Fr. Albert found the dog locked into the yard and the house ransacked.[7]

August 20 saw the final service of the summer program with Bishop Rath conducting it and baptizing some of the children. Fr. Albert played the organ. There was an exhibit in the parish hall showing the work done during the summer program, and there were refreshments too—fruit juice, coffee and cookies. At 12:30 there was staff dinner attended by Bishop Rath and his wife. Next day all the helpers left for the summer break and so did the Sisters. The Jersey City Record Book noted that "four Sisters, one dog, one dog basket and many bags" left for the convent, Fr. Albert driving them there in the bus and returning by train.

On September 23, 1972, Bishop Paul Moore was installed as Bishop of New York and the service was attended by Mother Margaret Helena and the Jersey City and New York Sisters. As the Fall season began, a new experiment in co-operation with St. Matthew's, Jersey City, was launched. The annual report published in December gave details. "This Fall we initiated a Children's Mass at 9:30 on Sundays, followed by Sunday School at St. Matthew's for the children who live in that area of the city. Our own Grace Church classes for downtown children meet on Saturday mornings 9:30 to 11:30." The first Children's Mass was on September 24 with Fr. Pederson presiding and 35 present, mostly children.

The annual report continued with news of another venture. "On November 29, we began a weekday afternoon program at the Marian [sic] Gardens Project.[8] Marian Gardens is the most isolated and most run-down of the city's housing projects. Many of the children are rough and disruptive in ordinary class groups; but they are children of God, many of them are members of Grace Church, and they are very much in need of the ministry of the Church. We are experimenting with taking the Church to them. The Housing Authority has made one of the vacant apartments available for our use; the community center will also be available as we need it for religious instruction and activities for the children, and a Mass for everyone each Wednesday evening. We made our beginning with 38 children and are expectant that it will grow and develop into a much broader program."

St. Martin's House saw some new occupants in November. Firstly there was a man who called himself "Brother Thomas."[9] And secondly, two men who were Asian refugees from Uganda arrived under a scheme organized by the Church World Service to give a safe refuge to people of Indian or Asian origin expelled from Uganda by President Idi Amin.

In the midst of all these new ministries, the well-established ones continued and in particular, the sales, bazaar and parties masterminded by the Sisters. By this time there were four Sisters at St. Christopher's: Sr. Elizabeth Anne, Sr. Eleanor Lucy, Sr. Susinne Paula and Sr. Ellen Marie. All four were at the convent on January 1, 1973, for Choral Mass. There was the usual tea party at 3:45pm and in the evening Sr. Laura Katharine showed her slides of Hawaii, where family members lived. Next day, Sr. Barbara Jean and Christine Brodeur took the four Sisters back to Jersey City. Once back, the Sisters were immersed in preparations for the Epiphany party attended by 150 children in spite of bitterly cold weather, and then there was the pageant in which about 50 children took part.

The Marion Gardens Project, centered on Dales Avenue, continued into 1973. On January 24 the Sisters noted in the Record Book that 41 children had attended the Church School there: "strenuous, but not impossible." Usually one of the clergy would go too, and also Br. Thomas, but much of the work fell on the Sisters. On Ash Wednesday 1973 (March 7) Sr. Eleanor Lucy and Sr. Ellen Marie accompanied both priests to Dales Avenue only to discover that the key had been forgotten! However, there is always a solution. "We distributed ashes from the car," noted the Record Book. The Sisters' own schedule for Ash Wednesday was rigorous: 6:25am Lauds and Prime; 7:00am Mass and ashes in church; breakfast; 9:30am Terce followed by Litany and Penitential Office; 11:30am Way of the Cross, Sext and Nones; 12:30 lunch; 3:30pm Vespers; 4:00pm bread and tea; 4:30pm to Marion Gardens; supper on return; 8:00pm Mass; Compline on return. And so to bed.

The good news that the Clewer Chapter had voted unanimously for re-affiliation with Mendham was sent to Mother Margaret Helena by cable on March 12, 1973. Mother telephoned the Sisters in New York and Jersey City immediately. It would be a few months before the formal re-affiliation but it was good news and there was much rejoicing on both sides of the Atlantic.

Trinity Institute was still meeting, and on March 22 Fr. Albert, Fr. Pederson and the Sisters attended a meeting of the Institute held at Riverside Church, NYC. These were still ecumenical times, and the meeting was addressed by Cardinal Suenens.[10]

On March 27 the Sisters from New York and Jersey City went to the convent to discuss the Clewer Rule. Later that day there was a birthday tea party, with cake, for Sr. Barbara Jean, Sr. Eleanor Lucy, Sr. Elizabeth Marion and Sr. Agnes Genevieve.

Grace Church had its annual retreat at the convent on April 6, which was attended by seventeen people. The conductor was Fr. Donahue, the Ecumenical Officer for the [RC] Archdiocese of New York.

On April 11 there was a big service to give thanks for the newly painted church. At the same service there were 39 baptisms by Bishop Rath and three priests stationed in four different locations in the church. Also six people were confirmed and received their first Holy Communion.

Next day there was a calamity! "A fire in the parish hall basement which the firemen felt was caused by malicious mischief. They broke the sky-lights and the vestibule roof and the parish hall floor was ruined by water from hoses and rain! Luckily we got our insurance."[11] The damage was estimated at $3,000–$4,000.

On May 11, 1973, Bishop Stark gave an address at the Diocesan Convention and then had a stroke at the end of the evening. He was taken to the Presbyterian Hospital. He had been Bishop of Newark since 1959[12] and retired later in 1973. But he recovered sufficiently to be at the convent on June 25.

As noted in Chapter 11, the Warden General, Fr. F. P. Coleman, visited Mendham during the month of June. The Sisters from Grace Church were able to go to the convent for the retreat which he conducted from June 4–8, also for Commemoration Day on June 24, when he preached. He visited Jersey City over the weekend of June 30–July 1, and upon his arrival in the late afternoon had tea with the Sisters and Fr. Albert. But the Sisters saw less of him than they had hoped as Fr. Albert took him out to dinner. "They were to come back for us to talk with the Warden General. At 9:30 they hadn't come so we three said Compline. At 10:00 they came. The Warden talked with us to 11 o'clock." Next day was not much better. "Fr. Coleman celebrated and preached all morning. Fr. Albert took him out to dinner after various adventures … We saw the Warden briefly and Fr. Albert decided to drive him to the convent." July 3 was the day of Fr. Coleman's departure and the Sisters, together with the New York Sisters, went to the convent for the July 4 celebrations. They arrived in time to have a final tea with Fr. Coleman before he left for England about 2:45pm. On July 4 there was a Choral Mass, lunch on the cloister, a tea party, early supper and then back to Grace Church and New York.

Once home, it was full steam ahead for the summer program. Sr. Suzanne Elizabeth came over from the convent to help, and there was the usual band of secular helpers. A new "Brother" (Br. Gilbert) also joined the ranks, working alongside Br. Thomas and living at St. Martin's House.

Fr. Coleman had asked the Sisters to write an account of their work at Grace Church for the Mother and Sisters at Clewer. Time did not allow them to write until well into the summer program but they gave a good description of the work, and of the great effort it took to make it a success. "So far things have gone very well. There have been two long bus trips a week lasting all day, two craft and sports days here, a Church School session on Saturday followed by staff dinner and discussion, and one free day each week. The Police have given us a Police bus trip three times … We have usually sent a Sister especially on the Police trips because our groups are sometimes difficult to manage. Fr. Albert is working with some of the Puerto Rican boys. He has bought a boat and hopes to have them help him scrape and paint and then enjoy trips on the Hudson River. In the meantime four of them are going on each trip. This is to help with the children in the water and teach them responsibility. So far that lesson hasn't been well learned and problems come up." Then of course there was the question of feeding all these children. "Five days a week we receive 300 government lunches for children and teenagers. Sr. Susinne Paula is carrying out the noon distribution. The children must eat in the room, they may not carry anything out, no food may be given to adults. Sister really enjoys giving out lunches, but it is a real chore some of us think. If the children throw meat into the rubbish Sister takes it out and gives it to various dog owners in the neighborhood. Some of [the dogs] are pretty thin for they are fed on scraps from the table."

In the midst of all the summer program, on Sunday July 15, there was another calamity! "About ten minutes past seven Sr. Elizabeth Anne called to me, 'We're having a flood!' She was dragging boxes out of the linen cupboard and tossing them to me [Sr. Eleanor Lucy]. There had been a cloudburst, the drain pipe was stopped and there were two holes in the roof! The water was pouring in to our fourth floor apartment. We called Fr. Albert! It was too much for us to cope with! In the end we had a big piece of plastic spread all over the roof held down by all the iron frying pans we could find in the house. From our house the rainwater dripped way down to the first floor where they make the altar bread! We worked on clearing up most of the day."[13]

But life went on and so did the summer program. Next day the Sisters sent off a group of campers in the Church van and about 50 children for the last Police trip. And Religious Life went on too. Neither fire nor flood would prevent the Sisters from living out their vowed life. So it was that on Monday Sr. Suzanne Elizabeth and Sr. Eleanor Lucy had their retreat, and next day the other two Sisters. Without the power of prayer the Sisters would not have been living an authentic life; nor would they have had the spiritual strength to cope with all the problems of inner city life.

Sr. Eleanor Lucy wrote very frankly in her letter to Clewer about the housing work. "We are not actually involved in the Housing Work except that it takes so much of Fr. Albert's time and energy that we are left to carry on with many administrative problems here. Just last Wednesday the Grace Church Foundation (separate from Grace Church, the Rector, Wardens, and Vestry), had a celebration to mark the purchase of some apartment houses through a bank instead of through Government banking which has been cut off by Washington. We all went up. The Mayor was there and spoke. He also cut the ribbon to show that the Foundation had taken over. There were various speeches … including from a Sister. Afterwards there was a reception. Father is continuing to buy houses to rehabilitate."[14]

The death of Jenny Moore, wife of Bishop Paul Moore, on October 3, 1973, though not unexpected, was still a great sadness. Sr. Elizabeth Anne and Sr. Eleanor Lucy traveled to Washington, DC, for the funeral on October 5 in the Cathedral. Ten days later, on October 15, eight Sisters attended the memorial service in the Cathedral of St. John the Divine, NYC.

And so the year proceeded on its way with the usual combination of joyful celebration as at Thanksgiving, and times of stress such as when one of the parish vehicles was stolen and another wrecked just before Christmas. If the clergy and Sisters wondered why such things happened to them when they were trying to help the perpetrators, they did not voice it aloud. But Fr. Albert had a lucky escape on December 26 when he was bringing the black car home from the garage. It stalled on the railroad track but the engineer saw him in time and managed to stop.

After their brief respite at the convent for Christmas it was back to Jersey City for the Sisters and another year of ministry and mission amongst some of the most deprived families.

Nineteen seventy-four was the centennial year of the Sisters' arrival in New York City from Clewer, and there would be celebrations during the year, and the re-affiliation of the two houses. Meanwhile, the year started with a combination of bad weather, transport problems with breakdowns and further thefts, and difficulties with organizing the Epiphany pageant which the Sisters felt had not gone very well. Fr. Albert continued to be frequently absent from the parish and Fr. Pederson was left holding the fort. Also, attendance at St. Matthew's and the Bible School at Dales Avenue was dropping in numbers. On January 27, Fr. Albert left for New Salem, MA, after the 9:30 Mass, and during his absence the rectory was broken into and the doors smashed.

There were some bright spots! Three Sisters from Clewer arrived at the end of January for the centennial celebrations. These were Sr. Jane Olive, Sr. Letitia and Sr. Catherine Mary. On January 30 the Sisters from Grace Church and New York attended the Trinity Institute and once again met the Archbishop of Canterbury and Cardinal Suenens. Also present this year was Prior Roger Schutz of Taizé. The Institute continued until February 1, and then next day the Sisters went to the Cathedral of St. John the Divine, NYC, for the consecration of Harold Louis Wright as Suffragan Bishop of New York.[15]

Bad snow storms did not deter members of Religious Communities attending a seminar at Mendham on February 4; and then on February 5, the centennial anniversary, there was a Mass of Thanksgiving for one hundred years of mission and ministry in the United States. The American Founders—Sr. Helen Margaret and Sr. Frances Constance—would have rejoiced at the achievement. On February 12, the three English Sisters came to Jersey City for a two-day visit, having been in New York for several days. They were shown all the varied work including some of the renovated housing. They returned to Clewer on February 20.

Things were coming to a head in the parish and a vestry meeting (which the Sisters did not attend) was called on February 19, 1974, at which Fr. Albert announced his forthcoming resignation on health grounds by permission of the bishop. The reason given was diabetes. The resignation would take effect from March 15. The possibility of a merger with St. Matthew's church was announced by Fr. Pederson but this came to nothing. And there were more tenement fires and some fire victims to shelter. At a vestry meeting on March 5, Fr. Albert asked to keep the black car and pay the expenses on it, though it would still be church property. He also said he would be "Rector Emeritus." This caused some controversy amongst the church and vestry members as it was not normal procedure. On Fr. Albert's last day he signed the station wagon over to himself. There was no farewell service. On March 18, Bishop Rath and Archdeacon Grant had a meeting with the vestry and according to the Sisters' Record Book "the motions about 'station wagon' and 'pastor emeritus' were rescinded." Next day Fr. Pederson took the number plates off the black car and canceled the insurance. On April 1, the vestry members voted for an application to the bishop for a new rector and expressed their preference for Fr. Pederson.

All this upheaval had taken place during Lent. The services from Maundy Thursday until Easter followed the usual pattern with a few exceptions, Fr. Pederson being single handed. On Good Friday (April 12), there was no service until 12:00 noon, when the Sisters led the Way of the Cross in church followed by a time of quiet. Fr. Pederson arrived by 2:00pm and led a meditation following the Mass of the Pre-sanctified. In the evening there was a service at St. Matthew's at 8:00pm.

On April 25 there was a fire in the basement of St. Martin's House, next door to St. Christopher's. Some children told the Sisters, who called the fire department. Smoke was coming from behind the basement door but fortunately it was only a small fire and there was no damage. Even so, the Sisters evacuated both houses and took Judy the dog out to safety. A few days later, on May 1, there was a second fire in the basement which was put out by Pablo, one of the Puerto Rican members of the church.

As already noted in Chapter 11, the highlight of summer 1974 was the visit from Clewer of Mother Annys, Sr. Eudora, Sr. Monica and Sr. Marjorie. Although they had celebrated the centennial of the Sisters' arrival on the actual day (February 5), it was also celebrated on Commemoration Day, June 23, when more than 200 people came. And it also celebrated the re-affiliation of the two halves of CSJB. All the Sisters had been present but next day, the Feast of the Birth of St. John Baptist, the Sisters in Jersey City had their own usual festivities. Although Sr. Monica and Sr. Marjorie left for England on June 27, Mother Annys and Sr. Eudora extended their visit until July 7, during which time they visited Jersey City. On the Sunday, after attending 8:00am Mass, Mother Annys, Sr. Eudora and Sr. Eleanor Lucy went to the 11:00 Mass at St. Matthew's. The two

English Sisters were still at the convent on July 4 when the Sisters from New York and Jersey City went to join in the celebrations. Mother Annys, Sr. Eudora and several others went to the parade in Mendham. At dinner there was strawberry shortcake and later an outdoor picnic. Then soon after, it was back to England for the Sisters from Clewer, but with the bonds of friendship and affiliation firmly forged. It is a bond which has lasted into the 21st century.

The summer program sped by, as did the summer vacation, and on September 12 the Sisters re-opened St. Christopher's for the Fall season. A highlight was the celebration at the Cathedral of St. John the Divine, NYC, of the 90th anniversary of the Order of the Holy Cross on September 14 (Holy Cross Day). The Jersey City Record Book had a lengthy entry for the day. "Sr. Elizabeth Anne, Sr. Eleanor Lucy, Sr. Susinne Paula all went to the Holy Cross Celebration in New York. Sr. Elizabeth Anne and Sr. Laura Katharine took up the elements in the procession at the offertory. All of us in the Big Procession. Mention was made of CSJB's help at the time of Holy Cross' foundation. Everyone very cordial."

Another great day soon followed—the installation of Fr. Pederson as Rector of Grace Church. Much preparation was done, and a good deal of it by the Sisters with help from Fr. Pederson. The installation took place on September 29 (St. Michael and All Angels). The Mass was bi-lingual. Bishop Anand officiated and about 125 people came to the service. The only representative from the convent was Muriel Blue, the resident Associate. The Mass and installation was followed by an open house and blessing of the rectory. Hopefully it was a new beginning—but on October 14, the parish hall was vandalized during the night.

The Grace Church School won an award for its banner at the centennial celebration of the Diocese of Newark on November 10. This was a real affirmation not only for the school but also for the parish.

The death of Sr. Agnes Genevieve on December 8 was a sadness for all.[16] As Sister in Charge of the work at St. Luke's Chapel, NYC, her death was a shock for the people of the parish as well as for the Sisters. It would also be a factor in the decision-making process about the future of the work at St. Luke's. All Sisters were present for the funeral on December 12.

Nineteen seventy-five began in much the same way as in former years with the usual Epiphany-tide activities. There was a bomb scare on January 18 at 6:00pm and another at 9:00pm. Both were hoaxes but they traded on people's fears.

The death of Sr. Waldine Lucia on March 26, 1975, while not entirely unexpected, was still a great loss to the Community, as already noted in Chapter 12. The Sisters returned to the convent on Holy Saturday and were taken to the nave of the main chapel to make their farewell visit. "We, the Sisters from Jersey City and New York, said a litany there." They were present at the funeral requiem, followed by the committal in the Community cemetery on Easter Monday. In the afternoon, after lunch, there was a discussion with the Warden over the growing problems with the branch work.

There were a number of lay people who were faithful helpers to the Sisters in all their work, especially with fund-raising and assisting with the numerous sales, parties and summer activities. One such was Mrs. Jessie Bober, who died on June 10 from a massive heart attack at the Medical Center where she had been since June 4. Her funeral was at Grace Church on June 13, and was attended by the Jersey City Sisters, and also Mother Margaret Helena, Sr. Agatha Louise and Sr. Barbara Jean, who came from the convent. Other faithful helpers at this time were Marion Burger, Muriel Unwin and Jean Hoppin.

The summer camp program went ahead as usual with Fr. Pederson playing a large part in transporting the children. And on August 3 there was the annual parish picnic at the convent. Three buses took 167 people there for this annual treat. Mass, celebrated outdoors, was followed by lunch. But the day was clouded by irresponsible behavior. The Sisters' Record Book noted: "No trouble at St. Marguerite's, but in orchard, at pond and in the woods, beer cans and other litter left. Absolutely no beer drinking allowed." There was more trouble on August 7 at the Saturday Church School, when fighting broke out. Sr. Eleanor Lucy thought it was a microcosm of race-related problems. Racial tension was still rife and later the same day there was a Mass in church for a man who was stabbed to death on Railroad Avenue.

As the year 1975 unfolded and the Sisters returned to Jersey City following the summer vacation, life was about to become more difficult with what Canon Carter would have called "a complication of circumstances." September 24 and 25 saw heavy rain and the newly fixed roof leaked in two places. On the same day, Inspectors from the Department of Missions of the Diocese of Newark made an inspection of St. Martin's and St. Christopher's and dropped a bombshell. They decided they were fire risks and must be closed as they were unsafe for habitation. As already noted in Chapter 12, the decision had been made to withdraw from St. Luke's Chapel, NYC, because of the change in parish status and the shortage of Sisters. This decision was difficult enough but under the present circumstances it was inevitable. Now, it seemed as if the solution to give up the house in New York and move Sr. Katharine Veronica to St. Christopher's, from whence she would commute to New York, could not proceed. A complication of circumstances indeed. Even so, the Sisters continued their work and ministry, and apart from one-line entries such as that for October 16: "Meeting with Bishop and Department of Missions," the Record Books show very few clues as to finding a solution.

On October 29, Bishop Paul Moore came to Grace Church with his new wife. He preached at the Mass at 7:00pm and about 120 people attended. Afterwards there was a reception in the parish hall. Before the service, at dinner in the rectory, the Sisters were able to talk to Bishop Moore and told him that the whole work was threatened. Even though he was not their bishop he always maintained an interest in Grace Church, having been one of the pioneering team there in the early 1950s.

The Sisters were not without strong supporters who would fight their case. Thus both Fr. Pederson and Muriel Unwin wrote strongly worded letters to Bishop Rath in protest about the condemnation by the Department of Missions. Fr Pederson's letter dated November 10 made the point that the Sisters' commuting from New York "is a blow to us ... We recognize two very different problems: one the safety of the Sisters, and two, the availability of the Sisters." Regarding the safety of St. Christopher's House, Fr. Pederson challenged the decision to close it. "We believe that the element of danger that exists is no more than in any other house in Jersey City. St. Christopher's House is in basically good condition." One of the recommendations had been to move Br. Thomas out of St. Christopher's by January 1st. "We believe there are good reasons for keeping him there. Unoccupied buildings are especially vulnerable to burglars and vandals ... We strongly believe that St. Martin's House and St. Christopher's House are not the burdens that the committee of the Department of Missions seems to think they are. However, we have found it is useless to debate this question as long as another question is being raised about the overall strategy of the work at Grace Church (Van Vorst)." The letter was copied to Archdeacon Grant, the Sisters, the Wardens and Vestry members, and others.

A week later, on November 16, 1975, Bishop Rath received a letter from Muriel Unwin in affectionate support of the Sisters' work.[17] "This letter is to let you know of my deep concern over the recent decisions of the Department of Missions with regard to the future of Grace Church (Van Vorst). For the past three years Jean Hoppin and I have spent every Wednesday from 10 to 3 at St. Christopher's House. We have responsibility for the used clothing rooms, but also to help the Sisters with other special events and programs. You can well imagine how familiar we are with all phases of the work there. I have served on the Commission of Evangelism and in many capacities at Calvary, Summit, including the President of the Women. However, none of these has even come close to the true spirit of Christianity when compared to the literal acts of mercy extended to desperate people at Grace Van Vorst. The summer program including camp, and the Christmas toys are of obvious benefit to many children. However, the food given to a hungry man, a sick child admitted to hospital, a woman in fear of abuse from a drunk husband— these are not statistics to be evaluated on the same basis as a suburban church."

She continued and highlighted an internal problem at the church. "I am fully aware that the Vestry has concern over the church proper, as well they might. Being poor themselves, their attitude towards some of the help extended is bound to be quite different from ours. In addition, it is hard for them to realize that the money used to fund special help to individuals, the summer program, the toys at Christmas etc., comes from special donations specifically for this use from church women in the Diocese … The Department of Missions has worked hard to come to a decision on the future of Grace Church … In all honesty I might have come to the same conclusions had I not been an intimate part of the work. First, we cannot judge the condition of St. Martin's House and St. Christopher's House on the same physical standards we expect in Summit or Montclair. Secondly, as an Associate of St. John Baptist, and a friend of the Sisters, I must speak in their behalf. This comes as a great blow to them. They felt they could continue to be of service to the people of Grace Van Vorst and community until either younger Sisters could take over the work or lay people like myself would fill their place. I'm afraid they feel set aside and unneeded to carry on their life's work. Father Pederson has dedicated his life to others with little remuneration for himself. His wife and family have been content to follow where he feels he can carry on the Lord's work. I have deep respect and love for this man."

She continued, "I plead for reconsideration of the plans that are now in progress. I would suggest that the Sisters be moved to the second floor of St. Christopher's House so their safety from fire be insured [sic] as the first step … With the cooperation of Father Pederson, Brother Thomas and the Vestry, any changes deemed necessary would be carefully thought out and executed over a period of time. I hope it will be possible to continue meeting the basic human needs of people as they arise from day to day. The accomplishments of the last 25 years at Grace Church are deserving of a more considered and gradual change … It is of the utmost concern to me, and I want to do everything I can not only for the Grace Van Vorst staff but for the people of the church."

A solution of sorts had been arrived at, whereby St. John Baptist House in Barrow Street, NYC, would not be closed and the Jersey City Sisters would move there and commute daily. Thus on December 10, 1975, the Jersey City Record Book states sadly: "St. Christopher's House closed as our residence. Sr. Susinne Paula went to the convent to stay. Sr. Elizabeth Anne and Sr. Eleanor Lucy went over to St. John Baptist House to live." On December 11, they noted: "First day of commuting … left at 9:30 for Jersey City. Had Mass in St. Christopher's chapel at 11:00 … Left for New York about 4:00 or 4:30 to be there to say Vespers with Sr. Katharine Veronica." Sr. Katharine Veronica was now the only Sister working in St. Luke's parish, Sr. Agnes Genevieve having passed to her rest, and Sr. Agatha Louise had returned to the convent permanently after a fall.

Bishop Rath replied to Muriel Unwin on December 11, promising to share with her the findings of the survey being carried out on the buildings. He continued: "There must also be some appraisal and study of the program that has been carried on at Grace Van Vorst through these later years to determine what facilities are necessary to carry on the work of the church in that area of Jersey City. Certainly the most important of the facilities are the people involved, the Sisters, the clergy, and volunteers like yourself. I can assure you that we have an abiding concern for Grace Van Vorst, and are not making any arbitrary decisions as to its future."

All the usual pre-Christmas activities took place, such as the toy sale, when up to 120 families were assisted. Sr. Susinne Paula, Sr. Laura Katharine and Sr. Suzanne Elizabeth all came to help, and because the sale spilled over into a second day, they all stayed overnight at St. Christopher's.

And on Christmas Eve, Sr. Elizabeth Anne and Sr. Eleanor Lucy stayed over in order to attend Midnight Mass at Grace Church. About 100 people were there, but only a handful at St. Matthew's. On Christmas Day Sr. Suzanne Elizabeth came for the Sisters and took them to the convent. Bad weather kept them there until December 27, when they returned in the school van driven by Sr. Barbara Jean.

So the year 1975 ended with a measure of uncertainty, but also with grounds for hope. While "the powers that be" within the diocese deliberated about the future of Grace Church, the Sisters continued to faithfully fulfill their vowed life and their commitment to the people of Jersey City, even if it meant commuting daily from New York. They would not willingly walk away from such important humanitarian work, and with strong supporters they carried their ministry into another year—and indeed several more years.

Nineteen seventy-six opened with a proposal from the Department of Missions for the appointment of a Governing Board for Grace Church. Its purpose would be to manage the parish and to appoint an administrator, "and to investigate with him the potential of continued work at Grace Church and to present a five-year plan in writing to the Bishop, the Department and the Council by June 30, 1977." Muriel Unwin's letter to the bishop must have struck the right note because the second proposal was "that a capital campaign be undertaken to rehabilitate St. Martin's and St. Christopher's Houses, accepting the offer of Mesdames Wilson and Unwin to chair such a drive with the clear understanding that the renovation of these buildings is undertaken on an emergency basis in order to permit the continuation of the program while a full planning process takes place covering the program and physical facilities." The proposals were approved by the Vestry members at Grace Church on February 10, 1976.

Meanwhile, Muriel Unwin was leaving no stone unturned in her efforts to raise funds for the renovation of the two houses. On January 26, 1976, she appealed to the Wilk's Fund, a charitable fund administered by St. Peter's, Morristown. And on March 25, she received word that a grant of $4,000 was being given towards the renovation of St. Martin's. The Sisters were "elated" at the good news.

In an appeal letter dated February 28, 1976, and written on Diocese of Newark notepaper, Muriel Unwin and Kathryn Wilson graphically described the situation. The appeal was aimed at individuals and Episcopal

Church Women groups with the sanction of the bishop and Department of Missions. "There is a crisis at Grace (Van Vorst) … which threatens to bring to an end the work of the Sisters of the Community of St. John Baptist there. This centers around two houses owned by Grace Church, one of which is in need of immediate renovation—for which funds are not available …" They went on to describe how the two houses had a common wall and that St. Martin's was solely heated by space heaters which were not properly ventilated. Also, the wiring was a fire hazard and consequently the Sisters were commuting from New York. "This is a hardship they undertake without complaint but surely cannot continue for long. In a period when problems of poverty, vandalism, and civil unrest have escalated in our major 'inner cities,' the Sisters have provided a program of compassionate understanding for the daily needs of the people in the parish and the neighborhood. In order for them to continue this Christian work in the home they have occupied for twenty-five years, it is imperative that these repairs be made."

Meanwhile, parish life went on. On January 6, the Feast of the Epiphany, there was the usual pageant. Sr. Suzanne Elizabeth and Sr. Susinne Paula came to help. Dressing the children in their costumes was always something of a challenge but all went well. Mass followed and then all went to the parish hall for movies. There were three Walt Disney movies and according to the Sisters' Record Book, "the children squealed all through. Afterwards the teenagers passed [around] refreshments—cookies and ice cream sticks. Presents were given out—38 families, 65 ladies each had stockings with 3 presents each. Children had bags as usual." On January 10 it was all repeated at St. Matthew's, though in fewer numbers, but there were presents for children and mothers—and some fathers too.

By February the Sisters were increasingly staying overnight in Jersey City because of the amount of work there or events ending late. On March 15, 1976, the Governing Board met for a long meeting lasting until 11:30pm. During the meeting the Sisters were given permission to return to St. Christopher's unconditionally—a great relief to all, even though the repairs still had to be done. As a precaution, Mr. Grier came over from Mendham and installed four smoke detectors. Their Record Book has a triumphant entry for April 7: "!! St. Christopher's re-opened!!" This made life so much easier for the Sisters, to be back where they felt called to be. Their spring appeal letter spelled out how they perceived their mission. "We have a mission to fulfil … Our Lord has sent us here—to witness to Him here; to show His love to His children in this city; to those who have not known Him; to those whose faith is weak; to those who have lost sight of Him; to those who would help in this mission here in this city where there is so much that would lead men [sic] astray or drive the Spirit from them … We must labor on in His strength and in His love doing the work He has given us to do that His Will may be accomplished in us and through us." Fr. Pederson added his own affirmation of the Sisters and their work. "Just a few words to witness to the joy that it is to work, pray and give with the Sisters and all the rest of the people on Second Street at the task of helping to put God's love into action … and to urge you to continue to work, pray and give with us for the spread of His Kingdom." And Br. Thomas added a note to say that there were 33 teenagers active in the Youth Group, plus others who attended Mass but not Youth Group activities. Three of the youths sat on the Vestry and two were elected delegates to the Diocesan Convention. The Sisters noted that there were two appeals, one for the repair of St. Martin's House to ensure the safety of St. Christopher's; and the usual annual appeal for the children's and youths' summer program. A sum of $11,900 was needed for the summer program.

The end of June and beginning of July 1976 was a combination of celebration and sadness. Celebration because of St. John Baptist Day, followed two days later by Commemoration Day. The centennial history *Stars in His Crown* was on sale and each Sister received her own copy.

July 4 was a particularly great celebration, being the bi-centennial of the Declaration of Independence.[18] The Jersey City Sisters walked down to the Hudson River and saw the end of the parade of boats. Next day they went to the convent for the day to continue the celebrations. In between all of this there was a degree of sadness, but tinged with thanksgiving. As noted in Chapter 12, on June 27 there was a service at Trinity Wall Street to give thanks for the ministry of several Communities within the large parish, including CSJB at St. Luke's Chapel. The Jersey City Record Book noted on July 1: "St. John Baptist House closed permanently." Sr. Katharine Veronica, Mrs. Marion Burger, and Alex the cat came home to the convent. It was the ending of an era, part of the Community's second spring, but as the Newsletter for Trinity Wall Street noted, the Sisters left enriched lives behind them.

The summer program proceeded but was hindered because the City Council decided St. Christopher's was not safe for the classes. That meant having everything in the parish hall, i.e. classes, activities, and lunch. Some of the boys were disruptive, which made hard work for the Sisters and helpers. Also, the acoustics in the hall made it very difficult to hear individuals over the collective noise! If the Sisters were disheartened, they needn't have been: the total enrollment of 130 was the largest they had on record.

Fall 1976 saw the installation of Fr. Laughlin as Rector of the newly independent parish of St. Luke's in the Fields, formerly St. Luke's Chapel, NYC. Mother Margaret Helena, Sr. Katharine Veronica, Sr. Eleanor Lucy, the Sisters from Jersey City, and several Associates attended. On November 20–22, Bishop Spong came for his Visitation and included Jersey City, where he preached and confirmed at Grace Church and preached at St. Matthew's. On Thanksgiving Day there was an evening Mass followed by an inspection by the architect's assistant. Meanwhile, the church was found to have structural problems and the altar was set up opposite the baptistery. A crack had been found in a major support beam under the front of the church and the Vestry decided to move services to the back.

But as the year passed into the Advent and Christmas seasons, the Sisters continued their ministry with the familiar parish activities undeterred by all these setbacks. Indeed the morale of the congregation was high. Members of the congregation including some of the teenagers had raised $1,800 for repairs to the organ, and the December bazaar brought in another $1,100. Mr. Sanchez, the Senior Warden, had painted the interior of the church and had inspired other members to join the project. He was also making the smaller rooms off the parish hall ready for the Saturday Church School and other activities that usually took place in St. Christopher's.

Nineteen seventy-seven opened as usual with the Epiphany pageant with more than 50 neighborhood children taking part in it. Parts had to be found for all, resulting in a dozen shepherd boys! The Sisters had to do an exercise in logistics in order to make the pageant "work" with the re-arranged church, but all was well. In a Newsletter to friends and supporters, Sr. Eleanor Lucy remarked that "the singing was the best we have ever had thanks to the 'Singing Sisters' our Reverend Mother sent to help us." The pageant was followed by the usual party in the parish hall, with cartoon movies, ice cream sticks, and presents for children, mothers and friends. There were about 175 persons present.

Sr. Eleanor Lucy continued her Newsletter on a more serious note. "Many friends brought us food as well as presents. The Pantry Shelf is well-filled now. It won't be for long. Yesterday a Family Services worker came to us for food because the Food Center sponsored by the City and other Churches was without food. She already contacted the Mayor's Action Committee and the Food Center in vain. We keep frozen sandwiches in the freezer at all times. Vagrant men come and ask for them. Sometimes we feel sorry about giving a frozen sandwich on a freezing day, and yet if we did not freeze them they would not always be on hand. The men surely need them when they care to come for them."

In the midst of all the parish activities, the Sisters were still in great demand to give talks in other parishes about their life and work. Sisters would also come frequently from the convent to help out at busy times. One such was Sr. Suzanne Elizabeth, who was frequently commuting between the convent, where she was Novice Mistress, and Jersey City. And also, she was visiting parishes to help their altar guilds.

By the end of March 1977, the decision had been made to sell St. Martin's House and concentrate on essential improvements to St. Christopher's. The City authorities were insisting on a complete fire escape in the front of the building from the fourth floor down, as well as essential repairs to the existing one in the rear of the building. Fire retardant doors also had to be added. The grant of $4,000 from the Wilk's Fund would now be used for this work. Roof repairs were also urgently needed and negotiations were ongoing to obtain a realistic and achievable estimate.

The connection with St. Matthew's Church was loosening and the Sisters noted in their Record Book that on March 27, 1977, Fr. Pederson had his last Sunday there. The Vestry there elected Fr. Keithly Warner in his place. On Palm Sunday (April 3), Sr. Eleanor Lucy and Sr. Suzanne Elizabeth attended Fr. Warner's first Sunday at St. Matthew's. There were 40 people in the congregation. Although the Sisters no longer visited St. Matthew's after June 12, they still continued the Sunday School work there, resuming in October after the summer break.

The Sisters' compassion to all was shown when at the beginning of May a woman and her four children arrived on their doorstep at 9:00pm. She had been to the Sisters for clothes the previous evening, having lost everything in a fire. Then, after leaving the Sisters, she had been arrested but was due to go to Court for resisting arrest. No one would take her and her children in, and so she turned to the Sisters once again. They gave the family food and allowed them to sleep in the front office on the first floor at St. Christopher's. She finally got help from the Mayor's Action Committee and they all went to the YWCA after being with the Sisters all day.

Work was continuing on the roof sporadically as there was a good deal of wet weather during the month of May. But on May 12 Muriel Unwin came with the good news that the City authorities had granted the building permit. Further good news followed with the completion of the roof on May 19.

On May 25 all the Jersey City Sisters went to the convent, where Lynne Pfitzinger was received as a postulant. (There were others in the novitiate at this time but they did not stay the course.) But so often times of joy have been followed by sadness; and on June 1, news came of the death of Fr. Templeton, Chaplain at the convent, after an illness of about four hours. The Sisters returned to the convent on June 4 for his funeral.

"House dismantled" was the alarming entry in the Jersey City Record Book for July 5, 1977. But it was all in a good cause, as the work on St. Christopher's now proceeded in earnest. It was not until August that the closing papers were signed for the sale of St. Martin's House. But the summer program was about to begin. It was carried out "in a somewhat complicated situation," as Sr. Eleanor Lucy explained in her Fall Newsletter to the Friends of Grace Church. The parish hall was used instead of St. Christopher's but "seven classes amounting to nearly one hundred children, frequently with no divisions, are difficult to teach." The City authorities helped by giving four all-day bus trips, and they opened the swimming pool in a nearby High School, so the Sisters sent the boys there in the morning and the girls in the afternoon. The Sister noted wryly, "The only use we were able to make of St. Christopher's House was a backyard sprinkler which provided water sports for the fives and sixes."

Apart from natural boisterousness and excitement, the children in the summer program usually gave no trouble. But on August 1, about twenty 11- and 12-year-old girls got into church because someone had left the door into the parish hall unlocked. It is not clear from the Sisters' Record Book whether these were girls taking part in the program, or girls from the neighborhood who wanted to make trouble. Sr. Elizabeth Anne and Sr. Eleanor Lucy took the matter in hand. They locked the door, and, after the girls had run around in a "disorderly fashion," managed to get them into the back pews in the church. The Sisters then attempted to lead them round to the parish hall but the girls pushed past Sr. Susinne Paula and ran down to the basement to tell ghost stories in the dark room. Sr. Eleanor Lucy "routed them out. They yelled in the parish hall for a long time. Then they tried the basement again but Sr. Eleanor Lucy stood at the foot of the stairs and they retreated at once." Finally the girls were removed one at a time. Their "adventure" or misdemeanor was over and for the Sisters it was all in a day's work, though hopefully there would not be too many like that!

The summer program closed on August 12. The parents had been invited to come between 2:00 and 3:00pm to receive the gifts the children had made for them. There were ice cream sticks for all! One hundred and fifty children had enrolled and the highest attendance in a single day was 96.

Next day, the Sisters began packing to return to the convent for the summer vacation, but also packing and moving things ready for the workmen to begin the repairs to the house. On August 16, "We left for the convent in the van—four Sisters, much baggage and Judy [the dog]." Work on the house took longer than expected and was still not ready when Sr. Eleanor Lucy wrote her Newsletter to the Friends of Grace Church. "Our own young men are in the process of painting the halls and multipurpose rooms. Our Associates, Mrs. Unwin and Mrs. Hoppin … are caring for the painting of the three rooms involved. The Clothes Room has been closed since the work began in early July. They plan to open one room which is finished this coming week. The Pantry Shelf is already painted and ready to be filled again. As soon as the multipurpose rooms on the first floor are finished Saturday Church School will begin." Many friends of the Sisters helped with the work, painting, sanding, preparing walls, scrubbing floors and generally cleaning up. The work was not completed until November and the Certificate of Occupancy was finally issued by the City authorities on December 8.

Lynne Pfitzinger's clothing as a novice took place on November 7, and all the Sisters were present at the convent for the 11:00am Mass at which the new novice took the name Mary Lynne.

The Advent and pre-Christmas activities went ahead as usual and the bazaar over two days at the beginning of December raised over $1,500— the best ever. Sr. Eleanor Lucy was busy with all the plans for the parish activities, but on December 13 she became ill with what was thought to be influenza, which was prevalent in Jersey City at the time. Even so, she helped finish the mailing for the thrift sale. As her condition worsened she was admitted to Morristown Memorial Hospital on December 16. She passed to her rest in the early hours of Saturday December 17. This was a great shock to all who knew her and loved her, but in a letter to the Friends, Sr. Elizabeth Anne wrote: "We knew that Sr. Eleanor Lucy would have expected us to go ahead and carry on the program she had been planning. This we are trying to do as well as we can." Thus the thrift sale of toys went ahead as usual on Tuesday December 20. An "army" of helpers was present to see to the smooth running of the event. It was, in a sense, a great tribute to Sr. Eleanor Lucy that the work went on, so that none of the children who would benefit from the toys would be neglected or disappointed. But there was sadness too—inevitably. As *The Jersey Journal* for December 19, 1977, noted: "Sister Eleanor knew literally thousands of people through her work in the church's food and clothing distribution programs."

The Sisters left the thrift sale at 4:00pm so as to drive to the convent in time for Litany, Vespers and Matins of the Dead. The funeral Mass took place next day, December 21, 1977, at 11:00am, preceded by a Watch from 9:00am. Bishop Rath officiated and Fr. Weed celebrated, assisted by numerous clergy. Bishop Moore, Bishop Spong and Fr. Laughlin were in the congregation. One person missing was Mother Margaret Helena, who was in Morristown Memorial Hospital recovering from surgery. Forty people from Grace Church, including children, came for the funeral as well as many other friends and Associates. Sr. Eleanor Lucy was laid to rest in the convent cemetery. Christine Brodeur and her mother drove the Sisters back to Jersey City, stopping at the hospital on the way in order to visit Mother. At 7:30pm there was a Memorial Mass at Grace Church attended by about 50 people.

A graduate of Radcliffe College and the Sorbonne in Paris, Sr. Eleanor Lucy was a born scholar and began what would have been a promising teaching career, except that she heard a call from God to dedicate her life to Him. Writing in a personal memoir she described how hard she resisted! She had been advised by a priest to consider the Religious Life, which he said was the highest vocation for a woman. "I said that I couldn't possibly do that. I had been brought up as a Congregationalist, before my confirmation. On the way home I had a vivid experience in the streetcar. I heard very clearly, 'You say you won't, but you will.'" Time passed and then ... "I had another distinct experience. 'Here is your second chance,'"—the inner voice again. This time she did not argue and wrote to Mother Florence Teresa. She was clothed as a novice on November 7, 1933, and professed on June 16, 1937. Sr. Eleanor Lucy worked in all the Community branch works including St. Helen's Hall, Portland, Oregon and St. John's School, Corsicana, TX, but it is for her work in Jersey City that she is best remembered. She went there for the first time in September 1951 along with Sr. Agatha Louise. In 1955 she went to work at St. Luke's, NYC, until 1957. Upon returning to Jersey City, she was made Sister in Charge in December 1957 and spent the rest of her Community life there. Mother Margaret Helena described her as "joyous" and there can be little doubt that this joyousness in the face of all the difficulties and complications at Jersey City was what endeared her to so many people.

As the year 1977 passed away, the Sisters' Record Book had a hopeful note for December 30. "Sr. Elizabeth Anne, Sr. Suzanne Elizabeth and Marion [Burger] went to buy toys and ice cream for party, and food for the house—in the *new van!*" The old van had given much trouble and Sr. Eleanor Lucy was hoping to have it replaced but it was so costly that it seemed like a pipe dream. She did not live to see it replaced, but would doubtless have shared the Sisters' joy that the summer outings would now be much easier.

Nineteen seventy-eight dawned at the convent with several Sisters, including those from Jersey City, keeping the traditional Watch until midnight. Next day, the Sisters from Jersey City returned there in the middle of the morning and it was full steam ahead for the usual Epiphany activities. Bad weather—deep snow and ice—presented a difficulty but did not stop activities such as Saturday Church School even though fewer children attended.

On February 13, 1978, the Warden, Fr. Weed, had his Visitation at the convent during which Sr. Katharine Veronica was appointed Assistant Superior and Sr. Elizabeth Anne Sister Superior at St. Christopher's House. Back in Jersey City, the new van was vandalized—three tires were slashed beyond repair and a tire on the car of a helper. Two days later, a window in the gym in the parish hall was pushed in and broken. Renovation work was still in progress at St. Christopher's, Fr. Pederson doing some of it himself, assisted by other volunteers including teenagers. On Holy Saturday, March 25, seventeen Church School children came and helped with polishing and dusting in church from 9:30 until 11:00.

Then Sr. Suzanne Elizabeth gave them candy and sent them home. At 6:00pm there was the lighting of the Paschal Candle and the baptism of two babies. At 7:30pm there was the Spanish First Mass of Easter, after which the Blessed Sacrament was brought to the Sisters' chapel in procession with Fr. Pederson, acolytes and the Sisters.

Sr. Susinne Paula was due to fly to England, but not having been out of the U.S. before, required a passport. She was rather concerned to discover there was no record of her birth! Finally, proof of her existence was traced through the Census. The passport came through on March 30, and the Record Book noted that "she feels it is 'for real now'." Indeed it was, and on April 26, Mother Margaret Helena, Sr. Susinne Paula and Sr. Elizabeth Marion flew to England for their three-week visit.

"Grace Church is always a place of joy and hard work," wrote Mother Margaret Helena in her letter to the Associates at the end of 1978. "The renovation of St. Christopher's was finally completed and the Sisters had an 'open house' in the first week of May.[19] It was a joyous occasion. The changes in the house have made some good places for meetings and Church School etc. The weekday services are being held in the largest classroom, thus saving fuel by not heating the church." The open house didn't just happen. It took a great deal of preparing. After so much work there was much cleaning to be done and faithful helpers Muriel Unwin and Jean Hoppin did a great deal of it. It had not simply been a case of painting and decorating, but in the words of Muriel Unwin in a letter to the Friends,[20] "... The Sisters carried on their summer and winter programs through unbelievably chaotic conditions as workmen hammered, sawed, broke through walls and rewired electric outlets ... Some of the improvements include a new roof, an additional fire escape, and lowered ceilings with recessed fluorescent lighting, all new windows with storm sash and screens, and a back door exit on the first floor. With the help of many volunteers the walls have been freshly painted or papered so that all four floors are now in top condition."

The open house took place on Sunday, April 30 in the afternoon and the Sisters' Record Book noted about 50 people from "outside," i.e. not parishioners, and 25–30 parishioners came. Sr. Katharine Veronica, Sr. Mary Lynne and Marion Burger came from the convent. Bishop Rath arrived at 3:30pm and at 4:00 he held an informal thanksgiving service, blessing each room throughout the house, ending in the chapel. Two little girls carried candles. Everyone seemed very pleased with all they saw.

The Sisters remarked that "it was a very successful and lovely occasion thanks to the help of Muriel Unwin, Jean Hoppin, Kay Wilson, Mary Willow, the Pederson's and various parishioners." Next day Fr. Pederson received a letter from Bishop Spong, setting a target date of December 3 for terminating his ministry at Grace Church.

After all the excitement of the open house and settling back into St. Christopher's with no workmen around, the summer proceeded in the usual manner with groups being sent off to the various camps, as well as the Vacation Bible School. Also, some Vietnamese refugees were taken in at this time. Brother Thomas, who had been at Grace Church for several years, finally moved out of his apartment in St. Christopher's at the beginning of July and it was used for more refugees.

At the end of August a Newsletter was sent to Friends and parishioners. Amongst the several items was the news that the funds collected by the parish in memory of Sr. Eleanor Lucy amounted to $289 and the check was sent to Mother Margaret Helena. She used it to purchase a reconditioned piano, which was placed in the chancel at Grace Church. It was dedicated at the closing service of the summer program on August 15, and was used at that service to accompany the musical pageant presented by about 75 children.

No sooner was the summer program over than plans were being made for the Fall and pre-Christmas activities. Thus the Newsletter contained an appeal for people to help financially or in other ways. "Help with taking care of buildings and grounds, of altar and vestments, with sewing and making articles for the bazaar, with running flea markets. What can you do? And, remember your regular worship with your parish family on Sundays. Show your love of God and your care and concern for His and your Church!" A group of young people planned a special "homecoming" day which took place on October 15. About 270 people attended and everyone was very enthusiastic. Many people came who had not been around for some time.

The end of October 1978 found all the Sisters at the convent for the installation of Fr. Paul Wessinger, SSJE, as Warden. Fr. Weed, who had been Warden for so many years, was to continue his link with the Community by becoming an Associate.

A letter to Fr. Pederson from Archdeacon Grant gave cause for concern at the beginning of November. It advised him to apply for mission status for Grace Church as there would be no funding for it as a parish after

December 31. This seemed to be a regression to the situation in the early 1950s. The Newsletter of August had stated that the church was behind in payment of Public Service bills, and much-needed repairs still had to be carried out. There was a congregational meeting on November 16, to apply for mission status, attended by 36 people. At another congregational meeting on December 17, a special Executive Committee was elected.

It was against this background of uncertainty that the work in Jersey City passed from 1978 into 1979. There may have been uncertainties about the parish, and the weather predictably turned to snow, but the Epiphany pageant went ahead without hesitation. There were 85 costumed children and around 200 people present. The Sisters had "a hearty tea" beforehand and reinforcements came to help from the convent in the shape of Sr. Katharine Veronica, Sr. Barbara Jean, several Associates including Marion Burger, and three girls from St. John Baptist School. Such help was greatly appreciated by the three Sisters based at Grace Church—Sr. Elizabeth Anne, Sr. Susinne Paula and Sr. Suzanne Elizabeth. In early February Fr. Pederson was still at Grace Church but attending interviews for another appointment.

The Sisters continued to engage in pastoral work. Thus when a member of the congregation died in February 1979, Sr. Elizabeth Anne accompanied Fr. Pederson to visit the family and make arrangements for the funeral. All the children were at home and were "glad to see Sister." The Sisters attended the Mass and burial service and assisted by reading the lessons and the intercessions. Sr. Elizabeth Anne also administered the chalice.

The Sisters' love of animals was stretched when they returned to the convent for Fr. Coleman's retreat in March. As usual they had taken Judy their dog with them. Their Record Book related what happened next. "Monday morning early, Judy came in contact with a skunk so she could not be let into the house. After breakfast Sr. Elizabeth Anne took a large can of tomato juice and washed her off on the back driveway. She was pretty good, but became impatient—difficult to rinse her off properly so she was pink for several days."

In between all their parish commitments and the frequent returns to the convent for confession and retreats, the Sisters also attended conferences. Nineteen seventy-nine saw them attending conferences on urban ministry and related subjects. Thus on March 10, Sr. Elizabeth Anne accompanied Fr. Pederson and other parishioners to Cathedral House in Newark for a

Hispanic Conference on Urban Christianity. It was led by Bishop Reus-Froylan of Puerto Rico[21] and was bi-lingual. Fr. Luce (priest in charge of Grace Church [Van Vorst] 1962–65) was amongst the delegates. The Sisters declared it was good to see him again. Next day, Sr. Elizabeth Anne, Sr. Suzanne Elizabeth, Fr. Pederson and Spanish members of the congregation went to a Spanish rally at Grace Church, Union City, NJ, with Bishop Reus-Froylan. A few days later, on March 17, Bishop Reus-Froylan came for a Spanish Mass in the parish hall. Forty-five people were present and afterwards there were refreshments, plus music and singing—the bishop played his guitar.

On April 21, 1979, Fr. Pederson's daughter Sigrid was married in Grace Church and the Sisters attended the wedding. Fr. Pederson took part of the service and the groom's cousin, a Methodist minister, assisted, as well as some Jesuit priests. It was a truly ecumenical occasion. Sr. Elizabeth Anne assisted in administering the chalice, and there were about 120 people present at the service.

Fr. Pederson was still looking for another appointment and also other priests were looking at Grace Church. One such hopeful priest did not make a good impression. He was late arriving for his interview, and the Sisters had to leave early to go to Hudson Ecumenical Church Women at the Church of the Incarnation, NYC. He further ruined his chance of appointment by referring to the area as "a ghetto"! The Sisters' Record Book noted that "this did not sit well" with the parishioners.

The newly renovated St. Christopher's House was now available for meetings. For instance, on April 25, 1979, the Department of Missions met and, following Mass in church at noon, had lunch and a meeting in the first-floor conference room. Hopefully they were impressed with the transformation of the building, which had cost in the region of $40,000, much of which had been raised through the efforts of Muriel Unwin and Jean Hoppin. Next evening, 40 people met for a Convocation meeting. Several of the young adults came and helped with refreshments. Archdeacon Turnbull attended and settled the rumors that the diocese was planning to close Grace Church.

On May 22, Fr. Elisha John Gwynn was interviewed and stayed overnight. He was elected as Rector at a special meeting of the Executive Committee on June 22, but would not take up his duties until the Fall. Back at the convent on Ascension Day, May 24, Fr. Gross (Chaplain since Fr. Templeton's death) received Sr. Martha Clare's first renewal of her vows.

Meanwhile on Sunday May 25 Fr. Pederson began to feel ill at the 11:30 service and asked Sr. Elizabeth Anne to give the sermon.

Sometimes the Sisters could not resist "treats"! The Jersey City Record Book notes that on June 14, upon their return from a meeting, a neighbor's child "had cotton candy. Sr. Suzanne Elizabeth 'ooh'ed' and 'ah'ed' about it so much that Fr. Pederson went and got three big balls of cotton candy for us, i.e. Father, Sr. Suzanne Elizabeth and Sr. Elizabeth Anne. Judy liked it too."

The summer program, including the camps, was a success as usual. Writing in the Fall Newsletter to Friends of Grace Church, the Sisters acknowledged the support they received. "You made it possible through your prayers, your interest, your support, and your many gifts of food, clothing and money." Ninety-one children had been sent to camp. The Sisters also paid tribute to the summer helpers. "Our staff was excellent—one college girl from Illinois who lived with us, five local college students, three mothers from the parish, and three teenage helpers. Their cooperation and attitude were exceptional, and they worked up another very good musical for the closing of the program."

The Sisters were also providing a scholarship for a young boy to attend a Church Farm School in Pennsylvania. His mother was a member of Grace Church and she was training to be a teacher. "We think she will be an excellent teacher, as she was one of the best we have had in our summer Bible School."

Fall 1979 saw a number of changes that would directly affect the work in Jersey City. Firstly, Fr. Pederson had finally left the parish at the end of the summer program. Fr. Gwynn had been in residence since early September and the Sisters had written in their Fall Newsletter that he had "already done much to strengthen and develop the life of the congregation." On October 2, the Sisters returned to the convent for the election of the Superior. They already knew that Mother Margaret Helena was not standing for re-election. Sr. Elizabeth Anne was elected and installed next day. Sr. Suzanne Elizabeth was appointed Sister Superior of St. Christopher's House. She returned to Jersey City the same day along with Sr. Susinne Paula and Sr. Martha Clare—and Judy the dog.

In their Fall Newsletter the Sisters wrote of the changes being made. "Plans are being made to extend the clothing room operations and the winter programs for children. Scout program, a children's choir, and an adult choir are a few of the many changes which are taking place—exciting changes with new hope and vision for the congregation of Grace Church." Girl Scouts had their first meeting at Grace Church with ten girls present, plus Fr. Gwynn, on October 4. (Boy Scouts began on October 11.) On October 6, there was a reception in the Church grounds to welcome Fr. and Mrs. Gwynn. This was organized by the Spanish congregation and neighborhood people. They gave them three presents—a Spanish dictionary, a Spanish Bible and a wallet. The Sisters helped set up and attended for two hours. Clearly Fr. Gwynn did not speak Spanish!

Although some painting and decorating had been done in the church it was largely cosmetic and there were problems still outstanding. On October 9, the "Bishop's Committee," i.e. the Executive Committee, met with Fr. Gwynn, Sr. Suzanne Elizabeth and Mother Elizabeth Anne, to vote on plans to heat and make renovations in the church. It was so cold in the church that it was decided to have all weekday Masses in the Sisters' chapel at St. Christopher's. There were many requests for food and clothing by the needy, and these were given in exchange for work being done. On October 28, 1979, the heating was turned on in the church for the first time in a long while.

On October 30, the Sisters received a phone call in the evening to say that Fr. Albert, past Rector of Grace Church, had died and next-of-kin were being sought. A strange request. Fr. Pederson was contacted and he offered to help find contacts. Also, the Sisters had some telephone contacts for his family in Massachusetts.

On November 1, 1979, the Sisters were back at the convent for Sr. Mary Lynne's profession in first vows. "It was a beautiful day," noted Sr. Suzanne Elizabeth in the Record Book. Back in Jersey City there was the Girl Scout Hallowe'en Party at 6:30pm and a bazaar meeting at the rectory at 8:00.

Mother Edna Frances and Sr. Gina were visiting the convent from Clewer and on November 3–4 they came to Jersey City. There had been more upheaval at St. Christopher's with work on the floors and a big "turn out" of things left by Fr. Pederson. Also, some rooms had changed use, so the Sisters worked hard to prepare the house ready for the English visitors. On Sunday November 4, "corn on the cob was cooked for the Sisters to sustain them through the pot luck luncheon after the 11:30 Mass, about 1:30pm. Also they had some sherbert—both foods never tasted before and enjoyed very much."[22] The English Sisters seemed to enjoy meeting the people of Grace Church and felt very welcome. They left for the convent in the afternoon and returned to England on the following Sunday.

On Thanksgiving Day, November 22, Fr. Gwynn celebrated Mass at 10:00am in the Sisters' chapel with 18 attending. But the major project at this time was the bazaar and all the various groups were involved in the preparations. On the second day of the bazaar Sr. Susinne Paula and Marion Burger came back to St. Christopher's after walking the dog and found the TV that had been on the Community Room table at the foot of the stairs. Further investigation found the roof trapdoor open and broken off. Somebody had clearly come in that way and intended to take the TV but on hearing someone return to the house fled back through the roof leaving the TV at the foot of the stairs.

On December 15, 1979, there was a pre-installation celebration with Bishop Spong at Grace Church Parish Hall from 7:30 until 11:30pm. The vestry and staff, including the Sisters, ate with the bishop, but the Sisters returned to St. Christopher's at 8:00 as people began arriving for the evening party. Next day, December 16, Bishop Spong celebrated, preached and installed Fr. Gwynn as Vicar of Grace Church. Mother Elizabeth Anne, Sr. Laura Katharine, Sr. Mary Lynne and other friends came from Mendham for the service, which began at 11:30am. Drums, two horns, a bass and piano, plus "star singers" provided the music. It was a long service, finishing at 2:00pm. Coffee hour was provided by the Sisters in the gym. Then they just about had time for a quick cup of soup with "the convent delegation" in St. Christopher's House before the latter left.

On December 17 the Sisters had a visit from Fr. Wessinger, newly appointed Warden—his first visit to Jersey City.

After all the celebrations and excitement of a new regime at Grace Church, it was back to work with the toy sale. Two Sisters came to help from the convent, eleven parishioners, and seven CSJB Associates and staff all helped, including Mrs. Gwynn, and it was a "pleasant day." Amongst the Associates who helped was Marion Burger. Much to her surprise a birthday cake was produced at 7:00pm for her 89th birthday the following day.

There were over 100 people at Midnight Mass, a great improvement on former years. There was a candlelight procession and recession, and music provided by flute and piano. The Mass was over by 1:30am and Fr. Gwynn invited the parishioners into the rectory for cocoa and bread and butter. The Sisters said Lauds in St. Christopher's chapel, and finally got to bed at 2:15am. Even so, they were up at 7:00am and left for the convent at 10:00am. But they were back in Jersey City on the 27th, having planning meetings with Fr. Gwynn and not ending until 11:00pm.

The Fall Newsletter had concluded, "Amidst the many changes, Grace Church continues to minister to the needs of the people in the neighborhood—clothing, food, furniture, some financial help, and counselling and guidance in the many problems that the people of the city must face. We go on in the assurance of your support and prayers; for ministering to God's children here in the city is your work as well as ours."

A Newsletter in December, which promised to be the first of a monthly letter, stated that "extensive repair work was begun on our deteriorated church building, and by mid-December, we had a beautiful structure we're all proud of. Church attendance has picked up considerably, and we're seeing many new faces each week."

None of the Sisters' work and ministry could be done without the dedication in their vowed life, and the prayer that undergirded it all. Thus on December 31, Sr. Suzanne Elizabeth, Sr. Martha Clare and other Sisters were to be found in the chapel at Mendham praying the old year out and the New Year in. It was a time-hallowed Community custom which the departed Sisters from former years would have recognized immediately.

As ever, fund-raising had to be done in order to make ends meet. With so many programs to run, and so many needy people to care for, the problem of funding was a never-ending story. Bake sales and flea markets brought in a regular, though sometimes small, income. At St. Christopher's House the clothes room had been reorganized to give more space, and Mrs. Barbara Gwynn was now helping Muriel Unwin and Jean Hoppin. And as always, there were needy men who asked for food. In January 1980 the Sisters were giving dinner to two men as part of the Crisis Center–Value exchange scheme.

It was important to inform the wider church about Grace Church. Many parishes knew about it because they were supporters through donations of toys, clothing and food. But there can never be too much publicity. Thus on Friday February 1, 1980, Sr. Suzanne Elizabeth went to Diocesan Convention and set up a table with flyers about the various programs at Grace Church. Packets of flyers were placed on the delegates' tables. The Diocesan newspaper had recently run an article on Grace Church so this was displayed, together with a large picture of the lych gate, which was placed on the wall. It was a long day and Sister and her helpers did not get home until 11:30pm. Convention continued next day and three Sisters and a helper left at 9:00am, arriving home at 5:30pm.

No matter how difficult the situation, the Sisters coped with it. When their doorbell rang at 4:30am on February 4, 1980, they found a distressed lady. They took her in, gave her breakfast and after a rest, took her to the train station to return to Newark. At 4:30pm she was back at St. Christopher's, lame from wandering about all day. She was given supper and a bed for the night. Two days later the lady wandered away before breakfast leaving a thank you note. At 4:30pm she was back again and was given a room to sleep in. As a precaution, her hat and coat were taken away for the night and returned to her after breakfast next morning. She was then taken to the train station in Newark and put on the train to Wilmington.

Fr. Pederson was still around and on February 5, 1980, the anniversary of the Sisters' first arrival in New York, he celebrated Mass in the Sisters' chapel at St. Christopher's House. The Sisters had remained on friendly terms with him, and had visited him in hospital when he had been seriously ill with pneumonia a few weeks previously. On the same day, the Sisters interviewed three Cambodian refugees. The Jersey City Record Book noted that "they seemed to be good prospects for 'renting' one of the apartments here and working in cleaning and maintenance, and the [altar] bread room." Next day, a Spanish family living nearby was also interviewed and they cleaned and painted the third-floor apartment before moving in. A few days later Fr. Pederson phoned to say he had found a job as a chaplain in a jail. The Sisters were all very happy for him.

The Sisters' ministry of sheltering the needy was well known, and that they would not turn anyone away. They had a phone call from the Palace Drug store on February 9, saying that a 66-year-old black woman who was nearly blind needed a place to stay for the night. She used to live in Jersey City, and had some money on her but not enough for a hotel. As usual, the Sisters came to the rescue and put her up in the guest room. Such rescue operations could only be temporary as the Sisters did not have many rooms to spare in the house. Sometimes there were dilemmas, as in the case of a lady they took in who, they discovered, was well known to all the senior citizens agencies, who described her as a "very difficult person." She had need of custodial care, but one of her daughters said she would take care of her. Then she changed her mind and no one in the family would take her in, nor would any agency. Three police officers were called and they spent an hour looking for some place for her to stay the night. Finally, the YMCA took her in for $16 and next day the agencies promised to investigate housing and care.

The bright start to Fr. Gwynn's ministry was faltering. The scout groups were not flourishing numerically, nor was the children's choir. The main problem was lack of leaders. Meetings took place frequently, but meanwhile the Sisters continued their ministry. They were a stable presence in a sea of uncertainty. The children who came to sing in the choir were rewarded with a trip to the American Museum of Natural History and Planetarium. Sr. Suzanne Elizabeth took twelve children and some adult helpers. "A great time was had by all!" The Spanish Masses also were struggling. When he was available, Fr Pederson celebrated, but numbers had seriously fallen off and sometimes no one came at all.

At the convent, Mother Elizabeth Anne phoned to say that their Associate Marion Burger had died in the evening of February 27. On February 29, the Mass at St. Christopher's was a requiem for Marion Burger. The funeral took place at the convent on Monday March 3, 1980, at 11:00am. Fr. Weed and Fr. Laughlin took part in the service, after which she was interred in the Associates' plot in the convent cemetery. It was a cold, sunny day, and as well as the Jersey City Sisters, there were many people from New York City present. On Monday, March 17, there was a memorial service at St. Luke's in the Fields, NYC.

On March 20, Sr. Suzanne Elizabeth and Sr. Martha Clare went to New York to the WOR Radio Station on Broadway, where they taped three programs to be aired the following Saturday, Sunday and the Sunday after that. And Sr. Suzanne Elizabeth revealed a hidden talent in the Record Book when she noted that she had tutored a young student in Spanish for one-and-a-half hours, and gave him further lessons.

Holy Week and Easter took their usual course: the Sisters went to the convent from Wednesday until Holy Saturday, thus ensuring that they would have the benefit of the Holy Week liturgy they were accustomed to. They returned to Jersey City in time to prepare the church and their chapel for Easter. On Easter Day about 200 people were present at the Mass at 11:00am. Afterwards the Sisters returned to the convent until Tuesday morning.

Relations between Fr. Gwynn and the Sisters had become tense. On April 16, Mother Elizabeth Anne and Sr. Katharine Veronica came over from the convent for a meeting with Fr. Gwynn and the Sisters. But he simply set out his agenda for the Sisters' work—to manage the Value-Exchange program, food and clothes and telephone calls for four hours a day, plus children's programs, and one Sister to do secretarial work for him. A further meeting was scheduled for a week's time.

On April 23, Mother and Sr. Katharine Veronica returned for the follow-up meeting with Fr. Gwynn together with the Sisters. Mother told Fr. Gwynn that the Community was no longer able to continue the ministry in Jersey City as the Sisters were needed at the convent to re-form and re-vitalize their life together. They would withdraw by June 1, unless the vicar really wanted the summer program. He said that he did want it and so Mother then said the Sisters would complete their work at Grace Church by August 15, 1980. He then said he hoped the Sisters would continue to give assistance in the parish in any way they could, especially with future summer programs. This of course would have been totally unfeasible. The future withdrawal was not publicized to the parish or to the Community until the bishop had spoken to Fr. Gwynn. Another meeting was scheduled for May 7, in order to discuss details.

On May 7, Mother Elizabeth Anne came for the meeting with Fr. Gwynn and Sr. Suzanne Elizabeth. No commitment was made to continue assistance after their withdrawal, which was settled for August 15. The announcement would be made when their formal written letter of resignation had been received by the bishop, the Archdeacon of Mission and Fr. Gwynn. On May 13, at the end of a busy day, Sr. Suzanne Elizabeth and Sr. Mary Lynne went to the Executive Committee meeting. Fr. Gwynn read out Mother Elizabeth Anne's letter concerning the resignation of the Community from Grace Church as of August 15. "People were quiet but expressed surprise and sorrow." On Sunday May 18, Fr. Gwynn announced the Sisters' resignation from the parish. He allowed people to respond and about seven did so, including a child. They all said how much the Sisters would be missed; how different it would be without them; and how important the Sisters were in their lives.

The imminent departure of the Sisters did not mean their work stopped as soon as it was made public. All the usual children's activities went ahead including the mammoth task of registration for summer camp, for which the Sisters had help as usual. The last Saturday Church School of the season took place on May 31, with twenty children present. Next day at Mass, the green altar frontal, chasuble, stole, and pulpit fall all had colorful paper flowers made by the children and used for the service. About 25 children sang, four were baptized and Archdeacon Turnbull preached. Afterwards there was a trip to Liberty State Park for a parish picnic. They left there at 5:00pm and were home by 6:00. "It was a beautiful sunny day 90°F, but breezy. A good time was had by all."

On Saturday, June 7 all the Sisters and Judy the dog went to the St. John Baptist School graduation at St. Peter's Morristown. It was the 100th graduation and was well attended, on a sunny, warm day. Later in the evening, four Sisters went to the alumnae dinner and dance and met many "old girls." Next day there was a Mass in the convent chapel for Sisters and SJBS graduates. About 30 of them attended.

The summer program went ahead despite teachers and helpers letting the Sisters down at short notice. Somehow, everyone got off to camp and all were taught at Vacation Bible School. The government lunches were late but everyone waited patiently and they arrived eventually. About 80 children enrolled. By this time it was mid-July and the Sisters were entering their last month at Grace Church. On July 26 they started packing books and china ready for the move back to the convent. After thirty years in Jersey City there would be much to do.

The end-of-program musical went ahead on Friday, August 1, and although only half the children turned up all went well. Fr. Pederson helped set up the microphones, and there was a good congregation including people from the neighborhood. However, Fr. Gwynn was absent, although his wife was there.

In the midst of all the packing up Mother Elizabeth Anne telephoned on August 5 to say that Sr. Winifred Agnes had died. She had been received as a novice in March 1925 but her great work was at St. Luke's Chapel, NYC. It was said in her Community Biography that "she was very fond of people and could talk with the lonely people, thus making her contribution to the mission of the Sisters at St. Luke's." Her requiem Mass was on Saturday, August 9, followed by burial in the convent cemetery. The Sisters came from Jersey City and returned there later the same day.

The closure of St. Christopher's House would also mean the people living in the apartments would have to be rehoused. Thus on August 11 the Sisters helped the Cambodians look at an apartment across the street. The Sisters had plenty of helpers with their preparations to leave and also received some media publicity. An illustrated article in the *Jersey Journal* on August 12, 1980, showed Sr. Suzanne Elizabeth, Sr. Susinne Paula and Sr. Mary Lynne packing books. On the same day a Eucharist and supper was held at St. Matthew's Church in honor of the Sisters' work in Jersey City. Dinner was served at 10:00pm! About 70 people were present and it was "a very joyous occasion." Mother Elizabeth Anne and Sr. Laura Katharine were also present.

On August 15, the Sisters' last day, Fr. Pederson said Mass in their chapel. Friends and helpers were present. Two hymns were sung and at the end Fr. Pederson emptied the tabernacle and consumed the Blessed Sacrament. Then all stayed for a talking breakfast. There was no sign of Fr. Gwynn. Later, Mother drove in with Sr. Katharine Veronica in the school van which was then loaded up with some of the Sisters' belongings. They left Jersey City by 4:00pm and were home at the convent in time for dinner.

Next day, August 16, they returned to St. Christopher's to pack up the house ready for the removal men. On Monday, August 18 the removal men arrived by 10:00am and "worked carefully and constantly." Fr. Gwynn was called but did not come over to get the keys or say goodbye. The Sisters led the removal van out of Jersey City and arrived at the convent in time for Vespers. All was unloaded by 9:00pm and the rain held off until 10:00pm.

Sr. Suzanne Elizabeth made the final entry in the Jersey City Record Book on August 22, 1980, after the Sisters had picked up the last of the summer campers and delivered them back to the church. "Work now completed for St. Christopher's House with the Sisters. Many thanks for a successful summer program and 29 years in Jersey City at Grace Church (Van Vorst)."

But it's not quite the end of the story. When I was making my annual research visit to Mendham in 2015 I asked whether a visit to Jersey City would be possible. Sr. Suzanne Elizabeth took Sr. Pamela, Sr. Monica Clare and myself to see Grace Church on Wednesday, May 6. We didn't know what we would find. Would the church be dilapidated, or closed? It was many years since Sr. Suzanne Elizabeth had been working in Jersey City.

When we arrived the church was locked but we made our way round the corner to the parish hall. There sitting on the doorstep were some homeless men. Sister spoke to them and they explained they were waiting to be called in to have lunch. A hopeful sign. When we went inside we found the hall buzzing with activity. There was a senior citizens' lunch club (after which the homeless would be fed). In a different part of the large hall there was a keep fit class, and elsewhere a group of ladies were doing handicrafts. Someone took us into the church. The fixed pews had been removed to make a large space for weekday activities. There were chairs for Sunday worship. One part of the nave of the church was used for a pre-school play area with all the toys ready for next day. In another part of the nave a dance group were just finishing their rehearsal. Clearly the whole church and hall were being used by the wider community for a variety of activities. We walked along the street and looked across at the former St. Christopher's House. It looked the same as ever.

When in 2018 I asked Sr. Suzanne Elizabeth which of the many ministries in her long Community life she felt was the most rewarding, she was unhesitating in her reply. "Jersey City with hundreds of children and Vacation Bible School—to teach and play and feed and clothe; fire victims and refugees to re-settle, counsel, teach and learn."

Jersey City is no longer a place of urban deprivation but somehow on that day in 2015 it seemed as if the Sisters were still there. And indeed this is their legacy, that the people in the neighborhood—the people on Second Street—still regard Grace Church as being there for them. This is the lasting legacy of the Sisters—that their work continues in other hands.

---

[1] Article in *Jersey Journal* August 14, 1970, by Prudence Wear 'Grace Church has Recipe for Joy.'

[2] The Margaret Hague Maternity Hospital finally closed in 1979.

[3] The booklet commemorating Grace Church's 125th anniversary noted: "Fr. Albert has labored assiduously to protect and better the living conditions of the minority people who largely make up our congregation … He has publicly protested against the landlord neglect and official indifference to housing problems, on one occasion by means of a street procession headed by a large cross made from charred timber taken from one of the holocausts in which members of our congregation perished. And, perhaps the most enduring accomplishment of all, he planned, enlisted public cooperation, and won federal financing for a housing project involving the rehabilitation of six large run-down tenement buildings on the same block as Grace Church. These apartment houses, containing a total of 44 apartments, were opened for the first tenants in June 1971, and dedicated last October 29th as the Rev. William Albert Houses."

[4] This is not to be confused with the St. John the Baptist Foundation.

[5] Trinity Institute continues into the 21st century with annual theological conferences, welcoming participants from all faith traditions.

[6] The Armenian massacre of 1915, also known as the Armenian Genocide, was the Ottoman Government's systematic extermination of 1.5 million Armenians, mostly civilians, within the Ottoman Empire. As of 2018, 29 countries have officially recognized the mass killings as genocide, but the Turkish government still refuses to do so. Source en.m.wikipedia.org

[7] The Sisters' Record Book is unclear whether it was the Rectory or St. Christopher's House. But has the comment "He (Fr. Albert) went to New Salem just the same."

[8] Marion Gardens was one of several housing projects begun in Jersey City in 1940 by the Jersey City Housing Authority to provide affordable housing to low-paid workers. By the 1970s Marion Gardens was a very run down and deprived area.

[9] Sr. Suzanne Elizabeth remembers Br. Thomas as one of a number of men at that time who lived an independent Religious Life unattached to any formal Community. He joined the Sisters for Offices and Mass in the chapel at St. Christopher's House and helped in the parish with visiting the sick and shut-ins. Eventually he joined a Christian Community.

[10] Cardinal Leo Joseph Suenens (1904–96) was Belgian by birth. He served as Archbishop of Mechelen-Brussel 1961–79 and was made a Cardinal in 1962. He was a strong supporter of renewal in the Catholic Church, took a leading role in Vatican II and was a leading ecumenist.

[11] Letter to the Mother and Sisters at Clewer, summer 1973.

[12] Bishop Stark died on May 8, 1986, at age 78.

[13] Letter to Clewer op. cit.

[14] Ibid.

[15] Bishop Wright was the first black priest in the Episcopal Church to become a bishop. He was told in 1952 by his college guidance counselor that "there's no place for blacks in the Episcopal Church." Source: *New York Times* February 3, 1974. Fortunately, times have changed.

[16] The Community Record Book stated that Sr. Agnes Genevieve had returned to the convent from NYC because of heart trouble and that on December 8 *after Vespers* she was found on the floor of her cell having died suddenly and peacefully. But the Jersey City Record Book states that she died "instantly of a heart attack *during Vespers*." It goes on to state that "Mother went directly afterwards to check how she was and found her lying dead on the floor."

[17] Muriel Unwin kept a file of appeal letters and other correspondence relating to the Sisters' work and ministry at Grace Church (Van Vorst). In July 2009 she deposited this material in the Sisters' archives at Mendham. She described in her covering letter how she and Jean Hoppin, both members of Calvary Church, Summit, had been volunteers at Grace Church from 1972–81. "It was the high light of our lives," she wrote. She also mentioned another volunteer, Kay Wilson from St. Gregory's Church, Parsippany. This material has been used in this chapter, and so her work goes on. Muriel Unwin died on July 21, 2018, at age 92.

[18] Some of the early US CSJB Sisters were descended from signers of the Declaration. See BONHAM, Valerie *Living Stones: The Community of St. John Baptist in America. Appendix 3 Sisters' families and American history*. Mendham, NJ, 2016.

[19] In fact the open house was on Sunday, April 30, in the afternoon.

[20] Letter from Muriel Unwin and Kathryn Wilson to Friends of Grace Church, February 28, 1978.

[21] The Right Revd. Francisco Reus-Froylan was bishop of the Episcopal Diocese of Puerto Rico, 1964–89.

[22] We English are so unadventurous with our food!

SHOWING FORTH THE KINGDOM OF GOD

The Community 1980–84

A S 1979 GAVE birth to a new decade, the Community of St. John
Baptist would face many changes, some already anticipated and
others less so. In the wider World there would be conflicts, political coups,
and hostage crises, but the end of the decade would see the Berlin Wall
collapse at the beginning of a new era—the end of the Cold War.

Meanwhile CSJB faced its own great change with the election of Sr.
Elizabeth Anne as Mother Superior in October 1979, already mentioned
in Chapter 12. Sr. Margaret Helena had been Mother Superior for 30
years, the longest in CSJB history. After her "retirement" she questioned
whether she had remained in office for too long. This would only be so
if her long tenure had damaged the Community, but she had guided the
Sisters through those years with wisdom and foresight. In her early years
as Superior she had, with Community agreement, considered moving
from the large convent on its hilltop site at Mendham, but this had been
thwarted by external forces, and it was perceived as God's will that the
Sisters should stay at Mendham. She had continued Mother Waldine
Lucia's policy of closing outdated institutional work and took on the
challenge of the inner city. That work was soon to end, but its value
in terms of showing forth the Kingdom of God was beyond measure.
Mother Margaret Helena fostered the vocations to the priesthood of a
number of young men. She also heartily supported the priestly vocation of
women, and specifically of some known to the Community. Relinquishing
office after so many years could not have been easy and she would live for
another 23 years within the Community, lovingly cared for by the Sisters
as she grew increasingly frail. But frailty was not a problem at first and
she continued to visit and nurture the Associates in Oregon for many
years, as well as conducting retreats and quiet days and giving spiritual
direction nearer home.

In January 1980 Mother Elizabeth Anne, Sr. Mary Lynne and the Sisters
from Jersey City attended the Diocesan ACTS/VIM (A Commitment
to Serve/Venture in Mission) rally at Seton Hall, NJ. This was attended

by about 1,000 Episcopalians. Former Presiding Bishop John Hines and retired Bishop of Newark George Rath were among the speakers. The aims were to aid community development and outreach, to promote collaboration and cooperation, and to foster and broaden clergy and lay leadership in the congregation. Funds were available upon application to help parishes fulfill their mission.

Ecumenical relations were still flourishing, with the Mendham Interchurch Service for the Octave of Prayer for Christian Unity being held at the Mallinckrodt convent in Mendham, home of the RC Sisters of Christian Charity. Two carloads went from CSJB, and Sr. Barbara Jean and Fr. Gross, the Community Chaplain, took part in the service, which was well attended. Fr. Donworth from St. Joseph's RC Church preached at the CSJB Sisters' 7:00 am Mass on the following Sunday.

St. John Baptist School students were eagerly anticipating the school's Centennial anniversary, 1880–1980. Former alumnae were being approached for their school memories for a Centennial history. There were a number of overseas students, including a girl from Liberia and two from Thailand. But there were clouds on the horizon—numbers of students were falling and a financial crisis was looming. The future of this, the Sisters' oldest work, was under threat.

The Community has always had the faithful support of Associates and friends, and one of the longest serving was Marion Burger, who, as noted in Chapter 13, died at Morristown Memorial Hospital on February 27, 1980, after a short illness, at age 89. In her Weekly Letter to the Sisters, Mother Elizabeth Anne wrote: "Marion will be much missed by many friends as well as by all of us. May she rest in peace."[1]

Sr. Winifred Agnes was by now a patient at Morris View Nursing Home. Mother Elizabeth Anne noted in her Weekly Letter to the Sisters on April 17 that "Sr. Katharine Veronica and I spent a few hours helping to feed the patients. All the nurses, except one, were out on strike; and families of the patients were asked to give some volunteer help. Fortunately the nurses were back on duty next day."

On Friday May 2 the four Sisters (including one novice) of the Community of the Way of the Cross[2] arrived for a two-week visit to the convent. A full schedule of visits was arranged for them. Sr. Barbara Jean took three of them to an Interchurch Hymn Sing at Mallinckrodt convent in Mendham, and then they attended the program at St. John Baptist School for parents' day. Sr. Katharine Veronica took them to Jersey City to see the work there, and this was followed the next day with a visit to the Cathedral of St. John the Divine, NYC. The visiting Sisters were very appreciative of their visit and of the hospitality they received.

The 75th anniversary celebration at St. George's, Maplewood, NJ, was attended by Mother Elizabeth Anne, accompanied by Sr. Margaret Helena. The celebration included a Eucharist, Baptism and Confirmation, followed by a reception and luncheon. There was then a special program of speeches, reminiscences and tributes.

St. Marguerite's retreat house was in great demand, as Mother Elizabeth Anne noted in her Weekly Letter to the Sisters on Monday May 12. "A group of Methodist ministers come this evening until Wednesday morning. The Prayer Group from St. Peter's, Mountain Lakes, will be here for a Quiet Day on Wednesday, and a group from Morris Plains for a Quiet Day on Thursday. Members of the Interior Life seminar group will be here on Thursday evening through Sunday noon. Next Sunday afternoon we expect two groups of Sunday school children for picnics—from St. John's-on-the-Mountain, Bernardsville, and the Church of the Savior, Denville." The first group of children came with their teachers, but the group from Denville were "rained out."

The important work at Jersey City had become untenable and Mother Elizabeth Anne submitted the Community's resignation with effect from August 15. A sad but necessary decision. Meanwhile on the eve of Ascension Day a postulant was received at First Vespers, and two weeks later, Sr. Martha Clare came in from Jersey City to make her second annual renewal of her vows.

There may have been concerns for the future of St. John Baptist School but they were put aside on the Centennial weekend of June 6–7, 1980. Commencement was held at St. Peter's, Morristown, on Saturday June 7, and was attended by about 400 people. Mother wrote: "It was a lovely service. The weather cleared, so it was an almost perfect day for a June graduation." Bishop Spong preached and celebrated the Eucharist as well as presenting thirteen diplomas and three certificates to the graduates. Mother Elizabeth Anne presented the awards. At the reception afterwards there were Centennial anniversary cakes. Twelve alumnae stayed at St. Marguerite's from Friday through Saturday. On Saturday night Sr. Katharine Veronica, Sr. Suzanne Elizabeth, Sr. Barbara Jean, and Mother attended the Alumnae banquet at the Bedminster Inn. Next day at 10:00am there was a Mass of Dedication in the main chapel at the convent attended by about 40 people including Sisters, alumnae, and other guests. Afterwards there was a brunch in the Sisters' dining room. "Everyone felt it was a successful Centennial weekend," wrote Mother to the Sisters.

The revised *Book of Common Prayer* for the Episcopal Church had been authorized by the General Convention, and the Sisters now decided to use it on a regular basis. At the beginning of June they began using Rite 1 for all Masses in preparation for Commemoration Day on June 28. They decided also to use the *Missa de Angelis* plainsong setting on Sundays and festivals. A further liturgical change came as the outcome of a discussion on points raised by the Warden General at Clewer regarding the offices of Sext and None. The Sisters at Mendham began the experimental use of the Noonday Office from the new Prayer Book in place of these two offices, while continuing to follow their three-week psalm cycle.

St. John Baptist Day, closely followed by Commemoration Day 1980, was joyous as usual. Writing to the Sisters on Thursday, July 3, Mother Elizabeth Anne recalled that "the weather was perfect on Saturday for our outdoor Commemoration Day luncheon. The temperature and humidity had dropped a bit from the previous days ... and the sky was clear and sunny. Around 200 guests were here for the service and luncheon, [and] ten new Associates were received. The Warden celebrated, and the Chaplain [Fr. Gross] and Fathers Weed, Cromey, Hummel and Pederson assisted in the sanctuary."

Sr. Margaret Helena had been for her annual family visit to Oregon. When she returned home to the convent she brought with her some volcanic ash from Mount St. Helen's, which had erupted on May 18, 1980. An earthquake below the north face of the volcano had resulted in the largest landslide in recorded history, and a major volcanic eruption that scattered ash across a dozen states. It took 1,300 feet off the top of the mountain, and fifty-seven people lost their lives. It was the first major eruption since 1857. Many years previously it had been predicted by Sr. Mildred Eleanor, who had a degree in geology from M.I.T. Apparently Sr. Margaret Helena was disappointed not to have seen the volcano as there were so many clouds, probably ash clouds. But on July 22, the day after she returned to the convent, it erupted again. Mother Elizabeth Anne told the Sisters, "She feels disadvantaged!" But maybe she had a lucky escape.

After all the excitement of the festivals many of the Sisters took their summer rests in July, some at the beach house at Manasquan, and others visiting their families. But August brought forth the usual spate of Vacation Bible Schools and summer camps which involved several Sisters.

Sr. Winifred Agnes died suddenly on August 5 at Morris View Nursing Home. Her connection with CSJB went back to her youth when she resided for a time at Holy Cross House, NYC, when young women were being taken in as boarders. Sr. Virginia Dorothea and Sr. Emma Gabriel were her mentors and it was while residing there that she was prepared for baptism and confirmation. Indeed, she always said that she had found her Religious vocation through Sr. Emma Gabriel's nurturing. After her profession in 1926, Sr. Winifred Agnes had a ministry at St. Anna's where she taught the girls typing and bookkeeping. Her later ministry was at St. Luke's Chapel, NYC. Thus she had worked and ministered in some of the original institutional work and later in the work of the second spring of the Community. While in the nursing home she had received Holy Communion from the Community Chaplain every week. Sr. Winifred Agnes' requiem was held at the convent on Saturday, August 9, with Bishop Stark officiating. This was followed by burial in the convent cemetery, and a buffet lunch was served afterwards.

As noted in Chapter 13, the Sisters finally withdrew from Jersey City as from August 15. Moving back to the convent required a finely tuned exercise in logistics. But both before and after their departure there were several farewells. On August 12 at St. Matthew's Church there was a farewell Eucharist and supper. As well as the "Jersey City" Sisters this was attended by Mother Elizabeth Anne and Sr. Laura Katharine. Later in the Fall, on October 19, the Hudson Convocation held a thanksgiving service at St. John's Church, Jersey City.

St. John Baptist School opened for the new academic year at the beginning of September with 61 students and three more expected from Liberia and two from Venezuela. Sr. Barbara Jean and Sr. Laura Katharine were now to work there, with Sr. Suzanne Elizabeth as school nurse once more, following the closure of St. Christopher's House in Jersey City. The school history had been well received[3] and two former teachers from the 1920s were delighted with it when they visited earlier in the year. Towards the end of October Marjorie Robinson, an Associate, visited the convent with Mrs. Elizabeth Scovil Karsten, a graduate from the school in the class of 1909. The Sisters thought she was the oldest living alumna!

A shock was dealt to the school in October when Fr. Cromey the Headmaster announced his forthcoming resignation as from

December 19. He was to become rector of St. Mary's Church, Tuxedo Park, New York. It was decided that after the Christmas vacation Sr. Margaret Helena would act as Head of the School (not for the first time). Mr. Max Whittam would be the interim Headmaster until the end of the school year. He had been teaching mathematics, so he knew the school and the students. Fr. Cromey celebrated and preached at the Sisters' Mass on Sunday November 9, his last Sunday.

And so the year ran its course with many activities involving the Sisters—altar guild meetings, retreats, conferences, talks and addresses in the parishes and welcoming guests to the convent. None of it could have functioned effectively without the Sisters' life of prayer, sacrament and regular retreats. It was the "holy oil" which ensured that all ran smoothly and which made the Sisters' vowed life something authentic. It was what people saw when they visited and what made them want to return.

The Christmas festivities were kept in the usual way, with a midnight Choral Mass. Lauds was sung at 7:30 in the morning instead of after the Midnight Mass and all the Sisters made their Communions at the 8:00am Low Mass. Sr. Agatha Louise was in hospital but received her Communion there, and it had been hoped that she would be able to come to the convent for Christmas dinner. However, the weather was so cold that it was thought best not to bring her out in it. She returned to the convent on December 28, but following a fall had to return to hospital at the end of January.

On the last Saturday of the old year, there was a wedding in the chapel at St. Marguerite's, possibly a "first" in its long history. The bride was Debbie Corrigan.

Mother and several Sisters attended the institution of Fr. Cromey as Rector of St. Mary's Church, Tuxedo Park, New York on Sunday January 4, 1981. But the real highlight of January 1981 was the visit for three weeks by Sr. Annys from Clewer. She had undergone a period of poor health and bouts of surgery which had prevented her from visiting for some time. So it was an occasion of great joy to welcome her back to Mendham. She accompanied various Sisters to meetings and sightseeing trips.

In her Weekly Letter of Saturday, January 24, Mother Elizabeth Anne told the Sisters that "last night and today, Fr. Robert Morris's 'Interweave' group is having a retreat at St. Marguerite's."[4] On February 3, Mother Elizabeth Anne and Sr. Suzanne Elizabeth attended the Diocesan Convention, during which they were presented with a plaque from the people of Grace Church (Van Vorst) in appreciation of all the years of service at Jersey City by the Community. On February 5 they both flew out to Israel on a ten-day study tour with a group led by Fr. Bruce Bramlett.

Although St. John Baptist School had reached its centennial in 1980, there was growing concern about its future. The Sisters had a discussion on February 10, 1981, when anxieties were expressed about the financial state of the school. Some Sisters had the idea that Community capital was being used to subsidize the school, but Mother Elizabeth Anne said that except for one specific legacy that was turned over to the school account, all funding had been from income. Furthermore, she maintained that three quarters of what the Community gave to the school was in the form of scholarships to help girls from urban areas (and possibly from overseas) to get an education. It was to be regarded as "one of our big 'charity' works." The question was also raised about the amount of time some Sisters had spent on school work. The time since Christmas had been difficult with the interim headmaster and another teacher off sick, but Mother was confident that under new leadership the school would go from strength to strength, and the Sisters would be released from some of the time spent there.

During the month of March 1981 there were a number of discussions with parents of the school girls who were concerned about the future and anxious to help. Also, there was a discussion with the teaching faculty and Board of Trustees to set up guidelines for a search committee for a new headmaster. The school was not attracting enough new girls and four more students did not return after the spring vacation.

There was some sad news when the Sisters learned that St. Luke's in the Fields Church in New York City, where they had worked for 26 years, had burned to the ground on March 9. The church was completely destroyed, leaving only blackened walls. A new organ costing $200,000 had been recently installed and was now destroyed. St. Luke's was the third oldest church building in New York. Undaunted, the parish planned to rebuild. An undated news cutting from the *New York Times* in the Community archives shows Bishop Paul Moore and Fr. Laughlin standing in the ruins of the church after a service to dedicate the materials to be used in the rebuilding. It was thought that the fire was caused by a rare chemical reaction in the beams that caused them to ignite through spontaneous combustion. Mayor Koch told those gathered for the ceremony that the fire had not destroyed "the dedication, vision or initiative" of the church community. So far $300,000 had been contributed to the cost of rebuilding. The total cost was expected to be in the region of $5 million.

On March 29, 1981, eight Sisters went to the Cathedral of St. John the Divine, NYC, for a service of Solemn Evensong in thanksgiving for the work of Religious Communities in the metropolitan area. About 110 Religious from eleven different Communities were in choir. The preacher was Fr. Eric Simmons, CR, from the Community of the Resurrection, Mirfield, UK. There was a number in the congregation which included between fifteen and twenty CSJB Associates.

The search continued for a new Headmaster for St. John Baptist School. Several clergymen were interviewed before the announcement was made that the Revd. Colley Bell would be the new Head, beginning on July 1. There was more good news at the beginning of May when the school received approval from the New Jersey State Education department following its evaluation. School life went on despite all the anxieties about the future, and the girls may have been unaware of all the question marks hanging over it. An appeal for $50,000 was made at around this time but by the Fall only $8,000 had been donated. On May 12, several Sisters attended the "moving up" dinner at the school for the eighth graders, and on Thursday May 14 there was the school Confirmation. Archbishop Trevor Huddleston, CR,[5] officiated at the Confirmation. He had dinner with the Sisters beforehand and stayed overnight at St. Marguerite's.

St. Marguerite's was as busy as ever with many different groups and individuals seeking a place to explore their journey in faith. Monday May 25 through Wednesday May 27 saw a group of Methodist Ministers, the Order of St. Luke,[6] having a retreat. Next day there was a one-day seminar conference of the Middle States Independent Schools, and Friday night through Saturday the Confirmation class from All Saints', Princeton. The next few days would see groups from Martinsville; St. Paul's, Morris Plains; Calvary, Summit; and the Department of Christian Education. There was, as the saying goes, "never a dull moment"! And as spring gave way to summer, there were the usual parish picnics for groups from far and wide, all enjoying the beautiful hilltop site and the Sisters' warm welcome as they gave tours of the convent.

Commemoration Day was on Sunday June 28, with Vespers at 4:00pm followed by supper—a reversion to the former timetable presumably because of its happening on a Sunday. About 200 guests came and the preacher was the Very Revd. James Parks Morton, Dean of the Cathedral of St. John the Divine. He was an old friend of the Sisters, having been one of the clergy at Grace Church (Van Vorst) in their early days at Jersey City. Fourteen new Associates were received.

St. John Baptist School opened on September 8, 1981, with 47 students, thirteen of whom were day students. There was an international flavor, with girls from Liberia, Zaire, Tanzania, Venezuela, Ecuador, China, and Korea, some of whom would need financial assistance with fees. There was tea at the convent for the parents of the boarders, and next day the students and faculty came to the convent for tea. An "Open House" and reception at the school was planned for Sunday, November 8, from 3:00pm to 5:00pm, so that people from northern New Jersey could meet Fr. and Mrs. Bell and the teaching faculty and see the school. After the event Mother reported to the Sisters that "it was a lovely affair and was well attended."

Sunday, October 4, 1981, was the eighth centennial of St. Francis of Assisi, and for the offertory at Mass the Sisters sang the prayer of St. Francis with Sr. Barbara Jean accompanying on guitar. This was probably the first time guitar accompaniment had been used in the convent chapel, although Sr. Barbara Jean taught guitar to the girls at the school and was frequently photographed with the guitar group. After the Mass at the convent, four Sisters and the Chaplain attended the Franciscan ecumenical celebration at the cathedral of St. John the Divine, NYC. Mother Elizabeth Anne reported that the service was "two and a half hours long with three sermons! I was asked to read the Epistle." On the previous day at First Vespers of St. Francis, a postulant had been admitted, but alas, she left five weeks later "for lack of vocation." On October 7, Mother, Sr. Katharine Veronica, and Muriel Blue left for a three-week visit to Clewer. All went well.

People have long memories when they have received kindness in a time of need. This is why so many "old girls" from the days of the Sisters' institutional work kept in touch or visited long after they had left. The Sisters were pleasantly surprised when they received "a small legacy" to help with the school. The amount was not specified in the Weekly Letter to the Sisters dated December 4, 1981. It came from the estate of Julia Jakobeck Crosby, who as a child was in the Sisters' care at Christ Church Home, South Amboy.[7]

Nineteen eighty-two began on a busy note with Sisters being appointed to various offices within the Community and attending meetings outside the convent: Sr. Margaret Helena attended a meeting of the Diocesan Commission on Christian Education; Mother Elizabeth Anne, Sr. Barbara Jean and Sr. Mary Lynne attended the Mendham Interchurch meeting; Mother and Sr. Suzanne Elizabeth were appointed as Community representatives on the Morris Convocation with Sr. Katharine Veronica as the alternate representative. Additionally, Sr. Suzanne Elizabeth attended the Diocesan Altar Guild meeting in Newark. Icy roads resulted in the cancellation of her meeting with the Commission on Women's Ministry, also at Newark. Snow and ice also saw the postponement of other meetings.

The school was still in straitened circumstances financially and on Friday January 25 the University Glee Club presented a benefit concert in aid of the school at St. Peter's, Morristown. The Sisters were the guests of the Parents' Association and Mother Elizabeth Anne reported to the Sisters in her Weekly Letter of February 3, 1982, that it was "a happy occasion" and that a sum of between $1,700 and $1,800 was raised.

There was a farewell tea at the convent on Sunday January 31 for Mrs. Marjorie Almy, who had taught at St. John Baptist School for the past thirteen years. A candlelit dinner in her honor took place at the school on the following Wednesday (February 3).

In addition to welcoming groups to St. Marguerite's, the Sisters continued to welcome individual guests, some of whom were old friends. Thus Dorothy Templeton, widow of a former Chaplain, made a visit at the end of January. She visited from time to time as did some family members too. On Wednesday, February 3, Mary Ellen Appleton arrived for a few days visit. Mother Elizabeth Anne gives no more details about her, but she is likely to have been a member of the family of Sr. Virginia Dorothea (Appleton) who died in 1950 and whose sister, Helena, was an Associate and benefactress of the convent.

Sr. Agatha Louise was admitted to Morristown Memorial Hospital on February 11 for treatment for fractures in her pelvis and back, but surgery was not considered necessary. She was brought home to the convent on February 24, but was readmitted a few weeks later, finally coming home on May 28. And on March 4, Sr. Margaret Helena went into hospital for knee replacement surgery which was initially successful but required much physical therapy and further surgery. She was not allowed to drive until the middle of August.

Springtime and early summer came and went in the usual manner with retreat groups, courses, conferences, and meeting friends old and new. Sisters continued to visit parishes, spreading the word about the Religious Life; but while many expressed interest, few came forward to offer themselves for a vowed life, and of those who did, even fewer found it to be their vocation. Even so, the Sisters continued to faithfully live theirs; and however much they went out and about to meetings and parish visits, it was all in the context of prayer. They also had the benefit of attending courses on the Bible and aspects of theology given by their Chaplain or other visiting clergy. Such courses were often open to people from the local parishes.

On Sunday June 6, 1982, St. Margaret's House, NYC, was dedicated and Mother Elizabeth Anne attended. She reported in her Weekly Letter to the Sisters on June 10 that it was "a glorious occasion. In spite of rain, everyone processed from Trinity Church across town, carrying balloons and preceded by a band of bagpipers, to St. Margaret's House at Fulton and Pearl Streets. After the dedication by the Rector there was a luncheon. Olive Anderson, one of our Associates who lives there, showed us her apartment."[8]

St. John Baptist School had its Commencement on Saturday June 5, and it was described as "lovely" by Mother Elizabeth Anne. Fr. Maitland, a member of the Board of Directors, gave the sermon and presented the diplomas. Little did people know that this would be the penultimate Commencement ceremony, but maybe the Sisters had an inkling, because they knew the school was having financial difficulties and there were fewer students. Nevertheless, during the coming academic year the Sisters did their best for the school. Sr. Mary Lynne was to work at the school and Sr. Margaret Helena was to teach religious studies.

About 160 guests came for Commemoration Day on June 26, for the Mass and luncheon. Five new Associates were received and there were four house guests over the weekend. Afterwards, there were activities involving the Sisters outside the convent. For instance on June 27, Sr. Suzanne Elizabeth, Sr. Barbara Jean, Sr. Laura Katharine and Sr. Mary Lynne left for the Christian Education Conference in Rutherford, NJ, returning on Wednesday 30 June. On July 6, the Mendham Interchurch Vacation Bible School opened, with Sr. Barbara Jean teaching music and Sr. Mary Lynne teaching crafts. The enrollment was smaller than previously because of other summer programs elsewhere.

There was a sad note in the Weekly Letter of July 20, 1982. Judy, the dog acquired by the Sisters when they were in Jersey City and subsequently brought to the convent, had to be put to sleep. She was unwell and the vet found a serious health issue. A month later, Pucker came to live with the Sisters and was well loved.

For some time the Sisters had not been using the beach house at Manasquan as much as when they first bought it. It had been used by Associates and friends of the Community on a fairly regular basis, but at the end of July the Sisters decided to sell it. They already had a buyer and the sale was in process.

On September 28, 1982, Sr. Elizabeth Marion passed to her rest in Morristown Memorial Hospital. On June 17 she had celebrated the 50th anniversary of her profession. Her brother and sister-in-law came for the celebration and were overnight guests. Over in England Sr. Sheila, writing to the Clewer Associates, remarked that "in 1978 we had the happiness of having a visit from her here, though she was rather frail at the time. It was good that so many of us were able to get to know her here." Sr. Elizabeth Marion's long Community life spanned almost every aspect of the Community work, beginning at St. Helen's Hall in Portland, Oregon, where her Community Biographer noted that "she had a great gift for organizing people and work, and was a great help to Sr. Mildred Eleanor and Mrs. Farris in organizing the Junior College." After the withdrawal from Oregon she taught Latin at St. John Baptist School, then worked at St. Marguerite's, did secretarial work for the Community, and was Novice Mistress. Later she was Sister in Charge at St. Luke's Chapel for a short time and then went to Jersey City. She was Assistant Superior until her death. Sr. Elizabeth Marion was a versatile and talented Sister who could turn her hand to anything, and whose life in Community spanned the older work as well as that of the second spring. After the usual requiem she was laid to rest in the convent cemetery.

On All Saints' Day, November 1, 1982, Sr. Mary Lynne was professed in final vows. From November 3–20 Mother General Edna Frances and Sr. Elizabeth Jane visited Mendham from Clewer. Writing in the December 1982 Newsletter to the Clewer Associates, Mother Edna Frances reported that "this was a very happy occasion, and we hope that next year some of [the American Sisters] will come over to visit us."

As the year 1982 drew to a close, Sr. Agatha Louise passed to her rest on December 15. Professed in 1927, she had been a teacher at St.

Marguerite's before joining the Community and she was the first novice to be sent to Oregon. After profession she remained in Oregon and became Sister in Charge of the Lower School at St. Helen's Hall. Her Community Biographer said that "she was a gifted teacher and had the enthusiasm and ability to inspire others. [Under her] the school flourished." From 1946–49 she was at St. John Baptist School in Corsicana, TX, and after a brief spell at St. Andrew's Hospital, Poughkeepsie, helped open St. Christopher's House in Jersey City and worked there until her health failed. Later she worked at St. Luke's Chapel, NYC. After being invalided home on health grounds once more, she found the last two years of her life with no particular ministry to be a difficult time. But she died peacefully in the 55th year of her profession, and was buried in the Community cemetery. Her Community Biographer wrote that "she was much loved wherever she went."

Sr. Agatha Louise played a part in the vocation of the future Sr. Suzanne Elizabeth. While nursing at St. Luke's Hospital, NYC, and feeling a growing call to the Religious Life, Nurse Suzanne Jackson met Sr. Agatha Louise, who was a patient there. They talked and corresponded for a few years, during which time she also visited other Communities. "I kept thinking that to be fair to the Sister I had met I ought to see her Community. So I came to visit Mendham and I knew it was the place for me. In 1962 I began making frequent visits, sometimes spending the weekend, and in 1963 I became a postulant."[9] And the rest, as the saying goes, is history!

Alas, no records for 1983 have survived at Mendham except for a newspaper article from the *Sunday Star Ledger* dated April 3, 1983. This gave a general outline of the life of the Sisters and their ministry together with their history. Several Sisters were interviewed about the Religious Life. Despite the lack of records, it is not difficult to imagine that the life of the Sisters was very similar to former years, with those who served on boards and committees fulfilling those roles. An important aspect of her extended Community life for Sr. Suzanne Elizabeth was her role in the Altar Guild movement at local, diocesan and national levels. "The National Altar Guild connected CSJB to groups across the country, teaching and giving retreats, workshops and fellowship—witnessing as a Religious and Christian. Several joined as CSJB Associates because of these connections."[10]

March 25, 1983, saw the centennial anniversary of the death of Mother

Harriet Monsell, foundress with the Revd. T.T. Carter of CSJB. At Clewer the day was kept as a family festival followed in June by a pilgrimage to Folkestone where Mother Harriet had died. Visits were made to the places where the Community had once ministered, concluding with a Mass at the church of St. Mary and St. Eanswythe, the ancient parish church of Folkestone. Doubtless at Mendham the anniversary was also observed with a mixture of solemnity, joy and thanksgiving.

It was with great sadness that the decision to close St. John Baptist School, after more than a century of existence, had to be made. But numbers of students were not increasing and financially it was getting harder to make ends meet. The school closed its doors after the Commencement and graduation in June 1983. "I think we feel badly, but we have to be realistic," Mother Elizabeth Anne told the *Sunday Star Ledger*. In the same interview Sr. Margaret Helena commented, "the students are sad. They feel it is a home. To many, it is very much a family." The overseas students had certainly regarded it as a "home from home" and during vacations a few had stayed at the convent because they could not get to their far-off families. But memories do not fade, and at the time of writing, the school alumnae still keep in touch with each other and with the Sisters both via the Community News and by meeting up. A few go back as far as the 1940s.

Sr. Barbara Jean and Sr. Jane Patricia had arrived at Clewer in time for July 4, the latter staying for her usual summer study visit. Sr. Jane Olive, writing in the Clewer Associates' Newsletter, commented that "we celebrated American Independence Day by having tea in the garden, while our American Sisters entertained us with some of their folk songs, many of which were familiar to us, so that we were able to join in."

In July 1983 Anglo-Catholics world-wide celebrated the 150th anniversary of the beginning of the Oxford, or Tractarian, Movement. The main celebration in the UK centered on a conference at Keble College, Oxford, from July 11–16, culminating in a great open-air Mass in the University Parks at which the Archbishop of Canterbury, the Rt. Revd. Robert Runcie, was the preacher. Several Sisters from Clewer attended as well as Sr. Barbara Jean, who estimated 12,000 people present, and there were about 200 priests concelebrating, all wearing matching chasubles, on what was a swelteringly hot day.

Sr. Barbara Jean had returned home before the re-election and installation of Sr. Edna Frances as Mother General. Mother Edna Frances was installed at Clewer on August 30 by the Bishop of Oxford, the Rt. Revd. Patrick Rodger, Visitor to the Clewer Community.

On July 12, 1983, Mother Elizabeth Anne underwent major surgery, after which she was in a great deal of pain. Her death on September 12, 1983, came as a shock to the Sisters because of the rapid progress of her illness. Mother General Edna Frances wrote in her Associates' Newsletter of September 1983: "Mother had only been ill for about ten weeks—our love and prayers go out to [the Sisters] in their bereavement and indeed in this enormous change in their lives."[11]

Like Sr. Agatha Louise, but not at the same time, the future Sr. Elizabeth Anne had taught for a time at St. Marguerite's. She then trained as a nurse at St. Luke's Hospital, NYC, and came to the Community in 1949. After profession in 1951 she worked at St. Luke's Chapel, NYC, and then in Jersey City, where she was Sister Superior until she was elected Mother Superior of the Community in 1979. Following her requiem she was laid to rest in the convent cemetery. Sr. Margaret Helena, writing her Community Biography, described her as "a hardworking, conscientious Sister who could fill in any place and do it well, and was loved by those with whom she worked."

It was a great bereavement for the Sisters, but in the midst of it, a successor as Mother Superior had to be elected in order for the life and work of the Community to continue. Sr. Suzanne Elizabeth was elected and installed in September 1983. Sr. Margaret Helena was appointed Assistant Superior, and Sr. Barbara Jean, Novice Guardian—note the change of title. Mother General Edna Frances informed the Clewer Associates in her letter of March 1984 about the leadership changes. She also noted that "the Sisters at Mendham have adopted a new cap and collar and we are trying it out at the moment experimentally."[12] A diary for 1984 kept as an unofficial Record Book by Sr. Barbara Jean noted that on December 27, 1983, "Sr. Barbara Jean modelled the new habit. Today Elsa came to adjust scapulars and collars. Sr. Katharine Veronica and Sr. Barbara Jean went shopping for red cord for habits."

"Times they were a-changing," but not in every way. On December 31, Mother Suzanne Elizabeth, Sr. Laura Katharine and Sr. Mary Lynne kept the Watch until midnight to pray the old year out and the New Year in. Nineteen eighty-four was welcomed at 8:00am with a Choral Mass, and in the afternoon the Sisters were invited to the Griers' for tea. Several guests came for dinner at the convent in the evening and there was a birthday cake for Sr. Katharine Veronica, who was 78. Next day the Grier family came to the convent for afternoon tea. There were some more changes, with the rearrangement of the refectory tables, the result of a Community conference. And Mary Basilion began her work for the Community as business manager and used the office formerly used by the Assistant Superior. She had previously been the treasurer at St. John Baptist School.

More change was in the air with the revision of the Constitution. Indeed, during Mother Suzanne Elizabeth's fourteen-year tenure of office, the Rule, Constitution, Office Book and Customary would all be revised. Looking back on that work, Sr. Suzanne Elizabeth has commented that it was the most challenging aspect of her time as Superior. It was necessary "in order to meet the needs of the present day, legally, spiritually and practically."[13] Also, there was the question of how to release those who found they had no vocation. Until this time there was no mechanism except dismissal, which was unpastoral. Reform was overdue. "We had to have loving ways to release postulants, novices and junior- and life-professed. With personal and Community psychotherapy facilitators meeting weekly for a year, I feel we laid firm ground for future situations other Superiors have had to deal with. We were able to remain in friendly contact after their departure rather than bearing grief over the necessary decision made in prayer for the health of all concerned."[14] All this work would take the Community several years but it laid the foundation for CSJB as it is in the 21st century. Work on the new habits continued and Monday February 20, 1984, the public holiday to celebrate George Washington's birthday was marked by the Sisters wearing their new habits for Mass.

Nineteen eighty-four saw Sisters attending various courses and workshops. For instance, Mother and Sr. Katharine Veronica attended workshops on manuscript illumination. This had long been an accomplishment of members of the Community. Later, Sr. Mary Lynne, who was already a talented artist, attended water-coloring classes. The ecclesiastical embroidery class continued to meet at the convent, led by Mother Suzanne Elizabeth. In January Sr. Barbara Jean began a course on spiritual direction at the General Theological Seminary, NYC, and soon after, Sr. Laura Katharine registered for it too. The course lasted until the end of April. Sr. Mary Lynne and Sr. Barbara Jean attended the Trinity Institute in New York, and on February 1, Mother traveled to

San Francisco for a meeting of the Trinity Institute there. At the end of February, Mother, Sr. Katharine Veronica and Sr. Mary Lynne began a course at Morris County Community College on calligraphy.

Old friends continued to keep in touch. Muriel Unwin and Jean Hoppin, who had been such staunch supporters in Jersey City, now came to the convent to help there from time to time. Marian Wysong, a former student and teacher at St. John Baptist School in the 1940s, kept in touch and came for lunch at the convent on March 15. She was presented with a birthday cake.

For a number of years the Sisters had been connected with Heath Village, a retirement community founded in Hackettstown, NJ, in 1962. In February 1984 Sr. Margaret Helena attended a Committee meeting there as part of her ministry. Sisters also visited at Holly Manor, a nursing home in Mendham. Sr. Katharine Veronica had a particular ministry there. And Sr. Barbara Jean conducted Bible study sessions at Alcott Manor, an assisted living facility in Mendham. Also, Sisters continued to work in the Church Bible schools, give talks on the Religious Life to parish groups, host retreat groups at St. Marguerite's as well as Interweave meetings, and carry out the ministry of hospitality in all its many forms. The fact that there were no branch houses and no school had enabled the Sisters to take on these many and varied new forms of ministry.

There was a burglary at St. Mark's, Mendham, on April 10, 1984, and several silver vessels were stolen. Other churches had also been broken into recently. On April 11, Mother and Sr. Barbara Jean began as a precaution to remove things from St. John Baptist School. When the school had closed in 1983 the Community had decided to open the building to any organization so long as it would benefit young people. Various organizations had applied, but the Community chose "The Shire," founded by Judith Knowlton of St. Peter's, Morristown. This was a 28-day program for young people with drug and alcohol addiction. The ethos of The Shire, named from J.R.R. Tolkien's *The Lord of the Rings*, evoked fellowship among the participants.[15]

As Holy Week dawned in 1984 there were some liturgical changes. On Palm Sunday the blessing of the palms took place in the library. On Maundy Thursday and Good Friday the usual rites took place, but the major change came on Holy Saturday and Easter Sunday. Sr. Barbara Jean noted in her unofficial Record Book: "Easter Even 5:30 Vespers from Office Book; 7:30 recreation; 8:00pm retire to dormitory. This was the first time we didn't have the New Fire in the evening. April 22, Easter 5:30am Rising bell; 6:00 Angelus. Great Vigil of Easter—Procession from Hall near the confessional. The day was lovely with a bit of sunshine after much rain. We called Clewer in the morning. We had six guests for dinner." It was around this time that the Easter Vigil at Clewer began to be celebrated early on Easter morning.

On Tuesday in Holy Week, all the Sisters, except Sr. Margaret Helena who was unwell, visited the German Sisters of the Brotherhood of Jesus in Plainfield for dinner and a slide show on the Passion of Christ, followed by Compline in the Sisters' chapel. Clearly ecumenical relationships were still flourishing.

There was a Chapter meeting on May 24 which was preceded by a Mass of the Holy Spirit. Fr. Cure the Sub Warden attended. Also present was Sr. Jane Patricia, who was still a member of the Community and therefore had a vote in Chapter, even though she was on extended leave of absence in order to pursue her studies. The Chapter was mostly concerned with the revised Constitution, Calendar and habit, and the discussions extended into the afternoon. On May 25, 1984, Sr. Mary Lynne and Christine Brodeur left for England and Scotland, calling in at Clewer on June 9.

Amongst all the groups and individuals who visited and stayed at St. Marguerite's or at the convent, there were a good number of former students from St. John Baptist School. Clearly they wished to keep in touch with the Sisters—a sign they had happy memories and a good start in life.

The Order of the Holy Cross was keeping its Centennial year in 1984. On June 2 they had a Mass at the Cathedral of St. John the Divine, NYC. Fourteen bishops and members of thirteen Anglican Religious Orders were present. Mother Suzanne Elizabeth, Sr. Barbara Jean and Sr. Laura Katharine attended and walked in the procession. There were other celebrations too, later in the year. On June 9, Mother, Sr. Margaret Helena, and Sr. Barbara Jean attended the ordination of deacons in Trinity Cathedral, Newark. Nancy Talmage, a CSJB Associate, was ordained at 73 years of age, along with three others. The weather was very hot, the thermometer reaching 99°F with high humidity.

On June 12, Sr. Margaret Helena and Sr. Katharine Veronica drove to Gaylordsville, CT, for a meeting of the Oratory of the Little Way, a Christian retreat and healing center. There they saw Fr. Weed, who was making some progress healthwise. June 24, St. John Baptist Day, was also Commemoration Day. After Mass at 8:00am the Sisters had a "talking breakfast" for the first time. More than 165 Associates and friends came for Evensong and supper. Earlier it had rained hard, but they had supper in the cloister. Also, there were several addresses: Sr. Margaret Helena spoke about the Sisters' activities; Sr. Katharine Veronica gave news of the Associates; and Mother Suzanne Elizabeth gave greetings to all and made an appeal for help in the library. There was a new Community Chaplain for the summer, Fr. Ramsey. He arrived on June 23, ready to take up his duties on the 29th. A few days later, on July 10, Sr. Katharine Veronica flew to England for a visit to Clewer until August 1. She had been ill with an ear infection shortly before leaving for England and during her visit was ill for a week.

At the end of July the Paulist Press came to the convent to make a video film of the play "Julian," about the life of Julian of Norwich. Filming took place in the chapel and Alex the convent cat found fame by having a part, even though he had to be renamed "Isaiah"! Meanwhile, St. Marguerite's was as busy as ever, hosting a two-week International Educational Workshop from Montclair State College. And indeed it *was* international, with students from Chile, Peru, Brazil, Mexico, Taiwan, Australia, West Germany, Norway, England, Ireland, Holland, Jordan, Israel, Lebanon and the U.S. The subject being studied was teaching philosophy to children.

Mother Suzanne Elizabeth's appeal for help in the Community library was bearing fruit. A number of Associates and other friends came to lend a hand including Muriel Unwin, Jean Hoppin, Laura Jonassen and Carolyn Dunham. Also, the Search program was going ahead with five "searchers." Christine Brodeur came towards the end to take them into New York to the Cloisters and to the Cathedral of St. John the Divine.

On September 4, 1984, Sr. Barbara Jean registered at Drew University and attended her first lectures next day. "I was thinking of being a deacon someday."[16] The course was part-time, i.e. non-residential, and would last five years, during which time Sr. Barbara Jean continued to take a full part in the life and work of the Community. Mother and Sr. Barbara Jean attended the Centennial celebrations of the Community of the Transfiguration in Toronto over the first weekend of September.

A highlight of October 1984 was the visit of Mother General Edna Frances from Clewer from the 4th until the 24th. Mother Edna Frances wrote enthusiastically about her visit in the Clewer Associates' Newsletter of December 1984. She described her visit as a "privilege and a joy." Apart from what she described as a "mammoth trip" to South Duxbury, MA, for a conference at St. Margaret's Conference Center with six other Superiors, she spent the whole time with the Sisters, "sharing their lives to the full" and joining in their ongoing Community discussions about the Rule, Constitutions, Customary and Calendar. The Fall colors on the long journey to Duxbury impressed her greatly. There were visits to nearby parishes, including St. John's-on-the-Mountain, Bernardsville; St. Mark's, Mendham; St. Luke's, Gladstone; and to St. Peter's, Essex Fells, where Bishop Desmond Tutu was speaking. Also, there was a tea for Associates and friends so that they could meet the Mother General, and about 50 attended.

After all the excitement of the Mother General's visit, the remaining two months of 1984 passed fairly quietly. On October 30, Sr. Katharine Veronica attended the marriage blessing of "Betsy," a former St. Anna's girl, and on November 3, several Sisters attended a service of blessing on a new ministry at Grace Church (Van Vorst), Jersey City. The new priest, Fr. Scott Kallstrom, visited the convent a few days later.

November 5 was Sr. Margaret Helena's birthday. Mary Basilion made cheese and apple cake for afternoon tea, and a margin note in Sr. Barbara Jean's Record Book states that "the 'working crew' from St. Marguerite's came with a cake at 6:30." On November 8, Founder's Day was held for the first time and there was a Choral Mass. On November 19, Margo Kolkebeck (the future Sr. Margo Elizabeth) came for a private retreat.

On November 23, 1984, some of the brethren from the Order of the Holy Cross came to the convent and celebrated the Eucharist in the main chapel, at the altar (formerly at St. John Baptist House, East 17th Street, NYC) which had been used for Fr. James Otis Sargent Huntington's profession 100 years previously. They wore the same High Mass vestments that were worn on that day by the Bishop of Central New York, the Rt. Revd. Frederic Dan Huntington, Fr. James's father. The vestments had been made by the English Sisters of CSJB in their Church workroom in Gower Street, London. Two days later, on November 25, the Sisters attended Mass in the chapel at the former St. John Baptist House on East 17th Street, NYC, where Fr. Huntington was professed. Then on December 15, Mother Suzanne Elizabeth, Sr. Margaret Helena and Sr. Mary Lynne went to Nancy Talmage's ordination to the priesthood at

St. Dunstan's, Succasunna, NJ. Mother sang the Ave Maria at the offertory.

As Christmas approached there were a number of pageants and carol services at local churches, several of which were attended by the Sisters. And as usual, the Sisters shared their Christmas festivities with several Associates, friends and helpers, as always receiving all as Christ.

---

[1] Weekly Letter to the Sisters, Wednesday March 5, 1980.

[2] The Community of the Way of the Cross was founded in March 1939 when several women bound themselves to a definite rule of life while still carrying on their work in the world. Their convent chapel in Buffalo, New York State, was blessed by the Bishop of Western New York, the Rt. Revd. Cameron Davis, on March 28, 1940, and the first two professions were made on August 29, 1943. The Sisters followed a modern rule but recited the Day Hours from the Benedictine Breviary. At the beginning of their second year, novices resumed their work in the world and the Community was supported by their earnings. The Sisters also gave quiet weekends and retreats, in the convent or out in the parishes, and religious instruction in schools, as well as visiting the sick and poor. Source: ANSON, Peter F. *The Call of the Cloister* 2nd rev. ed. 1964 pp.570–571. The Community is not mentioned in *Anglican Religious Life 2018–19*.

[3] PRICE, Margaret M. *St. John Baptist School 1880–1980*.

[4] Interweave was founded in 1979 by the Revd. Robert Morris to form an Interfaith educational center in northern New Jersey. Its incorporation as a non-profit organization was completed in 1980, and by 1981 membership had grown to 60. A grant from the Episcopal Diocese of Newark allowed Robert Morris to undertake Interweave work full time. By 1985 membership had grown to more than 200 and while the majority of events were held at Calvary Episcopal Church, Summit, other events took place at Christ Church, Short Hills, and at the Community of St. John Baptist, Mendham. Source: www.interweave.org

[5] Trevor Huddleston, CR, was a controversial man who, as Bishop of Masasi (Tanzania) 1960–68, was a leader in the anti-apartheid movement. He was a friend of both Nelson Mandela and Desmond Tutu. In 1978 Huddleston became Bishop of Mauritius and later the same year was elected as Archbishop of the Province of the Indian Ocean. He retired in 1984, and died at the Mother House of the Community of the Resurrection, Mirfield, UK, on April 20, 1998.

[6] The Order of St. Luke still visit St. Marguerite's at the time of writing (2019).

[7] For details of Christ Church Home, South Amboy, see BONHAM, Valerie *Living Stones: The Community of St. John Baptist in America* 2016 Chapter 3, p.40. Various Sisters worked there but Sr. Fanny Helen was Sister in Charge. The Admission Roll for Christ Church Home lists Julia Jakobek and her older sister Matilda. Julia was born on February 15, 1892, and Matilda on May 17, 1886. Their parents were Joseph and Mary Jakobek, but a note stated that their

mother was dead, which is probably why they came to the Home. Another note states that the father had married again and "comes occasionally to see the children." Both girls were admitted to the Home on March 12, 1895. Matilda was Confirmed on Whitsunday 1898 and had her first Holy Communion on July 3, 1898. She left on September 13, 1902, and was sent to "a place" at Redbank, i.e. to domestic service. Julia was Confirmed on May 8, 1904, and had her first Holy Communion on Whitsunday that year. A note in different handwriting states that Julia was "sent to Home" in 1905. This may refer to St. Hilda's Morristown, also run by CSJB, where children were transferred after Christ Church closed. Or it may mean she was sent to her family home. Clearly she never forgot the Sisters, hence her "small bequest" all those years later when she would have been in her 90th year of age.

[8] St. Margaret's House was founded by the Rector of Trinity, Wall Street, the Revd. Dr. Robert Parks, who had provided affordable housing for the elderly in his last parish at Jacksonville, FL. Trinity Church vestry proposed naming the New York project in honor of the Sisters of the Society of St. Margaret, who had a ministry to the elderly in the parish. Trinity provided the Sisters with a residence at 50, Fulton Street, named Neale House after their UK founder, the Revd. Dr. John Mason Neale.

[9] Sr. Suzanne Elizabeth, quoted in SIMPSON, James B. & STORY Edward M. *Stars in His Crown* p.272 Ploughshare Press NJ 1976.

[10] Sr. Suzanne Elizabeth in a written note to me in 2018.

[11] Sr. Suzanne Elizabeth has recalled: "Mother Elizabeth Anne was not well for the last six months, but finally found the cause of her pain. She had a fast growing tumor on her liver. She was nursed at home by her Sisters until she needed hospice care. Sr. SE was visiting family in Montreal but returned in time for Sr. Elizabeth Anne's funeral. In the midst of the Sisters' grief, [and] closing the last branch house, the Sisters turned to the process of electing a new Superior out of the seven Professed Sisters." Note written to me in 2018.

[12] The only Sister at Clewer who did not adopt the new simplified habit was Sr. Catherine Mary.

[13] Sr. Suzanne Elizabeth in a written note to me in 2018.

[14] Sr. Suzanne Elizabeth ibid.

[15] Information from a conversation with Sr. Barbara Jean 2017.

[16] Sr. Barbara Jean in conversation with Valerie Bonham.

TO RECEIVE ALL AS CHRIST

The Community 1985–89

NINETEEN EIGHTY-FIVE OPENED as usual with hospitality. After Vespers and Benediction on New Year's Day, five guests were present at dinner. It was also Sr. Katharine Veronica's birthday so there was a special cake. On January 6 there was an Epiphany Party and about 40 Associates and friends enjoyed carols, dessert and fellowship. On January 9 Fr. Gross, the Sisters' Chaplain, kept the 25th anniversary of his ordination with a Choral Mass.

Meanwhile, over at St. Marguerite's, the Montclair State College was having a conference. Some of the students were from South America and they had never seen snow before! They took photographs. The cold weather continued, and on January 21, the thermometer dropped to -13°F with a chill factor of -35°, cold enough to freeze the anti-freeze in cars. Even so, a postulant was received at Vespers on January 18, and was given a warm welcome.

There were many meetings to attend such as Diocesan Convention, ecumenical meetings and services. From January 28–30, Mother Suzanne Elizabeth and Sr. Laura Katharine went to St. Helena's convent for a conference on Holistic Community conducted by Scott Peck, author of *The Road Less Traveled*. Eighteen Religious Communities were represented. Two weeks later Mother attended a conference at Mount Holyoke, MA, conducted by the Trappist monk Fr. Basil Pennington, author of *Centering Prayer*.

The bitterly cold weather lasted through February but the Sisters continued with their varied work and ministry. Sr. Laura Katharine was in charge at St. Marguerite's and there continued to be a busy schedule there. Sisters continued to help at Sunday Schools such as at St. John's-on-the-Mountain, and at St. Luke's, Gladstone, where Mother assisted until the end of January. At the beginning of February new Saturday work began at the House of Prayer, Newark. Mother, Sr. Mary Lynne and the new postulant attended the service on Sunday February 3 and met the parishioners. Sr. Barbara Jean was still studying at Drew University but also led workshops and attended meetings. February 5, 1985, was observed by the Sisters as their Dedication festival as it was the anniversary of the first Sisters arriving in New York City from Clewer in 1875. The month ended on a hopeful note with the reception of another postulant, the second since the beginning of the year.

The Sisters were in great demand, with requests coming from far and wide for retreats, talks about Community life and conducting workshops. Thus on March 1, Sr. Barbara Jean had a blessing for her journey to Youngstown, Ohio, where she was to conduct a Lent mission. After her return on March 4 she gave a report to the Sisters. Two days later she went to Trenton, PA, to confer with a priest about the diaconate. New groups were coming to St. Marguerite's for retreats and conferences, such as the Diocesan postulancy group, i.e. those considering ordination. They stayed overnight on March 8. Mother Suzanne Elizabeth was also in demand for Altar Guild talks and workshops. Now that the Sisters had no external parish or institutional work they were free to use their gifts in many ways.

On Wednesday, April 10, 1985, all the Sisters went in two cars to St. Michael's Cemetery, Astoria, "to visit where our New York Sisters were buried before we had the New Jersey property. We found the plot nicely kept, and photographed and sketched the lovely large white Cross in the middle of sixteen Sisters' and four Associates' smaller Crosses in two rows on either side of the large Cross. We had lunch there bought at the corner deli. It was like visiting a Shrine."[1]

The diocese of New Jersey had its bi-centennial Eucharist on May 16 at Garden State Arts Center, and this was attended by Mother Suzanne Elizabeth, Sr. Barbara Jean, Sr. Mary Lynne, and Cynthia (one of the postulants). The guest speaker was the Archbishop of York, the Most Revd. John Habgood. On May 22, Mother, Sr. Mary Lynne and both postulants went to the Episcopal Church Women's Spring Ingathering at Trinity Cathedral, Newark. Sr. Mary Lynne was elected Chairperson of the affiliated organization of the ECW of Newark.

On June 9 Fr. Wessinger came to the convent to conduct the Sisters' retreat, which lasted until June 16. There was a different format with just one meditation each day. The Sisters were divided into two groups, each group meeting with Fr. Wessinger on alternate days for discussion. Sisters from other Communities joined the retreat, as in former years.

On June 22, 1985, a postulant was clothed as a novice, taking the name

Sr. Margaret Joan. Commemoration Day, Sunday June 23, saw 175 guests and the reception of eleven new Associates.

Next day (the Birth of St. John Baptist) all the Sisters spoke on the telephone to Mother General Edna Frances at Clewer. In the evening there was a picnic supper by the carport with "all the hilltop people" and employees. Then there was an electric storm which struck the convent transformer, causing loss of power. Even so, Sr. Barbara Jean noted that afterwards "it was lovely, clear and cool. We said Compline by flashlight." On Sunday June 30, Fr. Watters had his retirement service at St. Mark's, Mendham, attended by about 300 people.

The busy month of June with its familiar festivals gave way in July to something entirely new—the visit to Clewer by all the Sisters from Mendham. Sisters had visited before of course, but never the entire Community. Indeed, as Mother Edna Frances commented, "It had never happened before that the whole of CSJB had been together in one place at the same time."[2] Nor would it ever happen again, but in July 1985 it was, in Mother Edna Frances' words, "like planning a dream."

"We left at 3:00pm for Kennedy Airport in a limousine," was Sr. Barbara Jean's comment in her unofficial Record Book on Wednesday July 3. "Arrived at Clewer about 11:00am, July 4." After that entry there is nothing until the Sisters arrived home on Wednesday July 24! Fortunately, Mother Edna Frances wrote a full account to the Clewer Associates. Seven Sisters, one novice and a postulant flew into Heathrow airport on July 4, and when they arrived at the convent they found the entrance lodge decorated with the Stars and Stripes to welcome them. It was, after all, US Independence Day. Mother Edna Frances wrote, "You can imagine there was great excitement and we realized at last that the dream was beginning to come true."

The Sisters' visit was well organized by the Sisters at Clewer and included a visit to Hereford where the Warden General, Fr. Austin Masters, SSM, was a residentiary Canon; a day in Canterbury where they sang Vespers in the Chapel of Our Lady Undercroft; and a day in Folkestone, where years previously the Community had much work and ministry, and where Mother Harriet had spent the final eight years of her life. The vicar of the ancient parish church of St. Mary and St. Eanswythe, Canon Cole, showed the Sisters all the places associated with CSJB including Mother Harriet's grave. A visit to St. George's Chapel, Windsor Castle, was organized by Kenneth Harland, the Sisters' deputy organist, and they were entertained to tea by Canon White. Various Sisters from Clewer accompanied their guests on these excursions, one of which, to London, involved a boat trip down the Thames.

Mother Edna Frances noted that "there was a lot of work and sharing between us on all matters affecting our lives." And there were visiting speakers too. "Mrs. Valerie Bonham spoke to us about the history of the Community, which she is researching and in due course is planning to write a book.[3] The Revd. Dr. Paul Rampton came to talk about Canon Carter on whom he did his thesis for his doctorate." And the Revd. Alan Harrison conducted a Quiet Day for all the Sisters. On a different note, Roberta Nobleman did a performance of "Julian" in the Chapel of St. John Baptist. This depicted the life and times of Julian of Norwich. Local Associates and friends of the Community were invited too.

The time flew by and soon it was time for the Sisters to return to Mendham. Mother Edna Frances concluded her account to the Clewer Associates with characteristic humor. "The weather was perfect the whole time and the Sisters who had brought umbrellas wondered why people always complained about the weather in England. However, immediately after they had left for home the weather broke, and Sr. Barbara Jean, who stayed on to go with Sr. Gina to the Novice Guardians' Conference, knew why."

The convent at Mendham had not been left unattended. Associates and friends had stayed there to "hold the fort." The outside of the convent was re-stuccoed while the Sisters were away, but on their return they found the wrong color had been put on the arches. It was to be done again at no extra cost. Also during the summer new copper guttering was installed at St. Marguerite's, and improved lighting in the convent.

Once they were home the Sisters were soon immersed in the busy summer program of welcoming groups to St. Marguerite's, including delegates from Montclair State College there for a conference. Various Sisters were assisting at St. Mark's Vacation Bible School, which finished on August 16, and then next day there was the Search Program attended by four searchers. There were celebrations, too. On August 20, the postulant was clothed as a novice, taking the name Sr. Mary Elizabeth, and on August 24, Fr. Pederson celebrated the fortieth anniversary of his priestly ordination. He presided at a Choral Mass in the convent chapel.

The 68th General Convention of the Episcopal Church met for its triennial session in Anaheim, California, from September 7–14. Mother and Sr. Mary Lynne attended as observers, having first of all attended a Conference on the Religious Life. The Rt. Revd. Edmund Browning, Bishop of Hawaii, was elected Presiding Bishop. When they returned home the Sisters were kept busy making reports on the proceedings.

The Community was small in numbers at this time but their life as Religious was lived to the full in accordance with their vows and rule. All the activity was within this context. And indeed there was much activity. Sr. Barbara Jean was studying two days a week at Drew University and was student assistant at St. John's-on-the-Mountain,[4] which involved preaching from time to time and being in charge of the Sunday School, which she took over from Sr. Katharine Veronica. She was also Novice Mistress. Sr. Laura Katharine was in charge of St. Marguerite's Retreat House and was also studying Christian Spirituality at Drew. Sr. Mary Lynne, in addition to attending meetings and conferences, was also having art lessons. Sr. Katharine Veronica was the Associates' Sister and also had a ministry in various retirement homes, including Heath Village. And the Sisters gave talks, quiet days, and had preaching engagements at a variety of churches including the House of Prayer, Newark; All Saints, Princeton; and St. James, Edison, to name but a few.

In September Sr. Margaret Helena visited her relatives in Oregon and attended the Associates' meeting in Portland. There was Mass at Trinity Church, Portland, during which a new Associate was received—Mary Elizabeth Aldrich, a former student at St. Helen's Hall from the class of 1941. Afterwards there was lunch attended by 27. Sr. Margaret Helena wrote that it was "a little like a mini Commemoration Day."[5] Also in September, Sr. Gina arrived from Clewer for a two months' visit, returning on November 29. During that time she shared in Community life to the full. "Her visit was wonderful and it was hard to part with her."[6]

The Church of St. Luke's in the Fields, NYC, where the Sisters had worked for many years, was rededicated in the Fall of 1985 following the disastrous fire four years previously. Sr. Margaret Helena wrote that "five of us attended … The parish has raised over five million dollars to rebuild. It is a glorious triumph. As you enter you know it is the old church with differences, but the dear St. Luke's feeling is there."[7] Mrs. John Scott, a friend of Fr. Ledlie Laughlin, the Rector, presented an altar for the Lady Chapel at St. Luke's in memory of the Sisters' 26 years' service there. She had known CSJB Sisters in India when she was a little girl and her father was a missionary priest.

On Monday October 7, 1985, the Sisters began to hold a weekly Sabbath Day, but it was not at this time a complete "day off." On this first day there was Angelus at 7:00am, Lauds at 7:30, conference at 10:00, music practice at 11:00, Eucharist after the noonday office, and a talking lunch.

Following a discussion on Monday October 21, the altar in St. Michael's Chapel was moved forward (to its present position) so that the celebrant would face the congregation.

On October 9, Mother, Sr. Margaret Helena, Sr. Barbara Jean, Sr. Katharine Veronica and the two novices went to Grace Church (Van Vorst) for a celebration Mass and "pot luck" supper. Bishop Paul Moore was the celebrant and preacher. November 2 saw Mother Suzanne Elizabeth honored by the John Dewey Consortium, an organization of International Colleges, for her work in Jersey City and Newark. She was presented with a citation and a medal by Dr. Edward Leigh. The Sisters were present at the ceremony. The Community had always engaged with social issues, hence the early institutional work and later parish work in Jersey City and in New York. Thus on November 12, Sr. Gina, Sr. Mary Lynne and Sr. Mary Elizabeth went to a service and program at Grace Church (Van Vorst) on "family violence." This was sponsored by the Episcopal Church Women and the Commission on Women's Issues and Ministry. It took a closer look at the abuse of women in the context of marriage and family.

Sr. Margaret Helena left for Portland, Oregon, on December 5, her second visit that year. It was meant to be a short visit for Founders' Day at the Oregon Episcopal Schools, the successor to St. Helen's Hall.[8] However, her planned return on December 9 was held up due to a blizzard in Denver, CO. She finally arrived home at the convent on December 11.

As Christmas approached, Mother Suzanne Elizabeth, Sr. Margaret Helena, Sr. Laura Katharine and Sr. Katharine Veronica were pleased to attend the Eucharist and luncheon for their old friend Bishop Stark's 50th ordination anniversary on December 21. Next day some of the Sisters went with the Mendham Interchurch Choir for carols at the jail and at the senior citizens' center.

Sr. Barbara Jean noted in her unofficial Record Book: "The chapel and crèche are beautiful with poinsettia and floral arrangements, holly and green. Midnight Mass was lovely—several guests came. We telephoned Clewer and each of us had greetings with Mother Edna Frances." Mother Suzanne Elizabeth summed up the message of Christmas in the

Newsletter to the Associates. "This Christmas it is my prayer for all of us that we will really take and make the space to receive and feel God's love showering down and enfolding us, energizing us and flowing out to those around us, and that this truly will be the most blessed Christmas abounding in love and life and joy."

The Christmas Newsletter had contained an invitation to the Epiphany party. "You are invited for cakes—carols—celebration on Friday January 4, 1986, 7:30pm. Associates—Friends—Co-workers. Bring yourself and loved one. Bring pot luck dessert. Bring your talent." Thus began a fairly routine, if busy, year, although there were some highlights and a few sadnesses. It began well, when Friday January 10 saw Mother Suzanne Elizabeth and Sr. Laura Katharine attending the installation service of the Presiding Bishop, the Rt. Revd. Edmund Browning, at the National Cathedral in Washington DC. They stayed over with an Associate, Dick Downing. And on January 21, Sr. Laura Katharine and Sr. Mary Lynne flew from Kennedy Airport for a visit to Israel.

On Sunday February 9, 1986, Fr. Paul Weed died. He had been the Community Warden for 27 years, and Vicar of St. Luke's in the Fields, NYC, where the Sisters had worked for many years. There was a Requiem for him at the convent on February 11, and his funeral Requiem was celebrated on the following Saturday at St. Andrew's Church, Kent, CT, where he had lived in retirement. He was buried at Holy Cross Monastery, West Park, NY. On Wednesday February 19 there was a memorial service at St. Luke's in the Fields, attended by Sr. Margaret Helena, Sr. Katharine Veronica and Sr. Mary Lynne.

The work and ministry of the Community left memories long after the Sisters had withdrawn, and many people kept in touch. Sr. Margaret Helena's annual visits to Portland, Oregon, were the main reason why there was a strong body of Associates there. But this was not all. Former residents at St. Anna's Home, Mendham, kept in touch, as did women from other homes run by the Sisters. And after such a long passage of time it was not unusual for children and grandchildren of those girls and women to write or visit. This was surely a testimony to the kindness they experienced there and the good start in life they had been given. Alumnae of St. John Baptist School, which had closed just a few years previously, also maintained links, some of which have lasted into the 21st century.

Sr. Margaret Helena celebrated her 50th anniversary of profession on March 25, 1986. Bishop Spong celebrated the Eucharist, which was attended by many friends. Mother General Edna Frances telephoned to congratulate Sister on behalf of all the Sisters at Clewer. In addition, there were many cards and flowers. It was a very happy occasion, full of joy.

The Easter Vigil and first Mass of Easter were celebrated at sunrise, making a beautiful start to the Easter season. Next day, the Community organist, Gus Bittrich, led the Sisters in their first practice with the new 1982 Hymnal. Writing to the Sisters in her Weekly Letter of Wednesday April 2, Mother noted: "We will meet once a week during recreation to learn the new hymns. We will start using [the new Hymnal] this Sunday."

An old friend of the Community, the Rt. Revd. Leland Stark, died on May 8, 1986. As Bishop of Newark he was close to the Community and had been an Associate for 20 years. His requiem at Trinity Cathedral, Newark, was attended by Mother, Sr. Margaret Helena, Sr. Barbara Jean, and their Chaplain, Fr. Gross.

Several Sisters attended the priestly ordination of the Revd. Ninon Hutchinson at Trenton Cathedral on May 27. She had been staying at the convent to prepare for ordination and celebrated her first Mass in the chapel at St. Marguerite's. The Sisters were present, and also Fr. Wessinger and other guests. The Warden General, Fr. Austin Masters, SSM, arrived on May 30 for two weeks.

Sr. Katharine Veronica was diagnosed with bone cancer and was in hospital for treatment by chemotherapy and radiotherapy. Thanks to these wonders of modern medicine she was able to return home to the convent in mid-July. By that time she was able to walk with a "walker" and came to meals and offices. She received many visitors from New York City over the next few months.

At the end of July, Mother Suzanne Elizabeth and Margo Kolkebeck went to Ireland for a workshop. This was followed by a visit to Clewer until mid-August. Mother Edna Frances wrote: "We were very happy to have Mother Suzanne Elizabeth to stay with us for two weeks in August. It is always a great joy to have our Sisters from across the Atlantic with us, when we can personally exchange our thoughts and doings, so you can imagine there was a great deal we had to talk about!"[9]

The Mendham Community Newsletter had changed format from that of years past, and was now produced "in house" with articles, photographs of Community life and line drawings. The line drawings were produced by Dora Kapp, who was an Associate and often visited the convent. There was also a Newsletter for alumnae of St. John Baptist School. At the end of August 1986 Mother told the Sisters in her Weekly Letter: "Sr. Barbara Jean is rejoicing because Dora Kapp will undertake the editing and producing of the Alumnae letter. Dora is the mother of an alumna."

Many individual people, as well as groups, visited the convent. On Friday, September 12, 1986, Mother Suzanne Elizabeth wrote in her Weekly Letter that "Deborah Scott is expected to visit this weekend." This was the future Sr. Deborah Francis and was the first of a number of visits that would lead to her seeking admission as a postulant.

On October 14, Fr. Cure was installed as the Community Warden. He had previously been sub-Warden. At this time there were many meetings attended by the Sisters, in particular the Diocesan Altar Guild and Mendham Interchurch group. They also attended talks on various aspects of spirituality, especially talks on centering prayer by Abbot Thomas Keating and Fr. Basil Pennington. The Revd. Robert Morris and his Interweave group were also frequent visitors to the convent. A new rector, Fr. Carr Holland, was installed at St. Mark's, Mendham, on Saturday, October 25, and several Sisters attended.

At the end of November Mother Suzanne Elizabeth attended a conference in California on the Religious Life. There were about thirty people present from six Christian Communities and eight Religious Orders. "We met in a R.C. Benedictine Retreat Center in the beautiful high desert lending wonder and peace to our conference, attempting communication and mutual support to and with each other in a broken and stressful world where we work and minister. After the meeting of three days, the Society of St. Paul drove me to their monastery in Palm Desert where we shared with the Brothers about Novitiate training and life in Community."[10]

As Christmas approached, Sr. Susinne Paula celebrated the 50th anniversary of her profession on December 17. There was a Choral Eucharist with several guests. Fr. Gross gave "a lovely homily" and the flowers in the chapel were beautiful. On Christmas Day, The Shire came for Christmas dinner along with other guests. Mother noted that "a good time was had by all." Then the Griers invited the Sisters to their house in the convent grounds for carols on the 30th. Thus passed another year, full of service and dedication.

The New Year, 1987, saw the withdrawal from the novitiate of Elizabeth Hamilton on January 13. She had been an Associate before becoming a postulant, and upon leaving had requested to be admitted as an Oblate.[11] She was received at the Noonday Office on January 21, before returning to Ohio on the 23rd. Another postulant was received on Saturday February 7, at Vespers, but she left at the beginning of May. There were seven Searchers for the February weekend Search Program.

After further discussion it was decided that each Sister should have a "personal day," i.e. a day off from Community activities, from time to time. This was begun on February 12.

Close links were maintained with The Shire, and at the beginning of March Sr. Barbara Jean prepared a weekly Mass for them to be held in the chapel of the former school. Three girls there had requested baptism and Sr. Barbara Jean was preparing them. She was also elected to the Board of Directors of The Shire.

On Friday, May 8, Mother Suzanne Elizabeth preached at Newark Cathedral at a service celebrating Women's Ministry. She was accompanied by Sr. Barbara Jean, who assisted in the offertory procession. On the following Sunday Mother preached at St. Luke's Episcopal Church, Hope, NJ, and talked at the Coffee Hour. Sr. Laura Katharine went with her.

A distinguished visitor came to the convent on Wednesday, May 13, 1987. The Rt. Revd. Dinis Sengulane had been consecrated as the Anglican Bishop of Lebombo in Mozambique in 1976. He was currently visiting the USA and was assisting in the Diocese of Newark. He and his wife, Berta, visited the convent and after being shown round, stayed for lunch.[12]

Since October 1986 Sr. Barbara Jean and the novices had begun a weekly visit to Grace Church (Van Vorst) in Jersey City in order to conduct a Bible School. This ended on June 27, 1987. Sr. Margaret Helena noted in her letter to the Community Associates and Friends: "It ended on a sad note because the little boys were naughty and didn't get any doughnuts."[13] She gave no further details of the extent of their naughtiness, but to be denied doughnuts must surely indicate something serious!

As ever, June was a busy month. The Sisters' long retreat, from Sunday, June 7 through Saturday, June 13, was conducted by Abbot Benedict Reid, OSB, from the Benedictine Community at Three Rivers, Michigan. Sr. Margaret Helena noted that it was "exceptionally beautiful." After the peacefulness of the retreat it was full steam ahead for Commemoration Day on Saturday June 27. It had rained during the night but by the morning the sky was clear and 130 people came for the Mass, followed by lunch on the cloister. Sr. Margaret Helena thought it was "unusually nice" and that everyone "seemed to be happy." The "excellent sermon" was preached by the Revd. Nancy Talmage. On July 4, Dahlia Mazengia was received as an Oblate after spending two weeks as a guest at the convent. Sr. Barbara Jean, as Director of Oblates, wrote: "As a social worker and an active member of her church in Albany, New York, Dahlia hopes to carry her connection with our Community life into her daily environment."[14]

The ending of the academic year in the summer saw Sr. Laura Katharine finish her spiritual direction course at General Theological Seminary. Sr. Barbara Jean's course at Drew was longer, spread over one day a week, but in addition over the summer she took a course at Princeton Theological Seminary. During the Fall semester she attended General Theological Seminary three days a week.

The summer Search Program in the last two weeks of August was attended by four women. Sr. Barbara Jean wrote: "Each Sister had a part in sharing her life experience with the Searchers ... We prayed together, sang, worked, and slowly tried to discern with each person what God's direction for life might be."[15] Fr. Maitland and Fr. Gross assisted with the classes and discussions. But Sr. Margaret Helena remarked that although the women felt the program had been very helpful, "three at least had no idea of a religious vocation."[16]

With the coming of the Fall much work was done to improve the facilities at St. Marguerite's. The outside was freshly painted before the storm season made such work impossible. New chairs and carpets were installed in the chapel and the halls and stairways were painted. In addition, the second- and third-floor hallways were carpeted and new beds provided throughout. Up to Commemoration Day, 990 people had attended retreats and programs.

Work was proceeding on the revision of the Associates' Manual. Sr. Margaret Helena, writing to the Associates in October 1987, told them: "We have just revised the [Associates'] lists and find that we have 70 Priest Associates and 320 lay Associates, all of whom we keep in our prayers collectively and individually. We have a new system of intercessions for you. At Terce we pray for priests (2 or 3 by name), at the Noonday Office we pray for Religious Orders and the lay Associates (4 or 6 a day). The Sisters sing many of the Offices, usually Terce, Vespers and Compline."

The ministry of the Sisters had undergone considerable change during the decade of the 1980s. As Mother Suzanne Elizabeth explained in the Associates' Newsletter of October 1987, "Today the Community of St. John Baptist finds its main ministry to be *hospitality* ... To receive all as

Christ; feed the hungry, clothe the naked, visit those in prison—perform all the works of mercy. Over the past thirty years we went *out* into parishes and to the inner city to do much of this. Today we find that the world is coming to us *to be fed spiritually*, to find a firm foundation on which to stand up to the crises of this world." She went on to explain that in order to be prepared for this ministry the Sisters themselves need to cultivate hospitality in their own lives. And the way to do this was to "open our hearts, minds and souls daily to receive Christ into our lives. We must know that God comes to us every day, every moment ... If we can imagine our God coming to us for a cup of cold water or for a place to rest awhile, we will reach out of ourselves and take in this God and give a place of rest and *hospitality* ... *Then* we will find the energy to reach out to those who come to us." She quoted from the Rule of St. Benedict, who instructed his monks to receive others as Christ. And finally: "Thank you for coming to visit us and allowing us the opportunity to provide *hospitality*. We give thanks for all you do for us, most especially for your loving prayers ... And so we go on from glory to glory to the eternal praise of the most Blessed Trinity." It was a vision of ministry for the Community which could be truly lived even though numbers were smaller and less energized.

On October 26, 1987, Sr. Mary Elizabeth was professed in First Vows at 8:00am. Her vows were received by Bishop Spong. Twelve members of her family were present, including her newest grandson, who was baptized later in the morning. About 75 people came, including Fr. Wessinger. Breakfast was provided for all and lunch for the family and Sisters.

Another year drew to a close; a year full of activity and hospitality, undergirded as always by prayer. Ten guests came for Christmas dinner and there was Christmas mail to be shared from Clewer. In her Weekly Letter to the Sisters, dated December 30, 1987, Mother noted that "we had a very peace-filled Christmas, thanks be to God."

In time-honored custom some of the Sisters kept the Watch until 12:00 midnight to pray the old year out and to pray the New Year, 1988, in. The Feast of the Epiphany, January 6, was celebrated with a Choral Mass at 7:00am and a tea party by the fire in the library at 3:30pm. On the following Saturday evening the Epiphany party was quite well attended despite heavy snow on the previous day. The extreme cold with snow and ice continued into the following week, disrupting travel plans.

On Sunday, January 17, the Sisters heard news that the Church of the Resurrection at Elizabeth, NJ, together with the rectory, had burned down overnight. True to its name, the Church of the Resurrection rose again on December 19, 1988, by merging with the newly refurbished Trinity Church and becoming from that time St. Elizabeth's Church.

Winter weather continued and on January 25 there was more snow. A power line broke under the weight of it, causing a fire on the ground behind St. Marguerite's. The electricity company turned the power off and the fire was extinguished, but the Sisters were then without power in the convent. A generator was brought in for the heating and freezer. Dora Kapp lost her home to a fire on January 30, and sought temporary refuge at the convent. Mid-February saw yet more snow but it did not deter three "searchers" coming for the weekend Search Program.

As well as offering hospitality to groups and individuals, the Sisters also continued with a phenomenal amount of active ministry. This was in addition to Sr. Barbara Jean pursuing her theological studies. Thus on March 18, 1988, Mother flew to San Antonio, TX, to give a retreat and workshop, returning on the following Wednesday, and on Monday, April 11, Mother and Sr. Laura Katharine flew to Toronto for a Religious Life Conference, returning on Friday.

The Community Warden, Fr. Cure, SSJE, was leaving and made his last visit to the convent on Sunday April 10, 1988. During their Community Day discussions the Sisters considered the qualities they hoped for in a Warden. Fr. Robert Maitland Jr. was duly appointed and was instituted by Bishop Spong on Tuesday June 21.

Many years previously Sr. Olive Frances had perfected the art of writing illuminated manuscripts. She left the Community in 1927 but much of her work remained at the convent. The high humidity was not good for the manuscripts as they were written on vellum, and so Mother had taken them to the Morgan Library in NYC for restoration. After several months she was able to bring them home to the convent, where they remain on view.

The Community, through its ministry of hospitality and through the Sisters who went out into the parishes, was also having what may be called a "ministry of presence" in the wider Episcopal Church. This was by means of attending the meetings of organizations such as the Episcopal Church Women, the Diocesan and National Altar Guild, the local Diocesan Convention, and the triennial General Convention. The 69th General Convention of the Episcopal Church took place at Detroit, MI, from July 2–11, and was attended by Mother Suzanne Elizabeth and Sr. Laura Katharine as observers from the 7th until the 9th. The presence of Sisters at these meetings gave a visible message that Religious Communities had an integral part of the life of the wider Church.

The links with Clewer remained very strong and on July 26, Sr. Barbara Jean flew from Newark airport for a visit. Her flight had been delayed due to bad storms and did not take off until 4:00 am, but on July 27, Mother Edna Frances phoned to tell of her safe arrival.

On Monday, October 3, there was a Chapter of Election and Mother Suzanne Elizabeth was re-elected as Mother Superior. She was installed by Bishop Spong at 8:00am Mass on Thursday October 6. Fr. Maitland, Fr. Gross and Fr. Holland from St. Mark's, Mendham, were also present. Next day, Sr. Barbara Jean and Sr. Mary Lynne received their blessings for the offices of Assistant Superior and Novice Mistress respectively. Deborah Scott had been visiting the convent frequently. On Monday, October 10, 1988, she was received as a postulant at Vespers.

On this positive note, Sr. Barbara Jean's unofficial Record Book peters out—there are no more entries for 1988. But Community life continued even if the records were not kept, or have been lost sight of. Similarly, few records have survived for most of 1989, but even so, good things were happening both in the Community and in the wider World. The Cold War was coming to an end: the Berlin Wall had fallen; hardline Communism was ending; and the USSR had a new leader, Mikhail Gorbachev, who was willing to talk to Western leaders.

On April 25, 1989, Deborah Scott was clothed as a novice, taking the name Sr. Deborah Francis. Sr. Deborah Francis was raised as a secular Jew and during childhood lived on Long Island, NY. She graduated from NY State University College in 1974 with a BA in art history and fine arts. While at college she converted to Christianity under the sponsorship of the Intervarsity Christian Fellowship. She was baptized, and attended Baptist and Assemblies of God churches. She moved to NYC in 1975 to take part in a Church of the Nazarene mission in Times Square and in 1982 began attending Grace Episcopal Church, where she was confirmed in 1984. While working as a paralegal in Manhattan in 1987, she began to sense a call to the Religious Life. She corresponded with several Communities, but CSJB was the one she felt drawn towards. As an accomplished needlewoman, making cards and samplers by means of cross stitching, Sr. Deborah Francis meditated on this activity in the Christmas 1989 Community Newsletter. "Cross-stitching is where design and individual creativity meet … In the creative process what I stitch into this pattern is myself. I make this pattern my own by being faithful to the design laid out before me. In my life, with God and in Community, it is much the same. The basic pattern of the Religious has been laid out by another but I make it my own as I creatively stitch myself into it and watch the pattern of the Community emerge."

Sr. Barbara Jean, having ascertained that ordination as a deacon would not cause difficulties between Clewer and Mendham, was ordained to the diaconate at Trenton Cathedral on June 10, 1989. It was a great day for the Community—the first Sister to be ordained to holy orders. The usual time between ordination as deacon and priest was a year, but Sr. Barbara Jean opted for an extended diaconate out of respect for the Sisters at Clewer, some of whom did not agree with the ordination of women to the priesthood. Mother Edna Frances, who was a strong supporter of women's ordination, came over for Sr. Barbara Jean's ordination and was then able to take part in discussions about Community life.[17]

Sr. Sheila and Sr. Zoë arrived from Clewer for a visit on October 2. They stayed until the 17th, during which time they enjoyed various trips to New York and the Jersey shore. Sr. Margaret Helena remarked to the Associates: "We tried to show them what nice places New York and New Jersey have … We enjoyed their visit very much because *they* enjoyed everything."[18]

As the summer gave way to the Fall, new ministry was embarked upon. Sr. Barbara Jean wrote excitedly in the Newsletter for Christmas 1989: "This Fall has been a new adventure for Sr. Mary Elizabeth and me, as we both began parish work in the city of Elizabeth. She is in charge of the Church School at St. Elizabeth's on North Broad Street, and I am Deacon Assistant at St. John's. The two churches are about a mile apart. There is much to be done as both congregations cope with the needs of a changing neighborhood. It has been my privilege to visit many sick and shut-ins of St. John's congregation, and to assist at the Thursday healing Eucharist. I am also working with the Church School which is growing." As Advent and Christmas preparations escalated, Sr. Barbara Jean noted, "Both of these churches are struggling to help the needy, particularly at this time of year. We are glad to share in this ministry." Sr. Barbara Jean worked at St. John's on Tuesdays, Thursdays and Sundays, and Sr. Mary Elizabeth worked on Sundays at St. Elizabeth's.

Sr. Deborah Francis attended a three-day conference for novices in

November, at the Community of St. Helena in Toronto. Sr. Mary Lynne attended for an overnight stay. Also in November, Sr. Susinne Paula celebrated her 94th birthday—only two other Sisters had reached that age in the American Community. And on November 25 there were wedding bells! Fr. Gross, the Community Chaplain, and Virginia Brown Keener were married in the main chapel. Sr. Margaret Helena commented that "it was a beautiful occasion with a solemn Mass sung to Missa Marialis in a Chapel full of friends."

In her Christmas 1989 Newsletter, Mother Suzanne Elizabeth wrote of the importance of waiting and of "befriending the time, not killing it." She continued: "More things have been wrought by prayer than anyone can imagine. Let us keep the prayers going for peace in the world. Amazing, startling things are happening, wonderful, fearful, and powerful. Let us befriend the issues in prayer ..."

Meanwhile the Sisters still had strong links with The Shire. Sr. Laura Katharine joined the tutoring program, working with those who did not qualify for assistance from their school districts. She was helping slow readers to do their AA step work, and also assisted others in preparation for their General Education Development tests. The Sisters had appealed to Associates and friends for Bibles, and as a result each of the young people had been given a New Testament to keep. Sr. Barbara Jean wrote: "We have been asked again this year to have the staff and residents over on Christmas afternoon for Carol singing and refreshments. The young people are excited about coming—it brightens what is a very hard day away from family ... It is a joy to all of us to be involved in their lives and recovery programs, and we look forward to continued growth in 1990."[19]

The year and the decade ended in the usual way of the Community, welcoming the coming of the Christ-child and hospitality to friends.

[1] Quoted from Sr. Barbara Jean's unofficial Record Book for 1985. The Sisters' burial plot in St. Michael's Cemetery, Astoria, is a very peaceful place even though La Guardia airport and a busy road are nearby. I was taken there in 2013 by Sr. Suzanne Elizabeth along with Sisters Linda Clare, Victoria Michelle and Monica Clare. It was very moving to see where the early Sisters, including Sr. Helen Margaret, the American Foundress, and Mother Frances Constance, the first Superior, lay at rest.

[2] Clewer Associates' Newsletter, September 1985. By the early 20th century, there were over 300 Sisters in 40 branch houses in the UK, including Sisters in India and America. It would have been impossible to gather them all together.

[3] Strange as it may seem, I have no recollection of this talk! But "the book" ended up as a trilogy, the first of which was *A Joyous Service*, published in 1989 and revised in 2012. I also attended Dr. Rampton's talk and, with my family, the performance of "Julian," which was both moving and informative—and so graphic that one could almost see Julian's cell in Norwich. Roberta Nobleman was well known to the US Sisters as she lived in America and had performed several times at the convent in Mendham, including a performance of "Julian" which was videoed.

[4] St. John's-on-the-Mountain is in the Diocese of New Jersey, which, unlike the Diocese of Newark at this time, had retained the vocational diaconate.

[5] Mendham Community Newsletter Christmas 1985.

[6] Ibid.

[7] Ibid. I have been unable to discover the exact date of the rededication, but it was certainly in the last few months of 1985.

[8] In 1972 St. Helen's Hall had merged with Bishop Dagwell Hall to become Oregon Episcopal School. Over the succeeding years it was greatly extended, and at the time of writing in 2019 serves 870 students from pre-kindergarten through 12th grade and includes day school and boarding programs.

[9] Clewer Associates' Newsletter September 1986.

[10] Mother Suzanne Elizabeth, Weekly Letter to the Sisters, Wednesday, November 26, 1986.

[11] The Sisters at Clewer had introduced Oblates at the end of the 1940s when they had made many changes to the Community, and the first two were admitted as probationers in September 1949. The admission of Elizabeth Hamilton as an Oblate is the first mention in the records at Mendham of the introduction of Oblates there. The Community Manual for Oblates explained that "the object of the Oblate Rule is to admit to a close affiliation with the Community those who wish to dedicate their lives to God within this special bond of fellowship … while being in the secular state and discharging the normal duties of that state." Some common requirements were: regular attendance at the Eucharist; the recitation of at least one Office daily; spiritual reading, meditation, spiritual direction or confession and an annual retreat; and service to the Church and to CSJB.

[12] Bishop Sengulane became well known as a leading figure in the Peace and Reconciliation Campaign which led to the ending of the civil war in Mozambique. His wife, Berta, was killed in a car crash in 1998 at age 43. She had been a major supporter of his ministry and had herself founded several congregations. Bishop Sengulane retired from office in 2014.

[13] Mendham Community Newsletter October 1987.

[14] Ibid.

[15] Ibid.

[16] Ibid.

[17] In 1985 the Church of England's General Synod had voted in favor of women being ordained as deacons. The first were not ordained until 1987 because the Church of England's status as the Established Church meant that the Synod's decision had to gain Parliamentary approval. (It would be several years before the Synod allowed women to be ordained to the priesthood.)

[18] Mendham Community Newsletter, Christmas 1989.

[19] Ibid.

ALL GIFTS DIFFERING

The Community 1990–94

T HE FINAL DECADE of the twentieth century had been declared a "Decade of Evangelism" by resolution 43 of the 1988 Lambeth Conference, a gathering of all bishops from throughout the Worldwide Anglican Communion. Similarly, in the Catholic Church, Pope John Paul II had declared a "Decade of Evangelization." The great hope behind both similarly titled ideals was that Christians of all denominations would endeavor to proclaim the Gospel wherever they happened to be during the closing years of the 20th century. On a pragmatic level it was hoped that the fall in numbers in many churches of the developed World would stall, and that congregations would increase just as they were increasing spectacularly in parts of the developing World (known at that time as the "Third World").[1]

On February 5, 1990, the Community celebrated the 116th anniversary of the Sisters coming from Clewer to establish the Community work in New York. Writing to the Associates, Sr. Margaret Helena commented: "I have always wondered what the weather was like on that day in February 1874. This year Dora Kapp went to the library and got out the *New York Times* on microfilm and found out. The sidewalks and the middle of the street had been cleared in lower Manhattan. Snow was piled three feet deep on the sides. People were enjoying their horses and sleighs on the streets of upper Manhattan. It was a bright, sunny day."

Meanwhile, the Sisters were continuing their many ministries both at the convent and further afield. Mother Suzanne Elizabeth gave an Altar Guild workshop at St. Mark's, Mendham, on January 9. Since then she had preached at a World Day of Prayer service at Nutley, NJ, and given a Lent evening prayer workshop at Grace Church, Madison, a slide show about the Religious Life at Grace Church, Westwood, and an evening of flower-arranging meditation at Grace Church, Haddonfield. She also represented the Conference on Religious Life at an Ecumenical Conference of Religious at the Catholic University in Washington, DC. Other Sisters were busy too. Sr. Laura Katharine and Sr. Deborah Francis attended a Conference for Religious at St. Helena's Convent, and Sr. Mary Lynne and Sr. Deborah Francis attended a Conference for the Novitiate, also at St. Helena's. Sr. Barbara Jean and Sr. Mary Elizabeth continued their ministry at St. John's-on-the-Mountain in Bernardsville. This latter ministry had its poignant moments, such as when Sr. Barbara Jean asked the children to think of something that made them sad. A little girl aged four said, "When people make fun of your color and your name."

So much ministry to others could be exhausting but the Sisters continued to be nurtured by the Sacraments, by prayer and by their regular times of retreat. Thus their long retreat was looked forward to as a time to lay aside outside work and ministry and just "be." Also, the Sisters had been led by a Roman Catholic Sister exploring the Myers-Briggs personality type indicator. Under the heading "All gifts differing," Mother Suzanne Elizabeth wrote in the Easter 1990 Community Newsletter to Associates. "We learned how better to appreciate and respect ourselves and others when we feel 'different' or think ourselves 'different.'"

In May Fr. Wessinger kept the fiftieth anniversary of his ordination to the priesthood at the SSJE monastery at Boston, MA. Some of the Sisters remembered his first visit to Mendham in 1945, soon after his life profession in the Society of St. John the Evangelist. He always said he found his vocation through meeting CSJB Sisters in Portland, Oregon.

By 1990 the number of Oblates had risen to nine, consisting of two social workers, two hospital workers, a priest, a nurse, a mother, and two retired people. Sr. Barbara Jean was the Director of Oblates, and two of them contributed articles to the Community Newsletter of Easter 1990. Both emphasized how their commitment to the Community had deepened and grown and how they were using this gift in their everyday working life to show forth Christ's love in the workplace. Mary Adebonojo explained how "the life and ministry of all Oblates and other Associates is meant to be an extension of the work of the Community … It is prayer, the presence of Christ in us, which enables us to bring to our work the love and sympathy which promote healing and wholeness." As a hospital chaplain, she had found that the commitment as an Oblate was a source of strength in her own personal Christian journey. Dahlia Mazengia had overcome the challenges of how to bring Christ to her workplace as a staff development officer and had gradually managed to improve the morale of the staff, especially those at the lower end of the system. She had been told by a work colleague that she had "brought humanity into the workplace."

Associates of the Community were important too, and at the last Community Chapter meeting the decision was made to admit non-Episcopalians as Associates. Writing in the Autumn 1991 Newsletter, Sr. Laura Katharine noted: "Your being Associates and friends is most special and wonderful in so many ways … It is your free-will offering, it is the sharing in and the extension of our Community Life."

In July 1990 Mother Suzanne Elizabeth and Sr. Mary Lynne visited Clewer for three weeks. They had been asked before their arrival if there was anything they specially wanted to do and Sr. Mary Lynne said she would like to visit Iona. The visit to Iona was planned for July 9–12, with Sr. Sheila accompanying them. At the last minute, i.e. at 6:50 on the morning of departure, Sr. Sheila, who had a bad cold, decided she felt too ill to go. Who would take her place at such short notice? As Sr. Eudora related to the Clewer Associates in their Newsletter of September 1990: "I, Sr. Eudora, having a rest morning until 7:00am, was in bed at 6:50 when the Infirmarian came to say, 'There's a crisis, Sr. Sheila cannot go. Will you—leaving at 8:15? Me (aloud) Yes, (under my breath) not half! Forthwith a Blitz descended on my room. Mother appeared from nowhere and began to pack. Sr. Zoë produced breakfast. Mother and Sr. Zoë made the bed. Managed the end of Lauds and finished breakfast. Then 'booted and spurred' I stood by the car at 8:15am. The others came along with packs on their backs and grips in their hands and with Mother at the wheel—'poop, poop' like Toad we were off…"[2]

It was a very short visit to Iona, but as Mother General Edna Frances noted to the Clewer Associates, "They also spent as much time as possible at home with us, for Clewer is as much their home as it is ours, and their roots also go back to Mother Harriet and Canon Carter." During the Clewer visit, Sr. Mary Lynne went with Sr. Gina to the Novice Guardians' Conference at the Community of St. John the Divine, Birmingham. Also, the two Mothers and Sr. Mary Lynne attended a Thanksgiving Service and prize-giving at St. Stephen's College, Broadstairs.[3]

Nineteen ninety-one was heralded on January 6 (the Feast of the Epiphany) with the reception of Margo Kolkebeck as a postulant, and on May 31 (the Feast of the Visitation of Our Lady) she was clothed as a novice with the name Sr. Margo Elizabeth. Many family members were present as well as a good number of Quaker friends. Sr. Margo

Elizabeth came from a Quaker tradition. She had a varied background in music, art and psychology, receiving both undergraduate and graduate degrees from Farleigh Dickinson University, and later, a Master's degree in human development. In the early 1980s she used her skills as an artist and photographer to illustrate a number of books. She was also an accomplished musician and teacher of the flute, having played professionally for several years in a number of symphony orchestras. But it was during time spent at Pendle Hill, a Quaker center for study and contemplation, that she wrote in her journal, "I want prayer as the primary focus of my life." This realization eventually led her to Mendham.

The Shire was having financial difficulties and welcomed their last client in March. Mother Suzanne Elizabeth was concerned about this and asked prayers from the Associates "that the doors of our school will once again open to young people." The organizers of the rehabilitation program were negotiating with a new group that the Governor of New Jersey wanted to bring to the State. Because of "red tape" the final contracts had not yet been signed.

In April there were two first professions. Sr. Ora Mary had been a professed Sister from 1949 until March 4, 1968, when she left the Community. Now, in 1991, she sought re-admission and was professed in first vows on April 8. Writing to the Associates in autumn 1991, Sr. Margaret Helena said, "It was a very simple service but we hoped it was for life. Not so, she left the Community on July 27." There had been many changes in the years since 1968 and she found adapting difficult. A further request for re-admission was turned down. She died on November 6, 2009, at the age of 84.

On St. Mark's day, April 25, 1991, Sr. Deborah Francis made her first vows at a lovely service in the main chapel. And at Clewer, on August 5, Mary Britt was clothed as a novice, taking the name Sr. Mary Stephen.

On April 20, 1991, four Sisters went to the consecration of Jack McKelvey as Bishop of Newark. He would remain in office until June 1999, when he became Bishop of Rochester, NY. A few days later, three Sisters went to Peekskill[4] for the fiftieth anniversary of the profession of Sr. Mary Basil and Sr. Anastasia.

Sr. Pamela and Sr. Doreen visited from Clewer, arriving on May 27, and stayed for three weeks. Sr. Margaret Helena noted: "We tried to give them a bird's eye view of life in Mendham. It was a pleasure to have them here." Later in the year, Beryl Askew, a Clewer Oblate, came for a visit and was taken to many places of interest by Dora Kapp, who was now residing at the convent and was an Oblate too. Sr. Margaret Helena with characteristic humor noted that Beryl had been given "a good view of life in the Colonies!"

Community life in all its fullness continued, with Sisters using their gifts and exercising their many ministries throughout the summer season. Thus, guests were welcomed to the convent for Commemoration Day, and for events at St. Marguerite's. Further afield, Mother and Sr. Barbara Jean went to Phoenix, AZ, in July for a Conference on the Religious Life, followed by acting as volunteers at the 70th General Convention of the Episcopal Church, also at Phoenix. During the Convention they attended the meeting of the National Altar Guild. August saw Mother accompany Sr. Margaret Helena to Oregon, where they had a busy schedule with the Associates.

On July 26, 1991, Sr. Katharine Veronica was admitted to the nursing unit at the House of the Good Shepherd in Hackettstown, having become totally helpless and needing round-the-clock care. She had been diagnosed with bone cancer five years previously but had continued to live her vowed life as much as was possible. The last two years, when she became totally bedridden, had been difficult for her. Now, on August 10, 1991, she passed peacefully to her rest having been given "exquisite care" at the nursing home. Her funeral was at the convent on August 13 and she was laid to rest in the convent cemetery.

Sr. Katharine Veronica had trained as a nurse at St. Luke's Training School, NYC, and graduated in 1927. It was while she was visiting at Bergen Pines that she met Sr. Lillian Christine, CSJB, and a friendship was formed. She entered the convent in June 1937, and was professed by Bishop Washburn in November 1940. Her time in Community spanned the last years of the old institutional work, when she worked mostly at St. Anna's home (and kept in touch with many of the girls and women after they left), and at St. Marguerite's Home. But mostly her work in Community was part of the Second Spring—St. John Baptist School at Corsicana, TX, and St. Luke's Chapel, NYC, where she organized a lunch program for seniors living in the area. In 1966 she joined Deaconess Brown's mission to the Navajo Indians. Her letters from the Indian reservation are in Appendix 3. Also, she was school nurse at St. John Baptist School from 1939–40 and 1955–62. She was a Sunday School teacher at St. John's-on-the-Mountain in Bernardsville as well as Assistant

Superior of CSJB 1950–55, and Secretary from 1978–83. She did not leave her nursing skills behind when she joined the Community. She was on the Visiting Nurse staff and was Visiting Nurse Supervisor and acting director of the Visiting Nurse Association in Brooklyn, NYC. Her Community Biographer, Sr. Margaret Helena, wrote that "she had a wonderful gift for making friends. All ages loved her, from little children in the primary grades and girls at St. John Baptist School, to the parishioners at St. Luke's and Bernardsville. She kept up by letter with many people, some were childhood friends." Tributes flowed in from many whose lives she had touched and who would continue to remember her with thankfulness and love.

As the trees reddened in the Fall season, a huge problem for Mother Suzanne Elizabeth reared its head. Strict fire code regulations had been imposed on the convent and St. Marguerite's retreat house. "If we are to continue our life and ministry in these buildings, we must enclose stairwells and install a unified smoke detector system etc., etc. I had hoped that I would be able to report a resolution in this newsletter but I now realize that this is a slow, cumbersome process which *may* eventually work in our favor … What I *do* know is that we will need a great deal of assistance from you … We need your prayers, we need your donations, and we need your expert direction. Do you know organizations and/or corporations that make grants for such renovations? Do you know people that are adept at fund raising; do you know 'grant' writers? ... If CSJB ever meant anything to you, please tell us now by lending your support to these huge concerns."[5] It was indeed a huge concern, taking hours of negotiation, acres of paperwork, and a process that was emotionally and spiritually exhausting, for if the case failed to convince the "powers that be" it would mean the end of CSJB at Mendham. And then where would they go? The case dragged on for several years, of which there will be more later.

At the Chapter on October 26, 1991, Sr. Mary Elizabeth was not elected for final profession. Sr. Margaret Helena informed the Associates in the Christmas Newsletter. "We miss her and wish her well," she wrote.

Mother Suzanne Elizabeth had some good news to share about the former school buildings. "In time for Thanksgiving, Daytop has been granted the funds to open a new facility in our School buildings. They are presently organizing new staff to welcome teenagers to their program of rehabilitation from chemical dependency."

Nineteen ninety-two brought a sense of optimism in spite of

the challenges. Looking back on the year in the October Associates'
Newsletter, Mother Suzanne Elizabeth wrote: "Since Eastertide we have
had marvelous things happen, so grand that they are at once fearful and
wonderful." During Easter week the Sisters had the idea of a fund-raising
house tour. "Gathering a handful of Associates, we brainstormed and
quickly decided what we had to do. In two days we had 1,300 letters in the
mail. The newspaper and TV coverage was great (and free)." The event
was called "Monastery in May" and it took place on May 24, 1992. "It
was the only nice day of the Memorial Day weekend [and] we welcomed
1,000 people who patiently waited to tour the convent and St. Marguerite's.
Truly it was amazing." The purpose of the open day was to raise funds
for work needed for the fire code regulations. And the response to the
appeal had been very encouraging. "By July we had received a grant from
St. Martin's Retreat House, a once active retreat house nearby. For many
years the governing board has been making grants to retreat programs
from the income of the inherited estate. They offered a grant of $50,000
if we could match that amount. We matched it! Rather, YOU matched
it! How overwhelmed we are in gratitude. Surely God has heard our
prayers."

This was not the end of the saga. The Sisters had been unable to reach
any final agreement with "the powers that be" on the work that needed
to be done. They hoped it would be resolved by July 1993, but it would in
fact take far longer. Sr. Margaret Helena shed a bit more light on it. "The
frustrating thing is that we have not been able to make the alterations at
St. Marguerite's—we have not had a firm plan or approval from the Fire
Official and we cannot go ahead without knowing what we are to do!"

The Sisters had kept pets, usually cats and dogs, for many years, but
around Eastertide 1992 the Sisters found they had been "adopted" by a
small brown-and-white Indian pony. He just wandered into their grounds
and, liking the look of their grass, decided to stay! The owner was
eventually found but was not keen to take him back, so Pony stayed. He
lived for 28 years in his specially fenced-in paddock. Sr. Margo Elizabeth
soon established a rapport with him and remained his principal care giver.

There were changes at Clewer. Mother General Edna Frances had
decided to retire from office after fourteen years, a year earlier than the
end of her term of office. Sr. Jane Olive was elected in her place and
was installed by the Bishop of Oxford, the Rt. Revd. Richard Harries,
in August 1992. Sr. Deborah Francis was present, having been staying at

Clewer since July 7. She returned to Mendham on August 31. Sr. Elizabeth Jane had spent three months at Mendham from June 4 and returned home to Clewer on August 27.

Fr. Gross, the Community Chaplain for the past 15 years, decided to take early retirement and left on September 8. He moved with his wife to upstate New York. Meanwhile, a number of local clergy were celebrating the Eucharist in the Sisters' chapel until a new Chaplain could be appointed.

Things were moving in the right direction regarding the school occupancy. After months of planning, Daytop's residency became official. Daytop had begun its program at Mendham in January 1992 with teenagers aged 14–18, gradually increasing in numbers until all 50 places were filled. Fr. Joseph Hennen, Director of Daytop, had given an inspiring address at the Sisters' Commemoration Day in June. The Mendham work, the latest in a number of Daytop facilities, was dedicated on September 24, 1992, and was attended by four Sisters and a large crowd. Mother Suzanne Elizabeth gave the invocation. Sr. Barbara Jean described the event in the Community Newsletter for October 1992. "The young residents had worked hard for weeks with painters, carpenters, and gardeners to make the buildings and grounds shine and sparkle. A tent was erected near the circle for refreshments. A video on the program was produced and shown. A choir from another Daytop facility came to sing. The most dramatic moment came when Monsignor O'Brien, one of the founders, and honored guest Mary Tyler Moore, arrived on the front lawn in a helicopter!" The dedication ceremony took place in the gym with speeches, including one from the actress Mary Tyler Moore, who shared her own struggle with addiction. Sr. Barbara Jean went on to describe the daily schedule, which included tutoring time when teachers worked with the students on their high school courses, work around the facility in teams, and group time. Individual counseling was given, and family therapy. She wrote: "Families are an important part of the healing process, which can take up to a year in residence and then more time in after-care. Each resident is encouraged to take responsibility for his or her own life. This involves a gradual building up of trust. We will be starting a series of Bible studies at Daytop. They will be voluntary, but already there is a waiting list. I ask your prayers that this study of the Scriptures will enable these young people to find help from God in their struggle to rebuild relationships with their families, their world and within themselves."

The Community retained ownership of the school, now Daytop, and simply asked an annual rent of one dollar! While not directly involved in the rehabilitation program, the Sisters remained closely interested through their prayerful support, and Sr. Barbara Jean remained on the governing body. There is a parallel between the works of firstly The Shire, then Daytop, and the earlier institutional work of the Community, in that all were trying to help people from troubled backgrounds with many personal problems. Such work in its earlier form became untenable, but Daytop, endeavoring to answer modern needs with modern methods, answered a very much-needed cry for help. The early Sisters, now departed, would have seen the parallels between their work with the disadvantaged and the needs of those who came to Daytop.

On November 11, 1992, the General Synod of the Church of England at last legislated in favor of women being ordained to the priesthood, sixteen years after the General Convention had voted in favor of women priests in the Episcopal Church. It would be another two years before the first priestly ordinations took place in England in April 1994.[6]

As the year 1992 drew towards its close, a postulant was received on November 29, just before Vespers. The Community was still without a permanent Chaplain, but the Revd. Robert Morris came to celebrate the Midnight Mass, and on Christmas morning all the Sisters went to the 9:00am Mass at St. Mark's, Mendham. The Epiphany party, by this time a Community tradition, was attended by 40 people who enjoyed the sing-along followed by food and fellowship.

Mother Suzanne Elizabeth's Easter message to the Associates in 1993 reflected the huge strain both she and the Community were under due to the ongoing saga of the fire code regulations. "We have no answers, no matter how hard we've tried to get them, so we keep waiting … It has been a very active waiting and we feel now as if we are on a pinnacle when everything is just about ready to come forth. We are feeling a bit battered … we feel like we are standing in a time of chaos but we have worked hard to stay rooted and grounded in our life." She went on to comment on the huge changes in the nation and in society. And indeed those changes presaged the shape of things to come. On March 29, 1993, there was a terrorist attack on the World Trade Center in New York City. Little damage was done by the truck bomb in the underground carpark, and five men were arrested with a sixth still being sought. But it was a warning which mostly went unheeded. Eight years later, a far greater attack would be launched on the same site, and the world would never be the same again.

Mother Suzanne Elizabeth concluded her Easter letter on a positive note. "I don't think CSJB has ever been more dependent upon or more grateful for the support, love and prayers of our friends and Associates. You have all moved mountains, or at least enabled us to work confidently through heaps of red tape. You have told us by your support that our life and work are important and must continue. You have renewed our energies and our confidence. Truly we are ready for transformation and new life. Let us give thanks for this hope that is in us."

Sr. Margaret Helena informed the Associates in the Easter Newsletter for 1993 that construction work at St. Marguerite's would begin shortly after Easter. "It has been a long and anxious time. When the work is finished the Fire Commissioner tells us we have to begin at the convent!" Despite all the stress and anxiety, the Sisters continued their ministry far and wide. Mother had traveled to Washington, DC, twice for meetings as she was co-chair on a committee planning an Ecumenical Conference for Religious, due to take place May 7–9 in Milwaukee, Wisconsin. In February Mother and Sr. Barbara Jean went to Florida for a Superiors' meeting. Then Sr. Barbara Jean gave a retreat at Ocean City for the congregation of Trenton Cathedral, attended by about 50 people. And Sr. Laura Katharine had welcomed many people to St. Marguerite's.

On March 24, 1993, four new Associates were received, including Janet Thomas. She had been making regular retreats since August 1991. Sr. Deborah Francis renewed her first vows on April 28, 1993. The postulant who had been received at the end of November 1992 left on May 1, 1993, having no vocation. This meant that for the time being there was no one in the novitiate, Sr. Margo Elizabeth having made her profession in first vows on May 25, 1992.

On May 20, 1993, Sr. Susinne Paula had a mild stroke which affected her memory, sight, and ability to walk. She was admitted to Morristown Memorial Hospital for tests and as she did not improve she was moved to a nursing home, the House of the Good Shepherd, Hackettstown. She died peacefully on August 3, in the 98th year of her life and the 58th year of her profession.[7] Sr. Barbara Jean and Sr. Mary Lynne were staying at Clewer, but returned home upon hearing of Sister's death. Sr. Susinne Paula was greatly loved by many people whose lives she had touched during her long Community life and ministry. Tributes poured into the convent from many quarters: Bishop Moore, Associates, visitors to the convent, people who remembered her in Jersey City, and the nurses who had cared for her. A former postulant wrote: "We know she is not going to miss music practice—she thought it was worse than going to the dentist!" Sr. Susinne Paula was laid to rest in the convent cemetery. Her passing meant that Sr. Margaret Helena was the last remaining Sister to have been professed before 1940.

In July there was a special Chapter meeting to commend Sr. Barbara Jean to the Bishop and Standing Committee of New Jersey for ordination to the priesthood. Bishop Belshaw[8] set February 19, 1994, for the ordination to take place at the convent.

The Sisters had been without a resident Chaplain from September 1992 and many local clergy had celebrated the Eucharist and taken care of the Sisters pastorally. In August 1993, Fr. Philip Ramstad was appointed Chaplain, now to be known as "resident priest," and took up residence in the priest's apartment.

On September 14, Mother accompanied Sr. Margaret Helena, firstly to Vancouver in Washington State where Sister had family, and then across the Columbia River into Oregon. There they visited the Oregon Episcopal School, "and Mother saw many things that had come from the old St. Helen's Hall, especially the Chapel furniture."[9] There was the usual meeting of the Portland Associates, at which thirteen were present. "Another day Mother and I borrowed my niece's car and drove ninety-five miles into the wilderness to a place where you can look across the valley right into the crater of Mt. St. Helen's. It was a thrill indeed. On the last day we drove across Portland to the Riverview cemetery where we have a plot and where Sr. Katharine Angela and Mother Alice Ursula are buried."[10]

On October 18, 1993, Mother Suzanne Elizabeth was re-elected as Superior for a further five-year term. She was installed by Bishop Spong next day. There was a re-arrangement of Community offices: Sr. Barbara Jean continued as Assistant Superior, Sr. Laura Katharine was appointed Novice Mistress and Bursaress, and Sr. Mary Lynne became Sister in Charge of St. Marguerite's Retreat House. Sr. Margaret Helena was given a blessing as "Mother Emeritus" and Fr. Ramstad as "Eucharistic Minister." On November 26, there was a Chapter for the election of a new Warden, Fr. Maitland having resigned. Br. Robert Hugh, of the Society of St. Francis, was elected and was installed by Bishop Spong on December 7. On December 15, Douglas Freer, a CSJB Associate and former "Mendham boy," was ordained to the priesthood. Mother Suzanne Elizabeth had prepared him for Confirmation some years previously.

Nineteen ninety-four dawned with an air of excitement as Sr. Barbara Jean's ordination to the priesthood drew near. But first, there were the usual speaking commitments and hospitality to visitors and retreatants. And then there was the snow. The Sisters were accustomed to severe winters, but January 1994 was particularly severe and there were many cancellations. On January 29, there was a visit by Mr. Peter Stevens, the headmaster of the Oregon Episcopal School, accompanied by a lady who had graduated from St. Helen's Hall. On February 1, a committee of junior professed Religious met at the convent to plan a conference. Sr. Deborah Francis and Sr. Margo Elizabeth were members of the committee.

On February 8, Mother General Jane Olive and Sr. Marjorie flew from Heathrow for a visit, principally to attend Sr. Barbara Jean's priestly ordination. The snow began in earnest at Mendham and when the Sisters telephoned Clewer to warn them, they discovered they had already left for Heathrow airport. After seven hours their flight was diverted to Boston, MA, all the New York airports having closed due to the weather. The Sisters finally arrived at the convent at midnight on February 9. Next day the two Mothers flew to Las Vegas for the Conference on the Religious Life, while back at Mendham Sr. Barbara Jean taught Sr. Marjorie how to ski, this being a necessary means of getting around, since another eight inches of snow had fallen. On February 17 and 18 two bulldozers were brought in to clear the convent road so that two cars could pass.

February 19, 1994, dawned cold but sunny. The piled snow showed no sign of a thaw, but as Sr. Margaret Helena wrote in her letter to the Associates, "Inside the Chapel there was a warm sense of expectation and happiness," for this was Sr. Barbara Jean's ordination day. She continued: "The Community had considered this step carefully. [Sr. Barbara Jean] would be a Sister of CSJB *first*, she belonged to the Community but she would be enabled to fulfil her call in a fuller way. We were all supporting her in this step …[11] This is the first ordination in either part of the Community, and a very solemn step for both the English and American branches."[12]

About 300 people filled the main chapel and Lady chapel to capacity for the ordination. Sister Barbara Jean was presented to the Bishop of New Jersey by the Revd. Robert Maitland, Jr., and Sr. Margaret Helena, representing the Community, and the Revd. Joseph R. Parrish, Jr., and Mr. Henry H. Carroll, representing the parish of St. John's, Elizabeth, NJ, where Sister served. Mother Jane Olive read a lesson and Mother Suzanne Elizabeth preached an inspiring sermon and delivered a charge. The gifts were presented by Sisters Marjorie, Laura Katharine, Mary Lynne, Deborah Francis and Margo Elizabeth. Sixteen priests laid hands at the moment of ordination. At the offertory the oblation bearers were Sr. Barbara Jean's sister, Martha Packer Hartman, and her aunt, Norma Geddes. At the Eucharist the bishop was the principal celebrant and the co-consecrators were Sr. Barbara Jean and the Revd. Mary Adebonojo. At the end of the service the bishop asked Sr. Barbara Jean to give the blessing. The service ended with the hymn "Lift High the Cross." The "Master of Ceremonies" was Fr. Carr Holland, Rector of St. Mark's, Mendham. There was a reception following the service, the food being provided by the women of St. John's Church and the CSJB Associates. Sr. Margaret Helena summed up the day as a "beautiful, awe inspiring and wonderful day."[13] It was a real milestone in the history of CSJB, paving the way for other Sisters who would become priests. Sr. Barbara Jean celebrated her first Mass next day in the convent chapel.

One person who was unavoidably absent at the ordination was the new Warden, Br. Robert Hugh, SSF. He had made his visitation a few days previously and had met Mother Jane Olive and Sr. Marjorie, but had to leave before the ordination. Mother Jane Olive and Sr. Marjorie went home to Clewer on February 24, this time with no travel problems or diversions.

Another joyous day followed on April 25, 1994, St. Mark's Day, when Sr. Deborah Francis made her profession in final vows.

Sr. Margaret Helena concluded her news article in the Community Newsletter for Easter 1994 with some good news. "The fire alarm system and all that goes with it, lights, doors, buzzers and fireproof paint on the chestnut wainscoting is completed. We are waiting for final approval. I hear it isn't as bad as it sounded. Gratis Deo." Alas, the thanksgiving was premature. Mother Suzanne Elizabeth informed the Associates[14] later in the year, "Last spring we thought we had completed work on our retreat house [costing] $150,000. However, we did not pass the Fire Official's inspection. Plans that were previously negotiated *and* approved by him were now rejected. Blueprints previously approved were now unacceptable!!! Furthermore, he is now bringing pressure on us to begin renovations on the convent building. These renovations have been estimated at ONE HALF MILLION DOLLARS! The convent structure could not possibly be changed to meet these requirements and the astronomical cost would totally deplete us." She went on to say that after much prayer and consultation the Community had decided to appeal. The Court of Appeals heard part of the case at the end of May 1994 but did not reach a decision, so the Sisters were directed to try to negotiate before the next hearing in August. By mid-July agreement was reached on the retreat house and additional work was being done. The Community had an attorney who was working hard to reach a compromise. But "our legal fees are hefty and our pockets are empty." Mother reminded the Associates how they had helped with fund-raising two years previously. "WE NOW NEED ANOTHER MIRACLE. We must have another fund raiser in the spring and funds to keep us solvent ... Please pray for us." Mother concluded her report by noting that the seven Sisters in the Community could sell up and move elsewhere, "but if we can continue our life and work in this setting that has brought peace, healing and love to generations, we would prefer to do that. Please pray for us as we continue to minister to those who need us. So many find this place in the woods so special and renewing."

Alongside the stress of the fire code regulations Community life went ahead as usual. There were familiar events such as Commemoration Day at the end of June and the Search Program in August. Also in June, Mother and Sr. Laura Katharine went to England, basing themselves at Clewer, though Mother also attended the Superiors' Conference with Mother Jane Olive. They were back home in time for Commemoration Day. On August 24, Sr. Barbara Jean and Sr. Deborah Francis attended the 71st General Convention of the Episcopal Church at Indianapolis, Indiana. They were there as representatives of the Religious Orders and also the Diocesan Altar Guild. Whilst there they had a pastoral and prayerful ministry.

At the end of August 1994 Sr. Margaret Helena, accompanied by Sr. Mary Lynne, traveled to Vancouver to visit Sr. Margaret Helena's family, followed by the annual visit to Portland, Oregon, and the meeting of the Associates, of whom thirteen were present. Among them was Beatrice Paget, the oldest living CSJB Associate. Sr. Margaret Helena noted: "She will be 98 on her birthday in October. There she was, walking with her two canes, bright and cheerful as usual. I don't know when she was graduated from St. Helen's Hall, but it must have been seventy years ago.

She remembers Sr. Elisa Monica and Sr. Sara Josephine as well as the other Sisters who were there with me in the early days. On the day before we left, we were invited to be present at the opening day at the Oregon Episcopal School, the successor of St. Helen's Hall. It was a special occasion, the 125th anniversary of the opening of St. Helen's Hall. There was a big ceremony on the grounds with 700 students in attendance along with faculty, parents and guests. The fifth graders rang the bell one hundred and twenty-five times and the school was in session! It was thrilling to see the large student body and the new campus with its many buildings. I thanked God for it and remembered it has been fifty years since the Sisters withdrew."[15]

During the 1990s, the *Spiritual Exercises of St. Ignatius Loyola* were being rediscovered on both sides of the Atlantic and many people from all walks of life were asking for individually guided retreats using the Exercises. Thus Sisters from CSJB at Clewer and Mendham were being trained in spiritual direction. Mother Suzanne Elizabeth told the Associates: "Other Sisters and I are continuing our study here and in England to equip ourselves in spiritual direction so that we may better serve the many who come to us with this need." She returned in August from a thirty-day Ignatian retreat and in September accompanied Sr. Margo Elizabeth to England for a two-week long seminar in spiritual direction. During the UK visit they were able to spend a week on Iona and a further week at Clewer. Nearer home, Sr. Deborah Francis began a course on spirituality at General Theological Seminary in NYC. And a Conference for Religious was being planned at Mendham to take place on Thanksgiving weekend. In the midst of all the new ministries and challenges Religious Life went on. "We continue to say five offices a day, get our meditation time, have our daily Communion and pray for you. It is by your prayers we are strengthened to do all of this," wrote Sr. Margaret Helena.

The year 1994 drew onwards with a great celebration for Sr. Margaret Helena's 90th birthday on November 5. Three generations of her family were present, the youngest (Robert Thomas Haar) being just 13 months old. He was baptized in the Sisters' chapel on the Saturday. Local friends also came and 64 people, young and older, sat down for lunch on the Sunday. One young man (John Michael aged four) took quite a shine to the Sisters, telling his grandmother that yes, he would like to come back again but "not with all those other people, just 'the black and whites.'" Such is the witness of the Religious Life!

Bill and Shirley Grier had lived on the Community property since 1946, occupying what had once been the coach house in the days before the Sisters had a car. He was the property manager in addition to serving with the Mendham Township Fire Department. Shirley had a musical ministry to senior citizens. As well as being CSJB Associates they were active members of St. Luke's Church, Gladstone. They had celebrated their Golden Wedding anniversary in January 1993. Eric Grier, their grandson, had been working on the convent grounds for several years. Now, in October 1994, he was married at St. Bernard's Church in Bernardsville. Several Sisters attended the wedding.

Mother Suzanne Elizabeth was much more hopeful in her Advent letter to Associates. She told them that on the eve of Thanksgiving, a negotiating meeting lasting five hours, with the fire official, the town lawyer, and the Sisters' team of consultant, architect and lawyer, had reached a possible satisfactory agreement that everyone felt comfortable with. A plan was to be devised for smoke detectors to give early warning of problems and safe exits for the occupants. "It was," she said, "indeed a very special Thanksgiving Day." In addition, she also received a verbal approval of fire code renovations that had been completed on the retreat house and was assured that written approval was forthcoming. A heavy burden had been lifted from her shoulders but it would be necessary in the coming year to continue fund raising.

The Conference for Religious over the Thanksgiving weekend was one full of hope. The conductor, the Revd. Robert Morris, a CSJB Associate, had given new hope and insight to all present. Mother wrote, "Part of the exciting thing I felt was that CSJB appears to be moving into the future alive and in step. We have in place an active group of Associates, Oblates, residents and co-workers who all help to carry out the mission of the Sisterhood which they have joined, each in their own way. We also have an active Search Program … some of the former 'Searchers' are now Oblates, Associates and Sisters …"

She continued: "We feel new hope and energy surging out of our time of crisis and chaos, pain and sacrifice. We feel that a bright future is upon us built on the solid core of our absolute trust in God and our active search for God's will in all of this. Never before have I known the Sisters to prepare themselves so actively and thoroughly for our future ministry while dedicatingly [sic] tending to the works of the present moment in prayer and a very active apostolate. We know that the hard times are not over but we come into this new Christian Year open to the mighty acts of God, the whole meaning of which is LOVE."

Thus it was with renewed energy and hope the Sisters prepared themselves not only for the new Christian Year but also for the final years of the decade and of the twentieth century.

---

[1] The First World was the prosperous West; the Second World was those countries under the yoke of Communism; the Third World was those parts of Asia, sub-Saharan Africa and other countries where people struggled to exist amidst poverty, starvation and under oppressive regimes.

[2] I have already recorded this story in the revised edition (2012) of *A Joyous Service* but it is such a typical Sr. Eudora story to those who knew her that I felt it would bear repetition here.

[3] A year later, in July 1991, after 123 years of its existence in several locations, St. Stephen's College closed. The Community had withdrawn from teaching in 1965 but continued to own the property and remained on the Governing body. Financial problems and falling numbers made the decision to close inevitable.

[4] The Community of St. Mary the Virgin was founded in New York State in 1865 and was the first Community for women in the USA.

[5] Community Newsletter Autumn 1991.

[6] This was because although the General Synod of the Church of England is a legislative body, as the Established Church it has to gain Parliamentary approval for matters of doctrine, which the ordination of women was deemed to be. It was not a foregone conclusion that such approval would be given and there were some "tricky" moments. Eventually Parliament sanctioned it and then H.M. the Queen gave her Royal Assent. The amended Canons were promulgated, i.e. proclaimed, in General Synod in February 1994.

[7] Sr. Susinne Paula's Community Biographer wrote that at almost 98 she had attained the greatest age of any American Sister. This was probably written by Sr. Margaret Helena, who lived to an even greater age. In a memoir Sister Susinne Paula had written, she noted: "During World War 1 I worked in Washington for the Red Cross Headquarters at the U.S. Military Intelligence Offices for over a year."

[8] The Rt. Revd. George Phelps Mellick Belshaw, 9th Bishop of New Jersey, serving from 1983–94.

[9] Community Newsletter October 1993.

[10] Ibid.

[11] Sr. Barbara Jean has spoken to me of how supportive Mother Suzanne Elizabeth had been.

[12] Community Newsletter Easter 1994. There were at least two Sisters at Clewer who did not support women's ordination to the priesthood, but they did not raise objections to Sr. Barbara Jean's ordination. Later, when a Clewer Sister felt a calling to the priesthood, Sr. Zoë told me that she accepted it in obedience to the will of the Community.

[13] Community Newsletter Easter 1994.

[14] Community Newsletter October 1994.

[15] Ibid. Sr. Margaret Helena also noted that the bell had been brought around Cape Horn by ship to the original school and had been rung for the start of school in all the previous locations.

WORK FOR THE LORD

The Community 1995–99

NINETEEN NINETY-FIVE WAS ushered in with a carol service before Compline and the traditional vigil from Compline until midnight. Most of the house guests joined the Sisters, including one from England, who then returned and was received as a postulant at Clewer. However, she did not make it through to the novitiate.

On January 6, the Feast of the Epiphany, Sr. Barbara Jean and Sr. Deborah Francis attended the installation of the Rt. Revd. Joe Morris Doss as Bishop of the Episcopal Diocese of New Jersey.[1] St. John's, Elizabeth, was where the two Sisters were serving in that diocese.

Next day, in addition to the now traditional Epiphany party, there was an Oblates' meeting; a workshop on angels sponsored by Interweave; and two groups at St. Marguerite's. Sylvia Honeycutt, a resident Oblate for the past two years, moved to Richmond, VA, to care for her father. She renewed her Oblation before leaving. Other Oblates who also renewed their Oblation included Muriel Snyder and Lily Altamura. New Associates continued to be received, including the Revd. Dr. Charles Rice, assistant priest at St. Peter's, Morristown, and lecturer at Drew University seminary. He would become a good friend to the Sisters. Older Associates passed to their rest, including Doris West, who had been received in the 1940s when the Sisters worked at Corsicana in Texas. Sr. Laura Katharine continued to have pastoral care of the Associates and Oblates.

A new venture sponsored by Interweave called "Seminary for a day" took place on February 25, 1995, even though eight inches of snow had fallen. It was a good program much appreciated by the forty participants. On March 11, the Confirmation group from St. John's, Elizabeth, came and stayed overnight at St. Marguerite's, with Janet Thomas serving as House Mother.

Ecumenical links remained strong as ever. Thus from March 24–26, Sr. Deborah Francis and Sr. Margo Elizabeth gave a retreat at St. Marguerite's for a group from a Presbyterian church in Wallingford, PA. They attended all the offices and Mass in the convent chapel throughout their stay.

At the beginning of the year the fire code plan was at last accepted by the Fire Officer. Much time had been lost because the Sisters' plans were continually being rejected by one "body" whilst accepted by another. It was not simply a matter of time, but also of money. Mother Suzanne Elizabeth gave an update in her letter to the Oblates and Associates for Easter 1995. "We are deeply grateful to all who have given of their abundance to help us continue our ministry and hospitality. We thought a once-in-a-lifetime fund raiser would take care of the problem of fire code renovations on the convent <u>and</u> retreat house. As you know, just the retreat house renovations took more money than was raised. However, we are confident that one more fund raiser will take care of the convent renovations as now set before us and the Court of Appeals Board. We hope that $50,000 will cover the expenses of renovations that we are mandated to complete by August 1, 1995."

In order to cover these expenses the Sisters had decided to organize a second "Monastery in May," scheduled for Sunday, May 28, during the Memorial Day Weekend. Much help would be needed but Mother was confident it would be forthcoming. So much depended on getting the renovation work done in time before the August deadline—it was not simply a question of making the buildings safe, it was also a question of being able to continue ministry in a place so well loved and appreciated by the many groups and individuals who came there year after year. Mother wrote, "We who live here at the convent everyday are thankful for this beautiful place and abundance that we have been given to enjoy, as we also care for it, and open the place to many who come for refreshment of body, mind and spirit."

A major event such as "Monastery in May" needed a great deal of organizing, more than the Sisters could do by themselves. Thus on St. Mark's Day (April 25) ten Associates came to the convent and between them got 2,000 items of mail ready for posting, and on May 3 a committee of volunteers met to plan the event. The weather was perfect on the day itself. About 65 Associates and other friends came to help and 300 people came to see the convent and retreat house. Sr. Margaret Helena wrote in the October Community Newsletter[2] that all 125 chairs in the main chapel were occupied by guests who stayed for Vespers. Many gifts were also received from Associates who could not attend. During the following week Jean Hoppin, an Associate from Jersey City days, and Ethel Dennis, a former St. Marguerite's resident, came to help with "thank you" letters.

In the midst of all the preparation for "Monastery in May" and its aftermath, the real work of the Sisters continued with welcoming guests for retreats, giving spiritual direction, and attending conferences far and wide, in addition to prayer and sacraments. The Sisters' long retreat took place in the week beginning June 5, led by Sr. Ruth Fox, OSB. Amongst the groups coming during the summer was the National Embroidery Workshop, attended by about 12 ladies and led as usual by Edith Feisner, who taught the group 'white work' for altar linens. Three members of the group were admitted as Associates before they left.

On June 25, Sr. Barbara Jean and Sr. Deborah Francis had their last Sunday at St. John's church, Elizabeth. There was a farewell reception after the service. Sr. Margaret Helena wrote: "We were very sad about giving it up but we had six happy years there for which we are thankful, but we really need the Sisters at the convent."

Early in July 1995 the work began to bring the convent building up to the standard required by the new fire code regulations. No guests came during this time, and several Sisters took their summer vacations. Sr. Margaret Helena wrote in the October Community Notes: "WORK BEGAN AT THE CONVENT!!! At 7:30am workmen were all over the convent and it was moving day for the Sisters that were here. We had lunch at St. Marguerite's and were busy getting oriented. Mother, Sr. Laura Katharine, Sr. Margaret Helena, Sr. Deborah Francis and Sr. Margo Elizabeth had moved to St. Marguerite's. Our clergy Associates came to say Mass for us and either Sr. Laura Katharine or Sr. Deborah Francis cooked. Mother made many trips a day to supervise the work at the convent. August 7 we moved back to the convent. The work was almost finished. It looks nice, they had done a good job." The Sisters who had stayed at St. Marguerite's took their vacations once all had moved back to the convent. And at last the fire code renovations received final approval in the middle of October.

The fire code "battle" had been long and exhausting. Mother Suzanne Elizabeth, as the Superior, had borne most of the weight of it over four years and several rejections, and it must have been a tremendous relief to have the work completed. Mother wrote to the Associates in the October Community Notes that she had given much thought and prayer to what the Community should now be doing. She wrote: "I must think beyond Fire Code into the future of the Community and what the Lord would be having us do ... And now what would the Holy Spirit do in us today is to have us dream dreams and have visions—and <u>that</u> we all have been actively doing. We have come to the end of an era of parish ministry and now <u>all</u> the Sisters will be at the convent working full time in our ministry of hospitality and spiritual direction. We must expand our program at St. Marguerite's and not only will we be organizing the programs here but expect to be directing many of them as well. Each Sister has been quietly preparing herself with education programs, as well as having an individually guided spiritual life to equip her for her part in the ministry … As our Foundress Mother Harriet would say, 'we must meet the need of the day.' Please pray for us that we will have the strength and vision to carry on this ministry, [and] please pray for new vocations to join us …'"

In September Sr. Susan came to live with the Sisters for three months in order to learn to speak English. She came from a Syrian Orthodox Community from South India which had begun an affiliated house in Boston, MA. Mother Magdalene, the Superior, had studied at St. Margaret's convent, Boston, 18 years previously to prepare for the opportunity to open a house in the USA.

St. Marguerite's retreat house was in need of refurbishment. The fire code work had entailed huge expense and so the decision was made to seek practical help from Oblates, Associates, and other friends in order to refresh and renew the retreat house. Under the heading "Work for the Lord" the weekend of November 11–12 was earmarked. "It was a most successful event," wrote Sr. Laura Katharine in the December Community Notes. "A tremendous amount of work was accomplished by our many friends." These included Sam and Lily Altamura, Ethel Dennis, Janet Thomas, Dot Barkus and many others. Windows were cleaned, furniture was stripped down and polished, chairs re-upholstered, new curtains were made and new bedding provided. There was a great communal spirit of working together for the Lord and for the ministry of the Sisters. More work needed to be done, and it would be an ongoing project.

In England, Canon Austin Masters, SSM, was recovering from a slight stroke and retired as Warden General on October 1, 1995, several months earlier than had been expected. Fr. Lister Tonge had already agreed to be the new Warden but was unable to take up his new duties immediately due to other commitments.

Sr. Philippa Irene arrived from Clewer on October 23, and was to have been accompanied by Sr. Edna Frances. But Sr. Edna Frances had a slight stroke two days before take-off and was advised by her doctor not to fly. It was Sr. Philippa Irene's first visit to Mendham[3] and she was taken out and about. Thus she went to New York City, to Philadelphia where she saw the Liberty Bell and to Princeton where she saw Nassau Hall where the Declaration of Independence was signed. Also she was able to attend the Order of St. Helena's 50th anniversary. "She seemed to enjoy all our life and we enjoyed her," wrote Sr. Margaret Helena in the December Community Notes.

As 1995 drew to a close, Mother Suzanne Elizabeth wrote: "…You have encouraged us in our ministry, not only by making things like new, but by reminding us how valuable this place is for people to be able to come and in beautiful and comfortable surroundings, find Christ in their lives that when they leave us, they may bring Christ to the center of their world."

Nineteen ninety-six was welcomed as usual with a vigil of prayer. Then on New Year's Day, Sr. Susan returned to her Community and was replaced by Sr. Deborah who was to receive some training in the Religious Life as well as to learn to speak English. What Sr. Deborah thought of American winters has not been recorded, but that of 1996 was particularly harsh. There was a heavy snowfall on the evening before the Epiphany party, which went ahead despite the slippery conditions. Next day another twenty inches of snow fell, resulting in the cancellation of planned events. A man came to widen the driveway and dig out the garage and parking lots—he worked from 3:00pm until 3:00am to get it done. The week between New Year and Epiphany was a "Chapter week" with no guests, and the Sisters were fully occupied re-writing the Community Rule. The Sisters at Clewer had been through a similar experience a year previously.

On February 1, 1996, a postulant was received at Vespers, and on February 5, the Community kept its Feast of Dedication, remembering the day when the first three Sisters arrived in New York from Clewer in 1874 in order to establish the work in the USA. Even though there was more snow on February 14, the winter Search Program went ahead with three searchers. On February 18, the Warden, Br. Robert Hugh, SSF, arrived and was present at the Chapter which elected Sr. Margo Elizabeth for life profession to take place after Easter. The Warden stayed over Ash Wednesday, celebrated Mass and gave the Sisters a retreat. On the Sunday evening, February 25, Fr. Charles Rice, who had become an Associate in the previous year, led an evening of Taizé worship in the main chapel. This was attended by about 50 people who enjoyed this new style of praise and worship. At the beginning of March Fr. Rice conducted the Sisters' long retreat. They were joined by three Sisters of the Society of St. Margaret and three of the South Indian Sisters.

There were some changes at Clewer around this time. Fr. Lister Tonge was licensed as Chaplain at Clewer by the Bishop of Oxford, the Rt. Revd. Richard Harries, at a Sung Eucharist on February 19, 1996. During the period between Canon Austin Masters' retirement and Fr. Tonge's arrival, the Sisters at Clewer had decided to dispense with the title of Warden and thus Fr. Tonge was appointed as Chaplain.

March 25, 1996, marked the 60th anniversary of Sr. Margaret Helena's profession. No one in CSJB had celebrated 60 years before. She had known the Community even longer, having worked as a secular teacher at St. Helen's Hall in Portland, Oregon, for five years under Sr. Waldine Lucia, before being received as a postulant at Mendham in the Fall of 1933. Mother Suzanne Elizabeth had invited former Superiors, friends of long standing and people Sister had served with on the various committees in her long Community life. Amongst those present was Sr. Marjorie Raphael, SSM, from Boston, a former student of St. John Baptist School, and Sr. Edna Frances, CSJB, now recovered from her stroke. Other Communities represented were the Poor Clares, the Community of the Holy Spirit, the Order of St. Helena (and next day the Order of the Holy Cross). The Mass was in the main chapel and was celebrated by Br. Robert Hugh, SSF, and the preacher was Fr. Wessinger, SSJE. In his homily he recalled his long association with Sr. Margaret Helena and the Community. He recalled an encounter with one of the Sisters (now long departed) when he was just four years old! And he paid tribute to the great influence Sister Margaret Helena had on his life when he was a young priest. Lunch followed at St. Marguerite's and a good day was had by all.

Sadly, the Sisters' faithful dog, Pucker, had to be put to sleep. She was about sixteen years old and was lame and very sick. The Sisters soon decided they needed another dog, as on two occasions strangers had walked into the convent and found their way upstairs. In the words of Sr. Margaret Helena, Pucker had been a "very good barker." The decision was made to have another female dog, weighing not more than thirty pounds. In fact the Sisters fell in love with Petie, a male Border Collie/Springer Spaniel who was just over a year old and weighed in at sixty pounds! Sr. Margaret Helena with characteristic humor told the Associates that "one dog and eight Sisters have gone to obedience school!"

On April 25, 1996, Sr. Deborah Francis finished her Spirituality course at General Theological Seminary and received a certificate and commendation.

On May 24, Sr. Margo Elizabeth began her retreat to prepare for her life profession. Next day came news that her father had died unexpectedly after a long illness. Sister went to be with her family and it was decided to hold a private memorial service after the profession. She returned to the convent and resumed her retreat, after which the profession service went ahead on May 31, 1996. Many of her friends and relatives came; and in the words of Sr. Margaret Helena,[4] "The service was very beautiful and we are thankful to have another 'life-professed' Sister."

Three weeks later, on June 22, the Warden, Br. Robert Hugh, SSF, received the Revd. Francoise Ray as a novice, taking the name Sr. Frances Marie. Next day was Commemoration Day and the Warden preached and received seven new Associates. The first two weeks of June had seen the Embroidery Workshop take place for the National Altar Guild. This year's project had been "white work" for altar linens. Before they left, three of the ladies were admitted as Associates. Thus the work and ministry of CSJB was disseminated throughout the Episcopal Church by means of those who came into contact with the Sisters.

Mother Suzanne Elizabeth was very enthusiastic about making the Community work more visible through the many people who came to the convent or the retreat house. In the Michaelmas Community Notes she referred to the ways in which the Community had worked for the Lord in the past. Now, in a different age, it was equally important. She wrote: "Today our chief way of making Christ known and the power of Jesus' resurrection is in our ministry of hospitality and in spiritual direction." In order to make the work better known and for people to feel more welcome, the Community Notes now contained lists of all the events and activities available for people to attend. "We now turn to you for help in making people aware of the abundant opportunity here, the opportunity to know Christ in this beautiful and quiet setting so that they too may have the fullness of joy."

Work with young people was another aspect of the Sisters' ministry. Sr. Margo Elizabeth had taught a Confirmation Class at St. Mark's, Mendham, earlier in the year and the group had visited the convent. Sr. Barbara Jean noted: "I have been challenged by my continuing relationship with the youth at Daytop, through a series of Sunday afternoon Bible studies.

As they share their lives and experiences, I am reminded of the great pressures on our young people today. Daytop has made national news by being the first long-term treatment center for adolescents in the country to receive accreditation from the Joint Commission on Accreditation of Healthcare Organizations."

Although regular parish work had been given up, Sisters did parish work from time to time: thus in August, Sr. Barbara Jean and Sr. Deborah Francis conducted a Bible School at St. John's Church in Elizabeth. "As always," wrote Sr. Barbara Jean, "these inner-city children delight and exhaust us!"

Meanwhile at Clewer there were two professions. On July 6, Sr. Mary Stephen made her profession in life vows. The Bishop of Reading, the Rt. Revd. John Bone, received her vows, and about 120 people were present for the service and for the buffet lunch in the convent garden. Six weeks later, on August 24, the Chaplain received the first vows of Sr. Anne. Once more the sun shone and there were about 50 family and friends present, plus a good number of people from Clewer St. Stephen, where Sr. Anne had a ministry as a licensed lay reader.

Back at Mendham, one of the many photographs in the Michaelmas Community Notes was of Shirley and Bill Grier, with the caption "50 Golden Years with CSJB. Thank you. God Bless."

On September 8, 1996, Mary Neale Berkaw was received as a postulant, and a few weeks later, on November 1, Sr. Frances Marie withdrew from the novitiate.

The main event of the Fall season was the attic sale. Mother Suzanne Elizabeth had already explained to the Associates: "We need your ongoing support to endow St. Marguerite's Retreat House to continue the renovations and expand our programs." The date for the sale was fixed for October 12, 1996, and much help was needed to prepare for it. The Sisters and helpers spent days bringing things down from the attics at the convent and at the retreat house. Sr. Margaret Helena, writing in the Christmas Community Notes, described it all. "There were trunks, washstands and basins and pitchers, chairs and tables of all sizes, benches and bedframes, pictures and frames all sizes, three little red scooters (pre-dating skateboards) which little girls at St. Marguerite's had enjoyed and much more." All these hundreds of items had to be cleaned, dusted or polished. Also, a sale catalog was produced and on the day itself, which thankfully was sunny, many helpers came to prepare hot dogs and rolls, bagels, doughnuts, candy bars, and gallons of coffee. The saying "one person's rubbish is another's treasure" proved to be true. The front lawn was filled with guests, and in the words of Sr. Margaret Helena: "At eleven o'clock the Auction began and, without stopping for breath, went on until three o'clock … With the addition of gifts and donations from friends who couldn't be at the event, the money box had approximately $36,000 in it. We now have a good foundation for the Retreat House Endowment Fund." More than 60 volunteers had helped in various ways to make the day so successful.

Sr. Barbara Jean and Sr. Deborah Francis made an interesting "journey into history" when they received a letter from Fr. David Hoopes, OHC, rector of St. Thomas Church, Farmingdale, Long Island. They were invited to attend the re-dedication of the parish house, which would be named St. John Baptist House in memory of the work at Farmingdale by CSJB.[5] When the Sisters gave up the work in 1898 they offered their buildings to the parish, which was about three miles away. Church members came and dismantled the main cottage and chapel and rebuilt them next to their church as a parish house. This was the structure that after recent renovation was being rededicated. The two Sisters felt as if they were stepping back into history and noted that "it is good to remember our roots."

On December 9, 1996, news came that Muriel Blue had passed to her rest during the Fall. She first knew the Sisters in 1926 when, at age 13, she came to St. Michael's Home, Mamaroneck. She stayed five years, after which she left to work for the Sisters at St. Andrew's Convalescent Hospital, NYC. After several years on her own, she came to work at the convent in 1962 until she retired in 1980 and moved to senior citizen housing in Mendham. She had attended Sr. Margaret Helena's 60th Profession anniversary in March and recalled that she was there when Sister made her Vows.

The year 1996 drew to a close in the usual way. There was another year to look forward to in which to work for the Lord. The New Year, 1997, saw the Sisters working very hard to complete the revision of the Rule and Constitution. Similar work was being done at Clewer, with help from Sr. Agatha Mary of the Society of the Precious Blood at Burnham Abbey, a few miles from Clewer. In the summer of 1996 Sr. Agatha Mary had made a visit to Mendham to facilitate the Sisters in their revision of the Rule. Writing to the Associates in the Easter Community Notes,

Sr. Margaret Helena noted: "We made no basic changes but we brought some language up to date. 1850 language is a little different than 1997."[6]

In a course sponsored by Interweave, Sr. Barbara Jean began a class in Gregorian chant starting on February 4, 1997, taking up four sessions over four weeks. Members of the class came to the convent for Vespers on March 11, followed by a "pot luck" dinner. On February 10, Mary Neale Berkaw was received as a novice by the Warden, Br. Robert Hugh, SSF, taking the name Sr. Mary Neale. The service was attended by family members and was a happy occasion.

During Lent, Mendham Interchurch arranged for Wednesday noonday services at Mendham Lutheran church. On February 26 Sr. Barbara Jean conducted the service. Jim Stewart, the chef at St. Marguerite's, played the organ as well as making the soup! Sr. Margo Elizabeth played the flute and there was also a flute and organ duet during lunch. Sr. Deborah Francis and Sr. Mary Neale were the hostesses.

At Clewer, Sr. Eudora passed to her rest on March 11, 1997, eight weeks after a stroke which, according to Mother Jane Olive, had "left her totally helpless, but completely in her right mind." She was in her 96th year and during those weeks of her final illness had been faithfully cared for at the convent by the Sisters and a night nurse. She was well known at Mendham, having spent time there during the War (see Chapter 2), although by the time of her death Sr. Margaret Helena was the only Sister who would have remembered her from that time.[7] Sr. Eudora was the last Sister to have worked in India, America and Barbados.

Since Easter, two Roman Catholic Sisters of the Good Shepherd had come from Sri Lanka to study the program at Daytop as they were hoping to start similar work in Sri Lanka. They stayed at the convent until September 1. Also since Easter, a Roman Catholic Sister from Czechoslovakia stayed at the convent while attending a seminar of the I.A.P.C. (Institute for the Advancement of Philosophy for Children) from Montclair University. Ecumenism was still flourishing and several Sisters attended meetings and conferences throughout the summer.

Commemoration Day went well and seven new Associates were received, including Patrice McKenzie and two Methodist Pastors, Lisa and Eric Pridmore—the Associates' Rule had been changed in 1991 to allow non-Episcopalians to be admitted. At the time for reports Mother Suzanne Elizabeth announced that she would be resigning her office and there would be an election of a new Superior in the Fall. She had served the

Community as Superior for fourteen years and chose to resign in order to enable the new changes in the Rule and Constitution to be implemented.

Mother Suzanne Elizabeth had more to say about the revision of the Rule and Constitution in the Michaelmas Community Notes. "As you may know, since 1985 the Sisters have been revising our Rule and Constitution. For these documents to be alive and have any meaning, they must come out of our lived experience. We have basically completed this work and feel pleased with the product. Basically we have the same documents, but the changes reflect present thinking we hope will pass the test of time—or at least the next twenty years! One change you may notice is the title we have given the Superior, who is now called Sister Superior. We feel she is one among equals with a particular responsibility for the term elected. She also has a limited term that she can hold this responsibility ... No Sister may now serve more than twelve years at a time. In today's society, we feel this is a very important change. Another change we have made is in the title and role of the Warden. He is now the Presiding Minister and basically serves in an advisory capacity rather than one of authority. These changes are not unique to us but are what most other Religious Communities, including our English Sisters, have similarly done."

Another change was that Mondays would be a full Sabbath Day—a day of rest for the Sisters to spend however they wished. A few years previously the Monday Sabbath had been introduced but part of it was still taken up by meetings.

Several older Associates had passed to their rest including Doyle West, husband of Doris West who had known the Sisters in Texas. Betty Dormer had just retired from working at the convent for the past 39 years but kept in close contact with the Sisters.

Work for the Lord continued in practical ways with the continued renovation of St. Marguerite's Retreat House. An appeal earlier in the year for new chairs and carpeting at the retreat house library had been met and the exact amount of money needed had come in. The next stage was to renovate the bathrooms in order to double the facilities. The Sisters were applying for grants but also needed the help of Associates, Oblates and other friends.

September 29, 1997, saw the arrival from Clewer of Mother Jane Olive and Sr. Pamela, who had just one day to acclimatize to US time before the election on October 1 of Sr. Barbara Jean as Sister Superior. She was installed next day by Bishop Jack McKelvey. Sr. Laura Katharine was appointed Assistant Superior, Sr. Deborah Francis Novice Director, and Sr. Mary Lynne was re-appointed Bursaress. They were installed by Br. Robert Hugh, SSF, the Presiding Minister, who gave them a blessing and gave the other Sisters a blessing appropriate to their place in Community. Sr. Margaret Helena noted in the Christmas Community Notes that after the new appointments "there was much moving and changing of work places, but there wasn't enough suitable furniture for computers ... Sr. Pamela and our novice Sr. Mary Neale are very good at deciphering a drawing and knowing what goes where so new computer desks and chairs materialized." The English Sisters returned home on October 16, and as always the Sisters at Mendham were sorry to see them leave.

After an exhausting fourteen years in office, Sr. Suzanne Elizabeth took time out for a rest. Part of it was taken at the Community's log cabin, where various Sisters attempted to teach her how to use a lap-top computer. Such things were still in their early days but would soon "catch on" universally.

Parish ministry was revived, and at the end of October Sr. Deborah Francis and Sr. Mary Neale took up ministry at St. John's, Elizabeth, going on Sundays and Wednesdays when the Community schedule permitted. Sr. Barbara Jean and Sr. Deborah Francis had worked there from 1989 until 1995. Sr. Deborah Francis had written a Christmas play, to be performed on Christmas Eve, which involved children of all ages. Also, the two Sisters were helping with the Alpha Course, an adult Christian education program begun by Holy Trinity Church, Brompton, in London, England. On Wednesdays the two Sisters were very active in the parish through the food pantry. Between 30–100 people would come to obtain a bag of groceries. Many were women with young children and some were members of St. John's congregation.

Back at the convent, there was always maintenance work to be done. The four tall chimneys were repaired and the cross on top of the convent was replaced after blowing down in a bad storm the previous winter. St. Marguerite's had continued to be busy with many and varied programs, and at the convent the Stitchers' Workshop led by Carol Homer continued to meet twice a month, doing all kinds of ecclesiastical embroidery using silk and metal thread.

Writing her first letter to the Associates since her election as Superior, Sr. Barbara Jean paid tribute to Sr. Suzanne Elizabeth. "She has guided our Community into a new era, one in which our ministry of spirituality continues to grow." She continued, "At the turning of the year, let us all look forward as well as back, asking to be shown our part in God's plan, and courage to follow."

Thus the year 1997 moved towards 1998 and there was much for the Sisters to be thankful for, especially the 150 new Associates who had been received during the previous fourteen years. No doubt the remaining two years of the twentieth century would bring its own challenges but the Community moved forward with faith and hope for the future.

In her letter to the Associates and other friends in the Easter 1998 Community Notes, Sr. Margaret Helena wrote: "On New Year's Eve when we keep the long vigil from Compline to midnight, it is my practice to take the Associates' list and pray for you one by one and commend you all to God's care … We do like to hear from you anytime of the year, not necessarily only at Christmas." There was news in the Community Notes of former staff and students at St. John Baptist School. Father and Ruth Hummel, who had once been on the school staff, had written to say that he was teaching at the seminary in Alexandria and in time off had been traveling to Jerusalem and Oxford, as well as writing articles and books. On February 4, 1998, Dorothy Templeton Greenwood died in a car accident. She was the widow of Fr. Templeton, a former Chaplain at the convent and school, and had later remarried. She always kept in touch with the Sisters, having been an Associate since 1951. On February 13, the Revd. Nancy Talmage died after a few weeks of illness and was buried at Succasunna beside her husband on February 17. She had been an Associate since 1964 and both her daughters (Anne and Garland) were also Associates. Garland was a graduate of St. John Baptist School. And then on February 25, Rita Dennis Hanson died. She had been an Associate since 1966 but had known the Community for many years. There had been five sisters and two brothers in the Dennis family when their mother died. The boys went to Bonnie Brae Home and the girls came into the care of the Sisters. Rita and another sister were too old to go to St. Marguerite's with their younger sisters, so they went to St. Anna's in a wing of the convent. Another of the sisters, Ethel, had retired nearby by 1998 and came to help the Sisters with tasks such as mailing the Community Notes.

Community life went on with workshops, meetings, the long retreat and the ministry of hospitality at St. Marguerite's and at the convent, all undergirded by prayer and the sacraments. Sr. Suzanne Elizabeth was elected as a Trustee of the Board at the House of the Good Shepherd, an elderly care facility at Hackettstown, and was also accepted for a two-month course on Spiritual Direction at the Jesuit Retreat Center in Wernersville, PA. From March 13–15, 1998, Sr. Barbara Jean attended the New Jersey Diocesan Convention, and the Community received an award for long-time mission work in that diocese. And on March 20 a postulant was received.

As springtime gave way to summer, many practical works suddenly needed to be attended to. In the words of Sr. Margaret Helena: "We have had a busy summer making replacements of the mechanical parts of our living. First we had to replace a part of the chapel roof, and then the plumbing at St. Marguerite's. Then the organ in the main chapel refused to work—the wires had gotten wet. In preparation for Commemoration Day we had to have the wires replaced." There were other problems too—the lawnmower had to be replaced, the tractor broke down, the main chapel furnace had to be replaced, and finally the Sisters' car, having reached 120,000 miles, had to be replaced. With characteristic humor Sr. Margaret Helena finished her tale of woe. "Some of us have been away, but I'm glad to tell you that we have not needed replacement. We have been greatly blessed and helped by one novice and two postulants." The novitiate had grown in recent months. Eleanor Reynolds had been received as a postulant in May. She had previously been a member of a Vedanta Community[8] in California, and latterly a Sister in the Order of St. Helena. Looking ahead, the postulant who had been received in March was clothed as a novice on September 22, 1998, taking the name Sr. Janis Marie, and Sr. Mary Neale was now the senior member of the novitiate.

Commemoration Day 1998 was warm and sunny, but not too warm. The sermon was preached by the Rt. Revd. Vincent K. Pettit, former Suffragan Bishop of the Diocese of New Jersey.[9] Bishop Pettit was also received as an Associate. There was a report on the work at Daytop given by Fr. Joseph Hennen, the Director, who was also a Roman Catholic priest. It was also graduation day at Daytop and twenty-two young people had completed their high school courses and were receiving diplomas from their home schools. They would not leave Daytop until they had completed their prescribed time there, but to have graduated was a huge step forward.

In the nine months up to September 1998 ten Associates had passed to their rest, fourteen new Associates had been received and six Oblates came for their Fall meeting and renewed their promises.

In October Sr. Mary Stephen arrived from Clewer for her first visit to Mendham. She stayed sixteen days, during which time she was taken to Boston and Cambridge, MA, to meet the Society of St. John the Evangelist, a Community which had originated in Cowley, near Oxford, UK, hence the popular name the "Cowley Fathers." There was also a visit to New York City, and she took a full part in the life of the Sisters. "We sent her home exhausted but happy," wrote Sr. Margaret Helena in the Christmas 1998 Community Notes.

St. Marguerite's was attracting more weekend events and some weekday ones. Especially important was a Conference on Spiritual Direction conducted by Tilden Edwards, founder and director of the Shalem Institute in Washington, DC, and assisted by the Revd. Robert Morris. There were 40 participants and another session was promised, to be led by the Revd. Dr. Margaret Guenther.[10]

At the convent there was a daily Eucharist (except on Mondays) and various clergy came to celebrate. Also there were regular groups which met there such as E.F.M. (Education for Ministry), contemplative prayer and Bible study groups, and regular meetings of the ecclesiastical embroidery groups led by Edith Feisner, Marianna Klaiman, Mary Wagner and Carol Homer.

The Sisters ended the year 1998 in the usual manner and aware that the coming year would be the last of the twentieth century and of the second millennium. But before the year's ending Eleanor Reynolds was clothed as a novice on December 1, taking the name Sr. Eleanor Francis. Thus the Sisters entered the New Year with hope and a spirit of optimism.

The Sisters were also looking forward to the 125th anniversary of the first Sisters coming to New York from Clewer to establish Community work there. There was a Seminar for Religious on February 4–5, 1999, with the Revd. Robert Morris as Moderator, and representatives of nine other Communities, as well as CSJB, attended. There was a Mass of Thanksgiving on the actual anniversary (February 5) in the Chapel at St. Marguerite's where the Seminar was held. On Saturday, February 6, there was another Mass of Thanksgiving at 10:30am in the convent main chapel. Bishop Spong, the Community Visitor, celebrated, and clergy Associates and other friends took part. About 150 people attended the Saturday Mass and stayed for the reception at St. Marguerite's, where a large cake was cut by Sr. Barbara Jean. Sr. Elizabeth Jane came from Clewer to join in the celebrations. As well as representatives of other Communities, there were many Associates and other friends who had not visited for a long time. Dora Kapp had been refurbishing the Stations of the Cross in the main chapel and finished them in time for the anniversary. These had come from Holy Cross Church, NYC, following its closure in 1934/5. Others had helped with the preparations, including Christine Brodeur MacClellan and her husband Don, who came from Arizona for a month.

On the Feast of the Annunciation, March 25, 1999, Sr. Mary Neale was professed in first vows in the presence of Bishop Spong. Sr. Margaret Helena explained to the Associates in the spring 1999 Community Notes that "First vows are taken annually for at least three years. After annual vows the Sister is elected by Chapter for life vows. Our vows are the traditional monastic vows of poverty, chastity and obedience."

Sr. Margo Elizabeth had long felt an affinity with Ireland, having Irish ancestry. But it was not until 1986 that she made her first visit, repeated in 1996. "On both occasions, there was no doubt in my mind that I was on holy ground," she wrote in the Christmas 1998 Community Notes. Gradually the idea of leading a group on a pilgrimage matured and was planned for June 1999. Thus began a major part of Sr. Margo Elizabeth's ministry in the Community, which would eventually become "Celtic Journeys."

As summer took its course, Commemoration Day brought old and new faces who were all welcomed unconditionally. There was, however, a note of sadness in that Gus Bittrich was retiring as organist after fifteen years faithful service.

Then came time for Sisters' vacations before the August Search Program. Sr. Eleanor Francis went to California for family time and also was able to attend the great celebration in San Francisco of the 150th anniversary of the Diocese of California. Sr. Laura Katharine and Sr. Mary Neale went to Clewer for just over two weeks and were present at Sr. Anne's profession in final vows on August 10. Also at Clewer, Sr. Jane Olive was re-elected as Mother Superior for a further five years and was reinstalled on August 17 by the Bishop of Reading, the Rt. Revd. Dominic Walker, OGS.

Mother Jane Olive appealed for prayers in the autumn 1999 edition of the Clewer Associates' Newsletter. "Please remember us as we go forward into a rather uncertain future. The [UK] Community is growing smaller and older, and we have decided that we do need to move from our beautiful but very large building. This not likely to happen for some time yet, but it will mean the closing of our present works.[11] We are however, in good heart and believe that God still has work for us to do."

Reviving a long ago custom, there was a picnic on August 19 for members of Religious Communities. Sisters from the Order of St. Helena and from the Society of St. Margaret, Brothers from the Order of Holy Cross and a Franciscan Brother all attended and had supper on the cloister.

For perhaps the first time, Sr. Margaret Helena felt unable to make the long journey to Oregon. Sr. Mary Lynne represented her at the annual Associates' meeting at the Oregon Episcopal School in Portland on September 1, 1999.

A short notice with a photograph in the Michaelmas Community Notes told of the arrival at the convent of Sr. Jane Mankaa from Cameroon. She would be living with the Sisters for several months in order to gain experience of different forms of the Religious Life. Her great hope was to found an ecumenical Community for women working with the many homeless children back home. There will be more about Sr. Jane in succeeding chapters, but suffice it to say now that she had an enormous impact on CSJB and in particular Sr. Mary Lynne.

September 1999 brought torrential rain from Hurricane Floyd out in the Atlantic, and a seminar led by the Revd. Dr. Margaret Guenther at St. Marguerite's had to be cut short as people were concerned for the safety of their homes. Sr. Margo Elizabeth had found many new groups who came to St. Marguerite's for retreats and other meetings, not just at weekends but in the week too. The improvements to the bathrooms still needed to be made and Sr. Suzanne Elizabeth renewed her appeal for funds to replace sinks, toilets, showers and for upgrading the floors. The work was scheduled for July 2000, and $20,000 was needed. The $35,000 raised for the Endowment fund had been invested and the interest used to fund ongoing work at St. Marguerite's. But this was a major project and extra funds were greatly needed.

On September 23, 1999, Sr. Barbara Jean traveled to Maciene in Mozambique with a group from the Diocese of Newark as the guests of the Bishop of Lebombo, the Rt. Revd. Dinis Sengulane.[12] The Diocese of Newark had committed itself to helping install wells and pumps for clean water, and to begin a fund to combat malaria. A new Religious Order, the Community of St. Paul, had been founded there by two Sisters of the

Holy Name from South Africa. Sr. Barbara Jean returned to Mendham on November 9 after a memorable and life-changing trip.

Shortly before Sr. Barbara Jean returned from Africa, Sr. Janis Marie withdrew from the novitiate. On a happier note, Sr. Margaret Helena celebrated her 95th birthday on Friday November 5. There was a party, and in Sister's own words, "What a party it was—we celebrated the entire weekend!" Twenty-one of her relatives arrived on the day and stayed through Sunday. There was a festal Eucharist of Thanksgiving celebrated by Bishop Spong, his last "official" duty for the Community before retiring in the New Year. Sister continued: "The immediate family had time with this 'birthday girl' in the afternoon as well as on Sunday morning. After all the relatives left, the Sisters held an open house birthday tea party with 75 of my 'close friends.' I received over a hundred birthday cards and will cherish each one of them and their messages."

Early in December 1999, the Sisters received a letter from Bishop Spong telling them of the death of an old friend and Associate, the Revd. Arthur Pederson, at age 79. He had been ill for some time. Sr. Suzanne Elizabeth paid tribute to him in the Christmas Community Notes. "The Revd. Arthur Pederson was a faithful Associate of our Community as well as a parish priest with whom we worked in Jersey City for eighteen years. In those days Fr. Pederson not only conducted all the church services (in two churches), but also accompanied church members to court hearings, helped refugees find jobs, schooling and housing, fixed the boiler when the heat wouldn't go on, shoveled the sidewalk when it snowed, and supervised the gym activities. When the building that the Sisters lived and worked in was condemned and had to be restored, Fr. Pederson not only helped to raise the money, but worked side by side with the workers and parishioners putting in new ceilings, painting walls and generally doing most of the work while continuing to teach young people in government funded jobs. He was a locksmith and made all our keys to fit the locks …"

On December 5, 1999, Sr. Pamela flew to Mendham to work with the Sisters there for a year. An accomplished musician who had played violin in several orchestras before joining CSJB at Clewer, Sr. Pamela had more recently collaborated with Dr. Mary Berry and others in producing *An English Kyriale* (1991), consisting of Plainchant music for the Eucharist. The Christmas 1999 Community Notes welcomed Sr. Pamela, saying, "We hope, during her time with us, to complete a revision of our Office Book."

And so the year 1999, along with the 20th century and the 2nd millennium, drew to a close. Reflecting on the 125th anniversary in the spring 1999 Community Notes, Sr. Barbara Jean had written of the early Sisters and how the present Community shared their values. "In all that they did, there were two guiding principles that brought them strength and stability: their spirituality and life in Community. Through the changes of the last century and a quarter, these principles have been at the heart of our calling. The ministry of the Community has varied greatly in the past 125 years … We ourselves have changed. Our new members bring a variety of gifts to the Community, and our future work will be more varied. Each succeeding generation has brought new challenges and opportunities … Throughout the many transitions we have experienced … we have always tried to maintain our spirituality and Community life. These are an essential part of the Rule of St. Augustine and of the vision of our foundress, Harriet Monsell. As we enter the new millennium, there will be unique visions and challenges. We will continue to evolve according to the need of the day …" It is a fitting conclusion to this chapter in the Community life.

---

[1] The Rt. Revd. Joe Morris Doss (born 1943) was consecrated in 1993 and served as Coadjutor Bishop of New Jersey until 1994. He served as Diocesan Bishop from 1995–2002.

[2] It was about this time (1995) that the Community Newsletter was renamed Community Notes.

[3] And her last as she did not make final vows.

[4] Community Notes, Michaelmas 1996.

[5] See BONHAM, Valerie *Living Stones* Chapter 5.

[6] The Community was not founded until 1852. The earliest Rule was dated 1854 and was written in Mother Harriet Monsell's handwriting. The first printed Rule was dated 1869 and the Rule and Constitution were closely interwoven. The two were separated in the 1874 edition.

[7] Sr. Eudora was a great help to me when I was writing *Sisters of the Raj* and she allowed me to use the Indian chapter of her memoirs. She died the day before the book went to press.

[8] Vedanta is a Hindu movement founded in New York in 1896 by Swami Vivekananda, a disciple of Sri Ramakrishna. Organized on Western lines and combining Western and Hindu methods of instruction, the Vedanta Society teaches a philosophy derived from the

Upanishads (Hindu texts). The Vedanta Society has many centers in the West, particularly in the Western USA. (Source: *The Oxford Dictionary of World Religions* Ed. John Bowker 1997.)

[9] The Rt. Revd. Vincent King Pettit served as Suffragan Bishop of New Jersey from January 1984 until September 1990. He chaired the Standing Liturgical Committee that resulted in the 1979 revision of *The Book of Common Prayer*. He died from cancer on March 10, 2006.

[10] The Revd. Dr. Margaret Guenther was a long-time Associate Rector of St. Columba's Episcopal Church, Washington, DC. She was ordained priest in New York in 1979, and was married for 60 years. She was Professor Emerita of Ascetical Theology at General Theological Seminary, NYC, where she served for many years as Director of the Center for Christian Spirituality. Dr. Guenther was the author of several books on Christian spirituality. She died peacefully on December 11, 2016, at age 87 years.

[11] These were St. John's Convent Home for women with learning difficulties; the Clewer Spirituality Center; the Church Workroom; and St. Anne's House for elderly ladies.

[12] The Rt. Revd. Dinis Sengulane was Bishop of Lebombo from 1976–2014.

❧ 18 ❧

SHARE THE VISION

The Community 2000–2004

JANUARY 1, 2000, BROUGHT in a new year and also a new century and a new millennium. The Sisters were very much aware that it was 148 years since the Community had been founded at Clewer by Harriet Monsell and the Rector of Clewer, the Revd. Thomas Thellusson Carter.[1] On March 25 they celebrated the anniversary of the death of Mother Harriet Monsell, giving thanks for her life and the vision shared with Carter which brought forth CSJB. Perhaps neither of them could have imagined that the Community which had such small beginnings in the 19th century would still be alive, active and praying in the 21st.

Sr. Barbara Jean had been to a number of parishes, equipped with a slide show, talking about her visit to Mozambique. Sr. Margaret Helena commented in the Spring 2000 Community Notes: "The pictures show a dry and dusty country but she and other members of the group are very enthusiastic about the vitality of the Church there." Meanwhile, Sr. Jane Mankaa had finished her six-month stay at the convent and had gone to a small Benedictine monastery in Madison, Wisconsin. While at Mendham she had visited several parishes to share with them her ideas for starting a Community in Cameroon. But she had another year in the USA before her planned return.

Sr. Pamela was excited about a new ministry at Christ Hospital, Jersey City, and shared news of this in the Spring Community Notes. "It all began after a phone call from the Chaplain of the hospital asking if anyone would like to help with voluntary Chaplaincy work. Sr. Mary Lynne and I decided we would like to do this and asked for more information ..." It took a while to actually exercise any ministry but eventually they began their weekly visits. "Each week we report in and gather up information about new patients and any others whom the regular Hospital Chaplains want us to see ... Although the patients we visit come from a variety of cultures and faiths, most wish to talk and request our prayers. We also have a ministry to some of the relatives, but we experienced immense joy when asked by a Muslim to pray with him—truly a great privilege. The hospital provides a beautiful Chapel in memory of Bishop George Rath,[2] which is always open for prayer and services for the major denominations, which are relayed to all floors."

The February Search Program had produced an Oblate and two Associates. On Commemoration Day three new Associates were received, and also during the summer three new Oblates including Margaret Johnson. But also, several Associates had died during the past year, including Fr. Robert Maitland. The Revd. Canon John R. Ramsey, a long-time Associate and former summer Chaplain, passed to his rest during 2000. Sr. Margaret Helena missed Commemoration Day owing to a seven-week stay in hospital. She was visited regularly by the Sisters and also by her nephew John and his wife, who had come for Commemoration Day. They reported to her that the Mass was beautiful, the sermon excellent, the lunch very good and the cookies even better!

The summer season was busy. Sr. Laura Katharine and Sr. Mary Neale went to the 73rd General Convention, which met in Denver, CO, in July. Bishop Croneberger appointed Sr. Mary Neale coordinator of EFM (Education for Ministry) groups around the Diocese of Newark.

A labyrinth was being constructed in the convent grounds based on those at Chartres Cathedral in France and Grace Episcopal Cathedral in San Francisco. Bricks in the grass were being laid by members of Interweave and the project was being coordinated by Associate Patrice McKenzie.

Sr. Barbara Jean had an important piece of news in the Fall Community Notes. "As the years have passed since 1852 when we were founded in England, our Community has gone through several phases. Along with many Religious orders today, we are being called daily to respond to the spiritual needs of those who are seeking healing and wholeness in a fractured world … We are called to serve in a similar capacity in the wider Church. As we enter the new millennium we invite you to join us in our *SHARE THE VISION* project. It has several parts. The first is *Sanctuary Support*. This project will help us to maintain our property as a place of spiritual outreach. This aid is not all financial. There are times when volunteer work on the property is greatly needed. Another part is *Aid for Education*. This will enable us to offer scholarship aid to groups and individuals who cannot afford the full cost of a program. Our third project is called *Community Growth*. We pray that God will send us new members so that we can continue to answer calls for help that come so frequently

... Another area of Community growth is education for the Sisters, as we attend courses to qualify us for our work in Christian education and spiritual direction ... We pray that we may be guided to continue to serve God's people in the twenty-first century. We invite you to join us."

Renovation work at St. Marguerite's retreat house was continuing and the bathrooms now had new fixtures, freshly painted walls and clean tiles. The next project would be the convent bathrooms, which were overdue for renovation.

During the summer of 2000, Sisters from Mendham were visiting Clewer for the last time. The English Sisters had very reluctantly come to the decision that they must move away from their great Victorian mother house after 148 years there. In January they had purchased from the RC Servite Order the former priory and convent at Begbroke near Oxford. The priory dated from the time of the 17th century English Civil War, but the neighboring convent had been built in 1975. (The brothers had needed nuns to look after them, hence the convent!) This was a traumatic time for the English Sisters as they prepared to put the convent at Clewer on the market—and to sell by auction the contents. In July Sr. Barbara Jean and Sr. Pamela visited, followed in August by Sr. Deborah Francis and Sr. Eleanor Francis. Other Sisters would visit before the final move. But it was not all sadness at Clewer. On September 30, Sr. Anne was ordained as a deacon at Christ Church Cathedral in Oxford. Mother Jane Olive and several Sisters attended the service and Mother placed the stole on her immediately after she was ordained.[3]

Sr. Margo Elizabeth took a group to Ireland from September 1–11, rescheduled from June. Celtic Journeys were becoming an integral part of the ministry from the convent. The smooth running of these journeys was due to the immense preparation and planning by Sr. Margo, unseen by those who took part. Ireland was the "first love," but soon journeys to other Celtic destinations such as Northumbria, Scotland, Wales and the west of England would be offered.

At Mendham, Sr. Suzanne Elizabeth had organized a Needlework Pilgrimage to England from September 25–October 4, 2000. The co-leader, Mary Wagner, wrote enthusiastically in the Community Notes for Christmas 2000: "Sister Suzanne Elizabeth's Needlework Pilgrimage to England this past Fall, was a memorable journey for all those who went. In every place we had informative tour guides and lecturers and saw many fascinating types of stitchery ... It started with our long-awaited visit to

Clewer. Sister Doreen had prepared a wonderful collection of patterns and stitchery work that had been produced here in the [almost] 150 years of its existence. Sister Mary Steven [sic] took us on a tour of the convent and gave a talk on many of the Clewer frontals ..." Before leaving Windsor the group visited St. George's Chapel at the Castle and they were shown altar frontals, still in use, made by the Clewer Sisters. The tour then went to Salisbury, Canterbury, and Winchester Cathedrals before moving on to London to the Victoria and Albert Museum, Westminster Cathedral, and Watts and Co., the well-known firm of ecclesiastical suppliers. Writing to the Associates in the Christmas 2000 Community Notes, Sr. Margaret Helena commented: "They saw much more than beautiful vestments: there were beautiful buildings, beautiful countryside and beautiful people."

Sr. Margaret Helena reported that several former students from St. John Baptist School had visited the Sisters in recent months. Dorothy Keedwell Whiteside was from the class of 1934; Charlotte Urquhart Van Stolk, 1943; Doreen Madrell Boynton, 1955; and Jane Bramhall Carter from the class of 1960.

On November 30, 2000 (St. Andrew's Day), Sr. Eleanor Francis made her first vows. The Community was mindful of the fact that it was on St. Andrew's Day that Harriet Monsell had made her vows for life. Now, 148 years later, another Sister would take that momentous step. Sr. Eleanor Francis's vows were received by the Rt. Revd. Herbert Donovan, an old friend of the Community and newly elected Visitor. This was his first official duty. Sr. Margaret Helena declared that he celebrated and preached and then received the vows "with great grace."[4]

There was just a dusting of snow for Christmas but the New Year of 2001 brought a very harsh winter. A total of 48.6 inches of snow fell during January and February, which brought down several of the ageing trees around the convent, including one which fell across the main driveway. But the Sisters were in good heart because during the winter season two new postulants had been received. These were Shane Phelan, formerly a professor of political philosophy at the University of New Mexico, Albuquerque; and Julia Ruff, who had been director of a group home for the mentally ill in North Carolina. They were already Associates and, after attending the two-week Search Program in August 2000, felt called to test their vocations.

A third "new face" was that of Sr. Cecilia (Kim Hye Rim) from Seoul, South Korea. For the past fifteen years she had been a member of a

Roman Catholic Religious Order, the Sisters of St. Paul de Chartres, with a particular ministry in a child guidance center. She had come to the USA to study the methods at Daytop and would be living with the CSJB Sisters for a year. She said she had "especially enjoyed the kindness and openness of the Sisters."[5] For their part, the Sisters declared Sr. Cecilia to be "a whirlwind of energy. When she's not at Daytop she's cleaning, helping with the plants, and filling in anywhere we need it. Her sense of humor and her energy make us sure that her Community misses her, but we're glad she's here with us. Welcome Sr. Cecilia!"[6]

In January, despite the bad weather, Sr. Eleanor Francis began what would become a three-year ministry at the Church of the Redeemer in Morristown. At first she sang in the choir and did instrumental work. The rector at that time was the Revd. Phillip Wilson, who envisaged Redeemer as a "liberation" church welcoming all irrespective of race, color, or sexual orientation, and also people in recovery from addiction, people who had been abused, and those who questioned traditional church dogma. He was ahead of his time and also had devised an "unofficial" inclusive-language liturgy. Sr. Eleanor Francis commented in the Easter Community Notes: "To me there is no feeling of having lost the core traditions of the Episcopal Church. The centrality of the Eucharist remains, the beauty remains, the awe and mystery remains. I feel privileged to be able to extend the scope of my ministry to include the Church of the Redeemer."

February 2001 saw the first vestment conservation workshop. This was organized by Sr. Suzanne Elizabeth, assisted by Mary Wagner, Carol Homer, Clare Bonome and Marianna Klaiman. Much was achieved, including learning how to clean copes and the need to line the cope closet with special acid-free material. The Community cherished many special vestments made by Sisters, including the famous black cope made in 1918. Such treasures were now ageing and needed specialist conservation, which these workshops aimed to provide.

Sisters continued to make farewell visits to Clewer before the English Sisters moved to Begbroke. Thus on March 14, Sr. Laura Katharine arrived at Clewer and stayed for two months. Sr. Anne made a visit to Mendham on May 3, returning on May 26.

The Share the Vision project was making progress. Thanks to a very generous donation by an Associate in memory of his sister, a wheelchair lift had been installed to give easy access to the main chapel, and Sr. Margaret Helena was the first to use it at her 65th anniversary of profession on March 25. This was truly a Community milestone as no other Sister had reached such an auspicious anniversary. Before the service of Solemn Vespers, at which Bishop Herbert Donovan officiated, there was a festive tea party.

Other projects included building a ramp at St. Marguerite's. The tunnel under the front lawn connecting both wings of the convent was showing its age and work needed to be done to seal it from moisture. Estimates were $2,000 for the architect's plans and building permit and $12,800 for the work. The construction of fourteen extra parking spaces was in process at a cost of $10,600, and finally, the cost for clearing the road of fallen trees had been $1,000. It was all very challenging for the Sisters and they urgently needed the help of their Oblates, Associates and other friends.

Summer 2001 passed in the customary way, one of the highlights being the clothing in June of the two postulants as novices. They took the names Sr. Shane Margaret and Sr. Julia Ann. St. John Baptist-tide and Commemoration Day all went well.

At Clewer, the Sisters were still overcoming obstacles to their move to Begbroke. There were delays in getting planning permission for alterations to the buildings at Begbroke, and delays caused by trying to pack up the essentials after a century-and-a-half of living at Clewer. Eventually all obstacles were removed and the Sisters finally moved on September 8, 2001.

Three days after the English Sisters moved to Begbroke, the World was changed forever. The morning of Tuesday, September 11, 2001, dawned bright and clear in New York City. At 8:46am people were hurrying to work in the many offices in Manhattan when suddenly a plane appeared just a bit too close to the towers of the World Trade Center. Then it crashed into the north tower. Reporters on the TV news channels compared it with a B-25 Mitchell bomber which crashed into the Empire State Building in thick fog in 1945.[7] That was an accident. Then at 9:03am another plane crashed into the south tower and people realized with horror that this was no accident. It was a terrorist attack. News broke very quickly that a third plane had crashed into the Pentagon and a fourth, heading for Washington, DC, possibly for the White House, had been brought down by passengers who overpowered the hijackers before reaching its target. Within an hour and forty-two minutes both towers had collapsed.

Sr. Mary Lynne saw it all. She was sitting on a plane at Newark airport waiting for take-off. The New York skyline is just a short distance away and as she waited she saw both planes career into the towers. Her flight along with all others was immediately canceled.

Back in England, Mother Jane Olive tried in vain to communicate with the Sisters at Mendham. It was several days before she was able to speak to Sr. Barbara Jean and be reassured that the Sisters were safe.[8]

A week later, on September 17, Sr. Margo Elizabeth's Celtic Journey to Scotland was scheduled to take off from Newark. A lot of planning had gone into the visit and it looked as if it would be canceled. Fortunately they were allowed to go and Sr. Suzanne Elizabeth, who accompanied them, wrote about it in the Christmas 2001 Community Notes. "After hours of watching these endless unthinkable events raping our country's freedom to life, Sr. Margo started contacting each of the pilgrims and gradually everyone was able to confirm their desire to go if the plane was flying." Their first destination was Iona, a place of peace and healing. Sr. Suzanne Elizabeth continued her account: "Every place we went candles were lit, flowers offered and prayers said for the victims of the terrorist attack … Love poured out to us as representatives of a country under attack. All this only heightened the sense of our pilgrimage as being a journey made with sacred intent, searching for meaning and inspiration. If I thought I was wanting to bring a sense of hope, courage and faith to these places, I was greeted with overwhelming compassion and inspiration. Resting in the 'thinness' of these places gave us a sense of 'peace that passes all understanding' and brought balm to our aching spirits."

Sr. Mary Neale, Sr. Shane Margaret and Sr. Eleanor Francis were amongst the many who volunteered to help at Ground Zero, as the site of the ruined towers came to be known. Sr. Eleanor Francis went on Fridays for several months. "Our job was to be Chaplains and we had Red Cross training. It was mainly just listening to people—firemen, police, and operatives [clearing the debris]. I was [at the place] where the body parts were, working with the policemen and firemen. One fireman said 'it is so admirable the work you do.' It was like hell with the smoke and the stench. Later I went to the rehab centers where people could go to claim compensation. St. Paul's Church [Chapel] was nearby."[9]

Sr. Shane Margaret wrote about her experience, and that of Sr. Mary Neale, in the Community Notes for Christmas 2001. "One of the most valuable experiences of my life has been the opportunity that Sr. Mary Neale, Sr. Eleanor Francis and I have had to volunteer at the World Trade Center site. This is really 'Ground Zero' for Christian faith and love. The Episcopal Church and the Red Cross set up respite centers to provide for the workers at the 24-hour-a-day work site. Many churches volunteered to staff shifts at the centers. In October St. John's Church in Boonton, where Sr. Mary Neale serves, was chosen to work an 8:00pm to 8:00am shift at St. Paul's Chapel. They fed the workers and offered support to them and to the public … At St. Paul's we worked primarily with the public who walk by, stop and stare at the destruction down the street, and look at the candles, flowers, and messages that people have left. By inviting people to write something themselves we let them express their pain, their love, and their faith. At the Red Cross centers we make ourselves available to workers and to other Red Cross staff who need to be heard and to feel God's grace. I have received much more than I have given in this work … The workers on the site are just wonderful … There are people searching for God in the rubble and finding Him in the gentleness of their fellow workers … The people at Ground Zero are the finest example of humanity I've been privileged to work with. Sr. Mary Neale remembers looking at Ground Zero at night, when the smoke rose and the whole area was flooded with light, and seeing it as a light of life. That is how I see it in my prayers, radiating the light of God's love and healing for the whole country. God lives in the rubble there, binding and comforting those who continue to grieve and those doing the dangerous and tragic work of finding victims and clearing a wasteland."

On a happier note, Sr. Barbara Jean and Sr. Pamela had traveled to England for Sr. Anne's ordination to the priesthood on Sunday, September 30, by the Bishop of Dorchester, the Rt. Revd. Colin Fletcher, in St. Mary's Church, Kidlington, not far from Begbroke. Sr. Anne was the first Sister to be ordained in the English CSJB. Sr. Barbara Jean and Fr. Lister Tonge (the UK Sisters' Chaplain) were amongst those who laid their hands on Sr. Anne at the moment of ordination. Later, at 5:00pm, Sr. Anne celebrated Mass for the first time in the chapel at Begbroke Priory. She wore a chasuble made by UK Oblate Nancy Leslie, and a stole made by another Oblate, Barbara Evans.

Two weeks later, on October 11, Sr. Suzanne Elizabeth arrived ready for the blessing of Begbroke Priory on October 19. The service of blessing was conducted by the Bishop of Oxford, the Rt. Revd. Richard Harries, who went from room to room with appropriate prayers. Mother Jane Olive commented in the Christmas 2001 issue of their Newsletter: "Like Sr. Barbara Jean and Sr. Pamela, Sr. Suzanne Elizabeth did a good deal of moving furniture and sorting things out, so that we were reasonably tidy for the Bishop's visit considering we had only been here for six weeks." Fr. Lister Tonge traveled back to Mendham with Sr. Suzanne Elizabeth on October 22 and conducted a three-day workshop for the Sisters.

On December 12, 2001, Fr. David Bryan Hoopes,[10] Superior of the Order of the Holy Cross, was installed as Presiding Minister by Bishop Donovan. On December 21, 2001, Linda Riley was received as a postulant.

The year ended as usual with prayer for the coming year. The year 2001 had been one of great national anxiety and grief, but the Sisters continued in their vowed life, responding to all who needed their ministry, and all undergirded by prayer, their Rule and the Sacraments.

New Year 2002 came in with rain, snow and ice that resulted in only four people coming to the Epiphany Party on the Feast of the Epiphany (January 6). The preceding week had been Chapter Week and Sr. Margaret Helena noted in the Easter Community Notes that the Sisters had "worked very hard" in their meetings. On three Thursdays in January Bishop Donovan came for conferences with each Sister; it was a good way to get to know them better.

Two thousand and two was the 150th anniversary of the founding of the Community at Clewer by Harriet Monsell and the Revd. Thomas Thellusson Carter. Sr. Barbara Jean informed the Oblates and Associates: "We invite you to celebrate with us. We also ask your prayers as we embark on a new era with new members and new ministries. We ask your special help this year, so that the Community's outreach to retreatants, persons in need, parishes where we serve, Daytop, and Sr. Jane's mission in Africa can continue. Our vision for the future is similar to that of 150 years ago, but relevant to the needs of today. We hope you will share this vision with us, so that together we can carry the good news of the resurrection to God's people."

The Easter 2002 Community Notes carried an update on Sr. Jane Mankaa. "Sr. Jane, who came to live with us two years ago, has been studying at Assumption College for Sisters here in Mendham. She plans to return to her native Cameroon in May to begin her Ecumenical Community of Bethany. Last spring she was confirmed by Bishop Brome of the Diocese of Newark, and she will return to her city of Bamenda as an Anglican.[11] She has received a warm welcome from Bishop Jonathan Ruhumuliza, Supervising Bishop of the Anglican Church of Cameroon. She and several young women will open a home in Bamenda to take in children whose parents have died of AIDS. Sr. Jane has been raising money for this project, and has been speaking in local churches about her work. As her sponsors, we would welcome invitations for her to speak in your church, or a donation for her cause. She will be returning [here] in September to complete her education."

On March 15, 2002, Lura Lane was received as a postulant. Sr. Margaret Helena noted: "We now have two Junior Professed Sisters, two novices and two postulants. We are grateful for new faces."

Sr. Barbara Jean made an appeal for help in the Easter Community Notes. "Ten years ago in 1992 and again in 1995, you helped us raise the funds needed to renovate our buildings to meet the fire code. Now we need your help again, as we receive new applicants into our Community. Our numbers have doubled in the last six years, and our new members need support and education, so that they can be prepared for future service in the Church."

So it was that another Monastery in May was planned to take place on May 25 from 1:00–5:00pm. Helpers were needed and were duly signed up. It was a good day, with a craft fair, tea at St. Marguerite's, tours of the convent led by the Sisters, and at 5:00pm Vespers in the main chapel. Monastery in May raised $45,000 after expenses and was declared "a wonderful day." It was arranged and took place under the heading of Share the Vision, which was an ongoing project. Money was still being raised to renovate the tunnel and also to repair the stucco coating on the walls of the convent and cemetery. The chapel roof had lost some of the shingles and it was hoped repairs would be made soon. Education programs were ongoing.

Linda Riley was clothed as a novice on June 11, 2002, the Feast of St. Barnabas, taking the name Sr. Linda Clare. Two weeks later, on June 23, Commemoration Day was very well attended. The weather was beautiful, which was always a help, and more Associates and friends arrived than had been expected! The Eucharist was celebrated by Bishop Donovan and the sermon was preached by Br. David Bryan, OHC. He recalled the early days in New York when Fr. Huntington worked with the Sisters at the Holy Cross Mission and at Holy Cross Church where the Order was founded, with Fr. Huntington making his profession in the Chapel of St. John Baptist House. In the present day, bagpipes led the procession in and out of the chapel to the cloister for lunch. There were greetings and reports after lunch, including a report from Daytop, which would celebrate its tenth anniversary at Mendham on September 27.

The Sisters' many and varied ministries were highlighted in the Easter 2002 Community Notes with an illustrated feature titled "Meet the Sisters." Against a small photograph of each Sister there was a short resumé of her work and ministry. Thus: Sr. Barbara Jean, Superior, priest, editor of the Community Notes, spiritual director; Sr. Suzanne Elizabeth, former Superior, infirmarian, spiritual director, gives individually guided retreats (IGR), President of Diocesan Altar Guild; Sr. Laura Katharine, Assistant Superior, spiritual director, gives Quiet Days, arranges for groups and individual retreats at the convent; Sr. Deborah Francis, Novice Director, in charge of the refectory, spiritual director and retreat conductor; Sr. Pamela has written much of the music used in chapel, Chaplain at Christ Hospital, Jersey City, at present taking a Clinical Pastoral Education Course (CPE); Sr. Mary Lynne in charge of the "Nun Better Shop," bursar and works with the business manager; Sr. Margo Elizabeth, in charge of St. Marguerite's retreat house, organizes Celtic tours to Ireland and parts of the UK, has a large spiritual direction ministry; Sr. Mary Neale works in the convent chapel, maintains the Community database, assists at St. John's Church, Boonton; Sr. Eleanor Francis, in charge of the convent kitchen, gives workshops for Interweave, assists at the Church of the Redeemer, Morristown; Sr. Shane Margaret, a novice, works in the convent chapel, a member of the EFM group; Sr. Julia Ann, a novice, works in the chapel and with convent staff, and the guest ministry; Sr. Linda Clare, a novice, works in the pantry; Lura Lane, a postulant, works in the pantry and library.

Ministries would change over time and not all of those in the novitiate would proceed to final vows, but this "snapshot" of the Community in 2002 shows just how far-reaching the Sisters' ministries were. The untold story is of just how many lives they touched, inspired and healed. The ministry of the Sisters echoed the words of Mother Harriet Monsell: "You come to make the gift of yourselves."

As noted above, Sr. Mary Lynne had the idea of starting the "Nun Better Shop"—"Mementos from the Community created by the Sisters." It was an instant success, with visitors buying Anglican Prayer beads (similar to the rosary), bookmarks, cards, bracelets and many other items as time went on.

On September 10, 2002, Lura Lane was clothed as a novice, taking the name Sr. Lura Grace. This brought the numbers up to four novices. Two new postulants were received in the Fall season—the Revd. Barbara

Seras on October 3, and Diane McCarthy on October 29. Sr. Barbara Jean commented in the Christmas Community Notes: "Each one brings great gifts to the Community." Meanwhile, Sr. Mary Neale returned home to South Carolina, not having been elected to life vows.

On October 1 Sr. Barbara Jean was re-elected Superior and was re-installed next day. Sr. Suzanne Elizabeth was appointed Assistant Superior. And there was a new venture: Sr. Laura Katharine and Sr. Deborah Francis were appointed Novice Directors, to work as a team with the Superior and Assistant Superior. Sr. Margaret Helena commented to the Associates that this was working out well for all.

For perhaps the first time ever, none of the Sisters were able to attend the meeting of the Portland Associates on October 8, but new Associates were still being received there, bringing the total to twenty-seven. Sr. Margaret Helena's great-niece, Beth Blair, and B. Mary Inkster, Beatrice Paget's daughter, were both received as Associates. And the Rt. Revd. Hal Gross, former Suffragan Bishop of Oregon, and a long-standing Associate, had died on August 13. Also in Portland, Beatrice Paget, the oldest Associate, died on June 1 at the age of 105. She gave up riding when she was 90 because she thought her horse "Snowball" was too old!

The great event at the end of the year was the 150th Anniversary of the Community's founding at Clewer by Mother Harriet and the Revd. T. T. Carter. Sr. Barbara Jean described the Eucharist on November 30 in the main chapel as "glorious." About 180 people attended, including Mother General Jane Olive from Begbroke, UK. Bishop Donovan was the celebrant and Bishop Croneberger of Newark preached. Sr. Margaret Helena described the day in the Christmas 2002 Community Notes. "We had a marvelous procession with a thurifer followed by a Sister carrying the Sisters' cross. The Community of St. John Baptist, including Mother Jane Olive, came next, and then there were Religious from other Communities. Another processional cross, and the visiting clergy and four bishops completed the procession ... The Daytop choir sang an offertory anthem. At the end of the service the bagpiper piped us all out of the chapel and into the convent for the reception, leaving us with the memory of a beautiful service and a challenge for the next 150 years." Sr. Barbara Jean commented: "This event has given us the opportunity to reflect on our heritage from the past, the gifts of the present time, and the challenges of the future."

Members of the visiting Religious Communities had been invited to stay Friday through Sunday for a conference on "Building Foundations." On Friday evening the topic was "Cornerstones," presented by Mother Jane Olive, CSJB, and Br. David Bryan, OHC. On Saturday evening the theme was "Keystones," presented by Sr. Beryl, SSJD Canada (Society of St. John the Divine), and Br. Derek, SSF (Society of St. Francis). And on Sunday evening (Advent Sunday) Br. Gregory, OJN (Order of Julian of Norwich), and Sr. Ellen Stephen, OSH (Order of St. Helena), gave a presentation titled "Stepping Stones: Foundations for the Future." The Sisters found the conference helpful, "confirming and strengthening us all." Mother Jane Olive and Mother Ann Verena, CJGS,[12] arrived back in England on December 3.

"Share the Vision" was given an update in the Christmas Community Notes. Plans were being made to engage a contractor to repair the stucco on the convent and cemetery walls in the spring. $100,000 was needed and the Sisters were appealing for financial help under the heading "Rebuilding the Walls." A generous grant had been received for repairing the chapel roof and work would proceed as soon as the weather permitted. Under the heading of "Education," Sr. Eleanor Francis was currently attending Drew Theological Seminary; Sr. Pamela was training for chaplaincy at Christ Hospital, Jersey City; and members of the novitiate were enrolled in Education for Ministry. Sr. Barbara Jean also announced: "Next year there will be no major fundraisers, but we will be forming a Development Board to help us with planned giving and other funding sources."

A piece of good news that Sr. Margaret Helena did not write about herself was that she had recently been honored by the Episcopal Church Women of the Diocese of New Jersey for her retreat ministry there over many years. She had also celebrated her 98th birthday on November 5.

The Sisters' love for animals was reflected in their care of pets over many years. Alas, 2002 saw the death of Patches, their much-loved cat, who had lived with the Sisters since 1989. Towards the end of 2002, Jack, a black-and-white rescue cat, arrived and was soon well loved. There was also a companion for Petie. Mandy, a golden Labrador, had arrived in 2001, having come to the convent following the death of her owner, Sr. Mary Lynne's father. Alas, Mandy died on June 7, 2003. But Pony was contentedly grazing in his paddock, as he would for many more years.

The final event of 2002 was the Winter Art Show, December 14–20. Local artists were invited to display their work at St. Marguerite's. The Sisters' estate manager Richard Bradley won the first prize in sculpture with a beautiful wood carving of the Blessed Virgin Mary and Child Jesus.

The new year, 2003, opened in the usual way with the Epiphany party, but as Sr. Barbara Jean noted in the Easter Community Notes, it was a time of "great uncertainty: for our country, for our Church, and for each of us as individuals." The Iraq War was raging, and Sr. Barbara Jean quoted words from Thomas Paine at the time of the Revolutionary War[13] two hundred years previously: "These are times that try [our] souls." But she also added that "In the midst of uncertainty, spring has come again … There is a cycle of life that continues regardless of our human condition."

And indeed the Community had much to hope for and look forward to. There had been three months of snow and ice, but on March 7, 2003, the Revd. Barbara Seras was clothed as a novice, taking the name Sr. Barbara Catherine. She had been working at the convent for some months. There had been snow the day before her clothing, but the ceremony went ahead with Bishop Donovan celebrating the Eucharist; Br. David Bryan, OHC, preached. There were 75 guests at the service and reception, including Bishop Robert W. Ihloff, Bishop of Maryland. There were now five novices, with another postulant waiting to join.

Sr. Pamela had completed her Clinical Pastoral Education course at Christ Hospital, Jersey City, and was currently in the UK visiting family, and also the Sisters at Begbroke. While in England she renewed her Visa in order to return to the United States.

Meanwhile the Sisters were experimenting with a new look! There had been "new looks" before as the Victorian habit was gradually adapted to modern times, but they had always retained the veil, although in simpler form. Now they were experimenting with the option of retaining the habit but not the veil. The Easter 2003 Community Notes commented: "Some of our friends like us one way, and some the other. Either way, we continue to live our life of prayer and service to the people of God. We haven't really changed!"

On May 13, Diane McCarthy was clothed as a novice, taking the name Sr. Diane Jeannette, but she left the novitiate on December 17 in order to join the Episcopal Carmel of St. Teresa which was being founded by Sr. Teresa Irene in the Diocese of Maryland. On May 26, Sr. Linda Clare and Sr. Lura Grace arrived at Begbroke for a visit and to attend the Novices Conference at All Hallows Convent, Ditchingham, in the Diocese of Norwich. They were joined on June 8 by Sr. Deborah Francis, who had been on Sr. Margo Elizabeth's Irish Celtic Journey.

Although they had all been to England before, this was their first visit to Begbroke.

Many good things had evolved from the "Building Foundations" Conference at the end of the 150th anniversary celebrations. Under the heading "Paths of Spirituality," a program of activities was planned in which every Sister would take part. It took many forms, including activities listed on the calendar of coming events in each issue of the Community Notes. It also included ministry to the many groups who visited St. Marguerite's and the convent every week, and to individuals who came for spiritual direction. All the many and varied ministries exercised by the Sisters came under the Paths of Spirituality heading, from Celtic Journeys to hosting ecclesiastical embroiderers, to presentations on ikons, Taizé services, leading retreats, Quiet Days, and talks about keeping a Rule of Life. Many of these activities and ministries were in parishes, some familiar and some new. The novices too were included in this ministry.

Although the Sisters were not involved in the day-to-day program at Daytop, they retained a close relationship with it. Since coming to the Community, Sr. Shane Margaret had developed a ministry there. She wrote in the Easter 2003 Community Notes: "The spirituality groups that I have begun are focusing less on the idea of God, or the creeds about God, and more on the *experience* of God that changes our lives. Along with discussion, we also spend time learning to pray—sitting still, saying 'help' and 'thank you', listening for God—and in exercises in gratitude, honesty, and service. In this we follow the injunction to 'trust God, clean house, serve others' that has led so many from addiction to new life … I am finding that staff members also have spiritual needs that they bring to me. The Sisters are also meeting more parents, and praying actively for the clients and for their families."

Some older Associates had passed to their rest, including Jean Hoppin, who had been a tower of strength in the work at Jersey City and later at the convent. Also, Bill Lariviere died suddenly. He had given and installed the elevator at the convent in memory of his sister, Lena. New Associates received on Commemoration Day included Barbara Harriman and the Revd. Margaret Otterburn.

On June 28, 2003, Sr. Shane Margaret made her first vows. During the summer Sr. Barbara Catherine and Sr. Julia Ann covered Fr. Michael Delaney's parish during his absence. And Sr. Eleanor Francis spent three weeks visiting West Virginia in Appalachia as part of a seminary course on the work of the Church in an area of rural poverty. Also during the summer, trees were cleared from the woods, and thanks to a generous grant of $20,000 from St. Martin's Retreat House Board, the repairs to the roof of the main chapel had been finished, and the cottage behind St. Marguerite's, the garage and carport had all been re-roofed.

The 74th General Convention of the Episcopal Church met at Minneapolis, Minnesota, from July 28–August 8, and amongst its priorities were youth and young adults, reconciliation and evangelism, congregational transformation, justice and peace, and partnerships with other churches both inside and outside the Anglican Communion.[14] The theme of the Convention was "Engage God's Mission," challenging all to live out their baptismal vows and to develop a deep spiritual discipline. The theme at the daily Eucharist was "receive, repent, reconcile, restore" and was addressed in sermons by a wide variety of clergy.

Three Sisters attended the General Convention from July 30 onwards—Sr. Suzanne Elizabeth as part of the National Altar Guild Association, representing the Newark Diocesan Altar Guild; Sr. Laura Katharine, who worked at the Religious Life booth; and Sr. Shane Margaret, who went to assist Margaret Landis of the Church Historical Society. Sr. Suzanne Elizabeth wrote in the Fall 2003 Community Notes: "It is always exciting to see the governing body of the church at work together. Personally I felt proud of the way the work was being done maturely. It was grace-filled interaction of Christians at their best, listening and sensitive to the other with mutual respect … There was caring and dignity with which decisions were made and received." And of the National Altar Guild Association she wrote: "In 1976 I was asked to attend the NAG meeting during General Convention … It was wonderful meeting some of the most gracious women, and the exchange of information and mutual support was wonderful. I'm delighted to see that develop and grow over the years."

On September 28, 2003, Sr. Julia Ann made her first vows. They were received by the Bishop of Newark, the Rt. Revd. John P. Croneberger. Sisters were engaged in various external ministries at this time. Thus Sr. Julia Ann was taking training classes at the Jersey Battered Women's Shelter; Sr. Lura Grace was attending St. Mark's, Mendham, and was visiting elderly members there; and Sr. Barbara Catherine had celebrated the Eucharist in several local churches. Also, Sr. Suzanne Elizabeth had conducted several Altar Guild Workshops, and the annual Needle

Workshop was held at St. Marguerite's with Edith Feisner. Sr. Laura Katharine was taking an Enneagram Mastery course in New York and Sr. Eleanor Francis was studying for a Master's degree in Divinity at Drew University. In October the Rt. Revd. Jane Dixon, retired Suffragan Bishop of Washington, visited the convent, and on October 18, Sr. Barbara Jean and Sr. Linda Clare attended the Consecration of the new Bishop of New Jersey, the Rt. Revd. George Councell.

A quiet, but no less essential, ministry was that of the care and conservation of the vestments. On October 16, 2003, the New York Times had run an article titled "Stitching, Fabric and the Tapestry of a Convent's Faith." The article captured the spirit of the work done by Sr. Suzanne Elizabeth and her small team of dedicated needlewomen. "The response was amazing, far surpassing anything else we have had printed about us," wrote Sr. Suzanne Elizabeth. "We were put to the test the following week [when] St. Bernard's Church, Bernardsville burned down. Sunday morning one of the ladies from the parish delivered to me linen and silk altar hangings she was able to take out of the church. They appeared totally ruined, but I called one of our volunteers, Carol Homer, to do something with them … She took them home, hosed them down and dried them out on her back porch. The silks miraculously shone almost like new." A miracle indeed! "I was pleased that the church would have this preserved for the fabric of their faith in the future." This quiet ministry has transformed many pieces of sacred embroidery which might otherwise have been destroyed. It also involved much traveling as Sr. Suzanne Elizabeth went far and wide talking to parish and diocesan altar guilds, demonstrating and instructing them how to preserve and conserve their precious things.

There was news of Sr. Jane Mankaa, who had now returned to the U.S. to complete her education in the Religious Life. She had gone home to Cameroon in 2002 to establish her Community, to be known as the Benedictine Sisters of Bethany. Six young women had joined her and were presently living in the house she had bought. Now, with the help of the Diocese of Newark, Calvary Church, Summit, and the Connemara Foundation, a second house had been bought and named "The Good Shepherd Home." Now back in America, there was an article in the Christmas 2003 Community Notes about Sr. Jane. "Sr. Jane Mankaa felt called by God to serve the poor, but she was not sure how. Then one evening in 1997, she saw a small boy sleeping on a street in Yaoundé, the capital of Cameroon. 'I asked him why he was sleeping there, and he told me that's where he lived,' she said. 'I brought him some rice, and when I came back to see him the next morning there were ten other boys with him.' She learned that the street children were all orphans whose parents had died of AIDS. 'I knew then that caring for these children was what God wanted me to do.'" The article continued: "It has taken years of hard work, but Sr. Jane's vision is being realized. The first children have arrived at the Good Shepherd Home in Bamenda, Cameroon, to be cared for by the Benedictine Sisters of Bethany. Two brothers, Gilbert and Claude aged 9 and 13, came in September, Collin arrived shortly thereafter. Ten more will come to stay at Christmas time. Sr. Jane has worked tirelessly over the years traveling between Cameroon and the United States to seek education and funding while buying property, organizing the Community and the orphanage, and finding and training young women … The Good Shepherd Lutheran Church in Florham Park, NJ, for whom the orphanage is named, was the first congregation to become involved in Sr. Jane's work … A gift from Calvary Episcopal Church in Summit in May 2003 enabled the Sisters of Bethany to purchase land and a building that could be used for an orphanage. Donations from other congregations, individuals and foundations made it possible for the Sisters to bring electricity to the area, repair the building, construct a latrine, buy beds, and begin farming maize, cassava and potatoes … 'It is crucial that we care for these children. They are the hope and future of Africa,'" concluded Sr. Jane. So the work began in earnest, and anyone who thinks Sr. Jane is an African Mother Teresa will not be mistaken.

Sr. Margaret Helena was looking forward to her 99th birthday on November 5, and so were many other people. A birthday party had been planned, invitations sent out, and then on October 10 she was taken ill and admitted to Morristown Memorial Hospital. She returned home to the convent on October 18, but never regained her strength. She had "bounced back" so many times after illness that it came as a great shock and sadness when she passed to her eternal rest in the early hours of October 30. Her funeral was held on November 4, a day before her 99th birthday. She was laid to rest in the Community cemetery with so many other Sisters she had known and loved. In the words of Sr. Suzanne Elizabeth, "Perhaps we were the most surprised that Sr. Margaret Helena actually died. She had had so many 'close calls' that we began to feel she would always be with us, always there for us. We can only be grateful that she *was* there for so long, and at so many crucial times. Whether we had known her for forty years or for two, in our various ways we came to know and rely upon this most formidable of women. The sharp mind and indomitable will that kept this Community going for 30 years continued after her 'retirement' to support and guide us all. The end of an era has come; behold, God is doing a new thing. We pray we can be as vigorous and dynamic in spreading the Good News to all in need as Sr. Margaret Helena did during her 70 years in the Community ..."

Tributes poured in from far and wide. She was variously described by friends, Oblates and Associates as "a blessing," "a calm, loving center for us," "a great leader, while being so down-to-earth," "a gracious host [who] always made us feel so welcome." An unsigned tribute by a Sister in the Christmas 2003 Community Notes declared: "Sr. Margaret Helena was a remarkable combination of opposites. Profoundly conservative, a lifelong Republican, she supported women's ordination and oversaw some of the first ordinations of women in the State ... As she got older and the world—and the Community—changed in ways she would not have chosen, she was graceful and loving in her acceptance. Blessed with a long life, she strove to face the challenges of old age. She lived to the fullest the Community's motto—'He must increase, but I must decrease'—as she accepted her physical limitations. Rather than make them a source of bitterness or withdrawal, she focused her ministry on correspondence with Associates and friends, praying for those in need and for all of us. She was truly an alchemist of the soul, transforming pain into love." Not only did she correspond with Associates and pray for them, she also brought up to date the Sisters' Biography file, which is a valuable record of all the life-professed Sisters after their death.

Sr. Margaret Helena's time as Mother Superior has been assessed in Chapter 14. The word "formidable" has been used several times to describe her, especially in earlier life as Mother Superior. But it should be remembered that when she came into Community, Religious Sisters *were* formidable. It was a much more formal age with Sisters being much less accessible to visitors (who dined in a separate refectory), and even the habit was different to that of today. As times changed so did she, and she mellowed with age.

One more thing remains to be said. Comparisons were made at Begbroke between her death and that of Sr. Eudora, who was roughly contemporary with Sr. Margaret Helena and who died in 1997 at age 96.

A far more appropriate comparison would be with Canon Carter. Sr. Margaret Helena had been in CSJB for 70 years from the time of her reception as a postulant. Canon Carter had been alongside Mariquita Tennant when she founded the Clewer House of Mercy in 1849, and his prayers for someone to take over when illness forced her to give up were answered with the arrival of Harriet Monsell. Thus in 1852 together they began the Community of St. John Baptist, and Carter was there as Warden throughout the life of the Community until his death in 1901 at age 93. He had a number of health "scares" throughout his life, but like Sr. Margaret Helena, he always "bounced back." The day before he died he was at the re-installation of Mother Betha. The Sisters at Clewer could not imagine what life would be like without "the Warden." As with Sr. Margaret Helena, he seemed to go on forever. When he died it was the end of an era, as it was with Sr. Margaret Helena's death. Without doubt Sr. Margaret Helena was one of the "great Sisters" of the Community of St. John Baptist, and her memory and the legacy of her ministry is like a golden thread which still runs through the life and work of the Community.

At Christmas 2003 there was what Sr. Suzanne Elizabeth described as "witnessing a Christmas miracle." An Associate suffered a life-threatening illness and after Mass on Christmas morning Sr. Suzanne Elizabeth and Sr. Barbara Catherine hurried to Ridgewood Hospital. They arrived at ICU at 11:00am hoping and praying she would not have already gone for surgery. When they reached the ward they found her sitting up in bed, saying that the "tide had turned" and there was no need for surgery. Sr. Barbara Catherine gave her Holy Communion and anointed her with the oil of the sick. "We all felt we had witnessed a Christmas miracle," commented Sr. Suzanne Elizabeth in the Community Notes for Spring 2004.

In the same article, Sr. Suzanne Elizabeth wrote: "We Sisters seem to have taken on a new life of prayer for healing. The needs of the sick are on our lips and hearts, but we have also been called to visit the sick and walk with them and their families. Healing has come in whatever way our compassionate God has deemed. I sense CSJB's mission and ministry growing in new and real ways. Now may we all know this Eastertide the power of Jesus' resurrection, and the purpose of our life for which we have been grasped, forgetting all that we have done, and remembering only what we have to do to God's glory and praise." It was with this new vision of life and ministry that the Sisters went forward into 2004.

A former member of the Community died on January 26, 2004. Sr. Jane Patricia had been admitted as a postulant in 1939 and was life professed in 1941. She spent most of her life in Community at St. John Baptist School where she taught Latin.[15] But she was a real academic and her first love was the translating of Medieval Latin texts, especially the work of Peter Abelard. She had long leaves of absence from the Community to visit libraries in the UK, staying at Clewer each summer, and was finally released from her vows in 1985. After this she went to live with her sister in Amherst, MA, and became an Oblate of St. Gregory's Abbey at Three Rivers, Michigan, an Episcopal Benedictine monastery. She continued to wear a habit similar to that of CSJB and a different silver Cross. While her life in Community was difficult, she was an inspiration to many of her students at the school, who sent tributes to the Sisters. Her funeral requiem was on January 31, at Grace Church, Amherst, and was attended by Sr. Suzanne Elizabeth, Sr. Laura Katharine and Sr. Mary Lynne. She was buried at St. Gregory's.

Sr. Julia Ann wrote about her ministry at the Jersey Battered Women's Shelter of Morris County in the Community Notes for Easter 2004. After an eight-week training program she volunteered to work there on Fridays, playing games with the children and working on social skills. "Coming from violent families, many of them don't know any other way to solve a problem. I am blessed to work with staff members who are truly dedicated to the mission of supporting women and children in a time of crisis." She noted that in the facility there were women from all races and economic backgrounds. "Domestic violence happens everywhere."

Sr. Jane Mankaa had been attending the Diocesan Convention in Newark, NJ, with Sr. Barbara Jean and Sr. Linda Clare. This had led to a number of speaking engagements, especially amongst children, who in turn began fundraising and learning about AIDS in Africa. In Bamenda the first orphanage building was full and the Sisters there had begun a second building. In addition to providing food and shelter to the resident orphans, the Sisters were also feeding local children whose parents had died but who now found themselves to be heads of their households. These children had no money and would have to leave school and find work, but thanks to the food provided by the Sisters they were able to continue at school. It was hoped that the Sisters might eventually be able to build a school.

Ever since Sr. Jane had come to stay with CSJB, Sr. Mary Lynne had shared her vision for the work. Now on May 23, 2004, Sr. Mary Lynne was at last able to visit Bamenda with Sr. Jane, staying for a month. They were accompanied by Poul Bertelson, an architect who specialized in building churches in developing countries, and Lillian Cochran, a member of Calvary Church, Summit. Land for a future building had been bought by Calvary Church, Summit, and Sr. Jane hoped eventually to have an orphanage for 60 children, a clinic and a school. The visitors were greeted by the children with songs and poetry, and were also visited by the All Saints' Anglican Church choir and their rector, who walked five miles uphill to greet them. Sr. Jane and Sr. Mary Lynne went to the church there on the Sunday. The service, which was full of dancing, music and joy, lasted several hours! Sr. Mary Lynne became godmother to more than one baby and was honored to receive a live chicken! She in turn had brought over 200 crosses on cords and everywhere they went she gave them out to children and adults until they were all gone. She also taught people how to make prayer ropes and to crochet cinctures. Asked what stood out in her visit, she said, "These people live their faith. They love their Lord and pray from their hearts. God is real there." The article in the Fall issue of the Community Notes concluded: "This trip made even clearer just how important and life-changing Sr. Jane's work is ... God is working a wondrous thing in Cameroon, and we are all privileged to be a part of it."

There were some changes in the novitiate and amongst the junior professed members of the Community during 2004. Sr. Diane Jeannette, who had left the previous December to test her vocation with the Carmelites, returned to CSJB early in 2004 and was received back into the novitiate. Sr. Barbara Catherine left the novitiate in the summer, and on May 15, Lori Varney was received as a postulant. On June 11 (the Feast of St. Barnabas) Sr. Linda Clare made her first vows. The Rt. Revd. Martin Townsend, Suffragan Bishop of Newark, preached and received her vows. Many people from her former parish, St. Thomas's, Pittstown, Alexandria Township, NJ, came to the service.

Sr. Linda Clare had a varied background before entering the Community, having worked for Prudential Insurance, and four years with Merrill Lynch. But her longest occupation was as manager of a foxhunting stable for 21 years. Although she was a "cradle Episcopalian," working with horses meant she was unable to attend church on a regular basis. The conviction grew within her that she needed to go back to church and she found St. Thomas's church and a welcome there. A woman deacon there knew the Community and told Linda about it. She came to see for herself, stayed for supper and felt out of her depth. Then she talked to Sr. Margo Elizabeth and within a month came for spiritual direction. Her workplace was relocating further away—"it seemed like all the doors were closing except here." Torn between the attraction of the place and not knowing what it was about, she took three months' leave of absence from work—and didn't go back.[16]

A further change occurred when Sr. Julia Ann left the Community on September 10. Then on September 29 (the Feast of St. Michael and All Angels) Sr. Lura Grace made her first vows. Bishop Donovan celebrated the Eucharist and received her vows, and Br. David Bryan Hoopes, OHC, preached. Sr. Lura Grace also had a varied journey from clerical worker to business manager to Chamber of Commerce Director, to banker, to book store owner, to novelist, and finally to the CSJB novitiate. Books were a great passion, and animals too. Her vocation in the Community would soon lead her to a pastoral ministry at Daytop, and to St. Mark's, Mendham, where she visited the elderly and those who could not leave their homes to come to church.

There were changes at Begbroke too. July 2004 saw Mother Jane Olive reach the end of her term as Mother Superior and Mother General. She had served for twelve years and had steered the Community through major changes, not least moving from Clewer, and all the upheaval both practical and emotional that would entail. The decision was made not to elect another "Mother Superior" but instead to have a "leadership team." This consisted of Sr. Mary Stephen and Sr. Anne, with Sr. Ann Verena, CJGS. Also, since moving to Begbroke, the Sisters had acquired a "new look." They had put off their traditional black CSJB habit and large silver Cross in favor of a new, simplified blue habit and smaller silver Cross.

As part of her preparation for ordination, Sr. Eleanor Francis had participated during the summer in a program called Clinical Hospital Ministry Training, at San Francisco General Hospital. The nine seminarians who took part in the program were seeking to complete their Clinical Pastoral Education (CPE). Sr. Eleanor Francis wrote about her experience in the Fall 2004 issue of the Community Notes. "San Francisco General Hospital cares mostly for the poor and marginalized. Many are homeless or live in cheap dilapidated hotels. Some are in jail. Many are drug and/ or alcohol abusers. Mental illnesses are common. The Chaplains in my program spent most of our time in three areas of emphasis: emergency room and trauma, ICU and terminal illness, and the psychiatric units. In addition to visiting patients we spent six hours a week in class going over records of visits and case studies … The patients at San Francisco General taught me more than I can yet absorb. They gave me details of what it is like to live on the street or in a park or abandoned car. They taught me about the courage and wisdom it takes to go on when all the odds are against you … I loved all the patients at San Francisco General, but most of all I loved the psychiatric patients. I would walk onto a unit (they are all locked) and they would gather around me, 'Sister, do you have rosaries today? May I have a Bible? Please pray for me. Please bless me.' I was moved by their simple openness. Many had spiritual questions, some quite sophisticated … I am so grateful to the Sisters of the Community of St. John Baptist who allowed me to participate in this program …"

Sr. Pamela, having now permanently transferred from the UK Sisters to Mendham, was also continuing her Chaplaincy ministry. She wrote in the Fall Community Notes: "Who would have thought, nearly five years ago when I came to this country, that I would be Hospice Chaplain for the Visiting Nurse Association of Northern New Jersey? Sr. Mary Lynne and I had volunteered to visit patients in Christ Hospital, Jersey City. This then led me to take two units of the Clinical Pastoral Education course training to be a Chaplain. Since March I have been working for the VNANNJ Hospice, which covers the whole of Morris County … Most patients live in their own homes or those of relatives; a few are in nursing homes. So travelling around Morris County is very much part of the job. I have visited many patients whose faith backgrounds differ from my own. This has not hindered my ministry or relationship with them; in fact it may have helped in strengthening the bond and trust between us … I do not, however, minister only to patients who are dying. Much of my work is with their families and caregivers …"

Sisters continued in parish work too. After several years at the Church of the Redeemer in Morristown, Sr. Eleanor Francis was about to begin as a seminarian at St. Bernard's Church, in Bernardsville. Sr. Shane Margaret was now pastoral assistant at the Church of the Redeemer, involving adult education, retreats and healing prayer. And Sr. Lura Grace continued her ministry at St. Mark's, Mendham, as a Eucharistic minister bringing Holy Communion to those who could not travel to church.

There was good news in the "Share the Vision" project. The Sisters had been given $50,000 from the New Jersey Historic Trust for a planning grant to make a survey of the repairs and restoration needed. The study would begin in the spring of 2005 and after its completion the Community would be raising funds to make the much-needed repairs. "Our goal is a convent that is a treasure to all who live, work and visit here; not just a historic site, but a vibrant source of new life." The Sisters' second Annual Appeal in October, organized by the Development Board, had by the end of the year brought in $16,985.50, which in addition to the $34,475 raised in the previous year had been a great help towards all the renovation work. And the second Winter Art Show had also been a success.

A number of Associates had passed to their rest during 2004, including Nancy Pederson and Gus Bittrich. He had been the organist for the Community for a number of years as well as playing at churches throughout New Jersey. Sr. Barbara Jean was amongst the priests at his funeral. On a happier note, 17 new Associates had been received during the year. And the memory of Sr. Margaret Helena lived on. On November 4, 2004, the Oregon Associates held a celebratory Eucharist at the Oregon Episcopal School. A plaque describing her contribution was unveiled, and a copy of it was given to the Sisters at Mendham. This was placed in St. Michael's Chapel as a constant reminder of her great work for God in CSJB. Sr. Suzanne Elizabeth and Sr. Mary Lynne flew out to Portland for the Eucharist and spent several days with the local Associates.

The first half of the first decade in the new century closed with the keeping of Advent in preparation for the celebration of Christmas. Time-honored Community traditions were observed in the midst of what had been a busy year of active ministry. But it was those time-honored traditions of prayer, the Daily Office and the Eucharist which "oiled the wheels" of all the active ministry. The Community had reached out to many in need both near and far, and had opened the doors of their house to give hospitality and a warm welcome to all. The new year, 2005, would bring new challenges, but nothing that the Sisters were not equal to accept.

----

[1] T. T. Carter did not become a Canon of Christ Church, Oxford, until 1870.

[2] The Rt. Revd. George Edward Rath (1913–1995) was the seventh Bishop of Newark. He served as Suffragan Bishop of Newark 1965–70, Coadjutor Bishop 1970–74 and as Diocesan Bishop 1974–78. He was a good friend to the Sisters.

[3] Of the ten candidates for ordination, four were from Windsor—Sr. Anne, CSJB; Robert Langton, the Clewer Spirituality Center Administrator; Prue Dufour who had lived and worked at the convent for a time; and John Quick from Clewer St. Stephen.

[4] Bishop Donovan was the retired Bishop of Arkansas (1981–93). Before he was elected bishop he was the Rector of St. Luke's, Montclair. His wife, Dr. Mary Sudman Donovan, is a distinguished church historian specializing in the history of women's ministry in the Episcopal Church, and has greatly encouraged me in my work for CSJB since the late 1980s.

[5] Community Notes, Easter 2001.

[6] Ibid.

[7] The accident carved an 18x20-foot hole in the Empire State Building but the structure remained sound. Three crewmen from the aircraft and eleven people in the building lost their lives. The damage was estimated at $1 million, equivalent to about $14 million in 2018.

[8] I was a curate at Cookham on Thames in the Diocese of Oxford at this time, and on the day that became 9/11 I had been invited to afternoon tea with two elderly parishioners. As we sat enjoying tea and scones the telephone rang and a voice at the other end said, "Switch on your TV. Something dreadful has happened in New York." What we saw was like a scene from a disaster movie, except that this was real. The TV was switched on just after the north tower had collapsed and we watched in horror as the south tower went down just like a pack of cards. I went home soon afterwards and as I walked along I had never felt so afraid in all my life. I feared it meant war, as indeed it did. But it has turned out to be a different kind of war from which no one is safe. The twenty-first century, a century of terror, had begun.

[9] Conversation with Valerie Bonham, May 2018.

[10] There was a family connection between Fr. David Bryan Hoopes, OHC, and the late Mother Florence Teresa, CSJB, whose family name was also Hoopes.

[11] Sr. Jane had a Presbyterian background.

[12] The Companions of Jesus the Good Shepherd had been living at Clewer alongside CSJB since 1996 when they sold their large Victorian convent at West Ogwell, Devon. Sr. Ann Verena had become their Mother Superior in the same year. This was Mother Ann Verena's first visit to Mendham.

[13] Known in the UK as the American War of Independence.

[14] Much of the ground covered at the Convention was submerged in a welter of worldwide publicity concerning the confirmation of the Revd. Gene Robinson as Bishop-elect of New Hampshire—the "supposedly" first gay bishop in a non-celibate relationship. I regret that much of the invective thrown at the Episcopal Church for making this decision came from my own Church of England.

[15] See Chapter 4.

[16] Conversation with Valerie Bonham, May 2018.

RENEWING OUR MINISTRY

The Community 2005–2009

THE YEAR 2005 brought some unforeseen challenges to the Sisters. They had weathered the storms and winter snow as usual, but just when they thought springtime was on the way there was a cold spell early in March. A broken water pipe somewhere under the floor of the basement resulted in the loss of heating for four days. Sr. Barbara Jean wrote in the Easter Community Notes: "While workmen were searching for the leak, Sr. Linda Clare with David and George Ruff performed many miracles, keeping the fireplaces stocked with wood and the pipes above freezing. Every Sister had a part in the effort to keep the convent going." The exception was Sr. Barbara Jean herself, who was in Florida fulfilling preaching engagements. Three companies were called in before the broken pipe was found. "We will need to have a full examination of our heating pipes to ascertain whether more repairs are necessary."

The heating problem had underlined the fact that the system was old, possibly as old as the convent itself, and it brought the Sisters face to face with a bigger challenge. "This experience has led us to explore our commitment to our ministry in this place," wrote Sr. Barbara Jean. "The convent is 90 years old this year, and major renovation will be needed for us to continue our work of hospitality and spirituality here. We are already in a process of application to both the state and the county for preservation of our exterior walls. We will need to explore new sources of funding, as we face the future with vision and courage. We ask you to join in prayer as we seek God's call at this time of new directions. A miracle is needed!"

Sr. Barbara Jean's visit to Florida early in March was inspired by the needs of Sr. Jane's Good Shepherd Home. A longtime Associate, the Revd. Mary Willow, had read about Sr. Jane in the Community Notes and had shared the story with her parish. Sr. Barbara Jean and Lillian Cochran flew out to Hudson, FL, as guests of Mary Willow, and they were invited to speak about Sr. Jane's work in a number of parishes, all of which pledged their support. The journey to Florida also made a link with Associates who lived at a distance from Mendham. As Sr. Barbara Jean commented, "Many of you are serving faithfully in your parishes around the country and beyond, and your work is an extension of our ministry."

Meanwhile, Sr. Mary Lynne had gone back to Cameroon for the spring. She was working with children who were too young for school, telling stories and making pictures. Also, she was teaching a young postulant to read and write English, and was assisting in her formation as a Sister. Construction of a new two-room guest house was in progress, thanks to the generosity of supporters.

Sr. Mary Lynne was not the only member of the Community who was traveling in the spring of 2005. Sr. Lura Grace had spent two-and-a-half months with the English Sisters at Begbroke, returning early in April. The English Sisters had extended their hospitality by building the Harriet Monsell Center, which was used by groups for Diocesan training days and quiet days. And closer to home, Sr. Suzanne Elizabeth and Sr. Eleanor Francis were helping the people of St. Bernard's Church, Bernardsville, to collect the vestments and vessels needed to conduct services after the fire.

Sisters continued to attend conferences far and wide. In mid-April, Sr. Barbara Jean, Sr. Deborah Francis and Sr. Laura Katharine attended the Leaders' Meeting of the Conference of Anglican Religious Orders in the Americas (CAROA), held that year in Toronto. On the way they stayed at the new St. Mary's Convent (Eastern Province) in Greenwich, NY, and saw the Christ the King Spiritual Life Center for the Diocese of Albany there.

On May 7 there was a spring "work day" during which Sr. Pamela and Sr. Linda Clare organized a group of volunteers who worked in the woods, and groups to tidy everything up after the ravages of winter. The Sisters met with the Revd. Louis Sogliuzzo during May for a week of reflection, and a week later, on May 25, Sr. Margo Elizabeth took a group to Ireland. The Celtic Journeys were by now a well-established feature in the Community diary.

Interweave had been in existence for twenty-five years and several Sisters attended the anniversary celebrations early in June. Sisters also attended Daytop's high school graduation later in June. It was a busy month, mostly filled with joyful events, but the Sisters were saddened when Mary Basilion retired. She had been business manager at the school and convent for over thirty years and was very much missed. The Sisters now welcomed a new business manager, Sheila Fredericks. Graduates of

St. John Baptist School had their annual picnic on June 18, with the class of 1965 holding its 40th reunion.

The two major events of June 2005 were the profession in life vows of Sr. Eleanor Francis on the 22nd and Commemoration Day on the 26th. The Rt. Revd. Vincent Pettit[1] received Sr. Eleanor Francis's vows, and Br. David Bryan Hoopes, OHC, preached. Friends and family came for the service, including friends from her former parish of St. Mary the Virgin, San Francisco. On Commemoration Day, the Revd. Donald Shearer celebrated the Eucharist at 4:00pm, and the sermon was preached by the Revd. Dr. Diana L. Beach. Both were Associates of the Community. Several new Associates were received, including Lillian Cochran, the Revd. Victoria McGrath, and the Community's organist, Margaret Erath. Departed Associates were remembered, including longtime friend and employee Hilde Fischer. The day could not have brought better weather and it concluded with supper on the cloister. At both events in the main chapel a new free-standing altar was used which enabled the celebrant to face the congregation. It was designed and made by Oliver Puig, an EFM (Education for Ministry) member and friend of the Community, who was received as an Associate on Commemoration Day.

The Sisters in England had appealed for help because several of their number were elderly and needed nursing care. Their infirmarian, Sr. Zoë, needed vacation time and also time for a retreat. Thus they appealed to Sr. Suzanne Elizabeth, a trained nurse, to spend two months with them at Begbroke. She flew to England on July 3 and stayed until the end of August. Knowing that July 4 is an important day for Americans, two of the English Sisters took her out to tea in honor of the Boston Tea Party! Writing in the Fall issue of the Community Notes, Sr. Suzanne Elizabeth commented, "My occasional dream of returning to work in a hospital with all the new medications and treatments came to a reality." It was not all work, as there were some visits to Oxford and other places nearby. And also Sr. Anne was commissioned as Chaplain to the Oxford homeless at a service of blessing led by the Bishop of Oxford, the Rt. Revd. Richard Harries. Sr. Suzanne Elizabeth summed up her experience: "I am very grateful for this opportunity to live and work and pray alongside my English Sisters and to be so welcomed into their hearts and lives. They are a marvelous witness of Religious living life to the fullest in prayer and hospitality and such other works as they are called and able to do to God's glory and honor."

Sr. Suzanne Elizabeth arrived home in time to take part in five days of meetings with Sr. Ellen Stephen from the Order of St. Helena, to discern the Community's future mission and commitment to continuing at Mendham, despite the challenges it was presenting.

During the summer of 2005, Historic Building Architects LLC, under the leadership of Annabelle Radcliffe-Trenner, surveyed the grounds and convent buildings. The survey included the roofs, walls and interior as well as the electrical, heating and plumbing systems. This "in-depth" survey was made possible by grants from the State and County Historic Commissions. An interim report was presented to the Sisters at the end of August. In the words of Sr. Barbara Jean, "The GOOD NEWS is that our convent is sound and has many more years of life in it. The CHALLENGE is that it will need a complete new heating system and upgrades to the electricity and plumbing ... After careful consideration and much prayer, we have decided that we are FULLY COMMITTED to staying on this property and continuing our mission ... to all who come here."[2] She concluded her news with an appeal to Oblates, Associates and friends to identify possible sources of funding. The Development Board would soon be planning a Capital Campaign to raise funds, "so that we can keep our acres of land green and free of development, and provide a facility for Daytop as we renovate our buildings."

Sisters had been taking part in Vacation Bible Schools during the summer. Sr. Lura Grace was working at St. John's in Dover, NJ, and the children visited the convent to make T-shirts and hats. Sr. Mary Lynne and Sr. Linda Clare went to the Church of the Holy Spirit in Lebanon, NJ, wearing African clothes, to talk about Sr. Jane's work.

At the end of August 2005 Sr. Lori Joan left the novitiate. Sr. Barbara Jean commented, "We are grateful for her time with us, especially for her work in the kitchen and garden, and her presence at St. Luke's, Gladstone." And at the end of September, Sr. Diane Jeannette left the novitiate again to return to Washington, DC. She was hoping to soon be working as a caregiver to the mentally disabled at L'Arche in Arlington, VA.[3] On a happier note, Sr. Mary Stephen from Begbroke was ordained deacon at Christ Church Cathedral, Oxford, England, on September 24.

Sr. Deborah Francis had a ministry with the Oblates and wrote in the Fall Community Notes how she helped each of them to formulate a Rule of Life including the Daily Office, regular spiritual direction, an annual retreat and service to CSJB and to their church communities. Many of the Oblates had leadership roles in their local churches and had invited the Sisters to give quiet days and retreats. "It's a great joy to share our experience of prayer and spiritual life with the wider church in this way, and to get to know so many wonderful parishes."

The attic sale held a few years previously had been such a success that the Sisters decided to repeat it in the form of a "yard sale" on October 7 and 8, 2005. There was some good publicity in the local newspapers and no shortage of helpers on the day. The proceeds were enough for a new truck, which arrived in time for use by Ken McCurdy, the new estate manager.

On November 6, Oblate Lily Altamura gave a birthday party which was attended by Sr. Barbara Jean and Sr. Deborah Francis. All the gifts were to benefit the children at the Good Shepherd Home and they totaled $1,000. The Oblates had made the Good Shepherd Home their outreach project.

As the year 2005 drew to a close, Sr. Deborah Francis had embarked on a new ministry which would flourish in the years ahead. On Wednesdays she had begun holding an informal lunch after the 12:10 Mass at the Church of St. Mary the Virgin in New York City. This would evolve into a ministry amongst the many homeless people who sought refuge there and in the vicinity of Times Square. Sr. Lura Grace had also begun a new ministry at St. John's, Dover, NJ, and had organized World AIDS Awareness Day at Hope House in Dover. Together with the Rector of St. John's, Sr. Lura Grace was exploring new ways of reaching out to the homeless.

Sr. Barbara Jean summed up the Sisters' work in the Christmas 2005 Community Notes. "The Community of St. John Baptist, now 153 years old, is entering a new time in its history, and you are all a part of our transition. Our Sisters today provide a place of spiritual nurture and growth here on the convent grounds, as well as a unique outreach in the larger community … As we reach out to all of these people of God, it is important to have a strong center where we and others may be spiritually nurtured. You can help us to keep that center strong through your support. We need your ideas, your time, and your talent, but most of all, your prayers. We look forward to working with many of you in the coming year." Thus the Sisters ventured forth into a new year of mission and ministry, strengthened as always in their vowed life by prayer, the sacraments, and the support of their Oblates, Associates, and many friends.

In February 2006 Sr. Shane Margaret went with a group from Drew University to the 9th Assembly of the World Council of Churches, meeting in Porto Alegre, Brazil. She recounted her experience in the Easter issue of the Community Notes. "The WCC is the largest ecumenical group in the world. They also do a lot of interfaith work, and we met Hindus, Jews, Muslims and Sikhs, as well as Christians of all sorts. Every day we began and ended with prayer in a big circus tent—the only structure that could hold 4,000 people! During the day there were meetings. Delegates met in formal sessions, and made decisions by consensus (among 1,500 delegates, that's impressive!) Observers like my group met in sessions on refugees, spiritualty, interfaith dialog, economic justice, liberation theologies from all over the globe, on youth and on Orthodox issues."[4] Over coffee Sr. Shane Margaret met many people "whose lives are impacted by ours, by our country and its policies, and by our church's decisions. It is humbling to hear personally how big our footprint is in the world." This visit was an enormous privilege for Sr. Shane Margaret, but also for CSJB. As a Sister, she represented not only Drew University but also, unofficially, her Community. It was yet another example of CSJB's "long reach" into the wider church and world. After she returned home, Sr. Shane Margaret was elected by the Community on March 14 to life vows. Her profession would take place later in the summer.

On March 30, Sr. Barbara Jean, Sr. Laura Katharine, and Sr. Pamela attended a meeting of the New Jersey Historical Review Board of Historic Sites, along with architect Annabelle Radcliffe-Trenner. The Community's nomination for the New Jersey and National Registers of Historic Places was accepted by the Board, thus making the Community eligible for grants toward the renovation of the buildings. The Community Development Board had worked hard to make this decision possible, especially Myles Varley, David Sullivan, and Board secretary Lynn Wilder Mullin. The way was now clear for the Sisters to embark on their "Renewing our Ministry" campaign. This was not just about renewing the buildings, it would encompass all the ministries of the Community—spiritual growth, outreach to youth, ministry to those in need, environmental protection and preservation of the historic buildings.

In May, Sr. Eleanor Francis graduated from Drew University as a Master of Divinity. Sr. Lura Grace, Sr. Shane Margaret, Sr. Linda Clare, and Sr. Barbara Jean attended the graduation ceremony.

At the Good Shepherd Home in Cameroon several children had

suffered from malaria, and donations to the home had paid for their medical care. Gilbert, Sr. Jane's first orphan, was growing up and was about to take his exam to qualify him for secondary school. He would have to travel a distance as there was no secondary school nearby. Sr. Jane hoped to build a secondary school to accommodate several hundred pupils on the Good Shepherd Home property. At the moment it was a dream, but plans had been drawn up and were being presented to churches in New Jersey. On April 19, 2006, Sr. Mary Lynne set out for another visit, taking many things for the children, including medicine, which was so badly needed. At the Home, Sr. Mary Lynne was given an African name, "Ayumbi," meaning "Hear from the World." It was Sr. Jane's grandmother's name and was considered a blessing. Sr. Barbara Jean wrote that Sr. Mary Lynne "has been a blessing to the people of Bamenda and they have been a blessing to us."

Sr. Mary Lynne returned home on June 22 in time for Commemoration Day on June 25. The celebrant and preacher was the Rt. Revd. Carol Gallagher, Assisting Bishop of Newark. Five new Associates were received—the Revd. Philip Carr-Jones, the Revd. Kay Locke, the Revd. Timothy Mulder, Lynn Wilder Mullin, and LindaLee Mundy. During the service, Associates who had died in the past year were remembered, including the Rt. Revd. Vincent K. Pettit, retired Bishop of New Jersey, who had officiated at Sr. Eleanor Francis' profession in life vows. Three days later, on June 28, 2006, Sr. Shane Margaret was professed in life vows. Bishop Herbert Donovan was the celebrant and the preacher was Br. David Bryan Hoopes, OHC.

On July 3, Sr. Suzanne Elizabeth traveled to England for two months to assist in nursing care at Begbroke. She was accompanied by Sr. Margo Elizabeth, who returned after a three-week visit. August 24 saw the reception of Mary Fennelly as a novice, taking the name Sr. Mary Julian. She would assist Sr. Shane Margaret in ministry at Daytop.

In July Sr. Linda Clare took part in a project called RISE (Risingville Intercommunity Service Effort). She had heard about it through friends at Chatham United Methodist Church and learned that it was a program that repaired homes for those who needed it but could not help themselves because of physical disability or economic circumstances. The program aimed to help residents throughout Steuben County, NY. Although it was primarily a program for youth volunteers, each summer a week was set aside for adult helpers. Sr. Linda Clare went for a week in July, staying in a church, sleeping in a Sunday School classroom and taking showers at a nearby camping site. Each day began with prayer, then each team of volunteers went to a site for their week's work. Sr. Linda Clare's team helped a woman who was a wheelchair user and lived in a trailer with her three dogs. The team repaired her wheelchair ramps and built extensions, repaired her shed and poured a new concrete sidewalk which would increase her mobility and thus her independence. Sr. Linda Clare noted in the Fall 2006 Community Notes that the project was about building community, seeking to serve others and working with them to improve their quality of life. She hoped to return as a volunteer the following year.

Sr. Linda Clare continued to have responsibility for the buildings and grounds on the convent site, a responsibility which would increase as the restoration work got under way. Meanwhile during the summer of 2006, with the help of Ken McCurdy, much hard work was done to improve the property, including removing fallen trees. He had moved into the caretaker's house on June 29 together with his family. A grant of $175,000 by Morris County had helped to restore and upgrade the convent heating system which had broken down the previous year.

At a time of war and unrest in many parts of the world, the Sisters were turning their thoughts and prayer to ways in which they could work for peace in the wider community. Sr. Lura Grace had a heart for the homeless and during the summer had been a volunteer at "Our Place," a homeless shelter situated in the basement of the First Baptist Church in Morristown. It was the only Monday-through-Friday drop-in center in Morris County, and ministered to the homeless and marginalized, and those with mental illness or substance abuse, victims of domestic violence, and the lonely. Sr. Lura Grace wrote an account of the work in the Fall 2006 Community Notes. "To all we offer a comfortable and friendly place where people can chat, read the newspaper, have free coffee and snacks, or receive counseling. We refer them to appropriate agencies [and] also provide hygiene products and emergency clothing, short-term storage of personal belongings, companionship and support … Since August 1995, Our Place has served over 6,100 people and I am heartsick to report that we're seeing an increase in daily numbers. The center is funded solely by donations from individuals, churches and foundations. Every cent goes into running the program and keeping the door open. It is a constant struggle that the staff and volunteers face daily."

There was good news from Begbroke. Sr. Mary Stephen was to be ordained to the priesthood on September 24. Sr. Mary Lynne, Sr. Pamela and Sr. Barbara Jean traveled to England for the ordination by the Rt. Revd. Colin Fletcher, Bishop of Dorchester, in Dorchester Abbey. Sr. Mary Stephen celebrated the Eucharist for the first time later that day in the Sisters' chapel at Begbroke.

Many of the people who lived in the vicinity of the convent at Mendham had never visited the Sisters, and so on November 19 there was a Tea and Tour. Families came for cider, doughnuts and cookies and all enjoyed their time with the Sisters.

There was more good news at Mendham when Sr. Eleanor Francis was accepted for candidacy for ordination in the Diocese of Newark. And on December 5, 2006, she was blessed as Assistant Superior.

As the year 2006 proceeded, the Sisters continued in their varied ministries. Sr. Suzanne Elizabeth had been busy speaking to Altar Guilds and hosting workshops on the care of vestments and church linens. Some of these had been outside the diocese, for instance at the 75th General Convention in Columbus, Ohio, in June, when she had given a prayer workshop for the National Altar Guild. Sr. Margo Elizabeth was developing new Celtic Journeys and in September took a group to Cornwall for the first time. In October she took a group of retreatants to Iona and Lindisfarne. Sr. Deborah Francis and Sr. Laura Katharine were attending the Church of St. Mary the Virgin, NYC, on Sundays, in addition to Sr. Deborah Francis's weekly visits. Negotiations were under way with the Rector, the Revd. Stephen Gerth, for the Sisters to begin a branch house there. In addition, Sr. Laura Katharine had given several Enneagram workshops in parishes and at the convent. Sr. Pamela had been made Bursar in addition to her work as hospice Chaplain and website manager. As the Capital Campaign progressed, she would withdraw from the Chaplaincy ministry. Sr. Shane Margaret was in her second year of seminary in addition to her ministry at Daytop and at the Church of the Redeemer in Morristown.

The Good Shepherd Home in Cameroon now had a chapel. This was blessed on December 5, 2006, by the Rt. Revd. Justice O. Akrofi, Archbishop of the North-West Province of the Anglican Church of Africa. He was welcomed by the children with songs and verses recited by them. The Archbishop celebrated the Eucharist and blessed the chapel, assisted by Fr. Joseph Ngijoe, the Chaplain.

On December 26, 2006, Mary Basilion died after a short illness. She had worked as business manager at St. John Baptist School from 1974 until its closure in 1983, after which she transferred to the convent as business manager there until her retirement in 2004. At the school she had taught the students how to manage money and was a good listener when they had problems. At the convent she worked with the Community's Boards, helping with insurance plans and contractors. She put the Community's business onto computer in the early years of computing. She was Greek by birth and Greek Orthodox by religion.

The new year, 2007, would bring fresh challenges and new opportunities for ministry. A former resident at the convent, Dora Kapp, died on January 23, 2007. She had lived at the convent from 1988–2003 and had illustrated the Community Newsletters, as they were then called, with her pen-and-ink drawings. Also, and more lastingly, she had renovated and repainted the Stations of the Cross in the main chapel. These had been brought from Holy Cross Church, NYC, following its closure in 1934. Among her other occupations, Dora had served on the Diocesan Education Commission and had also worked for Interweave. Her memorial service was held at the convent on January 27. The celebrant was the Revd. Robert Morris, founder of Interweave, and the preacher was Sr. Barbara Jean.

In January 2007 there was a diocesan celebration to mark the retirement of Bishop Croneberger as Bishop of Newark, and another for the consecration of his successor, the Rt. Revd. Mark Beckwith. Sr. Suzanne Elizabeth wrote in the Eastertide Community Notes: "As President of the Diocesan Altar Guild I was responsible along with Sue Bennett and Carol Homer, for the altar arrangements. We arrived in three pick-up trucks with vestments, sacred vessels etc., for each of these services, which were a week apart! We set up and took down six to fifteen altar tables in the two locations where the Concelebrations took place. All went extremely well, but we sure do hope that the new Diocesan lasts a long time!"[5] Preparing for such major celebrations was only part of the work of the Diocesan Altar Guild. The recycling of vestments and vessels was a big part of it, and many stoles that were no longer needed were given to Sr. Mary Lynne to take to Cameroon, where the clergy had nothing.

Also in January 2007 seven people went from the Church of the Redeemer in Morristown to visit Sr. Jane's work in Cameroon. They took dozens of suitcases filled with medicines, toiletries, books, toys, and gifts for the children. Upon their return they declared it to have been a "life changing experience." Following their visit they started their "Water for life" campaign, aiming to raise $38,500. By the time all the pledges came in the church had raised $83,000 for Good Shepherd Home. The main project was a water tank to provide the Home with clean water and by the time the church members returned home in June it was nearly complete. Sr. Jane was also determined that some of the water would go to the nearby village.

The really exciting venture for the Community in 2007 was the beginning of the new work at the Mission House next to the Church of St. Mary the Virgin, NYC, just off Times Square. Sr. Laura Katharine and Sr. Deborah Francis moved in on March 15, greatly assisted in the logistics by Sr. Pamela. Fr. Lister Tonge, Chaplain to the Sisters at Begbroke, came for the opening. Sr. Deborah Francis wrote in the Eastertide Community Notes: "When the Community was approached by the Church of St. Mary the Virgin to start a branch house there, I jumped at the opportunity." The prelude to establishing the branch house was Sr. Deborah Francis's weekly visit on Wednesdays. Once they had moved into the Mission House the Sisters found plenty of work, preparing and assisting at the many services, and getting to know the congregation as well as the many homeless who sought daytime refuge in the church. Sr. Laura Katharine became responsible for the smooth running of the sacristy and preparing for the many services, as well as the conservation of the many older vestments. Sr. Deborah Francis continued the weekly lunches following the Wednesday Eucharist. She also helped in the parish office and continued to make embroidered greetings cards. The presence of the Sisters in New York also enabled Sr. Lura Grace to volunteer one day a week at John Heuss House, a homeless facility run from Trinity, Wall Street, in addition to working at Our Place. Sr. Lura Grace wrote: "Everyone is welcome there, and the house is open day and night, all year. They serve two hot meals a day, and offer shower and laundry facilities. Social workers guide the clients to seek housing and a job. The welcoming atmosphere makes the house a very healing place. I hope to serve for several months there in order to learn more about effective ministry to the homeless."

Also in March, Sr. Linda Clare and Sr. Mary Julian went to New Orleans to assist people at the Church of the Annunciation, Sr. Mary Julian's home parish. The city had been devastated by Hurricane Katrina in August 2005, and efforts were still being made to recover and rebuild. Along with the parish priest, Fr. Jerry Kramer, the Sisters helped set up a dormitory for volunteers. The upper floor of the parish house had been transformed into Resurrection House to shelter work groups coming to the area. They toured the most devastated areas and assisted with a weekly outdoor supper for hundreds of needy people. Sr. Linda Clare wrote of the "extent of the devastation that still exists and the enthusiasm and generosity of the volunteers and residents. Those residents who have enough continue to reach out to provide for those who are still in financial and emotional need."

Sr. Mary Lynne had returned to Cameroon for her annual two-month visit and was able to report that Sr. Jane now had the care of 50 orphans and that a new home had been founded nearby for children with HIV/ AIDS. The people of St. Peter's, Essex Fells, had begun a project to raise $165,000 for a secondary school.

There had been some re-assigning of duties within the Community. For instance, Sr. Eleanor Francis was to be the Oblates' Sister due to Sr. Deborah Francis moving to New York. Sr. Linda Clare, in addition to her responsibility for the buildings and grounds, had now taken over as kitchen Sister in succession to Sr. Deborah Francis. Sr. Margo Elizabeth had been working on her forthcoming book *Sometimes a Star*, consisting of a dialog between herself and various people she had met in Ireland. It would soon be ready for publication.

The fourth "Monastery in May" took place on May 27, 2007. Sr. Barbara Jean gave some advance advertising in the Eastertide Community Notes. "The day will include tours by the Sisters, who will show the Community's vestments, artwork and illuminations, as well as some of the nooks and crannies of this historic building. At St. Marguerite's, refreshments will be served. We will need our friends and Associates to help us as hosts and hostesses." There would also be a craft fair in the cloister, where many items would be displayed and for sale, including Sr. Mary Lynne selling items from the "Nun Better" shop. The day was planned by a Committee consisting of Lynn Wilder Mullin (Chair), Carolyn Dunham, Joanne Painter, Eileen Kennedy and Judy Kerr. The event was a success, with many new people attending. Nearly $20,000 was raised towards the renovation of the buildings. There was some good news coverage of the event, but the *Morris Daily Record* outdid them all by videoing Sr. Linda Clare's tour of the convent. Sr. Barbara Jean commented, "We now have a film star in the house!"

Although St. John Baptist School had closed in 1983, the alumnae had kept in touch with the Sisters and one another. School reunions had taken place regularly at St. Marguerite's and there had been a Newsletter for some years. Now, in 2007, Lynn Wilder Mullin from the class of 1965 gathered together news of former students, which was included in the Community Notes. This means of keeping in touch and circulating information has continued. News of an alumna from as far back as 1937 (Margaret Clarke McWelthy) made its way into the Eastertide 2007 Community Notes.

On June 10, 2007, Sr. Linda Clare made her profession in life vows. Bishop Herbert Donovan received her vows and celebrated the Eucharist. Fr. Gerald MacIntyre, SJ, preached. The main chapel was packed with family and friends.

In July, the Sisters received the good news that the convent, retreat house, garden wall and cemetery had been entered on the New Jersey and National Registries of Historic Places, which would enable them to apply for grant aid for the renovation projects. The Morris County Board of Chosen Freeholders had given a grant to assist with the new heating system at the convent and it was hoped that work would begin in the following spring. Also, the St. Martin's Retreat House Board had given a grant of $50,000 towards handicapped access and a handicapped access bathroom at St. Marguerite's. The Capital Campaign was still at the planning stage and the Development Board was preparing for it. The Graham Pelton Company was giving guidance in the process and a Campaign Committee had been formed. The Community was still very much involved but had wisely sought expert guidance. Sr. Pamela and Maureen Woods, the convent business manager, were on the steering Committee, and advance work was being done by Eileen Kennedy and Diana Wilcox. Sr. Pamela had also spent the summer renovating the guest apartment, formerly known as the priest's apartment in the days when the Sisters had a resident Chaplain.

Sr. Shane Margaret had spent the summer on a Clinical Pastoral Education program at Overlook Hospital in Summit, NJ. There were six students in her group including four Korean and Korean-Americans. "Together they taught me about Korean culture, and about being a minority."[6] She covered two general medical/surgical wards and an intensive care unit. Also there were field trips to a residential center for people with developmental disabilities and to the Holocaust Center at Brookdale Community College. She described the latter trip as "a day of profound sorrow." The whole CPE experience was "life-changing."

"Suddenly you're with new people, in a new setting, for 48 hours a week. Suddenly you're facing new situations and expectations. The first two weeks were very hard, but gradually we all got in a rhythm." [7]

Sr. Suzanne Elizabeth made her usual summer visit to Begbroke in July, but it was tinged with sadness. Sr. Zoë had been failing in health for some time and Sr. Suzanne Elizabeth's help was greatly needed during her two-month visit. As things turned out, Sr. Zoë's final illness was rapid and she was only in hospital for five days before her death at the beginning of October. It was a shock for the Sisters both in England and America. Sr. Mary Stephen described her as "part of the backbone of our Community." Since the English Sisters had moved to Begbroke their numbers had continued to diminish and it would not be very long before they began to consider their future there.

In September, Sr. Shane Margaret's application to the Diocese of Newark had been accepted and she was now a postulant for ordination to the priesthood. She had begun working with a new congregation at St. David's Church, Kinnelon, NJ. And on November 4 Sr. Lura Grace made her final vows at an afternoon Eucharist celebrated by Bishop Mark Beckwith. The preacher was Br. David Bryan, OHC. It was a joyful occasion.

By December $1,400,000 had been promised for the Capital Campaign, which was more than half the $2,500,000 target for the first phase of renovation. It was a good start, and the Development Board was planning to "go public" with a special event early in 2008. Readers of the winter issue of the Community Notes were urged to "watch for the date." Meanwhile, Sr. Barbara Jean and Sr. Linda Clare had been working with the Historic Building Architects, and the new heating system was planned for installation in 2008. But—the cost would be $800,000 and the County of Morris would only fund up to $175,000.

As the year 2007 drew to a close, Sr. Barbara Jean wrote in the Winter Community Notes: "We at the convent of St. John Baptist have been discerning together, attempting to chart our path with the help of the scriptures and trusted counselors. We have embarked on a journey of hope. We have begun to implement the dream of restoration of our buildings, so that many more people may come here to worship and find the peace of Christ. We do not know when or how the journey will be completed. We have gifts to give to the world … These include a holy place, prayer and worship, and ministry to those in need."

So it was on this note of faith and hope that the Sisters began the new year of 2008. Familiar, and by now traditional, events heralded the New Year, such as the Epiphany party, which was enjoyed by all. February brought a long-anticipated visit from Sr. Jane Mankaa, her first since 2004. Her time was taken up by visiting many schools and churches to spread the news of the Good Shepherd Home. The home now had 50 children and it was hoped that the new building would soon be finished. Three-quarters of the cost had been supplied by the Rosenberg Foundation[8] but the rest had to be raised in order to complete the building. A school called the Redeemer Nursery and Primary School, accommodating 25 children from ages three to eleven, had opened thanks to the Church of the Redeemer, Morristown. And St. Peter's Church, Essex Fells, were fundraising for a secondary school. Cows, pigs, and rabbits provided food for the children and for the six Sisters and ten employees. When Sr. Jane returned to Cameroon on May 19 she was accompanied by Sr. Mary Lynne, who would stay for two months. Upon her return, Sr. Mary Lynne was able to report that the new building now had a roof, but donations were still needed to complete the building, which would hold 80–100 children. And the Redeemer Nursery and Primary School was now in operation. The latest project was to develop a house for children with HIV or epilepsy. A property had been bought two years previously and now a man had been appointed as director.

Sr. Margo Elizabeth's book, *Sometimes a Star*, was published in the spring of 2008. It consisted of conversations and dialogs between Sr. Margo and "the real people of Ireland." Written under the pen-name of M. E. Colman,[9] the book endeavored to ask those who were interviewed, "What sustains you?" and "What do you feel is life-giving?"

On April 22, 2008, there was a special event to celebrate 100 years of ministry at St. Marguerite's, first as an orphanage for girls, then as a home school and finally as a retreat house.[10] The Community chose this special anniversary to publicly announce the Capital Campaign "Renewing Our Ministry." There were tours of St. Marguerite's, organized by Sr. Pamela, and a number of former residents and teachers were present, including Ethel Dennis, who told stories of her life and that of her sisters as young girls at the home, and also Judith Smith, a former teacher. Elfie Larkin, another former teacher there whom Sr. Eleanor Francis had met in California in 2006, was unable to be present but had told Sr. Eleanor Francis how happy she had been working there.[11] In the evening there was a gala reception at Daytop with the Presiding Bishop, the Most Revd. Katharine Jefferts Schori, as guest of honor. She spoke of the importance of retreats and of the need for grounding as we go about God's work. There were several other bishops present: Bishop Herbert Donovan, Bishop Mark Beckwith, Bishop George Councell (of New Jersey), and Bishop Mark Sisk (of New York). A Committee of the Development Board, chaired by Diana Wilcox, had planned the day and much hard work had gone into it.

The alumnae of St. John Baptist School were also keen to embrace the Capital Campaign. Writing to them in the Spring Community Notes, Lynn Wilder Mullin commented: "I am proud to say [the Capital Campaign Committee] have asked me to represent you, the Alumnae, as a member of this Committee … Whereas this is a campaign to raise the necessary funds to rebuild and restore these old and special structures, the real heart of this project is that we, you and I, have an opportunity to give the Sisters the ability to continue their ministries, [and] to allow others to follow in their steps for years to come."

Daytop had opened a new wing. A new classroom had been added to the end of the gym and was dedicated as the "Revd. Joseph Hennen Daytop Preparatory School" after the founder of Daytop, NJ. The Sisters attended the dedication on Friday May 9, 2008. The new wing had two large classrooms on two floors and a meeting room that would hold 50 people. Alongside the gym ten single bedrooms had been provided for residents who had completed the program and who might come and go to work or college. Also, the new wing included special classes for those with learning disabilities.

On June 7, 2008, Sr. Eleanor Francis was ordained deacon by the Rt. Revd. Mark Beckwith at Trinity and St. Philip's Cathedral in Newark. She had by now fully recovered from a serious car accident in September 2006, and was now looking forward to serving as a deacon at All Saints', Millington, NJ.

Next day the Sisters began their annual retreat, which was led by the Revd. Barbara Crafton. This was quickly followed by Commemoration Day on Saturday June 21. The celebrant was Bishop Herbert Donovan and the Revd. Barbara Crafton was the preacher. Twelve new Associates were received, including the Revd. John Negrotto, Diana Wilcox, the Revd. Cathy Brunson and Douglas McKenzie. At the outdoor luncheon the guest of honor was the Mayor of Mendham Township, Phyllis Florek.

She presented the Community with a framed certificate congratulating the Sisters on 100 years of ministry at St. Marguerite's.

Betty Dormer was specially honored at the annual employees' picnic in June. She had originally been a teenage girl at St. Anna's Home at the convent. After leaving, she married and in 1948 returned to work at the convent, helping with housekeeping and in the laundry, where she was an expert in ironing the heavily starched collars, caps and bands worn by the Sisters at that time. After "retiring" about ten years previously, she had returned as a volunteer! Now she was retiring again, this time with a certificate to mark 60 years of service to the Sisters.[12] Early in the following year she celebrated her 90th birthday and the Sisters gave a special dinner in her honor.

In July 2008 the Revd. Elizabeth Geitz, Lillian Cochran, and Nan Curtis set out on a life-changing journey to visit the Good Shepherd Home in Cameroon. Lillian Cochran had previously visited the orphanage, but it was a new experience for the others. It led Elizabeth Geitz to make a lasting commitment to support the work once she was home, as well as leading her to write an account of Sr. Jane and her work.[13] She wrote, "Was it a pilgrimage, or an adventure that my traveling companions and I made to the Good Shepherd Home? We learned about the orphans' lives, our own childhoods in the segregated South, and the bonds of affection that develop across cultural boundaries."

At last! The new heating system had been installed at the convent. It was a major work involving removal of asbestos, followed by the removal of old, rusted pipes and the dismantling of the furnace. A new energy-efficient water tank, a new water treatment system and new pipes were installed. Sr. Barbara Jean wryly commented, "Needless to say, this work was not done in silence. Our dedicated crew of workers arrives each weekday at 7:00am, and the sounds of drilling and welding are a new addition to our daily offices. They have been wonderful to work with and have around. Still we look forward to the anticipated September completion of this project."

The road from Daytop to the convent had also been resurfaced.

In the Fall, the Community sold fifteen acres of land bordering the old road to the Schiff Natural Land Trust, a large tract of woodland adjoining the convent property. Former Development Board member Frank Parker had a trail named after him, and Sr. Barbara Jean attended the ceremony.

St. Marguerite's retreat house was as busy as ever. Sr. Margo Elizabeth and Sr. Suzanne Elizabeth were responsible for taking the bookings, and even though there had been an economic downturn, there was still a busy schedule. Some of the retreats were led by the Sisters, and others by visiting clergy or lay leaders. And the Sisters also traveled far and wide to give parish retreats. Sr. Barbara Jean had been leading Labyrinth Walks in the spring and fall. Sr. Pamela had organized a weekend on the writing of ikons and the creation of illuminated manuscripts, both led by Patricia Miranda. And whilst not strictly retreats, the ecclesiastical embroidery workshops were led in a prayerful and reflective way. Sr. Mary Lynne and Sr. Linda Clare had led bead workshops which included instruction on the Anglican rosary. In New York, Sr. Laura Katharine had given Enneagram workshops and Sr. Deborah Francis had given ikon retreats.

In November Sr. Mary Julian withdrew from the novitiate and moved to Summit to study hospital Chaplaincy at Overlook Hospital. Also in November, the Sisters elected Fr. Lister Tonge as their new Community Pastor (note the change of title). He already ministered to the English Sisters as their Chaplain.[14]

On November 30, 2008, Sr. Deborah Francis participated in the Rededication of the Cathedral of St. John the Divine, New York. There had been a serious fire in the unfinished north transept on December 18, 2001. Although the fire was contained, much damage had been done by the smoke, but it was not until January 2005 that restoration work was begun.

On December 13, 2008, Sr. Eleanor Francis was ordained to the priesthood by Bishop Mark Beckwith, following a retreat at Holy Cross Monastery. Two hundred people crowded into the main chapel. The combined choirs of the Church of the Redeemer and All Saints', Millington, sang anthems, and Bishop Donovan preached. Sr. Suzanne Elizabeth and Sr. Laura Katharine presented the stole and chasuble specially made by Colleen Hintz. The stole depicted a river flowing down both sides. On one side was the Golden Gate Bridge in San Francisco and on the other, the George Washington Bridge in New York, symbolizing her life in California and now in the East. Along the river there were symbols of her spiritual journey.

It was on this note of excitement at a new ministry that the year 2008 drew to a close and the Sisters looked towards the new year, 2009.

There was a "new look" to the Community Notes beginning with the Spring 2009 issue—a colored cover and more photographs. Nor did the content disappoint, with many positive news items.

Despite the economic downturn, the Development Board was still meeting monthly, and the Capital Campaign total was slowly increasing, thanks to grant aid and fundraising efforts by Oblates, Associates and other friends. The convent heating system had been completed and work was almost finished on a barriers-free ramp for St. Marguerite's. Also at St. Marguerite's, the floor in the solarium had been raised and some of the window leads had been restored. It was hoped that a barrier-free access ramp would be installed at the convent very soon, including a walkway from the parking lot to the cloister. Sr. Pamela had withdrawn from her Chaplaincy ministry in order to assist with the Capital Campaign now that fundraising was being done in earnest.

The Sisters had begun a community garden in order to grow vegetables for the Morris County food pantry. Those Sisters who visited parishes had been moved by the increased needs of people suffering poverty and economic hardship. Local soup kitchens and food pantries were reporting record numbers of individuals and families seeking help. Sr. Linda Clare managed the new initiative, which was known as the "Garden of Hope."

On February 11, 2009, Sr. Deborah Francis traveled to South Africa for a mission trip. She was invited to accompany Dr. Michael McNett, a member of the Church of St. Mary the Virgin, NYC. He, together with his team, assisted in a community project in Richmond in the high desert known as the Karoo, between Johannesburg and Cape Town. Sr. Deborah Francis wrote about her visit in the Spring issue of the Community Notes. "Richmond is a typical rural South African town and township. There is a small downtown with shops, restaurants, a library … and a huge Dutch Reformed Church. This section is owned by the Afrikaners, descendants of the original Dutch settlers. Across the stream are the "colored" [sic] and Xhosa (native African) areas in the township. In the days of apartheid, guards were stationed on the bridge separating the township from the town … The guards have been gone for fourteen years, but there is still a great social distance between these two parts of Richmond." Dr. McNett and his team had founded "Hope for Richmond" as an attempt to bridge the gap. With grants from Rotary International they had transformed a former Afrikaner property in the township into a multi-purpose community center with a soup kitchen, an HIV clinic, a soccer program and a community hall. The soup kitchen alone served about 300 children a day.

Sr. Deborah Francis accompanied Michael and Moses, two members of the team, around the township. She wrote: "I was stunned by the number of persons with chronic diseases. Diabetes, hypertension, and edema of the legs are some of the most common. There is a 70% illiteracy rate, and unemployment and alcohol consumption compound the problem. Reflecting on my time in Richmond, what impressed me was the vibrant faith of the people that I met. Genuine Christian love and hospitality greeted us everywhere, not only in church services, but in gracious dinners in the homes of the Afrikaner farmers. I will never forget the people at St. Matthew's Anglican Church, whose joy in their worship was so moving … the Dutch Reformed and the Evangelical churches were equally welcoming. I was inspired by the courage and perseverance of these people as they surmount the deep divides in their town and township."

Sr. Mary Lynne returned to Cameroon for her annual two-month visit on April 14, 2009. At the main home in Bamenda the convent building had been damaged by a heavy rainfall and needed extensive repairs. There was better news about the new dormitory, which was almost completed, thanks to help from the Diocese of New Jersey and the Revd. Elizabeth Geitz. This would accommodate 80 children. The new home at Batibo was for children with HIV/AIDS or epilepsy. Some of these children had formerly been left in the jungle to die, but Mr. Chi, a Cameroonian, had begun to search for them and provide them with medication. Now Sr. Jane and her Sisters and staff were working with him.

Fr. Paul Wessinger died on May 22, 2009, at age 95. As already mentioned in earlier chapters, he had known the Sisters since he was a small boy in Portland, Oregon. Sr. Waldine Lucia had introduced him to the Society of St. John the Evangelist (known in the UK as the Cowley Fathers). He was a member of SSJE for 65 years including time as Superior. He served CSJB as Warden for many years. Sr. Barbara Jean paid tribute to him in the Fall 2009 issue of Community Notes: "We remember him with great affection and give thanks for his life and memory."

On June 6, 2009, Sr. Shane Margaret was ordained deacon at Trinity and St. Philip's Cathedral in Newark. She was currently assisting at St. David's Church, Kinnelon, NJ, as well as being the chapel Sister at the convent. But her bonds with CSJB were loosening, as later in the year it was announced that she would be living away from the convent in order to explore working full time in parish ministry.

Commemoration Day on June 27 followed closely on the ordination. Bishop Donovan was the celebrant and the preacher was the Rt. Revd.

Mark Fisk, Bishop of New York. Six Associates were received including Bishop Donovan and Susan Negrotto. There was a display on the lawn about the Capital Campaign, and in the parlor Sr. Mary Lynne had many items to sell in the Nun Better Shop, some of which had been made by the children in Cameroon.

In July, Sr. Suzanne Elizabeth and Sr. Eleanor Francis traveled to California to attend the 76th General Convention meeting at Anaheim.[15] Sr. Suzanne Elizabeth attended the National Altar Guild meeting during the Convention and introduced Marilyn Doyle, who gave a workshop on "Theology in Fabrics and Threads." Sr. Eleanor Francis assisted at the booth of the Conference of Anglican Religious Orders in the Americas (CAROA). She also co-led a service of Taiz worship, open to delegates, and about 100 people attended. "Both Sisters found the experience of the Convention to be inspiring, as they witnessed the Episcopal Church at a crucial moment in its history."[16]

In addition to her other ministries with the homeless, Sr. Lura Grace was serving on the Board of Trustees of the Interfaith Council for Homeless Families of Morris County, and in the Fall had joined their staff as part-time case manager in their Permanent Supportive Housing Program. This program worked with homeless children and their families after they had moved out of Interfaith's Emergency Shelter Program. The main goal was to help the homeless with whatever they needed to remain permanently housed. Sr. Lura Grace had a special ministry of counseling those in need.

Fr. Joe Hennen, Founder of Daytop NJ, retired in the Fall after eighteen years at the Mendham site. Since 1991 over 3,000 young people had passed through the program, and he had been an inspiration to them, their families and the staff. There was a farewell luncheon with a Hawaiian theme, as he would now be serving a parish in Hawaii. The luncheon was attended by Sr. Pamela, Sr. Eleanor Francis and Sr. Barbara Jean.

August 29, 2009, through early September saw another fundraising event for the renovation of the buildings. This was named the "Treasure Sale," and the Fall Community Notes showed a photograph of Sr. Suzanne Elizabeth and Sr. Linda Clare selling an item to an interested customer.

On October 19, 2009, "Bill" Grier passed to his rest at Holly Manor Nursing Home in Mendham after a long illness, at age 91. He had been estate manager for the convent and St. Marguerite's from 1945 until 1995, and had lived on the grounds with his family. After retiring he and his wife

Shirley moved to Mendham. There was a tribute in the Winter Community Notes: "Bill was always on call as a consultant in maintenance matters. He knew every inch of our property above and underground, and was a great resource. We celebrate his life of service to us and to the township of Mendham, where he served on the Fire Department for many years."

Sr. Barbara Jean made a visit to the Good Shephard Home in Cameroon beginning on November 1, All Saints' Day. She was very impressed by all that Sr. Jane was doing to help 100 children. As she noted in the Winter 2009 Community Notes, the numbers shifted frequently, and not all the children were in the same place, but all came under Sr. Jane's care. She wrote, "The challenges are great, as the Sisters strive to keep each one safe, clothed, fed and educated … It employs nannies for the babies, [and] teachers and workers for the property and farm animals. All of these people eat from Sr. Jane's kitchen, where great pots of rice, corn, and other staples are prepared each day … My experience was eye-opening about conditions of life in the third world and the challenges that people there must tackle every day." Sr. Barbara Jean also visited the Good Shepherd annex in Batibo for those with special health needs. A registered nurse known as "Mama Mary" cares for them. All attend school and receive medical care. One Sunday Sr. Barbara Jean celebrated the Eucharist at the main home and the children came up for a blessing at the end. She wrote, "I will not forget this moment." Also, the children put on a play based on St. Matthew 25 where Jesus showed how people should reach out to those in need. The children ended by thanking all and saying, "If you had not reached out to us, where would we be now?"

The Winter Community Notes announced the passing of Carman Ora Synnes, who as Sr. Ora Mary was a member of the Community from 1948 until 1968 and again briefly in the early 1990s. She died at La Mesa Healthcare Center in California at age 84. While in the Community she worked at St. John Baptist School for several years as a teacher and House Sister. Her funeral was at St. Andrew's Church in La Mesa, where she was a member.

From November 9–13 the Sisters hosted a workshop at St. Marguerite's for CAROA. Twenty-six members of eleven different Communities from the US and Canada attended. The workshop was led by the Revd. Barbara Crafton, who took as her theme "How to lead a Retreat."

On December 12, 2009, Sr. Shane Margaret was ordained to the priesthood at St. David's Church, Kinnelon, where she had served as a deacon. She was presented by Sr. Barbara Jean and Bishop Donovan, and the service was attended by many people from the Church of the Redeemer, Associates and Sisters of CSJB, as well as friends and members of St. David's church. It was noted that she would continue to serve at St. David's until called to a new parish.

Sr. Barbara Jean's term of office as Sister Superior came to an end in December, and on the 15th, Sr. Eleanor Francis was elected to succeed her as Superior. Sr. Barbara Jean wrote, "I look forward to another page in my life, serving the Community of St. John Baptist in whatever way I am asked." Sr. Eleanor Francis's installation would take place in a private ceremony on January 5, 2010. Thus the Community moved prayerfully from the first decade of the 21st century into a new phase in its life and ministry, open as always to new challenges.

---

[1] The Rt. Revd. Vincent Pettit was Suffragan Bishop of New Jersey 1984–90. He died on March 10, 2006.

[2] Community Notes, Fall 2005.

[3] L'Arche (French for The Ark) was founded in 1964 by Jean Vanier when he invited two men with disabilities into his home in Trosly-Breuil, France. By 2019 it had grown into an international organization of 153 communities in 38 countries and on five continents. Jean Vanier died on May 7, 2019, at age 91.

[4] The Eastern Orthodox Churches are not members of the WCC.

[5] He sure did! Bishop Beckwith was Bishop of Newark from 2007 until 2018.

[6] Community Notes, Fall 2007, Sr. Shane Margaret "A Life-Changing Experience."

[7] Ibid.

[8] The Rosenberg Foundation was established in 1935 by the bequest of California businessman Max L. Rosenberg, and since then almost 2,800 grants totaling nearly $80 million had been made to regional, statewide and national organizations advocating for racial and economic justice. Source: rosenbergfound.org

[9] Perhaps it's no coincidence that Sr. Margo Elizabeth chose the name Colman as her pen-name. Colman was Abbot of the holy island of Lindisfarne at the time of the Synod of Whitby in 664. When the Synod voted in favor of the Roman calendar instead of the Celtic he returned to Iona, and then in 668 he settled in Ireland at Inishbofin where he founded a monastery on Celtic lines. He died there in 674.

[10] For details of St. Marguerite's as an orphanage see BONHAM, Valerie *Living Stones* Chapter 13.

[11] Op. Cit. Chapter 19, pp. 320–21.

[12] In September 2019 I met Betty's daughter Kathy Kopec and we enjoyed tea together at the convent with Sr. Suzanne Elizabeth.

[13] GEITZ, Elizabeth *I am that child* Morehouse Publishing, New York and Harrisburg, PA, 2012.

[14] Fr. Lister Tonge had been Chaplain to the English Sisters since 1996 both at Clewer and Begbroke. He now served as Community Pastor to the US Sisters, visiting them two or three times a year.

[15] This was another crucial moment in the history of the Episcopal Church as it called for "an open process for the consideration of theological and liturgical resources for the blessing of same gender relationships …"

[16] Community Notes, Fall 2009.

FROM CORNERSTONES TO LIVING STONES

The Community from 2010 Onwards

T HE NEW YEAR, 2010, heralded a new beginning with the installation on January 5 of Sr. Eleanor Francis as Sister Superior. Bishop Donovan officiated at the private ceremony and Bishop Mark Beckwith also took part. This was followed by a luncheon to celebrate the event. The Spring 2010 Community Notes showed a photograph of the new Superior with both bishops and the two former Superiors, Sr. Suzanne Elizabeth and Sr. Barbara Jean. As Superior, Sr. Eleanor Francis would take an active part in the Capital Campaign and the renovation projects. Sr. Lura Grace was appointed Assistant Superior and Sr. Barbara Jean became the novice director.

Also in early January, the Community was presented with a plaque by the Morris County Freeholders, acknowledging the historic contribution made by the Community to Morris County by preserving the heating system of the building. The project had been made possible by the Morris County Historic Preservation Fund, which had contributed a significant grant towards it. Sr. Barbara Jean and Sr. Linda Clare went to the presentation, and the plaque is displayed on the lower floor of the convent.

The renovation project still had much work ahead and Sr. Linda Clare, along with architect Annabelle Radcliffe-Trenner, had just completed a grant application to Morris County for a barrier-free ramp to access the convent. The Carvel Foundation, a charitable organization in NYC, had given some financial help towards this, too. A new interior corridor to the main chapel, to replace the underground tunnel, was also included in this phase of the project. Some of the leaded glass windows at St. Marguerite's had already been replaced, but all the windows needed restoration, and this was to be the next stage of the project. Georgia Stained Glass, of Dover, NJ, had been chosen for the work. Morris County had approved the work and agreed to pay 80% of the cost, leaving the Community to raise the remaining 20% ($37,596). And clearly, the tiles on the convent roof were in dire need of replacement. These were the original tiles imported from England 95 years earlier, when the convent was built.

All these renovation projects took time and planning and much fundraising. The Sisters could not have done it alone, but fortunately they had a faithful group of Oblates, Associates, and friends, as well as the commitment of the Development Board and Morris County, the New Jersey Historic Trust, and other charitable organizations. And in this way the Sisters were able to continue their work of prayer and hospitality.

On March 17, the Revd. John Negrotto was received as an Oblate, bringing the number to seventeen. During their annual retreat the Oblates had been introduced to ikon writing, learning the process and also using them for meditation.

A spectacular exhibit called "The Glory of Orthodoxy" took place in the main chapel over the Pentecost weekend, May 22–23, 2010. It was hosted by the Sisters, and the 17th–19th-century ikons were lent by a private collector. The event was organized by an Associate, Timothy Carr, assisted by Sr. Pamela, who produced a lavish catalog to accompany the exhibit. Two lectures were given each day, one by the curator of the collection, Dr. Corrado Altomari, and one by Dr. Gary W. Jenkins. Orthodox Vespers was sung (in English) on the Saturday, led by Fr. Thomas Edwards of St. Gregory Palamas Orthodox Church of Glen Gardner, NJ. All proceeds from the event were donated to the Capital Campaign. Lily Altamura, Oblate and Development Board member, had introduced Dr. Altomari to the Sisters, thus making the event possible.

An estimated 85 people attended Commemoration Day on June 26, 2010. The celebrant was the Revd. Stephen Gerth, Rector of St. Mary the Virgin, NYC, and the preacher was Sr. Eleanor Francis. Five new Associates were received. After the Eucharist, luncheon was served on the cloister on what was a beautiful summer's day.

July 2010 saw Sr. Suzanne Elizabeth journeying to Begbroke, UK, for the sixth and last time. Although the English Sisters had only been at Begbroke for nine years, they were diminishing in numbers and the Priory was now too large for them. Sr. Suzanne Elizabeth wrote of this in the Fall 2010 issue of Community Notes. "The Priory is up for sale. Realtors[1] are showing prospective buyers around and the Sisters are preparing to downsize once again as they await approval of building plans for their new residence and chapel at Cuddesdon Seminary on the other side of Oxford, where they will take up their new Ministry of Presence among the seminarians, faculty and clergy there. It cannot be a reality for at least eighteen months … The Sisters plan to move as soon as their new house is ready."

Sr. Mary Lynne returned from Cameroon on July 22 full of news of new developments there. The chicken farm was thriving, providing not just food for the children, but also a surplus of chickens which could be sold for $6 to $8 dollars each. The Grace Bakery, provided by Grace Church, Madison, NJ, was a traditional outdoor oven providing daily bread for the children with some left over to sell to needy neighbors. Each day about 150 people were fed at the Good Shepherd Home and the annex in Batibo. Thirty of the children were now in secondary school, and two of the earliest orphans, Gilbert and Maribel, were planning to attend medical school in the following year. These and others who were reaching adulthood were assured of a home by Sr. Jane until they were ready to live in homes of their own. Younger children from nursery to fifth grade were attending Redeemer School, named for the Church of the Redeemer in Morristown. The new 80-bed dormitory was now complete and in use.

Back at Mendham, the summer Search Program hosted two "searchers," one of whom (Jean Marie Du Hamel) would become a convent resident. Centering Prayer, a form of meditation, was a feature of Thursday evenings at the convent from 7:15–8:30, concluding with Compline with the Sisters. And Sr. Margo Elizabeth's Celtic Journeys were going from strength to strength, with the usual Irish journey in May, followed by journeys to other Celtic sites in the Fall—Wales and the north of England featuring in 2010.

On November 28, 2010, Fr. Joseph Gross departed this life. He had been the Community Chaplain from 1977–92. After retirement he served in two parishes in Schenectady, NY. He was survived by his widow, Virginia. Nearer home, Judith McCurdy, wife of estate manager Ken McCurdy and mother of their two sons Ryan and Brandon, died suddenly on December 3, 2010. Her memorial service was conducted at the convent by the Sisters and was attended by 100 people. A reception followed at St. Marguerite's.

On November 30, 2010, Bishop Herbert Donovan retired as Bishop Visitor to the Community. Earlier in the month a special tea had been held by the Sisters for him and his wife, Mary. He was to continue as an Associate and a member of the Development Board. Also on November 30, the Rt. Revd. Prince Singh, Bishop of Rochester, NY, was installed as the new Bishop Visitor.[2] Assisting at the installation service were Bishop Donovan and Bishop Mark Beckwith.

The departure from the Community for full-time ordained ministry by Sr. Shane Margaret had meant that the valuable connection with Daytop had undergone a change. But the connection was not lost. In the words of Sr. Eleanor Francis in the Winter 2010–11 Community Notes, "It is a blessing for all of us to have a continuing relationship with Daytop … The students there help us as volunteers in various projects throughout the year and Sr. Barbara Jean serves on the Daytop Board." The article showed a picture of some of the young people at the convent's annual Christmas-tree-decorating evening. Sr. Eleanor Francis and Sr. Pamela helped with decorations and refreshments and Sr. Suzanne Elizabeth gave each of the student helpers a piece of "Nun Better" jewelry. Earlier in December Sr. Barbara Jean had attended the Daytop Holiday Brunch and musical program.

And so the year 2010 gave way to a new year, 2011, with the Sisters living out their vowed life, welcoming all, and always open to new ministries.

At this time there were three residents in the convent household. Janet Thomas had lived there for fifteen years and had been an Oblate since 1994. As a professional nanny she had served with several families as well as working at the convent as a part-time housekeeper and driver. Donna MacKenzie came to live and work at the convent in 2009, serving in housekeeping. She had expertise with growing plants and helping with the Garden of Hope; and she was also an expert at spinning and weaving. Jean Marie Du Hamel was the most recent resident, having moved to the convent towards the end of 2010. She worked for the Tewkesbury, NJ, Police Department in addition to ministry as a life coach.

Spring 2011 saw the introduction of Phase 2 of the Capital Campaign. The Sisters had reached the goal of $2.5 million in pledges for the first stage, but not all had been redeemed financially. The Community was responsible for 20% of all County grants and 50% of all State grants, and they had not yet raised the full $500,000 to match the grant from the State. Thus the goal for Phase 2 had been set at $1.5 million. Work to be done in Phase 2 included a ramp along the south cloister leading to the front door; preservation and restoration of all the convent roofs and chimneys; restoration of the stucco to the convent exterior; and repair of the roof at St. Marguerite's. Also, the electricity cabling was to be re-routed underground and a new electrical transformer provided. There had been much speculation about the underground tunnel connecting the south wing of the convent to the main chapel and providing easy access. It was a historic part of the convent, but had fallen into such disrepair and dampness that it was decided to infill it, and provide an internal barrier-free passageway to the main chapel which did not go under the lawn. One of the fundraising projects was the publication early in 2011 of the *Nun Better Cookbook*, the brainchild of Sr. Pamela, consisting of 380 recipes contributed by a large number of people.

In New York, both Sr. Laura Katharine and Sr. Deborah Francis had been teaching a class for adults on the Apocrypha. Sr. Laura Katharine was kept very busy preparing with volunteers for the many services at St. Mary's. Sr. Deborah Francis had started a food program in collaboration with St. Clement's Episcopal Church, nearby.

At St. Mark's, Mendham, the Rector had recently retired at the end of 2010 and Sr. Barbara Jean was acting as supply priest and also assisting in the Sunday School. And several Sisters had attended the Newark Diocesan Convention—Sr. Pamela to manage the CSJB table, and Sr. Suzanne Elizabeth and Sr. Mary Lynne to manage the Good Shepherd Home table.

Amongst those who passed to their rest early in 2011 was Samuel Altamura, husband of Oblate Lily, who died on February 11. He was 83. He had helped the convent with many of their projects. And on February 26, Dorothy Keedwell Whiteside, who had graduated from St. John Baptist School in 1934, passed to her rest shortly before her 95th birthday. She had been an Associate since 1960. She had volunteered at convent events for many years before moving to Virginia. She was buried in the convent cemetery next to her son, Craig, who had predeceased her.

Petie, the Sisters' beloved dog, died early in 2011. A few months later, Jennie, a short-haired black-and-white dog, came to live with the Sisters. She would let them know very loudly when any visitors came to the door! After carefully inspecting the Sisters' stalls in chapel to make sure everyone was there, Jennie would then take up her own place.

There was a new Associates' Manual, and Sr. Eleanor Francis was urging the large number of Associates (almost 400) to spread the good news of the presence of Religious Communities in the Episcopal Church. It was part of the new Associates' Rule that they should do so whenever the opportunity arose. In keeping with the times, there was an online version as well as the printed one.

During June, Michelle LaFrage arrived from Georgia. She had worked in a hospital as a nurse's aide, and later worked at a Christian Women's Center. Feeling called to do mission work, she joined a Christian drama group called the Covenant Players and their tour brought them to stay at St. Marguerite's, where they performed in local churches. She picked up a brochure about the Community and the Search Program, but it was sometime before she attended one. Now, in 2011, she planned to attend the August program, but when a tornado struck the facility where she lived and worked she asked the Sisters if she could come early. They readily agreed and it was noted in the Fall Community Notes that "she has been a welcome addition to our household at a time when many Sisters are on vacation and helpers are few."

In the UK, the Sisters were having a frustrating time regarding their proposed move from Begbroke. They had made an interim move from the Priory to the neighboring Priory House in May 2011 because the sale of the main house was about to reach completion. Then the sale fell through and the Priory was once again on the market. But at Cuddesdon things were moving forward. Sr. Jane Olive had signed a provisional contract for the work to proceed on their new accommodation and the new chapel, and this had begun in July 2011.

Sr. Mary Lynne arrived home from Cameroon in July and was able to report that the children, of whom 80 lived in Bamenda and 35 in Batibo, were healthy, happy and anticipating the opening of a new school year in September. Several were now old enough to start secondary school and three would be going to university. A video about the home had been made and would be for sale early in 2012—proceeds would help fund a secondary school with priority for orphans. Sr. Jane's ministry was not confined to the children in her care, but was also for her neighbors in need, whether that need was for advice, prayer, food or medicine.

The Fall season was a time of activity, always grounded in prayer. Much work was going ahead with the renovations and the Sisters opened their doors to the public and led a series of tours around the buildings and grounds. Guests of honor were State Senator Anthony Bucco and State Assemblyman Anthony Bucco, Jr. The Sisters led tours of the convent and St. Marguerite's, and architect Annabelle Radcliffe-Trenner led tours of the renovation project. As the Sisters' aim was to make the convent more accessible to local people, it was a good opportunity to greet neighbors who were visiting for the first time. Meanwhile, the final inspection of the restored windows at St. Marguerite's had been completed and deemed to be of excellent quality. At the convent, roof repairs continued, but the repointing of the chimneys was complete. All the leaded glass windows had been restored and were being held at the glass studio, awaiting installation once the dormers were repaired. The underground tunnel had been filled in with concrete, a task taking two days. One of the skylights had been removed and used as the entrance point for the pumping. It would be restored and replaced, as requested by the New Jersey Historic Trust.

Michelle LaFrage, having been resident since June and having participated in the Search Program, had applied to join the Community. As a Southern Baptist she was required first of all to join the Episcopal Church. She began attending the Church of the Messiah in Chester and was confirmed at the convent by Bishop Prince Singh after being prepared by Sr. Suzanne Elizabeth. On December 15, 2011, Michelle was received as a postulant.

The relationship with Daytop continued in a positive way, with many of the members coming to help the Sisters in various ways. This included helping with the mailing of the Community Notes, directing traffic on open days, and helping create a garden. Their pre-Christmas Holiday Brunch was again attended by Sr. Barbara Jean, who received the token rent of $1.00.

As the old year passed into 2012, the Sisters again had much to give thanks for, many to welcome and many to pray for. It was a mercifully mild winter and this had enabled the roofers to work almost every day. The rear roof had been renewed up to the ridge and work had now commenced on the south roof. Some of the original tiles were re-usable, but others had to be made to order using the original specification. The next major project was the restoration of the front roof. The electrical service had been re-routed and installed following the infilling of the tunnel.

One of the first Oblates, Dorothy "Dot" Bartkus, died at age 91 on January 24, 2012, at the House of the Good Shepherd, Hackettstown. She had belonged to the Diocesan and National Altar Guilds for many years and served the latter as secretary. During World War II she had served in the US Navy as a WAVE.[3]

Sr. Jane Mankaa arrived at Mendham in February 2012, hoping to stay until the end of July. Together with Sr. Mary Lynne she had been visiting churches to talk and show slides about her work. Also, she had spoken at the New Jersey Diocesan Convention at the invitation of Bishop George Councell and the Revd. Canon Elizabeth Geitz. The book *I am that child*, written by Elizabeth Geitz, recounting the visit she made to Cameroon with Nan Curtis and Lillian Cochran, had just been published, and Sr. Jane attended a book signing at the Episcopal Church Center in New York, hosted by Bishop Sisk. Elizabeth Geitz had begun a fundraising project to build a secondary school in Cameroon.

Funding was greatly needed in order to continue with the restoration projects and on March 18, 2012, the Capital Campaign Committee under Sr. Pamela organized its first benefit concert. The performers were Brian Harlow on the organ and cellist Robert Deutsch. About 70 people attended the concert in the main chapel.

Sr. Pamela, in addition to her work on the Capital Campaign Committee, was also in charge of refurbishing St. Marguerite's. The Community now had a website and she was responsible for this, updating it regularly. Sr. Margo Elizabeth was in her fourteenth year of organizing Celtic Journeys and there was no lack of support or interest in them, many people coming back to them year after year. But her ministry also encompassed spiritual direction and, as part of the guest ministry, welcoming groups and individuals. Sr. Linda Clare was responsible for coordinating with the architect on the restoration projects. Also, as a member of the Development Board she was responsible for grant applications, and worked with the estate manager, Ken McCurdy, on property maintenance.

The original idea of building a convent at Cuddesdon had been revised, and now the English Sisters were looking forward to moving into the new Harriet Monsell House, part of which would provide them with accommodation, and part of which was for the college. The Bishop Edward King Chapel was a separate building to be shared by all. On June 6, 2012, the "topping out" ceremony (the placing of the final piece of the roof) took place at Cuddesdon. Prayer capsules had been placed behind the foundation stones of both buildings.

On June 8, 2012, the Feast of the Dedication of the convent at Mendham, Michelle LaFrage was received as a novice, taking the name Sr. Victoria Michelle. This was a lovely occasion and once more the Community had an active novitiate. A few years previously there had been six novices—three had been professed in life vows, and three had left. Now Sr. Victoria Michelle took her place in choir and worked in the chapel, attended classes and made items for the Nun Better shop.

Also in the summer, Sr. Lura Grace had graduated from a three-year program in Spiritual Direction, held by the Sisters of Christian Charity in Mendham. She would now be available to serve in this much-needed ministry.

Commemoration Day 2012 was held on June 23, and the celebrant and preacher was the Rt. Revd. Prince Singh, Visitor to the Community. One hundred people attended, including the oldest Associate, Grace Terwilliger, aged 103. The Eucharist and Community notices was followed by an outdoor luncheon in the glorious sunshine. A week later, on June 30, sixteen alumnae of St. John Baptist School attended their annual reunion picnic at St. Marguerite's. The newly renovated solarium and patio made it a good meeting place.

In July, Sr. Suzanne Elizabeth and Sr. Pamela attended the 77th General Convention in Indianapolis in order to support the National Altar Guild Convention meeting alongside it. Sr. Pamela mainly attended the exhibit hall booth on Religious Orders. Sr. Suzanne Elizabeth led Morning Prayer for the National Altar Guild Association and acted as Chaplain to them. She was elected to be the Nominating Chair for Officers to be elected in 2015. There was much work to be done preparing for the daily Eucharist attended by several thousand delegates and observers. Also, both Sisters were able to attend some of the debates as observers and NAGA received a standing ovation in appreciation of many years of service and ministry to the General Convention and the National Church.

Sr. Jane Mankaa returned to Cameroon on August 1, 2012, after a busy time giving talks to parishes near and far. On her return home she found ten new children in the orphanage, bringing the total to 150. Back in the USA, the Revd. Canon Elizabeth Geitz had held a major fundraising event in aid of the proposed Good Shepherd Academy and later in the year she made another visit to Cameroon accompanied by Brenda Ruello from Milford, PA. A new Board of Directors was formed to govern the creation of what would be the first Anglican secondary school in Cameroon. This would now be a separate business from the orphanage. Architectural plans had been drawn up and it was hoped that the first phase of the building would begin soon. A further project was the creation of a clinic near the Good Shepherd Home. Dr. Nche Zama, of Pocono Medical Center in Pennsylvania, who was a native of Bamenda, was giving much support to the venture.

The August Search Program was attended by Sr. Victoria Michelle,

Catherine Colleson and Claudette Powell. The group was "an enthusiastic addition to our household."

In August 2012 a new offer for the Priory at Begbroke was made and accepted, and Harriet Monsell House was completed towards the end of September. Further delays meant that the Sisters did not move until November, and at the same time the newly revised and enlarged edition of *A Joyous Service* was delivered. Amongst the Sisters who did not move to Cuddesdon were Sr. Sheila, who was Mother Harriet's great-great-niece, and Sr. Edna Frances. Sr. Sheila had died in August 2010 but had known of the proposed move. Sr. Edna Frances died on May 22, 2012, at St. Mary's convent and nursing home, Chiswick, West London, where [UK] Sr. Monica had been living since January 2010.

In New York, Sr. Laura Katharine and Sr. Deborah Francis had been busy with parish activities and their own particular ministries. And on October 3 they participated in the ordination to the priesthood of the Revd. Mary Jett. This was the first ordination of a woman at St. Mary the Virgin.

On October 16 Claudette Powell, who had attended the August Search Program, was received as a postulant. A native of Georgia, she had studied in New York before spending 22 years as a photo editor in motion picture advertising in Hollywood, four years of which was with Paramount pictures. The most rewarding aspect of her work had been graphic design, and this would be an asset in Community life. She had always wanted to join a Religious Community, and now in 2012 she was at last able to test her vocation.

On October 22, a tropical storm in the Caribbean was upgraded by meteorologists to hurricane status and named "Sandy." It raged its way through Jamaica and Cuba before turning up the east coast of the US. New Jersey caught the full force and many trees fell in the convent grounds. The Community was fortunate in that none of the buildings were damaged, but electrical power was lost for two weeks. Ken McCurdy and some of the Sisters drove as far as Pennsylvania to find gasoline, which was needed to power generators which gave some heat and kept the freezers going. The Sisters noted that without Ken they could not have coped with the practicalities of the emergency. The hurricane finally dissipated on November 2. Then came the "cleanup," and many friends and Associates came to help clear the fallen trees. But throughout it all, the Sisters' life of prayer continued uninterrupted.

As winter approached, several programs and concerts were held in the main chapel: a concert of "ambient" music, a Meditation Workshop co-sponsored by Interweave, and a Brazilian guitar concert. There was an Advent retreat led by Sr. Margo Elizabeth, called "Seeking the Holy," and a vestment tour conducted by Sr. Suzanne Elizabeth. Also, regular events took place such as Labyrinth walks, centering prayer, and Fabric of Faith with the "Stitchers."

There was an air of excitement as 2012 passed into 2013. For some time the Sisters had been planning to celebrate the Centennial of the laying of the Cornerstone of the new convent on April 30, 1913. As the great day drew nearer, the Sisters' preparations began to be a reality as sponsors were found to help with the funding. But convent life went on as usual amid all the "busyness" attached to the celebrations. There was an ikon-writing retreat led by Patricia Miranda at St. Marguerite's on February 20–22. A long-term program began at the convent, on Thursday evenings from February 21 through May 16, on Quantum Physics and Theology, led by the Revd. Dr. Douglas Bendall. And on Sunday March 10, there was a concert in the main chapel by the Spirit of Orthodoxy Choir, called "The Season of Lent in Song." On April 9, Claudette Powell was clothed as a novice, taking the name Sr. Monica Clare.

Cornerstone Day was held on April 27, 2013, and was attended by 180 people. The Bishop of Newark, the Rt. Revd. Mark Beckwith, presided at the Eucharist in the main chapel and the preacher was the Very Revd. Lister Tonge, Dean of Monmouth in the Church in Wales, who had recently been appointed Community Pastor. Two of the hymns sung at the Eucharist, "When morning gilds the skies" and "Jerusalem the Golden," had been sung on April 30, 1913, when the Cornerstone was laid and blessed.

At the end of the Eucharist everyone joined a procession to the Cornerstone, which was blessed by the Community Visitor, Bishop Prince Singh. Prayers of thanksgiving and recommitment were offered. Amongst the other guests were the Rt. Revd. Dominic Walker, Bishop of Monmouth in the Church in Wales, Bishop Herbert Donovan, Dr. Mary Donovan, and Ethel Dennis, a former resident at St. Marguerite's Home, who had traveled all the way from Tennessee. Sr. Mary Stephen, CSJB, and Sr. Anne, CSJB, had come from Cuddesdon, UK. And there were other members of Religious Communities, including Br. Robert Hugh, SSF, former Warden of the Community.[4]

During lunch in the great marquee on the front lawn of the convent, there were speeches. Bishop Mark Beckwith spoke of the Community's ministry in the diocese of Newark. Then the Mayor of Mendham, Richard Merkt, presented the Community with a framed "proclamation." Finally, I spoke about my work for CSJB in the UK and plans to research and write the history of CSJB in the USA. There was an exhibit in the cloister of ten large posters of archive photographs showing the Community history from 1874 until 2013. Also, there were special displays of ice sculptures, made by "Jimmy's Creations," one of which showed the convent. On display in the Community Room there were many of the treasured vestments including the famous black cope. Finally, signed copies of the new edition of *A Joyous Service* were on sale in the cloister.

During my two-week stay, Sr. Suzanne Elizabeth took Sr. Linda Clare, Sr. Victoria Michelle, Sr. Monica Clare, and myself on a tour of CSJB sites in New York City. We began at St. Michael's cemetery, Astoria, where the early Sisters lie at rest, and then proceeded to the Cathedral of St. John the Divine, the former St. John Baptist House, now apartments, the former Holy Cross Mission House, also now apartments, then past St. Luke's Chapel and the later St. John Baptist House at 90, Barrow Street. It was a valuable experience to see places where the Sisters had once lived and worked.

On June 6, 2013, Mary Mulholland, tireless worker against substance abuse, passed to her rest. Sr. Barbara Jean wrote a tribute to her in the Fall 2013 Community Notes. "I first got to know Mary when we welcomed 'The Shire,' the first drug treatment center to lease our school building in 1985. The Sisters had stipulated that the new center be devoted to helping teens on the road to recovery. I was invited to serve on the board and met Mary, who was ready to aid this new venture … Several years later, it was clear that 'The Shire' and its successor 'The Steps' were unable to continue here. Mary took the lead in the effort to bring Daytop New York to Mendham. Daytop began here as a very small program and has grown into a successful facility … Without her efforts this might not have happened. During the many years that I served on the Daytop board with Mary, and after her retirement, I learned much from her … She faithfully supported our Community by serving on our Development Board in its early days and offering assistance whenever possible. We are grateful for her encouragement and assistance [and] our prayers go out for her family."

On June 18, 2013, Ellen Kohn-Perry, an Associate and former student at St. John Baptist School in its final years, and Associate Timothy Carr were ordained deacon by Bishop Mark Beckwith at Trinity and St. Philip's Cathedral, Newark. They were to serve at Christ Church, Short Hills, and St. John's, Boonton, respectively.

Commemoration Day took place on June 22, 2013, and was attended by almost 100 people. The celebrant at the Eucharist was the Rt. Revd. Andrew Dietsche, Bishop of New York, and Bishop Donovan preached. Six new Associates were received during the service. Lunch was served on the cloister following the Eucharist.

The joy of Cornerstone Day and Commemoration Day gave way to deep sadness on the death of Sr. Lura Grace on July 14, at age 64. Her health had been failing for some time but it was only at the end of May that advanced cancer was diagnosed. The funeral took place on July 26, attended by over 100 people consisting of Sisters, family, friends, Oblates, Associates and many whom she had befriended in her work amongst the homeless and in the parishes. Bishop Donovan was the celebrant and preacher. Later, her ashes were buried in the convent cemetery. She was the first Sister to be cremated. The Sisters' grief at the loss of a Sister at a comparatively young age and having a wide ministry, especially to the poor and needy, cannot be over-estimated. Her death was the first from the Community since that of Sr. Margaret Helena ten years previously.

During the summer Sr. Victoria Michelle volunteered for two projects with members of the Church of the Messiah in Chester. In July she spent a week in New Dorp, Staten Island, where a team was helping rebuild houses destroyed by Hurricane Sandy. Fifteen houses were restored over the summer months. In August, Sister helped at the Vacation Bible School and worked with young children doing artwork.

Back at the convent, the renovation work on the roof was making real progress. Some of the old tiles were still usable along with new ones made to the same specification. New deep gutters and ice and water shields were being installed, and the stucco on the dormers was being repaired. But the renovation work was not finished: the cemetery walls urgently needed attention, as well as the lych-gate and cemetery altar roofs. This would be a major project rather than patching up. More funding would be needed. During the Fall season, the top portion of the most unstable part of the wall was removed so that it did not fall and damage the memorial stones. The Construction Committee was headed by Oblate Fr. John Negrotto, who was a great help and support to Sr. Linda Clare.

Later in the year Sr. Deborah Francis traveled to Israel with a group from Christ Church, Short Hills, led by Associate the Revd. Robert Morris. They stayed at a kibbutz by the Sea of Galilee and visited all the holy places. She wrote in the Winter 2013/14 Community Notes: "There are so many memories that I will treasure. The most moving part of the pilgrimage was the opportunity to meet so many people who are looking for reconciliation and understanding among Palestinians and Israelis. One almost never hears about such people in the news. So often, one hears only about conflict and bloodshed … All of these persons and organizations seemed to me to be signs of hope in the midst of a seemingly interminable conflict … These are ordinary people doing extraordinary things. Shalom-Salaam-Peace."

On December 14, 2013, Ellen Kohn-Perry was ordained to the priesthood at Christ Church, Short Hills, NJ. She was the second alumna of St. John Baptist School to be ordained, the first being the Revd. Martha Blacklock from the year 1957, who was ordained in 1977. Sr. Barbara Jean preached at Ellen's ordination service.

And so the year 2013 passed into 2014. There had been sadness, but also joy, and the Sisters now looked forward to the new year of ministry and prayer.

On January 2 they had to bid farewell to Jack, their cat, who was 15 years old, but had been ill for some time.[5]

January 12, 2014, saw the arrival at the convent of Sr. Mary Ruth Akuphe from Sr. Jane's Benedictine Sisters of Bethany in Cameroon. She hoped to stay for a year and during that time would learn accounting and business management, as well as learning more about the Religious Life and spreading the word in the parishes about the Good Shepherd Home. She had been in charge of the annex at Batibo where children with special health needs lived.

Despite a cold winter with much snow, Sr. Linda Clare was able to report in the Spring/Summer 2014 Community Notes that the whole of the convent roof had now been completely restored. The leaded glass windows had been repaired and re-leaded, and new gutters, downspouts and underground drainage had been installed. But the renovation project never stopped! In addition to the cemetery walls mentioned above, St. Marguerite's was in dire need of a new boiler and removal of asbestos in the boiler room. And while on the subject of St. Marguerite's, there was a new venture. Oblates Patrice and Douglas McKenzie had converted part of the basement into an apartment at their own expense, where they hoped to live and have a part in the ministry of the Community. A blessing ceremony had taken place. A further piece of renovation work was done by the Revd. Philip Carr-Jones (the Sisters' Wednesday celebrant), who brought a team of volunteers from his parish, the Church of the Holy Spirit, Lebanon, NJ, and between them they tiled the concrete floor in the Lady Chapel. It took several weeks but the finished work would prevent ground water seeping into the low-lying chapel.

Often the question was asked, "What do the Sisters do?" Those who knew them well or whose lives had been touched by them had no need to ask. Even so, the question was asked by new visitors to the convent or St. Marguerite's, or people taking part in fundraising, or those in parishes visited by the Sisters. Sr. Barbara Jean endeavored to answer the question in an article in the Spring/Summer 2014 Community Notes. She began by telling the story of a distressed woman who rang the doorbell late one night, and having nowhere to go, asked for refuge. The Sisters agreed to her staying and after some weeks she was able to return home, having found peace and healing. That was the kind of ministry few people would know about, but Sr. Barbara Jean then described other ministries over the 161 years of the Community in America, some of which had been superseded by more modern examples. She summed it all up by describing the life of prayer which undergirded it all. "It ... provides the bedrock for our ministry of presence." The woman to whom the Sisters had given shelter returned to thank them. She said, "You opened the door when I had nowhere to go. I will always be thankful for your prayers and encouragement." The article was accompanied by photographs of the Sisters' ministry. These included a reunion at Grace Church (Van Vorst), Jersey City, with Sr. Suzanne Elizabeth; Sr. Barbara Jean, Sr. Linda Clare and Sr. Monica Clare with former worker Betty Dormer; Sr. Victoria Michelle, Sr. Mary Ruth and Sr. Mary Lynne at St. Paul's, Morris Plains; and Sr. Eleanor Francis leading hymn singing at the Epiphany party.

The two Sisters were still at St. Mary the Virgin, NYC, and Sr. Deborah Francis was carving out a ministry amongst the homeless. There were always homeless people, mostly men, sleeping in the pews, a place where they felt safe. When the church closed for the night some would sleep on the front steps. Through befriending one man Sister learned how he had lost a good job through illness. She also learned which subway stations were friendly to homeless people, letting them sleep there at night. This particular man managed to find work and then to be able to rent a room. In Sr. Deborah Francis's words, "I miss him. It makes me wonder how many [others] there are on the streets and how much difference a few friendly words and a welcoming community can make … Most people walk by them as if they weren't there. Almost no one talks to them."

On June 10, 2014, Sr. Victoria Michelle made her first vows in the presence of Bishop Prince Singh at a joyous Eucharist in the main chapel. About 100 people were present. Sr. Victoria Michelle was still working at the Church of the Messiah in Chester, where she served on the Altar Guild and Sunday School. Back at the convent, she worked in the sacristy and made jewelry for the Nun Better Shop.

Sr. Suzanne Elizabeth offered the invocation at the Daytop graduation ceremony that year. Twenty-seven students graduated from high school, and others received a diploma from the Joseph H. Hennen Preparatory School at Daytop.

On June 14 Joyce McGirr, an Associate and an alumna of St. John Baptist School, was ordained deacon at Trinity and St. Philip's Cathedral, Newark. Several Sisters were present and Sr. Barbara Jean was a presenter. Joyce was to serve as deacon at the Church of the Atonement, Tenafly, NJ.

The Fall season was a busy time for the Community, welcoming visitors, retreatants and conference delegates. From October 7–10 a conference for members of Religious orders and Christian communities was held at St. Marguerite's. The conductor was the Revd. Barbara Crafton.

October 13–16 saw a reunion of the St. John Baptist School class of '61. They stayed at St. Marguerite's and spent happy hours reminiscing, but also found time to visit Daytop, in the former school building, and St. Mark's, Mendham, where they saw the original school altar. Still on the subject of the school, when the new chapel was built in 1965 a stone altar top, known as a mensa, was provided. After some years when it was kept in storage following the school's closure, Lily Altamura had made it possible for the altar to be erected on the lawn near St. Marguerite's in memory of her late husband, Sam. It was used by groups at the retreat house, but there was no cross. Now in 2014 a limestone cross, carved by Rudy Miller and donated by Leber Funeral Home, was installed.

In November, Sr. Eleanor Francis and Sr. Victoria Michelle visited the English Sisters at Cuddesdon, staying with them at the newly built Harriet Monsell House. They were also able to see the splendid new chapel, dedicated to the memory of Bishop Edward King.[6] They also visited

Sr. Monica, CSJB's oldest Sister, who was living at St. Mary's Convent and nursing home in Chiswick, West London, under the care of the Society of St. Margaret.

Sr. Eleanor Francis had not finished her traveling for 2014, because in December she journeyed to Portland, Oregon, at the invitation of the Revd. Canon Robert Bryant, rector of St. John Baptist Episcopal Church in Portland. The main purpose of the visit was to conduct a Quiet Day, but Sister also preached at the Sunday services and led an adult forum. Whilst there she received Fr. Bryant as an Associate and they both hoped to revive the relationship between CSJB and Portland.

The Very Revd. Lister Tonge, Dean of Monmouth, had reached the end of his five-year term as Community Pastor. On December 3, 2014, Bishop Prince Singh, the Community Visitor, installed Fr. Bernard (Bernie) Poppe as Community Pastor. He had served as rector of St. George's, Maplewood, NJ, for twelve years.

Sr. Mary Ruth returned to Cameroon on December 11, 2014, but soon afterwards left the Community, having no vocation. But the Community in Cameroon continued to slowly grow and by the end of 2014 there were six Sisters at various stages in their formation as Religious. Sr. Jane had sent news that the Roberto Revere Clinic, named for a departed supporter, was almost completed. A small bathroom had been installed and more furnishings and equipment were needed to complete the project.

It was with a sense of deep shock and sorrow that the sudden death on December 13, 2014, of Fr. John Negrotto was announced. He had served in both the Diocese of New Jersey and Newark, and had been Rector of Holy Trinity Church, Hillsdale, NJ, for 27 years. In 2008 he became an Associate of CSJB and an Oblate in 2010. Also he had served on the Capital Campaign Committee and on the Construction Committee. Fr. John had been hoping to begin a new ministry as Chaplain to Daytop.

The Community entered the New Year of 2015 in the customary way with the Epiphany party, which took place on January 3, preceded by Vespers. Four new Associates were admitted at Vespers: the Revd. Wade Renn and his wife Mary Ann, the Revd. Deacon Barbara Jenson, and the Revd. Shawn Carty, Rector of St. Mark's, Mendham, since 2014. About 50 people attended the Epiphany party.

On February 3, 2015, Sr. Eleanor Francis was elected as Sister Superior for a second five-year term. She was re-installed on Wednesday, February 11, by Bishop Prince Singh, the Community Visitor, assisted by the

Community Pastor, the Revd. Bernie Poppe. Sr. Deborah Francis was appointed Assistant Superior while still working in New York, and Sr. Barbara Jean continued as Novice Director.

On March 7, the Revd. Deacon Barbara Harriman was received as an Oblate of the Community. She had known about CSJB for many years, having met Sr. Suzanne Elizabeth at a mission in West Milford. This brought the number of Oblates up to nineteen.

On April 4, 2015, Shirley Grier died. She was the wife of the late Bill Grier, Jr., who had died a few years previously. They had been Associates since 1985 and, as noted earlier, he had been caretaker of the convent and grounds for 50 years from 1945–95. They were members of St. Luke's Episcopal Church in Gladstone. Shirley had driven the school bus for many years and later in life became recreation director for Holly Manor nursing home, Mendham.

Sr. Monica Clare was using her skills to restore the many historic archive photographs of the Community, and had discovered many that had lain forgotten for decades. Amongst these was a series depicting the construction of the convent, which was of particular interest in this centennial year of the Sisters' moving into the still-to-be-completed building in 1915. She also discovered the original plans for the convent, which gave valuable insights into how the various rooms had changed use over the past 100 years; and Sr. Linda Clare discovered many photographs of the interior of the convent from that time.

On March 20 Sr. Suzanne Elizabeth welcomed the Second Province II Altar Guild workshop. The theme was "Care and Restoration of Soul and Vestments." Some participants arrived a day early in order to avoid the snow which fell all night, but it did not deter others from arriving next day—30 in all. It was not simply a practical session but also prayerful, the participants having been given a booklet of prayers prepared by Sister and used to begin and end each part of the day, thus providing a pattern for prayer at home. Many said this was the highlight of their day. Sr. Suzanne Elizabeth was assisted by Carol Homer, who demonstrated how vestments and frontals are made. A tour of the sacristy to see articles used for Benediction of the Blessed Sacrament and home Communions, and then a visit to the Church Workroom to see the historic copes, completed the day.

Sr. Mary Lynne made her annual visit to Cameroon from April until June, and was able to report that the work was going well. The medical clinic was being furnished and Sr. Jane was asking for donations for medical supplies. Funds had been set aside for salaries for a nurse and nursing assistants. Some of the older children would be graduating from school, and while a few would go into higher education, others would work on the farm to help provide food for the growing numbers of children.

On April 27, 2015, a new fundraising event took place—the Nun Better Golf Outing. This was the idea of Sr. Pamela, and she was assisted by Sheila Mulholland (daughter of the late Mary Mulholland), and aided by a Committee. It took place at the Spring Brook Country Club near Morristown, and fortunately the weather was kind. Forty-seven golfers played and many more sent sponsorships. Lynn Wilder Mullin spent many hours gift wrapping the raffle prizes, which were all donated, Sr. Pamela having toured shops and other businesses. The day was deemed a great success and all profits went to the Capital Campaign.

The approach to St. Marguerite's had been resurfaced with pavers donated by families and friends, bearing the names of their departed loved ones. The project had taken longer than had been hoped for, but now in springtime 2015 they were installed, and all were pleased with them. More work needed to be done at St. Marguerite's including the installation of a new boiler, the repainting of the window frames and replacement of woodwork.

On May 26, 2015, Bishop Prince Singh received the first vows of Sr. Monica Clare. The service was attended by members of her family and other friends. During the service she received the silver profession Cross, cincture and veil of a professed Sister. She had been serving at All Saints', Millington, as well as managing the CSJB Facebook page.

Commemoration Day came round again on June 20, with a good number of people attending the Eucharist and staying for lunch. Bishop Mark Beckwith preached at the Eucharist and had a special message for the Sisters. "Through the history of this Community there has been a pairing of prayer and mission: for women in distress, girls in school, kids daring to live in recovery at Daytop, orphans in Cameroon, and seekers from northern New Jersey and beyond. Your prayer has been deep, consistent and honest. You know about illusion, distraction and disappointment. You have chosen—over and over again, to go out rather than stay in, to pair prayer and mission … That is why there are over 400 plus Associates … We are grateful for your commitment and witness. Thank you and God bless you." As was the custom, at the end of the Eucharist there were reports on the Community's ministry, including updates on Daytop, the work in Cameroon, the Capital Campaign and a summary of each Sister's ministry. Five new Associates were received, including the Revd. Bernie Poppe and Christine Brodeur MacClellan. Then everyone processed to St. Marguerite's, where Bishop Beckwith blessed the memorial pavers.

The 78th General Convention of the Episcopal Church met at Salt Lake City from June 25 through July 3, 2015, attended by up to 10,000 people! Sr. Eleanor Francis and Sr. Suzanne Elizabeth were there too but with different roles. Sr. Eleanor Francis assisted at the booth for Religious Orders and Sr. Suzanne Elizabeth had her usual ministry with the National Altar Guild Association, which included setting up the altar and Communion stations for the daily Eucharist. Also Sister gave an interview to a radio station on the ministry of altar guilds, which she later described as "a wonderful experience."[7] The highlight of the Convention was the election of the Rt. Revd. Michael Curry as the new Presiding Bishop.

The Community was ever seeking and praying for more vocations, hence the Search Program, held twice a year. A new approach was being pioneered by some English Communities as well as a Community in Toronto. This was the Alongsider program, where a person interested in the Religious Life might live alongside a Community, sharing their life and work for an extended period, at the end of which they would either be admitted to the novitiate or leave to resume secular life. Sr. Eleanor Francis was enthusiastic about the idea and a brochure was prepared inviting interested people to come to Mendham.

The idea of Alongsiders was not the only innovation in the Religious Life at this time. New forms of monasticism were being lived, and in mid-July Sr. Barbara Jean and Sr. Suzanne Elizabeth traveled to Arkansas to visit Little Portion Hermitage in Berryville. They had previously read *The Universal Monk*, written by the founder, John Michael Talbot. The two Sisters met the founder and members of the Community, and shared in their life of worship, prayer, work, and fellowship. "We found this meeting very helpful, as we begin a new program in CSJB with 'Alongsiders.'"[8]

Back at the convent, Sr. Deborah Francis had returned from St. Mary the Virgin, New York, in August, and Sr. Monica Clare replaced her on September 10, 2015. She would continue the ministry to the homeless which Sr. Deborah Francis held dear, and was collecting knitted scarves for them. Over the coming months she, together with one of the parishioners, would expand this work. St. Mary's now had a clothes closet stocked with items donated from other local parishes. The church had connected up with the Breaking Ground Initiative, which had a ministry to the homeless in Times Square. Sr. Monica Clare was now able to put homeless people in touch with soup kitchens, shelters and mental health facilities. Meanwhile, Sr. Laura Katharine continued her ministry as sacristan and also cataloged the many antique vestments, some of which were too fragile to use but needed careful conservation. The great advantage for the Sisters was that the Daily Office of Morning Prayer, Noonday Prayer, Evening Prayer or Evensong, and Compline was celebrated at St. Mary's. In addition, Mass followed Morning Prayer and Noonday Prayer. On major feast days the Mass was sung; and on Sundays, Benediction of the Blessed Sacrament followed Evensong. The Sisters also had their own times for private prayer.

Celtic Journeys led by Sr. Margo Elizabeth were still going well, thanks to her organizing skills and support from Margaret Johnson. The usual journey to Ireland had taken place in May, followed in September by a journey to the West of England. Bookings were ongoing from one year to the next, proof, if any was needed, of the popularity of those journeys. In between, Sr. Margo Elizabeth was responsible for taking the bookings for St. Marguerite's and the convent guest house.

Sr. Eleanor Francis was honored with an invitation to offer a prayer in the Chapel of the United Nations on the International Day of Peace on September 21. She was there as the representative for Christianity of the United Religions Initiative which supports peace and understanding between nations and religions.

As well as the proposed Alongsider program, Oblates and Associates were still a valued part of the Community's extended family. On November 14, 2015, Catherine (Cathy) Harris was received as an Oblate at Noonday Prayer, having been an Associate since June 2011. Another friend of the Community, John Van Dine, was ordained to the vocational diaconate at St. John's Church, Dover, on December 12, 2015, by Bishop Mark Beckwith. He had served there as a Vestry member, Warden and Eucharistic minister, and had been an Associate of CSJB since 2008 and an Oblate since 2009.

In Cameroon, Sr. Jane had several postulants and a house had been opened in Kuflu where they would receive their training in the Religious Life. Local people had given them a warm welcome. Back at the Good Shepherd Home, all was well and the children were rejoicing that a group of supporters had delivered a large consignment of oatmeal, an important part of their diet. No child was ever put up for adoption, and no child was ever turned away. They were fed, clothed, given safe shelter, and educated in a loving family environment. Their motto was "May we all be one."

St. Mary the Virgin, NYC, was celebrating its 120th anniversary on its present site, and Sr. Monica Clare was able to design literature for the church's Capital Campaign, which was launched on December 8, the Feast of the Conception of the Blessed Virgin Mary. The Rt. Revd. Frank Griswold, former Presiding Bishop, celebrated the Mass and was assisted by the Rt. Revd. Allen Shin, Suffragan Bishop of the Diocese of New York.

Advent and Christmas came round in their familiar pattern. On December 23, several of the young people from Daytop came to the convent to help decorate the Christmas tree, an event which was enjoyed by all. On Christmas Day, the Sisters were joined for dinner by several Associates and other friends.

As the new year, 2016, dawned, the Sisters welcomed guests to the Epiphany Party on January 3. This started with Vespers, and three Associates were received—Ellen Bateman, who had attended a Search Program, and Louis and Carol Berry from All Saints', Millington, where Sr. Monica Clare had ministered before transferring to New York. Several Sisters attended the annual Convention of the Diocese of Newark, which met from January 29–30. Soon it was Chapter Week, and Pastor Fred Shilling from the Lutheran Church attended from February 17–19 to help facilitate the discussions.

At the convent, in addition to work at St. Marguerite's, the Sisters continued their efforts to put the buildings in good order. In addition to the cemetery walls, the replacement of gutters and downspouts on the main chapel and improving the underground drainage system were top priorities. Water ingress was cracking the external buttresses, and inside the chapel, rising damp was damaging the walls. Also, when the pitched roof had been built on the main chapel, the supporting walls had not been sufficiently reinforced. Now, over 40 years later, urgent work needed to be done to avert a disaster. A grant for all the work had been applied for from the Morris County Historic Trust.

On March 6, 2016, the Newark Boys' Apprentice Choir gave a concert in the main chapel which was followed by a meal in the refectory. Sr. Pamela organized it in aid of the Capital Campaign. But life at the convent was by no means all fundraising and activity. The aim of the renovation project was to put the buildings in good order so that they would be available to all who came to seek God, to find peace and to deepen their spiritual lives, as well as providing a safe and secure home for the Sisters. And the Sisters could not do this renovation work if their own lives were not undergirded by prayer, the Rule and the sacraments. In this way, they were spiritually empowered to face the challenges of a hundred-year-old building, and to be a welcoming presence for all who came to the convent and to St. Marguerite's.

Sr. Anne, CSJB, visited Mendham from the UK in May 2016 and was able to visit St. Mark's, Mendham, the Church of the Messiah in Chester, and the Church of St. Mary the Virgin, NYC. While in New York she went to East 17th Street to see the original Mother House, now apartments. The other important event was the second Nun Better Golf Outing on May 2, organized by Sr. Pamela with help from others. A misty, drizzly day did not deter the team of Sisters and volunteer helpers as they arrived at Spring Brook Country Club early in the morning. By 1:00pm tee-off the rain had stopped, and all the players had completed the round before the reception and dinner for 70 people. All money raised was for the repair work on the main chapel, which was estimated at $81,000 for the roof and $134,550 for the other work.

Commemoration Day was held on Saturday, June 25, and I was honored to preach at the Eucharist. The celebrant was the Community Pastor, the Revd. Bernie Poppe, and the guest of honor was Bishop Mark Beckwith, who was received as an Associate along with several others. About 110 people attended the Eucharist, followed by lunch on the cloister.

After Commemoration Day, the Sisters took their summer vacations, but out in the parishes Vacation Bible Schools were held. Sr. Victoria Michelle assisted with the Bible School at the Church of the Messiah in Chester and then joined a group of volunteers from the church to assist at a similar Bible School at the Church of the Good Shepherd in Ringwood, NJ. The Revd. Margaret Otterburn from Messiah and the Revd. Stephen Rozelle of Good Shepherd (both Associates) led the week-long program. About 50 children and teenagers from the Ramapough Lenape Nation of Native Americans attended, and the group also had a visit from Bishop Mark Beckwith.

The main event of the Fall season was Monastery in Mendham, held on Sunday October 9. It was the first since May 2007 and took a great deal of planning. Fortunately the Sisters had about 50 helpers who manned [sic] the craft stalls on the cloister, helped with tours and refreshments and hospitality. In this Centennial year of the Sisters moving into the convent it was an important way to celebrate, to share with others—and to raise funds and raise awareness of the ongoing renovation project. St. Marguerite's was open to the visitors too, and the day ended with a concert by the Adelphi Chamber Ensemble in the main chapel. Works by Handel, Bach, Scarlatti and Vivaldi were performed. The goal of $20,000 for the day had been met.

As the year moved towards its ending, the Sisters were able to report in the Fall 2016 Community Notes that generous donations had enabled more work to be done at St. Marguerite's. The chapel had been repainted and the carpet replaced, and carpets had been laid on the central staircase and second-floor hallway. Also, thanks to donations from St. John Baptist School Alumnae, the Carvel Foundation, and private donors, as well as the Golf Outing, work could now go ahead on strengthening the walls supporting the roof of the main chapel. This would cost $81,000 and work would begin in spring 2017.

In Cameroon the work was flourishing. All the children were in school and twelve young adults were attending university. The Good Shepherd Home Advisory Committee at Mendham had decided that sponsors must be found for further education in college or university, as the Home had been founded to support orphans through to secondary school. The Good Shepherd Academy, the brainchild of the Revd. Canon Elizabeth Geitz, had recently been opened as a residential school for sixth- and seventh-grade children. However, the ongoing political unrest in Cameroon brought uncertainty to the short-term future of the Academy.

On December 15, 2016, Bishop Mark Beckwith installed the Rt. Revd. Allen K. Shin, Suffragan Bishop in the Diocese of New York, as Bishop Visitor of the Community in succession to Bishop Prince Singh. During his visit, Bishop Shin was able to meet each Sister and to learn about the life and work of the Community.

As 2016 drew to a close the Sisters took delivery of *Living Stones*, the first of two books chronicling the history of CSJB in the USA since their arrival in 1874 (of which this is the second). The research and writing had taken me since my first visit for Cornerstone Day in 2013, and I had soon realized that it would take more than one volume. *Living Stones* told the story from 1874 until 1939, when the mission and ministry of the Community began to change. I traveled to Mendham in January 2017 for the launching of the book at the Epiphany Party on Sunday January 8.

Sr. Linda Clare was able to report in the Spring 2017 Community Notes that the structural upgrade to the interior buttresses and walls in the roof space over the main chapel had been completed. New rafters had also been installed to support the cross beams. The contractor had finished within the scheduled two-month time-frame, and the cost was less than had been budgeted. This was all very good news and the roof space and chapel were now safe. Alas, there was sad news a few months later when the Morris County Historic Preservation Trust failed to approve the Community's grant request for help with re-shingling the roof of the main chapel and improvements to the gutters and downpipes. This was a real blow and left the Sisters with a shortfall of over $200,000. The reason for the refusal was that the roof was the only part of the convent and retreat house buildings that was less than a hundred years old and therefore did not qualify for a Historic Preservation Trust grant.

The Sisters had a visit over three weeks in April and May 2017 from the Revd. Canon Joseph Ngijoe, former Chaplain to Sr. Jane's Community at the Good Shepherd Home in Cameroon. While at the convent he preached at Trinity and St. Philip's Cathedral in Newark. Meanwhile in Cameroon, there were 100 children in the main orphanage in Bamenda. The farm kept them busy in between school lessons, and also the older children helped care for the very young ones, assisted by hired housemothers. At the annex in Batibo the only source of water was from a stream and there was the risk that it might be polluted. The urgent need, therefore, was for a well to bring pure water to the Home. But it would cost $10,000. The new clinic was now supplied with equipment and medicines but Sr. Jane was looking to appoint a nurse and nursing assistants. Once it was staffed, the clinic would serve the Home at Bamenda and local residents. The Kuflu Mission Hall had been approved by the bishop for use as a church of the Diocese of Cameroon. A priest visited to conduct services for the village people and to give classes to the postulants at the adjoining convent. Two American Sisters from the ecumenical Community of Jesus in Orleans, MA, were helping to guide the postulants in the Religious Life.

Sr. Monica Clare was able to report that the ministry to the homeless at St. Mary the Virgin, NYC, was flourishing. The work was being coordinated with a social work agency called Breaking Ground. A monthly visit from a representative helped the homeless find shelter. Most of those who sought refuge in the church were men with mental health issues and about 90% were military veterans. Sr. Monica Clare also had contacts with Bellevue Hospital for assistance with the mentally ill. Clothing was given to both men and women at St. Mary's and a "Drop In" day was organized for April 28. Soon, there were regular "Drop In" days and volunteers came to help sort the donated clothing. Sr. Laura Katharine had started a project for the sale of used candles. The church had many services and the used candles were mounting up. Sister cleaned them up, trimmed them and sold them by the bagful. It was hugely successful and the money raised paid for repairs to the cabinet doors which housed the altar frontals.

The Third Annual Golf Outing was held on May 8, 2017, at Spring Brook Country Club in Morristown. The weather was kind to the 50 golfers and as usual the proceeds, after expenses, assisted the Community ministries and renovation projects.

Also in May, Sr. Eleanor Francis attended the Vedanta Society's Annual Spiritual Festival in San Francisco. She was invited to give a talk on a woman saint and chose St. Teresa of Avila. The audience numbered 800 people. As a former member of a Vedanta Community in California, Sr. Eleanor Francis maintained a great interest in interfaith dialog and often gave talks on Eastern religions. Later in the summer she served for a week as Episcopal Chaplain at Chautauqua, a cultural center in western New York State. She was able to attend the events and lectures during her time as Chaplain.

On Sunday June 11 Gay Grier, a CSJB Associate, was honored at the Senior Ministries Evensong, an annual event in the Diocese of Newark. Several Sisters attended. Gay had been active at St. Mark's Church, Mendham, since the 1960s, especially with the Altar Guild.

Commemoration Day on June 24, 2017, was a great day as usual with about 100 people attending the Eucharist celebrated by Bishop Allen Shin, assisted by the Revd. Deacon Cathy Brunson. After reports on the Sisters' ministries, lunch was served on the cloister. It was, as always, one of the occasions when the main chapel comes into its own. The altar was dressed and ablaze with candles and flowers, and the chapel contains items which tell the story of CSJB from its earliest days. The memorial boards to departed Sisters, many from Clewer as well as New York and Mendham, surround the walls of the choir; the memorial brass to Sr. Helen Margaret, the American Foundress, brought from Holy Cross Church, NYC, is set in the floor between the choir stalls; the Stations of the Cross, also from Holy Cross Church, surround the walls of the nave, and in the Lady Chapel, on the wall facing the altar, there is the beautiful carved Cross from the screen in the chapel of the original St. John Baptist House, NYC. Two stained glass windows, above the stairs leading from the chapel to the Lady Chapel, one of St. Anne teaching the Blessed Virgin Mary, and another of St. Helena, were brought from the chapel at the summer rest house at Farmingdale after its closure. The main chapel is a treasure house of history, of prayer, of devotion and of faithfulness.

The great event of the Fall season was the profession in life vows of Sr. Victoria Michelle on September 29, 2017, the Feast of St. Michael and All Angels. Her vows were received by Bishop Mark Beckwith in the presence of a congregation of about 130 Sisters, Oblates, Associates and other friends. After making her vows she was received as a full member of the Community by Sr. Eleanor Francis, assisted by Sr. Deborah Francis, Assistant Superior, and the Revd. Diana Wilcox. Amongst those present were Bishop Herbert and Dr. Mary Donovan, and former Community Pastor the Very Revd. Lister Tonge. The Fall 2017 Community Notes said of Sr. Victoria Michelle that "She has brought the faith learned in the Baptist Church of her Youth, and the heart of an evangelist into the Community."

On October 27, 2017, Margaret Price, a CSJB Associate and former English teacher at St. John Baptist School (1969–80), passed to her rest at the age of 93. She had collaborated in writing the history of the school. Her funeral was held at St. Peter's, Morristown, where she had served on the altar guild for many years. Sr. Barbara Jean and former student the Revd. Ellen Kohn-Perry (year of 1980) attended.

On November 11, 2017, the Revd. Peter Savastano, a priest in the Old Catholic Church, was received as an Oblate. He had first met the Sisters through Interweave, which continued to meet regularly at St. Marguerite's and at the convent. A further Interweave Course called "Emergent Spirit" was currently being held in the Chapter room of the convent.

The Sisters were saddened in mid-November when Bob their young cat failed to return early in the morning after staying out all night. The sadness was worsened by the uncertainty of his fate, but the general opinion was that he had fallen prey to a hungry predator in the night. At first he had been a house cat, but eventually began walking outside with Jennie, the convent dog, and the Sisters, and then became more adventurous. Alas, he ventured too far. A new seven-month-old kitten came to live at the convent in the following January which the Sisters named Clara Elizabeth. She was to be strictly a house cat, living with Oblate Janet Thomas in the fourth-floor apartment at the convent.

The year closed with the Sisters appealing for new chairs for St. Michael's Chapel. The fixed monastic seating had served for around fifty years, but it was now thought that chairs and prayer desks would make the space more flexible. The appeal soon brought in the required sum and the new furnishings were installed early in 2018, the fixed seats having been removed.

The 2017 Christmas festivities and hospitality concluded as usual with the Epiphany party on Sunday, January 7, 2018. At Vespers Gina Mercurio-Brown, a divinity student at Drew Theological School, was received as an Associate. About 40 guests attended and Vespers was followed by the usual hymn singing and buffet supper. The winter Search Program followed during Presidents' Weekend, February 16–19, with three searchers attending.

It was a hard winter with a severe storm which the Sisters reckoned had been more destructive in their grounds than Hurricane Sandy. Over 20 trees suffered major damage, some were completely felled and the approach road to the convent was blocked by a large fallen tree. Fortunately, none of them damaged the convent or adjacent buildings, but professional tree arborists had to be engaged in order to make everything safe. It was an unexpected extra expenditure. On a more positive note, work was able to go ahead to replace the shingle roof of the main chapel. The shingles, which are thinner than tiles, had suffered much damage due to bad weather since the 1990s. At the same time, larger gutterings and downspouts were fitted, and it was hoped soon to repair the underground drainage to connect with these. The work on the roof was completed before the summer rains and a contractor was hired to install the underground drainage. But there was always another renovation task ahead. The slate roof at St. Marguerite's was the original one dating from 1908. Regular maintenance work was done but now it needed replacing. Further fundraising would be needed before the work could be done.

There was sad news from Cuddesdon in April 2018. Sr. Elizabeth Jane, who had been living in a care home in Hampshire, passed to her rest on April 11. And Sr. Monica, who had been living at St. Mary's Convent Home, Chiswick, in West London, passed to her rest on April 29.

On May 8, 2018, another Nun Better Golf Outing took place at Spring Brook Country Club in Morristown. Sr. Pamela wrote in the Community Notes for Fall 2018: "We had beautiful weather … The Golf Course and welcome from Spring Brook Country Club was lovely as usual and everyone had a wonderful time."

At the end of May, Sr. Anne, CSJB, and Carol Wotherspoon, UK Associate, visited the convent and were present for Sr. Monica Clare's profession in life vows on June 8. Her vows were received by Bishop Allen Shin, Visitor to the Community, assisted by Sr. Eleanor Francis, Sr. Barbara Jean, the Revd. Diana Wilcox and the Revd. Victoria McGrath. Family members, friends, Oblates and Associates attended the profession service in the main chapel.

Commemoration Day on June 23, 2018, was attended by about 100 people. Bishop Mark Beckwith was the celebrant and preacher for the last time as he was about to retire as Bishop of Newark. Six new Associates were received including Marnie Robinson and Meghan Gibson.

The 79th General Convention of the Episcopal Church met at Austin, TX, from July 5–18, 2018. Sr. Eleanor Francis attended to help with the Religious Life booth, and Sr. Pamela was part of the National Altar Guild.

The winds of change were blowing through the Community in the second half of 2018. In July, the Revd. Shawn Carty, formerly rector of St. Mark's, Mendham, moved with his wife, Jeanne, into the apartment in the basement of St. Marguerite's in order to take up the position of Retreat House Director. Until this time the managing of the retreat house had been undertaken by the Sisters.

The Sisters had also decided that after eleven years at St. Mary the Virgin, NYC, the time had come to withdraw from this ministry. It had never been a branch house in the traditional sense. The two Sisters had returned to the convent on Monday evenings for the Community discussions on Tuesdays, for Chapter meetings and the Community retreat. Now it was time to hand over to others who would continue the work, especially the ministry to the homeless. Two Franciscan Brothers took up the work soon after the Sisters left. There had been calls for the Sisters to work in the Diocese of Newark and this could not be answered while two of them were in New York. Thus it was that Sr. Monica Clare returned to the convent on August 28, 2018, and Sr. Laura Katharine returned on August 30, along with Kookie, the New York cat, who would be a house cat at the convent. During her time at St. Mary the Virgin, NYC, and in addition to her ministry there, Sr. Monica Clare had completed a course in spiritual direction.

Now once more at full strength, the Sisters accepted a new ministry at All Saints' Church, Millington, where the Revd. Victoria McGrath was Rector. This began in September 2018 with Sr. Deborah Francis and Sr. Monica Clare joining the Sunday congregation. Sr. Monica Clare was no stranger to All Saints', having sung in the choir there as a novice before going to New York. In addition to Sunday attendance the two Sisters had a healing prayer ministry, served at the food pantry and ran a "Blessings to go" stall at the rummage sale, where people could request prayers. In addition to this ministry, Sr. Barbara Jean had been at St. Mark's, Mendham, as a supply priest and parish member. During clergy vacancies she did Sunday duty, conducting the parish Eucharist. Also, Sr. Victoria Michelle was still serving at the Church of the Messiah in Chester, where she taught in Sunday School, was an altar guild member and helped with parish projects. Thus at this time in the life if the Community, Sisters had ministries in three parishes.

On September 22 the Revd. Carlye Hughes was consecrated as the 11th Bishop of Newark at the New Jersey Performing Arts Center in Newark. Bishop Carlye was the first woman and the first African American to serve as Bishop of Newark. Sr. Eleanor Francis was one of the presenters and Sr. Suzanne Elizabeth was there with the Diocesan Altar Guild. Several other Sisters attended and two sang in the choir. On November 20, Bishop Carlye visited the convent, where she had lunch and a tour.

In October 2018 Sr. Victoria Michelle and Sr. Monica Clare visited the English Sisters at Ripon College, Cuddesdon, near Oxford, staying with them at Harriet Monsell House. On October 18 they attended the launch at Lambeth Palace of the second phase of the "Clewer Initiative," a project funded by the UK Sisters to help fight modern-day trafficking and slavery. They visited the House of Lords, where they had lunch with the Rt. Revd. Alistair Redfern, the Church of England's lead bishop in the campaign against modern slavery. At a presentation at Cuddesdon by the Revd. Rachel Carnegie from the Anglican Alliance, the two Sisters learned how the Alliance is attempting to stop human slavery throughout the world. Finally, they visited a drop-in center for sex workers in Bristol, called One25. This was followed by a visit to Mariquita House, named after Mariquita Tennant, who started the rescue work in the parish of Clewer in 1849.[9] Mariquita House was bought by the English Sisters as a safe house for former trafficking victims. Their visit gave the two Sisters much food for thought, and they returned home to Mendham hoping that similar work could be started in the USA. They wrote in the Winter 2018 Community Notes: "It is so inspiring to see these works being supported by the English Community in the spirit of Mariquita Tennant and of our Mother Foundress Harriet Monsell, who sought all her life to give women strength, dignity and hope." In this way the original rescue work of the Sisters at Clewer had come full circle in these last years of their ministry. The sadness was that 166 years later women and girls were still being led into prostitution, and both women and men were being trafficked into human slavery, not only in the developing World but also in the UK in plain sight.

The Fall 2018 Community Notes reported the deaths of several Associates and friends with many years' service to the Community. The Revd. Henry Folsom, a sixth cousin of Sr. Helen Margaret Folsom, the American Foundress, died on May 8. In recent years the Sisters had been in touch with him and he had visited them at the convent. On June 30, 2018, Gloria Spencer Crowson passed away at the age of 87. She had graduated from St. Helen's Hall in 1949 and had been a student there when it was still being run by CSJB. She became a registered nurse and the mother of five children. In 1964 she became an Associate and served on several diocesan and national organizations. She kept in touch with the Sisters and made visits from time to time. Dorothy (Dottie) Gruber died on July 10, and had been an Associate since 1979 along with her friend Gerrie Dressler. Both had served as volunteers at the convent. On July 21, Muriel Unwin died at the age of 92. She had been an Associate since 1974 when she lived in Summit, NJ. Together with her friend Jean Hoppin she had helped the Sisters at Grace Church (Van Vorst), Jersey City, and had helped save St. Christopher's House, where the Sisters lived. Betty Dormer died on July 23 at the age of 99. A former St. Anna's girl, she had served the Community for over 60 years as an employee and as an Associate. The Revd. Charles Rice, former Community Pastor died on October 8, at age 81.

On December 6, 2018, the Revd. John Beddingfield was installed as Community Pastor in succession to the Revd. Bernie Poppe, who had left New Jersey for a new parish. Fr. Beddingfield was Rector of the Church of the Holy Trinity, NYC,[10] and had worked with the Sisters at the Church of St. Mary the Virgin, NYC. A former Presbyterian minister, he was ordained in the Episcopal Church in 2003, and was also a member of the Franciscan Third Order.

The Winter 2018 Community Notes had news of the Good Shepherd Home and related work. "The Good Shepherd Home in Cameroon is doing well. Although there has been a civil conflict in the English-speaking provinces, the Home has not been involved. The greatest challenge has been education for the children, since the schools are closed. During this period, the younger children have received instruction in reading, writing and arithmetic from older children and friends of the Sisters on an informal basis … Some of the children have been taken to Yaoundé for schooling since there is no fighting there. Sr. Jane reported recently that an effort is being made to restore peace." Meanwhile Sr. Mary Lynne was advised by Sr. Jane not to visit Cameroon due to the civil unrest.

Christmas 2018 came and there were twenty at dinner, consisting of Sisters, Oblates, Associates and friends. Next day, the Sisters welcomed Nancy Monk on an overnight visit. She was the great-niece of William Cordingley, architect of the convent.[11]

The first event of 2019 was the Epiphany Party on the Feast of the Epiphany, Sunday January 6, and about 40 Associates and friends gathered for what was a Community tradition. Two new Associates were received at Vespers. Earlier that day the Sisters had celebrated the festival with a Choral Mass.

On January 21, 2019, another old friend of the Sisters passed to his eternal rest. The Very Revd. Ledlie Laughlin died at the age of 88. He had been an Associate since 1960, but his links with the Community went back to the 1950s, when he had worked with the Sisters at Grace Church (Van Vorst) in Jersey City. He became Dean of Trinity Cathedral, Newark, from 1963 until 1969. This was followed by ministry at St. Luke's in the Fields, NYC. The years of his active ministry coincided with the civil rights movement, which he supported, and later he supported the LGBT community.

St. John Baptist School alumnae continued to keep in touch with the Sisters and one another. There was usually an alumnae picnic around St. John Baptist-tide. The Revd. Ellen Kohn-Perry had recently become a member of the St. John Baptist School Corporation Board, which manages the accounts and awards education grants to young women.

The Spring 2019 Community Notes had short profiles of the Sisters and their varied ministries, most of which have been the substance of this book. But one of those ministries may not be quite so obvious. Regular visitors to the convent chapel would be familiar with the Plainchant settings to the Daily Office and Choral Eucharist. These settings were the work of Sr. Pamela, formerly a professional musician, who, since her arrival from Clewer in 1999, had arranged the psalms and canticles of the Book of Common Prayer of the Episcopal Church for Plainchant singing.

Sr. Margo Elizabeth was well known for her popular Celtic Journeys, and during 2019 she had introduced a new journey—a retreat in February to the holy island of Lindisfarne, off the Northumberland coast, UK. And another ministry undertaken by many of the Sisters was spiritual direction.

Groups and individuals who came to the retreat house and convent continued to be many and varied—too many to enumerate. But two events stand out. A group from St. Thomas' Church, Mamaroneck, met at St. Marguerite's from March 15–17, 2019. The Sisters had worked at St. Michael's Home, Mamaroneck, next to St Thomas' Church, from 1887 until 1938.[12] In October the Women's Group from Trinity Lutheran Church, Manasquan, NJ, came to St. Marguerite's. Many years previously, the Sisters had owned a holiday house at Manasquan.

On March 22, 2019, Sr. Pamela and Sr. Monica Clare attended the tribute to Women's Service Award annual luncheon. Sheila Mulholland, daughter of the late Mary Mulholland, and a friend of the Community, was an honoree.

Sr. Eleanor Francis continued her interest in interfaith matters, and at the end of March Rabbi Deb Smith and her husband, Neil, a Cantor, gave a program for the Sisters on Judaism. They brought a Torah for the Sisters to see. On April 1, Sr. Eleanor Francis and Sr. Barbara Jean attended the 19th annual Jewish Film Festival, sponsored by St. Elizabeth College, near Morristown. The film and the discussion that followed it were about the Holocaust. This was of particular interest to Sr. Eleanor Francis, whose Jewish mother and grandmother were Holocaust survivors.

The political situation in Cameroon was causing concern to the Sisters. The uprising was in the western part of the country where Bamenda is situated, but the orphanage had not so far been disturbed. The houses at Batibo and Kuflu were closed for the time being and the children were mostly in Bamenda, though some were in Yaoundé, the capital, with two of the postulants. Some families displaced by the uprising were also at

Bamenda, Sr. Jane having giving them refuge. Although education was now intermittent, there was enough food as the Sisters and children were able to run the farm.[13]

April brought Holy Week and Easter, and as usual the Sisters celebrated the Easter Vigil and First Mass of Easter at 6:00am. The new fire was lit on the cloister, and Easter candles lit from it. Then Sisters and guests walked in procession to St. Michael's Chapel for the Mass. Later, Sisters, residents, Oblates, Associates and friends, numbering 23 in all, had Easter dinner. On April 25, still in the Octave of Easter, Sr. Deborah Francis celebrated the 25th anniversary of her profession in life vows.

A month later, on May 26, 2019, Sr. Suzanne Elizabeth celebrated the 50th anniversary of her profession in life vows. The Weekly Letter to the Sisters for May 31–June 14 described the celebrations as "a glorious occasion." Forty-five people squeezed into St. Michael's Chapel for the Eucharist, which was celebrated by Bishop Allen Shin. The preacher was the Revd. John Beddingfield, Community Pastor, and the Revd. Deacon Barbara Harriman was the liturgical deacon. Friends spanning Sr. Suzanne Elizabeth's life were present, ranging from nursing friends, clergy, former members of the Community, and friends from the many Altar Guilds which she had helped and guided. The Eucharist was followed by a reception in the refectory, the centerpiece of which was a large cake, shared by all.

St. Mark's, Mendham, had a new Rector, the Revd. Lorna Erixson. Although she was the first female Rector at the church, the congregation was accustomed to having a woman celebrant, Sr. Barbara Jean having been the interim minister since the Revd. Shawn Carty left. And indeed Sr. Barbara Jean was a well-known and well-loved Sunday School teacher and member of the congregation. With the advent of the new Rector at St. Mark's, Sr. Barbara Jean began attending St. John's Church, Dover, NJ. On May 30, the Revd. Lorna Erixson came to the convent to meet the Sisters, staying for noon-day Office and lunch.

Over the decades the Sisters had cared for many pets—mainly dogs and cats. They were mourned when they died and in due course replaced by new ones to love and care for. But Pony, despite frail health which required a special diet, seemed to go on forever. On June 11, 2019, Pony's life came to an end, much to the distress of the Sisters, especially Sr. Margo Elizabeth, who had been his principal care giver. His exact age was uncertain but likely to have been between 30 and 35 years. He had been at the convent for over 25 years, grazing contentedly in his paddock, except for the odd occasion when the grass on the front lawn or at Daytop seemed greener!

The Community Notes always had news of St. John Baptist School alumnae. One of the oldest of them, Katherine (Kit) King Rockwell from the class of 1941, had just published a book of prayers and meditations called *Love Letters to Jesus*. Though she was over 90 years old, she still attended Oblate meetings when possible.

From time to time, descendants of girls who had lived in homes run by the Sisters in past times came to visit. On June 19, 2019, the Sisters received a visit from the descendants of Anna Loretta Wagner, who had lived at St. Anna's from 1917 until 1920. These were Anna Loretta's daughter and two granddaughters. Anna Loretta's sisters Esther and Ethel had also been in the care of the Sisters at the same time.[14] The three visitors were given a tour of the convent and St. Marguerite's by Sr. Monica Clare and Sr. Linda Clare. Also they were shown photographs from the early 20th century.

Commemoration Day, June 22, 2019, was a glorious day with perfect weather. The celebrant and preacher was the Rt. Revd. Robert Ihloff, former Bishop of Maryland and presently Assisting Bishop in Virginia. Four new Associates were received, including Sheila Mulholland, friend and supporter of Daytop. About 100 people attended the Eucharist and stayed for lunch on the cloister.

Sr. Victoria Michelle had a new ministry helping the homeless at the Morristown Homeless Solutions. She attended twice a month, when the Church of the Messiah, Chester, and Grace Lutheran Church, Mendham, had their days. About 30 homeless people are housed and fed for about three months, until permanent housing can be found for them.

On March 27, 2019, Doris Thompson Myers died at age 85 in Denton, TX. She was the widow of Fr. Thompson, at one time Chaplain to the Sisters. After his death she married again and became an expert in the life and work of C. S. Lewis.

A long-term Associate, Bill Hermann, died on July 13 at 91 years of age. His last visit to the convent had been on Easter Sunday. Sr. Suzanne Elizabeth and Sr. Barbara Jean attended his funeral on September 19. A memorial service was held at the convent in September, after which his ashes were buried in the Associates' area of the convent cemetery.

On September 7, 2019, Oblate Peter Savastano was ordained to the priesthood in the Episcopal Church, having previously been a priest in the Old Catholic Church. Bishop Carlye Hughes officiated at the ordination and was also both celebrant and preacher. The service was held at Christ Church, Short Hills, NJ, where he had served as deacon. Sr. Eleanor Francis, Sr. Barbara Jean, Sr. Pamela, Sr. Monica Clare, Sr. Linda Clare, and myself attended the service and the reception afterwards.

The Society of St. Francis celebrated the centennial of its founding in the USA on September 14. The Eucharist took place at the Church of St. Luke's in the Fields, where the preacher was the Presiding Bishop, the Most Revd. Michael Curry. Sr. Monica Clare, Sr. Pamela, and Sr. Eleanor Francis attended the service, which also included a life profession.

On September 30, Sr. Eleanor Francis, Sr. Deborah Francis, and Sr. Monica Clare attended the Rosh Hashanah services at the Jewish Renewal Congregation Or Ha Lev at the Presbyterian church in Parsippany, as guests of Rabbi Debra Smith and her husband Dr. Neal Smith. In addition to sharing friendship with Rabbi Debra Smith, Sr. Eleanor Francis had also been working with Dr. Shabiha Sheik, who co-leads with Rabbi Debra a Jewish–Muslim Sisterhood that works to build relationships with women of the two faiths.

On October 4, the feast of St. Francis of Assisi, the Sisters held the annual blessing of the animals living at the convent, and those of friends (minus the convent cats, who were strictly house cats). A small memorial stone in memory of Pony was blessed and placed in his paddock. It had a picture of a pony and the inscription "PONY" June 11, 2019.

October 21 saw Sr. Monica Clare meeting a film crew from "State of Grace," a website news show, and being interviewed about gender and religion. Next day through October 27 she was on vacation, but on the 24th she hosted a forum at One Spirit in NYC on how to help the homeless. There were six panelists from various homeless services and 85 people attended.

There was some more sad news from Cuddesdon. On December 12, 2019, Sr. Ann Verena passed to her rest at St. Mary's Convent and Nursing Home, Chiswick, in West London. She was the last Sister and Mother Superior of the Companions of Jesus the Good Shepherd, a Community that had moved from Devon to Clewer in 1996, and thence to Begbroke and Cuddesdon. She had also been Community Leader of UK CSJB 2009–14. Sr. Ann Verena and Sr. Jane Olive, CSJB, had moved to Chiswick for extra care in 2018. Her funeral requiem was to be at

Chiswick on December 30. There were now just two active CSJB Sisters living at Cuddesdon—Sr. Mary Stephen and Sr. Anne.

There was bad weather at Mendham early in December, including an ice storm which made everywhere look lovely but made walking and driving treacherous. Some bookings at the retreat house had to be canceled. More importantly, the winds of change continued to blow in the Community and its work. A special Chapter was held for changes to the Constitution on November 12.[15] Fortunately, the bad weather did not prevent Bishop Allen Shin, the Community Visitor, from making his visitation from December 2–4. Sr. Eleanor Francis had reached the end of her second, and final, term of office as Sister Superior, and so on December 4, 2019, there was a Chapter of Election. Bishop Shin presided at the Mass of the Holy Spirit, assisted by the Revd. John Beddingfield, the Community Pastor. At the Chapter meeting which followed, Sr. Monica Clare was elected as the new Sister Superior. A week later, on December 11, Bishop Shin installed Sr. Monica Clare as Superior. In the afternoon he installed Sr. Laura Katharine as Assistant Superior and Sr. Pamela as Novice Director and Bursar.

A new manager, Brad Kalos, had been appointed at St. Marguerite's on December 9, to replace the Revd. Shawn Carty, who had resigned.

The year ended with the usual Christmas and Epiphany festivities and hospitality. The Sisters now entered the year 2020, the third decade of the 21st century, in good heart and with the prospect of new beginnings. Sr. Eleanor Francis took time out after leaving office as Superior to learn more about the Holocaust and the experience of her mother and grandmother.

The Revd. Lorna Erixson was the celebrant and preacher at the convent for the Eucharist on the Feast of the Epiphany, January 6, 2020. And on January 11, 2020, Sr. Monica Clare, Sr. Pamela, Sr. Eleanor Francis, Sr. Barbara Jean, and Sr. Linda Clare attended her installation by Bishop Carlye Hughes as Rector of St. Mark's, Mendham. Sr. Eleanor Francis was the preacher. So far, so predictable, but no one at the start of 2020 could have envisaged what challenges the year would bring.

Several years previously, Sr. Barbara Jean had spoken to me about her vision for the future of Religious Communities and said, "We stand on the edge of the future." By March 2020 her words took on a prophetic note because by that time the world was gripped in a pandemic that no one had anticipated, and no one knew how to eradicate. It would profoundly affect all walks of life throughout the world. At Mendham, the Sisters suddenly found themselves having to cancel groups and individuals from coming to the convent and St. Marguerite's.

This was a future no one had dreamed would happen. But the Sisters rose to the challenge. At first they concentrated on their life of prayer and sacrament which they offered for the needs of all in this time of crisis. And then thanks to modern technology they were able to communicate with Oblates, Associates and friends, holding meetings, prayers, services, workshops and all kinds of activity, including the Search Program, through Zoom. They also worked hard on the vegetable garden to help those in need through the local food pantry. And there were two joyous occasions, the first when Sr. Barbara Jean celebrated the 50th anniversary of her life vows on March 31, and the second when Sr. Laura Katharine celebrated her 50th anniversary on September 8. Many activities and ministries have continued via Zoom, email and telephone. It may be said with no exaggeration that even in these uncertain days, the Sisters have throughout the pandemic found new ways of ministry, of sharing and caring for others, and this has led to another Second Spring.

And finally …

February 5, 2024, will mark the 150th anniversary of the first three Sisters from Clewer arriving in New York in 1874. Mother Harriet was still the Superior when those three Sisters made what she called "your venture of faith." She was deeply interested in it and wrote encouraging letters to the Sisters. In 1874 neither she nor Canon Carter could have imagined just how great would be the work of the Sisters in the USA—great and varied. Nor could she have imagined just how many hearts and lives they would touch, how many broken lives they would mend, how many people they would bring to Christ or show His love to them. So it is right that Mother Harriet should have the last word. She wrote: "You have opened your soul to take in the life of God, and now He will lead you on, as and how He will." And that has been a template for the Sisters all down the years. Hurricanes and pandemics have not prevailed over them—and so their story will indeed continue.

[1] In the UK realtors are known as estate agents.

[2] The Rt. Revd. Prince G. Singh was born in Chennai, formerly Madras, in India. He was ordained to the priesthood in the Church of South India in 1990 and served congregations in rural south India. He served as Associate Rector at St. Peter's, Morristown, NJ, 1997–2000, and as Rector of St. Alban's Episcopal Church in Oakland, NJ, from 2000 until his election as eighth Bishop of the Episcopal Diocese of Rochester, NY, in February 2008.

[3] WAVES (Women Accepted for Volunteer Emergency Service) was the women's branch of the United States Naval Reserve during World War II.

[4] I was also present on that great day. Early in January, Sr. Eleanor Francis had emailed me with an invitation to attend the celebrations and be one of the speakers. I was also asked to prepare a booklet on the history of CSJB in America, to be given out on the day. Sr. Barbara Jean sent me some earlier booklets for source material and I duly produced a manuscript. I arrived for a two-week visit a few days before Cornerstone Day and subsequently began researching the Community archives.

[5] I was really sad when I heard of Jack's death. During my first visit in 2013 he would wander down to the Chapter Room where I was working on the archives and would come and sit on my lap—for a while. Then he would go and lie on one of the cushions used by the "centering prayer group."

[6] Edward King (1829–1910) was Principal of Cuddesdon Theological College 1863–73 and Bishop of Lincoln 1885–1910.

[7] Community Notes, Fall 2015.

[8] Ibid.

[9] Mariquita Tennant founded the Clewer House of Mercy in her home near St. Andrew's Church, Clewer, and later relocated to larger premises still within the parish. Ill health forced her to give up the work, which was subsequently re-founded by the Rector, the Revd. T. T. Carter, and Harriet Monsell. Together they founded the Community of St. John Baptist to take over the rescue work. See: BONHAM, Valerie *A Joyous Service* rev. ed. 2012 and *A Place in Life* 1992.

[10] Not to be confused with Trinity, Wall Street.

[11] Nancy Monk brought the Jive Yoga and Meditation Group to St. Marguerite's for a program from June 28–30, 2019.

[12] See BONHAM, Valerie *Living Stones* Chapter 7 and pp.325–326.

[13] On April 1, 2021 (Maundy Thursday), the Sisters at Mendham were shocked to receive news of Sr. Jane's death. For further details, see Appendix Four for Sr. Monica Clare's tribute.

[14] Anna Loretta Wagner, known at St. Anna's as Etta, was admitted on May 15, 1916, at age 15. She was sent there by the Children's Aid Society of Clinton County, Lock Haven, PA. After leaving St. Anna's on September 4, 1920, she went to St. John Baptist School to work as a servant. Her sister Esther Maria Wagner was also sent from the Children's Aid Society, because their mother was unable to look after them. Esther was admitted to St. Marguerite's on March 12, 1917, at age seven years. The Society paid $10 a month to provide clothing. Esther had survived meningitis as a baby but because of her frail health the Sisters were

unable to look after her and she was returned to the Society in August 1917. There is no entry for Ethel at St. Anna's, but there is an entry for Helen or Ellen Margaret Wagner who was admitted on May 5, 1919, at age 18 years. Maybe her name had been changed, a not uncommon occurrence. She was sent by Miss Day from the Children's Guardians, Jersey City. She left St. Anna's on July 14, 1919.

[15] A special Chapter for a second vote for changes in the Constitution was held on January 14, 2020.

APPENDIX 1

CSJB AMERICA (Mothers Superior, later Sisters Superior) during the period covered by this book

M. Alice Ursula, 1942, in succession to M. Florence Teresa

M. Waldine Lucia, 1943

M. Margaret Helena, 1949

M. Elizabeth Anne, 1979

M./Sr. Suzanne Elizabeth, Sister Superior, 1983

Sr. Barbara Jean, 1997

Sr. Eleanor Francis, elected December 15, 2009; installed January 15, 2010

Sr. Eleanor Francis, re-elected February 2015

Sr. Monica Clare, elected December 4, 2019; installed December 11, 2019

MOTHERS SUPERIOR CSJB UK during the period covered by this book

M. Dorothy Frances, July 7, 1939

M. Annys, September 15, 1958

M. Edna Frances, August 10, 1978

M. Jane Olive, August 1992–2004

Leadership team

Sr. Anne, Sr. Mary Stephen, with Sr. Ann Verena, CJGS, 2004–09

Community Leader

Sr. Ann Verena, CJGS, elected Community Leader of CSJB 2009–14

Community Co-ordinator

Sr. Jane Olive, February 2014–18

After 2018 the UK Sisters did not elect a Community Co-ordinator or Leader.

APPENDIX 2

SISTERS WHO HAVE ENTERED INTO REST SINCE 1940

Sr. Adela, d. Nov 16, 1940
Sr. Mary Katharine, d. Sept 28, 1942
Sr. Alice Ursula, d. May 26, 1943
Sr. Elisa Monica, d. Sept 14, 1946
Sr. Florence Teresa, d. Aug 1, 1948
Sr. Marie Elizabeth, d. Nov 10, 1949
Sr. Fanny Helen, d. Jan 31, 1950
Sr. Catherine Vera, d. May 25, 1950
Sr. Virginia Dorothea, d. July 7, 1950
Sr. Alice Madeline, d. Apr 16, 1951
Sr. Ada Marian, d. Dec 4, 1951
Sr. Laura Claire, d. Apr 22, 1952
Sr. Lillian Christine, d. May 6, 1952
Sr. Sara Josephine, d. Aug 19, 1955
Sr. Jeannette Louise, d. June 19, 1959
Sr. Beatrice Clare, d. Dec 16, 1961
Sr. Francina, d. Jan 13, 1962
Sr. Elisabeth Roberta, d. Mar 26, 1962
Sr. Julia Frances, d. May 27, 1965
Sr. Ellen Juliana, d. Jan 29, 1967
Sr. Mildred Eleanor, d. Mar 13, 1967
Sr. Mary Joan, d. Feb 9, 1970
Sr. Mary Barbara, d. Aug 2, 1971
Sr. Agnes Genevieve, d. Dec 8, 1974
Sr. Waldine Lucia, d. Mar 26, 1975
Sr. Eleanor Lucy, d. Dec 17, 1977
Sr. Margaret Raphael, d. Sept 2, 1978
Sr. Winifred Agnes, d. Aug 5, 1980
Sr. Elizabeth Marion, d. Sept 28, 1982
Sr. Agatha Louise, d. Dec 15, 1982
Sr. Elizabeth Anne, d. Sept 12, 1983
Sr. Katharine Veronica, d. Aug 10, 1991
Sr. Susinne Paula, d. Aug 3, 1993
Sr. Margaret Helena, d. Oct 30, 2003
Sr. Lura Grace, d. July 14, 2013

APPENDIX 3

AT THE END of Commemoration Day, June 24, 1966, Sr. Katharine Veronica and Sr. Agnes Genevieve arrived at the reservation of the Navajo Native Americans in Arizona to assist Deaconess Marian Brown (pictured below), who had ministered there for many years. They would stay for six weeks, and this was the second of what would be three visits. The previous year they had visited for two weeks, and in 1967 Sr. Katharine Veronica made her final visit, this time accompanied by Sr. Barbara Jean. The two Sisters were based at the Good Shepherd Mission at Fort Defiance, AZ, very close to the border with New Mexico, and kept in regular contact with Mother Margaret Helena at Mendham. Three letters to Mother, written by Sr. Katharine Veronica in July 1966, have survived and are reproduced here.

Deaconess Marian Brown

July 18, 1966.
Yatehey, Shma—How do you like my Navajo? Translation—A big hello, Mother. We began the Vacation Church Schools in the outstations this morning. The enrolment not so good for various reasons—Head Start programs,[1] migrations to other States for harvesting sugar beets, and no shoes. At Coalmine[2] we had 28—seven in my class. Deaconess Brown

was quite discouraged at Sawmill [Mission]. We averaged one hundred at the Mission.

Last Tuesday we travelled 914 miles to Durango [Colorado] and back. We left Tuesday at 2:00pm, in the heat of the day, but Dss. Brown is on Navajo time. She had an 11 o'clock service at Sawmill—thirteen for lunch, arrived at the Mission 1:30pm—passed the time until 2 o'clock when the Post Office was opened to mail an important letter. We drove to the Sawmill Mission at Farmington. My, what a forlorn place that is!! There are no beautiful red mesas or hills—just barren. We didn't see Fr. Ford but I remembered reading in *The Living Church* about the Revd. Judd Blaine and his family being there. They were, and we had a nice visit. The last time I saw them was in 1957 in Jersey City … Fr. Blaine worked with the Sioux Indians for four years, and is on a sabbatical leave …

After a chat over a cold drink of water, we proceeded to Durango. Dss. Brown was misled over making reservations for the train trip to Silverton [Colorado]. She was told it was not necessary to make reservations on a weekday. It was—so it meant getting up at 4:30am our time to be at the station by 5:00am. It was 6 o'clock their time. It was a case of first come first served for the benefit of cancellations and at 8:15 we received our tickets. It was a most beautiful ride up the mountains, some had snow on the peaks. The train went along the Animas River. I can't do justice to the scenic trip any more than I can paint a sunset. At one point, near the top, the train stopped. It had to produce more steam to reach the summit. I took pictures standing on the platform between the cars … I hope they turn out well … When we descended the Rockies, we drove to Farmington where Dss. Brown looked at trailers. (We have been in and out of trailers with her in various places. She plans to buy one to live in on the Mission grounds). Then we had some food and drove home—quite a jaunt.

The food has not been so good this summer and my stomach has been in perpetual turmoil—unusual for me. Sunday we did have roast beef and I perked up and got my second wind. Mrs. Blaine came with four Navajo girls from Shiprock for the service and stayed for dinner and Squaw dance. (You know she is the Revd. Young's daughter of NH [New Hampshire]. Sr. Mary Joan knows her from Manchester.)

Last Monday Dss. Brown conducted a burial service in the Church yard for a newborn baby, a Caesarian who lived only 50 minutes. Only the great grandparents and a great uncle were present. The father was at Prescott [AZ] on a job—probably didn't know about the baby's birth and death. Before the service we made some home visits in the neighborhood. What shacks! We found two women weaving rugs, the only beautiful thing in their rooms.

On Friday (July 8th) the evening after we returned to the Mission from Gallup with Dss. Brown we heard that there was a Sing and Squaw dance at Black Rock—so we went. What a sight! Navajos coming—a few mothers came. Many mothers have to work because the fathers are drunk most of the time.

Sunday, July 10th. The Stinsons left for Sewanee [Tennessee]. They were so happy on Saturday when the furniture arrived—6:45am. They worked like beavers all day, unpacking and arranging the furniture, retiring quite late. When I was up at 12 o'clock, I could see Mrs. S. placing garments in a trunk. As they drove out of the entrance at 9:40am (Sunday), Bishop Reed and family from Bogota, Columbia, drove in ... The Bishop came for the 10 o'clock service. In the afternoon, Dss. Brown took us to Old Oraibi[3] where we heard there was to be a Hopi dance. Some of the children were selling piki, the tissue thin bread made from red or yellow or blue corn. We bought some blue. The corn is finely ground and baked on a hot rock and rolled into bundles like papyrus ... We were too late for supper at the Mission so we bought some food at a grocery store in Window Rock and had a picnic under the Window.

A week ago on Friday night and Saturday we had two lovely Danish girls, one 21 and the other 20 years. They had spent a year in California and were returning to Denmark. One was interested in anthropology and was advised to visit Navajoland. Mr. Humphrey (the friend of the Stinsons, who is here for a year on volunteer basis), drove them to Gallup on Saturday morning to get a bus to Albuquerque—then another to cross the USA to NYC—then a ship.

What endurance Dss. Brown has! The day before the last day of the Vacation Church School she took groups of children home, then a teachers' meeting, [and] home visits in the wilderness, [then] home where she filled out 23 certificates for her children. She retired at 12 o'clock. She remarked one day how well Sr. Agnes Genevieve and I did—plunging in a VCS without an opportunity to adjust to the altitude. They say anything you do in this altitude takes three times as much energy as in any other place. That is probably what makes you feel so exhausted and hungry. Last week, after the Silverton trip, I made visits with her around Blue Canyon. It takes about two hours to make one because of the distance from the main road, and only a trail to travel over. In most places we had to get out and open hand made gates to get into the private lanes. I saw the place where I will teach the first week in August. It will be under some piñon trees. If it rains, we will have to make a beeline to the 2 by 4 shack where Ruby Mitchell lives. She is a dear old woman—no teeth—no English—hobbles on a cane. She lives two miles from the main road— beautiful wild flowers around her poor little hut. Oh—if you could see how some of these people live—far worse than any slum neighborhood in a big city. I can't begin to describe the poverty.

Last Saturday Fr. Davis took us to the Acoma Sky City[4] ... We had a private tour of this ancient pueblo village, high on a Mesa—most interesting, near Albuquerque. The church was built in 1629. Then to the Laguna Reserve which is adjacent—an old church there too. Fr. Davis mentioned one time that he might like to be an Associate. He had intercession for vocations for us at a Mass.

The young people this year are not on good lines—too much pairing off—misbehaving badly on the Grand Canyon trip, and lack of responsibility and interest in the Navajos. At the last staff meeting (they do not come) they talked about the possibility of not having young people another year.

Mrs. Stinson told us that they are thinking of adopting an Indian baby girl. Tomorrow morning I will go to Mass at Coalmine. Fr. Davis with some others will drive over. We will have breakfast there and I will stay on for the Vacation Church School.

It has been very hot here. It is so dry, I do not know where the humidity comes from. However, I perspire and feel the heat. It was lovely last year. Fr. Davis told us that the sheep at Black Mountain are dying from the heat. I know that New Jersey and New York must be worse, but it truly has been bad here. I feel as tho' I were burning up in the middle of the afternoon.

This brings much love from your loving child,
Katharine Veronica, Sister, CSJB
P.S. My class at Coalmine is up to 19. 55 children in VCS there.

July 22, 1966, at The Episcopal Mission
Dearest Mother,

What a missionary I am! I came out here to help the Indians and they waited upon me. During the time I was writing my last letter to you (July 18th), I was very nauseated, but thought it would pass away during my slumber. That was wishful thinking … You know the story of my admittance to the Presbyterian Mission Hospital.[5] They were just wonderful to me. The doctor from Buffalo, NY, was very nice. He said that it doesn't take long for one to become dehydrated out here … One of the young nurses is from Oregon City, another from Rochester, NY, also a Seneca Indian, and [another] Indian from Wyoming. The Navajo patients and visitors can't understand why they can't speak Navajo to them (they look like Navajos). There were Navajo nurses' aides—all very nice. Three young, smiling girls came in [on] Wednesday to bring some lovely cultivated flowers … I was in the Isolation Unit with children with diarrhea, pneumonia, measles etc. Yesterday, I recovered from the nausea (I had a "shot" for that). The Superintending Nurse of the Hospital is lovely. She came to see me. I am going to write her a little note of appreciation. The Blue Shield and Cross covered everything. I had an X-Ray of chest, blood analysis etc. All the starch is out of me right now. I asked about returning to the Good Shepherd Mission. They didn't seem eager in getting rid of me but the doctor agreed and said I needed to get my strength back and force fluids. The office clerks could not reach our Mission—some damage due to the storm the previous night. However, a nurse from the Government Hospital in Fort Defiance was there and she offered to drive me here. I do not know how she knew of my being stranded. She has been here only a short time from Riverside, California. So I rode back in a bright red Valiant, invited her to come to our Church service sometime. (She is a Presbyterian too.)

Last night Dss. Brown and Sr. Agnes Genevieve went to Fort Defiance to get me some soup. They were caught in a flash flood—quite a thunderstorm. What I long for is a nice juicy beefsteak. Today is Friday.

I hope my last letter made some sense. I tried to write about the things we did but I fear under the circumstances, it was not well organized. I forgot to tell you about the fish fry last Friday evening. We all went back of Standing Rock on the way to Navajo. This rock looks like a mitten for the most part but from the rear and at a certain angle it looks like a hand—even the wrinkles on the joints. I knew it last summer as the Mitten Rock. We had an ideal spot for a "fry"—surrounded by beautiful red rocks extending high up. The boys and girls climbed to the tops of them. They looked like human flies. Kenny, Mrs. Easton's nephew brought me some broken pieces of pottery found on top of these huge rock hills. (He was baptized on Sunday—was in my class at VCS.) Well, we had the best rainbow trout cooked over the coals. I ate two! We had cabbage, carrot and apple salad and watermelon. No can opener was put in, so no coffee tin could be opened. Going back to the rocks there were several shelves covered with straw—eagle nests. I was so eager to see a wild eagle, but none obliged.

Last Saturday afternoon there was an Indian wedding in the Mission Chapel. No invitations were rendered to us. Fr. Luxon from the Rosebud Reservation in one of the Dakotas [South Dakota] brought a Sioux male to marry a Navajo girl. They met at the Bureau of Indian Affairs. We saw the bride dressed in white. The reception was in the room under our bedrooms. Fr. Luxon worked here as a seminarian. Dss. Brown had him here for Friday dinner ...

[Sr. Katharine Veronica had some reservations about a male volunteer who made tactless remarks "right in front of the kids." When he was challenged about it "he was furious and drove the bus over the rugged hills like a hot-rodder."]

Her letter continued:

I was very pleased when Sister brought me your letter at the hospital ... [It was] an excellent tonic. I have done very little on that prayer Course but hope to catch up the week before the Youth Conference of August 14th. I am not worrying for I have a potential outline in my head ... As to visiting my aunt—that really was a surprise and I am most grateful. It really would be a charitable thing to do. If it is convenient with you, and she is at home, I would rather wait to go after the second Youth Conference. I feel I would need to get sorted out and cleaned up from the first one. Is the second one August 28th? ... Whatever is well for your plans is fine. I was just thinking there was only a week between the two conferences but there are two weeks—no—there is only one week—I sure am goofy. I haven't a calendar at hand and my head is not working mathematically. I think I would rather wait until after the Youth Conferences.

A letter came today from Dorothy [her younger sister]. She is flying to Scotland, Dutch Line, July 29th. Needless to say, she is very excited. She has Navy friends located at Holy Loch[6] and they are Godparents to my second nephew. She will return on an English plane ... I don't know where Holy Loch, Scotland is—have no map. If it is near Yorkshire, England, I hope she goes. It is where the Finch family came from.[7]

Thank you again for everything. With much love and prayers.
      Your loving child,
            Katharine Veronica, Sister, CSJB.
P.S. My love to all the Sisters.

July 26, 1966
Dearest Mother,

I had just finished reading the Associates' letter (very good) when
Deaconess Brown came and wanted me to go visiting with her up in Blue
Canyon. At one house—not larger than the convent kitchen—children
were pouring out of the door and windows. We were spreading the news
of the Vacation Church School for next week up there. My interpreter is
lined up—Habana, whom I know from last year. She was so happy to see
me after church last Sunday. [She] got out of her pickup truck and ran over
to greet me. On Saturday morning we went with Fr. Davis, Mrs. Easton
and two interpreters to Black Mt. for Mass. When we arrived—90 miles
away—most of the parishioners were asleep. Lucy Tome had a coming
out party. This affair occurs when a girl reaches puberty. It lasts for four
days with various activities. She was dressed in a wine color fluted skirt
with matching velveteen blouse, and much, much silver and turquoise
jewelry—necklace, pins, rings, belt. She is only thirteen. Well, we had a
picture with her in front of an adobe hogan[8]—and another one with the old
grandparents. The people are more primitive up here. We didn't have Mass.

We proceeded to Keams Canyon where we had our picnic lunch—very
good. Harriet Easton had fried chicken for it, and Mrs. Davis, French
potato salad. After lunch Fr. Davis went to change his clerical shirt to a
blue one, for we were on our way to the top of the First Mesa[9] on Hopi
Reservation. They still are not too friendly with priests—dating back to
the Spaniards.[10] I wish you could have seen this Mesa. When we reached
the top and looked down, you felt as tho' you were as high up as the
Empire State Building. We walked around through the streets and stopped
to talk to the children. Harriet bought some oven bread and some more
of that blue bread which I am bringing for Dr. Colmer. He likes it. It
tastes like tissue paper to me. The children had small pieces of pottery
for sale. The Hopis make beautiful pottery and baskets. The children
had tried to imitate the adults. Harriet bought a few pieces and let Sister
and I choose a piece each. It is quite crude to the beautiful work of the
adults. We heard that there was to be a Home Dance near Oraibi—so we

proceeded there. Many people gathered—Whites and Indians. You should have seen [us] climbing a ladder to the roof of a pueblo dwelling. While ascending and descending, Fr. Davis said, "Oh for a picture to send to the Mother Superior." Well—we at least didn't sit on the edge of [the] roof with our legs dangling as the majority of the spectators did. We sat properly on a small bench.

Finally, the dancers came—22 representing men and 9 as women (only men do the dance). The costumes alone made you think you were in the heart of Africa. You have seen Katcina [sic] dolls?[11]—the costumes were like them. A most elaborate headdress—evergreen boughs around neck and waist—naked from neck down to waist—handwoven apron rear and front with a very wide belt. A fox skin hung from the waist in the rear (all dressed alike). They wore turtle shells with rattles inside, near their knees. These make a weird noise during the dance. They wore the ankle height moccasins. The ones representing women wore wigs with hairdo looking like Japanese, and knee length dresses and leggings. There was a Master of Ceremonies—he had long hair with a fluffy feather on top [and] just a skirt, no moccasins. He went around calling off directions in Hopi and sprinkling corn pollen on them at regular intervals. There is not much activity to the dance—they chant and when it comes through the slit of their headgear, which covers the whole head, it sounds like a hum—like this Hu-hu-huhuhu. They brought various things in with them, such as cat tails about four feet long. Tied to these cat and nine tails were Katcina dolls or bows and arrows, baskets of colored eggs (like Easter ones), and beans, corn, bread, peaches, grapes. At a certain point in the dance the cat and nine tails with the dolls were given to the little girls, and bow and arrows to the boys. Some of the women received the food. This was not just put on for tourists—it really is a sacred dance for them—like Christmas with its gifts. They kept repeating the so-called dance. They say sometimes it goes on all day. The men dressed as women had large hollow gourds and used some kind of a stick on it like a rasp. The men had hand rattles.

After that performance we descended the ladders and came home. We went to the Davies' for dinner—homemade, ah I can't spell it. I need Sr. WL [Waldine Lucia], but the Spanish food with tortillas and cheese, and purée beans like the Mexicans have. All very delicious.

Sr. Anne Marie SSM[12] is Godmother to Becky Davis (age 10). I wrote Sr. Mary Barbara to send Fr. Davis a school catalog because they are planning ahead for Becky, and he requested one but it has not come. In course of conversation Fr. Davis spoke how [the bishop] really is not interested in the Indians. Fr. Luxon of Rosebud Reservation said the same thing. The missionaries trying to get anywhere with the Executive Council is like banging your head against a wall. He thinks they are "fixing" to close the boarding school here. He would like to see a retreat house at the mission—with Sisters. Of course he would like to have us—there are suitable quarters over the dining room. The Retreatants would be housed in the dormitory space where we are now. Mother Ruth[13] has been here a couple of times to give retreats. Over at the Presbyterian Mission—where I was—they have little rest houses and give retreats. Last summer they had 5,000 visitors and during the whole year, 8,000 people. They really have quite a set up over there.

Sunday evening we showed our slides. Everybody interested. Fr. Davis wished we had more on the school. All we had [was the] chapel [and] rear of school from the pond, [and] a view from the front of school and rear. A priest from a seminary in Atlanta, Georgia, is visiting Father and he saw the slides too. After Evening Prayer that night, Mrs. Davis invited us to come up for some watermelon. I saw a vivid blue lizard outside the chapel door. I was all for catching it for my collection. [!] I had never seen one that color. I wrote Muriel about the snake we encountered yesterday—hope she tells you about it. [Alas, Sister did not give any more details in this letter.]

When we first came out here, I wrote Betty Kennaugh[14] who is just beyond Santa Fe. We didn't hear from her. When Mrs. Brookshier, the House Mother here, left for her vacation near Santa Fe, she said that she would look them up. We had a letter—the Kennaughs are in Europe for the summer. She wrote that they have a beautiful home. Some priest is staying there.

Tomorrow night we are having a pot luck supper. Deaconess Brown is to be presented with a Two Grey Hills rug.[15] They are the best weavers over there, and rugs are very expensive. This is to be her retirement gift—then a movie—Big night.

About 6:15pm last night Fr. Davis came over to ask if I would be willing to go out on an emergency call. Harriet Easton had cut her hand and she wanted me to look at it.[16] We didn't leave for Navajo until around 8:00pm. I cleansed the wound and bandaged it but advised she see the doctors today. She put it off until late this afternoon. When I saw it again, I told her she must go to a M.D. She was scared from the appearance of it and made a beeline down to the Government Hospital at Fort Defiance. They gave her a shot for tetanus and she has to return for dressings etc.,—a nasty cut on top of thumb from a broken glass in dish water ...

I have 24 children in my class at Coalmine. Dss. Brown says I have more in my class than the whole VCS at Sawmill. They are 4, 5, 6, and 7th graders and I am busy. I had a nice get well card from Muriel. No more tonight—will write again on Sunday. (Harriet Easton has blown out 3 new tires in two and a half months—the roads are awful.)

With much love from your loving child.

Katharine Veronica, Sister, CSJB

No other letters from the reservation have survived, but the memory of her three summers there stayed with Sr. Katharine Veronica for many years. She recalled those visits in a personal memoir and gave an insight into the visit to the Grand Canyon which was a seven- to eight-hour drive from the Mission. She wrote: "A camping trip to the Grand Canyon with Deaconess [Brown] and college students [and] staff. We spent the first night in Tuba City in a horse pasture. I slept in the back seat of a car when I thought I wouldn't fit into a pup tent which had been given me for the occasion. The others were on the ground in sleeping bags. The other three nights were at a camping site by the Grand Canyon. I then had the pick-up truck for a motel. This truck had a canopy which made it look like a Conestoga wagon."[17]

Another memory was of "avoiding the mule train when walking down the Grand Canyon." Sister Katharine Veronica also recalled "attending a Navajo funeral and burial service, and later a fellowship with the family and friends." People kept in touch with her—"the joy of receiving Navajo mail from young and old." It was all a great experience, and as well as teaching in the Mission through an interpreter ("a slow process"), and attending the social events such as the Hopi dances, Sr. Katharine Veronica was greatly inspired by the scenery and handicrafts. "Seeing double rainbows for the first time; the beautiful rock formations; jewelry of turquoise and silver; gathering petrified wood at Fluted Rock and garnets from anthills on Snake Hill."

Deaconess Brown retired from her ministry to the Navajo in 1968. She had ministered amongst the Navajo and Arapahoe Native Americans for 29 years. An article in *The Morning News*, May 4, 1983 (Wilmington,

Delaware), reported that "In her Chevrolets, she has seen the USA at its grandest, climbed mountains and crossed plains in blizzards and blazing sun, and come as close to the Indian soul as is possible for one lone white woman. Her first seven years out West, she was a member of St. Michael's Mission at Ethete, Wyoming [where] she worked with the Arapahoe. The remaining 22 years, she was with Good Shepherd Mission on the 25,000 square mile Navajo reservation at Fort Defiance, Arizona." Deaconess Brown was commissioned as a deaconess in 1939 and was the last surviving member of the Deaconess Order in the Episcopal Church. The Order was discontinued following the ordination of women to the priesthood (something of which she did not approve). She died on May 11, 1990, at the Episcopal Church Home, Hockessin, Delaware, at the age of 88.

---

[1] Head Start is a program of the US Department of Health and Human Services that provides comprehensive early childhood education, health, nutrition, and parent involvement services to low-income children and families.

[2] Coalmine Canyon is a ravine near Tuba City at the edge of the Painted Desert in north Arizona.

[3] Oraibi or Old Oraibi is a Hopi village in the north-eastern part of Navajo County, AZ. It is located on Third Mesa on the Hopi Reservation. Founded before 1100 AD, it is one of the oldest continuously inhabited settlements in the United States. A series of severe droughts in the late 13th century forced the Hopi to abandon several villages and go to other settlements. Oraibi was one of these and its population grew considerably. It remained unknown to Europeans until 1540, when a Spanish explorer, Pedro de Tovar, looking for gold, discovered the Hopi people, who at first welcomed him. In 1629 the Franciscan Mission was established in the village, but a revolt by the Native Americans in 1680 resulted in the cessation of the Mission.

[4] Acoma Sky City stands on top of a 357ft. Mesa. It is another of the oldest continuously inhabited settlements in the US, having been built between 1100 and 1250 AD. Access was difficult until modern times when a hand-cut staircase was carved into the sheer sandstone rock face. In 1540 the pueblo (village) was discovered by the Spaniard Francisco Vasquez de Coronado, but because of its inaccessibility, the Acoma residents resisted the invaders. In 1598 the Spanish invaded New Mexico, raiding Native American pueblos, arriving at Acoma in the same year. At first the Spaniards were welcomed, but when the winter stores were raided, the Acoma residents resisted, killing 12 Spaniards. A battle on January 21–22, 1599, resulted in 500 Acoma men being slaughtered along with 300 women and children. Retribution by the Spaniards was brutal, and the memory remains a sore point.

[5] Sr. Katharine Veronica did not repeat the story here, so we do not know it.

[6] Holy Loch is a sea loch near the Firth of Clyde in Scotland. It takes its name from the 6th century AD when St. Munn landed there from Ireland and built a church. During World War II the loch was used as a British Royal Navy submarine base. During the Cold War, the loch was used as a United States Navy ballistic missile submarine base from 1961–92. Following the fall of the Soviet Union and ending of the Cold War, the base was closed in 1992. Sr. Katharine Veronica was unsure how far Holy Loch was from Yorkshire. It is 242 miles.

[7] Sr. Katharine Veronica's family name was Finch.

[8] An adobe hogan is the traditional dwelling of the Navajo.

[9] First Mesa is located on the Hopi Reservation, AZ. It consolidates three Hopi and Arizona Tewa villages—Hano, Sitsmovi and Walpi. Walpi is the oldest village, having been continuously inhabited for 1,100 years, and is still without running water or electricity.

[10] "… dating back to the Spaniards …" See notes 3 and 4 above.

[11] Katcina or Katsina dolls are figures carved by the Hopi people and given to young girls at a special ceremony.

[12] Sr. Anne Marie, SSM, entered St. Margaret's Convent, Boston, MA, in 1945 and was professed in life vows in 1948. In 1953 she went to Haiti, where she was in charge of Holy Trinity School, Port-au-Prince, until 1977. She succeeded Sr. Marjorie Raphael as Mother Superior at Boston in 1977 and remained in office until 1988, when she was succeeded by Sr. Adele Marie. She died quite suddenly on September 22, 1995, while visiting the SSM Community in Aberdeen, Scotland (known as the Convent of St. Margaret of Scotland). She was 75.

[13] Mother Ruth (Ruth Elaine Younger, 1897–1986) was a member of the Sisterhood of St. John the Divine, Toronto, and was professed in life vows on December 29, 1922. In 1950 she opened St. Hilda's School on Morningside Heights, which became St. Hilda's and St. Hugh's School. In 1952 she founded the Community of the Holy Spirit in New York and was elected Mother Superior, an office she held until 1976. She died on December 22, 1986.

[14] Betty Kennaugh was the wife of the Revd. Robert Kennaugh, parish priest of St. John Baptist Church, Corsicana, TX, until 1948. The Sisters undertook work there, helping to found a school from 1945–49. Sr. Katharine Veronica was the first Sister to go to Corsicana. After the Sisters withdrew from the work, the Kennaughs kept in touch with them. See Chapter 3.

[15] Two Grey Hills rugs are unique to the Navajo, using undyed wool, and are hand woven into intricate patterns.

[16] Sr. Katharine Veronica was a trained nurse.

[17] A Conestoga wagon was a heavy covered wagon, looking rather like the wagons used by settlers going west.

APPENDIX 4

TRIBUTE TO SR. JANE MANKAA

Sister Jane Mankaa EBSB, 1961–2021

For the Sisters of CSJB, this was a Holy Week like no other. On the afternoon of April 1, Maundy Thursday, we received news that our beloved Sister Jane Mankaa, founder of the Good Shepherd Home for Children in Cameroon, had died after a brave struggle with cancer. Words cannot possibly express the shock and grief which this loss has brought upon all of us who love Sister Jane. Even with all our theological and psychological perspectives and our certainty that we will see her in the next world, it is still almost unbearably painful to be deprived of her brilliant light and endless compassion in this world.

Sister Jane was born in 1961 in Cameroon, West Africa, and was the oldest of eight siblings. At age 16 she joined the Emmanuel Sisterhood, an ecumenical order in the Presbyterian Church. Years later she felt a calling to become Anglican and work with homeless children. She came to the US in 1999 and lived at CSJB for a year while studying convent management with us and with Roman Catholic Communities. While at CSJB, Sister Jane formed a close bond with Sister Mary Lynne, who had felt called to missionary work most of her life.

CSJB formed a partnership with Sister Jane and, with the assistance of several churches and many generous individuals, helped her to raise the funds to found the Benedictine Sisters of Bethany and the Good Shepherd Home for Children. Sister Jane faced seemingly insurmountable obstacles while building her ministry, but she was filled with the courage and determination of the Holy Spirit to help the many children who had been orphaned by the AIDS epidemic in her homeland.

Since its founding in 2003, the Good Shepherd Home has provided a loving, safe home for children who would have surely died abandoned and unloved without Sister Jane. The Home has grown to include a nursery school, the Good Shepherd Academy, the Roberto Rovere Health Clinic, a bakery, a chicken farm, a fish farm, and two branch houses. The Home has never made any of the children available for adoption due to the risk of trafficking but has instead committed to raising every child to adulthood and then providing them with a college education and a loving family for life. There is usually an average of 150 children living at the Home at any given time. Sister Mary Lynne made annual two-month trips to the Good Shepherd Home from its founding until the outbreak of the Cameroonian Civil War in 2017 and she continues to help raise funds and raise awareness of her dear friend's mission.

The work of the Good Shepherd Home will continue, even with its Mother Foundress in heaven. Many tireless workers and supporters are organizing the management of the Home and ensuring that it continues to serve the most vulnerable of children for many years to come.

If you would like to help continue the work of the Good Shepherd Home, go to www.goodshepherdhome.org to learn more.

I am the resurrection, and the life:
he that believeth in me,
though he were dead, yet shall he live:
And whosoever liveth and believeth in me shall never die.

(John 11:25–26)

Sr. Monica Clare

INDEX

Acosta, Revd. William, 58, 59
Adams, Mr. and Mrs., Jnr, 129
Adebonojo, Revd. Mary, 343, 354
Aitkins, Revd. Frank, 9, 93
Aitkins, Revd. James Fley, 9
Akrofi, Rt. Revd. Justice O., 414
Albany Cathedral, New York State, 35
Albert, Laura, 138
Albert, Mrs. Anne, 167, 169, 170, 258
Albert, Revd. William V., 136, 161–71,
   174, 190, 258–71, 291, 299, 300
Aldrich, Mary Elizabeth, 328
Alinsky, Saul, 164
All Saints, Millington, 142, 421, 423, 448,
   451, 459
All Saints, Princeton, NJ, 217, 309, 328
Allen, Jean, 62
Allin, Rt. Revd. John, 188, 192, 212
Almy, Deborah, 203
Almy, Marjorie, 311
Altamura, Lily, 360, 363, 410, 431, 434,
   445
Altamura, Sam, 363, 434, 445
Anand, Rt. Revd. Kenneth, 184, 186,
   188, 192, 263, 272
Anderson, Constance, 71
Anderson, Olive, 312
Appleton family, 74, 77, 87, 89, 311
Appleton, Miss Helena, 77, 87, 88, 91,
   311
Appleton, Revd. Richard P., 87
Ascension Church, Bogota, 110
Askew, Beryl, 345
Ayres, Revd., 13, 18

Bacon, Dom Francis Hilary, OSB, 21, 31
Bailey, Blythe, 71
Bailey, Margaret, 71
Baker, Revd. William Osborn, 7, 21, 122
Baptistine Sisters, 181
Barrow, Revd., 35
Bartkus, Dorothy, 436
Basilion, Mary, 317, 321, 407, 414
Bateman, Ellen, 451

Beach, Revd. Dr. Diana L., 408
Beckwith, Rt. Revd. Mark, 248, 415,
   419, 421, 423, 428, 430, 433, 440–42,
   448–9, 450, 452, 453, 456, 458
Beddingfield, Revd. John, 460, 463, 466
Begbroke, 382, 384, 385, 387, 391,
   393–4, 398, 402, 407, 408, 409, 412,
   413–14, 416, 419, 429, 431, 435, 439,
   465
Bell, Mrs., 310
Bell, Revd. Colley, 309, 310
Belshaw, Rt. Revd. George Phelps
   Mellick, 352, 358
Bennett, Sue, 415
Bennit, Revd. George Stephen, 100
Berry, Louis and Carol, 451
Berry, Dr. Mary, 377
Bigrigg, Revd. Roland, 149
Bishop. See surname + Rt. Revd.
Bishop Dagwell Hall, 60, 145, 340
Bittrich, Gus, 331, 375, 404
Blacklock, Revd. Martha, viii, 202, 207,
   208–9, 443
Blaine, Mrs., 473
Blaine, Revd. Judd, 473
Blair, Beth, 391
Blank, Archbishop Joost de, 113, 119
Blue, Muriel, 143, 153, 186, 272, 310, 368
Bober, Mrs. Jessie, 152, 259, 273
Boggess, Revd. Elwood, 199, 218
Bone, Rt. Revd. John, 367
Bonome, Clare, 384
Boynton, Doreen Madrell, 383
Br. Derek, SSF, 392
Br. Gregory, OJN, 392
Br. Thomas, 266, 268, 274, 279, 300
Bramlett, Revd. Bruce, 308
Britt, Mary, 345
Brodeur, Christine, xii, 176, 177–8, 191,
   194, 202, 205, 266, 284, 319, 320, 375,
   449
Brome, Rt. Revd., 388
Brown, Deaconess Marian, xiii, 135, 138,
   191, 346, 472, 472–82

Brown, Louise, 159

Brown, Revd., 124

Browning, Rt. Revd. Edmund, 328, 330

Brunson, Revd. Deacon Cathy, 421, 455

Bryan, Br. David, OHC, 389, 392, 393, 419

Bryan, Canon Henry, 100–101

Bryant, Revd. Canon Robert, 446

Burger, Marion, 198, 204, 207, 273, 279, 285, 286, 288, 292, 295, 303

Calvary, Summit, 275, 300, 309, 322, 396–7, 401

Campbell, Rt. Revd. Robert, OHC, 82

Carnegie, Revd. Rachel, 459

Carr, Timothy, 431, 442

Carr-Jones, Revd. Philip, 412, 444

Carroll, Revd. Henry H., 354

Carson, Revd. Thomas, 57

Carter, Canon T. T., xv, xx, 24, 38, 86–7, 167, 218, 273, 315, 327, 344, 380, 388, 391, 399, 404, 467, 468

Carter, Jane Bramhall, 383

Carty, Jeanne, 458

Carty, Revd. Shawn, 446, 458, 463, 466

Casey, Frances, 71

Castle, Revd. Robert, 158, 159, 167, 173, 174

Cathedral of St. John the Divine, NYC, 8, 24, 99, 116, 119, 148, 161, 182, 184, 187, 190, 259, 269, 270, 272, 304, 309, 310, 319, 320, 423, 441

Cato, Revd. Philip, 203

Celtic Journeys, iv, ix, *252*, 375, 382, 386, 390, 393, 394, 407, 414, 432, 437, 450, 462

Chambers, Revd., 128

Chapter, Clewer, xv, xxi, 2, 23, 24, 27, 32, 35, 36, 37, 38, 45, 179, 180, 182, 266

Chapter, Mendham, xxi, 2, 8, 14, 15, 25, 32, 33, 35, 36, 37, 38, 40, 41, 43–5, 72, 73–4, 75, 79, 88, 124, 136, 137, 138, 139, 140, 161, 165, 171, 179–81, 182, 184, 216, 258, 260, 319, 337, 344, 347, 352, 364, 375, 388, 451, 466, 469

Chi, Mr., 425

Christ Church Episcopal Cathedral, Indianapolis, 109, 119

Christ Church Home, South Amboy, xvii, 310, 322–3

Christ Church, East Orange, 166

Christ Church, Elizabeth, NJ, 85, 258

Christ Church, Glendale, 98

Christ Church, Hackensack, 121

Christ Church, Middletown, NJ, 212

Christ Church, Newark, 5, 33, 34, 39, 41, 76, 79, 81, 84, 109

Christ Church, Oxford, England, 382, 409

Christ Church, Short Hills, xii, 322, 442, 443, 465

Christ Hospital, Jersey City, 169, 380, 390, 392, 393, 403

Chrystal, Chris, xiii, 68–72, 123, 133

Church Army, 101, 105, 159, 162, 164, 166, 168, 169, 258

Church of the Annunciation, New Orleans, 416

Church of the Ascension, NYC, 65

Church of the Atonement, Tenafly, NJ, 445

Church of the Incarnation, NYC, 289

Church of the Messiah, Chester, xii, *257*, 436, 442, 445, 452, 459, 464

Church of the Redeemer, Morristown, 384, 390, 403, 414, 415, 420, 423, 428, 432

Church of the Resurrection, 175, 335, 336

Church of the Savior, Denville, NJ, 191, 304

Church of the Transfiguration, Towaco, NJ, 192

Church Workroom, 8, 92, 93, 98, 128, 321, 379, 447

Civil War, 172

Clayton, Revd. P. (Tubby), 105, 118

Cochran, Lillian, 401, 406, 408, 422, 437

Coleman, Revd. F. P., 183, 192, 214, 267–8, 288

Collett, Dom Martin, OSB, 21

Colon, Mr. and Mrs., 170, 259

Commemoration Day, xix, 94, 130, 135, 137–8, 140, 142, 156, 164, 171, 177,

188, 197, 203, 212, 215, *254*, 267, 271, 279, 305, 309, 312, 319, 326, 328, 333, 334, 346, 349, 355, 366, 369, 373, 375, 381, 385, 389, 394, 408, 412, 421, 425, 431, 438, 442, 448, 452, 455, 458, 464, 472

Commencement, 14, 49, 61, 62, 65, 79, 113, 137, 142, 177, 215, 304, 312, 315

Commission on Women's Ministry, 311, 329

Community cemetery, Mendham, 6, 36, 68, 75, 85, 93, 97, 125, 127, 134, 139, 273, 314, 397

Community of St. John Baptist, Clewer, viii, xv, xviii, xx, xxi, 2, 4, 8, 10, 11, 20, 21, 23–4, 26–8, 32, 35, 37, 45, 46, 81, 92, 98, 127–8, 131, 133, 136, 138, 145, 172, 178–82, 207–8, 209, 211, 214, 218, *241*, 266, 315, 323, 326–7, 338, 340, 348, 356, 359, 365, 368, 382, 384–5, 402, 405, 460

Community of St. Mary, 134, 135, 186, 194, 202, 358

Community of the Resurrection, 128, 309, 322

Community of the Transfiguration, 91, 98, 182, 184

Companions of Jesus the Good Shepherd, 405, 465

Constitution, 23, 26, 27, 31–3, 37, 41, 45, 87, 136, 179, 180, 213, 317, 319, 321, 368, 370, 378, 466, 469

Consultative Council, 16, 18, 25, 36–7, 106, 201, 260

Cordingley, William Wade, 29, 47, 63, 71, 126, 132, 136, *229*, 461

Cornerstone, xviii, 8, 60, 100, 136, 143, *224*, *251*, 440, 442, 453, 468

Corrigan, Debbie, 307

Councell, Rt. Revd. George, 396, 421, 437

Covid 19 Pandemic, v, xiii, 466–7

Crafton, Revd. Barbara, 421, 427, 445

Cromey, Revd. Edwin, 196–7, 198, 200, 205, 207, 210, 218, 305, 306–7

Croneberger, Rt. Revd. John P., 381, 391, 395, 415

Crossland, Mary, 62

Crowson, Gloria Spencer, 460

CSJB Associates, viii, ix, x, xix, 9, 12, 34, 41, 51, 52, 59, 61, 74, 77, 79, 80, 81, 82, 84, 85, 86, 87, 93, 94, 96, 97, 107, 115, 117, 119, 121, 123, 130, 131, 132, 135, 137, 138, 139, 141, 143, 146, 177, 183, 184, 186, 187, 188, 191, 197, 198, 199, 201, 202, 203, 204, 205, 206, 207, 208, 211, 212, 213, 215, 216, 217, 272, 275, 280, 283, 284, 286, 287, 288, 292, 295, 302, 303, 305, 306, 309, 310, 312, 313, 314, 315, 316, 319, 320, 321, 322, 324, 325, 326, 327, 328, 330, 331, 332, 333, 334, 338, 339, 342, 343–4, 345, 346, 347, 348, 350, 351, 352, 353, 354, 355, 356, 357, 360, 361, 362, 363, 364, 365, 366, 367, 368, 369, 370, 371, 372, 373, 374, 375, 376, 377, 381, 383, 384, 385, 388, 389, 391, 394, 398, 404, 406, 408, 409, 410, 412, 417, 421, 424, 426, 428, 431, 434, 439, 442, 446, 447, 448, 449, 450, 451, 452, 455, 456, 457, 458, 460, 461, 463, 464, 467, 478

CSJB Associates, Clewer, 193, 313, 315, 316, 320, 326, 327, 340, 344, 375, 458

Cullen, Mr., 1

Cure, Revd. Thomas, SSJE, 216, 217, 319, 332, 336

Curry, Most Revd. Michael, 449, 465

Curtis, Nan, 422, 437

Dagwell, Rt. Revd. Benjamin, 13, 15, 17, 49, 51–2, 83

Damuth, Revd. Warren K., 31

Davis, Revd., 475, 478–9, 480

Davis, Rt. Revd. Cameron, 322

Daytop, viii, 347, 349–50, 366–7, 369, 373, 384, 388, 389, 391, 394, 402, 407, 409, 412, 414, 421, 422, 426, 433, 436, 441, 445, 446, 448, 449, 451, 464

De Lagerberg, Ruth, 96

Declaration of Independence, 200, 279, 300, 364

Delaney, Revd. Michael, 394

Dennis, Alice, 145

Dennis, Ethel, 361, 363, 420, 440

Dennis, Marguerite, 96
Dennis, Rita, 372
Dennis, Roseanna, 198
Dietsche, Rt. Revd. Andrew, 442
Diocesan Altar Guild, 86, 190, 196, 206, 311, 314, 332, 336, 355, 390, 395, 396, 415, 436, 459
Dixon, Rt. Revd. Jane, 396
Doane, Rt. Revd. George Washington, 100
Doane, Rt. Revd. William, 118
Donahue, Revd., 267
Donovan, Dr. Mary Sudman, x, xiii, 405, 440, 456
Donovan, Rt. Revd. Herbert, 383, 385, 388, 389, 391, 393, 402, 405, 412, 418, 421, 423, 425–6, 428, 430, 432–3, 440, 442, 456
Dormer, Betty, 370, 422, 444, 460
Doss, Rt. Revd. Joe Morris, 360, 378
Downing, Dick, 330
Dressler, Gerrie, 460
Ducet, Revd. Luis, 163, 174
Dunham, Carolyn, 320, 417
Dunham, Revd. Clarence, 7

Earthquake, 200, 218, 305
Easton, Mrs. Harriet, 476, 478, 480, 481
Edler, Revd., 150
Edwards, Revd. Thomas, 431
Edwards, Tilden, 374
English Civil War, 382
Episcopal Church Women, xiii, 134, 139, 169, 204, 325, 329, 336, 392
Erath, Margaret, 408
Erixson, Revd. Lorna, 463, 466
Evans, Barbara, 387

Farris, Mrs., 313
Fearon, Dr., 217
Feisner, Edith, 362, 374, 396
Fennelly, Mary, 412
First Order, 2
Fischer, Hilde, 408
Fisher, Marian, 71
Fisk, Rt. Revd. Mark, 426
Fletcher, Rt. Revd. Colin, 387, 414

Florek, Phyllis, 421
Flores, Mrs., 259
Floyd-Jones, Louisa, 3
Folsom family, xv, xx, 90, 121, 188, 460
Folsom, George Winthrop, 90
Folsom, Helen Stuyvesant, xv
Folsom, Revd. Henry F., 121, 129, 133, 188, 460
Ford, Revd., 473
Forney, Colonel Frank, 78, 90
Fox, Revd. William, 58
Fox, Sr. Ruth, OSB, 362
Fr. See surname + Revd.
Freer, Douglas, 352
Frey, Revd. William, 163, 174
Friedley, Durr, 47

Gallagher, Rt. Revd. Carol, 412
Gardner, Mr., 8
Garfield, Revd., 160
Gates, Mrs. Florence Jayne, 77, 85
Geddes, Norma, 354
Geitz, Revd. Canon Elizabeth, xiii, 422, 425, 437, 438, 453
General Convention, 83, 146, 147, 202, 206, 208, 305, 327, 336, 346, 350, 355, 381, 395, 405, 414, 426, 438, 449, 458
George, Ruth, 128
Gerth, Revd. Stephen, 414, 431
Gibson, Meghan, 458
Gleckler, Ann, 121
Gleckler, Gertrude, 94, 115, 121
Good Samaritan Hospital, 4
Good Shepherd Church, Ringwood, NJ, 452
Good Shepherd Home, Cameroon, xiii, 396–7, 406, 410, 411–12, 414, 416, 420, 422, 432, 434, 438, 443, 450, 453, 454, 461, 484, 485
Good Shepherd Mission, Fort Defiance, AZ, 472, 476, 482
Grace Church (Van Vorst), Jersey City, vii, viii, xii, 79, 82, 85, 86, 97, 98, 100–118, 121, 123, 130, 131, 132, 136, 141, 148–9, 151, 153, 154, 155, 156, 158, 159, 161, 162–72, 173, 174, 190, 192, 197, 200, 203, 210–11, 212, 216,

217, *230*, 258–61, 262–4, 265, 267,
268, 270, 272, 273, 274–8, 280, 282,
283, 284, 286, 287–300, 308, 310, 321,
329, 333, 444, 460, 461
Grace Church, Amherst, 400
Grace Church, Haddonfield, 342
Grace Church, Madison, NJ, 342, 432
Grace Church, Monroe, LA, 174
Grace Church, Union City, NJ, 289
Great Depression, 1, 27, 48, 101
Greenwood, Dorothy Templeton. *See*
Templeton, Dorothy
Greey, Barbara, 71
Grier family, 94, 316–7, 332
Grier, Eric, 357
Grier, Gay, 455
Grier, Mr. Bill, 40, 112, 117, 195, 199,
204, 264, 278, 332, 356, 367, 426, 427,
447
Grier, Shirley, 356, 367, 447
Griswold, Rt. Revd. Frank, 451
Gross, Revd. Joseph, 289, 303, 305, 324,
331, 332, 334, 337, 339, 349, 432
Gross, Rt. Revd. Hal R., 205, 212, 391
Ground Zero, 385–7
Gruber, Dorothy (Dottie), 460
Guenther, Revd. Dr. Margaret, 374, 376,
379
Gunther, Mr., 33
Gwynn, Mrs. Barbara, 292–3, 297
Gwynn, Revd. Elisha John, 216, 217,
289, 290, 291, 292–3, 295–6, 297, 298

Habgood, Most Revd. John, 325
Hackman, Margaret, 186
Hall, Revd., 26
Hamilton, Elizabeth, 332, 340
Hanson, Rita Dennis, *see* Dennis, Rita
Harries, Rt. Revd. Richard, 348, 365,
387, 408
Harriet Monsell House, Ripon College,
Cuddesdon, UK, 437, 439, 445, 459
Harriman, Revd. Deacon Barbara, 394,
447, 463
Harris, Catherine (Cathy), 450
Harris, Emily, 71
Harrison, Revd. Alan, 327

Hartman, Martha Packer, 354
Harvey, Revd., 160
Hawkins, Joantre, 71
Hemsley, Revd. Bernard, 167, 175
Henderson, Judith Meylan, 64, 65, 72
Hennen, Revd. Joseph, 349, 373, 421,
426
Henry, Revd., 33
Hermann, Bill, 464
Hines, Rt. Revd. John E., 134, 303
Hobbie, Theo, 145
Hobbs, Revd., 258
Holland, Revd. Carr, 332, 337, 354
Holy Cross Church, NYC, xv, xvi, 29,
375, 389, 415, 455
Holy Cross Mission, xv, xix, 3, 75, 79,
82, 125, 306, 389, 441
Holy Cross Monastery, NY, xii, 131, 136,
330, 423
Holy Cross, North Plainfield, 110, 166
Holy Trinity School, Haiti, 206, 483
Holy Trinity, Brompton, London,
England, 371
Holy Trinity, Hillsdale, NJ, 446
Holy Trinity, NYC, 164, 460
Homer, Carol, 371, 374, 384, 396, 415,
447
Honeycutt, Sylvia, 360
Hoopes, Revd. David, OHC, 368, 388,
402, 405, 408, 412
Hoppin, Jean, 273, 275, 283, 286, 287,
289, 293, 300, 318, 320, 361, 394, 460
Hospital chaplaincy, 343, 380, 390, 392,
402, 403, 414, 418, 423, 424
House of Mercy, Clewer, 399, 468
House of Prayer, Newark, 324, 328
House of the Good Shepherd,
Hackettstown, 181, 346, 351, 373, 436
House of the Holy Comforter, 33, 46
Howell, Dorothy, 71
Huddleston, Most Revd. Trevor, CR,
309, 322
Hugh, Br. Robert, SSF, 352, 354, 364,
365, 366, 369, 371, 440
Hughes, Rt. Revd. Carlye, *253*, 459, 465,
466
Hughson, Revd. Shirley Carter, OHC, 32

Hummel, Revd., 305, 372
Hummel, Ruth, 372
Humphrey, Mr., 474
Huntington, Revd. James, OHC, 98, 321, 389
Huntington, Rt. Revd. Frederic Dan, 321
Hurricane Connie, 88
Hurricane Esther, 152, 173
Hurricane Floyd, 376
Hurricane Katrina, 416
Hurricane Sandy, 439, 442, 457
Hutchinson, Revd. Ninon, 331

Icke, Irene, 124
Ihloff, Rt. Revd. Robert W., 393, 464
Inkster, B. Mary, 391
Interweave, 307, 318, 322, 332, 360, 369, 381, 390, 407, 415, 440, 456

Jackson, Suzanne, 127, 130, 131, 314
Jakobek, Julia, 322
Jakobek, Matilda, 322
Jenson, Revd. Deacon Barbara, 446
Johnson, Margaret, 381, 450
Jonassen, Laura, 320
Jones, James S., 68, 72, 132
Julian, Mr. Raymond, 97

Kallstrom, Revd. Scott, 321
Kalos, Brad, 466
Kapp, Dora, 331, 332, 336, 342, 346, 375, 415
Karsten, Mrs. Elizabeth Scovil, 306
Keener, Virginia Brown, 339
Kelsey, Rt. Revd. Dr. Morton, 214, 219
Kennaugh, Betty, 480, 483
Kennaugh, Revd. Robert, 55, 56, 57, 58, 59, 483
Kennedy, Eileen, 417, 418
Kerr, Judy, 417
King, Rt. Revd. Edward, 437, 445, 468
Klaiman, Marianna, 374, 384
Kohn-Perry, Revd. Ellen, 441, 443, 456, 461
Kolkebeck, Margo, 321, 331, 344
Kramer, Revd. Jerry, 416
LaFrage, Michelle, 435, 436, 437

Lagerberg, Ruth de, 96
Lake House, Lake Oswego, 4
Lane, Lura, 389, 390
Lariviere, Bill, 394
Larkin, Elfie, 420
Laughlin, Very Revd. Ledlie, 108, 109, 112, 116, 121, 131, 149, 154, 155, 156, 181, 192, 197, 203, 207, 259, 280, 284, 295, 308, 328, 461
Leech, Revd. David, 145
Leslie, Nancy, 387
Lewis, Mildred, 108
Locke, Revd. Kay, 412
Luce, Revd. John B., 131, 154, 156, 158, 159, 160, 161, 173, 289
Ludlow, Rt. Revd. Theodore R., 106, 119
Luxon, Revd., 477, 480
Lyon, Gilberta, 71

Mother: see Sr. + name
MacAdie, Rt. Revd. Donald, 94, 98, 114, 119, 130, 148, 153, 156
MacClellan, Christine Brodeur. See Brodeur, Christine
MacClellan, Don, 375
MacIntyre, Revd. Gerald, SJ, 418
MacLaury, Revd., 39
Macurdy, Revd. David, 100
Magdalens at Clewer, 23
Mahan, Revd. Milo, 100, 118
Maitland, Revd. Robert, 177, 191, 201, 203, 312, 334, 336, 337, 352, 353, 381
Martinsville, 309
Mason, Rt. Revd., 84
Masters, Revd. Austin, SSM, 214, 326, 331, 363, 365
Mayo, Revd., OHC, 21
Mazengia, Dahlia, 334, 343
McCarthy, Diane, 391, 393
McConahay, Mary Ann, 71
McGirr, Joyce, 445
McGrath, Revd. Victoria, 408, 458, 459
McIlvaine, Alice, 71
McKelvey, Rt. Revd. Jack, 345, 370
McKenzie, Douglas, 421, 443
McKenzie, Patrice, 369, 381, 443
Mercurio-Brown, Gina, 457

Midnight Mission, xvii
Miller, Revd. Raymond, 85, 180
Milligan, Revd., 187
Miranda, Patricia, 423, 440
Mission Sisters, ix, 2–3, 23, 82, 125
Monastery in May, 348, 361–2, 389, 417
Monk, Nancy, 461, 468
Moore, Jenny, 98, 101, 104, 105, 109, 118, 119, 167, 184, 269
Moore, Mary Tyler, 349
Moore, Revd. Robert, 57
Moore, Rt. Revd. Paul, 79, 98, 101, 105, 106, 108, 109, 112, 119, 158, 161, 162, 173, 182, 184, 207, 210, 214, 259, 265, 269, 274, 284, 308, 329, 352
Morris Convocation, 214, 311
Morris County Community College, 318
Morris, Dom Augustine, OSB, 21
Morris, Dr. Stuyvesant Fish, 90
Morris, Revd. Robert, 307, 322, 332, 350, 357, 374, 415, 443
Morris, Rt. Revd. Benjamin Wistar, 60
Morton, Revd. James Parks, 108, 109, 111, 112, 116, 121, 123, 149–50, 154, 173, 207, 310
Mothers Superior. See Sisters, Mothers and Sisters Superior
Mulder, Revd. Timothy, 412
Mulholland, Mary, 441, 448, 462
Mulholland, Sheila, 448, 462, 464
Mullin, Lynn Wilder, xii, 126, 133, 411, 412, 417, 418, 421, 448
Mundy, LindaLee, 412
Myers, Doris Thompson, 464
Myers, Rt. Revd. Chauncey Kilmer (Kim), 99, 101, 108

Nancrede, Revd. Harry Walstane de, 195
National Cathedral, Washington, DC, 158, 184, 188, 209, 330
Navajo Native Americans, xiii, 95, 135, 138, 140, 191, 209, 346, 472–82, 483
Neale, Revd. Dr. John Mason, 98, 323
Negrotto, Revd. John, 421, 431, 442, 446
Negrotto, Susan, 426
Newark Cathedral, 128, 138, 155, 156, 165, 213, 333

Ngijoe, Revd. Canon Joseph, xiii, 414, 454
Noble, Mrs., 93
Noble, Revd. Edward, 8, 9, 10, 14, 26, 29, 30, 34, 80, 93
Nobleman, Roberta, 327, 340
Nun Better Golf Outing, xii, 252, 255, 448, 452, 453, 455, 458
Nun Better Shop, 390, 417, 426, 433, 434, 437, 445

O'Brien, Monsignor, 349
Oblates, ix, 333, 334, 340, 343, 346, 357, 360, 361, 363, 370, 374, 381, 385, 387, 388, 398, 409–10, 417, 424, 431, 433, 434, 436, 442, 443, 446, 447, 450, 456–7, 458, 461, 463, 464, 467
Oblates, Clewer, 345, 387
Ogden, Annie, 90
Oglesby, Mr., 168
Order of St. Anne, 94, 98
Order of St. Helena, 116, 364, 365, 373, 376, 392, 409
Order of St. Luke, 309, 322
Order of the Holy Cross, xv, 116, 190, 202, 245, 272, 319, 321, 365, 388
Oregon Episcopal School, 60, 246, 340, 352, 353, 356, 376, 404
Osborne, Judge and Mrs., 79
Otterburn, Revd. Margaret, 394, 452
Our Place homeless shelter, 413, 416

Packer, Barbara, 121, 131, 132, 134
Paget, Beatrice, 355, 391
Paine, Thomas, 393
Painter, Revd. Abigail, viii, 208
Painter, Joanne, 417
Parks, Revd. Dr. Robert R., 181, 197, 263, 323
Patterson, Revd. Albert C., 100
Pederson, Nancy, 404
Pederson, Revd. Arthur, 190, 203, 210, 262, 263, 264, 265, 266, 270–71, 272, 273, 274, 275–6, 279, 281, 285, 286, 287, 288–9, 290, 291, 294, 295, 297, 298, 305, 327, 377

Pegram, Revd. Robert, 84, 101, 102, 108, 109, 161
Pennington, Revd. Basil, 324, 332
Percival, Catherine, 24
Pettit, Rt. Revd. Vincent K., 373, 379, 408, 412, 428
Pfitzinger, Lynne, 204, 210, 282, 283
Phelan, Shane, 383
Pike, Rt. Revd. James, 95, 99
Pinckney, Celestine, 7, 62
Poppe, Revd. Bernard (Bernie), 446, 447, 449, 452, 460
Portland Academy, 50
Post, Revd. Norman, 132
Powell, Claudette, 439, 440
Price, Margaret, 456
Probation Service, 15
Puig, Oliver, 408
Pullman, Julie, 71
Purdy, Lawson, 9–10, 14, 29, 34, 68, 97

Rampton, Revd. Dr. Paul, 327, 340
Ramsey, Most Revd. Michael, 117, 263
Ramsey, Revd. Canon John R., 320, 381
Ramstad, Revd. Philip, 352
Ransom, Revd. James, 203
Rath, Rt. Revd. George, 131, 133, 137, 138, 164, 166, 169, 183, 187, 198, 199, 203, 210, 212, 213, 258, 265, 267, 271, 274, 275, 276, 284, 286, 303, 381, 404
Ray, Revd. Francoise, 366
Redeemer Mission, Brookhaven, MS, 174
Redfern, Rt. Revd. Alistair, 459
Reed, Rt. Revd., 474
Reid, Dom Benedict, OSB, 144, 333
Renn, Mary Ann, xiii, 446
Renn, Revd. Wade, 446
Reus-Froylan, Rt. Revd. Francisco, 289, 301
Revolutionary War, 393
Reynolds, Eleanor, 373, 374
Rice, Revd. Dr. Charles, 360, 364–5, 460
Riches, Rt. Revd. Kenneth and Mrs., 184
Riley, Linda, 388, 389
Ripon College, Cuddesdon, UK, 90, 459

Riverside Church, NYC, 267
Riverview Cemetery, Portland, 13, 49, 352
Roberts, Louise, 71
Robinson, Marjorie, 306
Robinson, Marnie, xiii, 458
Robinson, Mr., 123
Robinson, Revd. Gene, 405
Rockwell, Kitty King, xiii, 72, 464
Rodger, Rt. Revd. Patrick, 316
Rozelle, Revd. Stephen, 452
Ruff, Julia, 383
Ruhumuliza, Rt. Revd. Jonathan, 388
Rule, 20, 23, 26, 31, 33, 35, 36, 37, 41, 46, 102, 179, 180, 184, 213, 267, 317, 321, 322, 328, 335, 340, 364, 368, 369, 370, 378, 388, 394, 409, 434, 452
Runcie, Rt. Revd. Robert, 315
Runtz-Rees, Miss Caroline, 77

Sadley, Revd. William, 148
Savastano, Revd. Peter, 456, 464
Schlueter, Revd. Edward, 13, 32, 36, 40, 41, 42, 43, 77, 89, 92, 98, 112, 119
Schori, Most Revd. Katharine Jefferts, 421
Schwartzentruber, Revd., 217
Scott, Deborah, 332, 337
Seabury, Mrs. Katharine (Hovey), 61
Second Order, 2–3
Sengulane, Most Revd. Dinis, 333, 340, 376, 379
Seras, Revd. Barbara, 390–91, 393
Seton, St. Elizabeth Ann, 198, 218
Severance, Dom Paul, OSB, 7, 13, 21, 24, 30, 31
Sharf, Mr., 172
Shearer, Revd. Donald, 408
Shin, Rt. Revd. Allen K., *246*, 451, 453, 455, 458, 463, 466
Simmonds, Revd., 13
Simmons, Revd. Eric, CR, 309
Simpson, Revd. James, 181, 201, 203, 323
Singh, Rt. Revd. Prince, 432, 436, 438, 440, 445, 446, 448, 453, 468
Sisk, Rt. Revd. Mark, 421, 437

Sisterhood of St. John the Divine, Toronto, 483
Sisters, Mothers and Sisters Superior: *see listing below*
Smith, Dorothy Lyon, 9
Smith, Judith, 420
Smith, Margaret, 138
Smith, Neil, 462
Smith, Rabbi Deb, 462, 465
Snyder, Muriel, 360
Society of St. John the Evangelist, 26, 45, 47, 343, 374, 425
Society of St. John the Forerunner, 23
Society of St. Margaret, 38, 94, 98, 113, 116, 141, 161, 184, 192, 202, 218, 323, 365, 376, 446
Society of St. Paul, 332
Society of the Precious Blood, 368
Sogliuzzo, Revd. Louis, 407
Sontag, Frederick, 118
Sotolongo, Revd., 164
Spanish influenza, xviii, 13, 15, 44, 48, 195–6
Spong, Rt. Revd. John Shelby, 201, 203, 207, 210, 213–14, 215, 216, 217, 280, 284, 287, 292, 304, 330, 335, 336, 337, 352, 374, 375, 377
Sr. + *name*: *see under* Sisters, Mothers and Sisters Superior *below*
St. Alban's, Oakland, NJ, 468
St. Andrew's Hospital, Clewer, xvii, 128
St. Andrew's Hospital, NYC, xvii, xix, 5, 6, 9–10, 12, 19, 26, 30, 31–32, 33, 35, 39, 40, 47, 79, 82, 89, 129, 176, 368
St. Andrew's Hospital, Poughkeepsie, 33, 35, 39, 40, 41, 44, 75, 314
St. Andrew's, Kent, CT, 330
St. Andrew's, La Mesa, 427
St. Anna's Home, vii, xvi, xvii, xviii, xix, 3, 5, 7, 9, 11, 12, 14, 15–16, 19, 22, 82, 115, 123, 125, 127, 133, 140, 145, 187, 196, 204, 218, 306, 321, 330, 346, 372, 422, 460, 464, 468–9
St. Bernard's School, 79, 177
St. Bernard's, Bernardsville, 357, 396, 403, 407
St. Boniface Church, Jersey City, 166, 170, 175, 261
St. Christopher's House, Jersey City, 83, 102, 103–4, 105, 106, 107, 109, 110, 111, 113–14, 115, 116, 117, 124, 128, 148, 149, 150, 151, 152, 153, 154, 156, 159, 160, 162, 164, 165, 167, 169, 170, 171, 172, 189, 198, 199, 207, 211, 212, 216, *237*, 258, 259, 260, 261, 262, 266, 271, 272, 273, 274–6, 277, 278, 279, 280, 281, 282, 285, 286, 287, 289, 290, 291, 292, 293, 294, 295, 297–9, 300, 306, 314, 460
St. Clement's, Philadelphia, 21, 91
St. Columba's, Washington, DC, 379
St. David's, Kinnelon, NJ, 419, 425, 427
St. Dunstan's, Succasunna, NJ, 189, 322
St. Elizabeth's, Elizabeth, NJ, viii, 336, 338
St. George's, Maplewood, NJ, 304, 446
St. Gregory Palamas Orthodox Church, 431
St. Gregory's Abbey, 21, 144, 147, 189, 400
St. Gregory's Church, Parsippany, 300
St. Gregory's Priory, Valparaiso, 21
St. Helen's Hall, vii, xvii, xix, 3, 4, 6, 11, 12, 15, 17, 18, 22, 40, 41, 48, 49–50, 51–52, 54, 60, 63, 65, 69, 74, 76, 78, 83, 88, 96, 103, 104, 123, 127, 131, 140, 143, 145, 147, 176, 191, 195, 196, 207, 210, *246*, 285, 313, 314, 328, 329, 340, 352, 353, 355, 356, 365, 460
St. Hilda's, Morristown, xvii, 323
St. James, Edison, 328
St. James, Mount Airy, 161
St. James, Texarkana, 57
St. John Baptist Cathedral, Portland, Oregon, 196
St. John Baptist Church, Corsicana, TX, *221*, 483
St. John Baptist Church, Portland, 446
St. John Baptist House, xvi, 3, 76, 83, 95, 106, 108, 109, 113, 117, 124, 134, 140, 155, 159, 161, 176, 182, 195, *222*, *236*, *238*, *245*, 276, 279, 321, 389, 441, 456
St. John Baptist House, Corsicana, TX, *222*

St. John Baptist House, Farmingdale, 368

St. John Baptist Parochial School, Corsicana, TX, 5, 25, 30, 40, 53, 69, 76, 103, 285, 314, 346

St. John Baptist School, viii, xii, xiii, xvi, xviii, xix, 5, 7, 10, 11, 12, 13, 14, 15, 17, 19, 24, 30, 40, 43, 44, 48, 54, 61, 63, 64, 65, 66, 69, 71, 72, 74, 76, 77, 78, 82, 83, 85, 88, 92, 98, 104, 110, 113, 121, 122, 124, 126, 131, 132, 133, 134, 135, 136, 137, 142, 154, 161, 176, 177, 180, 185, 186, 187, 189, 191, 194, 196, 197, 198, 199, 200, 202, 203, 206, 207, 209, 212, 215, 218, *223, 224, 225, 229, 233, 234, 235*, 288, 297, 303, 304, 306, 308, 309, 310, 311, 312, 313, 315, 317, 318, 319, 322, 330, 331, 346, 347, 365, 372, 383, 400, 408, 415, 417, 421, 427, 434, 438, 442, 443, 445, 453, 456, 461, 464, 468

St. John Baptist School, Newport, UK, 128

St. John the Baptist Foundation, 7, 9, 10, 19, 21, 24, 30, 34, 85, 87, 95, 127, 130, 139, 299

St. John's, Boonton, NJ, 87, 199, 387, 390, 442

St. John's, Dover, NJ, 81, 409, 410, 450, 463

St. John's, Elizabeth, NJ, viii, 354, 360, 362, 367, 371

St. John's, Jersey City, 158, 173, 306

St. John's, Passaic, 121, 156

St. John's-on-the-Mountain, Bernardsville, 304, 321, 324, 340, 346

St. Luke's Chapel, NYC, vii, viii, 5, 13, 43, 47, 69, 73, 74, 75, 76, 79, 81, 85, 86, 89, 93, 95, 98, 99, 102, 103, 104, 106, 109, 119, 120, 124, 128, 139, 176, 181, 185, 190, 194, 197, 198, 201, 203, 204, 207, 262, 272, 274, 279, 280, 285, 297, 306, 313, 314, 316, 346, 441

St. Luke's Episcopal Church, Hope, NJ, 333

St. Luke's Hospital, NYC, 30, 79, 80, 115, 131, 314, 316

St. Luke's in the Fields, NYC, 47, 89, 207, 280, 295, 308, 328, 330, 461, 465

St. Luke's School, NYC, 95, 204, *236*

St. Luke's, Gladstone, 321, 324, 357, 409, 447

St. Luke's, Montclair, xii, 134

St. Margaret's House, NYC, 312

St. Marguerite's Home, vii, xviii, xix, 1, 3, 5, 6, 7, 9, 11, 14, 15, 16, 18, 19, 24, 25, 26, 30, 39, 54, 63, 76, 79, 96, 104, 108, 109, 124, 134, 145, 146, 190, 196, 198, 218, 313, 314, 316, 346, 361, 372, 420, 428, 440, 468

St. Marguerite's House, 27, 30, 34, 41, 42, 43, 44, 73, 80, 82, 89, 92, 94, 117, 120, 123, 132, 135, 139, 144, 145, 149, 180, 185, 186, 189, 196, 197, 200, 203, 206, 207, 212, *224*, 273, 304, 307, 309, 311, 318, 319, 320, 321, 322, 324, 325, 327, 328, 331, 334, 346, 347, 348, 351, 360, 362, 363, 365, 367, 369, 370, 371, 372, 373, 374, 376, 382, 385, 389, 390, 392, 394, 396, 417, 418, 420, 422, 424, 426, 427, 430, 432, 433, 435, 436, 437, 438, 440, 443, 444, 445, 448, 449, 450, 453, 456, 457, 458, 462, 464, 466, 467, 468

St. Mark's, Basking Ridge, 132

St. Mark's, Honolulu, 87

St. Mark's, Mendham, xii, 11, 77, 82, 119, 124, 170, 180, 183, 184, 186, 196, 199, 200, 201, 202, 204, 212, 218, *224*, 318, 321, 326, 332, 337, 342, 350, 354, 366, 395, 402, 403, 434, 445, 446, 452, 455, 458, 459, 463, 466

St. Mark's, Philadelphia, 100

St. Martin's House, 172, 259, 261, 266, 268, 271, 273, 274, 275, 277, 278, 279, 281, 282

St. Martin's Retreat House Board, 348, 395, 418

St. Mary the Virgin, NYC, viii, 21, 47, 88, 97, 123, 160, 214, *250*, 410, 414, 416, 424, 431, 439, 434, 439, 444, 449, 450, 451, 452, 454, 455, 458, 460

St. Mary the Virgin, San Francisco, 408

St. Mary's, Harlem, 173

St. Mary's, Tuxedo Park, 307

St. Matthew's, Jersey City, 258, 263, 265, 270, 271, 277, 278, 280, 281, 298, 306, 425

St. Michael's Cemetery, Astoria, 325, 340, 441

St. Michael's Chapel, 45, 89, 129, 156, 187, 200, 329, 404, 457, 463

St. Michael's Home, Mamaroneck, xvii, xix, 75, 125, 127, 135, 140, 205, 368, 462

St. Paul's Cathedral, Calcutta, 192

St. Paul's Chapel, NYC, ix, 167, 386–7

St. Paul's, Baltimore, 118

St. Paul's, Chatham, 110

St. Paul's, Morris Plains, viii, 81, 143, 169, 208–9, 309, 444

St. Paul's, Richmond, Virginia, 201

St. Paul's, Staten Island, 21

St. Paul's, Waxahachie, 57

St. Paul's, Westfield, 121

St. Peter's, Essex Fells, 321, 417, 420

St. Peter's, Morristown, 14, 61, 117, 188, 196, 202, 203, 214, 277, 297, 304, 311, 318, 360, 456, 468

St. Peter's, Mountain Lakes, 304

St. Peter's, Washington, NJ, 121, 133

St. Phillip's, Bronx, 86

St. Stephen's, Plainfield, 121

St. Stephen's, Portland, 26

St Stephen's College, Broadstairs, UK, 28, 128, 146, 196, 344, 358

St. Thomas, Farmingdale, 368

St. Thomas, Mamaroneck, 462

St. Thomas, Pittstown, 401, 402

St. Uriel's, Sea Girt, NJ, 33, 81, 84, 143, 180

Stark, Rt. Revd. Leland, 68, 95, 98, 106, 113, 115, 135, 137, 151, 152, 156, 158, 159, 167, 169, 177, 184, 185, 203, 210, 259, 260, 267, 300, 306, 329, 331

Stearly, Rt. Revd. Wilson Reiff, 8

Sterling, Rt. Revd. Chandler, 160, 174

Stevens, Peter, 353

Stewart, Jim, 369

Stinson, Mr. and Mrs., 474, 475

Stockwood, Rt. Revd. Mervyn, 161

Story, Revd. Edward, 181, 201, 203, 323

Strickland, Kenneth, 14, 19

Strong, Rt. Revd. Thomas Banks, 45

Stuyvesant, Judith, xx

Sisters, Mothers and Sisters Superior

Sr. Ada Marian, 78, 89

Sr. Adela, 5, 6, *221*

Sr. Agatha Louise, 18, 25, 32, 39, 44, 49, 50, 51, 54, 55, 56, 69, 70, 88, 91, 102, 103, 104, 106, 109, 125, 126, 130, 131, 135, 136, 143, 144, 145, 156, 158, 189, 194, 198, 202, 204, *226, 230, 231, 232*, 273, 276, 285, 307, 311, 313–14, 316

Sr. Agatha Mary, SPB, 368

Sr. Agnes Genevieve, 11, 14, 29, 54, 63, 64, 65, 75–6, 83, 88, 114, 116, 119, 124, 127, 128, 131, 135, 136, 138, 143, 144, 182, 189, 190, 197, *231, 236, 237*, 267, 272, 276, 300, 472, 474, 476

Sr. Agnes Jean, 208

Sr. Alice, xx

Sr. Alice Madeline, 5, 78

Sr./M. Alice Ursula, 6, 7, 8, 9, 11, 12–14, 19, 50, 51, 63, 177, *220*, 352

Sr. Amy Grace, 37, 46, 182

Sr./M. Ann Verena, CJGS, 392, 402, 405, 465

Sr. Anna Patience, 29

Sr. Anne, 367, 375, 382, 384, 387, 402, 405, 408, 440, 452, 458, 466

Sr. Anne Marie, SSM, 206, 479, 483

Sr./M. Annys, 94, 127, 128, 132, 140, 159, 178, 179, 181, 182, 185, 187, 188, 189, 193, 209–10, 211, 214, 216, 217, 219, *241*, 271–2, 307

Sr. Barbara Catherine, 393, 394, 395, 399, 401

Sr./Sr. Sup. Barbara Jean, viii, xii, 46, 121, 134, 139, 140, 142, 143, 144, 145, 146, 161, 162, 165, 166, 168, 169, 176, 183, 184, 185, 187, 189, 192, 195, 197, 200, 201, 204, 212, 215, *238, 242, 243, 245, 248, 253, 256*, 258, 259, 266, 267, 273, 277, 288, 303, 304, 306, 310, 311, 312, 315, 316, 317, 318, 319, 320, 321,

323, 324, 325, 326, 327, 328, 329, 331,
332, 333, 334, 336, 337, 338, 339, 340,
343, 346, 349, 350, 351, 352, 353–4,
355, 358, 359, 360, 362, 366, 367, 368,
369, 370, 371, 373, 375, 376–7, 378,
380, 381, 382, 386, 387, 388, 389, 390,
391, 392, 393, 396, 400, 404, 406, 407,
409, 410, 411–12, 414, 415, 417, 419,
422–3, 425, 426, 427, 428, 430, 433,
434, 436, 441, 443, 444, 445, 447, 449,
456, 458, 459, 462, 463, 464, 465–6,
467, 468, 472
Sr. Beatrice Clare, 89, 107, 125, 153
Sr. Beatrice Kitchener, SSJF, *241*
Sr. Beryl, SSJD, 392
M. Betha, 399
Sr. Catherine, 132, 133
Sr. Catherine Faith, 6
Sr. Catherine Mary, 185, 186, 270, 323
Sr. Catherine Vera, 23, 74, 75, 89, *226*
Sr. Deborah Francis, *250*, *251*, 332, 337,
338, 342–3, 345, 348, 351, 353, 354,
355, 356, 360, 362, 366, 367, 368, 369,
371, 382, 390, 391, 393, 407, 409, 410,
414, 416, 417, 423, 424, 434, 439, 443,
444–5, 447, 449, 456, 459, 463, 465
Sr. Diane Jeannette, 393, 401, 409
Sr. Doreen, 345
Sr./M. Dorothy Frances, 19, 23, 27, 28,
32, 36, 37, 38, 39, 46, 94, 183, 191,
218, 219, *238*
Sr. Dorothy Maude, 208
Sr./M. Edna Frances, 211, 214, 217, *241*,
291, 313, 315, 316, 320, 326–7, 329,
331, 337, 338, 344, 348, 363, 365, 439
Sr./Sr. Sup. Eleanor Francis, viii, xii, *248*,
249, *253*, 374, 375, 382, 383, 384, 386,
390, 392, 394, 396, 402, 403, 407, 408,
411, 412, 414, 417, 420, 421, 423, 426,
428, 430, 431, 433, 434, 444, 445–6,
449, 450, 455, 456, 458, 459, 462, 465,
466, 468
Sr. Eleanor Lucy, 18, 24, 32, 43, 54, 56,
59, 83, 102, 103–4, 106, 110, 111,
112–13, 114, 116, 117, 124, 143, 145,
151, 152, 156–7, 160, 161, 163, 165,
166, 167, 168, 169, 170, 171, 173, 179,

184, 185, 187, 199, 202, 203, 207,
210–11, *225*, 258, 259, 260, 262, 263,
264, 266, 267, 268, 269, 271, 272, 273,
276, 277, 280, 281, 282, 283–5, 287
Sr. Elisa Mary, 20
Sr. Elisa Monica, xix, xxi, 7, 9, 11, 12, 14,
17, 20, 23, 29, 30, 36, 45, 46, 48, 61,
62, 63, 64–6, 67, 68, 72, 97, 355
Sr. Elisabeth Roberta, 28, 107, 115, 127,
139, 154, 191
Sr. Eliza Faith, 9
Sr. Elizabeth, 30
Sr./M. Elizabeth Anne, 39, 74, 79, 92,
103, 109, 110, 112–13, 114, 116, 144,
145, 151, 152, 156, 157, 160, 161, 163,
165, 166, 167, 168, 169, 170, 171, 177,
182, 185, 187, 189, 198, 199, 200, 203,
206, 207, 211, 216, 217, *230*, *240*, 258,
260, 263, 264, 266, 268, 269, 272, 276,
277, 282, 284, 285, 288–9, 290, 291,
292, 295, 296, 297, 298, 302, 303, 304,
305, 306, 307, 308, 310, 311, 312, 315,
316, 323
Sr. Elizabeth Jane, *241*, 313, 349, 375,
457
Sr. Elizabeth Marion, 18, 26, 30, 40, 42,
69, 75–6, 88, 93, 102, 103, 104, 106,
114, 116, 126, 145, 156, 185, 187, 198,
202, 204, 208–9, 211, *225*, *231*, 267,
286, 313
Sr. Ellen Elisabeth, 31, 33, 42
Sr. Ellen Juliana, 11, 13, 107, 120, 127,
139, 140, 165, *231*, *232*
Sr. Ellen Marie, 147, 168, 169, 171, 266
Sr. Ellen Stephen, OSH, 392, 409
Sr. Emma, xv, xx, xxi
Sr. Emma Gabriel, 306
Sr. Esther Mary, CRJBS, *241*
Sr. Eudora, 6, 7, 8, 14, 17, 21, 22, 28, 31,
133, 146, 187, 188, 189, 191, 218, *241*,
271–2, 344, 358, 369, 378, 398
Sr./M. Evelyn, 10
Sr. Fanny, xv, xx
Sr. Fanny Helen, 8, 43, 74, 75, 89, 322
Sr. Florence Agatha, 45
Sr./M. Florence Teresa, xix, xxi, 2, 4, 6,
7, 8, 9, 11, 12, 13, 14, 23, 26, 35–6,

49, 50, 61, 62, 63, 125, 134, 205, *220*, 285, 405

Sr. Frances Agatha, 26

Sr./M. Frances Constance, ix, xv–xvi, xvii, 2–3, 23, 38, 48, 118, 134, 270, 340

Sr. Frances Marie, 366, 367

Sr. Frances Maude, 129

Sr. Francina, 2, 3, 89, 107, 125, 133, 153, *231*

Sr. Georgina, 28

Sr./M. Gertrude Verena, xvi, 44

Sr. Gina, 217, *241*, 291, 327, 328, 329, 344

Sr. Gladys, 128

M. Harriet, vi, xv, 11, 38, 98, 111, 119, 140, 149, 155, 201, 218, 315, 326, 344, 363, 378, 380, 383, 388, 390, 391, 399, 460, 467, 468

Sr. Helen Margaret, xv, xvi, 121, 188, 270, 340, 455, 460

Sr. Helen Muriel, 135, 146

Sr. Henrietta Mary, 3

Sr. Hilda Frances, 36, 37, 46

Sr. Hilda Mary, 20

Sr./M. Jane Frances, 29, 46

Sr. Jane Mankaa, EBSB ("Sister Jane"), ix, xiii, *250*, *252*, 376, 380, 388–9, 396–7, 400–401, 405, 406, 409, 412, 415–16, 417, 420, 422, 425, 427, 432, 435, 436–7, 438, 443, 446, 448, 450, 454, 461, 463, 468, 484–5

Sr./M. Jane Olive, viii, 185, 270, 315, 348, 353, 354, 355, 369, 370, 375, 382, 386, 387, 391, 392, 402, 435, 465

Sr. Jane Patricia, 7, 17, 33, 43, 70, 122, 126, 129, 177, 180, 183, 185, 187, 188–9, 194, 202, *226*, 315, 319, 400

Sr. Janis Marie, 373, 377

Sr. Jeannette Louise, 2, 3, 96–7, 106, 107, 116, *220*

Sr. Julia Ann, 385, 390, 394, 395, 400, 402

Sr. Julia Bernardine, 205

Sr. Julia Frances, 7, 11, 36, 42, 44, 46, 89, 96, 116, 119, 124, 134–5, 145, 146, 161, 195, *227*, *231*

Sr. Karen John, 203

Sr. Katharine Angela, 13, 49, 51, 75, 352

Sr. Katharine Veronica, 5, 32, 43, 54, 56, 69, 83, 95, 104, 106, 107, 109, 111, 113, 115, 116, 119, 121, 125, 131, 135, 138, 140, 142, 143, 145, 154, 160, 169, 180, 182, 185, 187, 189, 191, 194, 198, 202, 204, 205, 207, 209, 211, 212, 216, *231*, *236*, *237*, *238*, *245*, 259, 274, 276, 279, 280, 285, 286, 288, 295–6, 298, 303, 304, 310, 311, 316, 317, 318, 319, 320, 321, 324, 328, 329, 330, 331, 346, 472, 477–82, 483

Sr. Laura Claire, 82, 89

Sr. Laura Katharine, 135, 139, 141, 143, 144, 146, 162, 169, 171, 177, 187, 189, 197, 198, 199, 201, 202, 203, 204, 212, 215, *238*, *245*, *250*, *256*, 260, 263, 266, 272, 276, 292, 298, 306, 312, 316, 317, 319, 324, 328, 329, 330, 333, 334, 336, 337, 339, 342, 344, 351, 352, 355, 360, 362, 363, 370, 375, 381, 384, 390, 391, 395, 396, 400, 407, 411, 414, 416, 423, 434, 439, 450, 455, 458, 466, 467

Sr. Letitia, 185, *241*, 270

Sr. Lilian Mary, 28

Sr. Lillian Christine, 2, 3, 5, 23, 33, 46, 82, 346

Sr. Linda Clare, xii, *244*, *246*, *254*, 340, 389, 390, 393, 396, 400, 401, 406, 407, 409, 411, 412–13, 416–17, 418, 419, 423, 424, 426, 430, 437, 441, 442, 443, 444, 447, 454, 464, 465, 466

Sr. Lori Joan, 409

Sr. Lura Grace, *250*, 390, 393, 395, 402, 403, 407, 409, 410, 411, 413, 416, 419, 426, 430, 438, 442

Sr. Margaret, 29, 46

Sr./M. Margaret Helena, viii, x, 14–15, 17, 18, 20, 22, 23, 28–9, 30, 32, 33, 38, 40, 41, 42, 43, 44, 45, 47, 49, 55, 68, 71, 74, 75, 77, 78, 79, 80, 81, 83, 84, 85, 86, 87, 88, 90, 91, 92, 93, 94, 96, 102, 103, 105, 106, 107, 113, 114, 115, 116, 117, 120, 121, 123, 124, 125, 127–8, 129, 130, 131, 132, 133, 134, 135, 136, 137, 138, 139, 140, 142, 143,

144, 145, 146, 149, 150, 152, 154,
155, 156, 159, 161, 162, 165, 166,
177, 178–9, 181, 182, 183, 184, 185,
187, 188, 189, 190, 191, 194, 195, 197,
198, 199, 200, 201, 202, 203, 204, 205,
206, 207, 208, 209, 210, 211, 212, 213,
214, 215, 216, 217, *221*, *231*, *232*, *233*,
237, *244*, *246*, 260, 263, 264, 265, 266,
273, 280, 284, 285, 286, 287, 290, 302,
304, 305, 307, 311, 312, 315, 316, 318,
319–20, 321, 328, 329, 330, 331, 333,
334, 338, 339, 342, 345–6, 347, 348,
351, 352, 353, 354, 355, 356, 358, 359,
361, 362, 364, 365, 366, 367, 368, 369,
371, 372, 373, 374, 375, 376, 377, 380,
381, 383, 384, 388, 389, 391, 392,
397–8, 399, 404, 442, 472

Sr. Margaret Joan, 326

Sr. Margaret Raphael, 42, 62, 138,
140–41, 143, 170, 171, 187, 198, 213

Sr. Margo Elizabeth, *243*, *252*, 321, 344,
348, 351, 353, 356, 360, 362, 364, 366,
369, 375, 376, 382, 386, 390, 393, 402,
407, 412, 414, 417, 420, 422, 428, 432,
437, 440, 450, 462, 463

Sr. Marie Elizabeth, 44, 47

Sr. Marjorie, viii, 188, 189, 271, 353, 354

Sr./M. Marjorie Raphael, SSM, xiii, 72,
206, 218, 365, 483

Sr. Martha Clare, 203, 289, 290, 293,
295, 304

M. Mary Agnes, SSM, 38

Sr./M. Mary Angela, xvi, xviii, 21, 48

Sr. Mary Barbara, 30, 40, 42, 43, 44,
65–6, 67, 69, 83, 88, 114, 122, 124,
126, 129, 132, 177–8, 180, 194, *227*,
233, 479

Sr. Mary Carol, 88

Sr. Mary Elizabeth, 327, 329, 335, 338,
343, 347

Sr. Mary Joan, 42, 89, 106, 137, 176, 191,
231, *232*, 473

Sr. Mary John, OSB, 128, 133

Sr. Mary Julian, 412, 416, 423

Sr. Mary Katharine, 9, 10–11, 46

Sr. Mary Lynne, xiii, 22, 204, 212,
214–15, 217, *240*, *245*, *246*, *250*, *252*,
283, 286, 291, 292, 296, 297, 302, 311,
312, 313, 316, 317–18, 319, 321, 324,
325, 328, 329, 330, 337, 339, 343, 344,
351, 352, 355, 371, 376, 380, 385, 390,
392, 400–401, 403, 404, 407, 409, 412,
414, 415, 417, 420, 423, 425, 426, 432,
434, 435, 436, 444, 447, 461

Sr. Mary Neale, 369, 371, 373, 375, 381,
386–7, 390, 391

Sr. Mary Ruth, EBSB, 443, 444, 446

Sr. Mary Stephen, 345, 367, 374, 402,
409, 413–14, 419, 440, 466

Sr. Mary Theresa, *241*

Sr. Mildred Eleanor, 15, 18, 23, 25, 30,
32, 44, 50, 51, 54, 56, 57, 58, 59, 83,
93, 98, 102, 103, 104, 106, 109, 110,
111, 113, 140, 166, *226*, *231*, 305, 313

Sr. Moira, CRJBS, *241*

Sr. Monica, 188, 189, 214, 215, 271, 439,
446, 457

Sr./Sr. Sup. Monica Clare, vi, xii, xiii, 90,
246, *252*, *253*, 298, 340, 440, 441, 444,
447, 448, 449–50, 451, 454, 458–9,
462, 464, 465, 466, 468

Sr. Olive Frances, 10, 22, 123, 336

Sr. Ora Mary, 31, 39, 42, 104, 109, 111,
113, 115, 116, 119, 131, 141, 147, *231*,
345, 427

Sr. Pamela, xii, xiii, *241*, *246*, *252*, *253*,
298, 345, 370, 371, 377, 380, 382, 387,
390, 392, 393, 403, 407, 411, 414, 416,
418, 420, 423, 424, 426, 431, 433, 434,
437, 438, 448, 451, 452, 458, 462, 465,
466

Sr. Philippa Irene, 363–4

Sr. Sara Josephine, 88, 89, 355

Sr. Shane Margaret, 385, 386, 390, 394,
395, 403, 411, 412, 414, 418, 419, 425,
427, 428, 433

Sr. Sheila, 119, *241*, 313, 338, 344, 439

Sr. Sophia Agnes, 5

Sr. Susinne Paula, 70, 76, 103, 106, 110,
111, 112–13, 114, 116, 117, 128, 150,
152, 154, 156, 160, 163, 170, 171, 185,
199, 203, 211, *231*, *240*, *245*, 260, 266,
268, 272, 276, 278, 283, 286, 288, 290,
292, 297, 332, 339, 351–2, 358

Sr./M./Sr. Sup. Suzanne Elizabeth, ix, xii, 22, 72, 80, 89, 92, 98, 127, 131, 133, 137, 138, 140, 142, 143, 144–5, 146, 147, 160, 161, 162, 164, 171, 177, 179, 180, 181, 183, 184, 185–6, 187, 188, 189, 190, 192, 195, 196, 199, 200, 201, 202, 203, 204, 205, 206, 207, 215, 216, *240*, *241*, *245*, *253*, *255*, 262, 268, 269, 276–7, 278, 281, 285–6, 288, 289, 290, 291, 293, 295, 296, 297, 298, 299, 300, 304, 306, 307, 311, 312, 314, 316, 317, 318, 319, 320, 321, 323, 324, 325, 329, 330, 331, 332, 333, 334, 336, 337, 339, 340, 342, 343, 344, 345, 346, 347, 348, 349, 350–51, 352, 353, 354–5, 355–6, 357, 358, 361, 362, 364, 365, 366, 367, 369, 370, 371, 372, 376, 377, 382, 384, 386, 387–8, 390, 391, 395, 396, 397, 399, 400, 404, 407, 408–9, 412, 414, 415, 419, 423, 426, 429, 430, 431, 433, 434, 436, 438, 440, 441, 444, 445, 447, 449, 459, 463, 464

Sr. Victoria Michelle, xii, *252*, *257*, 340, 437, 438, 441, 442, 444, 445, 452, 456, 459, 464

Sr. Virginia Dorothea, 74, 75, 77, 87, 89, 306, 311

Sr./M. Waldine Lucia, 11, 13, 14, 15–16, 17–18, 19, 20, 23, 25, 26–8, 29, 30, 31, 32, 33, 34, 35, 36, 37, 39, 41, 42, 43, 44, 45, 46, 48, 49, 50, 51, 52–60, 65, 73, 78, 80, 83, 88, 89, 91, 93, 96, 106, 107, 113, 114, 115, 116, 117, 124, 125, 127, 128, 129, 130, 131, 134, 136, 137, 143, 144, 145, 146, 151, 152, 154, 155, 156, 162, 182, 183, 184, 185, 188, 189, 195, 196, 218, *220*, *231*, *232*, *237*, 273, 302, 365, 425, 479

Sr. Winifred Agnes, 194, 198, 205, *236*, *237*, 297, 303, 306

Sr. Zoë, *241*, 338, 344, 359, 408, 419

Talmage, Anne, 372
Talmage, Garland, 372
Talmage, Revd. Nancy, 319, 321, 334, 372
Templeton, Mrs. Dorothy, 188, 311, 372

Templeton, Revd. Elmer J., 80, 94, 124, 132, 137, 162, 189, 198, 202, 210, 282, 289, 372
Temporary vows, 20, 24, 27, 136, 146
Tennant, Mariquita, 399, 459, 460, 468
Terwilliger, Grace, 438
The Satura, 61, 62, 63, 64, 66, 67, 71, 121, 144
Third Order, 23, 461
Thomas, Janet, 351, 360, 363, 433, 457
Thompson, Revd., 464
Tonge, Very Revd. Lister, 363, 365, 387, 388, 416, 423, 429, 440, 446, 456
Townsend, Rt. Revd. Martin, 401
Trenton Cathedral, *242*, 331, 338, 351
Trinity Cathedral, 8, 114, 131, 319, 325, 331, 421, 425, 442, 445, 454, 461
Trinity Church, Easton, 160
Trinity Church, Irvington, 150
Trinity Church, Portland, 60, 328
Trinity Church, Princeton, 7
Trinity Church, Wall Street, 47, 89, 112, 119, 120, 133, 181, 184, 190, 192, 197, 198, 202, 204, 207, 263, 279, 312, 323, 416
Trinity Institute, 263, 266, 270, 299, 317–18
Tucker, Mrs. Allen, 138
Turnbull, Revd. Joseph, 53, 87, 90, 289, 297
Turner, George, 128
Turner, Ruth, 128
Tutu, Most Revd. Desmond, 209, 219, 321, 322

Unwin, Muriel, 273, 274, 275, 276, 277, 282, 283, 286, 287, 289, 293, 300, 318, 320, 460

Vacation Bible School, 76, 81, 82, 84, 97, 106, 107, 109, 113, 117, 138, 143, 158, 162, 167, 180, 189, 197, 204, 212, 215, 259, 264, 265, 287, 297, 299, 306, 312, 327, 409, 442, 452, 472, 474, 475, 478
Van Dine, John, 450
Van Stolk, Charlotte Urquhart, 383
Varney, Lori, 401

Venables, Revd. W. F., 106

Vocations, xvi, xviii, 2, 4, 5, 20, 21, 26, 36, 39, 42, 56, 60, 74, 98, 121, 127, 128, 131, 132, 140, 141, 176, 185, 191, 203, 216, 284, 302, 306, 310, 312, 314, 317, 334, 343, 351, 363, 383, 401, 402, 439, 446, 449, 475

Vowed life, xx, 39, 41, 85, 91, 94, 149, 169, 194, 202, 269, 277, 293, 307, 312, 346, 388, 410, 433

Wagner, Anna Loretta (Etta), 464, 468

Wagner, Ellen Margaret (Ethel?), 464, 469

Wagner, Esther Maria, 464, 468–9

Wagner, Mary, 374, 382, 384

Walker, Rt. Revd. Dominic, OGS, 375, 440

Wallis, Revd., 21

Walter, Revd. Francis Xavier, 156, 158, 159, 161, 173

Warden, xv, xx, 2, 7, 9, 12, 13, 14, 21, 24, 26, 30, 31, 32, 36, 38, 39, 40, 41, 43, 56, 73, 79, 83, 85, 86, 110, 114, 137, 138, 140, 150, 156, 178, 181, 182, 183, 192, 195, 198, 201, 203, 204, 210, 213, 214, 216, 217, 262, 267, 273, 285, 287, 292, 305, 319, 326, 330, 331, 332, 336, 352, 354, 363, 364, 365, 366, 369, 370, 399, 425, 440, 450

Warner, Revd. Keithly, 281

Washburn, Rt. Revd. Benjamin, 2, 13, 14, 16, 20, 21, 25, 34, 39, 78, 79, 80, 82, 83, 85, 87, 94, 96, 98, 101, 102, 112, 114, 119, 123, 138, 165, 346

Watters, Revd. Philip S., 210, 218, 326

Webster, Hamilton Fish, 89, 90

Webster, Mrs. Sydney, 3

Weed, Revd. Paul, 32, 33, 36, 40, 41, 42, 43, 56, 73, 76, 79, 83, 110, 114, 124, 137, 138, 140, 150, 156, 162, 166, 178, 181, 182, 189, 198, 199, 201, 203, 210, 213, *236*, 262, 284, 285, 287, 295, 305, 319, 330

Weller, Laura, 132, 135, 161

Wessinger, Revd. Paul, SSJE, 26, 45, 53, 213, 214, 216, 287, 292, 325, 331, 335, 343, 365, 425

West, Doris, 55, 57, 59, 108, 360, 370

West, Doyle, 55, 57, 58, 59, 84, 108, 129, 370

Westapher, Revd. Clarence, 57, 58

Whiteside, Dorothy Keedwell, 383, 434

Wilcox, Revd. Diana, xii, 418, 421, 456, 458

Williams, Revd. Granville Mercer, SSJE, 43, 47

Willow, Revd. Mary, 287, 406

Wilson, Ellen, 71

Wilson, Kathryn (Kay), 277, 287, 300

Wilson, Markie, 71

Wilson, Mrs. Teresa, 199

Wilson, Patricia, 71

Wilson, Revd. Phillip, 384

Wilson, Ruth, 71

Wipfler, Revd. William, 163, 174

Wood, Jean Mary, 62, 71

Woods, Maureen, xii, 418

Wotherspoon, Carol, 458

Wright, Rt. Revd. Harold Louis, 270, 300

Wysong, Marian, 62, 67, 71, 122, 133, 206, 318

Wysong, Marjorie, xiii, 72, 218

Wysong, Mr., 83

CPSIA information can be obtained
at www.ICGtesting.com
Printed in the USA
LVHW080708100622
720956LV00010B/220